Access 2013

the missing manual®

The book that should have been in the box®

Matthew MacDonald

Beijing | Cambridge | Farnham | Köln | Sebastopol | Tokyo

Access 2013: The Missing Manual

by Matthew MacDonald

Published by O'Reilly Media, Inc.,
1005 Gravenstein Highway North, Sebastopol, CA 95472.

O'Reilly books may be purchased for educational, business, or sales promotional use. Online editions are also available for most titles (*http://my.safaribooksonline.com*). For more information, contact our corporate/institutional sales department: (800) 998-9938 or *corporate@oreilly.com*.

April 2013:   First Edition.

See *http://http://oreilly.com/catalog/errata.csp?isbn=0636920028406* for release details.

ISBN-13: 978-1-449-35741-2

[LSI]

Contents

Part One: Storing Information in Tables

Part Seven: **Appendix**

The Missing Credits

ABOUT THE AUTHOR

 **Matthew MacDonald** is a four-time Microsoft MVP and a technology writer with well over a dozen books to his name. Office geeks can follow him into the world of spreadsheets with *Excel 2013: The Missing Manual*. Web fans can build an online home with him in *Creating a Website: The Missing Manual*. And human beings of all descriptions can discover just how strange they really are in the quirky handbooks *Your Brain: The Missing Manual* and *Your Body: The Missing Manual*.

ABOUT THE CREATIVE TEAM

Nan Barber (editor) has worked with the Missing Manual series since the previous millennium. She lives in Massachusetts with her husband and iMac. Email: *nanbarber@oreilly.com*.

Kara Ebrahim (production editor) lives, works, and plays in Cambridge, MA. She loves graphic design and all things outdoors. Email: *kebrahim@oreilly.com*.

Nan Reinhardt (proofreader) lives in the Midwest, where she enjoys summer weekends at the lake, boating, swimming, and reading voraciously. Nan is not only a freelance copyeditor and proofreader, but she's also a published romance novelist. Check out her work at *www.nanreinhardt.com*. Email: *nanleigh1@gmail.com*.

Ron Strauss (indexer) specializes in the indexing of information technology publications of all kinds. Ron is also an accomplished classical violist and lives in northern California with his wife and fellow indexer, Annie, and his miniature pinscher, Kanga. Email: *rstrauss@mchsi.com*.

Andrew Vickers (technical reviewer) has been building bespoke Access databases for his clients since Access 97 in 1999. He has also developed a number of database products for the property industry through his company Hartlebury Software in Worcestershire, UK (*www.hartleburysoftware.co.uk*).

Paloma Fautley (technical reviewer) is a student currently pursuing a degree in Robotics Engineering. She has used various versions of Access from 2003 on and has both developed and manipulated databases professionally for years. Email: *GFautley@gmail.com*.

ACKNOWLEDGEMENTS

Writing a book about a program as sprawling and complex as Access is a labor of love (love of pain, that is). I'm deeply indebted to a whole host of people who helped out with this edition and the two previous ones. They include Nan Barber, Brian Sawyer, and Nellie McKesson, and technical reviewers Andrew Vickers, Paloma Fautley, John Pierce, James Turner, Juel Bortolussi, and Michael Schmalz. I also owe thanks to many people who worked to get this book formatted, indexed, and printed—you can meet many of them on the Missing Credits page.

Completing this book required a few sleepless nights (and many sleep-deprived days). I extend my love and thanks to my daughters, Maya and Brenna, who put up with it without crying most of the time, my dear wife, Faria, who mostly did the same, and our moms and dads (Nora, Razia, Paul, and Hamid), who contributed hours of babysitting, tasty meals, and general help around the house that kept this book on track. So thanks everyone—without you, half of the book would still be trapped inside my brain!

—Matthew MacDonald

THE MISSING MANUAL SERIES

Missing Manuals are witty, superbly written guides to computer products that don't come with printed manuals (which is just about all of them). Each book features a handcrafted index and cross-references to specific pages (not just chapters). Recent and upcoming titles include:

Access 2010: The Missing Manual by Matthew MacDonald

Adobe Edge Animate: The Missing Manual by Chris Grover

Buying a Home: The Missing Manual by Nancy Conner

Creating a Website: The Missing Manual, Third Edition by Matthew MacDonald

CSS3: The Missing Manual by David Sawyer McFarland

David Pogue's Digital Photography: The Missing Manual by David Pogue

Dreamweaver CS6: The Missing Manual by David Sawyer McFarland

Droid 2: The Missing Manual by Preston Gralla

Droid X2: The Missing Manual by Preston Gralla

Excel 2010: The Missing Manual by Matthew MacDonald

Excel 2013: The Missing Manual by Matthew MacDonald

FileMaker Pro 12: The Missing Manual by Susan Prosser and Stuart Gripman

Flash CS6: The Missing Manual by Chris Grover

Galaxy S II: The Missing Manual by Preston Gralla

Galaxy Tab: The Missing Manual by Preston Gralla

Google+: The Missing Manual by Kevin Purdy

HTML5: The Missing Manual by Matthew MacDonald

iMovie '11 & iDVD: The Missing Manual by David Pogue and Aaron Miller

iPad: The Missing Manual, Fifth Edition by J.D. Biersdorfer

iPhone: The Missing Manual, Fifth Edition by David Pogue

iPhone App Development: The Missing Manual by Craig Hockenberry

iPhoto '11: The Missing Manual by David Pogue and Lesa Snider

iPod: The Missing Manual, Tenth Edition by J.D. Biersdorfer and David Pogue

JavaScript & jQuery: The Missing Manual, Second Edition by David Sawyer McFarland

Kindle Fire HD: The Missing Manual by Peter Meyers

Living Green: The Missing Manual by Nancy Conner

Mac OS X Lion: The Missing Manual by David Pogue

Microsoft Project 2010: The Missing Manual by Bonnie Biafore

Microsoft Project 2013: The Missing Manual by Bonnie Biafore

Motorola Xoom: The Missing Manual by Preston Gralla

Netbooks: The Missing Manual by J.D. Biersdorfer

NOOK HD: The Missing Manual by Preston Gralla

Office 2010: The Missing Manual by Nancy Conner and Matthew MacDonald

Office 2011 for Macintosh: The Missing Manual by Chris Grover

Office 2013: The Missing Manual by Nancy Conner and Matthew MacDonald

OS X Mountain Lion: The Missing Manual by David Pogue

Personal Investing: The Missing Manual by Bonnie Biafore

Photoshop CS6: The Missing Manual by Lesa Snider

Photoshop Elements 11: The Missing Manual by Barbara Brundage

PHP & MySQL: The Missing Manual, Second Edition by Brett McLaughlin

QuickBooks 2012: The Missing Manual by Bonnie Biafore

QuickBooks 2013: The Missing Manual by Bonnie Biafore

Switching to the Mac: The Missing Manual, Lion Edition by David Pogue

Switching to the Mac: The Missing Manual, Mountain Lion Edition by David Pogue

Windows 7: The Missing Manual by David Pogue

Windows 8: The Missing Manual by David Pogue

WordPress: The Missing Manual by Matthew MacDonald

Your Body: The Missing Manual by Matthew MacDonald

Your Brain: The Missing Manual by Matthew MacDonald

Your Money: The Missing Manual by J.D. Roth

For a full list of all Missing Manuals in print, go to *www.missingmanuals.com/library. html.*

Introduction

People have tried a variety of techniques to organize information. They've used Rolodexes, punch cards, cardboard boxes, vertical files, Post-it notes, 10,000-page indexes, and (when all else failed) large paper piles on flat surfaces. But after much suffering, people discovered that computers were far better at dealing with information, especially when that information is large, complex, or changes frequently.

That's where Microsoft Access comes into the picture. Access is a tool for managing *databases*—carefully structured catalogs of information (or *data*). Databases can store just about any type of information, including numbers, pages of text, and pictures. Databases also range wildly in size—they can handle everything from your list of family phone numbers to a ginormous product catalog for Aunt Ethel's Discount Boutique.

In this book, you'll learn how to design complete databases, maintain them, search for valuable nuggets of information, and build attractive forms for quick and easy data entry. You'll delve into the black art of Access *programming*, where you'll pick up valuable tricks and techniques that you can use to automate common tasks, even if you've never touched a line of code before. And you'll even explore the new *web app* feature that lets you put your database online so anyone can use it—provided you have a SharePoint server or an Office 365 hosting plan.

▩ What You Can Do with Access

The modern world is filled with information. A web search for a ho-hum topic like "canned carrots" nets more than a million web pages. As a result, it's no surprise that people from all walks of life need great tools to store and manage information.

It's impossible to describe even a fraction of the different databases that Access fans create every day. But just to get you thinking like a database maven, here are some common types of information that you can store handily in an Access database:

- Catalogs of books, CDs, rare wine vintages, risqué movies, or anything else you want to collect and keep track of.

- Mailing lists that let you keep in touch with friends, family, and coworkers.

- Business information, like customer lists, product catalogs, order records, and invoices.

- Lists of guests and gifts for weddings and other celebrations.

- Lists of expenses, investments, and other financial planning details.

Think of Access as a personal assistant that can help you organize, update, and find any type of information. This help isn't just a convenience—it also lets you do things you could never accomplish on your own.

Imagine you've just finished compiling a database for your collection of 10,000 rare comic books. On a whim, you decide to take a look at all the books written in 1997. Or just those that feature Aquaman. Or those that contain the words "special edition" in the title. Performing these searches with a paper catalog would take days. On an average computer, Access can perform all three searches in under a second.

Access is also the king of small businesses because of its legendary powers of customization. Although you can use virtually any database product to create a list of customer orders, only Access makes it easy to build a full *user interface* for that database (as shown in *Figure I-1*).

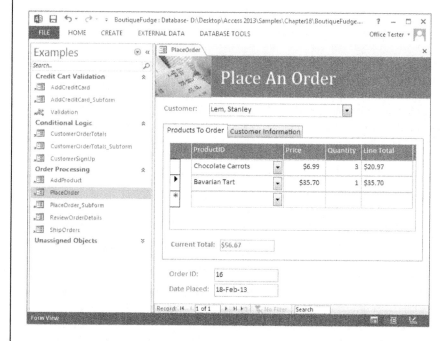

FIGURE I-1

This sales database includes handy forms that sales people can use to place new orders (shown here), customer service representatives can use to sign up new customers, and warehouse staff can use to review outgoing shipments. Best of all, the people who are using the forms in the database don't need to know anything about Access. As long as a database pro (like your future self, once you've finished this book) has designed these forms, anyone can use them to enter, edit, and review data.

The Benefits of a Good Database

Many people use an address book to keep track of close friends, distant relatives, or annoying coworkers. For the most part, the low-tech address book works great. But consider what happens if you decide to store the same information in an Access database. Even though your contact list isn't storing Google-sized volumes of information, it still offers a few features that you wouldn't have without Access:

- **Backup**. If you've ever tried to decipher a phone number through a coffee stain, you know that sometimes it helps to have things in electronic form. Once you place all your contact information into a database, you'll be able to preserve it in case of disaster, and print as many copies as you need (each with some or all of the information showing). You can even share your list with a friend who needs the same numbers.

- **Space**. Although most people can fit all the contacts they need into a small address book, a database ensures you'll never fill up that "M" section. Not to mention that you can cross out and rewrite the address for your itinerant Uncle Sid only so many times before you run out of room.

- **Searching**. An address book organizes contacts in one

way—by name. But what happens once you've entered everyone in alphabetical order by last name, and you need to look up a contact you vaguely remember as Joe? Access can effortlessly handle this search. It can also find a matching entry by phone number, which is great if your phone gives you a log of missed calls by number only, and you want to figure out who's been pestering you.

- **Sharing**. Only one person at a time can edit most ordinary files like Microsoft Word documents and spreadsheets. This limitation causes a problem if you need your entire office team to collaborate on a potluck menu. But Access lets multiple people review and change your data at the same time, on different computers. Chapter 19 has the full story.

- **Integration with other applications**. Access introduces you to a realm of timesaving possibilities like mail merge. You can feed a list of contacts into a form letter you create in Word, and automatically generate dozens of individually addressed letters.

All these examples demonstrate solid reasons to go electronic with almost any type of information.

The Two Sides of Access

As you'll see in this book, you'll actually perform two separate tasks with Access:

- **Designing your database**. This task involves creating *tables* to hold data, *queries* that can ferret out important pieces of information, *forms* that make it easy to enter information, and *reports* that produce attractive printouts.

- **Dealing with data**. This task involves adding new information to the database, updating what's there, or just searching for the details you need. To do this work, you use the tables, queries, forms, and reports that you've already built.

Most of this book is dedicated to task #1—creating and perfecting your database. This job is the heart of Access, and it's the part that initially seems the most daunting. It's also what separates the Access masters from the neophytes.

Once you've finished task #1, you're ready to move on to task #2—actually *using* the database in your day-to-day life. Although task #1 is more challenging, you'll (eventually) spend more time on task #2. For example, you might spend a couple of hours creating a database to keep track of your favorite recipes, but you'll wind up entering new information and looking up recipes for *years* (say, every time you need to cook up dinner).

Access vs. Excel

Access isn't the only Office product that can deal with lists and tables of information. Microsoft Excel also includes features for creating and managing lists. So what's the difference?

Although Excel's perfectly good for small, simple amounts of information, it just can't handle the same *quantity* and *complexity* of information as Access. Excel also falters if you need to maintain multiple lists with related information (for example, if you want to track a list of your business customers and a list of the orders they've made). Excel forces you to completely separate these lists, which makes it harder to analyze your data and introduces the possibility of inconsistent information. Access lets you set up strict *links* between tables, which prevents these problems.

Access also provides all sorts of features that don't have any parallel in the spreadsheet world, such as the ability to create customized search routines, design fine-tuned forms for data entry, and print a variety of snazzy reports.

Of course, all this isn't to say that Access is *better* than Excel. In fact, in many cases you might want Excel to partner up with Access. Excel shines when crunching reams of numbers to create graphs, generate statistics, or predict trends. Many organizations use Access to store and manage information, and then export a portion of that information to an Excel spreadsheet whenever they need to analyze it. You'll learn how to take this step in Chapter 23.

TIP Looking to polish up your Excel skills? Check out *Excel 2013: The Missing Manual.*

Access vs. SQL Server

Microsoft provides another database product—the industrial-strength SQL Server, which powers everything from Microsoft's own search engine to the NASDAQ stock exchange. Clearly, SQL Server is big business, and many Access fans wonder how their favorite database software compares.

One of the most important differences between Access and database products like SQL Server is that Access is a *client-side* database. In non-techie terms, that means that Access runs right on your personal computer. Database engines like SQL Server are *server-based*: They store the data on a high-powered server computer, which you access from a garden variety PC. (This interaction happens over a local network or over the Internet, depending on how you've configured SQL Server.)

Server-based databases are much more complex to set up and maintain, but they provide enhanced performance and rock-solid stability, even when thousands of people use them at once. However, the only people that require high-end databases like SQL Server are large organizations. Amazon.com wouldn't last 5 minutes if it had to rely on an Access database. But Access works just fine for most small and mid-sized businesses. It's also perfect for personal use. (If you still have lingering doubts about whether Access can meet your needs, check out the box on page 7.)

Another important difference between Access and server-side database products is that Access is an all-in-one solution for storing *and* interacting with data. Server-side database engines like SQL Server focus exclusively on storing data (and sending that data to other computers when they request it). However, this single-minded design has a sizable price. An ordinary person can't directly edit a database that's stored by SQL Server. Instead, you need to use yet *another* program that can talk to SQL Server and ask for the information it needs. In most cases, this program needs to be hand-built by a savvy programmer. In other words, if you're using SQL Server, you need to write a whole application before you can effectively use your database.

Sometimes, Access fans do turn into SQL Server gurus. You can start with a modest Access database and then step up to SQL Server when your needs exceed what Access provides. The process isn't always seamless, but it's possible. You can even keep using Access as a front end to manage your SQL Server database. You can learn about this trick in Chapter 21.

When Access Isn't Enough

If you've picked up this book, you probably have a good sense that Access will meet your needs. But if you're in any doubt, a quick reality check will confirm whether you're on the right path.

The following list describes a few warning signs that suggest you and Access just aren't a good fit. If you don't fall into any of these categories, congratulations—you're ready to use the most straightforward and productive database software anywhere!

- **You need to store huge volumes of information (more than 2 gigabytes of data)**. You're unlikely to hit this mark unless you're storing large pictures or other types of digital content inside a database. Even a big Access database is usually less than 100 megabytes (about 20 times smaller than the 2 GB limit).

- **You need to share your database over the Web**. Ordinary Access databases just aren't cut out for the Web. But Access 2013 introduces a new *web app* feature that uses Microsoft SharePoint behind the scenes, so your database can serve far more people than it could through Access alone. However, there are disadvantages—for example, some Access features don't carry over to the web application, and you must invest in SharePoint server or a SharePoint hosting service. Chapter 22 describes Access's web database feature in detail.

- **You're going to share your database on a network, and more than a dozen people need to use it at once**. It's difficult to correctly interpret this limit. It's perfectly fine for hundreds of people to use your database from time to time, but problems occur when many people are all jockeying to make changes to the same database file at the same instant. You need to test your database to figure out whether you can cross this limit without introducing problems, and you may need to switch to a web app (Chapter 20) or use Access in conjunction with SQL Server (Chapter 21). For more information about sharing Access—and for some help deciding what's the best way to satisfy large crowds of people—see page 641.

The Access Ribbon

The ribbon is a super-toolbar that replaces the various toolbars that clogged the window in the ancient days before Access 2007. It's clear, streamlined, and carefully organized into *tabs*—Home, Create, External Data, and so on. Initially, Access starts out with four tabs (although other tabs appear when you perform specific tasks).

When you create or open a new database, you start at the Home tab. Click the Create tab (as shown in *Figure 1-2*), and you get access to a slew of powerful commands that let you add new database components.

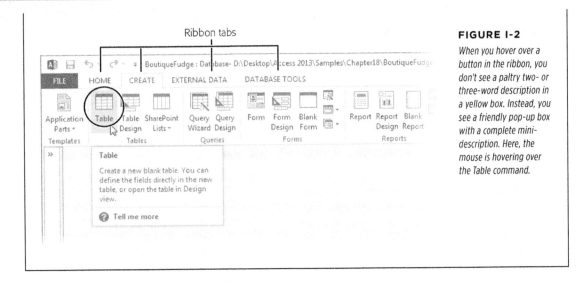

Ribbon tabs

FIGURE I-2

When you hover over a button in the ribbon, you don't see a paltry two- or three-word description in a yellow box. Instead, you see a friendly pop-up box with a complete mini-description. Here, the mouse is hovering over the Table command.

Here's a quick rundown of the basic ribbon tabs:

- **File** looks like a tab, but it's actually the gateway into backstage view. Page 11 explains how backstage view works.

- **Home** gathers together a variety of common commands including the familiar copy-and-paste tools and formatting commands for tweaking fonts and colors. You'll also find handy features like sorting, searching, and filtering, all of which you'll tackle in Chapter 3.

- **Create** has commands for inserting all the different database objects you'll learn about in this book (see page 24 for the lowdown). These include the tables that store data, the queries that search it, the forms that help you edit it, and the reports that help you print it.

- **External Data** has commands for importing data into Access and exporting it to other programs. You'll also find features for integrating with Microsoft SharePoint Server. You'll use these commands in Part Six.

- **Database Tools** features the pro tools you'll use to analyze a database, link tables, and scale up to SQL Server. You'll also find the commands for inserting Visual Basic code, which you'll explore in detail in Part Five.

TIP If you have a scroll mouse, you can breeze through the tabs by moving the mouse pointer over the ribbon, and then rolling the scroll wheel up or down.

One nice ribbon feature is the way it adapts to different window sizes. In a wide Access window, there's room to spread out, and text appears next to almost every button. But in a narrow Access window, where space is more limited, Access strips the text off less important buttons to make room (*Figure I-3*).

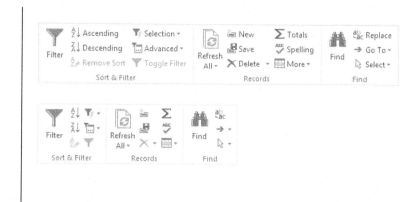

FIGURE I-3

Here are three sections from the Home tab in the ribbon (Sort & Filter, Records, and Find). When the Access window is wide, there's plenty of room to show buttons and text (top). But if you resize the Access window down to super-skinniness, the ribbon removes text so it can keep showing the same set of commands. If you want to know what a no-text button does, hover your cursor over it to see its name.

TIP Want to reclaim the screen real estate that the ribbon occupies? Just double-click the current tab, and the ribbon collapses, leaving only the row of tab titles visible. Double-click the tab again to pop the buttons back into sight.

Using the Ribbon with the Keyboard

If you're a diehard keyboard lover, you'll be happy to hear that you can trigger ribbon commands with the keyboard. The trick is to use *keyboard accelerators*, a series of keystrokes that starts with the Alt key (the same keys you *used* to use to get to a menu). When using a keyboard accelerator, you *don't* hold down all the keys at the same time. (As you'll soon see, some of them have enough letters to tie your fingers up better than the rowdiest game of Twister.) Instead, you press the keys one after the other.

The trick to keyboard accelerators is to understand that once you press the Alt key, you do two things, in this order:

1. **Pick the correct ribbon tab.**

2. **In that tab, choose a command.**

Before you can trigger a specific command, you *must* select the right tab (even if you're already there). Every accelerator requires at least two key presses after you press the Alt key. You'll need even more if you need to dig through a submenu.

By now, this whole process probably seems hopelessly impractical. Are you really expected to memorize dozens of different accelerator key combinations?

Fortunately, Access is ready to help you out with a feature called *KeyTips*. Here's how it works: Once you press the Alt key, letters magically appear over every tab in the ribbon. Once you press a key to pick a tab, letters appear over every button in that tab. You can then press the corresponding key to trigger the command. *Figure I-4* shows how it works.

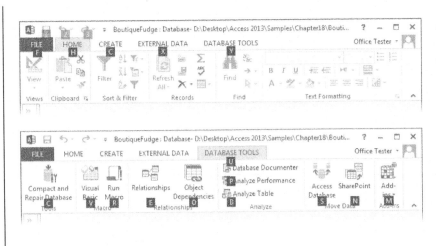

FIGURE I-4

Top: When you press Alt, Access pins KeyTips next to every tab, over the File menu, and over the buttons in the Quick Access toolbar.

Bottom: If you follow up by pressing Y (for the Database Tools tab), you'll see letters next to every command in that tab. Now you can press another key to run a command (for example, W moves your data to SQL Server).

> **TIP** Don't bother trying to match letters with tab or button names—the ribbon's got so many features packed into it that in many cases, the letters don't mean anything at all.

In some cases, a command may have two letters, and you need to press both keys, one after the other. You can back out of KeyTips mode at any time without triggering a command by pressing the Alt key again.

Some other shortcut keys don't use the ribbon. These key combinations start with the Ctrl key. For instance, Ctrl+C copies highlighted text, and Ctrl+S saves your current work. Usually, you find out about a shortcut key by hovering over a command with the mouse cursor. Hover over the Paste button in the ribbon's Home tab, and you see a tooltip that tells you its timesaving shortcut key is Ctrl+V. And if you've worked with a previous version of Access, you'll find that Access 2013 keeps most of the same shortcut keys.

The Quick Access Toolbar

Keen eyes will notice the tiny bit of screen real estate that sits just above the ribbon (*Figure I-5*). This bit of screen holds a series of tiny icons, and it's called the Quick Access toolbar (or QAT to Access nerds).

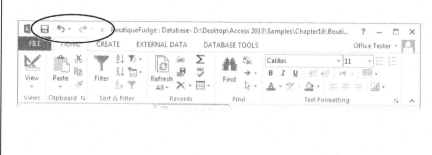

FIGURE I-5

The Quick Access toolbar puts the Save, Undo, and Redo commands right at your fingertips. Access singles out these commands because people use them more frequently than any other commands. But as you'll learn in the appendix of this book, you can add anything you want here.

If the Quick Access toolbar were nothing but a specialized shortcut for three commands, it wouldn't be worth the bother. However, the nifty thing about the Quick Access toolbar is that you can customize it. In other words, you can remove commands you don't use and can add your own favorites.

Microsoft has deliberately kept the Quick Access toolbar very small. It's designed to give a carefully controlled outlet for those customization urges. Even if you go wild stocking the Quick Access toolbar with your own commands, the rest of the ribbon remains unchanged. (And that means a coworker or spouse can still use your computer without suffering a migraine.) However, Access also lets you get more radical by revising the arrangement of tabs, sections, and buttons in the ribbon. To learn how to customize the QAT and the ribbon, check out the appendix.

Backstage View

Your data is the star of the show. That's why Access's creators refer to databases as being *on stage*. Sure, it's a strange metaphor, but the rationale for Access's backstage view makes sense: It temporarily takes you away from your database and lets you concentrate on other tasks that don't involve entering or editing data. These tasks include creating a new database, converting your database to a different format, printing part of its contents, and changing Access settings.

To switch to backstage view, click the File button that appears just to the left of the Home tab in the ribbon. To get out of backstage view, click the back arrow (shown in *Figure I-6*) or press Esc.

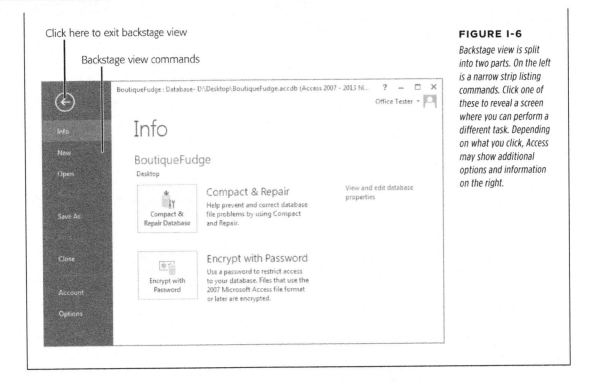

FIGURE I-6

Backstage view is split into two parts. On the left is a narrow strip listing commands. Click one of these to reveal a screen where you can perform a different task. Depending on what you click, Access may show additional options and information on the right.

Along with creating and opening databases, you can also use Access's backstage view to:

- Compact, repair, and encrypt your database file (choose Info)

- Save a copy of your database (choose Save As)

- Print some of the information in your database (choose Print)

- Quit Access (choose Close)

- Configure all sorts of Access options (choose Options) or change your user information (choose Account)

You'll return to backstage view to perform all of these tasks in the chapters ahead.

The Changes in Access 2013

Access 2013 doesn't bring the usual avalanche of new features. In fact, Microsoft took the exact opposite approach, and focused on streamlining and modernizing Access by kicking out some of its oldest and creakiest features. These changes have stirred up more than a little controversy among old-hand Access programmers, and much of it is justified. However, the ultimate goal—to make sure that Access remains a viable, thriving platform for businesses, individuals, and all kinds of data lovers—is a worthy one.

The most significant addition to Access 2013 is an Internet-enabled feature that Microsoft calls *web apps* (covered in Chapter 20). Web apps allow ordinary Access users to create databases that live on the Web, where hundreds or thousands of people can use them. Best of all, web apps require no extra skills beyond a basic knowledge of Access, and they are underpinned by Microsoft's SQL Server data engine, ensuring good performance and offering the sort of data integration possibilities that make programmers drool. However, the tradeoffs are significant. Web apps have far fewer features than traditional desktop apps, and they require a SharePoint 2013 server to host them. Businesses that aren't already using SharePoint 2013 may want to consider Microsoft's Office 365 subscription plan (described in the box on page 14), but the cost of licensing a team of people adds up quickly.

Beside web apps, the only other significant changes in Access are feature *removals*. Here are the key features that are no longer offered in Access 2013:

- **Access data projects.** This nifty feature let Access experts create and manage SQL Server databases without leaving the comfort of Access. Its removal is the most controversial change in Access 2013. Now, Access fans who want to link Access and SQL Server together need to master SQL Server's management tools, as described in Chapter 21.

- **The upsizing wizard.** In the past, the upsizing wizard could take an overtaxed Access database and convert it to a SQL Server database. To do that now, you need the help of another tool, called SSMA. Fortunately, it's free (page 758).

- **Support for Access 97 files.** Access 2013 can't open or convert Access 97 files. Sixteen years after Access 97 was first introduced, this shouldn't come as much of a surprise. But if you still have an extremely old database kicking around, make sure you convert it using an older version of Access, like Access 2010 or 2007. In a similar vein, Access 2013 has finally given up on dBASE, which means you can't import information from this long-dead database software either.

- **Pivot tables and pivot charts.** Pivot tables and charts provided a powerful way to analyze huge quantities of data. However, the Access pivot table feature only had a subset of the full pivot table capabilities found in Excel. Now, Microsoft recommends that people who want to analyze their data do so in Excel. (Excel has a handy data connection feature that can grab the latest information from a database and insert it into a workbook.)

- **Data collection through email.** This seldom-used feature let you send out an email form asking for data. Outlook would then take the replies and send the data to an Access table. The idea was good, but the implementation was awkward.

For the full list of discontinued features, including a few specialized, rarely used ones, go to *http://tinyurl.com/afwls36* for Microsoft's official rundown.

The Office 365 Subscription Service

Office 365 is a set of subscription services for businesses, educational institutions, and government workers. When a company signs up, they give each of their employees a separate Office 365 account that they can use to run Office (either online or on the desktop, if the subscription plan includes desktop use). The Office 365 plan also includes online services, such as email, messaging, document sharing, project tracking, and more. The exact set of features depends on the plan you use—higher-end plans include SharePoint and support Access's new web app feature.

The drawback to Office 365 is that each person who uses it needs a separate subscription plan, and each subscription plan entails a monthly payment to Microsoft (ranging from $4 to over $20 per month). For big businesses, the cost of giving their employees Office 365 subscriptions is often *less* than buying multiple copies of the shrinkwrapped Office software, and it saves them many of the administration, because Microsoft manages most of the administration, from spam filtering to setting up SharePoint. However, Office 365 probably won't interest families, hobbyists, or self-employed people.

To learn more about Office 365 and compare the different subscription plans, visit *http://office.microsoft.com*.

■ About This Book

Despite the many improvements in software over the years, one feature hasn't improved a bit: Microsoft's documentation. In fact, with Office 2013, you get no printed user guide at all. To learn about the thousands of features included in this software collection, Microsoft expects you to read the online help.

Occasionally, these help screens are actually helpful, like when you're looking for a quick description explaining a mysterious programming command. On the other hand, if you're trying to learn how to, say, create a summary with subtotals, you'll find nothing better than terse and occasionally cryptic instructions.

This book is the manual that *should* have accompanied Access 2013. In these pages, you'll find step-by-step instructions and tips for using almost every Access feature, including those you haven't (yet) heard of.

About the Outline

This book is divided into seven parts, each containing several chapters.

- **Part One: Storing Information in Tables**. In this part, you'll build your first database and learn how to add and edit *tables* that store information. Then you'll pick up the real-world skills you need to stop mistakes before they happen, browse around your database, and link tables together.

- **Part Two: Manipulating Data with Queries**. In this part, you'll build *queries*—specialized commands that can hunt down the data you're interested in, apply changes, and summarize vast amounts of information.

- **Part Three: Printing Reports**. This part shows you how to use *reports* to take the raw data in your tables and format it into neat printouts, complete with fancy formatting and subtotals.

- **Part Four: Building a User Interface with Forms**. In this part, you'll build *forms*—customized windows that make data entry easy, even for Access newbies.

- **Part Five: Programming Access**. Now that you've mastered the essentials of databases, you're ready to delve into the black art of Access programming. In this part, you'll use macros and Visual Basic programming to automate complex tasks and solve common challenges.

- **Part Six: Going Large: Access Databases for Many Users**. In this part, you'll learn to let groups of people use your database at the same time. You'll start by learning how to split your Access database and host it on a network. Then you'll consider other options, such as putting your database online in a web app, or linking your database to SQL Server or SharePoint. Finally, you'll learn about the import and export features that can transport data into your database and copy it to other types of files.

- **Part Seven: Appendix**. This book wraps up with an appendix that shows how to customize the ribbon to get easy access to your favorite commands.

About→These→Arrows

Throughout this book, you'll find sentences like this one: "Choose Create→Tables →Table." This method is a shorthand way of telling you how to find a feature in the Access ribbon. It translates to the following instructions: "On the ribbon, click the **Create** tab. On the tab, look for the **Tables** section. In the Tables box, click the **Table** button." (Look back to *Figure I-2* to see the button you're looking for.)

As you saw back in *Figure I-3*, the ribbon adapts itself to different screen sizes. Depending on your Access window's size, the button you need to click may not include any text. Instead, it shows up as a small icon. In this situation, you can hover over the mystery button to see its name before deciding whether to click it.

If you resize the Access window so that it's *really* small, you might run out of space for a section altogether. In that case, you get a single button that has the section's name. Click this button, and the missing commands appear in a drop-down panel (*Figure I-7*).

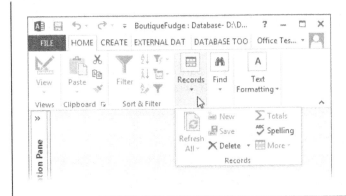

FIGURE I-7

In this example, Access doesn't have the room to display the Home tab's Views, Records, or Find sections, so they're all replaced with buttons. If you click any of these buttons, then a panel appears with the content you're looking for.

■ CONTEXTUAL TABS

Although nice, predictable tabs are a great idea, some features obviously make sense only in specific circumstances. Say you start designing a table. You may have a few more features than when you're entering data. Access handles this situation by adding one or more *contextual tabs* to the ribbon, based on your current task. These tabs have additional commands that are limited to a specific scenario (*Figure I-8*).

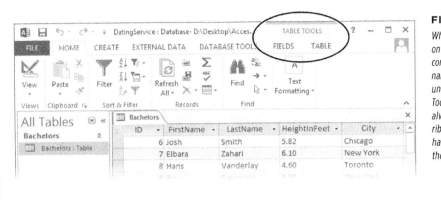

FIGURE I-8

When you're working on a table, two new contextual tabs appear, named Fields and Table, under the heading Table Tools. Contextual tabs always appear on the ribbon's right side and have the word "Tools" in their names.

When dealing with contextual tabs, the instructions in this book always include the title of the tab section (it's Table Tools in *Figure I-8*). Here's an example: "Choose Table Tools | Fields→Add & Delete→Text." Notice that this instruction's first part includes the contextual tab title (Table Tools) and the tab name (Fields), separated by the | character.

■ DROP-DOWN BUTTONS

From time to time you'll encounter buttons in the ribbon that have short menus attached to them. Depending on the button, this menu appears as soon as you click the button, or it appears only if you click the button's drop-down arrow, as shown in *Figure I-9*.

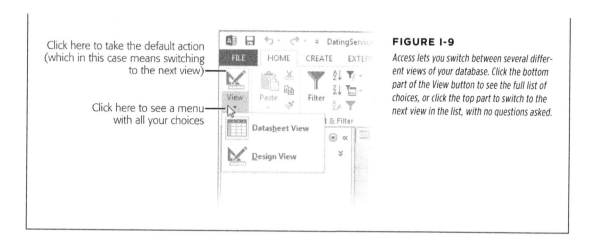

Click here to take the default action (which in this case means switching to the next view)

Click here to see a menu with all your choices

FIGURE I-9

Access lets you switch between several different views of your database. Click the bottom part of the View button to see the full list of choices, or click the top part to switch to the next view in the list, with no questions asked.

When dealing with this sort of button, the last step of the instructions in this book tells you what to choose from the drop-down menu. For example, say you're directed to "Home→Views→View→Design View." That tells you to select the Home tab, look for the Views section, click the drop-down part of the View button (to reveal the menu with extra options), and then choose Design View from the menu.

NOTE Be on the lookout for drop-down arrows in the ribbon—they're tricky at first. You need to click the *arrow* part of the button to see the full list of options. If you click the other part of the button, then you don't see the list. Instead, Access fires off the standard command (the one Access thinks is the most common choice), or the command you used most recently.

■ BACKSTAGE VIEW

When you see an instruction that includes arrows but starts with the word "File," it's telling you to go to Access's backstage view. For example, the sentence "Choose File→New" means click the **File** button to switch to backstage view, and then click the **New** command (which appears in the narrow list on the left). To take another look at backstage view and the list of commands it offers, jump back to *Figure I-6* on page 11.

■ ORDINARY MENUS

As you've already seen, the ribbon has taken the spotlight from traditional toolbars and menus. However, in a couple of cases, you'll still use the familiar Windows menu, like when you use the Visual Basic editor (in Chapter 18). In this case, the arrows refer to menu levels. The instruction "Choose File→Open" means "Click the **File** menu heading. Then, inside the File menu, click the **Open** command."

About Shortcut Keys

Every time you take your hand off the keyboard to move the mouse, you lose a few microseconds of time. That's why many experienced computer fans use keystroke combinations instead of toolbars and menus wherever possible. Ctrl+S, for one, is a keyboard shortcut that saves your current work in Access (and most other programs).

When you see a shortcut like Ctrl+S in this book, it's telling you to hold down the **Ctrl** key, and, while it's down, press the letter **S**, and then release both keys. Similarly, the finger-tangling shortcut Ctrl+Alt+S means hold down Ctrl, then press and hold Alt, and then press S (so that all three keys are down at once).

■ About the Online Resources

As the owner of a Missing Manual, you've got more than just a book to read. Online, you'll find example files so you can get some hands-on experience, as well as tips, articles, and maybe even a video or two. You can also communicate with the Missing Manual team and tell us what you love (or hate) about the book. Head over to *www.missingmanuals.com*, or go directly to one of the following sections.

Missing CD

As you read this book, you'll see a number of examples that demonstrate Access features and techniques for building good databases. Most of these examples are available as Access database files in a separate download. Go to to *www.missingmanuals.com/cds/access2013mm*, where you can download a Zip file that includes the examples, organized by chapter. And so you don't wear down your fingers typing long web addresses, the Missing CD page also offers a list of clickable links to the websites mentioned in this book.

Registration

If you register this book at oreilly.com, you'll be eligible for special offers—like discounts on future editions of *Access 2013: The Missing Manual*. Registering takes only a few clicks. To get started, type *http://oreilly.com/register* into your browser to hop directly to the Registration page.

Feedback

Got questions? Need more information? Fancy yourself a book reviewer? On our Feedback page, you can get expert answers to questions that come to you while reading, share your thoughts on this Missing Manual, and find groups for folks who share your interest in Access. To have your say, go to *www.missingmanuals.com/feedback*.

Errata

In an effort to keep this book as up to date and accurate as possible, each time we print more copies, we'll make any confirmed corrections you've suggested. We also note such changes on the book's website, so you can mark important corrections into your own copy of the book, if you like. Go to *http://tinyurl.com/acc2013-mm* to report an error and view existing corrections.

■ Safari® Books Online

Safari® Books Online is an on-demand digital library that lets you easily search over 7,500 technology and creative reference books and videos to find the answers you need quickly.

With a subscription, you can read any page and watch any video from our library online. Read books on your cellphone and mobile devices. Access new titles before they're available for print, and get exclusive access to manuscripts in development and post feedback for the authors. Copy and paste code samples, organize your favorites, download chapters, bookmark key sections, create notes, print out pages, and benefit from tons of other timesaving features.

Creating Your
First Database

Although Microsoft won't admit it, Access can be intimidating—intimidating enough to trigger a cold sweat in the most confident office worker. Even though Microsoft has spent millions of dollars making Access easier to use, most people still see it as the most complicated Office program on the block. They're probably right.

Access seems more daunting than any other Office program because of the way that databases work. Quite simply, databases need *strict rules*. Other programs aren't as obsessive. For example, you can fire up Word, and start typing a letter straight away. Or you can start Excel, and launch right into a financial report. But Access isn't nearly as freewheeling. Before you can enter a stitch of information into an Access database, you need to create that database's *structure*. And even after you've defined that structure, you'll probably want to spend more time creating other useful tools, like handy search routines and friendly forms that you can use to simplify data lookup and data entry. All of this setup takes effort and a good understanding of how databases work.

In this chapter, you'll conquer any Access resistance you have, and learn to create a simple but functional database. Along the way, you'll get acquainted with the slick Access user interface, and you'll learn exactly what you can store in a database. You'll then be ready to tackle the fine art of database design, which is covered in detail throughout this book.

Using Someone Else's Database

Can I use an Access database I didn't design?

Although every database follows the same two-step process: first somebody creates it and then people fill it with information, the same person doesn't need to perform both jobs. In fact, in the business world, different people often work separately on these two tasks.

For example, a summer student whiz-kid at a beer store may build a database for tracking orders (task #1). The sales department can then use the database to enter new orders (task #2), while other employees look up orders and fill them (also task #2). Warehouse staff can make

sure stock levels are OK (again, task #2), and the resident accountant can keep an eye on total sales (task #2).

If task #1 (creating the database) is done well, task #2 (using the database) can be extremely easy. In fact, if the database is well designed, people who have little understanding of Access can still use it to enter, update, and look up information. Amazingly, they don't even need to know they're running Access at all!

You'll learn more about sharing Access with groups of people in Part Six.

◼ Understanding Access Databases

As you already know, a database is a collection of information. In Access, every database is stored in a single file. That file contains *database objects*, which are the components of a database.

Database objects are the main players in an Access database. Altogether, you have six different types of database objects:

- **Tables** store information. Tables are the heart of any database, and you can create as many tables as you need to store different types of information. A fitness database could track your daily running log, your inventory of exercise equipment, and the number of high-protein whey milkshakes you down each day, as three separate tables.

- **Queries** let you quickly perform an action on a table. Usually, this action involves retrieving a choice bit of information (like the 10 top-selling food items at Ed's Roadside Diner or all the purchases you made in a single day). However, you can also use queries to apply changes.

- **Forms** are attractive windows that you create, arrange, and colorize. Forms provide an easy way to view or change the information in a table.

- **Reports** help you print some or all of the information in a table. You can choose where the information appears on the printed page, how it's grouped and sorted, and how it's formatted.

- **Macros** are mini-programs that automate custom tasks. Macros are a simple way to get custom results without becoming a programmer.

- **Modules** are files that contain Visual Basic code. You can use this code to do just about anything—from updating 10,000 records to firing off an email.

Access gurus refer to all these database ingredients as objects because you manage them all in essentially the same way. If you want to use a particular object, you add it to your database, give it a name, and then fine-tune it. Later on, you can view your objects, rename them, or delete ones you don't want anymore.

NOTE Designing a database is the process of adding and configuring database objects. For those keeping score, an Access database can hold up to 32,768 separate objects.

In this chapter, you'll consider only the most fundamental type of database object: *tables*. But first, you need to create a blank database you can work with.

■ Starting a Database

When you start Access, you begin at the welcome page. From there, you're just a few clicks away from generating a database of your very own.

In this chapter, you'll slap together a fairly straightforward database. This example is designed to store a list of prized bobblehead dolls. (For those not in the know, a bobblehead doll is a toy figure with an oversized head on a spring, hence the signature "bobbling" motion. Bobblehead dolls usually resemble a famous celebrity, politician, athlete, or fictional character.)

TIP You can get the Bobblehead database, and all the databases in this book, on the Missing CD page at *www.missingmanuals.com/cds/access2013mm*.

Here's how to create a blank new database:

1. **Start Access.**

   Access starts you out with what is, for Microsoft, a remarkably streamlined window (*Figure 1-1*). Here you can create a new database or open an existing one.

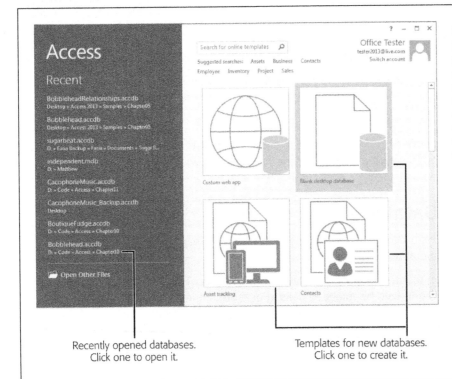

FIGURE 1-1

When you start Access, you see this two-part welcome page. On the left is a list of recently opened databases (if you have any). On the right is a list of templates that you can use to create a new database.

Recently opened databases.
Click one to open it.

Templates for new databases.
Click one to create it.

> **TIP** If you already have Access open and you've been working with another database, just choose File→New to create a new database. You'll get the same list of templates as when you first launch Access.

2. **Click the "Blank desktop database" template.**

When you choose to create a blank database, that's exactly what you get—a new, empty database file with no tables or other database objects. Starting from scratch is the best way to learn about Access. It's also the favorite choice of database experts, who prefer to create everything themselves so it's exactly the way they like it.

Other templates let you create databases that are preconfigured for specific scenarios and certain types of data. The box on page 27 has more information.

The cool-sounding "Custom web app" template is a special case. It lets you create a web-enabled database that runs on SharePoint. You'll explore this new feature (and its limitations), in Chapter 20.

No matter which template you click, Access pops open a new window that lets you choose a name and location for your new database (*Figure 1-2*).

UP TO SPEED

Templates: One Size Fits Some

The example in this section shows you how to create a blank database. However, if you scroll down (on the right side of the *Figure 1-1*), you'll find a long list of prebuilt databases, which are known as *templates*. Templates aim to save you the work of creating a new database and let you jump straight to the fine-tuning and data-entry stage.

As you might expect, there's a price to be paid for this convenience. Even if you find a template that stores the type of information you want to track, you might find that the pre-defined structure isn't quite right. For example, if you choose to use the Home Inventory template to track all the stuff in your basement, you might find that it's missing some information you want to use (like the projected resale value of your stuff

on eBay) and includes other details you don't care about (like the date you acquired each item). To make this template work, you'll need to change the design of your table, which involves the same Access know-how as creating one.

In this book, you'll learn how to build your own databases from the ground up and customize every square inch of them. Once you're an Access master, you can spend many fun hours playing with the prebuilt templates and adapting them to suit your needs. To give it a whirl, click one of a dozen or so templates that are shown in the main Access window. Or, even better, hunt for more by using the Search box at the top of the Access window, which scans through the thousands of templates available on Microsoft's Office website.

3. **Type a file name for the database you're about to create.**

   Access stores all the information for a database in a single file with the extension *.accdb* (which stands for "Access database"). Don't stick with the name Access picks automatically (like "Database1.accdb"). Instead, pick something more descriptive. In this example, Bobblehead.accdb does the trick.

   As with any other file, Access files can contain a combination of letters, spaces, numbers, parentheses, hyphens (-), and the underscore (_). It's generally safest to stay away from other special characters, some of which aren't allowed.

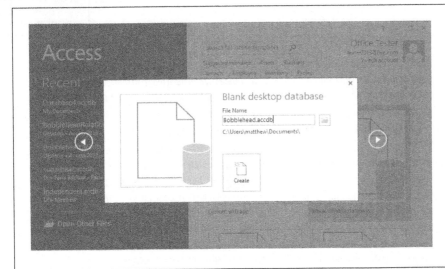

FIGURE 1-2

This database will be named Bobblehead.accdb. As you can see by the file path below the File Name box, it will be saved in the folder C:\Users\ matthew\Documents. You can edit the file name by typing in the File Name box, and you can browse to a different folder by clicking the folder icon.

NOTE Depending on your computer settings, Windows may hide file extensions. Instead of seeing the Access database file MyScandalousWedding.accdb in file-browsing tools like Windows Explorer, you may just see the name MyScandalousWedding (without the .accdb part on the end). In this case, you can still tell the file type by looking at the icon. If you see a small Access icon next to the file name, that's your signal that you're looking at an Access database.

4. **Choose the folder where you want to store your database.**

   Like all Office programs, Access assumes you want to store every file you create in your personal Documents folder. If this isn't what you want, click the folder icon to show the File New Database window, browse to the folder you want (*Figure 1-3*), and then click OK.

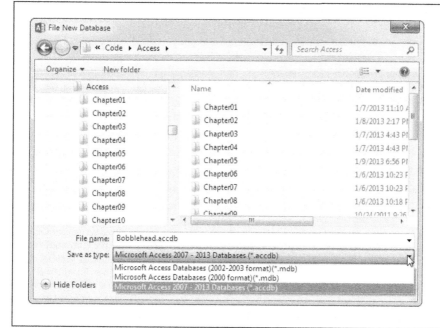

FIGURE 1-3

The File New Database window lets you choose where you'll store a new Access database file. It also gives you the option to create your database in the format used by older versions of Access (.mdb), instead of the more modern format used by Access 2007, Access 2010, and Access 2013 (.accdb). To change the format, simply choose the corresponding Access version from the "Save as type" list, as shown here.

5. **Click the big Create button (under the File Name box).**

   Access creates your database file and then shows a datasheet where you can get to work creating your first table.

Telling Access Where to Store Your Databases

Access always assumes you want to store databases in your Documents folder. And though you can choose a different location every time you save or open a database, if there's another folder you need to visit frequently, then it makes sense to make that your standard database storage location. You can configure Access to use this folder with just a few steps:

1. Make sure you've opened a database or created a new one. You can't make this change from the window you

see when you first start Access.

2. Choose File→Options. The Access Options window appears.

3. In the list on the left, choose General.

4. In the page on the right, look for the "Creating databases" heading. Underneath, you'll find a "Default database folder" text box. Type the path to the folder you want to use (like *C:\MyDatabases*), or click Browse to navigate to it.

When you're finished, click OK to save your changes.

Once you create or open a database, the Access window changes quite a bit. An impressive-looking toolbar (the *ribbon*) appears at the top of your screen, and a

Navigation Pane shows up on the left. You're now in the control center where you'll perform all your database tasks (*Figure 1-4*).

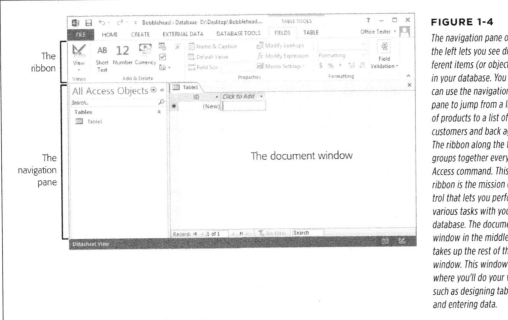

The ribbon

The navigation pane

FIGURE 1-4

The navigation pane on the left lets you see different items (or objects) in your database. You can use the navigation pane to jump from a list of products to a list of customers and back again. The ribbon along the top groups together every Access command. This ribbon is the mission control that lets you perform various tasks with your database. The document window in the middle takes up the rest of the window. This window is where you'll do your work, such as designing tables and entering data.

If you haven't used the ribbon before (either in Access or in another Office program), the Introduction covers the basics of how the ribbon works. Otherwise, carry on to the next section, where you'll learn how to add a table to your brand-new, empty database.

■ Building Your First Table

Tables are information containers. Every database needs at least one table—without it, you can't store any data. In a simple database, like the Bobblehead database, a single table (which we'll call Dolls) is enough. But if you find yourself wanting to store several lists of related information, you need more than one table. In the database BigBudgetWedding.accdb, you may want to keep track of the guests that you invited to your wedding, the gifts that you requested, and the loot that you actually received. In Chapter 5, you'll see plenty of examples of databases that use multiple tables.

Figure 1-5 shows a sample table.

The name of the table   A field named Character

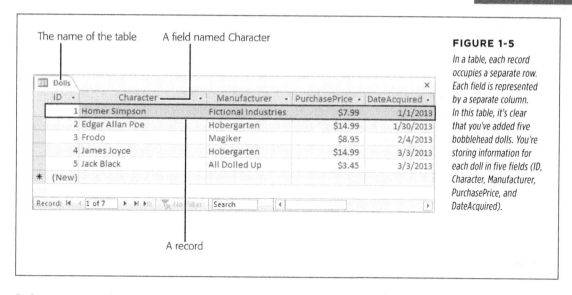

FIGURE 1-5

In a table, each record occupies a separate row. Each field is represented by a separate column. In this table, it's clear that you've added five bobblehead dolls. You're storing information for each doll in five fields (ID, Character, Manufacturer, PurchasePrice, and DateAcquired).

A record

Before you start designing this table, you need to know some very basic rules:

- **A table is a group of** *records*. A record is a collection of information about a single thing. In the Dolls table, for example, each record represents a single bobblehead doll. In a Family table, each record would represent a single relative. In a Products table, each record would represent an item that's for sale. You get the idea. When you create a new database, Access starts you out with a new table named *Table1*, although you can choose a more distinctive name when you decide to save it.

- **Each record is subdivided into** *fields*. Each field stores a distinct piece of information. For example, in the Dolls table, one field stores the person on whom the doll is based, another field stores the price, another field stores the date you bought it, and so on.

- **Tables have a rigid structure**. In other words, you can't bend the rules. If you create four fields, *every* record must have four fields (although it's acceptable to leave some fields blank if they don't apply).

- **Newly created tables get an ID field for free**. The ID field stores a unique number for each record. (Think of it as a reference number that will let you find a specific record later on.) The best part about the ID field is that you can ignore it when you're entering a new record. Access chooses a new ID number for you and inserts it in the record automatically. You'll learn much more about ID fields on page 83.

Database Planning for Beginners

Many database gurus suggest that before you fire up Access, you should decide exactly what information you want to store by brainstorming. Here's how it works. First, determine the type of list you want by finishing this sentence "I need a list of...." (One example: "I need a list of all the bobblehead dolls in my basement.")

Next, jot down all your must-have pieces of information on a piece of paper. Some details are obvious. For example, for the bobblehead doll collection, you'll probably want to keep track of the doll's name, price, and date you bought it. Other details, like the year it was produced, the company that created it, and a short description of its appearance or condition may require more thought.

Once you've completed this process and identified all the important bits of data you need, you're ready to create the corresponding table in Access. The bobblehead doll example demonstrates an important theme of database design: First you plan the database, and then you create it using Access. In Chapter 5, you'll learn a lot more about planning more complex databases.

Creating a Simple Table

When you first create a database, it's almost empty. But to get you started, Access creates your first database object—a table named Table1. The problem is, this table begins life completely blank, with no defined fields (and no data).

If you followed the steps in the previous section to create a new database, you're already at the *Datasheet view* (*Figure 1-5*), which is where you enter data into a table. All you need to do is customize this table so that it meets your needs.

You can customize a table in two ways:

- **Design view** lets you precisely define all aspects of a table before you start using it. Almost all database pros prefer Design view, and you'll start using it in Chapter 2.

- **Datasheet view** is where you enter data into a table. Datasheet view also lets you build a table on the fly as you insert new information. You'll use this approach in this chapter.

The following steps show you how to turn a blank new table (like Table1) into the Dolls table by using the Datasheet view:

1. **To define your table, simply add your first record.**

   In this case, that means choosing a bobblehead doll to add to the list. For this example, you'll use a nifty Homer Simpson replica.

NOTE It doesn't matter which doll you enter first. Access tables are *unsorted*, which means they have no underlying order. However, you can sort them any way you want when you need to retrieve information later on.

2. **In the datasheet's rightmost column, under the "Click to Add" heading, type the first piece of information for the record (see *Figure 1-6*).**

Based on the simple analysis you performed earlier, you know that you need to enter four fields of information for every doll. For the Homer Simpson doll, this information is "Homer Simpson" (the name), "Fictional Industries" (the manufacturer), "$7.99" (the price), and today's date (the purchase date). Although you could start with any field, it makes sense to begin with the name, which is clearly an identifying detail.

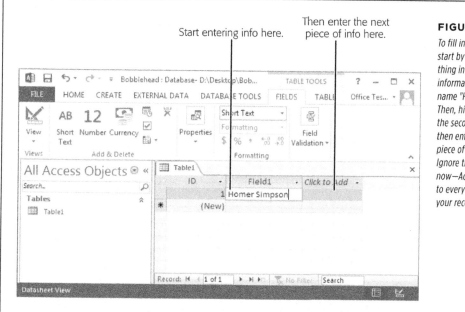

Start entering info here.

Then enter the next
piece of info here.

FIGURE 1-6

To fill in your first record, start by entering something in the first field of information (like the doll name "Homer Simpson"). Then, hit Tab to jump to the second column, and then enter the second piece of information. Ignore the ID column for now—Access adds that to every table to identify your records.

3. **Press Tab to move to the next field, and return to step 2.**

Repeat steps 2 and 3 until you've added every field you need, being careful to put each separate piece of information into a different column (*Figure 1-7*).

You may notice one quirk—a harmless one—when you add your first record. As you add new fields, Access may change the record's ID value of the record (changing it from 1 to 2 to 3, for example). Because the new record hasn't been inserted yet, every time you change the table's design by adding a new field, Access starts the process over and picks a new ID number, just to be safe. This automatic renumbering doesn't happen if you officially add the record (say, by moving down to the next row, or, in the ribbon, by clicking Home→Records→Save) and *then* add more fields to the table. However, there's really no reason to worry about the ID number. As long as it's unique—and Access guarantees that it is—the exact value is unimportant.

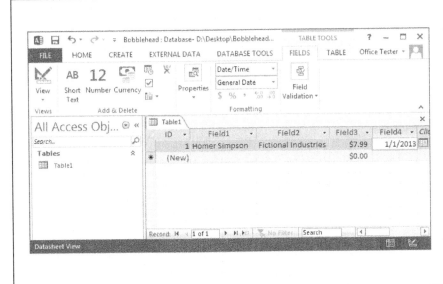

FIGURE 1-7

The only problem with this example so far is that as you enter a new record, Access creates spectacularly useless field names. You see its choices at the top of each column (they have names like Field1, Field2, Field3, and so on). The problem with using these meaningless names is that they may lead you to enter a piece of information in the wrong place. You could all too easily put the purchase price in the date column.

NOTE If you press Tab without entering any information, you'll move to the next row and start inserting a new record. If you make a mistake, you can backtrack using the arrow keys.

Putting Big Values in Narrow Columns

A single field can hold entire paragraphs of information. But if you have lengthy values, you may find yourself running out of viewing space while you're typing them into a narrow column. And although you're free to scroll forward and backward through your field, this gets annoying fast. Most people prefer to see the entire contents of a column at once.

Fortunately, you don't need to suffer in silence with cramped columns. To expand a column, just position your mouse at the right edge of the column header. (To expand a column named Field1, move your mouse to the right edge of the Field1 box.) Then, drag the column to the right to resize it as big as you want.

If you're just a bit impatient, there's a shortcut. Move the mouse over the right edge of the column, so it turns into a two-way arrow. Then, simply double-click the column edge. The column resizes itself to fit its largest piece of information (as long as doing so doesn't stretch the column beyond the edge of the Access window).

4. **It's time to fix your column names. Double-click the first column title (like Field1).**

   The field name switches into Edit mode.

5. **Type a new name, and then press Enter.**

Repeat this process until you've cleaned up all the field names. The proper field names for this example are Character, Manufacturer, PurchasePrice, and DateAcquired. *Figure 1-8* shows how it works.

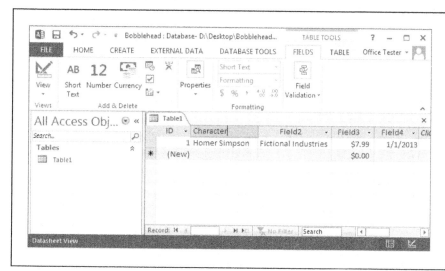

FIGURE 1-8

To specify better field names, double-click the column title. Next, type the real field name, and then press Enter. Page 90 has more about field naming, but for now just stick to short, text-only titles that don't include any spaces, as shown here.

TIP Don't be too timid about tweaking your table. You can always rename fields later, or even add entirely new fields. (It's also possible to *delete* existing fields, but that has the drawback of also clearing out all the data that's stored in the field.)

6. **Press Ctrl+S or choose File→Save to save your table.**

Access asks you to supply a table name (see *Figure 1-9*).

FIGURE 1-9

A good table name is a short text title that doesn't have any spaces (like Dolls here).

7. **Type a suitable table name, and then click OK.**

Congratulations! The table is now a part of your database.

NOTE Technically, you don't need to save your table right away. Access prompts you to save it when you close the datasheet (by clicking the X at the document window's top-right corner), or when you close Access.

As you can see, creating a simple table in Access is almost as easy as laying out information in Excel or Word. If you're itching to try again, you can create *another* table in your database by choosing Create→Tables→Table from the ribbon. But before you get to that stage, it makes sense to take a closer look at how you edit your table.

Editing a Table

You now have a fully functioning (albeit simple) database, complete with one table, which in turn contains one record. Your next step is filling your table with useful information. This often-tedious process is *data entry*.

To fill the Dolls table, you use the same datasheet you used to define the table. You can perform three basic tasks:

- **Editing a record**. Move to the appropriate spot in the datasheet (using the arrow keys or the mouse), and then type in a replacement value. You may also want to use Edit mode, which is described in the next section.

- **Inserting a new record**. Move down to the bottom of the table to the row that has an asterisk (*) on the left. This row doesn't actually exist until you start typing some information. At that point, Access creates the row and moves the asterisk down to the next row. You can repeat this process endlessly to add as many rows as you want (Access can handle millions).

- **Deleting a record**. You have several ways to remove a record, but the easiest is to right-click the margin immediately to the left of the record, and then choose Delete Record. Access asks you to confirm that you really want to remove the selected record, because you can't reverse the change later on.

WORD TO THE WISE

When in Doubt, Don't Delete

Most seasoned database designers rarely delete records from their databases. Every ounce of information is important.

For example, imagine you have a database that lists the products that a mail-order origami company has for sale. You might think it makes sense to delete products once they've been discontinued and can't be ordered anymore. But it turns out that it makes sense to keep these old product records around. For example, you might want to find out what product categories were the best sellers over the previous year. Or maybe a manufacturer issues a recall of asbestos-laced paper, and you need to track down everyone who ordered it. To perform either of these tasks, you need to refer to past product records.

This hang-onto-everything rule applies to any kind of database. For example, imagine you're tracking student enrollment at a top-flight culinary academy. When a class is finished, you can't just delete the class record. You might need it to find out whether a student has the right prerequisites for another course, which teachers she's had in the past, and so on.

The same is true for employees who retire, sales promotions that end, items that you used to own but you've sold, and so on. You need them all (and you probably need to keep them indefinitely).

In many cases, you'll add extra fields to your table to help you separate old data from the new. For example, you can create a Discontinued field in the Products table that identifies products that aren't available anymore. You can then ignore those products when you build an order-placement form.

■ EDIT MODE

You'll probably spend a lot of time working with the datasheet. So settle in. To make your life easier, it helps to understand a few details.

As you already know, you can use the arrow keys to move from field to field or row to row. However, you may have a bit of trouble editing a value. When you start typing, Access erases any existing content. To change this behavior, you need to switch into *Edit mode* by pressing F2; in Edit mode, your typing doesn't delete the stuff that's already in that field. Instead, you get to change or add to it. To switch out of Edit mode, you press F2 again. *Figure 1-10* shows a close-up look at the difference.

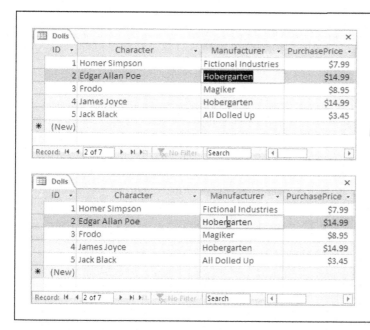

FIGURE 1-10

Top: Normal mode. If you start typing now, you'll immediately erase the existing text ("Hobergarten"). The fact that all the text in the field is selected is a big clue that you're about to wipe it out.

Bottom: Edit mode. The cursor shows where you're currently positioned in the current field. If you start typing now, you'll insert text in between "Hober" and "garten."

Edit mode also affects how the arrow keys work. In Edit mode, the arrow keys move through the current field. For example, to move to the next cell, you need to move all the way to the end of the current text, and then press the right arrow key again. But in Normal mode, pressing the arrow keys always moves you from cell to cell.

■ DATASHEET SHORTCUT KEYS

Power users know the fastest way to get work done is to use tricky keyboard combinations like Ctrl+Alt+Shift+*. Although you can't always easily remember these combinations, a couple of tables can help you out. Table 1-1 lists some useful keys that can help you whiz around the datasheet.

TABLE 1-1 *Keys for Moving Around the Datasheet*

KEY	RESULT
Tab (or Enter)	Moves the cursor one field to the right, or down when you reach the edge of the table. This key also turns off Edit mode if it's currently switched on.
Shift+Tab	Moves the cursor one field to the left, or up when you reach the edge of the table. This key also turns off Edit mode.
→	Moves the cursor one field to the right (in Normal mode), or down when you reach the edge of the table. In Edit mode, this key moves the cursor through the text in the current field.
←	Moves the cursor one field to the left (in Normal mode), or up when you reach the edge of the table. In Edit mode, this key moves the cursor through the text in the current field.
↑	Moves the cursor up one row (unless you're already at the top of the table). This key also turns off Edit mode.
↓	Moves the cursor down one row (or it moves you to the "new row" position if you're at the bottom of the table). This key also turns off Edit mode.
Home	Moves the cursor to the first field in the current row. This key brings you to beginning of the current field if you're in Edit mode.
End	Moves the cursor to the last field in the current row. This key brings you to the end of the current field if you're in Edit mode.
Page Down	Moves the cursor down one screenful (assuming you have a large table of information that doesn't all fit in the Access window at once). This key also turns off Edit mode.
Page Up	Moves the cursor up one screenful. This key also turns off Edit mode.
Ctrl+Home	Moves the cursor to the first field in the first row. This key doesn't do anything if you're in Edit mode.
Ctrl+End	Moves the cursor to the last field in the last row. This key doesn't do anything if you're in Edit mode.

Table 1-2 lists some convenient keys for editing records.

TABLE 1-2 *Keys for Editing Records*

KEY	RESULT
Esc	Cancels any changes you've made in the current field. This key works only if you use it in Edit mode. Once you move to the next cell, the change is applied. (For additional cancellation control, try the Undo feature, described next.)

KEY	RESULT
Ctrl+Z	Reverses the last edit. Unfortunately, the Undo feature in Access isn't nearly as powerful as it is in other Office programs. For example, Access lets you reverse only one change, and if you close the datasheet, you can't even do that. You can use Undo right after you insert a new record to remove it, but you can't use the Undo feature to reverse a delete operation.
Ctrl+"	Copies a value from the field that's immediately above the current field. This trick is handy when you need to enter a batch of records with similar information. *Figure 1-11* shows this often-overlooked trick in action.
Ctrl+;	Inserts today's date into the current field. The date format is based on computer settings, but expect to see something like "12-24-2013." You'll learn more about how Access works with dates on page 73.
Ctrl+Alt+Space	Replaces whatever value you've entered with the field's default value. You'll learn how to designate a default value on page 133.

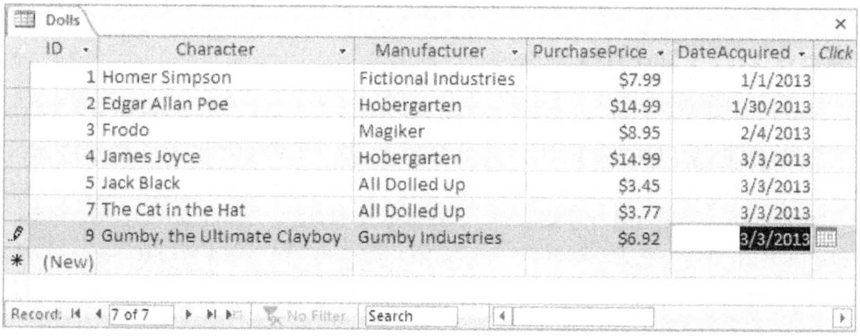

FIGURE 1-11

An Access user has been on an eBay buying binge and needs to add several doll records. With a quick Ctrl+" keystroke, you can copy the date from the previous record into the DateAcquired field of the new record.

CUT, COPY, AND PASTE

Access, like virtually every Windows program, lets you cut and paste bits of information from one spot to another. This trick is easy using just three shortcut keys: Ctrl+C to copy, Ctrl+X to cut (similar to copy, but the original content is deleted), and Ctrl+V to paste. When you're in Edit mode, you can use these keys to copy whatever you've selected. If you're not in Edit mode, the copying or cutting operation grabs all the content in the field.

Copying an Entire Record in One Step

Usually, you'll use copy and paste with little bits and pieces of data. However, Access has a little-known ability that lets you copy an *entire record*. To pull it off, follow these steps:

1. Click the margin to the left of the record you want to copy.

   This selects the record. (If you want to copy more than one adjacent record, hold down Shift, and then drag your mouse up or down until they're all selected.)

2. Right-click the selection, and then choose Copy.

This copies the content to the Clipboard.

3. Scroll to the bottom of the table until you see the new-row marker (the asterisk).

4. Right-click the margin just to the left of the new-row marker, and then choose Paste.

Presto—an exact duplicate. (Truth be told, one piece of data doesn't match exactly. Access updates the ID column for your pasted record, giving it a new number. That's because every record needs to have a unique ID. You'll learn why on page 88.)

Saving Databases

Unlike other programs, Access doesn't require that you save your data. It automatically saves any edits you make to the records in a table. This automatic-saving process takes place every time you change a record, and it happens almost instantaneously. It also takes place behind the scenes, and you probably won't notice anything. But don't be alarmed when you exit Access and it doesn't prompt you to save changes, as *any change to your data is saved the moment you make it*.

The rules are a bit different for database objects (page 24). When you add or edit a database object, Access waits until you finish and close the object, at which point it prompts you to save or discard your changes. If you're a bit paranoid and you can't stand the wait, just click the tiny Save icon in the Quick Access toolbar in the top-left corner of the window (it looks like a floppy disk) to save the current database object immediately.

NOTE Remember, when you click File, you enter Backstage view, which provides a narrow strip of commands (on the left) and a page with options for the currently selected command (on the right). You use Backstage view to open, save, and convert database files—see page 11 if you need a quick review about how it works.

Making Backups

The automatic save feature can pose a problem if you make a change mistakenly. If you're fast enough, you can use the Undo feature to reverse your last change (*Figure 1-12*). However, the Undo feature reverses only your most recent edit, so it's no help if you edit a series of records and then discover the problem. It also doesn't help if you close your table and then reopen it.

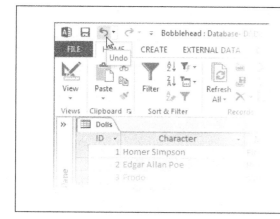

FIGURE 1-12

The Undo command appears in the Quick Access toolbar at the top left of the Access window, so it's always available.

For these reasons, it's a good idea to make frequent database backups. To make a database backup, you simply need to copy your database file to another folder, or make a copy with another name (like Bobblehead_Backup1.accdb). You can perform these tasks with Windows Explorer, but Access gives you an even easier option. First, choose File→Save As. Then, under the "File Types" heading, choose Save Database As. Finally, under the Save Database As heading, double-click Back Up Database. This opens a Save As window that offers to create a copy of your database, in the location you choose (*Figure 1-13*).

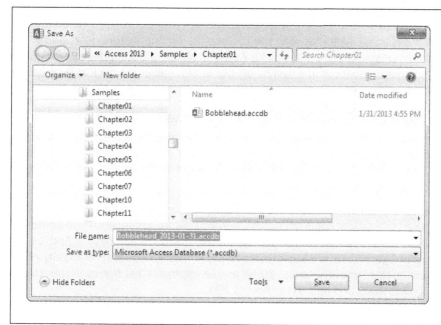

FIGURE 1-13

When you choose to create a backup, Access fills in a suggested file name that incorporates the current date. That way, if you have several backup files, you can pick out the one you want.

Of course, it's still up to you to remember to copy your database backup to another location (like a network server) or to a different type of storage (like a DVD or a USB memory stick), so you're ready when disaster hits.

What's with the .laccdb File?

I see an extra file with the extension .laccdb. What gives?

So far, you've familiarized yourself with the .accdb file type. But if you're in the habit of browsing around with Windows Explorer, you may notice another file that you didn't create, with the cryptic extension .laccdb. For example, if you're editing the Bobblehead.accdb database, you may spot a mysterious file named Bobblehead.laccdb.

Access creates a .laccdb file when you open a database file and removes it when you close the database, so you'll see it only

while you or someone else is browsing the database. Access uses the .laccdb to track who's currently using the database. The *l* stands for *lock*, and it's used to make sure that if more than one person is using the database at once, people can't make changes to the same record at the same time (which could cause all manner of headaches).

You'll learn more about how Access works with multiple users in Chapter 19, but for now it's safe to ignore the .laccdb file. You don't need to include it in your backups.

Saving a Database with a Different Name

Access makes this job easy. Just choose File→Save As and click the big Save As button. Access opens a Save As window, where you can browse to a different folder on your hard drive and type a new file name. When you're finished, click Save to seal the deal and create the newly named copy of your database.

Keep in mind that once Access creates the new database file, that file is the one it keeps using. In other words, if you create another table or edit some of your data, Access updates the *new* file. If you want to go back to the old file, you need to open it in Access again. (Alternatively, you can use the backup feature described in the previous section. Like the File→Save As command, the backup feature creates a copy of your database with a new name, but after it makes the backup it carries on using the original version.)

Saving a Database in a Different Format

When you create a new database, Access uses its modern *.accdb* format (which is short for "Access database"). Microsoft introduced the .accdb format with Access 2007, and it still works in Access 2010 and Access 2013. That makes it the go-to choice for new databases.

However, there may be times when you need to share your data with people who are using truly ancient copies of Access. Versions before Access 2007 use a different database format, called *.mdb* (which stands for "Microsoft database"). And, as you can see in *Figure 1-14*, the .mdb format actually comes in *two* versions: a really, really old version that supports Access 2000, and an improved that Microsoft introduced with Access 2002 and reused for Access 2003.

FIGURE 1-14

To change the format of your database, choose File→Save As (1), click Save Database As (2), and then pick the format you want from the "Database File Types" section (3). Use "Access 2002-2003 Database" or "Access 2000 Database" to save a .mdb file that works with very old versions of Access.

The standard .accdb format is the best choice if you don't need to worry about compatibility, because it has the best performance and a few extra features. But if you need to share databases with people running much older versions of Access, the .mdb format is your only choice.

> **TIP** Older database formats are less reliable and may not support all of the Access features you want to use. The best approach is to stick with the .accdb format and save a copy of your data in an older format for the people who need it. However, if possible, keep using the modern .accdb format as the master copy of your database—the one you'll use to enter new data and to create your Access queries, reports, and forms.

You can also use the old-style .mdb format when you first create a database. Choose File→New and then click the folder icon next to the File Name box. Access opens the File New Database window (which you saw back in *Figure 1-3*). It includes a "Save as type" box where you can choose the Access 2002-2003 file format or the even older Access 2000 format. (If you're set on going back any further, say the Access 95 format, your best bet is a time machine.)

Shrinking a Database

When you add information to a database, Access doesn't always pack the data as compactly as possible. Instead, Access is more concerned with getting information in and out of the database as quickly as it can.

After you've been working with a database for a while, you might notice that its size bloats up like a week-old fish in the sun. If you want to trim your database back to size, you can use a feature called *compacting*. To do so, just choose File→Info and click the big Compact & Repair Database button. Access then closes your database, compacts it, and opens it again. If it's a small database, these three steps unfold in seconds. The amount of space you reclaim varies widely, but it's not uncommon to have a 20 MB database shrink down to a quarter of its size.

NOTE If you compact a brand-new database, Access shows a harmless security warning when the database is reopened. You'll learn about this message, and how to avoid it, in the next section.

The only problem with the database-compacting feature is that you need to remember to use it. If you want to keep your databases as small as possible at all times, you can switch on a setting that tells Access to compact the current database every time you close it. Here's how:

1. **Open the database that you want to automatically compact.**

2. **Choose File→Options to get to the Access Options window.**

3. **In the list on the left, choose Current Database.**

4. **Under the Application Options heading, turn on the "Compact on Close" checkbox.**

5. **Click OK to save your changes.**

   Access tells you that this change has no effect until you close and reopen your database.

You can set the "Compact on Close" setting on as few or as many databases as you want. Just remember, it's not switched on when you first create a new database.

◼ Opening Databases

Once you've created a database, it's easy to open it later. The first step is go backstage; choose File→Open. There you'll see a list of all the databases you've viewed most recently (*Figure 1-15*). To open one, just click it. Incidentally, you see the same list of recent databases when you first start Access (*Figure 1-1*).

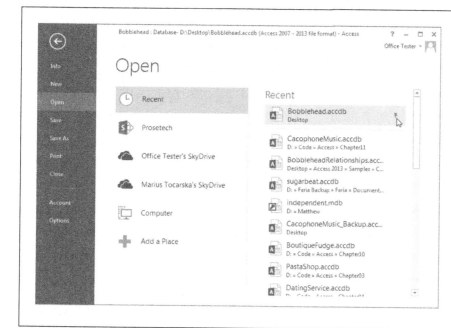

FIGURE 1-15

The Recent Databases's biggest advantage is the way it lets you keep important files at your fingertips by using pinning. To try it, click the thumbtack next to the database file you want to keep. Access moves your database to the top of the list and keeps it there. From this point on, that database won't leave the list, no matter how many databases you open. If you decide to stop working with the database later on, just click the thumbtack again to release it.

TIP Do you want to hide your recent work? You can remove any file from the Recent Databases list by right-clicking it and choosing "Remove from list." And if the clutter is keeping you from finding the databases you want, just pin the important files, right-click any file, and choose "Clear unpinned items." This action removes every file that isn't pinned down.

Ordinarily, Access tracks the previous 25 databases in the File→Recent list, but you can tell it to keep a shorter or longer list. To change this setting, choose File→Options, choose Client Settings, scroll down to the Display section, and change the number for "Show this number of Recent Documents." You can pick any number from 0 to 50.

If you want to open a database that's on your computer but not on the list of recent databases, you can browse your way to the file. Start by choosing File→Open, and, in the Places list, click Computer (*Figure 1-16*). Click one of the folders you've recently used, and Access shows an Open window listing the files in that location. Or, just click the big Browse button underneath to hunt around in the current folder. When you find the file you want, double-click it.

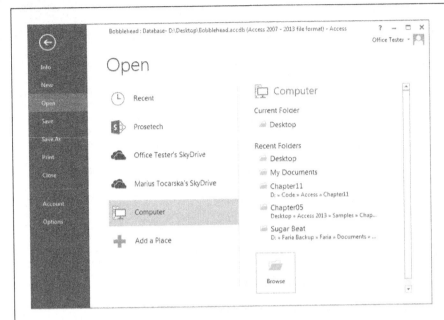

FIGURE 1-16

When you click Places, Access shows you a list of folders in which you've recently opened or saved databases. Click one, and Access shows you the familiar Open window for that folder.

TIP You can also grab files from your SkyDrive file-sharing account, if you've configured it in Access. However, this is strictly a one-way street: you can download databases from your SkyDrive folder, but you can't upload new ones from Access. In other words, you'll use SkyDrive as a way to transfer databases from one computer to another, not as a permanent home for your databases. If you want to keep your database on the Web, you need the web database feature described in Chapter 20. (And to learn more about Microsoft's SkyDrive service, visit *http://tinyurl.com/skydr.*)

Finally, as always, you can open a database file from outside Access by simply double-clicking it in Windows Explorer or on your desktop.

Designating a Database as Trusted

When you open a database for the first time, you'll notice something a little bizarre. Access pops up a message bar with a scary-sounding security warning (*Figure 1-17*).

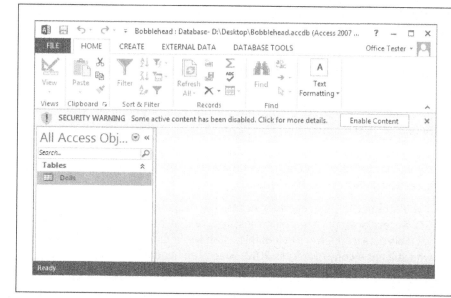

FIGURE 1-17

This security warning tells you that Access doesn't trust your database—in other words, it's opened your file in a special safe mode that prevents your database from performing any risky operations.

If you're opening your own recently created database, this security warning is a bit confusing, because right now your database doesn't even *attempt* to do anything risky. However, once you start building databases with code routines (as described in Part Five), or when you start using action queries (Chapter 8), it's a different story. In those situations, you need to know if Access trusts your database and will allow it to run code and action queries.

In the meantime, you're probably wondering what you should do about the message bar. You have two options:

- Click the X at the right side of the message bar to banish it. (But it'll reappear the next time you open the database.)

- Click Enable Content to tell Access that it can trust this database. Access won't bother you again about this file, unless you rename the database file or move it to a new folder. This arrangement is called *trusted documents*, and it's described in more detail on page 512.

Opening More Than One Database at Once

Every time you use the File→Open command, Access closes the current database and then opens the one you chose. If you want to see more than one database at a time, you need to fire up more than one copy of Access at the same time. (Computer geeks refer to this action as starting more than one *instance* of a program.)

It's almost embarrassingly easy. If you double-click another database file while Access is already open, a second Access window appears in the taskbar for that database.

You can also launch a second (or third, or fourth...) instance of Access from the Start menu, and then use File→Open to load up a different database in each one.

Opening a Database Created in an Older Version of Access

You can use the File→Open command to open an Access database created with a previous version of Access.

Access handles old database files differently, depending on just how old they are. Here's how it works:

- If you open an Access 2002-2003 file, you don't get any notification or warning. Access keeps the current format, and you're free to make any changes you want.

- If you open an Access 2000 file, you're also in for smooth sailing. However, if you change the design of the database, the new parts you add may not be accessible in Access 2000 anymore.

- If you attempt to open an older Access file (like one created for Access 95 or 97), Access presents a warning message...and gives up. If you need to rescue valuable data trapped in a Paleolithic database, your best bet is to find someone who still has a copy of Access 2010, which can handle older file formats.

TIP You can tell the current database's format by looking at the text in parentheses in the Access window's title bar. For example, if you open an Access 2002-2003 file, the title bar will include the text "(Access 2002-2003 file format)."

When you open an old-school Access database, you'll notice something else has changed. When you open a table, it doesn't appear in a tabbed window like the ones shown in *Figure 1-19*. Instead, the table opens in an ordinary window that can float wherever it wants *inside* the main Access window. This seems fine at first, until you open several tables at once. Then, you're stuck with some real clutter, as shown in *Figure 1-18*.

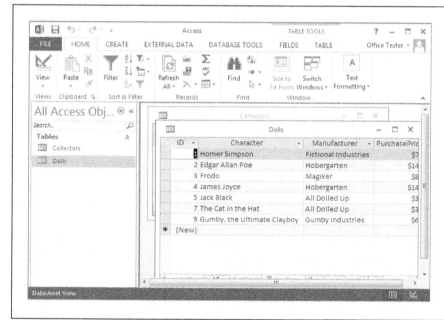

FIGURE 1-18

*In an old-style Access da-
tabase, different windows
can overlap each other.
It's not long before the
table you want is buried
at the bottom of a stack
of windows.*

This somewhat unfriendly behavior is designed to mimic old versions of Access,
like Access 2003. But don't worry—you can get back to the slick tabs even if you
don't convert your database to the new format. All you need to do is set a single
configuration option:

1. **Choose File→Options.**

2. **In the list on the left, choose Current Database.**

3. **Under the Application Options heading, look for the Document Windows
   Options setting, where you can choose Overlapping Windows (the Access
   2003 standard) or Tabbed Windows (the wave of the future).**

4. **Click OK.**

5. **Close and open your database so the new setting takes effect.**

For a retro touch, you can use the same setting to make a brand-new Access database use overlapping windows instead of tabs.

■ The Navigation Pane

It's time to step back and take a look at what you've accomplished so far. You've
created the Bobblehead database and added a single database object: a table

named Dolls. You've filled the Dolls table with several records. You don't have the fancy windows, reports, and search routines that make a database work smoothly, but you do have the most important ingredient—organized data.

One issue you haven't tackled yet is how you manage the objects in your database. For example, if you have more than one table, you need a way to move back and forth between the two. That tool is the navigation pane, shown in *Figure 1-19*.

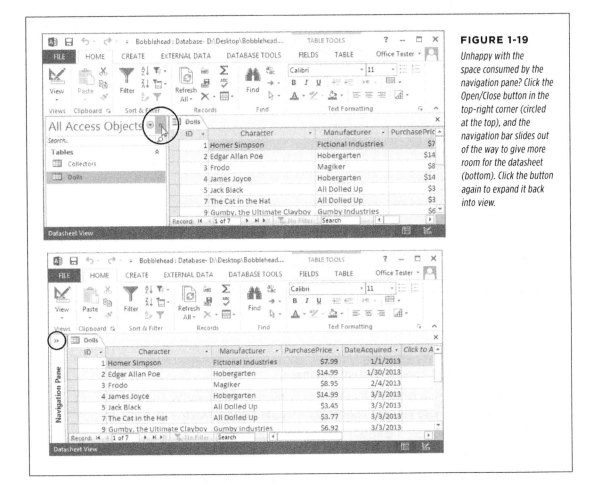

FIGURE 1-19

Unhappy with the space consumed by the navigation pane? Click the Open/Close button in the top-right corner (circled at the top), and the navigation bar slides out of the way to give more room for the datasheet (bottom). Click the button again to expand it back into view.

Browsing Tables with the Navigation Pane

The navigation pane shows the objects (page 24) that are part of your database, and it lets you manipulate them. However, you don't necessarily see all your database objects at all times. The navigation pane has several different viewing modes, so you can home in on exactly what interests you.

When you first create a database, the navigation pane shows only the tables in your database. That's good enough for now—after all, your database doesn't contain anything but the tables you've created. (You'll learn how to customize the navigation pane in Chapter 14.)

To try out the navigation pane, you need a database with more than one table. To give it a whirl, choose Create→Tables→Table from the ribbon to add a new blank table. Follow the steps starting on page 32 to define the table and insert a record or two.

> **TIP** Not sure what table to create? Try creating a Collectors table that tracks all the friends you know who share the same bobbleheaded obsession. Now try to come up with a few useful fields for this table (while remembering that there's no need to go crazy with the details yet), and then compare your version to the example in *Figure 1-20*.

Once you've added the new table, you see both the new table and the old in the navigation pane at the same time. If you want to open a table, then, in the navigation pane, just double-click it. If you have more than one datasheet open at once, Access organizes them into tabs (see *Figure 1-20*).

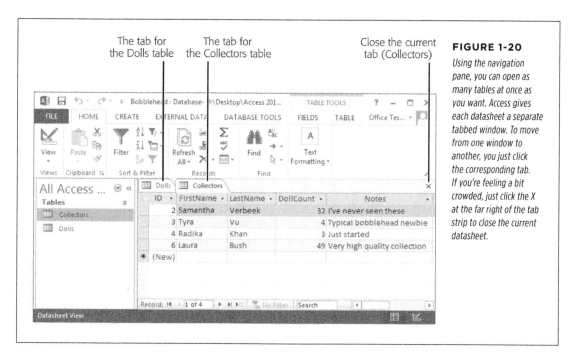

The tab for the Dolls table   The tab for the Collectors table   Close the current tab (Collectors)

FIGURE 1-20

Using the navigation pane, you can open as many tables at once as you want. Access gives each datasheet a separate tabbed window. To move from one window to another, you just click the corresponding tab. If you're feeling a bit crowded, just click the X at the far right of the tab strip to close the current datasheet.

If you open enough tables, eventually all the tabs won't fit. In this situation, Access adds tiny scroll buttons to the left and right of the tab strip. You can use these buttons to move through all the tabs, but it takes longer.

Collapsing the Ribbon

Most people are happy to have the ribbon sitting at the top of the Access window, with all its buttons on hand. However, serious data crunchers demand maximum space for their data. They'd rather look at another record of information than a pumped-up toolbar. If this preference describes you, you'll be happy to know you can *collapse* the ribbon, shrinking it down to a single row of tab titles, as shown in *Figure 1-21*. To do so, just double-click the current tab title.

Even when the ribbon is collapsed, you can still use all its features. Just click a tab. If you click Home, the Home tab pops up over your worksheet. As soon as you click the button you want in the Home tab (or click somewhere else in the Access

window), the ribbon collapses itself again. The same trick works if you trigger a command in the ribbon using the keyboard, as described on page 9.

If you use the ribbon only occasionally, or if you prefer to use keyboard shortcuts, it makes sense to collapse the ribbon. Even when collapsed, the ribbon commands are available; it just takes an extra click to open the tab. On the other hand, if you make frequent trips to the ribbon, or if you're learning about Access and you like to browse the ribbon to see the available features, don't bother collapsing it. The extra space that you'll lose is well worth it.

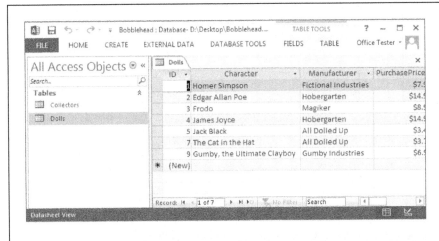

FIGURE 1-21

Do you want to use every square inch of screen space for your data? You can collapse the ribbon (as shown here) by double-clicking any tab. Click a tab to pop it open temporarily, or double-click a tab to bring the ribbon back for good. And if you want to perform the same trick without raising your fingers from the keyboard, you can use the shortcut key Ctrl+F1.

Managing Database Objects

So far, you know how to open a table using the navigation pane. However, opening tables isn't all you can do with the navigation pane. You can actually perform three more simple tasks with any database object that shows up in the navigation pane:

- **Rename it**. Right-click the object, and then choose Rename. Type in the new name, and then press Enter. Go this route if you decide your Dolls table would be better off named DollsInMyWorldRenownedCollection.

- **Create a copy**. Right-click the object, and then choose Copy. Right-click any-where in the navigation pane, and then choose Paste. Access prompts you to supply the new copy's name. The copy-an-object feature is useful if you want to take an existing table and try redesigning it, but you're not ready to remove the original copy just yet.

- **Delete it**. Right-click the object, and then choose Delete. Access asks you to confirm this operation, because you can't reverse it with the Undo command.

Access gives you a few more options for transferring database objects and tucking them out of sight. You'll consider these features later in the book.

TIMESAVING TIP

Creating a Shortcut to a Table

You probably already know that you can place a Windows shortcut on your desktop that points to your database file. To do so, just right-click your desktop, choose New→Shortcut, and then follow the instructions to pick your database file and choose a shortcut name. Now, anytime you want to jump back into your database, you can double-click your shortcut.

You probably don't know that you can create a shortcut that opens a database *and* navigates directly to a specific table. In fact, this maneuver is even easier than creating a plain-vanilla shortcut. Just follow these steps:

1. Resize the Access window so it doesn't take up the full screen, and then minimize any other programs. This way,

you can see the desktop behind Access, which is essential for this trick.

2. Find the table you want to use in the navigation pane. Drag this table out of Access and over the desktop.

3. Release the mouse button. Access creates a shortcut with a name like "Shortcut to Dolls in Bobblehead. Accdb." Double-click this shortcut to load the Bobblehead database and to open a datasheet right away for the Dolls table.

Building Smarter Tables

I n the previous chapter, you learned how to dish out databases and pop tables into them without breaking a sweat. However, there's bad news. The tables you've been creating so far aren't up to snuff.

Most significantly, you haven't explicitly told Access what *type* of information you intend to store in each field of your table. A database treats text, numbers, dates, and other types of information differently. If you store numeric information in a field that expects text, you can't do calculations later on (like find the average value of your bobblehead dolls), and you can't catch mistakes (like a bobblehead with a price value of "fourscore and twenty").

To prevent problems like these, you need to define the *data type* of each field in your table. You'll tackle this important task in this chapter. Once you've mastered data types, you're ready to consider some of the finer points of database design.

Understanding Data Types

All data is not created equal. Consider the Dolls table you created in Chapter 1 (page 30). Its fields actually contain several different types of information:

- **Text**. The Character and Manufacturer fields
- **Numbers**. The ID and PurchasePrice fields
- **Dates**. The DateAcquired field

You may naturally assume that the PurchasePrice field always includes numeric content and that the DateAcquired field always includes something that can be interpreted as a date. But if you haven't set the data types correctly, Access doesn't share your assumptions and doesn't follow the same rules.

When you create a new field by typing away in Datasheet view, Access makes an educated guess about the data type by examining the information you've just typed in. If you type *44*, Access assumes you're creating a number field. If you type *Jan 6, 2013*, Access recognizes a date. However, it's easy to confuse Access, which leads to the problems shown in *Figure 2-1*.

FIGURE 2-1

Here, Access doesn't recognize the date format used for the DateAcquired field when it was created. As a result, Access treats that field as ordinary text. There's nothing stopping you from entering dates in several different formats, which makes the DateAcquired information harder to read and impossible to sort. This field also lets in completely nonsensical entries, like "fourscore bananas."

To prevent invalid entries, you need to tell Access what each field *should* contain. Once you set the rules, Access enforces them rigorously. You put these requirements in place using another window—your table's Design view.

■ Design View

When you create a new database, Access starts you off with a single table and shows that table in Datasheet view. (As you learned last chapter, Datasheet view is the grid-like view where you can create a table *and* enter data.) To switch to Design view, right-click the tab name (like "Dolls"), and then choose Design View. (Or you can use the Home→Views→View command or the View buttons at the bottom of the Access window. *Figure 2-2* shows all your options. All of these commands do the same thing, so pick whichever approach seems most convenient.)

NOTE If you've opened a truly old Access 2003 database, you won't see any tabs. Instead, you'll get a bunch of overlapping windows. You can remedy this problem and get your tabs back by following the instructions on page 49. Or, if you want to keep the overlapping windows, just use the View buttons or the ribbon to change views (instead of the right-click-the-tab-title approach described above).

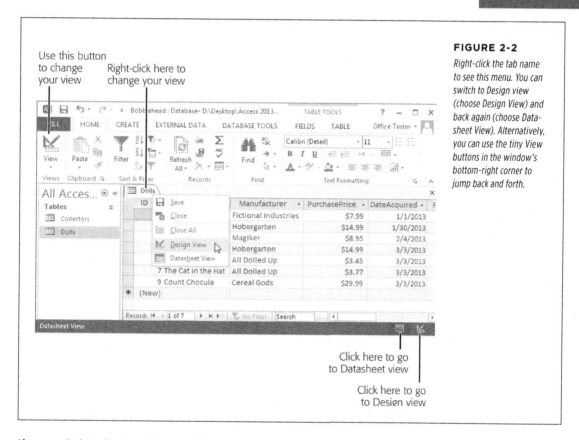

Use this button to change your view

Right-click here to change your view

Click here to go to Datasheet view

Click here to go to Design view

FIGURE 2-2

Right-click the tab name to see this menu. You can switch to Design view (choose Design View) and back again (choose Datasheet View). Alternatively, you can use the tiny View buttons in the window's bottom-right corner to jump back and forth.

If you switch to Design view on a brand-new table that you haven't saved yet, Access asks you for a table name. Access then saves the table before switching you to Design view.

TIP For a handy shortcut, you can create a new table and automatically start in Design view. To do this, choose Create→Tables→Table Design. However, when you take this route, your table doesn't include the very important ID column, so you need to add one yourself, as you'll see shortly.

While Datasheet view shows the content in your table, Design view shows only its *structure* (see *Figure 2-3*).

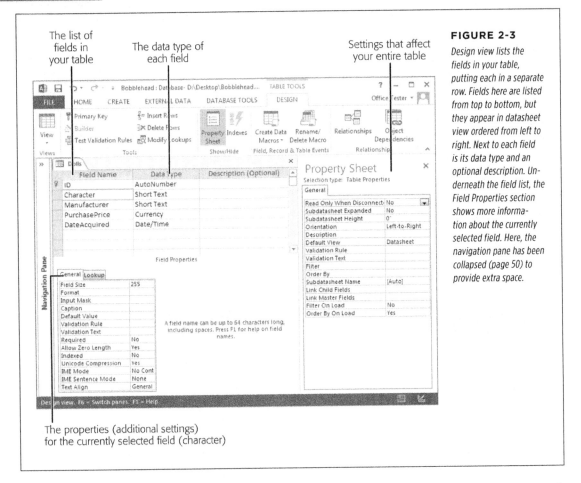

The list of fields in your table

The data type of each field

Settings that affect your entire table

FIGURE 2-3

Design view lists the fields in your table, putting each in a separate row. Fields here are listed from top to bottom, but they appear in datasheet view ordered from left to right. Next to each field is its data type and an optional description. Underneath the field list, the Field Properties section shows more information about the currently selected field. Here, the navigation pane has been collapsed (page 50) to provide extra space.

The properties (additional settings) for the currently selected field (character)

You can use Design view to add, rearrange, and remove fields, but you can't use it to add new records. In the Dolls table, you can use Design view to add a Quantity field to keep track of doll duplicates. However, you can't add your newly purchased Bono bobblehead without switching back to the Datasheet view. Design view isn't intended for data entry.

If the Property Sheet box is open on the window's right side, you may want to close it to reclaim more space. (The Property Sheet lets you set a few highly technical table settings, none of which you need to consider right now.) To banish it, choose Table Tools | Design→Show/Hide→Property Sheet. To bring it back later, just repeat the same command.

Organizing and Describing Your Fields

Design view lets you rearrange the order of your fields, add new ones, rename the existing ones, and more. You can also do all these things in Datasheet view, but Access gurus usually find it's easier to make these changes in Design view, without being distracted by the data in the table.

Here are a few simple ways you can change the structure of your table in Design view:

- **Add a new field to the end of your table**. Scroll to the last row of the field list, and then type in a new field name. This action is equivalent to adding a new field in Datasheet view.

- **Add a new field between existing fields**. Move to the field that's just *under* the place where you want to add the new field. Right-click the field, and then choose Insert Rows. Then, type a field name in the new, blank row.

- **Move a field**. Click the gray square immediately to the left of the field you want to move, and release the mouse button. This selects the field. Then, click the gray square, and drag the field to the new position.

> **NOTE** Remember, the order of your fields isn't all that important, because you can change the order in which you view the fields in Datasheet view. However, most people find it's easier to design a table if they organize the fields from the start.

- **Delete a field**. Right-click the gray square immediately to the left of the field you want to remove, and then choose Delete Rows. Keep in mind that when you remove a field, you also wipe out any data that was stored in that field. This action isn't reversible, so Access prompts you to confirm that it's really what you want to do (unless the table is completely empty).

- **Add a description for a field**. Type in a sentence or two in the Description column next to the appropriate field. (You might use "The celebrity or fictional character that this bobblehead resembles" as the description for the Character field in the Dolls table, as shown in *Figure 2-4*.)

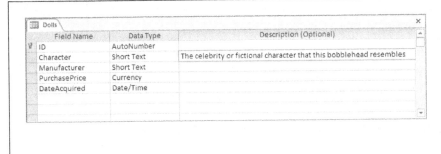

FIGURE 2-4

Descriptions can help you remember what's what if you need to modify a table later on. Descriptions are a great idea if more than one person maintains the same database, in which case you need to make sure your fields are as clear as possible. Descriptions also appear in the status bar when you're entering information in a table.

NOTE Previous versions of Access used the description for another purpose. When someone was editing a record, the description of the corresponding field appeared in the status bar. Access 2013 discontinues this practice, which was found to be relatively useless, because most people never think to look down in the status bar.

How Updates Work in Design View

Access doesn't immediately apply the changes you make in Design view. Instead, it waits until you close the table or switch back to Datasheet view. At that point, Access asks whether you want to save the table. (The answer, of course, is Yes.)

Sometimes, you may apply a change that causes a bit of a problem. You could try to change the data type of a field so that it stores numbers instead of text. (The box on page 64 discusses this problem in more detail.) In this situation, you won't discover the problem until you close the table or switch back to Datasheet view, which may be a little later than you expect.

If you've made a potentially problematic change and you just can't take the suspense, you're better off applying your update *immediately*, so you can see if there's a problem before you go any further. To do so, click the Quick Access toolbar's Save button (it's the diskette icon in the Access window's top-left corner), or just use the keyboard shortcut Ctrl+S. Access applies your change and saves the table. If it runs into a problem, Access tells you about it (and lets you choose how you want to fix it) before you do anything else with the table.

Access Data Types

Design view is a powerful place for defining a table. Design view lets you tweak all sorts of details without jumping around the ribbon (as you would if you were creating a table in Datasheet view).

One of the details is the *data type* of each field—a setting that tells Access what type of information you're planning to store in it. To change the data type, make a selection in the Data Type column next to the appropriate field (*Figure 2-5*). Here's where you separate the text from numbers (and other data types). The trick is choosing the best data type from the long list Access provides—you'll get more help for that in the following section.

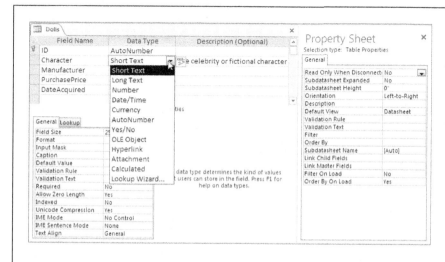

FIGURE 2-5

To choose a data type, click the Data Type column next to the appropriate field. A drop-down list box appears, with 12 choices.

Depending on the data type you choose, you can adjust other *field properties* to nail down your data type even more precisely. If you use a text data type, you use field properties to set the maximum length. If you choose a decimal value, you use field properties to set the number of decimal places. You set field properties in the Field Properties part of the Design view, which appears just under the field list. You'll learn more about field properties throughout this chapter (and you'll consider them again in Chapter 4).

The most important decision you make for any field is choosing its data type. The data type tells Access what sort of information you plan to store in that field. Access uses this information to reject values that don't make sense (see *Figure 2-6*), to perform proper sorting, and to provide other features like calculations, summaries, and filtering.

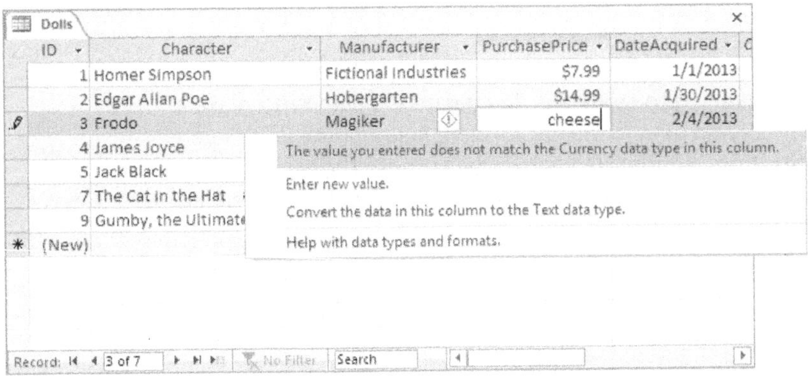

FIGURE 2-6

This currency field absolutely does not allow text. Access lets you fix the problem by entering a new value (the right choice) or changing the field data type to Text so that it allows anything (the absolutely wrong choice).

NOTE A field can have only one data type. You can't create a field that can store two or three different data types, because Access wouldn't have enough information to manage the field properly. (Instead, in this situation, you probably need two separate fields.)

As you learned earlier, there are three basic types of data in the world: text, numbers, and dates. However, Access actually provides a whopping *12* data types, which include many more specialized choices. Before you pick the right data type, it's a good idea to review all your choices. Table 2-1 shows an overview of the menu options in the Data Type list. (The Lookup wizard choice isn't included, because it isn't a real data type. Instead, this menu option launches the Lookup wizard, which lets you set a list of allowed values. You'll learn more about this on page 155 in Chapter 4.)

TABLE 2-1 *Access Data*

DATA TYPE	DESCRIPTION	EXAMPLES
Short Text	Numbers, letters, punctuation, and symbols, up to a maximum of 255 characters (an average-sized paragraph).	Names, addresses, phone numbers, and short product descriptions. This is one of the most commonly used data types.
Long Text (previously called Memo)	Large amounts of unformatted text, up to 65,536 characters (an average-sized chapter in a novel).	Long descriptions, articles, letters, arrest warrants, and other short documents. Unlike the Short Text data type, you can't sort records based on the data in a Long Text field.

DATA TYPE	DESCRIPTION	EXAMPLES
Number	Different kinds of numbers, including negative numbers and those that have decimal places.	Any type of number except currency values (for example, dollar amounts). Stores measurements, counts, and percentages.
Currency	Similar to Number, but optimized for numbers that represent values of money.	Prices, payments, and expenses.
Date/Time	A calendar date or time of day (or both). Don't use this field for time *intervals* (the number of minutes in a song, the length of your workout session)—instead, use the Number data type.	Birthdates, order dates, ship dates, appointments, and UFO sighting times.
Yes/No	Holds one of two values: Yes or No. (You can also think of this as True or False.)	Fields with exactly two options, like male/female or approved/unapproved.
Hyperlink	A URL to a website, an email address, or a file path.	www.FantasyPets.com, noreplies@antisocial.co.uk, C:\Documents\Report.doc.
Attachment	One or more separate files. The content from these files is copied into the database.	Pictures, Word documents, Excel spreadsheets, sound files, and so on.
AutoNumber	Stores a unique, identifying number that Access generates when you insert a new record.	Used to uniquely identify each record; typically set as the primary key (page 88). Usually, every table has a single AutoNumber field named ID.
Calculated	Generates the value automatically, based on an expression you supply. You can perform simple math and combine the values from other fields.	Values that depend on other fields. For example, if you already have a UnitCost and a Quantity field, you can add a TotalCost calculated field that multiplies them together.
OLE Object	Holds embedded binary data, according to the Windows OLE (object linking and embedding) standard. Rarely used, because it leads to database bloat and other problems. The Attachment field is almost always a better choice.	Some types of pictures and documents from other programs. Mostly used in old-school Access databases. Nowadays, database designers use the Attachment data type instead of the OLE Object data type, or they store the data in separate files outside of the database, and record the file name in a Short Text field.

The following sections describe each data type except for OLE Object, which is a holdover from the dark ages of Access databases. Each section also describes any important field properties that are unique to that data type.

Changing the Data Type Can Lose Information

The best time to choose the data types for your fields is when you first create the table. That way, your table is completely empty, and you won't run into any problems.

If you add a few records, and *then* decide to change the data type in one of your fields, life becomes a little more complicated. You can still use Design view to change the data type, but Access needs to go through an extra step and *convert* the existing data to the new data type.

In many cases, the conversion process goes smoothly. If you have a Short Text field that contains only numbers, you won't have a problem changing the data type from Short Text to Number. But in other cases, the transition isn't quite so seamless. Here are some examples of the problems you might run into:

- You change the data type from Short Text to Date, but Access can't interpret some of your values as dates.

- You change the data type from Short Text to Number, but

some of your records have text values in that field (even though they shouldn't).

- You change the data type from Short Text to Number. However, your field contains non-integer numbers (like 4.234), and you forget to change the Field Size property (page 70). As a result, Access assumes you want to use only whole numbers and chops off all your decimal places.

The best way to manage these problems is to make a backup (page 40) before you make any drastic changes, and to be on the lookout for changes that go wrong. In the first two cases in the list above, Access warns you that it needs to remove some values because they don't fit the data type rules (see *Figure 2-7*). The third problem is a little more insidious—Access gives you a warning, but it doesn't actually tell you whether a problem occurred. If you suspect trouble, switch to Datasheet view, and then check out your data before going any further.

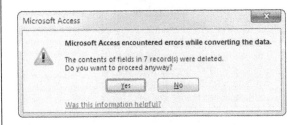

FIGURE 2-7

Don't say you weren't warned. Here, Access lets you know (in its own slightly obscure way) that it can't make the change you want—modifying the data type of field from Text to Date—without throwing out the values in seven records. The best course of action is to click No to cancel the change and then take a closer look at your table in Datasheet view to track down the problematic values.

Short Text

Short Text is the all-purpose data type. It accepts any combination of letters, numbers, and other characters. So you can use a Short Text field for a word or two (like "Mary Poppins"), a sentence ("The candidate is an English nanny given to flights of song."), or anything else ("@#$d sf_&!").

Sometimes it seems that the Short Text data type is just too freewheeling. Fortunately, you can apply some stricter rules that deny certain characters or force text values to match a preset pattern. For example, Access usually treats phone numbers like text, because they represent a series of characters like 123-4444 (not the single number 1,234,444). However, you don't want to let people put letters in a phone number, because they obviously don't belong. To put this restriction into action, you can use input masks (page 138) and validation (page 146), two features discussed in Chapter 4.

> **NOTE** Because Short Text fields are so lax, you can obviously enter numbers, dates, and just about anything else in them. However, you should use Short Text only when you're storing some information that can't be dealt with using another data type, because Access always treats the contents of a Short Text field as plain, ordinary text. In other words, if you store the number 43.99 in a Short Text field, Access doesn't realize you're dealing with numbers, and it won't let you use it in a calculation.

■ TEXT LENGTH

Every Short Text field has a *maximum length*. This trait comes as a great surprise to many people who aren't used to databases. After all, with today's gargantuan hard drives, why worry about space? Can't your database just expand to fit whatever data you want to stuff inside?

The maximum length matters because it determines how *densely* Access can pack your records together. For performance reasons, Access needs to make sure that an entire record is stored in one spot, so it always reserves the maximum amount of space a record might need. If your table has four fields that are 50 characters apiece, Access can reserve 200 characters' worth of space on your hard drive for each record. On the other hand, if your fields have a maximum 100 characters each, Access holds onto twice as much space for each record, even if you aren't actually using that space. The extra space isn't a major issue (you probably have plenty of room on your computer), but a spread-out database may experience slightly slower searches.

The most a Short Text field can hold, ever, is 255 characters. If you need to store a large paragraph or an entire article's worth of information, you need the Long Text data type instead (page 67).

When you add a new Short Text field, Access gives it a maximum capacity of 255 characters. This is a safe choice, but if you don't need that much space you can reduce the maximum of your field to something more fitting. (The box on page 67 has some guidelines.) To set the maximum length, go to the Field Properties section, and enter a number in the Field Size box (*Figure 2-8*).

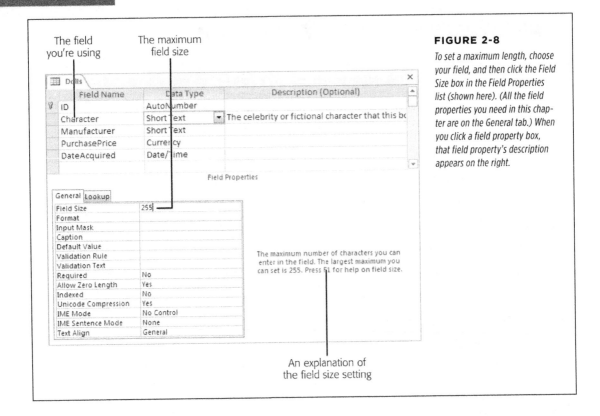

The field
you're using

The maximum
field size

FIGURE 2-8

To set a maximum length, choose your field, and then click the Field Size box in the Field Properties list (shown here). (All the field properties you need in this chapter are on the General tab.) When you click a field property box, that field property's description appears on the right.

An explanation of
the field size setting

TIP It's worthwhile being a little generous with maximum lengths to avoid the need to modify the database later.

Maximum Length Guidelines

Here are some recommended maximum lengths for the Short Text data type:

- **First names and last names**. Usually, 25 characters handles a first name, while 50 characters plays it safe for a long, hyphenated last name.

- **Middle initial**. One character. (Sometimes common sense is right.)

- **Email address**. Go with 50 characters. Email addresses closer to 100 characters have turned up in the wild (Google "world's longest email address" for more), but they're unlikely to reach your database.

- **Cities, states, countries, and other places**. Although a Maori name for a hill in New Zealand tops out at over 80 characters (see *http://tinyurl.com/longest-w*), 50 is enough for most practical purposes.

- **Street address**. A street address consists of a number, followed by a space, and then the street name, another space, and the street abbreviation (like Rd or St). Fifty characters handles it, as long as you put postal codes, cities, and other postal details in other fields.

- **Phone numbers, postal codes, credit card numbers, and other fixed-length text**. Count the number of characters and ignore the placeholders, and set the maximum to match. If you want to store the U.S. phone number (123) 456-7890, make the field 10 characters long. You can then *store* the phone number as 1234567890, but use an input mask (page 138) to add the parentheses, spaces, and dash when you *display* it. This approach is better because it avoids the headaches that result from entering similar phone numbers in different ways. And if you plan to accept international numbers, you'll need to allow for up to 15 digits.

- **Description or comments**. Specifying the maximum of 255 characters allows for three or four average sentences of information. If you need more, consider the Long Text data type instead.

Remember, if in doubt, opt for a bigger size, because accommodating your data is more important that squeezing out every last drop of performance.

Long Text

Microsoft designed the Long Text data type to store large quantities of text. If you want to place a chapter from a book, an entire newspaper article, or just several paragraphs into a field, you need the Long Text data type.

> **NOTE** In previous versions of Access, the Long Text data type was called Memo. The old name was a little odd—although a Long Text field can certainly store the information from an interoffice memorandum, it's useful anytime you have large blocks of text.

When creating a Long Text field, you don't need to supply a maximum length, because Access stores the data differently from other data types. Essentially, it stuffs Long Text data into a separate section, so it can keep the rest of the record as compact and efficient as possible, but accommodate large amounts of text.

A Long Text field tops out at 65,536 characters. To put it in perspective, that's about the same size as this chapter. If you need more space, add more than one Long Text field.

NOTE Technically, the 65,536-character limit is a limitation in the Access user interface, not in the database. If you program an application that uses your database, it could store far more—up to a gigabyte's worth of information in a Long Text field.

If you need to edit a large amount of text while you're working on the datasheet, you can use the Zoom box (*Figure 2-9*). Just move to the field you want to edit, and then press Shift+F2.

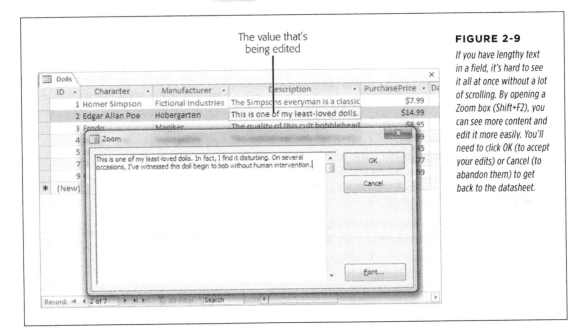

The value that's
being edited

FIGURE 2-9

If you have lengthy text in a field, it's hard to see it all at once without a lot of scrolling. By opening a Zoom box (Shift+F2), you can see more content and edit it more easily. You'll need to click OK (to accept your edits) or Cancel (to abandon them) to get back to the datasheet.

■ FORMATTED TEXT

Like a Short Text field, the Long Text field stores *unformatted* text. However, you can also store *rich text* in a Long Text field—text that has different fonts, colors, text alignment, and so on. To do so, set the Text Format field property to Rich Text (rather than Plain Text).

To format part of the text in a field, you simply need to select it (while editing the record in Datasheet view) and then choose a formatting option from the Home→Text Formatting section of the ribbon. However, most of the time you won't take this approach, because it's difficult to edit large amounts of text in the datasheet's narrow columns. Instead, use Shift+F2 to open a Zoom box, and then use the minibar (*Figure 2-10*).

TIP There's another, even easier way to get formatted text into a Long Text field. Create the text in a word processing program (like Word), format it there, and then copy and paste it into the field. All the formatting comes with it.

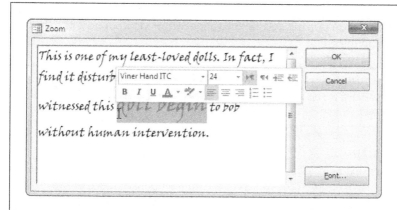

FIGURE 2-10

To show the minibar—a compact toolbar with formatting options—select some text. As soon as you release the mouse button, it pops into view.

NOTE The minibar is sometimes a little finicky, and you may need to reselect the text more than once to get it to appear. If you can't get the minibar to appear at all, you are probably attempting to format a Short Text field, or a Long Text field that has the Text Format property set to Plain Text.

As neat as this feature may seem at first glance, it's rarely worth the trouble. Database purists believe that tables should store raw information and let other programs (or fancy forms) decide how to format it. The problem is that once you've created your formatted text, it can be quite a chore to maintain it. Just imagine having to change the font in 30,000 different records.

If you really do want to store formatted content, consider linking your database to a separate document, like a Word file. In Access, you can do this in two ways:

- **Create a field that points to the file**. For example, you can place a value like *C:\myfile\BonoBobbleheadDescription.docx* in a field. For this trick, use the Short Text or Hyperlink data type (page 79).

- **Embed the file inside your database**. This way, it's impossible to lose the file (or end up pointing to the wrong location). However, you'll need to pull the file out every time you want to update it. To do this, you need to use the Attachment data type (page 80).

Number

The Number data type includes a wide variety of differently sized numbers. You can choose to allow decimal numbers, and you can use negative values (just precede the value with a – sign). You should use the Number data type for every type of numeric information you have—except currency amounts, in which case the Currency data type (page 72) is a better match.

When you use numeric fields, you don't include information about the units you're using. You may have a field that represents a Weight in Pounds, a Height in Meters, or an Age in Years. However, these fields contain only a number. It's up to you to know what that number signifies. If you think other people may be confused, consider explaining the units in the description (page 59), or incorporate it into the field name (like HeightInMeters).

> **NOTE** Your field should *never, ever* contain values like "44 pounds." Access treats this value as a text value, so if you make this mistake, you can't use all the important number-crunching and validation tools you'll learn about later in this book.

▓ NUMBER SIZE

As with a Short Text field, when you create a numeric field, you need to set the Field Size property to make sure Access reserves the right amount of space. However, with numbers, your options are a little more complicated than they are for ordinary text.

Essentially, numbers are divided into several subgroups, depending on whether they support non-integer values (numbers to the right of a decimal point) and on how many *bytes* of space Access uses to store them.

> **NOTE** A *byte* is a group of eight bits, which is the smallest unit of storage in the computer world. For example, a megabyte is approximately one million bytes.

Table 2-2 lists the different Field Size options you can choose for the Number data type and explains when each one makes most sense. Initially, Access chooses Long Integer for all fields, which gives a fair bit of space but requires whole numbers.

TABLE 2-2 *Field Size Options for the Number Data*

FIELD SIZE	CONTAINS	WHEN TO USE IT
Byte	An integer (whole number) from 0 to 255. Requires just one byte of space.	This size is risky, because it fits only very small numbers. Usually, it's safer to use Integer for small numbers and give yourself a little more breathing room.
Integer	An integer (whole number) from −32,768 to 32,767. Requires two bytes of space.	Useful if you need small numbers with no decimal part.
Long Integer	An integer (whole number) from −2,147,483,648 to 2,147,483,647. Requires four bytes of space.	The Access standard. A good choice with plenty of room. Use this to store just about anything without hitting the maximum, as long as you don't need decimals.

FIELD SIZE	CONTAINS	WHEN TO USE IT
Single	Positive or negative numbers with up to 38 zeroes and 7 decimal places of accuracy. Requires four bytes of space.	The best choice if you need to store non-integer numbers or numbers that are too large to fit in a Long Integer.
Double	Positive or negative numbers with up to 308 zeroes and 15 decimal places of accuracy. Requires eight bytes of space.	Useful if you need ridiculously big numbers.
Decimal	Positive or negative numbers with up to 28 zeroes and 28 decimal places of accuracy. Requires eight bytes of space.	Useful for numbers that have lots of digits to the right of the decimal point.

NOTE Table 2-2 doesn't include Replication ID, because you almost always use that option with the AutoNumber data type (page 83).

■ NUMBER FORMATTING

The Field Size determines how Access stores your number in the table. However, you can still choose how it's *presented* in the datasheet. For example, 50, 50.00, 5E1, $50.00, and 5000% are all the same number behind the scenes, but people interpret them in dramatically different ways.

To choose a format, you set the Format field property. Your basic built-in choices include:

- **General Number**. Displays unadorned numbers, like 43.4534. Any extra zeroes at the end of a number are chopped off (so 4.10 becomes 4.1).

- **Currency and Euro**. Both options display numbers with two decimal places, thousands separators (the comma in $1,000.00), and a currency symbol. These choices are used only with the Currency data type.

- **Fixed**. Displays numbers with the same number of decimal places, filling in zeroes if necessary (like 432.11 and 39.00). A long column of numbers lines up on the decimal point, which makes your tables easier to read.

- **Standard**. Similar to Fixed, except it also uses thousands separators to help you quickly interpret large numbers like 1,000,000.00.

- **Percent**. Displays numbers as percentages. For example, if you enter 0.5, that translates to 50%.

- **Scientific**. Displays numbers by using scientific notation, which is ideal when you need to handle numbers that range widely in size (like 0.0003 and 300). Scientific notation displays the first nonzero digit of a number, followed by a fixed number of digits, and then indicates what power of ten that number needs to be multiplied by to generate the specified number. For example, 0.0003 becomes 3.00 x 10^{-4}, which displays as 3.00E−4. The number 300, on the other hand, becomes 3.00 x 10^2, or 3E2.

NOTE When using Fixed, Standard, Percent, or Scientific, you should also set the Decimal Places field property to the number of decimal places you want to see. Otherwise, you always get two places.

- **A custom format string**. This cryptic code tells Access exactly how to format a number. You type the format string you need into the Format box. For example, if you type in the weird-looking code #,##0, (including the comma at the end) Access hides the last three digits of every number, so 1,000,000 appears as 1,000 and 15,000 as 15.

NOTE Custom number formats aren't terribly common in Access (they're more frequently used with Excel). Later on, you'll learn about expressions (page 237), which let you do pretty much the same thing.

Currency

Currency is a slight variation on the Number data type that's tailored for financial calculations. Unlike with the Number data type, here you can't choose a Field Size for the Currency data type—Access has a one-size-fits-all policy that requires eight bytes of storage space.

TIP The Currency data type is better than the Number data type because it uses optimizations that prevent rounding errors with very small fractions. The Currency data type is accurate to 15 digits to the left of the decimal point, and 4 digits to the right.

You can adjust the number of decimal places that Access shows for currency values on the datasheet by setting the Decimal Places field property. Usually, it's set to 2.

The formatting that Access uses to display currency values is determined by the "Region and Language" settings on your computer (see the box on page 75). However, these settings might produce results you don't want—for example, say you run an artisanal cereal business in Denmark that sells all its products overseas in U.S. dollars (not kroner). You can control exactly how currency values are formatted by setting the Format field property, which gives you the following options:

- **Currency**. This option is the standard choice. It uses the formatting based on your computer's regional settings.

- **Euro**. This option always uses the Euro currency symbol (€).

- **A custom format string**. This option lets you use any currency symbol you want (as described below). You need to type the format string you need into the Format box.

There's a simple recipe for cooking up format strings with a custom currency symbol. Start by adding the character for the currency symbol (type in whatever you want), and then add #,###.##, which is Access code for "give me a number with thousands separators and two decimal places."

For example, the Danish cereal company could use a format string like this to show the U.S. currency symbol:

```
$#,###.##
```

Whereas a U.S. company that needs to display a Danish currency field (which formats prices like *kr 342.99*) would use this:

```
kr #,###.##
```

NOTE Enterprising users can fiddle around with the number format to add extra text, change the number of decimal places (just add or remove the # signs), and remove the thousands separators (just take out the comma).

Date/Time

Access uses the Date/Time data type to store a single instant in time, complete with the year, month, day, and time down to the second. Behind the scenes, Access stores dates as numbers, which lets you use them in calculations.

Although Access always uses the same amount of space to store date information in a field, you can hide some components of it. You can choose to display just a date (and ignore time information) or just the time (and ignore date information). To do this, you simply need to set the Format field property. Table 2-3 shows your options.

TABLE 2-3 *Date/Time Formats*

FORMAT	EXAMPLE
General Date	2/23/2013 11:30:15 PM
Long Date	February 23, 2013 11:30:15 PM
Medium Date	23-Feb-13
Short Date	2/23/2013
Long Time	11:30:15 PM
Medium Time	11:30 PM
Short Time	23:30

NOTE Both the General Date and Long Date formats show the time information only if it's not zero.

The format affects only how the date information is displayed—it doesn't change how you type it in. Access is intelligent enough to interpret dates correctly when you type any of the following:

- 2013-2-23 (the international year-month-day standard always works)

- 2/23/2013 (the most common approach, but you might need to flip the month and day on non-U.S. computers)

- 23-Feb-2013

- 23-Feb-13

- Feb 23 (Access assumes the current year)

- 23 Feb (ditto)

To add date and time information, just follow the date with the time, as in 23-Feb-13 5:06 PM. Make sure to include the AM/PM designation at the end, or use a 24-hour clock.

If it's too much trouble to type in a date, consider using the calendar smart tag instead. The smart tag is an icon that appears next to the field whenever you move to it, as shown in *Figure 2-11*. You can turn this feature off by setting the Show Date Picker field property to Never.

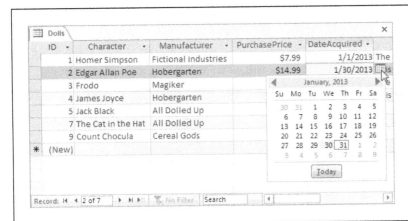

FIGURE 2-11

Access automatically pops up the calendar smart tag for all date fields. Click the calendar icon to pop up a mini calendar where you can browse to the date you want. However, you can't use the calendar to enter time information.

Dating Your Computer

Windows has regional settings for your computer, which affect the way Microsoft programs display things like dates and currencies. In Access the regional settings determine how the different date formats appear. In other words, on a factory-direct U.S. computer, the Short Date format shows up as 2/23/2013. But on a Canadian or British computer, it may appear as 23/2/2013. Either way, the information that's stored in the database is the same. However, the way it appears in your datasheet changes.

You can change the regional settings, and they don't have to correspond to where you live—you can set them for your company headquarters on another continent, for instance. But keep in mind that these settings are global, so if you alter them, you affect all your programs.

To change regional settings, click the Start button (in Windows 7) or go to the Start screen (in Windows 8) and type *region*. When the Region shortcut appears, click it. The Region and Language window will appear. The most important setting is in the first box, which has a drop-down list you can use to pick the language and region you want to use, like English (United States) or Swedish (Finland).

You can fine-tune the settings in your region, too. This makes sense only if you have particular preferences about how dates that don't match the standard options should be formatted. To do so, click the Additional Settings button. Then, click the Date tab in the new window that appears (*Figure 2-12*).

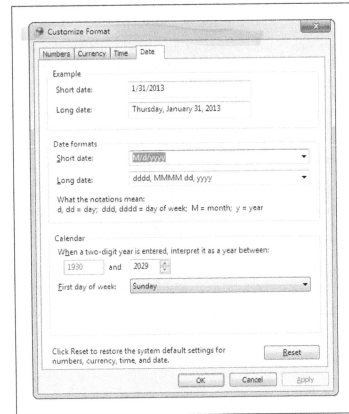

FIGURE 2-12

Your computer settings determine how dates appear in applications like Access. Use the drop-down lists to specify the date separator; order of month, day, and year components in a date; and how Access should interpret two-digit years. You can mix and match these settings freely, although you could wind up with a computer that's completely counterintuitive to other people.

■ CUSTOM DATE FORMATS

If you're not happy with the seven standard date options that Access provides, you can craft your own date format string and type in the Format property. This format string tells Access how to present the date and time information.

A date format string is built out of pieces. Each piece represents a single part of the date, like the day, month, year, minute, hour, and so on. You can combine these pieces in whatever order you want. For example, consider the following format string:

```
yyyy-mm-dd
```

This string translates as the following instructions: "Display the four-digit year, followed by a dash, followed by a two-digit month number, followed by another dash, followed by a two-digit day number." You're free to put these components in any order you like, but this example defines them according to the ISO date standard.

If you apply this format string to a field that contains the date January 1, 2013, you see this in the datasheet:

```
2013-01-01
```

You can control how to display the year, day, and month components. For example, if you replace mm with mmm, your dates will show three-letter month abbreviations instead of the month number:

```
2013-Jan-01
```

Remember that regardless of what information you choose to display or hide, Access stores the same date information in your database.

Table 2-4 shows the basic placeholders that you can use for a date or time format string.

TABLE 2-4 *Date and Time Formatting Codes*

CODE	DESCRIPTION	DISPLAYS (JANUARY 1, 2013, 1:05:05 P.M.)...
d	The day of the month, from 1 to 31, with the numbers between 1 and 9 appearing without a leading 0.	1
dd	The day of the month, from 01 to 31 (leading 0 included for 1 to 9).	01
ddd	A three-letter abbreviation for the day of the week.	Tue
dddd	The full name of the day of the week.	Tuesday
m	The number value, from 1 to 12, of the month (no leading 0 used).	1
mm	The number value, from 01 to 12, of the month (leading 0 used for 01 to 09).	01
mmm	A three-letter abbreviation for the month.	Jan
mmmm	The full name of the month.	January
yy	A two-digit abbreviation of the year.	13
yyyy	The year with all four digits.	2013
h	The hour, from 0 to 23 (no leading 0 used).	13
hh	The hour, from 00 to 23 (leading 0 used for 00 to 09).	13
:n	The minute, from 0 to 59 (no leading 0 used).	5
:nn	The minute, from 0 to 59 (leading 0 used for 00 to 09).	05
:s	The second, from 0 to 59 (no leading 0 used).	5

CODE	DESCRIPTION	DISPLAYS (JANUARY 1, 2013, 1:05:05 P.M.)...
:ss	The second, from 0 to 59 (leading 0 used for 00 to 09).	05
AM/PM	Tells Access to use a 12-hour clock, with an AM or PM indication.	PM
am/pm	Indicates a 12-hour clock, with an am or pm indication.	pm
A/P	Tells Access to use a 12-hour clock, with an A or P indication.	P
a/p	Tells Access to use a 12-hour clock, with an a or p indication.	p

Yes/No

A Yes/No field is a small miracle of efficiency. It's the leanest of Access data types, because it allows only two possible values: Yes or No.

When using a Yes/No field, imagine that your field poses a yes or no question by adding an imaginary question mark at the end of your field name. You could use a field named InStock to keep track of whether a product is in stock. In this case, the yes or no question is "in stock?" Other examples include Shipped (in a list of orders) or Male (to separate the boys from the girls).

> **TIP** Don't make the mistake of using the Yes/No data type for a field that may expand to accept more than two options in the future, because that change will force you to edit every record in your database. Instead, use a Lookup (page 155), which lets you limit a field to a small set of distinct values.

Although every Yes/No field is essentially the same, you can choose to format it slightly differently, replacing the words "Yes" and "No" with "On" and "Off" or "True" and "False." You'll find these three options in the Format menu. However, it doesn't make much difference because on the datasheet, Yes/No fields are displayed with a checkbox, as shown in *Figure 2-13*.

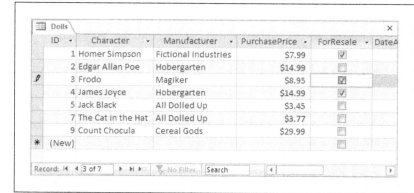

FIGURE 2-13

In this example, ForResale is a Yes/No field. A checked checkbox represents Yes (or True or On). An unchecked checkbox represents No (or False or Off).

Hyperlink

The Hyperlink data type comes in handy if you want to create a clickable link to a web page, file, or email address. You can mix and match any combination of the three in the same table.

Access handles hyperlinks a little differently in Datasheet view. When you type text into a hyperlink field, it's colored blue and underlined. And when you click the link, Access pops it open in your browser (*Figure 2-14*).

NOTE Access doesn't prevent you from entering values that aren't hyperlinks in a Hyperlink data field. This trait leads to problems if you click the hyperlink. If you put the text "saggy balloons" in a hyperlink field and click it, Access tries to send your browser to *http://saggy balloons*, which obviously doesn't work.

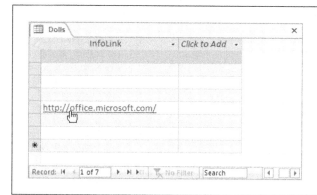

FIGURE 2-14

Click this hyperlink, and you'll head straight to the welcoming arms of Office Online.

One hyperlink field feature isn't immediately obvious. Hyperlink fields actually store more than one piece of information. Every hyperlink includes these three components:

- The text you see in the cell

- The text you see when you hover over the link with your mouse (the tooltip)

- The destination you go to when you click the cell (the URL or file path)

When you type a link into the datasheet, the first two are set to the same value—whatever you've just typed in. For example, when you type *www.FantasyPharmacologists. com*, the text you see and the tooltip are both set to hold the same content, which is *www.FantasyPharmacologists.com*.

To set the third piece of information—the URL or file path—Access examines your entry and makes a reasonable guess. For example, if you type *www.FantasyPharmacologists. com*, Access assumes you want the URL to be the web location *http://www. FantasyPharmacologists.com*, so it adds the *http://* sequence at the beginning. Similarly, if you type an email address like *dr.z@b-store.com*, Access creates the full email link *mailto:dr.z@b-store.com*. When you click a link like this in Access or in a web browser, your email program starts a new message. Finally, if you enter a file path or a URL that already starts with *http://* (or some other URL prefix), Access doesn't make any changes.

Most of the time, Access's approach gives you the result you want. However, you aren't limited to this strategy. You can set these three components to have different values—for example, so your URL has a website address (like *www.zyqcorp.com*) but your display text has a more approachable name ("The ZYQ Corporation"). To do so, move to the value, and then press Ctrl+K to pop up the Edit Hyperlink window (see *Figure 2-15*). Or right-click it, and then choose Hyperlink→Edit Hyperlink.

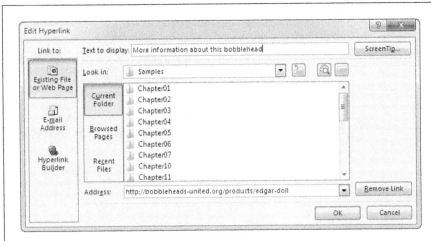

FIGURE 2-15

Using the Edit Hyperlink window, you can change the text that appears in the cell (at the top of the window) and the page that Access opens when you click it (at the bottom). You can also create links that use email addresses (in which case Access opens the email program that's configured on your computer) or links to file paths (use the folder browsing area to pick the file you want).

Attachment

The Attachment data type lets you add one or more files to your database record in much the same way that you tack on attachments to your email messages. Access stores the files you add to an attachment field as part of your table, embedded inside your database file.

The Attachment data type is a good choice if you need to insert a picture for a record, a short sound file, or even a document from another Office application like Word or Excel. You could create a People table with a picture of each person in your contact list, or a product catalog with pictures of the wares you're selling. In these cases, attachments have an obvious benefit—because they're stored inside your database file, you never lose track of them.

However, attachments aren't as graceful with large files, or files you need to modify frequently. If you place a frequently modified document into an Access database, it isn't available on your hard drive for quick editing, printing, and searching. Instead, you need to fire up Access and then find the corresponding record before you can open your document. If you want to make changes, you also need to keep Access open so it can take the revised file and insert it back into the database.

WARNING Think twice before you go wild with attachments. An Access database is limited to two gigabytes of space. If you start storing large files in your tables, you may run out of room. Instead, store large documents in separate files, and then record the file name in a field that uses the Short Text or Hyperlink data type.

When you use the Attachment data type, make sure you set the Caption field property, which determines the text that appears in the column header for that field. (Often, you'll use the field name as the caption.) If you don't set a caption, the column header shows a paper clip but no text.

You'll recognize an attachment field in the datasheet because it has a paper-clip icon next to it (*Figure 2-16*).

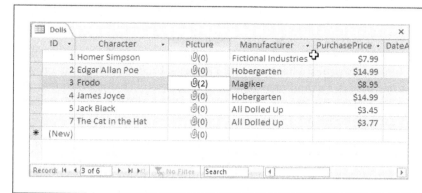

FIGURE 2-16

Attachments are flagged with a paper clip icon and a number in brackets, which tells you how many files are attached. In this example, all the values in the Picture attachment field are empty except Frodo, which has two.

To attach a file or review the list of attached files, double-click the paper-clip icon. You'll see the Attachments window (see *Figure 2-17*).

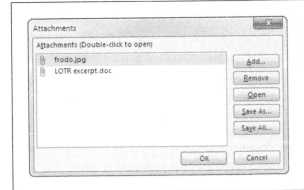

FIGURE 2-17

The Attachments window shows you all the files that are linked to your field.

Here's what you can do in the Attachments window:

- **Add a new attachment**. Click the Add button. Then browse to a new file and click OK. You'll see the file appear at the bottom of the list.

- **Delete an attachment**. Select the attachment in the list and then click Remove.

- **Save a copy of an attachment**. Select the attachment, click Save As, and then browse to a location on your computer. Or, click Save All to save copies of all the attachments in this field. If you change these copies, you don't change the attachment in the database.

- **Open an attachment**. Select the attachment and then click Open. Access copies the attachment to a temporary folder on your computer, where Internet content is cached, and then opens it in the associated program. For example, .doc files get opened in Microsoft Word.

When you open an attachment, Access copies it to the same place where it temporarily stores web pages while you surf. (The exact location depends on your user name and includes a randomly generated sequence of characters, but expect something like *C:\Users\matthew\AppData\Local\Microsoft\Windows\Temporary Internet Files\ACC4589*.)

Here's something nifty. If you keep the Attachments window open while you change, save, and close the temporary copy of your file, Access notices the update. Then, when you switch back to Access and close the Attachments window, Access offers to update your database by copying the updated file back into your database, and replacing the original (*Figure 2-18*). This feature sounds great, but it doesn't always work. For example, Word's security settings don't let you update the temporary file—instead, Word forces you to save a new copy of it somewhere else, which means Access won't notice any updates you make. To make sure your attachment gets updated, you need to remove the original and add the new version in the Attachments window. Or, avoid these headaches altogether by attaching only files that you don't plan to edit.)

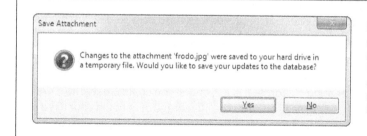

FIGURE 2-18

In this example, Access notices that you've updated the attachment file "frodo.jpg" in Paint. When you close the Attachments window, Access asks if you want to update the database with the new saved version. This system only works if you keep the Attachments window while you edit.

Unfortunately, the Attachment data type doesn't give you a lot of control. Here are some of its limitations:

- You can't restrict the number of attachments allowed in an attachment field. All attachment fields allow a practically unlimited number of attachments (although you can't attach two files with the same name).

- You also can't restrict the types of files used for an attachment.

- You can't restrict the size of the files used for an attachment.

AutoNumber

An AutoNumber is a special sort of data type. Unlike with all the other data types you've seen, you can't fill in the value for an AutoNumber field. Instead, Access does it automatically whenever you insert a new record. Access makes sure that the AutoNumber value is unique—in other words, it never gives two records the same AutoNumber value.

NOTE Every table can have up to one AutoNumber field.

Ordinarily, the AutoNumber field looks like a *sequence* of numbers—Access tends to give the first record an AutoNumber value of 1, the second an AutoNumber of 2, and so on. However, the truth isn't so straightforward. Sometimes, Access skips a number. This skipping could happen when several people are using a database at once, or if you start adding a new record, and then cancel your action by pressing Esc. You may also delete an existing record, in which case Access never reuses that AutoNumber value. As a result, if you insert a new record and you see it's assigned an AutoNumber value of 401, you can't safely assume that there are already 400 records in the table. The actual number is probably less.

An AutoNumber value doesn't represent anything, and you probably won't spend much time looking at it. The AutoNumber field's sole purpose is to make sure you have a unique way to point to each record in your table. Usually, your AutoNumber field is also the primary key for your table, as explained on page 88.

USING AUTONUMBERS WITHOUT REVEALING THE SIZE OF YOUR TABLE

AutoNumber values have one minor problem: They give a clue about the number of records in a table. You may not want a customer to know that your brand-new food and crafts company, Better Butter Sculptures, hasn't cracked 12 customers. So you'll be a little embarrassed to tell him he's customer ID number 6.

The best way to solve this problem is to start counting at a higher number. You can fool Access into generating AutoNumber values starting at a specific minimum. For example, instead of creating customer IDs 1, 2, and 3, you could create the ID values 11001, 11002, 11003. This approach also has the advantage of keeping your IDs a consistent number of digits, and it lets you distinguish between IDs in different tables by starting them at different minimums. Unfortunately, to pull this trick off, you need to fake Access out with a specially designed query, which you'll see on page 295.

Alternatively, you can tell Access to generate AutoNumber values in a different way. You have two choices:

- **Random AutoNumber value**. To use random numbers, change the New Values field property from Increment to Random. Now you'll get long numbers for each record, like 212125691, 1671255778, and -1388883525. You might use random AutoNumber to create values that other people can't guess. (For example, if you have an Orders table that uses random values for the OrderID field, you can use those values as confirmation numbers.) However, random AutoNumbers are rarely used in the Access world.

- **Replication IDs**. Replication IDs are long, obscure codes like 38A94E7B-2F95-4E7D-8AF1-DB5B35F9700C that are statistically guaranteed to be unique. To use them, change the Field Size property from Long Integer to Replication ID. Replication IDs are really used only in one scenario—if you have separate copies of a database and you need to merge the data together in the future. The next section explains that scenario.

Both of these options trade the easy-to-understand simplicity of the ordinary AutoNumber for something a little more awkward, so evaluate them carefully before using these approaches in your tables.

USING REPLICATION IDS

Imagine you're working at a company with several regional sales offices, each with its own database for tracking customers. If you use an ordinary AutoNumber field, you'll end up with several customers with the same ID, but at different offices. If you ever want to compare data, you'll quickly become confused. And you can't combine all the data into one database for further analysis later on.

Access gives you another choice—a *replication ID*. A replication ID is a strange creation—it's an extremely large number (16 bytes in all) that's represented as a string of numbers and letters that looks like this:

```
38A94E7B-2F95-4E7D-8AF1-DB5B35F9700C
```

This ID is obviously more cumbersome than an ordinary integer. After all, it's much easier to thank someone for submitting Order 4657 than Order 38A94E7B-2F95-4E7D-8AF1-DB5B35F9700C. In other words, if you use the AutoNumber value for tracking or bookkeeping, the replication ID is a bad idea.

However, the replication ID solves the problem described earlier, where multiple copies of the same database are being used in different places. That's because replication IDs are guaranteed to be *statistically unique*. In other words, there are so many possible replication IDs that it's absurdly unlikely that you'll ever generate the same replication ID twice. So even if you have dozens of separate copies of your database, and they're all managing hundreds of customers, you can rest assured that each customer has a unique customer ID. Even better, you can periodically fuse the separate tables together into one master database. (This process is called *replication*, and it's the origin of the term "replication ID." You'll learn more about transferring data from one database to another in Chapter 23.)

> **NOTE** A replication ID is also called a GUID (short for "globally unique identifier"). In theory, the chances of two GUIDs being identical are one in 2^{128}, which is small enough that you could set one billion people to work, ask them to create one billion GUIDs a year, and still be duplicate-free for the next decade or two. In practice, the real limitation is how good the random number generator is in Access.

Figure 2-19 shows a table that uses replication IDs.

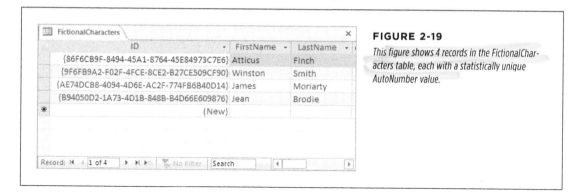

FIGURE 2-19

This figure shows 4 records in the FictionalCharacters table, each with a statistically unique AutoNumber value.

Calculated

A *calculated* field is one that shows the result of a calculation. You provide the formula (known as the *expression*) that produces the result. Access does all the calculating work. For example, imagine you have a table of products with a Price field and a CostToManufacture field. You can add a calculated field named Profit that uses the expression [Price] - [CostToManufacture] to arrive at its result. (Technically, the square brackets are required only for field names that have spaces in them, but Access likes to add them in every expression just to be safe.) When you create a calculated field, you type the expression into the Expression field property. It's impossible to create a calculated field without an expression—if you try it, Access won't let you save the table.

Like an AutoNumber field, a calculated field is a hands-off affair. In the current example, whenever you update a record's Price or CostToManufacture, Access automatically performs the profit calculation and stores the result in the Profit field. You don't need to—and can't—edit the Profit field by hand.

When you choose the Calculated data type, the Expression Builder window appears. You'll look at this window more closely on page 246. For now, all you need to know is that you can type your expression into the topmost text box, and click OK to seal the deal.

Before you get too excited and start adding calculated fields all over the place, here's a word of caution. Calculated fields like the Profit example usually aren't a good idea. If you need to have this sort of information easily at hand (and often you do), you're better off creating a *query* that can run the calculation. Using a query helps you avoid bulking up your table with unnecessary information. Instead, your query calculates the information whenever you need it. (Page 237 describes this technique in much more detail and shows you how to write many more advanced expressions for queries or tables.)

NOTE So if calculated fields make more sense in queries than in tables, why does Access offer the Calculated data type? It's for special situations where calculations are extremely slow, you have lots of records, and performance is critical. In this situation, it *may* make sense to use a calculated field to avoid the time-consuming calculating query when you need the calculated result. But unless you're a database pro and you're certain you need this frill, you're better off keeping your tables for raw data and letting other database objects handle the number crunching.

Setting Field Data Types in Datasheet View

Although Access pros favor Design view, it's not the only game in town. You can create exactly the same table, with exactly the same data types, using Datasheet view.

You can actually use two techniques to create fields with proper data types in Datasheet view. The first approach is to click the "Click to Add" column header, which appears on the right side of your table. When you do, Access pops open a list of the different field types (as shown in *Figure 2-20*). Choose one, type a field name, and you're ready to start entering information in the new field.

The second technique is to use the ribbon, which gives you more field-creation options. To try this approach, move to the column that falls just *before* the position where you want to insert the new field. Then, pick an option from the Table Tools | Fields→Add & Delete section of the ribbon. The most popular field types (for example, Short Text, Number, Currency, and Date & Time) have buttons of their own, but many more options are tucked just out of sight in the Table Tools | Fields→Add & Delete→More Fields list. In fact, the More Fields list is a bit cleverer than the Data Type list in Design view. Rather than just including the basic data types, it includes a much larger

collection of data type *presets*. For example, rather than seeing one Date/Time data type, you find a list of differently formatted date options, including Short Date, Medium Date, Long Date, Medium Time, and so on. These options all use the same Date/Time data type, but with the field properties adjusted to get the desired formatting.

At the very bottom of the More Fields list, under the Quick Start heading, are a small number of more unusual presets. These are field building blocks—readymade fields like Phone and Status—that pair a basic data type with some field properties tailored for a specific type of information. A few actually insert several related fields. (For example, choose Address and you get the following fields: Address, City, State Province, ZIP Postal, and Country Region.) Access fans are divided on whether this feature is a true timesaver or just another distraction. But if you like it, you can even create your own presets for the More Fields list. Just select your fully configured field (or group of fields), and choose Table Tools | Fields→Add & Delete→More Fields→Save Selection As New Data Type. Supply a name for your preset, and pick a category for the More Fields list.

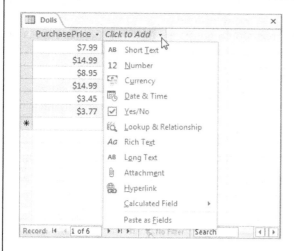

FIGURE 2-20

For quick field creation, use the data type list that pops up when you click the column header on the right side of the datasheet.

■ The Primary Key

Design view also lets you set a table's *primary key*, which is a field (or a combination of fields) that's unique for each record. Every table should have a primary key.

The purpose of a primary key is to prevent duplicate records (that is, records with *exactly* the same information) from slipping into your table. Databases are notoriously fussy, and they definitely don't like this sort of sloppiness.

The challenge of preventing duplicates isn't as easy as it seems. Access is designed to be blisteringly fast, and it can't afford to double-check your new record against every other record in the table to see if there's a duplicate. So instead, it relies on a *primary key*. As long as every record in a table has a unique, never-duplicated primary key, you can't have two identical records. (At worst, they'll be two almost-identical records that have the same information in all their other fields, but have different primary keys. And this is perfectly acceptable to Access.)

Choosing a primary key is trickier than it seems. Imagine you have a list of friends (and their contact information) in a table named People. You may logically assume that you can create a primary key by using a combination of first and last name. Unfortunately, that just won't do—after all, many are the address books that have two Sean Smiths.

Your best solution is to *invent* a new piece of information. For example, you can label every individual in your contact list with a unique ID number. Best of all, you can get Access to automatically create this number for you (and make sure that no two people get the same number), so you don't even need to think about it. That way, if you have two Sean Smiths, each one has a different ID. And even if Ferris Wheel Simpson decides to change his first name, the ID remains the same.

This approach is exactly the one Access uses when you create a table by using Datasheet view. Consider the Dolls table you built in Chapter 1. Notice that it includes a field named ID, which Access fills automatically. You can't set the ID value in a new record, or change it in an existing record. Instead, Access takes complete control, making sure each bobblehead has a different ID number. This behavior is almost always what you want, so don't try to change it or delete the ID field.

However, there's one exception. If you *create* a table in Design view by choosing Create→Tables→Table Design, Access assumes you know what you're doing, and it doesn't create an ID field for you. You need to add an ID field (or something like it).

Creating Your Own Primary Key Field

If your database doesn't have an ID field (perhaps because you created it using the Create→Tables→Table Design command), it's up to you to create one and set the primary key. Here's how to do it:

1. **Create a new field by typing a name in the Field Name column.**

   For automatically generated values, the name "ID" is a good choice. Some people prefer to be a little more descriptive (for example, BobbleheadID, CustomerID, and so on), but it's unnecessary.

2. **In the Data Type column, choose AutoNumber.**

   By choosing the AutoNumber data type, you make sure that Access generates a unique ID value for every new record you insert. If you don't want this process to happen, you can choose something else (like the Short Text or Number data type). You'll be responsible for entering your own unique value for each record, which is more work than it seems.

3. **Right-click the field and then choose Primary Key.**

   This choice designates the field as the primary key for the table. Access doesn't allow duplicate values in this field.

TIP   If you want to make a primary key that includes more than one field, you need to take a slightly different approach. Hold down the Ctrl key, and click each field you want to include, one after the other. Then, while holding down Ctrl, right-click your selection and choose Primary Key.

UP TO SPEED

Why It's Important to Be Unique

You won't completely understand why it's so important for each record to have a unique ID number until you work with the more advanced examples in later chapters. However, one of the reasons is that other programs that use your database need to identify a record *unambiguously*.

To understand why there's a problem, imagine that you've built a program for editing the Dolls table. This program starts by retrieving a list of all your table's bobbleheads. It displays this list to the person using the program and lets her make changes.

Here's the catch—if a change is made, the program needs to be able to apply the change to the corresponding record in the database. And to apply the change, it needs some unique piece of information that it can use to locate the record. If you've followed the best design practices described above, the unique "locator" is the bobblehead's ID.

◼ Six Principles of Database Design

With great power comes great responsibility. As a database designer, it's up to you to craft a set of properly structured tables. If you get it right, you'll save yourself a lot of work in the future. Well-designed databases are easy to enhance, simpler to work with, and lead to far fewer mind-bending problems when you need to extract information.

Sadly, there's no recipe for a perfect database. Instead, a number of recommendations can guide you on the way. In the following sections, you'll learn about a few of the most important.

> **NOTE** Few database rules can't be broken. Sometimes, there's tension between clear, logical design and raw performance. Other times, database designers adopt personal quirks and conventions that make their lives a little easier. But even though an experienced database designer can bend, warp, and—on occasion—limbo right under some of these rules, they're still an excellent starting point for newbies. If you follow them, they'll never steer you into a bad decision. Finally, remember this: Building a good database is an art that takes practice. For best results, read these guidelines, and then try building your own test databases.

1. Choose Good Field Names

Access doesn't impose many rules on what field names you can use. It lets you use 64 characters of your choice. However, field names are important. You'll be referring to the same names again and again as you build forms, create reports, and even write code. So it's important to choose a good name from the outset.

Here are some tips:

- **Keep it short and simple**. The field name should be as short as possible. Long names are tiring to type, more prone to error, and can be harder to cram into forms and reports. (Of course, you don't want a table name that's been abbreviated into nothingness either. The cryptic name FinCSalesReg isn't good for anyone.)

- **CapitalizeLikeThis**. It's not a set-in-stone rule, but most Access fans capitalize the first letter of every word (known as CamelCase), and then cram them all together to make a field name. Examples include UnitsInStock and DateOfExpiration.

- **Avoid spaces**. Spaces are allowed in Access field names, but they can cause problems. In SQL (the database language you'll use to search for data), spaces aren't kosher. That means you'll be forced to use square brackets when referring to a field name that includes spaces (like "[Number Of Guests]"), which gets annoying fast. If you really must have spaces, consider using underscores instead.

- **Be consistent**. You have the choice between the field names Product_Price and ProductPrice. Either approach is perfectly reasonable. However, it's not a good idea to mingle the two approaches in the same database—doing so is a recipe for certain confusion. Similarly, if you have more than one table with the same sort of information (for example, a FirstName field in an Employees table and in a Customers table), use the same field name.

- **Don't repeat the table name**. If you have a Country field in a Customers table, it's fairly obvious that you're talking about the Country where the customer lives. The field name CustomerCountry would be overkill.

- **Don't use the field name "Name."** Besides being a tongue-twister, Name is an Access keyword. Instead, use ProductName, CategoryName, ClassName, and so on. (This is one case where it's OK to violate the previous rule and incorporate the table name in the field name.)

Also give careful thought to naming your tables. Once again, consistency is king. For example, database nerds spend hours arguing about whether to pluralize table names (like Customers instead of Customer). Either way is fine, but try to keep all your tables in line.

2. Break Down Your Information

Be careful that you don't include too much information in a single field. You want to have each field store a single piece of information. Rather than have a single Name field in a table of contacts, it makes more sense to have a FirstName and a LastName field.

There are many reasons for breaking down information into separate fields. First of all, it stops some types of errors. With a Name field, the name could be entered in several different ways (like "Last, First" or "First Last"). Splitting the name avoids these issues, which can create headaches when you try to use the data in some sort of automated task (like a mail merge). But more importantly, you can more easily work with data that's broken down into small pieces. Once the Name field is split into FirstName and LastName, you can perform sorts or searches on just one of these two pieces of information, which you couldn't otherwise do. Similarly, you should split address information into columns like Street, City, State, and Country—that way, you can far more easily find out who lives in Nantucket.

The top of *Figure 2-21* shows an example of proper separation; the bottom shows a dangerous mistake—an attempt to store more than one piece of information in a single field.

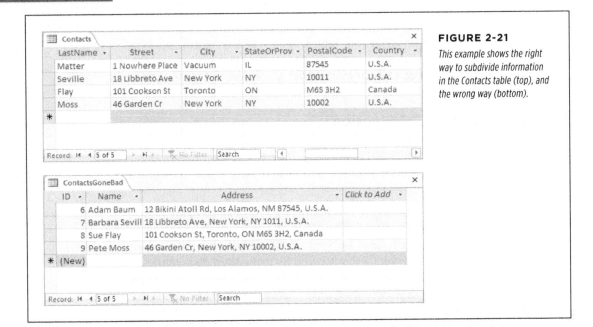

FIGURE 2-21

This example shows the right way to subdivide information in the Contacts table (top), and the wrong way (bottom).

Notice that it's technically still possible to take the information in the top table in and break it down still further. For example, the street address information in the Street field could be split into StreetNumber, StreetName, and StreetType fields. However, that added bit of complexity doesn't add anything, so database gurus rarely go to the extra trouble.

3. Include All the Details in One Place

Often, you'll use the same table in many different tasks. You may use the Dolls table to check for duplicates (and avoid purchasing the same bobblehead twice), to identify the oldest parts of your collection, and to determine the total amount of money you've spent in a given year (for tax purposes). Each of these tasks needs a slightly different combination of information. When you're calculating the total money spent, you aren't interested in the Character field that identifies the doll. When checking for a duplicate, you don't need the DateAcquired or PurchasePrice information.

Even though you don't always need all these fields, it's fairly obvious that it makes sense to put them all in the same table. However, when you create more detailed tables, you may not be as certain. It's not difficult to imagine a version of the Dolls table that has 30 or 40 fields of information. You may use some of these fields only occasionally. However, you should still include them all in the same table. As you'll see in this book, you can easily filter out the information you don't need from the datasheet, as well as from your forms and printed reports.

4. Avoid Duplicating Information

As you start to fill a table with fields, it's sometimes tempting to include information that doesn't really belong. This inclusion causes no end of headaches, and it's a surprisingly easy trap to fall into. *Figure 2-22* shows this problem in action with a table that tries to do too much.

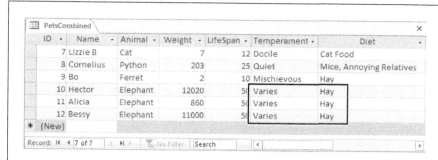

FIGURE 2-22

This table lists the available pets at an exotic animal breeder. It also lists some helpful information about the life expectancy, temperament, and meal requirements of each type of animal. Initially, this design seems fairly reasonable. However, a problem appears when you have several of the same type of animals (in this case, three elephants). Now the elephant-specific details are repeated three separate times.

Duplicate data like that shown in *Figure 2-22* is inefficient. You can easily imagine a table with hundreds of similar records, needlessly wasting space repeating the same values over and over again. However, this concern is minor compared to the effort of updating that information, and the possibility of inconsistency. What happens if you want to update the life expectancy information for every elephant based on new studies? Based on the current design of the table, you need to change each record that has the same information. Even worse, it's all too easy to change some records but leave others untouched. The overall result is inconsistent data—information in more than one spot that doesn't agree—which makes it impossible to figure out the correct information.

This problem occurs because the information in the Pets table doesn't all belong. To understand why, you need to delve a little deeper into database analysis.

As a rule, every table in a database stores a single *thing*. In the Pets table, that thing is pets. Every field in a table is a piece of information about that thing.

In the Pets table, fields like Name, Animal, and Weight all make sense. They describe the pet in question. But the LifeSpan, Temperament, and Diet fields aren't quite right. They don't describe the individual pet. Instead, they're just standards for that species. In other words, these fields aren't based on the *pet* (as they should be)—they're based on the *animal type*. The only way to solve this problem is to create two tables: Pets and AnimalTypes (*Figure 2-23*).

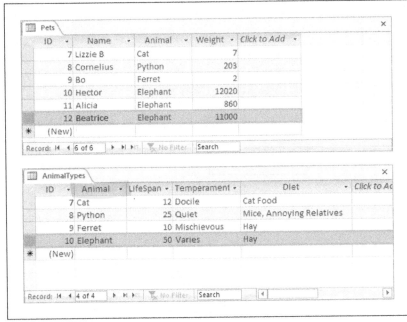

FIGURE 2-23

Now the animal-specific information is maintained in one place, with no duplicates. It takes a little more work to get all the pet information you need—for example, to find out the life expectancy for Beatrice (top), you need to check out the Elephant record in the AnimalTypes table (bottom)—but the overall design is more logical.

It takes experience to spot fields that don't belong. And in some cases, breaking a table down into more and more subtables isn't worth the trouble. You could theoretically separate the address information (contained in fields like Street, City, Country, and PostalCode) from a Customers table, and then place it into a separate Addresses table. However, it's relatively uncommon for two customers to share the same address, so this extra work isn't likely to pay off. You'll consider how to define formal relationships between tables like Pets and AnimalTypes in Chapter 5.

TIP Many database gurus find the best way to plan a database is to use index cards. To do this, start by writing down all the types of information you need in your database. Then, set aside an index card for each table you expect to use. Finally, take the fields you wrote on the scrap paper, and write them down on the appropriate index cards, one at a time, until everything is set into neat, related groups.

5. Avoid Redundant Information

Another type of data that just doesn't belong is redundant information—information that's already available elsewhere in the database, or even in the same table, sometimes in a slightly different form. As with duplicated data, this redundancy can cause inconsistencies.

Calculated data is the most common type of redundant information. An Average-OrderCost field in a Customers table is an example. The problem here is that you can determine the price of an average order by searching through all the records in the Orders table for that customer and then averaging them. By adding an Average-Or-derCost field, you introduce the possibility that this field may be incorrect (it may not match the actual order records). You also complicate life, because every time a customer places an order, you need to recalculate the average, and then update the customer record.

Here are some more examples of redundant information:

- **An Age and a DateOfBirth field (in a People table)**. Usually, you'll want to include just a DateOfBirth field. If you have both, the Age field contains redundant information. But if you have only the Age field, you're in trouble—unless you're ready to keep track of birthdays and update each record carefully, your information will soon be incorrect.

- **A DiscountPrice field (in a Products table)**. You should be able to calculate the discount price as needed based on a percentage. In a typical business, markups and markdowns change frequently. If you calculate 10 percent discounts and store the revised prices in your database, you'll have a lot of work to do when the discount drops to 9 percent.

> **NOTE** As you've already learned, Access gives you a more acceptable way to use calculated data: by creating a calculated field (page 85). This dodges the problems of inconsistency and maintenance, because Access maintains the calculated data for you. However, calculated data still makes for awkward database design. As a general rule, don't use calculated fields unless you're absolutely sure you need this particular compromise to boost performance, and you've ruled out the alternatives (like queries).

6. Include an ID Field

As you learned on page 31, Access automatically creates an ID field when you create a table in Datasheet view and sets it to be the primary key for the table. But even now that you've graduated to Design view, you should still add an ID field to all your tables. Make sure it uses the AutoNumber data type so Access fills in the numbers automatically, and set it to be the primary key.

In some cases, your table may include a unique field that you can use as a primary key. *Resist the temptation.* You'll always buy yourself more flexibility by adding an ID field. You never need to change an ID field. Other information, even names and Social Security numbers, may change. And if you're using table relationships, Access copies the primary key into other tables. If a primary key changes, you'll need to track down the value in several different places.

> **TIP** It's a good idea to get into the habit of using ID fields in all your tables. In Chapter 5, you'll see the benefits when you start creating table relationships.

Mastering the Datasheet: Sorting, Searching, and Filtering

I n Chapter 1, you took your first look at the *datasheet*—a straightforward way to browse and edit the contents of a table. As you've learned since then, the datasheet isn't the best place to build a table—Design view is a better choice for database control freaks. However, the datasheet is a great tool for reviewing the records in your table, making edits, and inserting new data.

Based on your experience creating the Dolls table (page 30), you probably feel pretty confident breezing around the datasheet. However, most tables are considerably larger than the examples you've seen so far. After all, if you need to keep track of only a dozen bobbleheads, you really don't need a database—you'll be just as happy jotting the list down in any old spreadsheet, word processor document, or scrap of unused Kleenex.

On the other hand, if you plan to build a small bobblehead empire (suitable for touring in international exhibitions), you need to fill your table with hundreds or thousands of records. In this situation, it's not as easy to scroll through the mass of data to find what you need. All of a sudden, the datasheet seems more than a little overwhelming.

Fortunately, Access is stocked with datasheet goodies that can simplify your life. In this chapter, you'll become a datasheet expert, with tricks like sorting, searching, and filtering at your fingertips. You'll also learn a quick-and-dirty way to print a snapshot of the data in your table.

> **TIP** It's entirely up to you how much time you spend using datasheets. Some Access experts prefer to create *forms* for all their tables (as described in Part Four). With forms, you can design a completely customized window for data entry. Designing forms takes more work, but it's a great way to satisfy your inner Picasso.

Datasheet Customization

Getting tired of the drab datasheet with its boring stretch of columns and plain text? You can do something about it. Access lets you tweak the datasheet's appearance and organization to make it more practical (or to suit it to your peculiar sense of style). Some of these customizations—like modifying the datasheet font—are shameless frills. Other options, like hiding or freezing columns, can genuinely make it easier to work with large tables.

NOTE Access doesn't save formatting changes immediately (unlike record edits, which it stores as soon as you make them). Instead, Access prompts you to save changes the next time you close the datasheet. You can choose Yes to keep your customizations or No to revert to the table's last look and feel (which doesn't affect any edits you've made to the *data* in that table).

Formatting the Datasheet

Access lets you format the datasheet with eye-catching colors and fonts. Do these options make any difference to the way the datasheet works? Not really. But if your computer desktop looks more like a '60s revival party than an office terminal, you'll enjoy this feature.

To find the formatting features, look at the ribbon's Home→Text Formatting section (see *Figure 3-1*).

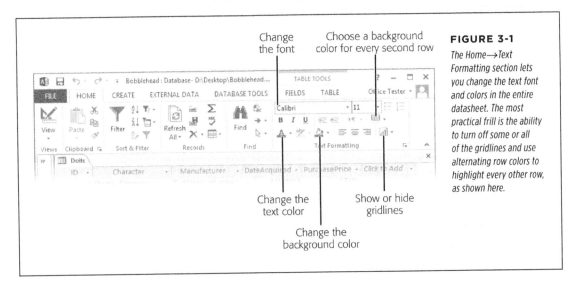

Change the font

Choose a background color for every second row

Change the text color

Change the background color

Show or hide gridlines

FIGURE 3-1

The Home→Text Formatting section lets you change the text font and colors in the entire datasheet. The most practical frill is the ability to turn off some or all of the gridlines and use alternating row colors to highlight every other row, as shown here.

Every formatting change you make affects the entire table. You may think it's a nifty idea to apply different formatting to different columns, but Access doesn't let you. If this limitation is frustrating you, be sure to check out forms and reports later in this book. Both are more complicated to set up, but give you more formatting power.

TIP There's one other way you can use the ribbon's Home→Text Formatting section. If you have a field that uses the Long Text data type and you've set your field to use rich text (page 68), you can select some text inside your field, and change its formatting using the ribbon.

GEM IN THE ROUGH

Customizing All Your Datasheets

Access lets you format only one table at a time. So if you find a formatting option you really like, you'll need to apply it separately to every table in your database.

However, you can set formatting options so that they automatically apply to every table in every database by configuring Access itself. To pull off this trick, follow these steps:

1. Choose File→Options to show the Access Options window.

2. Choose Datasheet from the list on the left.

3. On the right, you see the standard font, gridline, and column width options, which you can change to whatever you want.

When you change the datasheet formatting settings in the Access Options window, you change the *defaults* that Access uses. These settings determine the formatting that Access uses for new tables and any tables that aren't customized. When you customize a table, you override the default settings, no matter what they are.

Rearranging Columns

The fields in the datasheet are laid out from left to right, in the order you created them. Often, you'll discover that this order isn't the most efficient for data entry.

Imagine you've created a Customers table for a novelty pasta company. When a new customer registration ends up on your desk, you realize that the registration form starts with the name and address information, and then includes the customer's pasta preferences. Unfortunately, the fields on the datasheet are laid out in a completely different order. From left to right, they're arranged like this: ID, FreshPastaPreference, DriedPastaPreference, FirstName, LastName, Street, City, State, Country. This organization isn't as crazy as it seems—it actually makes it easier for the people filling pasta orders to quickly find the information *they* want. But because of this ordering, you need to skip back and forth just to enter the information from a single registration.

Fortunately, you can solve this problem without redesigning the table. Drag the columns you want to move to new positions, as shown in *Figure 3-2*.

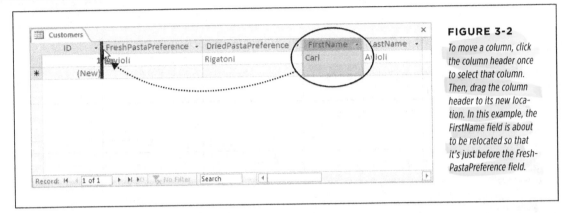

FIGURE 3-2

To move a column, click the column header once to select that column. Then, drag the column header to its new location. In this example, the FirstName field is about to be relocated so that it's just before the Fresh-PastaPreference field.

The best part of this approach is that you don't need to modify the database's actual structure. If you switch to Design view after moving a few columns, you'll see that the field order hasn't changed. In other words, you can keep the exact same physical order of fields (in your database file), but organize them differently in Datasheet view.

NOTE Rearranging columns is a relatively minor operation. Don't be afraid to shift columns around to suit a specific editing job and then switch them back later on. Your changes don't affect the data in the database. If you want to use a particular column order for a one-time job, simply refrain from saving your changes when you close the datasheet.

Resizing Rows and Columns

As you cram more and more information into a table, your datasheet becomes wider and wider. In many cases, you'll be frustrated with some columns hogging more space than they need and others being impossibly narrow.

As you'd expect, Access lets you tweak column widths. But you probably haven't realized how many different ways you can do it:

- **Resize a single column**. Move the mouse to the column's right edge, so that the mouse pointer changes into a vertical bar. Then click the edge and drag it to the left (to shrink the column) or to the right (to make it larger).

- **Resize a column to fit its content**. Double-click the right column edge. Access makes the column just wide enough to fit the field name or the largest value (whichever's larger). However, it doesn't make the column so wide that it stretches beyond the bounds of the window.

- **Resize several adjacent columns**. Drag the first column's header across the columns until you've selected them all. Then, drag the right edge of your selection to the left or the right. All the selected columns shrink or expand to fit the available space, sharing it equally. (A similar trick is to select several columns and then double-click the right edge of the last column. This resizes all the columns to fit their content.)

- **Resize a column with pinpoint accuracy**. Right-click the column header, and then choose Field Width. You'll see the Column Width dialog box, which lets you set an exact width as a number (*Figure 3-3*).

FIGURE 3-3

The Column Width window lets you set an exact width as a number. (The number doesn't actually have a concrete meaning—it's supposed to be a width in characters, but because modern Access uses proportional fonts, different characters are different sizes.) You can also turn on the Standard Width checkbox to reset the width to the standard narrow size, or click Best Fit to expand the column to fit its content (just as when you double-click the edge of the column).

TIP   Remember, a column doesn't need to be wide enough to show all its data at once. You can scroll through a lengthy text field using the arrow keys, and if that's too awkward, use the Shift+F2 shortcut to show the full contents of the current field in a Zoom box.

Just as you can resize columns, you can also resize rows. The difference is that Access makes sure all rows have the same size. So when you make one row taller or shorter, Access adjusts all the other rows to match.

You'll mainly want to shrink a row to cram more rows into view at once. You'll want to enlarge a row mostly to show more than one line of text in each text field (see *Figure 3-4*).

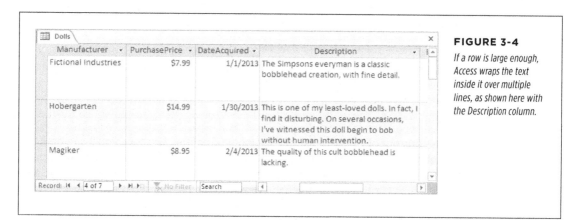

FIGURE 3-4

If a row is large enough, Access wraps the text inside it over multiple lines, as shown here with the Description column.

Hiding Columns

Many tables contain so many columns that you can't possibly fit them all into view at the same time. This quality is one of the drawbacks to the datasheet, and often you have no choice but to scroll from side to side.

However, in some situations, you may not need to see all the fields at once. In this case, you can temporarily hide the columns that don't interest you, thereby homing in on the important details without distraction. Initially, every field you add to a table is out in the open.

To hide a column, select the column by clicking the column header. You can also select several adjacent columns by clicking the column header of the first, and then dragging the mouse cursor across the rest. Then, right-click your selection and choose Hide Fields. The column instantly vanishes from the datasheet. (This sudden disappearance can be a little traumatic for Access newbies.)

Fortunately, the field and all its data remain just out of sight. To pop the column back into view, right-click any column header and choose Unhide Fields. Access then shows the Unhide Columns window (*Figure 3-5*).

> **NOTE** You'll notice that Access uses the words "column" and "field" almost interchangeably. This leads to strange cases where the command uses one word (like Unhide *Fields*) while the window uses the other (Unhide *Columns*). But don't let this quirk throw you off.

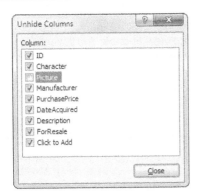

FIGURE 3-5

Using the Unhide Columns window, you can choose to make hidden columns reappear, and (despite the name) you can hide ones that are currently visible. Every column that has a checkmark next to it is visible—every column that doesn't is hidden. As you change the visibility, Access updates the datasheet immediately. When you're happy with the results, click Close to get back to the datasheet.

At the bottom of the field list in the Unhide Columns window, you'll see an entry named "Click to Add." This "field" isn't really a field—it's the placeholder that appears just to the right of your last field in Datasheet view, which you can use to add new fields (page 33). If you're in the habit of adding fields by using Design view, you can hide this placeholder to free up some extra space.

If you add a new record while columns are hidden, you can't supply a value for that hidden field. The value starts out either empty or with the default value (if you've defined one for that field as described on page 133). If you've hidden a required field (page 130), you receive an error message when you try to insert the record. All you can do is unhide the appropriate column, and then fill in the missing information.

Freezing Columns

Even with the ability to hide and resize columns, you'll probably need to scroll from side to side in a typical datasheet. In this situation, you can easily lose your place. You might scroll to see more information in the Contacts table, but then forget exactly which person you're looking at. Access has one more feature that can help you by making sure important information is always visible—*frozen* columns.

A frozen column remains fixed in place at the Access window's left side at all times. Even as you scroll to the right, all your frozen columns remain visible (*Figure 3-6*). To freeze a column (or columns), select them, right-click the column header, and then choose Freeze Fields.

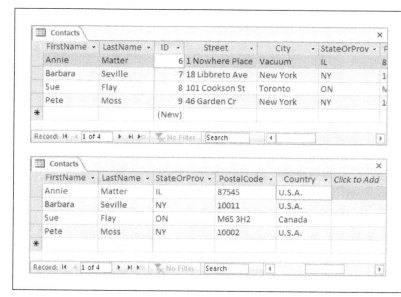

FIGURE 3-6

Top: In this example, the First-Name and LastName field are frozen. They appear initially at the left. (The ribbon is collapsed in this figure to make more room, as described on page 52.)

Bottom: When you scroll to the side to see more information, the FirstName and LastName columns stay put.

TIP If you want to freeze several columns that aren't next to each other, start by freezing the column that you want to appear at the very left. Then, repeat the process to freeze the column that you want to appear just to the right of the first column, and so on.

Frozen columns must always be positioned at the left side of the datasheet. If you freeze a column that's somewhere else, Access moves it to the left side and then freezes it. You can move it back after you unfreeze the column by using the column-reordering trick on page 99. Keep in mind that while a column is frozen, you can't drag it to a different place.

To unfreeze columns, right-click a column header, and then choose Unfreeze All Fields.

> **NOTE** Eventually, you'll discover that the customizations provided by the datasheet aren't enough, or you'll need to customize the same table different ways for different people. These signs tell you that you need to step up to forms, a more advanced data display option described in Part Four.

Datasheet Navigation

In Chapter 1, you learned the basics of moving around the datasheet. Using your mouse and a few select keystrokes, you can cover a lot of ground. (Refer back to page 37 for a review of the different keys you can use to jump from place to place and perform edits.)

However, you haven't seen a few tricks yet. One is the timesaving record navigation buttons at the bottom of the datasheet (*Figure 3-7*).

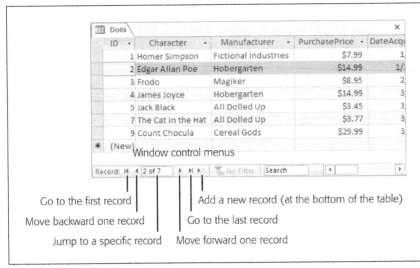

FIGURE 3-7

You could easily overlook the navigation buttons at the bottom of the datasheet. These buttons let you jump to the beginning and end of the table, or, more interestingly, head straight to a record at a specific position. To do this, type the record number (like "4") into the box (where it says "2 or 7" in this example), and then hit Enter. Of course, this trick works only if you have an approximate idea of where in the list your record is positioned.

Several more datasheet features help you orient yourself when dealing with large amounts of data, including *sorting* (which orders the records so you can see what you want), *filtering* (which cuts down the data display to include only the records you're interested in), and *searching* (which digs specific records out of an avalanche of data). You'll try out all these features in the following sections.

Sorting

In some cases, you can most easily make sense of a lot of data by putting it in order. You can organize a customer list by last name, a product catalog by price, a list of wedding guests by age, and so on. Sorting doesn't change how Access stores records, but it does change the way they're displayed.

To sort your records, pick a column you want to use to order the records. Click the drop-down arrow at the right edge of the column header, and then choose one of the sort options at the top of the menu (see *Figure 3-8*).

FIGURE 3-8

This Short Text field gives you the choice of sorting alphabetically from the beginning of the alphabet (A to Z) or backward from the end (Z to A). The menu also provides filtering options, which are described on page 107.

Depending on the data type of the field, you'll see different sorting options, as explained in Table 3-1. (You can also apply the same types of sort by using the commands in the ribbon's Home→Sort & Filter section.)

TABLE 3-1 *Sorting Options for Different Data Types*

DATA TYPE	SORT OPTIONS	DESCRIPTION
Short Text and Hyperlink	Sort A to Z Sort Z to A	Performs an alphabetic sort (like the dictionary), ordering letter by letter. The sort isn't case-sensitive, so it treats "baloney" and "Baloney" the same.
Number, Currency, and AutoNumber	Sort Smallest to Largest Sort Largest to Smallest	Performs a numeric sort, putting smaller numbers at the top or bottom.
Date/Time	Sort Oldest to Newest Sort Newest to Oldest	Performs a date sort, distinguishing between older dates (those that occur first) and more recent dates.
Yes/No	Sort Selected to Cleared Sort Cleared to Selected	Separates the selected from the unselected values.

TIP   Use the Home→Sort & Filter→Remove Sort command to return your table to its original, unsorted order.

Sorting is a one-time affair. If you edit values in a sorted column, Access doesn't reapply the sort. Imagine you sort a list of people by FirstName. If you then edit the FirstName value for one of the records, changing "Frankie" to "Chen," Access *doesn't* relocate the row to the C section. Instead, the changed row remains in its original place until you re-sort the table. Similarly, any new records that you add stay at the end of the table until the next sort (or the next time the table is opened). This behavior makes sense. If Access relocated rows whenever you made a change, you'd quickly become disoriented.

NOTE   The sorting order is one of the details that Access stores in the database file. The next time you open the table in Datasheet view, Access automatically applies your sort settings.

UP TO SPEED

Sorting with Special Characters

Text sorts can be a little counterintuitive, especially if you have a text field that includes numeric content.

Ordinarily, when you sort two numbers (like 153 and 49), the numbers are arranged from smallest to largest (49, 153). However, a text sort doesn't work this way. When Access performs a text sort, it examines the text character by character, which means it sorts numbers based on the first *digit*. If the first digit is the same, then it checks the second digit, and so on. As a result, if you sort 49 and 153 alphabetically, you get 153, 49, because 4 (the first digit in 49) is larger than 1 (the first digit in 153).

Life gets even more interesting if you throw punctuation and other special characters into the mix. Here's the order in which Access sorts everything (in a standard A-to-Z sort):

1. Blank (empty) values
2. Space
3. Special characters (like punctuation)
4. Numbers
5. Letters

■ SORTING ON MULTIPLE FIELDS

If a sort finds two duplicate values, there's no way to know what order they'll have (relative to one another). If you sort a customer list with two "Van Hauser" entries in it, you can guarantee that sorting by last name will bring them together, but you don't know who'll be on top.

If you want more say in how Access treats duplicates, you can choose to sort based on more than one column. The traditional phone book, which sorts people by last name and *then* by first name, is a perfect example of this. People who share the same last name are thus grouped together and ordered according to their first name, like this:

```
...
Smith, Star
```

```
Smith, Susan
Smith, Sy
Smith, Tanis
...
```

In the datasheet, sorts are *cumulative*, which means you can sort based on several columns at the same time. The only trick is getting the order right. The following steps take you through the process:

1. **Choose Home→Sort & Filter→Remove Sort.**

   Access reverts your table to its original, unsorted order.

2. **Use the drop-down column menu to apply the subsort that you want for duplicates.**

   This is the sort order that Access applies *second*. You haven't yet picked the order that Access applies first, which is the potentially confusing part of this technique.

   For example, if you want to perform the phone book sort (names are organized by last name, then first name), you need to turn on sorting for the FirstName field. Table 3-1 explains the sorting options you'll see, depending on the data type.

3. **Use the drop-down column menu to apply the main, top-level sort.**

   This is the sort order that Access applies *first*. In the phone book sort, this is the LastName field.

You can extend these steps to create sorts on more fields. Imagine you have a ridiculously large compendium of names that includes some people with the same last *and* first name. In this case, you could add a third sort—by middle initial. To apply this sort, you'd switch sorting on in this order: MiddleInitial, FirstName, LastName. You'll get this result:

```
...
Smith, Star
Smith, Susan K
Smith, Susan P
Smith, Sy
...
```

Filtering

In a table with hundreds or thousands of records, scrolling back and forth in the datasheet is about as relaxing as a pneumatic drill at 3:00 a.m. Sometimes, you don't even need to see all the records at once—they're just a finger-tiring distraction from the data you're really interested in. In this case, you should cut the datasheet down to just the records that interest you, with *filtering*.

To filter records, you specify a condition that the record must meet to be included in the datasheet. For example, an online store might pick out food items from a full product catalog, a shipping company might look for orders made last week, and a dating service might hunt down bachelors who don't live with their parents. When you apply a filter condition, you end up hiding all the records that don't match your requirements. They're still in the table—they're just tucked neatly out of sight.

Access has several different ways to apply filters. In the following sections, you'll start with the simplest, and then move on to the more advanced options.

■ QUICK FILTERS

A *quick filter* lets you choose what values you want to include and which ones you want to hide, based on the current contents of your table. To apply a quick filter, choose the column you want to use, and then click the drop-down arrow at the column header's right edge. You'll see a list of all the distinct values in that column. Initially, each value has a checkmark next to it. Clear the checkmark to hide records with that value. If you want to hide everything except for a few specific values, click to remove the checkmark next to "(Select All)," and then add a checkmark next to the ones you want. Click OK to apply your filter.

Figure 3-9 shows an example where a sort and filter are being used at the same time. When a column is using filtering, Access adds a funnel icon to the right side of the column header.

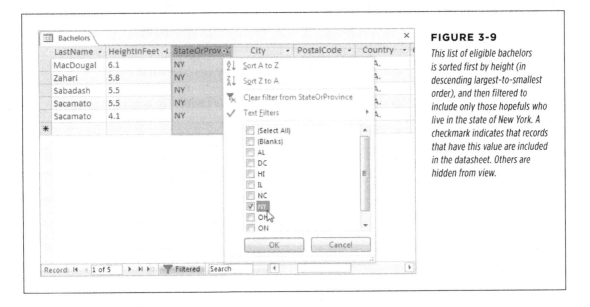

FIGURE 3-9

This list of eligible bachelors is sorted first by height (in descending largest-to-smallest order), and then filtered to include only those hopefuls who live in the state of New York. A checkmark indicates that records that have this value are included in the datasheet. Others are hidden from view.

> **TIP** To remove all the filters on a column (and show every record in the datasheet), click the drop-down button at the right edge of the column header, and then choose "Clear filter from."

Not all data types support filtering. Data types that do include Number, Currency, AutoNumber, Short Text, Hyperlink, Date/Time, and Yes/No. Long Text fields don't support quick filters (because their values are typically too large to fit in the drop-down list), but they do support other types of filters.

You can apply quick filters to more than one column. The order in which you apply the filters doesn't matter, because all filters are *cumulative*, which means you see only records that match all the filters you've set. You can even use quick filters in combination with the other filtering techniques described in the following sections. To temporarily remove a filter, choose Home→Sort & Filter→Toggle Filter. Click Toggle Filter again to put your filter back into action.

> **NOTE** Quick filters work best if you have a relatively small number of distinct values. Limiting people based on the state they live in is a great choice, as is the political party they support or their favorite color. It wouldn't work as well if you wanted to cut down the list based on birth date, height, or weight, because there's a huge range of different possible values. (You don't need to give up on filtering altogether—rather, you just need to use a different type of filter.)

■ FILTER BY SELECTION

Filter by selection lets you apply a filter based on any value in your table. This choice is handy if you've found exactly the type of record you want to include or exclude. Using filter by selection, you can turn the current value into a filter without hunting through the filter list.

Here's how it works. First, find the value you want to use for filtering in the datasheet. Right-click the value, and then choose one of the filter options at the end of the menu (see *Figure 3-10*).

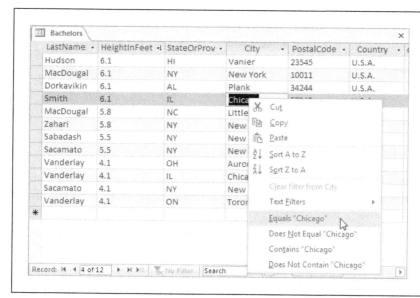

FIGURE 3-10

Depending on the data type, you see slightly different filtering options. For a Short Text field (like the City field shown here), you have the option to include only the records that match the current value (Equals "Chicago"), or those that don't (Does Not Equal "Chicago"). You also have some extra filtering options that go beyond what a quick filter can do—namely, you can include or exclude fields that simply contain the text "Chicago." That filter condition applies to values like "Chicagoland" and "Little Chicago."

All data types that support filtering allow you to filter out exact matches. But many also give you some additional filtering options in the right-click menu. Here's what you'll see for different data types:

- **Text-based data types**. You can filter values that match exactly, or values that contain a piece of text.

- **Numeric data types**. You can filter values that match exactly, or numbers that are smaller or larger than the current number.

- **Date data types**. You can filter values that match exactly, or dates that are older or newer than the current date.

Finally, to get even fancier, you can create a filter condition using only *part* of a value. If you have the value "Great at darts" in the Description field in your table of hopeful bachelors, you can select the text "darts," and then right-click just that text. Now you can find other fields that contain the word "darts." This ability is what gives the filter "by selection" feature its name.

Access makes it easy to switch filtering on and off at a moment's notice. *Figure 3-11* shows how.

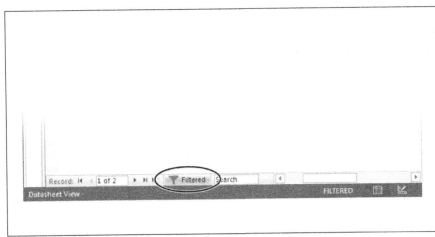

FIGURE 3-11

*Right next to the naviga-
tion controls at the bottom
of your datasheet is a
Filtered/Unfiltered indicator that tells you when
filtering is applied. You
can also use this box to
quickly switch your filter
on and off—clicking it once
removes all filters, and
clicking it again reapplies
the most recent set of
filters.*

FILTER BY CONDITION

So far, the filters you use have taken the current values in your table as a starting point. But if you're feeling confident with filters, you may be ready to try a more advanced approach: *filtering by condition*. When you use a filter by condition, you can define exactly the filter you want.

Imagine you want to find all the rare wine vintages in your cellar with a value of more than $85. Using the filter-by-selection approach, you need to start by finding a wine with a value of $85, which you can use to build your condition. But what if there isn't any wine in your list that has a price of exactly $85, or what if you just can't seem to find it? A quicker approach is defining the filter condition by hand.

Here's how it works. First, click the drop-down arrow at the right edge of the column header. But instead of choosing one of the quick filter options, look for a submenu with filtering options. This menu is named according to the data, so Short Text fields include a Text Filters option, number fields have a Number Filters option, and so on. *Figure 3-12* shows an example.

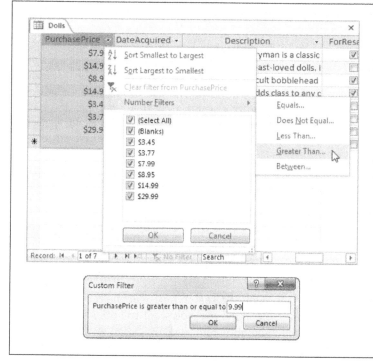

FIGURE 3-12

Top: With a numeric field like this Purchase-Price field, filtering by condition lets you look at values that fall above a certain minimum.

Bottom: Once you've chosen the type of filter you want, you need to supply the information for that filter. If you choose Greater Than, you need to supply the minimum number. Records that are equal to or larger than this value are shown in the datasheet.

Here's a quick overview that describes the extra options you get using filter by condition, depending on your data type:

- **Text-based data types**. All the same options as filter by selection, plus you can find values that start with specific text, or values that end with certain text.

- **Numeric data types**. All the same options as filter by selection, plus you can find values that are in a range, meaning they're greater than a set minimum but smaller than a set maximum.

- **Date data types**. All the same options as filter by selection, plus you can find dates that fall in a range, *and* you can choose from a huge list of built-in options, like Yesterday, Last Week, Next Month, Year to Date, First Quarter, and so on.

Filters vs. Queries

If you use filters frequently, you're sure to run into a problem. Access stores only one set of filters—the filters you're currently using. In other words, once you apply a different filter, your original filter is gone, and you need to reapply it from scratch the next time you need it. In most cases, reapplying a filter isn't difficult. But if you've spent a considerable amount of effort crafting the perfect set of filter conditions, and you know you want to use them later, it's frustrating.

If you find yourself in this situation, you're overusing filters. Instead of relying on filters to show the information you're interested in, you'd be better off creating a separate, reusable *query*. Like filters, queries let you see a subset of your data based on certain conditions. Unlike filters, queries can contain much more sophisticated logic, they can leave out columns you're not interested in, and Access saves them as separate database objects so you can always reuse them later. You'll start using queries in Chapter 6.

Searching

Access also provides a *quick search* feature that lets you scan your datasheet for specific information. Whereas filtering helps you pull out a batch of important records, searching is better if you need to find a single detail that's lost in the mountains of data. And while filtering changes the Datasheet view by hiding some records, searching leaves everything as is. It just takes you to the data you want to see.

The quickest way to search is through the search box near the record navigation controls (see *Figure 3-13*). Just type in the text you want to find. As you type, the first match in the table is highlighted automatically. You can press Enter to search for subsequent matches.

When performing a search, Access scans the table starting from the first field in the first record. It then goes left to right, examining every field in the current record. If it reaches the end without a match, it continues to the next record and checks all of its values, and so on. When it reaches the end of the table, it stops.

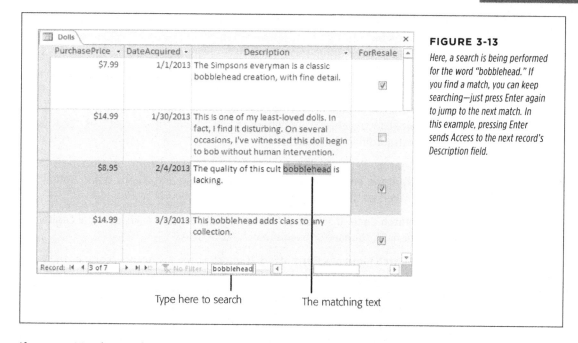

FIGURE 3-13

Here, a search is being performed for the word "bobblehead." If you find a match, you can keep searching—just press Enter again to jump to the next match. In this example, pressing Enter sends Access to the next record's Description field.

Type here to search   The matching text

If you want to change the way Access performs a search, you'll need to use the Find feature instead:

1. **Choose Home→Find→Find.** (Or, just use the shortcut Ctrl+F.)

   The "Find and Replace" window appears (*Figure 3-14*).

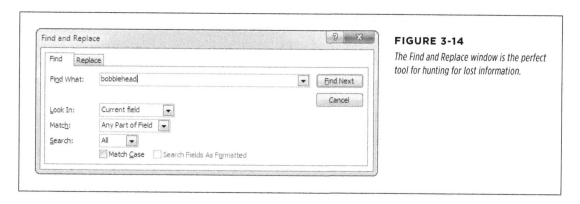

FIGURE 3-14

The Find and Replace window is the perfect tool for hunting for lost information.

2. **Specify the text you're searching for in the Find What box, and then set any other search options you want to use:**

- **Find What.** The text you're looking for.

- **Look In.** Lets you choose between searching a single field (choose "Current field") or the entire table (choose "Current document").

- **Match.** Lets you specify whether values need to match exactly. Use Whole Field to require exact matches. Use "Start of Field" if you want to match beginnings (so "bowl" matches "bowling"), or "Any Part of Field" if you want to match text anywhere in a field (so "bowl" matches "League of extraordinary bowlers").

- **Search.** Sets the direction Access looks: Up, Down, or All (which loops from the end of the table to the beginning, and keeps going until it has traversed the entire table).

- **Match Case.** If selected, finds only matches that have identical capitalization. So "banana" doesn't match "BANANA."

- **Search Fields As Formatted.** If selected, means Access searches the value as it appears on the datasheet. For example, the number 44 may appear in a Currency field as $44.00. If you search for 44, you always find what you're looking for. But if you search for the formatted representation $44.00, you get a match only if you have Search Fields As Formatted switched on. In extremely large tables (with thousands of records), searches may be faster if you switch off Search Fields As Formatted.

TIP To turn off Search Fields As Formatted, you must choose to search a single field in the Look In box. If you are searching the entire table, then you must search the formatted values.

3. **Click Find Next.**

Access starts searching from the current position. If you're using the standard search direction (All), Access moves from left to right in the current record, and then down from record to record until it finds a match.

When Access finds a match, it highlights the value. You can then click Find Next to look for the next match, or Cancel to stop searching.

Find and Replace

The search feature doubles as a powerful (but somewhat dangerous) way to modify records.

Initially, when the "Find and Replace" window appears, it shows the Find tab. However, you can click the Replace tab to be able to find specific values and replace them with different text. All the settings for a replace operation are the same as for a find operation, except you have an additional text box, called Replace With, to supply the replacement text.

The safest way to perform a replace operation is to click the Find Next button to jump to the next match. At this point, you can look at the match, check that you really *do* want to modify it, and then click Replace to change the value and jump to the next match. Repeat this procedure to move cautiously through the entire table.

If you're a wild and crazy skydiving sort who prefers to live life on the edge, you can use the Replace All button to change every matching value in the entire table in a single step. Although this procedure is ridiculously fast, it's also a little risky. Replace operations *can't be reversed* (the Undo feature is no help here because it can reverse only a single record change), so if you end up changing more than you intend, there's no easy way back. If you're still seduced by the ease of a Replace All, consider creating a backup of your database file before going any further.

Advanced Editing

In Chapter 1, you learned the essentials of editing, including how to add, delete, and modify records. However, Access has a few finer points that you haven't seen yet. In the following sections, you'll tackle two great conveniences in Access—the spell checker and AutoCorrect—and you'll learn a simple way to insert special characters in your fields.

The Spell Checker

The spell-checking functionality in Access is almost exactly the same as in other Office applications like Word—it uses the same dictionary, catches the same sorts of errors, and gives you the option to either ignore things it doesn't recognize or add them to the dictionary.

The difference is that when you perform a spell check with Access, it examines only the content in Short Text and Long Text fields. Numbers, dates, and everything else gets a pass. Of course, many of your fields are likely to contain text you don't want to spell check—like names, places, or product titles. You have two ways to handle this. You can perform a spell check on a single field, thereby ignoring everything else. Or, you can start a datasheet-wide spell check, but choose to ignore certain fields on the fly.

Here's how it works:

1. **Move to the field where you want to start the spell check.**

If you want to check the entire datasheet from start to finish, move to the first field in the first record.

If you want to check part of the datasheet, move to the location where you want to start checking. Keep in mind that when Access reaches the end of your datasheet, it loops around and starts again at the top, continuing until it's reviewed every field in every record. (Of course, you can cancel a spell check at any time.)

If you want to check just a single field, select that field before continuing by clicking the column header.

2. **Choose Home→Records→Spelling (or just press F7).**

If you're performing a datasheet-wide spell check, Access examines the current record and moves through the fields from left to right. When it finishes, it moves to the next record and repeats the process. If you've selected a single column, Access scans only the values in that field, from top to bottom.

When the spell check finishes, a window informs you that all your data has been checked. If your table passes the spell check, this window is the only feedback you receive. On the other hand, if Access discovers any potential spelling errors during its check, it displays a Spelling window (as shown in *Figure 3-15*), showing the offending word and a list of suggestions.

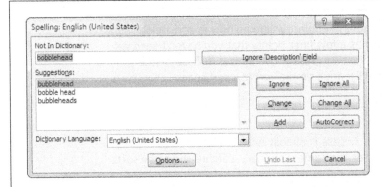

FIGURE 3-15

When Access encounters a word it thinks is misspelled, it highlights the word. At that point, you can click one of the options on the Spelling window—for example, click Change to replace the misspelled word with selected suggestion—or type your own correction into the "Not in Dictionary" box.

The Spelling window offers a wide range of choices. If the spell checker is complaining about a word that really is misspelled, you have three options:

- **Fix it once**. Click one of the words in the list of suggestions, and then click Change to replace your text with the proper spelling. You can also double-click the word in the list of suggestions, which has the same effect. Or, if you have your own correction in mind, type it into the "Not in Dictionary" box and then click Change.

- **Fix it everywhere**. Click one of the words in the list of suggestions, and then click Change All to replace your text with the proper spelling. If Access finds the same mistake elsewhere in your datasheet during the spell check, it automatically repeats the change, without bothering to alert you about the problem.

- **Fix it forever**. Click one of the words in the list of suggestions, and then click AutoCorrect. Access makes the change for this field, and for any other similarly mistaken words. In addition, it adds the information for the change to the AutoCorrect list. If you type the same unrecognized word into another record (or even another table), Access automatically corrects your entry. This option is useful if you've discovered a mistake that you make frequently.

On the other hand, if the spell checker is complaining about a word that you don't want to change, you have a few more possibilities available, by clicking the following options:

- **Ignore** skips this problem and keeps checking. If Access finds the same mystery word elsewhere in your spreadsheet, it prompts you again for a correction.

- **Ignore All** skips this problem and keeps checking. If Access finds the same mystery word elsewhere in your spreadsheet, it ignores the word. You might use Ignore All to force Access to disregard something you don't want to correct, like a person's name.

- **Ignore Field** ignores any errors in that field for the remainder of the spell check. This one is a handy way to filter out fields that contain a lot of names, places, or titles, so you don't waste your time reviewing bogus spell-checker suggestions.

- **Add** adds the word to the custom spell check dictionary. This step is a great one to take if you plan to keep using the word in this datasheet and many more. (A company name makes a great addition to the custom dictionary.) Not only does Access ignore any occurrences of this word, but if it finds a similar word in a field, it provides the custom word in its list of suggestions, letting you quickly clear up minor typos.

- **Cancel** stops the operation altogether. You can then correct the field and resume the spell check later.

> **NOTE** Every Office application on your computer shares the same custom dictionary. If you add a word in Access and then perform a spell check in Word, the same word is allowed. This convenience is timesaving, as long as you don't go overboard adding words that don't really belong.

▦ SPELL-CHECKING OPTIONS

You can control how the spell checker works by setting a few straightforward options. To set these options (or just take a look at them), choose File→Options to show the Access Options window. Then, choose Proofing in the list on the left (*Figure 3-16*). You can also find the same page of options if you click the Spelling window's Options button while a spell check is underway.

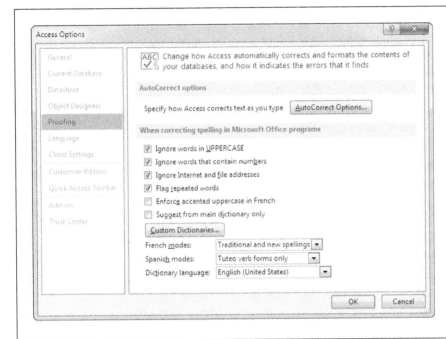

FIGURE 3-16

The spell checker options let you specify the language and a few other miscellaneous settings. All spell check settings are language-specific; the last box in the window indicates the language you're currently using.

Here are the most common spelling options:

- **Ignore words in UPPERCASE**. If you choose this option, Access doesn't bother to check any word in all capitals (which is helpful when your text contains lots of acronyms).

- **Ignore words that contain numbers**. If you choose this option, Access doesn't check words that contain numeric characters, like "Sales43" or "H3llO." If you don't choose this option, Access checks these entries and flags them as errors, unless you've specifically added them to the custom dictionary.

- **Ignore Internet and file addresses**. If you choose this option, Access ignores words that appear to be file paths (like *C:\Documents and Settings*) or website addresses (like *http://FreeSweatSocks.com*).

- **Flag repeated words**. This search finds errors where you inadvertently repeat the same word twice, like like this this.

- **Enforce accented uppercase in French**. Forces French words to take the accents they should have, even for capital letters (where they look a little weird). English speakers don't need to worry about this setting.

- **Suggest from main dictionary only**. If you choose this option, the spell checker doesn't use words in the custom dictionary as suggestions if it finds an unrecognized word. However, it still accepts a word that matches one of the entries in the custom dictionary.

You can also choose the file that Access uses to store custom words—the unrecognized words that you add to the dictionary while a spell check is underway. To do so, click the Custom Dictionaries button, which shows the Custom Dictionaries window (*Figure 3-17*).

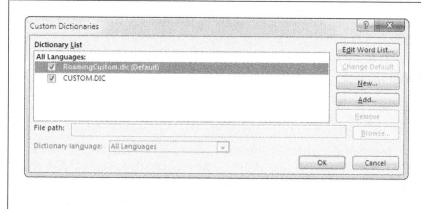

FIGURE 3-17

Access starts you off with two custom dictionary files: RoamingCustom.dic (the default) and custom.dic (for backward compatibility with old versions of Office). To add a custom dictionary that already exists, click Add and browse to the file. Or click New to create a new, blank custom dictionary. You can also edit the list of words a dictionary contains (select it and click Edit Word List). Figure 3-18 shows an example of editing the default dictionary.

FIGURE 3-18

When you click Edit Word List, you see all the words in your custom dictionary. You can add new ones or remove entries that no longer apply.

NOTE   Custom dictionaries are stored in an account-specific section of your hard drive. For example, if you're logged in under the user account mitt_romney, you'll probably find the custom dictionary in the folder *C:\Users\ mitt_romney\AppData\Roaming\Microsoft\UProof*. One side effect of this system is that custom dictionaries aren't shared between two people who use different accounts on the same computer (unless you manually add the other user's dictionary in the Custom Dictionaries window).

AutoCorrect

As you type text in a field, AutoCorrect cleans up behind you, correcting things like incorrectly capitalized letters and common misspellings. AutoCorrect is such a subtle feature that you might not even realize it's monitoring your every move. To get a taste of its magic, look for behaviors like these:

- If you type *HEllo*, AutoCorrect changes it to *Hello*.

- If you type *friday*, AutoCorrect changes it to *Friday*.

- If you start a sentence with a lowercase letter, AutoCorrect uppercases it.

- If you scramble the letters of a common word (for example, typing *thsi* instead of *this*, or *teh* instead of *the*), AutoCorrect replaces the word with the proper spelling.

- If you accidentally press Caps Lock, and then type *sMITH* when you really wanted to type *Smith*, Access not only fixes the mistake, it also switches off Caps Lock.

For the most part, AutoCorrect is harmless and even useful, because it can spare you from delivering minor typos in a major report. But if you need to type irregularly capitalized words (or just like to rebel against standard English), you can turn off some or all of the AutoCorrect actions.

To set AutoCorrect options, choose File→Options to show the Access Options window. Then, choose Proofing in the list on the left. In the page of settings on the right side, click the "AutoCorrect options" button.

Most of the settings are self-explanatory, and you can turn them off by unchecking them. *Figure 3-19* explains the "Replace text as you type" option, which is not just for errors.

TIP   For really advanced AutoCorrect settings, you can use the Exceptions button to define cases where Access doesn't use AutoCorrect. When you click this button, the AutoCorrect Exceptions window appears with a list of exceptions. This list includes abbreviations that include the period but shouldn't be capitalized (like "pp.") and words where mixed capitalization is allowed (like "WordPress").

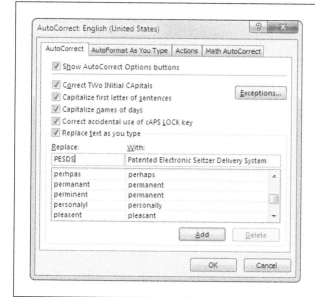

FIGURE 3-19

Under "Replace text as you type" is a long list of symbols and commonly misspelled words (the column on the left) that Access automatically replaces with something else (the column on the right). But what if you want the copyright symbol to appear as a C in parentheses? You can remove individual corrections (select one, and then click Delete), or you can change the replacement text. And you can add your own rules. You may want to be able to type "PESDS" and have Access insert "Patented Electronic Seltzer Delivery System." Simply type in the "Replace" and "With" text as shown here, and then click Add.

Special Characters

Text content isn't just about letters, numbers, and punctuation. You also have special symbols that you can't type directly on your keyboard. One example is the copyright symbol (©), which you can insert into a field by entering the text *(C)*, and letting AutoCorrect do its work. Other symbols, like the Greek theta (θ), aren't as readily available. To use a symbol like this, you'll need the help of the Character Map utility.

The Character Map is an often-overlooked tool that lets you see all the characters that a font provides. It's great for digging out the odd accented é and other non-English characters.

NOTE Other Office applications, like Word and Excel, provide far more special characters for you to use. They support all sorts of fonts, including the nifty Wingdings font that's packed with icons. However, Access has a more rigorous way of working. It accepts only plain-vanilla characters that are supported in any font. Databases store unformatted information. Short Text fields don't include font and formatting details. The only exception is the seldom-used rich text feature for Long Text fields (page 68).

Here's how you can use the Character Map to add a special character:

1. **Start the Character Map utility.**

   The Character Map utility is a part of Windows, not Access. As a result, you need to launch it outside of Access. To do that, click the Start button (in Windows 7) or go to the Start screen (in Windows 8) and type *charmap*. A single match appears, named *charmap.exe*. Click it to launch the Character Map program (*Figure 3-20*).

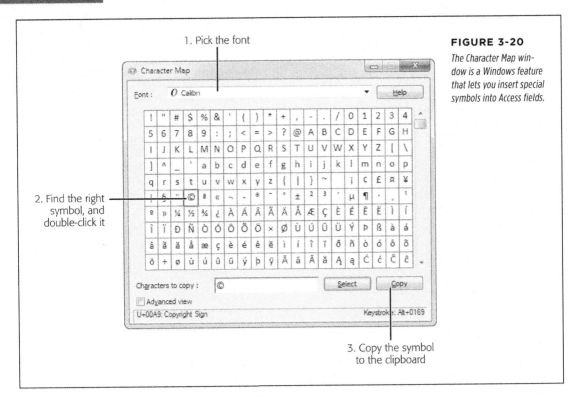

1. Pick the font

2. Find the right symbol, and double-click it

3. Copy the symbol to the clipboard

FIGURE 3-20

The Character Map window is a Windows feature that lets you insert special symbols into Access fields.

2. **In the Font list, select the Calibri font.**

   There's no point using an exotic font, because Access doesn't support it. However, you can find the supported special characters using any common font, including Arial, Times, and Tahoma. Calibri is the standard font that Access uses to display information in the datasheet, unless you've customized it (page 98).

3. **Scroll through the list of characters until you find the one you want.**

   If you need a letter character from another language, look hard—you'll almost certainly find it. If you want something a little more exotic but can't find it, you're probably out of luck. You'll need to use ordinary text instead.

4. **Double-click the character.**

   It appears in the "Characters to copy" box at the bottom of the Character Map window. You can repeat steps 3 and 4 as many times as you need to copy several characters in a row.

5. **Click Copy.**

   Windows copies the symbols in "Characters to copy" to the Clipboard.

6. **Switch back to the Access window.**

   If you aren't in the right field—the place where you want to insert the copied text—move there now. If you want to place the symbol between existing characters, make sure you move the cursor to the right place inside the field.

7. **Press Ctrl+V to paste the symbol.**

GEM IN THE ROUGH

Getting Quick Totals for a Column

Access has a nearly hidden feature that lets you make quick, basic calculations with an entire column of numeric values. For example, you can use this to get the average price from a table of products, or the total contributions from a table of donations. Here's how it works:

1. Choose Home→Records→Totals. An extra row appears at the bottom of the datasheet, with the word "Total" at the far left.

2. Click in the totals row, under the column you want to use for your calculation. A drop-down list appears with

different types of calculations (*Figure 3-21*).

3. Choose the type of calculation you want to perform. Access shows the calculated value under the column. If you add a record or modify a value in the column, Access updates the totals immediately. You can repeat step 2 and 3 to pick totals for as many columns as you want,

The totals row is a simple, straightforward tool. One nice feature is that it respects your filtering settings, so if you've filtered the table to show just five rows, only five rows are used to calculate the totals. However, the totals row is far less powerful than the totals queries you'll build on page 263.

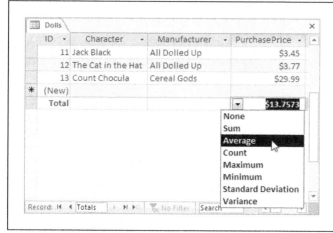

FIGURE 3-21

Here, the Total row shows the average price of all the records in the Dolls table.

Printing the Datasheet

If you want to study your data at the dinner table (and aren't concerned about potential conflicts with non-Access-lovers), nothing beats a hard copy of your data. You can dash off a quick printout by opening your datasheet, choosing File→Print to enter backstage view, and then clicking the big Print button. However, the results you get will probably disappoint you, particularly if you have a large table.

The key problem is that Access isn't bothered about tables that are too wide to fit on a printed page. It deals with them by splitting the printout into separate pages. If you have a large table and you print it using the standard Access settings, you could easily end up with a printout that's four pages wide and three pages long. Assembling this jigsaw is not for the faint of heart. To get a better printout, it's crucial that you *preview* your table before you print it, as described in the next section.

Print Preview

The print preview feature in Access gives you the chance to tweak your margins, paper orientation, and so on, before you send your table to the printer. This way, you can make sure the final printout is usable. To preview a table, open it (or select it in the navigation pane), choose File→Print, and then click the Print Preview button.

The print preview shows a picture of what your data will look like once it's committed to paper. Ordinarily, the print preview shows you a single page of your printout at a time. But to get an overall sense of what's going on—for example, to see whether all your columns can fit on a single page—it's a good idea to lay two or more sheets side by side. To see two pages at once, choose Print Preview→Zoom→Two Pages (*Figure 3-22*). To see more, choose Print Preview→Zoom→More Pages, and then choose the number of pages you want to see at once from the list.

If you decide you're happy with what you see, you can fire off your printout by clicking the Print button on the ribbon (Print Preview→Print→Print). The familiar Windows Print window opens so you can pick a printer and seal the deal.

When you're finished looking at the print preview window, click the ribbon's Close Print Preview button (Print Preview→Close Preview→Close Print Preview), or click one of the view buttons at the Access window's bottom-right corner to switch to Datasheet view or Design view.

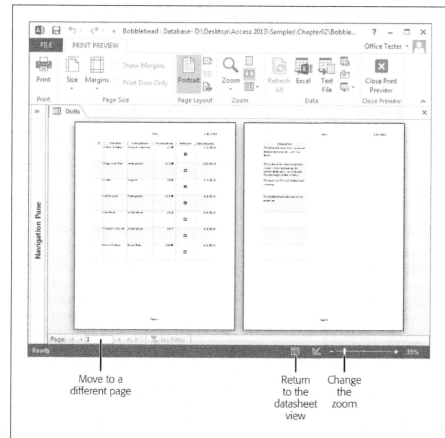

FIGURE 3-22

Unlike the datasheet view, the print preview paginates your data. You see exactly what fits on each page and how many pages your printout requires (and what content shows up on each page). Print preview shows you that this table is too wide to fit on one sheet of paper, so some of the columns will be relocated to a second page.

Move to a
different page

Return
to the
datasheet
view

Change
the
zoom

▨ MOVING AROUND THE PRINT PREVIEW

You can't change any data while viewing a table in the Print Preview window. However, you can browse through the pages of your virtual printout and see if it meets your approval.

Here's how you can get around in the preview window:

- Use the scroll buttons to move from one page to another. These buttons look the same as the scroll buttons in the datasheet, but they move from page to page, not record to record.

- To move from page to page, you can use the Page Up and Page Down keys.

- To jump in for a closer look, click anywhere on the preview page (you'll notice that the mouse pointer has become a magnifying glass). This click magnifies the sheet to 100 percent zoom, so you can more clearly see the text and details. To switch back to full-page view, click the page or click the mouse pointer again.

- To zoom more precisely, use the zoom slider that's in the status bar's bottom-right corner. Slide it to the left to reduce your zoom (and see more at once), or slide it to the right to increase your zoom (and focus on a smaller portion of your page).

■ CHANGING THE PAGE LAYOUT

Access provides a small set of page layout options that you can tweak using the ribbon's Print Preview→Page Layout section in the print preview window. Here are your options:

- **Size**. Lets you use different paper sizes. If you're fed up with tables that don't fit, you may want to invest in some larger stock (like legal-sized paper).

- **Portrait and Landscape**. Let you choose how the page is oriented. Access, like all Office programs, assumes you want to print text using standard *Portrait* orientation. In portrait orientation, pages are turned upright so that the long edge is along the side and the short edge is along the top. It makes perfect sense for résumés and memos, but it's pure madness for a wide table, because it guarantees at least some columns will be rudely chopped off and relocated to different pages. *Landscape* orientation makes more sense in this case, because it turns the page on its side, fitting fewer rows per page but many more columns.

- **Margins**. Lets you choose the breathing space between your table and the edges of the page. Margins is a drop-down button, and when you click it, you see a menu with several common margin choices (Normal, Narrow, and Wide). If none of those fit the bill, click the Page Setup button, which opens a Page Setup window where you can set the exact width of the margin on each side of the page.

Fine-Tuning a Printout

Based on the limited page layout options, you might assume that you can't do much to customize a printout. However, you actually have more control than you realize. Many of the formatting options that you've learned about in this chapter also have an effect on your printout. By applying the right formatting, you can create a better printout.

Here are some pro printing tips that explain how different formatting choices influence your printouts:

- **Font**. Printouts use your datasheet font and font size. Scale this down, and you can fit more in less space.

- **Column order and column hiding**. Reorder your columns before printing to suit what you want to see on the page. Even better, use column hiding (page 102) to conceal fields that aren't important.

- **Column widths and row height**. Access uses the exact widths and heights that you've set on your datasheet. Squeeze some columns down to fit more, and expand rows if you have fields with large amounts of text and you want them to wrap over multiple lines.

- **Frozen columns**. If a table is too wide to fit on your printout, the frozen column is printed on each part. For example, if you freeze the FirstName field, you'll see it on every separate page, so you don't need to line up the pages to find out who's who.

- **Sort options**. They help you breeze through data in a datasheet—and they can do the same for a printout. Apply them *before* printing.

- **Filter options**. These are the unsung heroes of Access printing. Use them to get just the important rows. That way, your printout has exactly what you need.

The only challenge you face when using these settings is the fact that you can't set them from the print preview window. Instead, you have to set them in the datasheet, jump to the print preview window to see the result, jump back to the datasheet to change them a little bit more, jump back to the print preview window, and so on. This process can quickly get tiring.

TIP Don't spend too much time tweaking the formatting options to create the perfect printout. If you have a large table that just can't fit gracefully on one page, you probably want to use reports, which are described in Part Three. They provide much more formatting muscle, including the ability to split fields over several lines, separate records with borders, and allow large values to take up more space by gently bumping other information out of the way.

Blocking Bad Data

E ven the best database designer has spent sleepless nights worrying about the errors that could be lurking in a database. Bad data is a notorious problem—it enters the database, lies dormant for months, and appears only when you discover you've mailed an invoice to a customer named "Blank Blank" or sold a $4.99 bag of peanuts for $499.

The best way to prevent these types of problems is to stop bad data from making it into your database in the first place. In other words, you need to set up validation rules that reject suspicious values as soon as someone types them in. Once bad data has entered your database, it's harder to spot than a blueberry in a swimming pool.

This chapter covers the essential set of Access data validation tools:

- **Duplicates, required fields, and default values** are the basics of data integrity.

- **Input masks** format ordinary text into patterns, like postal codes and phone numbers.

- **Validation rules** lay down strict laws for unruly fields.

- **Lookups** limit values to a list of preset choices.

There's one validation technique that this chapter doesn't cover: using *data macros*. Data macros are specialized routines that spring into action when someone makes a change in your database. They're remarkably powerful, but you can't use them until you learn the basics of macro programming. In the meantime, the validation tools you'll pick up in this chapter are simpler and easier to maintain.

NOTE You'll learn how to build macros in Chapter 15. You'll learn how to use macros to perform validation with data events in Chapter 16.

Data Integrity Basics

All of Access's data validation features work via the Design view you learned about in Chapter 2. To put them in place, you choose a field and then tweak its properties. The only trick is knowing which properties are most useful. You've already seen some in Chapter 2, but the following sections fill in a few more details.

TIP Remember, Access gives you three ways to switch to Design view. Once you right-click the table tab title, you can then choose Design View from the menu, use the Home→View button on the ribbon, or use the tiny view buttons at the Access window's bottom-right corner. And if you're really impatient, then you don't even need to open your table first—just find it in the navigation pane, right-click it there, and then choose Design View.

Preventing Blank Fields

Every record needs a bare minimum of information to make sense. However, without your help, Access can't distinguish between critical information and optional details. For that reason, every field in a new table is optional, except for the primary-key field (which is usually the ID value). Try this out with the Dolls table from Chapter 1; you'll quickly discover that you can add records that have virtually no information in them.

You can easily remedy this problem. Just select the field that you want to make mandatory in Design view, and then set the Required field property to Yes (*Figure 4-1*).

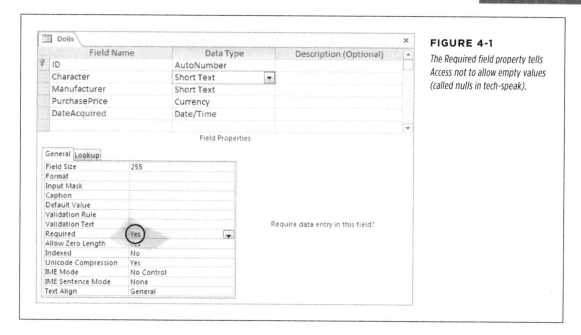

FIGURE 4-1

The Required field property tells Access not to allow empty values (called nulls in tech-speak).

Access checks the Required field property whenever you add a new record or modify a field in an existing record. However, if your table already contains data, there's no guarantee that it follows the rules.

Imagine you've filled the Dolls table with a few bobbleheads before you decide that every record requires a value for the Character field. You switch to Design view, choose the Character field, and then flip the Required field property to Yes. When you save the table (by switching back to Datasheet view or closing the table), Access gives you the option of verifying the bobblehead records that are already in the table (*Figure 4-2*). If you choose to perform the test and Access finds the problem, it gives you the option of reversing your changes (*Figure 4-3*).

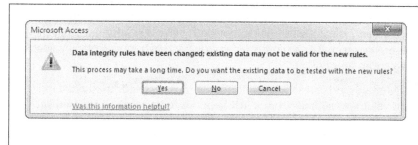

FIGURE 4-2

It's a good idea to test the data in your table to make sure it meets the new requirements you put into place. Otherwise, invalid data could still remain. Don't let the message scare you—unless you have tens of thousands of records, this check doesn't take long.

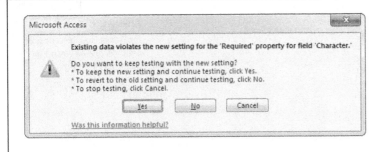

FIGURE 4-3

If Access finds an empty value, it stops the search and asks you what to do about it. You can keep your changes (even though they conflict with at least one record. After all, at least new records won't suffer from the same problem. Your other option is to reset your field to its more lenient previous self. Either way, you can track down the missing data by performing a sort on the field in question (page 104), which brings empty values to the top.

WORD TO THE WISE

Don't Require Too Much

You need to think very carefully about what comprises the set of values you need, at a minimum, to create a record.

For example, a company selling Elvis costumes might not want to accept a new outfit into their Products table unless they have every detail in place. The Required field property is a great help here, because it prevents half-baked products from showing up in the catalog.

On the other hand, the same strictness is out of place in the same company's Customers table. The sales staff needs the flexibility to add a new prospect with only partial information. A potential customer may phone and leave only a mailing address (with no billing address, phone number, email information, and so on). Even though you don't have all the information about this customer, you still need to place that customer in the Customers table so that he or she can receive the monthly newsletter.

As a general rule, make a field optional if the information for it isn't necessary or may not be available at the time the record is entered.

■ BLANK VALUES AND EMPTY TEXT

Access supports this Required property for every data type. However, with some data types you may want to add extra checks. That's because the Required property prevents only blank fields—fields that don't have any information in them at all. However, Access makes a slightly bizarre distinction between blank values and something called *empty text*.

A blank (null) value indicates that no information was supplied. Empty text indicates that a field value was supplied, but it just happens to be empty. Confused yet? The distinction exists because databases like Access need to recognize when information is missing. A blank value could indicate an oversight—someone may just have forgotten to enter the value. On the other hand, empty text indicates a conscious decision to leave that information out.

To try this out in your datasheet, create a Short Text field that has Required set to Yes. Try inserting a new record and leaving the record blank. (Access stops you cold.) Now, try adding a new record, but place a single space in the field. Here's the strange part: Access automatically trims out spaces, and by doing so, it converts your single space to empty text. However, you don't receive an error message because empty text isn't the same as a blank value.

The good news is that if you find this whole distinction confusing, then you can prevent both blank values *and* empty text. Just set Required to Yes to stop the blank values, and set Allow Zero Length to No to prevent empty text.

NOTE A similar distinction exists for numeric data types. Even if you set Required to Yes, you can still supply a number of 0. If you want to prevent that action, use the validation rules described later in this chapter (page 146).

Setting Default Values

So far, the fields in your tables are either filled in explicitly by the person who adds the record or are left blank. But there's another option—you can supply a *default value*. Now, if someone inserts a record and leaves the field blank, Access applies the default value instead.

You set a default value by using the Default Value field property. For example, for a numeric AddedCost field, you could set this to be the number 0. For a text Country field, you could use the text "U.S.A." as a default value. (When you use text for a default value, you must wrap the text in quotation marks.)

Access shows all your default values in the new-row slot at the bottom of the datasheet (*Figure 4-4*). It also automatically inserts default values into any hidden columns (page 133). But default value settings don't affect any of your existing records—they keep whatever value they had when you last edited them.

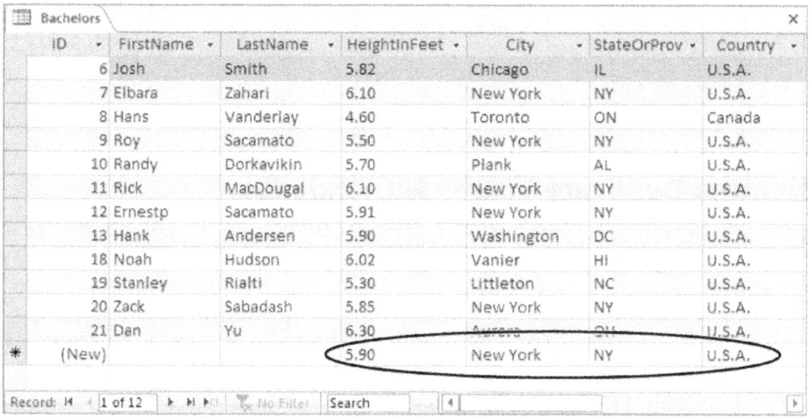
Bachelors

ID	FirstName	LastName	HeightInFeet	City	StateOrProv	Country
6	Josh	Smith	5.82	Chicago	IL	U.S.A.
7	Elbara	Zahari	6.10	New York	NY	U.S.A.
8	Hans	Vanderlay	4.60	Toronto	ON	Canada
9	Roy	Sacamato	5.50	New York	NY	U.S.A.
10	Randy	Dorkavikin	5.70	Plank	AL	U.S.A.
11	Rick	MacDougal	6.10	New York	NY	U.S.A.
12	Ernestp	Sacamato	5.91	New York	NY	U.S.A.
13	Hank	Andersen	5.90	Washington	DC	U.S.A.
18	Noah	Hudson	6.02	Vanier	HI	U.S.A.
19	Stanley	Rialti	5.30	Littleton	NC	U.S.A.
20	Zack	Sabadash	5.85	New York	NY	U.S.A.
21	Dan	Yu	6.30	Aurora	OH	U.S.A.
(New)			5.90	New York	NY	U.S.A.

Record: 1 of 12 No Filter Search

FIGURE 4-4

This dating service uses four default values: a default height (5.9), a default city (New York), a default state (also New York), and a default country (U.S.A.). This system makes sense, because most of their new entries have this information. On the other hand, there's no point in supplying a default value for the name fields.

Access inserts the default value when you create a new record. (You're then free to change that value.) You can also switch a field back to its default value by using the Ctrl+Alt+Space shortcut while you're editing it.

> **TIP** One nice feature: You can use the default value as a starting point for a new record. For example, when you create a new record in the datasheet, you can edit the default value, rather than replacing it with a completely new value.

You can also create more intelligent *dynamic* default values. Access evaluates dynamic default values whenever you insert a new record, which means that the default value can vary based on other information. Dynamic default values use *expressions* (specialized database formulas) that can perform calculations or retrieve other details. One useful expression, Date(), grabs the current date that's set on your computer. If you use Date() as the Default Value for a date field (as shown in *Figure 4-5*), Access automatically inserts the current date whenever you add a new record.

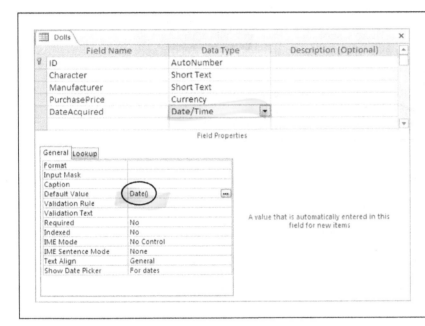

FIGURE 4-5

If you use the Date() function as the default value for the Date-Acquired field in the bobblehead table, then every time you add a new bobblehead record, Access fills in the current date. You decide whether you want to keep that date or replace it with a different value.

Preventing Duplicate Values with Indexes

In a properly designed table, every record must be unique. To enforce this restriction, you should choose a primary key (page 88), which is one or more fields that won't be duplicated.

Here's the catch. As you learned in Chapter 2, the safest option is to create an ID field for the primary key. So far, all the tables you've seen have included this detail. But what if you need to make sure *other* fields are unique? Imagine you create an Employees table. You follow good database design principles and identify every record with an automatically generated ID number. However, you also want to make sure that no two employees have the same Social Security number (SSN), to prevent errors like accidentally entering the same employee twice.

> **TIP** For a quick refresher about why ID fields are such a good idea, refer to page 95. In the Employees table, you certainly could choose to make the SSN the primary key, but it's not the ideal situation when you start linking tables together (Chapter 5), and it causes problems if you need to change the SSN later on (in the case of an error), or if you enter employee information before you've received the SSN.

You can force a field to require unique values with an *index*. A database index is analogous to the index in a book—it's a list of values (from a field) with a cross-reference that points to the corresponding section (the full record). If you index the SocialSecurityNumber field, Access creates a list like the following and stores it behind the scenes in your database file.

SOCIAL SECURITY NUMBER	LOCATION OF FULL RECORD
001-01-3455	...
001-02-0434	...
001-02-9558	...
002-40-3200	...

Using this list, Access can quickly determine whether a new record duplicates an existing SSN (see the box below for an explanation of how this works). If the SSN is a duplicate, then Access doesn't let you insert the record.

UP TO SPEED

How Indexes Work

It's important that the list of SSNs is *sorted*. Sorting means the number 001-01-3455 always occurs before 002-40-3200 in the index, regardless of where the record is physically stored in the database. This sorting is important, because it lets Access quickly check for duplicates. If you enter the number 001-02-4300, Access needs to read only the first part of the list. Once it finds the next "larger" SSN (one that falls later in the sort, like 001-02-5010), it knows the remainder of the index doesn't contain a duplicate.

In practice, all databases use many more optimizations to make this process blazingly fast. But there's one key principle—without an index, Access would need to check the entire table. Tables aren't stored in sorted order, so there's no way Access can be sure a given SSN isn't in there unless it checks every record.

So how do you apply an index to a field? The trick is the Indexed field property, which is available for every data type except Attachment and OLE Object. When you add a field, the Indexed property is set to No, which means Access doesn't create an index. To add an index and prevent duplicates, you can change the Indexed property in Design view to Yes [No Duplicates]. The third option, Yes [Duplicates OK], creates an index but lets more than one record have the same value. This option doesn't help you catch repeated records, but it can still help speed up searches (see the box below for more).

> **NOTE** As you know from Chapter 2, primary keys also disallow duplicates, using the same technique. When you define a primary key, Access automatically creates an index on that field.

When you close Design view after changing the Indexed field property, Access prompts you to save your changes. At this point, it creates any new indexes it needs. You can't create a no-duplicates index if you already have duplicate information in your table. In that situation, Access gives you an error message when you close the Design window and it attempts to add the index.

FREQUENTLY ASKED QUESTION

Indexes and Performance

Are indexes a tool for preventing bad data or a technique for boosting performance?

Indexes aren't just for preventing duplicate values. They also shine when you need to boost the speed of common searches. Access can use the index to look up the record it wants, much as you can use the index at the back of this book to find a specific topic.

If you perform a search that scours the Employees table looking for the person with a specific SSN, then Access can use the index. That way, it locates the matching entry much more quickly, and it simply follows the pointer to the full record.

For more information about how indexes can speed up searches, refer to page 215. However, it's important to realize that indexes enhance performance only for extremely large, complex tables. If you're storing a few hundred records, each of which has a handful of fields, you really don't need an index—Access already performs searches with blinding speed.

▓ MULTIFIELD INDEXES

You can also use indexes to prevent a *combination* of values from being repeated. Imagine you create a People table to track your friends and their contact information. You're likely to have entries with the same first or last name. However, you may want to prevent two records from having the same first *and* last name. This limitation prevents you from inadvertently adding the same person twice.

> **NOTE** This example could cause endless headaches if you honestly *do* have two friends who share the same first and last names. In that case, you'll need to remove the index before you're allowed to add the name. So think carefully about legitimate reasons for duplication before you create any indexes.

To ensure that a combination of fields is unique, you need to create a *compound index*, which combines the information from more than one field. Here's how to do it:

1. **In Design view, choose Table Tools | Design→Show/Hide→Indexes.**

    The Indexes window appears (*Figure 4-6*). Using the Indexes window, you can see your current indexes and add new ones.

2. **Choose a name for your index. Type this name into the first blank row in the Index Name column.**

The index name has no real importance—Access uses it to store the index in the database, but you don't see the index name when you work with the table. Usually, you'll use the name of one or both of the fields you're indexing (like LastName+FirstName).

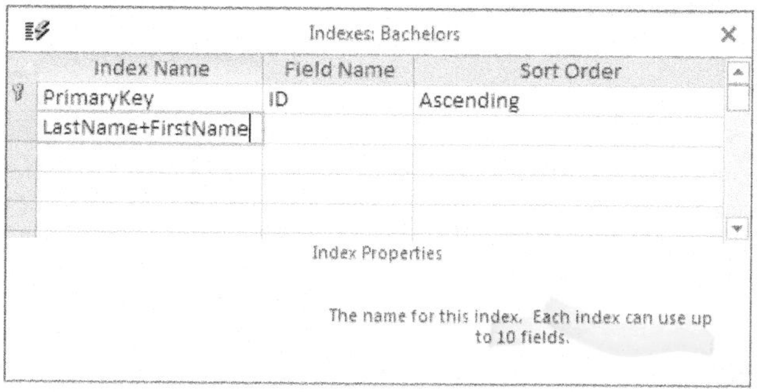

FIGURE 4-6

The Indexes window shows all the indexes that are defined for a table. Here, there's a single index for the ID field (which Access created automatically) and a compound index that's in the process of being created.

3. **Choose the first field in the Field Name column in the same row (like Last-Name).**

It doesn't matter which field name you use first. Either way, the index can prevent duplicate values. However, the order does affect how searches use the index to boost performance. You'll learn more on page 215.

4. **In the area at the bottom of the window, set the Unique box to Yes.**

This creates an index that prevents duplicates (as opposed to one that's used only for boosting search speeds).

You can also set the Ignore Nulls box to Yes, if you want Access to allow duplicate blank values. Imagine you want to make the SSN field optional. In this case, you should set Ignore Nulls to Yes. If you set Ignore Nulls to No, then Access lets only one record have a blank SSN field, which probably isn't the behavior you want.

TIP You can also disallow blank values altogether using the Required property, as described on page 130.

Ignore the Primary box (which identifies the index used for the primary key).

5. **Move down one row. Leave the Index Name column blank (which tells Access it's still part of the previous index), but choose another field in the Field Name column (like FirstName).**

If you want to create a compound index with more than two fields, then just repeat this step until you've added all the fields you need. *Figure 4-7* shows what a finished index looks like.

You can now close the Indexes window.

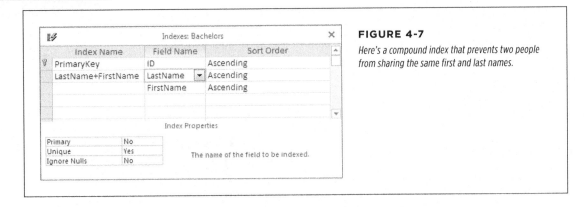

FIGURE 4-7

Here's a compound index that prevents two people from sharing the same first and last names.

Input Masks

As you've already learned, databases prize *consistency*. If you have a field named Height, you better be sure every value in that field uses the same type of measurements; otherwise, your data isn't worth its weight in sock lint. Similarly, if you have a PhoneNumber field, you better make sure every phone number has the same format. If some phone numbers are written with dashes, spaces, and parentheses (like *(844) 547-1123*), while others are a bit different (say, *847-547-1123*), and a few leave out the area code information altogether (*547-1123*), then you've got a small problem on your hands. Because of the lack of consistency, you'll have a hard time working with this information (say, searching for a specific phone number or sorting the phone numbers into different categories based on area code).

To help you manage values that have a fixed pattern—like phone numbers—you can use an *input mask*. Essentially, an input mask (or just *mask* for short) gives you a way to tell Access what pattern your data should use. Based on this pattern, Access changes the way values are entered and edited to make them easier to understand and less error-prone. *Figure 4-8* shows how a mask lets Access format a series of characters as they're being typed into a field.

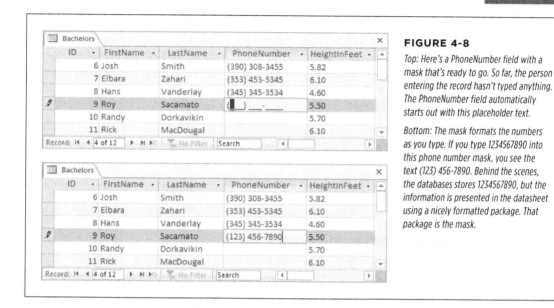

FIGURE 4-8

Top: Here's a PhoneNumber field with a mask that's ready to go. So far, the person entering the record hasn't typed anything. The PhoneNumber field automatically starts out with this placeholder text.

Bottom: The mask formats the numbers as you type. If you type 1234567890 into this phone number mask, you see the text (123) 456-7890. Behind the scenes, the databases stores 1234567890, but the information is presented in the datasheet using a nicely formatted package. That package is the mask.

You can add a mask to any field that uses the Short Text data type. Masks give you several advantages over ordinary text:

- **Masks guide data entry**. When empty, a masked edit control shows the placeholders where values need to go. A phone number mask shows the text "(_ _ _) _ _ _-_ _ _ _" when it's empty, clearly indicating what type of information it needs.

- **Masks make data easier to understand**. You can read many values more easily when they're presented a certain way. Most people can pick out the numbers in this formatted Social Security number (012-86-7180) faster than in this unformatted one (012867180).

- **Masks prevent errors**. Masks reject characters that don't fit the mold. For example, if you're using the telephone mask, you can't use letters.

- **Masks prevent confusion**. With many types of data, you have several ways to present the same information. You can enter phone numbers both with and without area codes. By presenting the mask with the area code placeholder, you're saying that this information is required (and where it goes). It's also obvious that you don't need to type in parentheses or a dash to separate numbers, because those details are already there. You'll see the same benefit if you use masks with dates, which can be entered in all sorts of different combinations (Year/Month/Day, Month-Day-Year, and so on).

Masks are best suited for when you're storing numeric information in a Short Text field. This scenario occurs with all sorts of data, including credit card numbers, postal codes, and phone numbers. These types of information shouldn't be stored in number fields, because they aren't meant to be interpreted as a single number. Instead, they're meant to be understood as a series of digits. (If you do make the mistake of storing a phone number in a number field, you'll find out that people can type in perfectly nonsensical phone numbers like 0 and –14 because these are valid numbers, even if they aren't valid phone numbers. But an input mask on a Short Text field catches these errors easily.)

Masks can't help you with more sophisticated challenges, like data values that have varying lengths or subtle patterns. For instance, a mask doesn't help you spot an incorrect email address.

NOTE Text and Date/Time are the only data types that support masks.

Using a Readymade Mask

The easiest way to get started with masks is to use one of the many attractive options that Access has ready for you. This method is great, because it means you don't need to learn the arcane art of mask creation.

Here's what you need to do to pick out a prebuilt mask:

1. **In Design view, select the Short Text field where you want to apply the mask.**

   For this test, try a PhoneNumber field.

2. **Look for the Input Mask field property.** Click inside the field.

   When you do, a small ellipsis (...) button appears at the right edge, as shown in *Figure 4-9*.

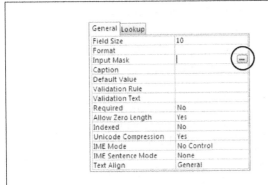

FIGURE 4-9

The ellipsis (...) button (circled) is just the way Access tells you that you don't need to fill in this value by hand. Instead, you can click the ellipsis and pop up a wizard (like the Input Mask Wizard) or some sort of helpful window.

3. **Click the ellipsis button.**

   The Input Mask Wizard starts (see *Figure 4-10*).

4. **Choose the mask you want from the list of options.**

   In this case, choose the first item in the list (Phone Number).

TIP Don't see what you want? You'll need to create your own, using the tips on page 143. If you see one that's close but not perfect, select it. You can tweak the mask in the wizard's second step.

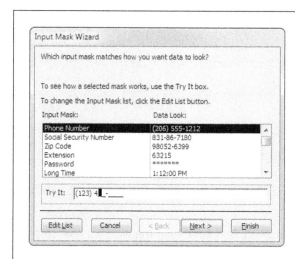

FIGURE 4-10

The Input Mask Wizard starts with a short list of commonly used masks. Next to every mask, Access shows you what a sample formatted value looks like. Once you select a mask, you can check it out in the Try It text box. The Try It text box gives you the same behavior that your field will have once you apply the mask.

5. **Click Next.**

   The wizard's second step appears (see *Figure 4-11*).

6. **If you want, you can change the mask or the placeholder character.**

   To change the mask, you'll need to learn what every mask character means. Page 144 explains it all.

   You use the placeholder to show the empty slots where you enter information. The standard choice is the underscore. Optionally, you can use a space, dash, asterisk, or any other character by typing it in the "Placeholder character" box.

FIGURE 4-11

The phone number mask is !(999) 000-0000. Each 9 represents an optional number from 0 to 9. Each 0 represents a required number from 0 to 9. So according to this mask, (123) 456-7890 is a valid phone number, as is 123-4567, but (123) 456 isn't.

7. **Click Next.**

If you're adding a mask to a Short Text field, then the wizard's final step appears (see *Figure 4-12*).

If you're adding a mask to a date field, then Access doesn't need to ask you how to store the information—it already knows. In this case, you can jump to step 9 and click Finish.

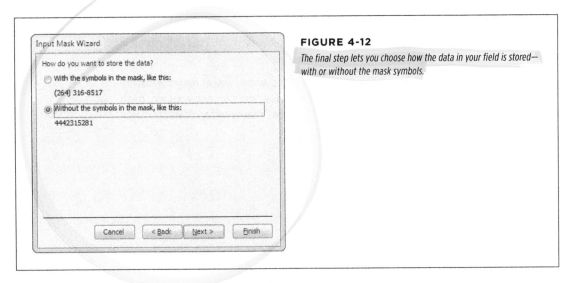

FIGURE 4-12

The final step lets you choose how the data in your field is stored— with or without the mask symbols.

8. **Choose how you want to store the value in this field.**

The standard choice is to store just the characters you've typed into the field. If you use this option, the placeholders aren't included. For example, the phone number (416) 123-4567 is stored as *4161234567*. This option saves a little space, and it also lets you change the mask later on to present the information in a slightly different way.

You could also store the mask complete with all the extra characters. Then a phone number is stored complete with hyphens, dashes, and spaces, like *(416) 123-4567*. This approach isn't nearly as flexible because you can't change the mask later.

9. **Click Finish.**

   The final mask appears in the Input Mask field property.

   Before going any further, you may want to make sure that the length you've reserved for your field matches the mask. In the phone number example, you need a Field Size of 10 if you've chosen to store unformatted values (because there are 10 digits), or a Field Size of 14 for the whole shebang, complete with placeholders (one dash, one space, and two parentheses).

10. **Switch back to the Datasheet view, and click Yes when Access asks you to save changes.**

    Your input mask is now in place.

NOTE Access uses the input mask information to control how information is entered into the datasheet. However, it's possible for someone to circumvent the mask by entering the information in other ways. (Things that can bypass a mask, either deliberately or accidentally, include an update query, a Visual Basic code routine, or a custom record-editing form.) In other words, a mask isn't an absolute guarantee against invalid data—if you want such a guarantee, then you need a validation rule instead (page 146).

Creating Your Own Mask

The Input Mask wizard provides a fairly limited set of choices. If you want to use a mask with your own type of information (like a special customer code that your business uses), then you have to create your own mask.

Creating a mask is fairly easy, but it can take a bit of fiddling before you nail down exactly the result you want. You have two basic options:

- Type or edit the mask directly in the Input Mask field property.

- Launch the Input Mask wizard, choose a mask to use as a starting point, and then tweak it in step 2. This approach has the advantage that you can test your mask in the Try It box before you save it as part of your table.

Every mask is built out of three types of characters:

- **Placeholders** designate where you type in a character.

- **Special characters** give additional instructions that tell Access how to treat a part of the mask.

- **Literals** are all other characters, which are really just decoration to help make the value easier to interpret.

In the previous example, the phone number mask was !(999) 000-0000. The characters 9 and 0 are placeholders—they represent where you type in the digits of the phone number. The parentheses, space, and dash are just formatting niceties—they're the literals. And the exclamation mark is the only special character. It tells Access that characters should be entered into the mask from left to right, which is the standard option and the only one that really makes sense for a phone number.

To help you sort all this out, refer to the following tables. Table 4-1 shows all the placeholders you can use in an input mask. Table 4-2 shows other special characters. Everything else is automatically a literal character.

TABLE 4-1 *Placeholder Characters for an Input Mask*

CHARACTER	DESCRIPTION
0	A required digit (0 through 9).
9	An optional digit (0 through 9).
#	An optional digit, a plus sign (+), or a minus sign (-).
L	A required letter.
?	An optional letter.
A	A required letter or digit.
a	An optional letter or digit.
&	A required character of any type (including letters, numbers, punctuation, and so on).
C	An optional character of any type (including letters, numbers, punctuation, and so on).

TABLE 4-2 *Special Characters for an Input Mask*

CHARACTER	DESCRIPTION
!	Indicates that the mask is filled from left to right when characters are typed in. This is the default, so this character isn't required (although the prebuilt masks include it).
<	Converts all characters that follow to lowercase.
>	Converts all characters that follow to uppercase.

CHARACTER	DESCRIPTION
\	Indicates that the following character should be treated as a literal. For example, the # character has a special meaning in masks. Thus, if you want to actually include a # in your mask, you need to use \#. Sometimes, this character is used before a placeholder even when it's not needed. You may see a phone mask that has the character sequence \- instead of just -. Both are equivalent.
Password	Creates a password entry box. Any character you type in the box is stored as the character but displayed as an asterisk (*). When using this option, you can't include anything else in your mask.

Here are a few sample masks to get you started:

- **(000) 000-0000**. A phone number that *requires* the area code digits. This mask is different from the phone number mask that the Input Mask Wizard uses. That mask replaces the first three 0 characters with 9, making the area code optional.

- **00000-9999**. A U.S. Zip code, which consists of five required digits followed by a hyphen and (optionally) four more digits.

- **L0L 0L0**. A Canadian postal code, which is a pattern of six characters that alternate between characters and digits, like M6S 3H2.

- **99:00 >LL**. A mask for entering time information into a Date/Time field. It's made up of two digits for the hour and two digits for the minute. The last two characters are always displayed in uppercase (thanks to the > character) and are meant to be AM or PM. (Technically, this mask doesn't prevent the user from flouting the system and typing in two different characters. However, if you enter a time like 12:30 GM, Access complains that it can't convert your entry into the Date/Time data type, as required for the field.)

- **099.099.099.099**. An IP (*Internet Protocol*) address, which identifies a computer on a network. An IP address is written as four values separated by periods. Each value must have at least one digit and can have up to three. This pattern is represented in the mask by 099 (one required digit, followed by two optional digits).

- **Password**. A mask that allows ordinary, unlimited text, with one difference. All characters are displayed as asterisks (*), to hide them from prying eyes.

Masks can also have two optional bits of information at the end, separated by semicolons (;).

The second section is a number that tells Access whether it should store the literal characters for the mask in the record. (This is the last question that the Input Mask Wizard asks.) If you leave this piece out or use the number 1, Access stores only the characters that someone types in. If you use the number 0, then Access stores the full text with the literals.

The third section supplies the placeholder character. If you leave this section out, Access uses the familiar underscore.

Here's a mask that uses these two extra bits of information:

```
(000) 000-0000;1;#
```

Here, the second section is *1*, and the third section is *#*. This mask is for phone numbers. It uses the number sign for a placeholder, and it includes the following literals: two parentheses, a space, and a dash. These literals aren't stored in the field.

POWER USERS' CLINIC

Adding Your Mask to the Mask List

Sometimes you may create a mask that's so useful you want to use it in many different tables in your database (and maybe even in different databases). While you can certainly copy your mask to every field that needs to use it, Access has a neater option—you can store your mask in its *mask list*. That way, the mask shows up whenever you run the Input Mask Wizard, right alongside all of Access's other standard masks.

To add your mask to the list, head to the Input Mask field property (for any field), and then click the ellipsis button to fire up the Input Mask Wizard. Then, click the Edit List button, which pops up a handy window where you can edit the masks that Access provides, and add your own (*Figure 4-13*).

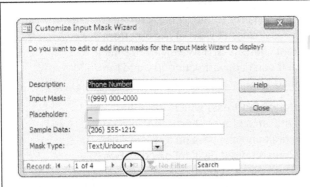

FIGURE 4-13

To add your own mask, use the "New blank" button (circled). Or you can use this window to change a mask. For example, the prebuilt telephone mask doesn't require an area code. If that's a liberty you're not willing to take, then replace it with the more restrictive version (000) 000-0000.

■ Validation Rules

Input masks are a great tool, but they apply to only a few specific types of information—usually fixed-length text that has a single, unchanging pattern. To create a truly bulletproof table, you need to use more sophisticated restrictions, like making sure a number falls in a certain range, checking that a date hasn't yet occurred, or verifying that a text value starts with a certain letter. *Validation rules* can help you create all these restrictions by drawing on the full power of the SQL language.

NOTE You'll get a more thorough introduction to SQL starting in Chapter 6. Fortunately, you need only a dash of SQL to write a validation rule. The key ingredient is a validation *expression*, and you'll see several practical examples of expressions that you can drop straight into your tables.

A validation rule's premise is simple. You set up a restriction that tells Access which values to allow in a field and which ones are no good. Whenever someone adds a new record or edits a record, Access makes sure the data lives up to your validation rules. If it doesn't, then Access presents an error message and forces you to edit the offending data and try again.

Applying a Field Validation Rule

Each field can have a single validation rule. The following steps show you how to set one up. You'll start out easy, with a validation rule that prevents a numeric field from accepting 0 or any negative number (and in the following sections you'll hone your rule-writing abilities so you can tackle other data types).

Here's how to add your validation rule:

1. **In Design view, select the field to which you want to apply the rule.**

   All data types—except Long Text, AutoNumber, and OLE Object—support validation. The validation rule in this example works with any numeric data type (like Number or Currency).

2. **In the Validation Rule field property, type a validation expression (*Figure 4-14*).**

   An expression is a bit of SQL that performs a check on the data you've entered. Access performs its validation check when you finish entering a piece of data and try to navigate to another field or another record. For example, *>0* is a validation rule that forces the value in a number field to be larger than 0. You'll learn more validation rules in the following sections.

3. **Type some error-message text in the Validation Text field property.**

   If you enter a value that fails the validation check, Access rejects the value and displays this error text in a window. If you don't supply any text, then Access shows the validation rule for the field (whatever you entered in step 2), which is more than a little confusing for most mere mortals.

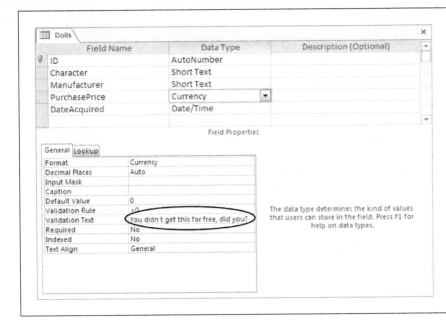

FIGURE 4-14

Here, the Validation Rule property prevents impossible prices, and the Validation Text provides an error message.

4. **Right-click the tab title and then choose Datasheet View.**

If your table has existing records, Access gives you the option of checking them to make sure they meet the requirements of your validation rule. You decide whether you want to perform this check, or skip it altogether.

Once you're in Datasheet view, you're ready to try out your validation rule (*Figure 4-15*).

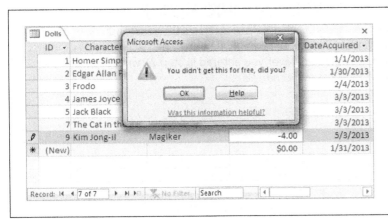

FIGURE 4-15

Here, a validation rule of >0 prevents negative numbers in the Price field. When you enter a negative number, Access pops up a message box with the validation text you defined, as shown here. Once you click OK, you return to your field, which remains in edit mode. You can change the value to a positive number, or press Esc to cancel the record edit or insertion.

NOTE Just because your table has validation rules doesn't mean the data inside *follows* these rules. A discrepancy can occur if you added records before the validation rules came into effect. To avoid these headaches, set up your validation rules before you start adding data.

Writing a Field Validation Rule

As you can see, it's easy enough to apply a validation rule to a field. But *creating* the right validation rule takes more thought. To get the result you want, you need to take your first step into the sometimes-quirky world of SQL.

Although validation is limited only by your imagination, Access pros turn to a few basic patterns again and again. The following sections give you some quick and easy starting points for validating different data types.

NOTE Access uses your validation rule only if a field contains some content. If you leave it blank, then Access accepts it without any checks. If this isn't the behavior you want, then just set the Required property to Yes to make the field mandatory, as described on page 130.

■ VALIDATING NUMBERS

For numbers, the most common technique is to check that the value falls in a certain range. In other words, you want to check that a number is less than or greater than another value. Your tools are the comparison signs < and >. Table 4-3 shows some common examples.

TABLE 4-3 *Expressions for Numbers*

COMPARISON	SAMPLE EXPRESSION	DESCRIPTION
Less than	<100	The value must be less than 100.
Greater than	>0	The value must be greater than 0.
Not equal to	<>42	The value can be anything except 42.
Less than or equal to	<=100	The value must be less than or equal to 100.
Greater than or equal to	>=0	The value must be greater than or equal to 0.
Equal to	=42	The value must be 42. (Not much point in asking anyone to type it in, is there?)
Between	Between 0 and 100	The value must be 0, 100, or somewhere in between.

■ VALIDATING DATES

As with numbers, date validation usually involves checking to see if the value falls within a specified range. Here, your challenge is making sure that your date is in the right format for an expression. If you use the validation rule *>Jan 30, 2013*, Access is utterly confused, because it doesn't realize that the text (Jan 30, 2013) is supposed to represent a date. Similarly, if you try *>1/30/2013*, then Access assumes the numbers on the right are part of a division calculation.

To solve this problem, use Access universal date syntax, which looks like this:

    #1/30/2013#

A universal date always has the date components in the order month/day/year, and it's always bracketed by the # symbol on either side. Using this syntax, you can craft a condition like *>#1/30/2013#*, which states that a given date must be larger than (fall after) the date January 30, 2013. January 31, 2013, fits the bill, but a date in 2012 is out.

The universal date syntax can also include a time component, like this:

    #1/30/2013 5:30PM#

> **NOTE** When comparing two dates, Access takes the time information into consideration. For example, the date #1/30/2013# doesn't include any time information, so it's treated as though it occurs on the very first second of the day. As a result, Access considers the date value #1/30/2013 8:00 AM# larger, because it occurs 8 hours later.

Once you've learned the universal date syntax, you can use any of the comparison operators you used with numbers. You can also use these handy functions to get information about the current date and time:

- Date() gets the current date (without any time information, so it counts as the first second of the day).

- Now() gets the current instant in time, including the date and time information.

> **NOTE** A *function* is a built-in code routine that performs some task, like fetching the current date from the computer clock. You'll learn about many more date functions, which let you perform advanced tasks like finding the day of the week for a date, on page 256.

Table 4-4 has some examples.

TABLE 4-4 *Expressions for Dates*

COMPARISON	SAMPLE EXPRESSION	DESCRIPTION
Less than	<#1/30/2013#	The date occurs before January 30, 2013.

COMPARISON	SAMPLE EXPRESSION	DESCRIPTION
Greater than	>#1/30/2013 5:30 PM#	The date occurs after January 30, 2013, or on January 30, 2013, after 5:30 p.m.
Less than or equal to	<=#1/30/2013#	The date occurs before January 30, 2013, or on the first second of January 30, 2013.
Greater than or equal to	>=#1/30/2013#	The date occurs on or after January 30, 2013.
Greater than the current date	>=Date()	The date occurs today or after.
Less than the current date	<Date()	The date occurs yesterday or before.
Greater than the current date (and time)	>Now()	The date occurs today after the current time, or any day in the future.
Less than the current date (and time)	<Now()	The date occurs today before the current time, or any day in the past.

■ VALIDATING TEXT

With text, validation lets you verify that a value starts with, ends with, or contains specific characters. You perform all these tasks with the *Like* operator, which compares text to a pattern.

This condition forces a field to start with the letter *R*:

```
Like "R*"
```

The asterisk (*) represents zero or more characters. Thus, the complete expression asks Access to check that the value starts with *R* (or *r*), followed by a series of zero or more characters.

You can use a similar expression to make sure a piece of text ends with specific characters:

```
Like "*ed"
```

This expression allows the values *talked*, *walked*, and *34z%($)#ed*, but not *talking*, *walkable*, or *34z%($)#*.

For a slightly less common trick, you can use more than one asterisk. The following expression requires that the letters *a* and *b* appear (in that order but not necessarily next to each other) somewhere in the text value:

```
Like "*a*b*"
```

Or consider this example, that tests for an email address by allowing any amount of text, followed by an @ sign, followed by more text, followed by a period, and then followed by the last bit of text:

```
Like "*@*.*"
```

Along with the asterisk, the Like operator also supports a few more characters. You can use ? to match a single character, which is handy if you know how long text should be or where a certain letter should appear. Here's the validation rule for an eight-character product code that ends in OZB:

```
Like "?????OZB"
```

The # character plays a similar role, but it represents a number. Thus, the following validation rule defines a product code that ends in OZB and is preceded by five numbers:

```
Like "#####OZB"
```

You can combine the ? or # with * to allow a variable amount of text, but require a certain number of characters. For example, the expression ?* tells Access to accept one character, followed by zero or more additional characters.

Using this technique, you can build a slightly smarter email expression that requires a minimum of four characters arranged around the special character @ and the period. (So a bogus value like @. is no longer allowed, but *a@b.cd* is good.) Here's what the expression looks like:

```
Like "*?@*?.*??"
```

And finally, you can restrict any character to certain letters or symbols. The trick is to put the allowed characters inside square brackets.

Suppose your company uses an eight-character product code that always begins with A or E. Here's the validation rule you need:

```
Like "[AE]???????"
```

Note that the [AE] part represents one character, which can be either A or E. If you wanted to allow A, B, C, D, you'd write [ABCD] instead, or you'd use the handy shortcut [A-D], which means "allow any character from A to D, including A and D."

Here's one more validation expression, which allows a seven-letter word and doesn't allow numbers or symbols. It works by repeating the [A-Z] code (which allows any letter) seven times.

```
Like "[A-Z][A-Z][A-Z][A-Z][A-Z][A-Z][A-Z]"
```

As you can see, text validation expressions aren't always pretty. Not only can they grow to ridiculous sizes, but there are lots of restrictions they can't apply. You can't, for instance, let the length of the text vary between a minimum and maximum that you set. And you can't distinguish between capitalized and lowercase letters.

TIP You can get around many of these limitations by using some of the functions that Access provides. On page 253, you'll learn how to use functions that can snip out bits of text, test lengths, check capitalization, and more.

■ COMBINING VALIDATION CONDITIONS

No matter what the data type, you can also *combine* your conditions in two different ways. Using the *And* keyword, you can create a validation rule that enforces two requirements. This trick is handy, because each field can have at most a single validation rule.

To use the And keyword, just write two validation rules, and put the word "And" in between. It doesn't matter which validation rule is first. Here's a validation rule that forces a date to be before today but later than January 1, 2000:

```
<Date() And >#1/1/2000#
```

You can also use the Or keyword to accept a value if it meets either one of two conditions. Here's a validation rule that allows numbers greater than 1000 or less than –1000:

```
>1000 Or <-1000
```

Creating a Table Validation Rule

Field validation rules always apply to a single field. However, database designers often need a way to compare the values in different fields. Suppose you have an Orders table that logs purchases from your monogrammed sock store. In your Orders table, you use two date fields: DateOrdered and DateShipped. To keep everything kosher, you need a validation rule that makes sure DateOrdered falls *before* DateShipped. After all, how can you ship a product before someone orders it?

Because this validation rule involves two fields, the only way to put it in place is to create a validation rule for the whole table. Table validation rules can use all the SQL tricks you've learned about so far, *and* they can pull the values out of any field in the current record.

Here's how to create a table validation rule:

1. **Switch to Design view, if you're not there already.**

   If the Property Sheet isn't visible, choose Table Tools | Design→Show/Hide→Property Sheet.

   A box with extra settings appears on the right side of the window (*Figure 4-16*).

FIGURE 4-16

The Property Sheet shows some information about the entire table, including any sorting (page 104) and filtering settings (page 107) you've applied to the datasheet, and the table validation rule. Here, the validation rule prevents orders from being shipped before they're ordered.

> **TIP** You can create only a single validation rule for a table. This limit might sound like a problem, but you can get around it by using the And keyword to yoke together as many conditions as you want. The validation rule may be a little difficult to read, but it still works without a hitch.

2. **In the Property Sheet tab, set the Validation Rule.**

   A table validation rule can use all the same keywords you learned about earlier. However, table validation rules usually compare two or more fields. The validation rule [DateOrdered] < [DateShipped] ensures that the value for the Date-Ordered field is older than the one used for DateShipped.

   When referring to a field in a table validation rule, you need to wrap square brackets around your field names. That way, Access can tell the difference between fields and functions (like the Date() function you learned about on page 134).

3. **Set the Validation Text.**

   This message is the error message that's shown if the validation fails. It works the same as the validation text for a field rule.

When you insert a new record, Access checks the field validation rules first. If your data passes the test (and has the right data types), then Access checks the table validation rule.

> **TIP** Once you set the table validation rule, you might want to close the Property Sheet to get more room in your Design window. To do so, choose Table Tools | Design→Show/Hide→Property Sheet.

Lookups

In a database, minor variations can add up to big trouble. Suppose you're running International Cinnamon, a multinational cinnamon bun bakery with hundreds of orders a day. In your Orders table, you have entries like this:

```
Quantity    Product
10          Frosted Cinnamon Buns
24          Cinnamon Buns with Icing
16          Buns, Cinnamon (Frosted)
120         FCBs
...
```

(Other fields, like the ID column and the information about the client making the order, are left out of this example.)

All the orders shown here amount to the same thing: different quantities of tasty cinnamon and icing confections. But the text in the Product column is slightly different. This difference doesn't pose a problem for ordinary human beings (for example, you'll have no trouble filling these orders), but it does create a small disaster if you want to analyze your sales performance later. Since Access has no way to tell that a Frosted Cinnamon Bun and an FCB are the same thing, it treats them differently. If you try to total up the top-selling products or look at long-range cinnamon sales trends, then you're out of luck.

> **NOTE** This example emphasizes a point that you've seen before. Namely, databases are strict, no-nonsense programs that don't tolerate minor discrepancies. For your databases to be useful, you need to make sure you store topnotch information in them.

Lookups are one more tool to help standardize your data. Essentially, a lookup lets you fill a value in a field by choosing from a readymade list of choices. Used properly, this tool solves the problem in the Orders table—you simply need a lookup that includes all the products you sell. That way, instead of typing the product name in by hand, you can choose Frosted Cinnamon Buns from the list. Not only do you save some time, but you also avoid variants like FCBs, thereby ensuring that the orders list is consistent.

Access has two basic types of lookup lists: lists with a set of fixed values that you specify, and lists that are drawn from a linked table. In the next section, you'll learn how to create the first type. Then, in Chapter 5, you'll graduate to the second.

> **NOTE** The only data types that support lookups are Short Text and Number.

Creating a Simple Lookup with Fixed Values

Simple lookups make sense if you have a simple, short list that's unlikely to change. The state prefix in an address is a perfect example. In this case, there's a set of just 50 two-letter abbreviations (AL, AK, AZ, and so on).

To try out the process in the following list of steps, you can use the Bachelors table included with the online examples for this chapter (look for the DatingService.accdb database file). Or, you can jump straight to the completed lookup by checking out the DatingServiceLookup.accdb file:

1. **Open the table in Design view.**

   If you're using the DatingService.accdb example, then open the Bachelors table.

2. **Find the field where you want to add the lookup.**

   In the Bachelors table, it's the State field.

3. **Make sure your field has the correct data type.**

   Short Text and Number are the most common data types that you'll use in conjunction with the lookup feature.

4. **From the data type list, choose Lookup Wizard.**

   This action doesn't actually change your data type. Instead, it tells Access you want to run the Lookup Wizard based on the current data type. When you select this option, the first step of the Lookup Wizard appears (*Figure 4-17*).

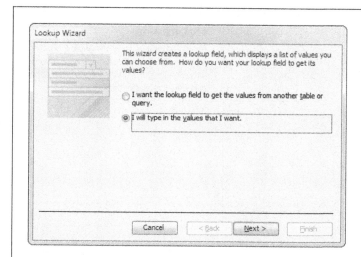

FIGURE 4-17

First you choose the source of your lookup: fixed values or data from another table.

5. **Choose "I will type in the values that I want."**

   Page 180 describes your other choice: drawing the lookup list from another table.

6. **Click Next.**

   The second step of the wizard gives you the chance to supply the list of values that should be used, one per row (*Figure 4-18*). In this case, it's a list of abbreviations for the 50 U.S. states.

   You may notice that you can supply multiple columns of information. For now, stick to one column. You'll learn why you may use more on page 180.

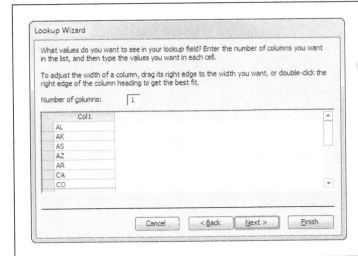

FIGURE 4-18

This lookup includes the abbreviations for all the American states. This list is unlikely to change in the near future, so it's safe to hardcode this rather than store it in another table.

7. **Click Next.**

   The final step of the Lookup Wizard appears.

8. **Choose whether you want the lookup column to store multiple values.**

   If you allow multiple values, then the lookup list displays a checkbox next to each item. You can select several values for a single record by choosing more than one item.

WARNING Once you configure a field to allow multiple values and you save your table, you can't back out. Access won't let you modify the field's Allow Multiple Values setting to convert it back to a single-value field.

   In the State field, it doesn't make sense to allow multiple values—after all, a person can physically inhabit only one state (discounting the effects of quantum teleportation). However, you can probably think of examples where multiple selection does make sense. For example, in the Products table used by International Cinnamon, a multiple-value lookup would let you create an order for more than one product. (You'll learn more about multiple-value selections and table relationships in Chapter 5.)

9. **Click Finish.**

   Switch to Datasheet view (right-click the tab title, and then choose Datasheet View), and then save the table changes. *Figure 4-19* shows the lookup in action.

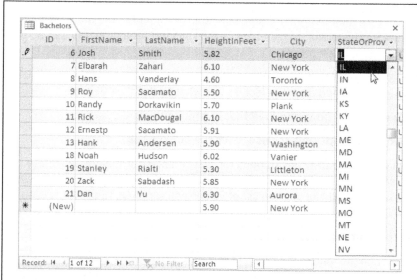

FIGURE 4-19

When you move to a field that has a lookup, you'll see a down-pointing arrow on the right side. Click this arrow, and a drop-down list appears with all your possibilities. Choose one to insert it into the field.

Creating a Lookup That Uses Another Table

In the lookup example in this chapter, you created a lookup list that's stored as part of your field settings. This is a good approach, but it's not the best solution. A much more flexible approach is to store the lookup list in a separate table.

You'll find several reasons to use a separate table:

- **It lets you add, edit, and remove items**, all by simply editing the lookup table. Even if you think you have a set of fixed, unchanging values, it's a good idea to consider a separate table. For example, the set of state abbreviations in the previous section seems unlikely to change—but what if the dating service goes international, and you need to add Canadian provinces to the list?

- **It lets you reuse the same lookup list in several different**

fields (either in the same table, or in different tables). That beats endless copy-and-paste operations.

- **It lets you store extra information**. For example, maybe you want to keep track of the state abbreviation (for mailing purposes) but show the full state name (to make data entry easier). You'll learn how to perform this trick on page 180.

Table-based lookups are a little trickier, however, because they involve a table *relationship*: a link that binds two tables together and (optionally) enforces new restrictions. Chapter 5 is all about relationships, which are a key ingredient in any practical database.

Adding New Values to Your Lookup List

When you create a lookup that uses fixed values, the lookup list provides a list of *suggestions*. You can choose to ignore the lookup list and type in a completely different value (like a state prefix of ZI), even if it isn't on the list. This design lets you use the lookup list as a timesaving convenience without limiting your flexibility.

In many cases, you don't want this behavior. In the Bachelors table, you probably want to prevent people from entering something different in the State field. In this case, you want the lookup to be an error-checking and validation tool that actually stops entries that don't belong.

Fortunately, even though this option is mysteriously absent in the Lookup wizard, it's easy enough to add after the fact. Here's what to do:

1. **In Design view, go to the field that has the lookup.**

2. **In the Field Properties section, click the Lookup tab.**

   The Lookup tab provides options for fine-tuning your lookup, most of which you can configure more easily in the Lookup wizard. In the Row Source box, for example, you can edit the list of values you supplied. (Each value is on the same line, in quotation marks, separated from the next value with a semicolon.)

3. **Set the "Limit to List" property to Yes.**

   This action prevents you from entering values that aren't in the list.

4. **Optionally, set Allow Value List Edits to Yes.**

   This action lets people modify the list of values at any time. This way, if something's missing from the lookup list, you can add it on the fly (*Figure 4-20*).

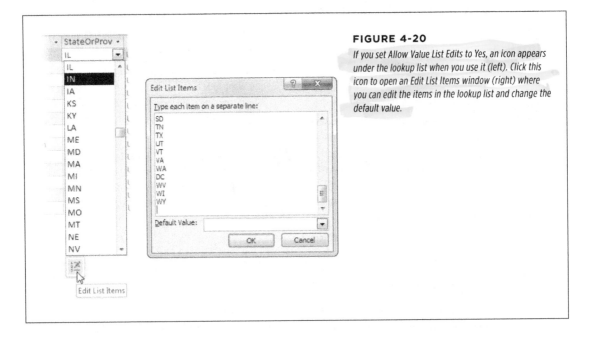

FIGURE 4-20

If you set Allow Value List Edits to Yes, an icon appears under the lookup list when you use it (left). Click this icon to open an Edit List Items window (right) where you can edit the items in the lookup list and change the default value.

Linking Tables with Relationships

The tables you've seen so far lead lonely, independent lives. You don't find this isolation with real-world databases. Real databases have their tables linked together in a web of *relationships*.

Suppose you set out to build a database that can manage the sales of your custom beadwork shop. The first ingredient is simple enough—a Products table that lists your merchandise—but before long you'll need to pull together a lot more information. The wares in your Products table are sold in your Orders table. The goods in your Orders table are mailed out and recorded in a Shipments table. The people in your Customers table are billed in your Invoices table. All these tables—Products, Orders, Shipments, Customers, and Invoices—have bits of related information. As a result, if you want to find out the answer to a common question (like, "How much does Jane Malone owe?" or "How many beaded wigs did we sell last week?"), you'll need to consult several tables.

Based on what you've learned so far, you already know enough to nail down the design for a database like this one. But relationships introduce the possibility of inconsistent information. And once a discrepancy creeps in, you'll never trust your database the same way again.

In this chapter, you'll learn how to *explicitly* define the relationships between tables. This process lets you prevent common errors, like data in different tables that doesn't sync up. It also gives you a powerful tool for browsing through related information in several tables.

Relationship Basics

One of any database's key goals is to break information down into distinct, manageable pieces. In a well-designed database, you'll end up with many tables. Although each table records something different, you'll often need to travel from one table to another to get all the information you want.

To better understand relationships (of the nonromantic kind, anyway), consider an example. The following section demonstrates two ways to add information to the bobblehead database: one that risks redundant data, and one that avoids the problem by properly using a relationship.

Redundant Data vs. Related Data

Think back to the Dolls table you created in Chapter 1 to store a list of bobblehead dolls. One of the pieces of information in the Dolls table is the Manufacturer field, which lists the name of the company that created each doll. Although this seems like a simple enough detail, it turns out that to properly assess the value of a bobblehead, you need to know a fair bit more about the manufacturing process. You may want to know things like where the manufacturing company is located, how long it's been in business, and if it's had to fight off lawsuits from angry customers.

If you're feeling lazy, you could add all this information to the Dolls table, like so (the shaded columns are the new ones):

ID	CHARACTER	MANUFAC-TURER	MANUFACTURER LOCATION	MANUFACTURER OPENING YEAR	MANUFACTURER LAWSUITS	PURCHASE PRICE
342	Yoda	MagicPlastic	China	2008	No	$8.99

Your first reaction to this table is probably to worry about the clutter of all these fields. But don't panic—in the real world, tables must include all the important details, so they often grow quite wide. (That's rule #3 of data design, from page 92.) So don't let the clutter bother you. You can use techniques like column hiding (page 102) to filter out the fields that don't interest you.

Although column clutter isn't a problem, another issue lurks under the surface in this example—redundant data. A well-designed table should list only one type of thing. This version of the Dolls table breaks that rule by combining information about the bobblehead *and* the bobblehead manufacturer.

This situation seems innocent enough, but if you add a few more rows, things don't look as pretty:

ID	CHARACTER	MANUFAC-TURER	MANUFACTURER LOCATION	MANUFACTURER OPENING YEAR	MANUFACTURER LAWSUITS	PURCHASE PRICE
342	Yoda	MagicPlastic	China	2008	No	$8.99
343	Dick Cheney	Rebobblicans	Taiwan	2010	No	$28.75
344	Tiger Woods	MagicPlastic	China	2008	No	$2.99

Once you have two bobbleheads that were made by the same company (in this case, MagicPlastic), you've introduced duplicate data, the curse of all bad databases. (You'll recognize this as a violation of rule #4 of good database design, from page 93.) The potential problems are endless:

- If MagicPlastic moves its plants from China to South Korea, you'll need to update a whole batch of bobblehead records. If you were using two tables with related data (as you'll see next), you'd have just one record to contend with.

- It's all too easy to update the manufacturer information in one bobblehead record but to miss it in another. If you make this mistake, you'll wind up with *inconsistent* data in your table, which is even worse than duplicate data. Essentially, your manufacturer information will become worthless because you won't know which record has the correct details, so you won't be able to trust anything.

- If you want to track more manufacturer-related information (like a contact number) in your database, you'll have to update your Dolls table and edit *every single record*. Your family may not see you for several weeks.

- If you want to get information about manufacturers (but not dolls), you're out of luck. For example, you can't print a list of all the bobblehead manufacturers in China (at least not easily).

It's easy to understand the problem. By trying to cram too many details into one spot, this table fuses together information that would best be kept in two separate tables. To fix this design, you need to create two tables that use *related data*. For example, you could create a Dolls table like this:

ID	CHARACTER	MANUFACTURER	PURCHASE PRICE
342	Yoda	MagicPlastic	$8.99
343	Dick Cheney	Rebobblicans	$28.75
344	Tiger Woods	MagicPlastic	$2.99

And a separate Manufacturers table with the manufacturer-specific details:

ID	MANUFACTURER	LOCATION	OPENING YEAR	LAWSUITS
1	MagicPlastic	China	2008	No
2	Rebobblicans	Taiwan	2010	No

This design gives you the flexibility to work with both types of information (dolls and manufacturers) separately. It also removes the risk of duplication. The savings are small in this simple example, but in a table with hundreds or thousands of bobblehead dolls (and far fewer manufacturers), the difference is dramatic.

Now, if MagicPlastic moves to South Korea, you need to update the Location field for only one record, rather than for many instances in an overloaded Dolls table. You'll also have an easier time building queries (Chapter 6) that combine the information in neat and useful ways. (For example, you could find out how much you've spent on all your MagicPlastic dolls and compare that with the amounts you've spent for dolls made by other manufacturers.)

> **TIP** Access includes a tool that attempts to spot duplicate data in a table and help you pull the fields apart into related tables. (To try it out, choose Database Tools→Analyze→Analyze Table.) Although it's a good idea in theory, this tool really isn't very useful. You'll do a much better job of spotting duplicate data and creating well-designed tables from the start if you understand the duplicate-data problem yourself.

Matching Fields: The Relationship Link

This bobblehead database shows you an example of a *relationship*. The telltale sign of a relationship is two tables with matching fields. In this case, the tip-off is the Manufacturer field, which exists in both the Dolls table and the Manufacturers table.

> **NOTE** In this example, the fields that link the two tables have the same name in both tables: Manufacturer. However, you don't have to do it this way. You can give these fields different names, so long as they have the same data type.

Using these linked fields, you can start with a record in one table and look up related information in the other. Here's how it works:

- **Starting at the Dolls table**, pick a doll that interests you (let's say Yoda). You can find out more information about the manufacturer of the Yoda doll by looking up "MagicPlastic" in the Manufacturers table.

- **Starting at the Manufacturers table**, pick a manufacturer (say, Rebobblicans). You can now search for all the products made by that manufacturer by searching for "Rebobblicans" in the Dolls table.

In other words, a relationship gives you the flexibility to ask more questions about your data and to get better answers.

Linking with the ID Column

In the previous example, the Dolls and Manufacturers tables are linked through the Manufacturer field, which stores the name of the manufacturing company. This seems like a reasonable design—until you spend a couple of minutes thinking about what might go wrong. And database experts are known for spending entire weeks contemplating inevitable disasters.

Here are two headaches that just may lie in store:

- **Two manufacturers have the same company name**. So how do you tell which one made a doll?

- **A manufacturer gets bought out by another company and changes its name**. All of a sudden, there's a long list of records to change in the Dolls table.

You might recognize these problems, because they're similar to the challenges you faced when you tackled primary keys (page 88). As you learned, it's difficult to find information that's guaranteed to be unique and unchanging. Rather than risk problems, you're better off just relying instead on an AutoNumber field, which stores an Access-generated ID number.

Interestingly enough, you use the same solution when linking tables. To refer to a record in another table, you shouldn't use just any piece of information—instead, you should use the unique ID number that points to the right record. Here's a redesigned Dolls table that gets it right by changing the Manufacturer field to ManufacturerID:

ID	CHARACTER	MANUFACTURER ID	PURCHASE PRICE
342	Yoda	1	$8.99
343	Dick Cheney	2	$28.75
344	Tiger Woods	1	$2.99

If you take a look back at the Manufacturers table (page 163), you can quickly find out that the manufacturer with the ID value 1 is MagicPlastic.

This design is the universal standard for databases. However, it does have two obvious drawbacks:

- The person adding records to the Dolls table probably doesn't know the ID of each manufacturer.

- When you look at the Dolls table, you can't tell what manufacturer created each doll.

To solve both these problems, use a *lookup*. Lookups show the corresponding manufacturer information in the Dolls table, and they also let you choose from a list of manufacturers when you add a record or edit the ManufacturerID field in the Dolls table. (You saw how to use lookups with value lists on page 156. You'll learn how to use lookups to bring together related tables, like Dolls and Manufacturers, on page 180.)

TIP For even more power, you can use a *join query* (page 227). A join query lets you fill in all the manufacturer details alongside the doll information so you can view them side-by-side.

The Parent-Child Relationship

No, this isn't a detour into feel-good Dr. Phil psychology. Database nerds use the labels *parent* and *child* to identify the two tables in a relationship and to keep track of which one's which.

Here's the analogy. In the real world a pare   n have any number of children. However, a child has exactly one set of parent   rule works for databases. In the bobblehead database, a single manufa   d can be linked to any number of doll records. However, each doll reco   single manufacturer. So according to the database world's strange so   ufacturers is a parent table and Dolls is a child table. They're linked b   ild relationship.

NOTE Don't think too hard about the parent-child analogy. It's not a perfect match with biological reality. For example, in the bobblehead database, you may create a manufacturer that doesn't link to any dolls (in other words, a parent with no children). But you still call that record a parent record, because it's part of the parent table.

It's important to realize that you can't swap the parent and child tables around without changing your relationship. It's incorrect to suggest that Dolls is the parent table and Manufacturers is the child table, since that would break the parent-child analogy: A single doll can't have more than one manufacturer, and a manufacturer isn't limited to creating a single doll. To prevent problems and all-around fuzzy thinking, you need to know exactly which table is the parent and which one is the child.

TIP If you have trouble identifying which table is the parent, there's a simple rule to steer you right. *The child table always contains a piece of identifying information from the parent table.* In the bobblehead database, the Dolls table contains the ManufacturerID field. On the other hand, the Manufacturer table doesn't have any doll information.

If you have database-savvy friends, you'll hear the term "parent-child relationship" quite a bit. The same relationship is also called a *one-to-many* relationship (where *one* is the parent and *many* represents the children, because a single parent record in one table can link to several child records in the other). It's the most common relationship, but not the only one—you'll learn about two other types later in this chapter.

NOTE Relationships are so common in modern-day databases that software like Access is often described as a *relational database management system* (RDBMS). A database without relationships is about as common as an oceanfront resort in Ohio.

Using a Relationship

The relationship between Dolls and Manufacturers is *implicit*, which is a fancy way of saying that you know the relationship exists, but Access doesn't. Database pros aren't satisfied with this arrangement. Instead, they almost always define their relationships *explicitly*. When you create an explicit relationship, you clearly tell Access how two tables are related. Access then stores the information about that relationship in the database file.

You have good reasons to bring your relationships out into the open. Once Access knows about a relationship, it can enforce better error checking. It can also provide handy features for browsing related data and editing linked fields. You'll see all these techniques in the following sections. But first, you need to learn how to define a relationship.

Defining a Relationship

You can try out the following steps with the Bobblehead.accdb file, which is included with the online examples for this chapter. It contains the Dolls and Manufacturers tables, in their original form (with no relationships defined). The Bobblehead-Relationships.accdb database file shows the final product: two tables with the right relationship.

Here's what you need to do to set up a relationship:

1. **Every relationship links two fields, each in a different table. Your first step is to identify the field you need to use in the parent table.**

   In a well-designed database, you use the primary-key field (page 88) in the parent table. For example, in the Manufacturers table, you use the ID column, which uniquely identifies each manufacturer.

2. **Open the child table in Design view. (The quickest way is to right-click it in the navigation pane, and then choose Design View.)**

   In this example, the child table is Dolls.

3. **Create the field you need in the child table if it's not there already.**

   Each child record creates a link by storing a piece of information that points to a record in the parent table. You need to add a new field to store this information, as shown in *Figure 5-1*.

NOTE   The fields that you link in the parent and child tables must have consistent data types. However, there's one minor wrinkle. If the parent field uses the AutoNumber data type, the child field should use the Number data type instead (with a Field Size of Long Integer). Behind the scenes, an AutoNumber and a Long Integer actually store the same numeric information. But the AutoNumber data type tells Access to fill in the field with a new, automatically generated value whenever you create a record. You obviously don't want this behavior for the ManufacturerID field in the Dolls table.

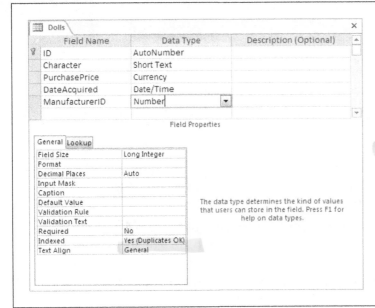

FIGURE 5-1

In the Dolls table, you need a field that identifies the manufacturer for that doll. It makes sense to add a new field named ManufacturerID. Set the data type to Number, and the Field Size to Long Integer, so it matches the ID field in the Manufacturers table. After you add this field, you need to fill it with the right information. (Each doll record should have the ID number of the corresponding manufacturer.)

4. **Close both tables.**

   Access prompts you to save your changes. Your tables are now relationship-ready.

5. **Choose Database Tools→Relationships→Relationships.**

   Access opens a new tab named Relationships. This tab is a dedicated window where you can define the relationships between all the tables in your database. In this example, you'll create just a single relationship, but you can use the Relationships tab to define many more.

   Before Access lets you get to work in the Relationships tab, it pops up a Show Table window for you to choose what tables you want to work with (see *Figure 5-2*).

6. **Add both the parent table and child table to your work area.**

   It doesn't matter which one you choose first. To add a table, select it in the list, and then click Add (or just double-click it).

   Access represents each table in the Relationships tab by a small box that lists all the table fields. If relationships are already defined between these tables, they'll appear as connecting lines.

FIGURE 5-2

*You can add as many tables as you want to the Relationships tab.
But be careful not to add the same table twice (it's unnecessary and
confusing).*

7. **Click Close.**

You can now arrange the tables in the Relationships tab (see *Figure 5-3*). The
Relationships tab shows a *database diagram*—it's the canvas where you add
relationships by "drawing" them on.

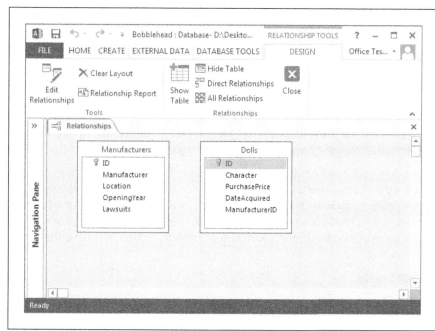

FIGURE 5-3

*The database diagram on
the Relationships tab lets
you drag the tables you've
added to any place in the
window. If you have a
database that's thick with
relationships, you can (and
should) arrange them so
the relationships are clearly
visible. To remove a table
from the diagram, right-
click it and then choose
Hide Table. To add another
table, right-click the blank
space, and then choose
Show Table to pop up the
Show Table window.*

TIP   Access gives you a shortcut if you need to rework the design of a table that's open in the Relationships tab. Just right-click the table box and choose Table Design.

8. **To define your relationship, find the field you're using in the child table. Drag this field to the field you want to link it to in the parent table.**

    In this case, you're linking the ManufacturerID field in the Dolls table (the child) to the ID field in the Manufacturers table (the parent). So drag ManufacturerID (in the Dolls box) over to ID (in the Manufacturers box).

    TIP   You can drag the other way, too (from the parent to the child). Either way, Access creates the same relationship.

    When you release the mouse button, the Edit Relationships window appears (see *Figure 5-4*).

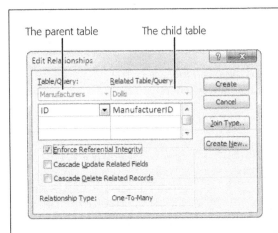

The parent table   The child table

FIGURE 5-4

Access is clever enough to correctly identify the parent table (shown in the Table/Query box) and the child table (shown in the Related Table/ Query box) when you connect two fields. Access identifies the field in the parent table because it has a primary key (page 88) or a unique index (page 134). If something isn't quite right in the Edit Relationships window, swap the tables or change the fields you're using to create the relationship before continuing.

9. **If you want to prevent potential errors, put a checkmark in the Enforce Referential Integrity option. (It's always a good idea.)**

    This setting turns on enhanced error checking, which prevents people from making a change that violates the rules of a relationship (like creating a doll that points to a nonexistent manufacturer). You'll learn more about referential integrity and the two settings for cascading changes on page 174. For now, it's best to switch on the Enforce Referential Integrity option and leave the others unchecked.

10. **Click Create.**

    This action creates the relationship that links the two tables. It appears in the diagram as a line (*Figure 5-5*).

If you receive an error that says "the database engine could not lock your table because it is already in use by another person or process," it means you still have your table—or a database object that uses your table—open in another tab. But in order to create a relationship, Access needs exclusive control over both tables. To fix this problem, cancel the current operation, close all the tabs except the Relationships tab, and repeat the process starting at step 8.

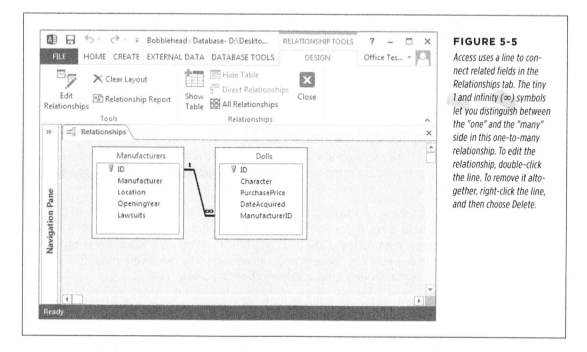

FIGURE 5-5

Access uses a line to connect related fields in the Relationships tab. The tiny 1 and infinity (∞) symbols let you distinguish between the "one" and the "many" side in this one-to-many relationship. To edit the relationship, double-click the line. To remove it altogether, right-click the line, and then choose Delete.

TIP If you chose Enforce Referential Integrity (in step 9), Access checks to make sure any existing data in the table follows the relationship rules. If it finds some that doesn't, it alerts you about the problem and refuses to continue. At this point, the best strategy is to create the relationship without referential integrity, correct the invalid data, and then edit the relationship later to turn on referential integrity.

11. **Close the Relationships tab.**

    You can click the X in the tab's top-right corner, or choose Relationship Tools | Design→Relationships→Close.

    When you close the Relationships tab, Access asks whether you want to save its layout. Access is really asking you whether you want to save the relationship diagram you've created. Whether or not you choose to save, the relationship remains in the database, and you can use it in the same way. The only difference is whether you'll be able to quickly review or edit the relationship in the Relationships tab.

If you choose to keep the relationship diagram, the next time you switch to the Relationships tab (by choosing Database Tools→Relationships→Relationships), you see the same arrangement of tables. This feature is handy.

If you choose not to keep the relationship diagram, it's up to you to recreate the diagram next time by adding the tables you want to see and arranging them in the window (although you won't need to redefine the relationships). This process takes a little more work.

TIP Many database pros choose to save their database diagram, because they want to see all their relationships at once in the Relationships tab, just the way they left them. However, real-world databases often end up with a tangled web of relationships. In this situation, you may choose *not* to save a complete diagram so you can focus on just a few tables at once.

Editing Relationships

The next time you want to change or add relationships, you'll follow the same path to get to the Relationship window (choose Database Tools→Relationships→Relationships).

Every database can store a single relationship diagram. If you chose to save the relationship diagram for your tables (in step 11 in the previous section), the tables will appear automatically, just as you left them. If you want to work with tables that aren't in any relationships yet, you can add them to the diagram by right-clicking anywhere in the blank area, and then choosing Show Table.

If you chose *not* to save your relationship diagram, you can use a few shortcuts to put your tables back on display:

- Drag your tables right from the navigation pane, and then drop them in the Relationships tab.

- Choose Relationship Tools | Design→Relationships→All Relationships to show all the tables that are involved in *any* relationships you've created previously.

- Add a table to the diagram, select it, and then choose Relationship Tools | Design→Relationships→Direct Relationships to show the tables that are linked to *that* table.

You can also use Relationship Tools | Design→Relationships→Clear Layout to remove all the tables from the current relationship diagram. This way, you have a clear surface and can add back just a few select tables. Clearing the layout doesn't remove the underlying table relationships; they remain even though they aren't on display in your diagram.

As you already know, you can use the Relationships tab to create new relationships. You can also edit the relationships you've already created. To do so, right-click the line that represents the relationship, and then choose Edit Relationships. (This takes some deft mouse clicking; if you don't see the Edit Relationships option in the menu, you've missed the line.) To remove a relationship, right-click the relationship line, and then choose Delete.

> **NOTE** Usually, you edit a relationship to change the options for referential integrity, which you'll learn about in the next section.

Referential Integrity

Now that you've gone to the work of defining your relationship, it's time to see what benefits you've earned. As in the real world, relationships impose certain restrictions. In the database world, these rules are called *referential integrity*. Taken together, they ensure that related data is always consistent.

> **NOTE** Referential integrity comes into action only if you switched on the Enforce Referential Integrity option (page 170) for your relationship. Without this detail, you're free to run rampant and enter inconsistent information. (There is, however, one situation where you may want to switch if off; see the box on page 174.)

In the bobblehead example, referential integrity requires that every manufacturer you refer to in the Dolls table must exist in the Manufacturers table. In other words, there can never be a bobblehead record that points to a nonexistent manufacturer. That sort of error could throw the hardiest database software out of whack.

To enforce this rule, Access disallows the following three actions:

- Adding a bobblehead that points to a nonexistent manufacturer.

- Deleting a manufacturer that's linked to one or more bobblehead records. (If that record were removed, you'd be left with a bobblehead that points to a nonexistent manufacturer.)

- Updating a manufacturer by changing its ID number, so it no longer matches the manufacturer ID in the linked bobblehead records. (This updating isn't a problem if you use an AutoNumber field, because you can't change AutoNumber values once you've created the record.)

> **NOTE** If you need to add a new doll made by a new manufacturer, you must add the manufacturer record first, and *then* add the doll record. There's no problem if you add manufacturer records that don't have corresponding doll records—after all, it's perfectly reasonable to list a manufacturer even if you don't have any of the dolls they've made.

Along with these restrictions, Access also won't let you remove a table if it's in a relationship. You need to delete the relationship first (using the Relationships window) and *then* remove the table.

Switching Off Referential Integrity

Are there any situations where you don't want to enforce referential integrity?

In most cases, referential integrity is the ultimate database safety check, and no one wants to do without it—especially if the database includes mission-critical information for your business. Remember, referential integrity prevents only inconsistent data. It still lets you leave a field blank if there's no related record that you want to link to.

The only time you may decide to dodge the rules of referential integrity is when you're using *partial copies* of your database. This situation usually happens in a large business that's using the same database at different sites.

Consider an extremely successful pastry sales company with six locations. When a customer makes an order at your downtown location, you add a new record in the Orders table and fill in the CustomerID (which links to a full record in the Customers table). But here's the problem: The full customer record may not be in your copy of the database—instead, it's in one of the databases at another site, or at company headquarters. Although the link in the Orders table is valid, Access assumes you've made a mistake because it can't find the matching customer record.

In this situation, you may choose to turn off referential integrity so you can insert the record. If you do, be sure to enter the linked value (in this case, the CustomerID) very carefully to avoid errors later on.

▨ BLANK VALUES FOR UNLINKED RECORDS

It's important to realize that there's one operation you can perform that doesn't violate referential integrity: creating a bobblehead that doesn't point to *any* manufacturer. You do this by leaving the ManufacturerID field blank (which database nerds refer to as a *null value*). The only reason you'll leave the ManufacturerID field blank is if the manufacturer record doesn't exist in your database, or if the information doesn't apply. Perhaps the bobblehead wasn't created by any manufacturer but was created by an advanced space-faring alien race and left on this planet for you to discover.

If this blank-value back door makes you nervous, you can stop it. Just set the Required field property (page 130) on the ManufacturerID field in the Dolls table. This setting ensures that every bobblehead in your Dolls table has legitimate manufacturer information. This technique is important when related information isn't optional. A sales company shouldn't be able to place an order or create an invoice without linking to the customer who made the order.

▨ CASCADING DELETES

The rules of referential integrity stop you cold if you try to delete a parent record (like a manufacturer) that other child records (like dolls) link to. However, there's another option—and it's much more drastic. You can choose to blow away all related child records whenever you delete a parent. For example, this would let you remove a manufacturer and wipe out all the dolls that were produced by that manufacturer.

WARNING Cascading deletes are risky. It's all too easy to wipe out way more records than you intend, and if you do, there's no going back. Even worse, the Undo feature can't help you reverse this change. So proceed with caution.

To turn on this option, you need to switch on the Cascade Delete Related Records setting when you create your relationship (*Figure 5-4*). You can also modify the relationship later on to add this setting.

Once you've switched on this option, you can try it by deleting a manufacturer, as shown in *Figure 5-6*.

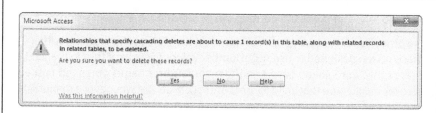

FIGURE 5-6

In this example, the Dolls-Manufacturers relationship uses the Cascade Delete Related Records setting. When you delete a manufacturer, Access warns you that you'll actually end up deleting every linked doll record.

WORD TO THE WISE

Use Cascading Deletes with Care

Cascade Delete Related Records is the nuclear option of databases, so think carefully about whether it makes sense for you. This setting makes it all too easy to delete records when you should really be *changing* them.

If you're dropping a customer from your customer database, it doesn't make sense to remove the customer's payment history, which you need to calculate your total profit. Instead, you're better off modifying the customer record to indicate that this record isn't being used anymore. You could add a Yes/No field named Active to the customer record, and set this field to No

to flag customer accounts that aren't currently in use, without removing them.

Also keep in mind that cascading deletes are just a convenience. They don't add any new features. If you don't switch on Cascade Delete Related Records, you can still remove linked records, as long as you follow the correct order. If you want to remove a manufacturer, start by removing any linked bobbleheads, or by changing those bobbleheads to point to a different manufacturer (or have no manufacturer at all) by modifying the ManufacturerID values. Once you've taken this step, you can delete the manufacturer record without a problem.

▓ CASCADING UPDATES

Access also provides a setting for cascading updates. If you switch on this feature (by going to the Edit Relationships window, and then choosing Cascade Update

Related Fields), Access copies any change you make to the linked field in the parent record to all the children.

With the bobblehead database, a cascading update lets you change the ID of one of your manufacturers. When you change the ID, Access automatically inserts the new value into the ManufacturerID field of every linked record in the Dolls table. Without cascading updates, you can't change a manufacturer's ID if there are linked doll records.

Cascading updates are safer than cascading deletes, but you rarely need them. That's because if you're following the rules of good database design, you're linking based on an AutoNumber ID column (page 83). Access doesn't let you edit an AutoNumber value, and you don't ever need to. (Remember, an AutoNumber simply identifies a record uniquely, and it doesn't correspond to anything in the real world.)

On the other hand, cascading updates come in handy if you're working with a table that hasn't been designed to use AutoNumber values for links. If the Dolls and Manufacturers table were linked based on the manufacturer name, you need cascading updates—it makes sure that child records are synchronized whenever a manufacturer name is changed. Cascading updates are just as useful if you have linked records based on Social Security numbers, part numbers, serial numbers, or other codes that aren't generated automatically and are subject to change.

Navigating a Relationship

Relationships aren't just useful for catching mistakes. Relationships also make it easier for you to browse through related data. In Chapter 6, you'll learn to create search routines that pull together information from related tables (page 227). But even without this technique, Access provides some serious relationship mojo in the datasheet.

Here's how it works. If you're looking at a parent table in the datasheet, you can find the related child records for any parent record by clicking the + box at the left of the row (*Figure 5-7*).

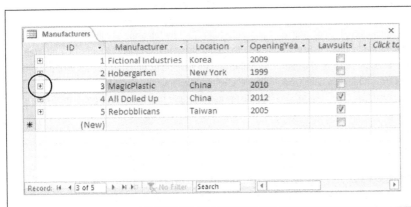

FIGURE 5-7

Curious to find out what dolls you have from MagicPlastic? Just click the plus box (circled).

This drops a *subdatasheet* into view, which shows just the related records (*Figure 5-8*). You can use the subdatasheet to edit the doll records here in exactly the same way as you would in the full Dolls datasheet. You can even add new records.

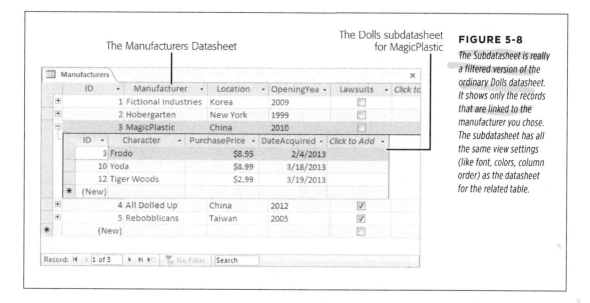

The Manufacturers Datasheet

The Dolls subdatasheet for MagicPlastic

FIGURE 5-8

The Subdatasheet is really a filtered version of the ordinary Dolls datasheet. It shows only the records that are linked to the manufacturer you chose. The subdatasheet has all the same view settings (like font, colors, column order) as the datasheet for the related table.

TIP You can open as many subdatasheets as you want at the same time. The only limitation is that the records in a subdatasheet don't show up if you print the datasheet..

A parent table may be related to more than one child table. In this case, Access gives you a choice of what table you want to use when you click the + box. Imagine you've created a Customers table that's linked to a child table of customer orders (Orders), and a child table of billing information (Invoices). When you click the + box, Access doesn't know which table to choose, so it asks you (see *Figure 5-9*).

FIGURE 5-9

When Access doesn't know which table to use as a subdatasheet, it lets you pick from a list of all your tables. In this case, only two choices make sense. Choose Orders to see the customer's orders, or Invoices to see the customer's invoices. When you select the appropriate table in the list, Access automatically fills in the linked fields in the boxes at the bottom of the window. You can then click OK to continue.

TIP You have to choose the subdatasheet you want to use only once. Access remembers your setting and always uses the same subdatasheet from that point on. If you change your mind later on, you'll need to tweak the table settings, as described in the box on page 179.

As you create more elaborate databases, you'll find that your tables are linked together in a chain of relationships. One parent table might be linked to a child table, which is itself the parent of another table, and so on. This complexity doesn't faze Access—it lets you drill down through all the relationships (see *Figure 5-10*).

The Orders
subdatasheet for
Lisa Limone

The OrderDetails
subdatasheet for
Order #2

The Customers Datasheet

FIGURE 5-10

There are two relationships at work here. Customers is the parent of Orders (which lists all the orders a customer has placed). Orders is the parent of OrderDetails (which lists the individual items in each order). By digging through the levels, you can see what each customer bought.

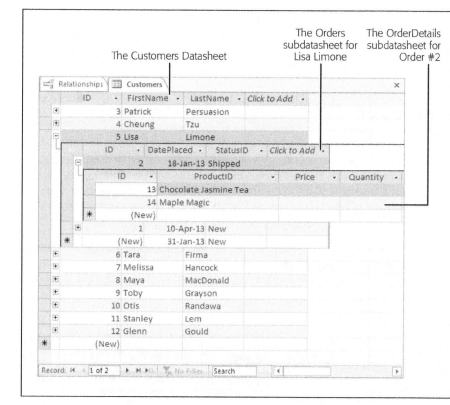

Changing Subdatasheet Settings

You can tweak a few more details that affect how subdatasheets are shown for your table. To show these settings, switch your table to Design view. Then, choose Table Tools | Design→Show/Hide→Property Sheet (assuming the Property Sheet isn't currently visible). This action shows the Property Sheet box at the right side of the window.

The Property Sheet has a collection of miscellaneous settings that apply to your whole table. Here are the ones that relate to subdatasheets:

- **Subdatasheet Name**. The linked table used for the subdatasheet. If you have several linked tables, you may choose to adjust this to the one you want to work with.

Or set it to "(Auto)" so that Access prompts you for the subdatasheet you want to use the next time you click the + box, as shown in *Figure 5-7*.

- **Subdatasheet Height**. Sets the height, in inches, given to the subdatasheet to display its data. If all the related rows don't fit into this space, you'll need to scroll through them. The standard setting is 0, which allows the subdatasheet to take as much space as it needs.

- **Subdatasheet Expanded**. Lets you choose whether the subdatasheets should start off hidden until you click the + box (the default setting), or automatically expand when you open the table (choose Yes).

Lookups with Related Tables

So far, you've seen how relationships make it easier to review and edit your records. But what about when you add your records in the first place? Relationships are usually based on an unhelpful AutoNumber value. When you create a new doll, you probably won't know that 3408 stands for Bobelle House O' Dolls. Access stops you from entering a manufacturer ID that isn't linked to anyone, but it doesn't help you choose the ID value you want.

Fortunately, Access has a technique to help you. In the previous chapter, you learned about *lookups*, a feature that provides you with a list of possible values for a column (page 155). When creating a lookup, you can supply a list of fixed values, or you can pull values from another table. You could create a lookup for the ManufacturerID field in the Dolls table that uses a list of ID values drawn from the Manufacturers table. This type of lookup helps a bit—it gives you a list of all the possible values you can use—but it still doesn't solve the central problem. Namely, the befuddled people using your database won't have a clue what ID belongs to what manufacturer. You still need a way to show the manufacturer name in the lookup list.

Happily, *lookup lists* provide just this feature. For this trick, you create a lookup that has more than one column. One column holds the information (in this case, the manufacturer name) that you want to display to the person using the database. The other column has the data you want to use when a value is picked (in this case, the manufacturer ID).

> **NOTE** Access is a bit quirky when it comes to lookups. It expects you to add the lookup, and *then* the relationship. (In fact, when you set up a lookup that uses a table, Access creates a relationship *automatically*.) So if you've been following through with the examples on your own, you'll need to *delete* the relationship between the Dolls and Manufacturers tables (as described on page 172) before you go any further.

The following steps show how you can create a lookup list that links the Dolls and Manufacturers tables:

1. **Open the child table in Design view.**

   In this example, it's the Dolls table.

2. **Select the field that links to the parent table, and, in the Data Type column, choose the Lookup Wizard option.**

   In this example, the field you want is ManufacturerID.

3. **Choose "I want the lookup column to get values from another table or query" and then click Next.**

   The next step shows a list of all the tables in your database, except the current table.

4. **Choose the parent table, and then click Next.**

In this case, you're after the Manufacturers table. Once you select it and move to the next step, you'll see a list of all the fields in the table.

5. **Add the field you use for the link and another more descriptive field to the list of Selected Fields (*Figure 5-11*). Click Next to continue.**

In this case, you need to add the ID field and the Manufacturer field.

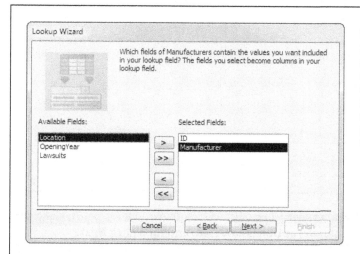

FIGURE 5-11

The secret to a good lookup is getting two pieces of information: the primary key (in this case, the ID field) and a more descriptive value (in this case, the manufacturer's name). The ID field is the piece of information you need to store in the doll record, while the Manufacturer field is the value you'll show in the lookup list to make it easier to choose the right manufacturer.

TIP In some cases, you might want to use more than one field with descriptive information. For example, you might grab both a FirstName and LastName field from a FamilyRelatives table. But don't add too much information, or the lookup list will become really wide in order to fit it all in. This looks a bit bizarre.

6. **Choose a field to use for sorting the lookup list (*Figure 5-12*), and then click Next.**

In this example, the Manufacturer field is the best choice to sort the list.

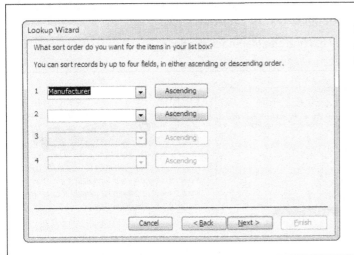

FIGURE 5-12

It's important to sort the lookup list, so that the person using it can find the right item quickly.

7. **The next step shows a preview of your lookup list (*Figure 5-13*). Make sure the "Hide key column" option is selected, and then click Next.**

Although the primary key field has the value that links the two tables together, it doesn't mean much to the person using the database. The other, descriptive field is more important.

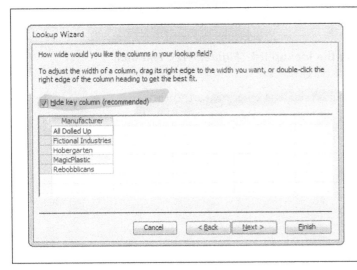

FIGURE 5-13

Here, the lookup list shows the manufacturer name (the Manufacturer field) and hides the manufacturer ID (the ID field).

8. **Choose a name for the lookup column.**

Usually, it's clearest if you keep the name of the field that uses the lookup—in this case, ManufacturerID.

The final step also gives you two additional options:

- **Allow Multiple Values.** If you turn on this option, the lookup list shows a checkbox next to each item, so that you can pick several at once. (In this example, you can create a doll that has more than one manufacturer.) You'll learn more about the Allow Multiple Values option on page 188.

- **Enable Data Integrity.** This choice plays the same role as the Enforce Referential Integrity setting in the Relationships tab. If you turn it on, Access prevents you from violating the rules of referential integrity (like creating a doll that points to a nonexistent manufacturer). You can also choose a suboption called Cascade Delete, which matches the Cascade Delete Related Records setting you learned about earlier (page 174).

9. **Click Finish.**

Now, Access creates the lookup for the field and prompts you to save the table. Once you do, Access creates a relationship between the two tables you've linked with your lookup column. Here, Access creates a parent-child relationship between Manufacturers and Dolls, just as you did yourself at the beginning of this chapter.

Now, if you switch to the datasheet view of the Dolls table, you can use your lookup when you're editing or adding records (*Figure 5-14*).

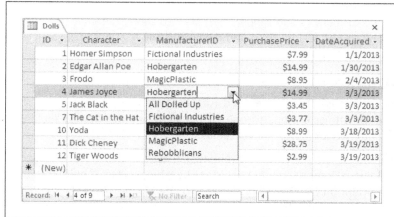

FIGURE 5-14

Even though the Dolls table stores an ID value in the ManufacturerID field behind the scenes, that's not how it appears on your datasheet. Instead, you see the related manufacturer name (both onscreen and in any printouts you make). Even better, if you need to add a new record or change the manufacturer that's assigned to an existing one, you can pick the manufacturer from the list by name.

Refreshing a Lookup

I just added a record, but it doesn't appear in my lookup. Why not?

Access fills in your lookup lists when you first open the table. For example, when you open the Dolls table, Access gets a list of manufacturers ready to go. However, sometimes you might have both the table that *uses* the lookup and the table that *provides* the lookup data open at the same time. In this situation, the changes you make in the table that provides the lookup won't appear in the table that uses the lookup.

To see how this works, open both the Dolls and Manufacturers tables at once. (They'll appear in separate tabs.) In the Manufacturers table, add a new manufacturer. Now, switch back to the Dolls table and try using the ManufacturerID lookup. You'll notice that the lookup list doesn't show the new record.

Fortunately, there's an easy solution. You can tell Access to refresh the lookup list at any time by choosing Home→Records→Refresh All. Try that out in the Dolls table, and you'll see the updated list of manufacturers appear in the lookup.

More Exotic Relationships

As you've learned, a one-to-many (a.k.a. *parent-child*) relationship that links a single record in one table to zero, one, or more records in another table is the most common relationship. A single manufacturer could be linked to one bobblehead, several bobbleheads, or no bobbleheads at all.

Along with one-to-many relationships, there are two subtly different types of relationships: one-to-one relationships and many-to-many relationships. You'll learn about both in the following sections.

One-to-One Relationship

A *one-to-one relationship* links one record in a table to zero or one record in another table. People sometimes use one-to-one relationships to break down a table with lots of fields into two (or more) smaller tables.

A Products table may include detailed information that describes the product and its price, and additional information that describes how the product is built. This information is important only to the people in the engineering department, so you may choose to split it into a separate table (named something like ProductsEngineering). That way, sales folks don't need to see engineering information when they're making an order. Other times, you might break a table into two pieces because it's simply too big. (Access doesn't let any table have more than 255 fields.) For more detail on when to (and when not to) use a one-to-one relationship, see the box on page 186.

You create a one-to-one relationship in the same way you create a one-to-many relationship—by dragging the fields in the Relationships tab (*Figure 5-15*). The only difference is that the linked fields in *both* tables need to be set to prevent duplicates. This way, a record in one table can (at most) be linked to a single record in the other table.

NOTE   A field prevents duplicates if it's set as the primary key for a table (page 88), or if it has an index that prevents duplicates (page 134).

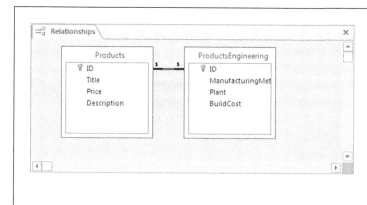

FIGURE 5-15

When you link two fields that don't allow duplicates (and you have the Enable Referential Integrity option switched on), Access realizes that you're creating a one-to-one relationship. Access places the number 1 at each side of the line to distinguish it from other types of relationships. In this example, the ID column in the Products table and the ID column in the ProductsEngineering table are both primary keys of their respective tables, so there's no way to link more than one record in ProductsEngineering to the same record in Products.

When you create a design like the one shown in *Figure 5-15*, make sure that the ID column is not configured to be an AutoNumber field in both tables. Otherwise, Access will try to generate a new AutoNumber when you insert the first record and when you insert the second, linked record.

If you want to use an AutoNumber ID field (and there's no reason you shouldn't), use it in the *parent* table. In this example, the Products table contains the AutoNumber ID. The ID field in the ProductsEngineering table uses the Number data type. That way, each record in the ProductsEngineering table can link itself to a record in the Products table using a matching ID value.

Approach One-to-One Relationships with Caution

One-to-one relationships are extremely rare in Access. Usually, features like column hiding (page 102) and queries (Chapter 6) are better choices if you want to see only some of the fields in a table.

Splitting a table into two pieces complicates the design of your database, and you'd generally do it only if you have other reasons to separate the tables. Some possible examples include:

- The two parts of the table need to be placed in separate databases (page 642) so that different people can copy them to separate computers and edit them independently.

- You want to stop prying eyes from seeing sensitive data. One way to do this is to put the information that should be secure into a separate table, and to put that separate table in a different, more secure database file.

- You have a table that stores huge amounts of data, like an Attachment field (page 80) with large documents. In this case, you might get better performance by splitting the table. You might even choose to put one half of the table in a separate database (page 642).

- Some of the data in your table is optional. Rather than include a lot of blank fields, you can pop it into a separate table. If you don't need to include this information, you don't need to add a record to the linked table.

If you don't have these requirements, you're better off creating a single large table.

Many-to-Many Relationship

A *many-to-many relationship* links one or more records in one table to one or more records in another table. Consider a database that tracks authors and books in separate tables. Bestselling authors seldom stop at one book (so you need to be able to link one author to several books). However, authors sometimes team up on a single title (so you need to be able to link one book to several authors). A similar situation occurs if you need to put students into classes, employees into committees, or ingredients into recipes. You can even imagine a situation where this affects the bobblehead database, if more than one manufacturer can collaborate to create a single bobblehead doll.

Many-to-many relationships are relatively common, and Access gives you two ways to deal with them.

▦ JUNCTION TABLES

Junction tables are the traditional approach for dealing with many-to-many relationships, and people use them throughout the database world (including in industrial-strength products like Microsoft SQL Server). The basic idea is that you create an extra table that has the sole responsibility of linking together two tables.

Each record in the junction table represents a link that binds together a record from each table in the relationship. In the books and authors database, a single record in the junction table links together one author with one book. If the same author writes three books, you need to add three records to the junction table. If two authors work on one book, you need an additional record to link each new author.

Suppose you have these records in your Authors table:

ID	FIRST NAME	LAST NAME
10	Alf	Abet
11	Cody	Pendant
12	Moe	DeLawn

And you have these records in your Books table:

ID	TITLE	PUBLISHED
402	Fun with Letters	January 1, 2013
403	How to Save Money by Living with Your Parents	February 24, 2011
404	Unleash Your Guilt	May 5, 2012

Here's the Authors_Books table that binds it all together:

ID	AUTHOR ID	BOOK ID
1	10	402
2	11	403
3	12	403
4	11	404

Authors_Books is a junction table that defines four links. The first record indicates that author #10 (Alf Abet) wrote book #402 (*Fun with Letters*). As you traverse the rest of the table, you'll discover that Cody Pendant contributed to two books, and two authors worked on the same book (*How to Save Money by Living with Your Parents*).

> **TIP** The junction table often has a name that's composed of the two tables it's linking, like Authors_Books.

The neat thing about a junction table is that it's actually built out of two one-to-many relationships that you define in Access. In other words, the junction table is a child table that has two parents. The Authors table has a one-to-many relationship with the Authors_Books table, where Authors is the parent. The Books table also has a one-to-many relationship with Authors_Books, where Books is the parent. You can define these two relationships in the Relationships tab to make sure referential integrity rules the day (*Figure 5-16*).

Although junction tables seem a little bizarre at first glance, most database fans find that they quickly become very familiar. As with the one-to-many relationships you used earlier, you can create lookups for the AuthorID and BookID fields in the

Authors_Books table. However, you'll always need to ad⟨...⟩hors_Books record by hand to link an author to a book.

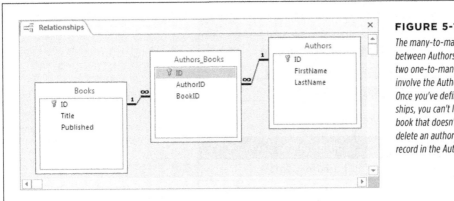

FIGURE 5-16

The many-to-many relationship between Authors and Books is really two one-to-many relationships that involve the Authors_Books table. Once you've defined these relationships, you can't link to an author or book that doesn't exist, and can't delete an author or book that has a record in the Authors_ Books table.

MULTI-VALUE FIELDS

For most of database history, junction tables were the only option for many-to-many relationships. But to support its SharePoint integration features (Chapter 22), Access added another approach, called *multi-value fields*.

As its name suggests, a multi-value field can store more than one value. This capacity neatly solves the problem of many-to-many relationships. The trick is to configure the linked field in the child table as a multi-value field. Reconsider the authors and books example. Without the junction table, you'd need to add an AuthorID column to the Books table to indicate which author wrote a given book:

ID	TITLE	PUBLISHED	AUTHOR ID
402	Fun with Letters	January 1, 2013	10
403	How to Save Money by Living with Your Parents	February 24, 2011	11
404	Unleash Your Guilt	May 5, 2012	11

But an ordinary field holds a single value. Thus, this table can indicate only one of the two authors for book #403.

However, if you change AuthorID to allow multiple values, you can enter a list of authors, like this:

ID	TITLE	PUBLISHED	AUTHOR ID
403	How to Save Money by Living with Your Parents	February 24, 2011	11, 12

Behind the scenes, a multi-value field actually uses a junction table. However, Access hides that detail from you, which makes it a bit easier to link related records.

To create a multi-value field, you need to use a lookup. As you've already seen (page 183), you can choose to turn on this option in the last step of the Lookup wizard. Alternatively, if you already have a lookup in a field, you just need to make one minor modification. Open the table in Design view, choose the field that has the lookup (like ManufacturerID), and then, in the Field Properties section, click the Lookup tab. Look for the Allow Multiple Values property, and change it from No to Yes.

> **WARNING** Once you change your field to support multiple values, you can't switch back, even if you haven't added more than one value to the field in any record.

Figure 5-17 shows a multi-value lookup list in action.

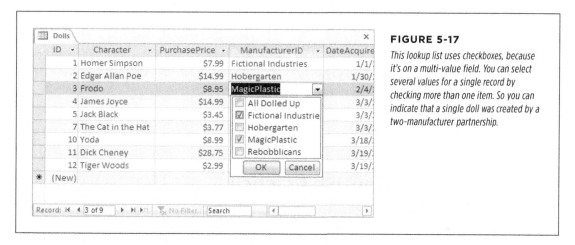

FIGURE 5-17

This lookup list uses checkboxes, because it's on a multi-value field. You can select several values for a single record by checking more than one item. So you can indicate that a single doll was created by a two-manufacturer partnership.

Multi-value fields cause headaches if you want to transfer your database to SQL Server (as described in Chapter 21), because SQL Server doesn't support them. So if there's a possibility that you'll need to share your database with lots of people (say, in a large company), and you might move your data to a high-powered SQL Server database someday, avoid multi-value fields.

FREQUENTLY ASKED QUESTION

Dealing with Many-to-Many Relationships

Which approach is better: junction tables or multi-value fields?

Most database purists will stick with junction tables for years to come. They're accepted, established, and don't hide your database's inner workings. Junction tables are particularly useful if you want to add extra bits of information about the relationship between these two tables. Suppose you create a Students_Classes table to keep track of the classes every student is taking at a popular school. In the Students_Classes table, you could insert additional fields like EnrollmentDate, ConfirmationLetterSentDate, and PrerequisitesChecked.

On the other hand, junction tables have a downside—you can't work with them as easily in the datasheet. If your database uses the Authors_Books junction table, you need to edit at least two tables just to add one new book to your system. First, you need to insert a record into the Books table. Then, you

need to open the Authors_Books table, and add a new record there that maps this book to an author. (You can use lookups in the Authors_Books table to make this process easy, but it still requires a separate step.) But if the Books table includes a multi-value Authors field, you can add the book and assign all the authors in one step, which is more convenient.

If you've decided to go with junction tables and you want to make your life a bit easier, Access has a great solution. You can build a customized *form* that deals with more than one table at once. You can create a form that lets the person using the database insert a record in the Books and Authors_Books tables at the same time. Best of all, your form can make it look like there's only one table involved. You'll learn how to pull this trick off in Part Four.

■ Relationship Practice

Every database designer needs to see the world in terms of tables and relationships. Savvy database designers can quickly assess information and see how it's related. With this ability, they can build just the right database for any situation.

The following sections provide two scenarios that help you practice more realistic relationship building. Both databases used in these scenarios are available with the samples for this chapter, and they'll turn up again in the following chapters, when you start to build more sophisticated database objects like queries, reports, and forms.

The Music School

Cacophoné Studios runs a medium-sized music school. They have a fixed series of courses in mind, and a roster of teachers that can fill in for most of them. They also have a long list of past and potential customers. Last year, a small catastrophe happened when 273 students were crammed into the same class and no teacher was assigned to teach it. (Next door, a class of 14 had somehow ended up with three instructors.) They're hoping that Access can help them avoid the same embarrassment this time around.

TIP   Want to play along with Cacophoné Studios? Try to make your own list of possible tables and their relationships before reading ahead.

■ IDENTIFYING THE TABLES

Every business is a little different, and it would take a long, detailed analysis to get the perfect table structure for Cacophoné Studios. However, even without knowing that much, you can pick out some fairly obvious candidates:

- **Teachers**. A table to store a list of all the teachers on their roster, complete with contact information.

- **Students**. A table to store all class-goers past, present, and potential. You don't need to distinguish between these different groups of people in the Students table—instead, you can sort out the current students from the others by looking for related data (namely, their class enrollments). So you can keep things simple in the Students table, and just store name and contact information.

- **Classes**. A table to store the classes that Cacophoné Studios is running. This table should include the class name, date it starts, date it ends, maximum enrollment number, and any other key information.

NOTE   Course requirements are stored using a multi-value lookup field named PreviousClassRequirements. This field contains the ID values of each required class. (In other words, every record in the Classes table has the nifty ability to point to *other* classes in the same table.)

Cacophoné Studios will certainly want many more tables before long. But these tables are enough to get started.

■ IDENTIFYING THE RELATIONSHIPS

It's fairly easy to pick out the relationships you need. Students take classes. Teachers teach classes. This suggests two relationships—one between Students and Classes, and one between Teachers and Classes.

But there's a bit of a hitch. Cacophoné Studios certainly doesn't want to stop a single student from taking more than one class, so you'll need a many-to-many relationship between the two tables. And even though Cacophoné Studios plans to have only one teacher in each class, they want to keep open the possibility that two or more teachers might co-teach. So Teachers and Classes are also locked in a more complex many-to-many relationship. To support these two relationships, you can create two junction tables, named Students_Classes and Teachers_Classes (respectively).

Figure 5-18 shows a snapshot of this arrangement.

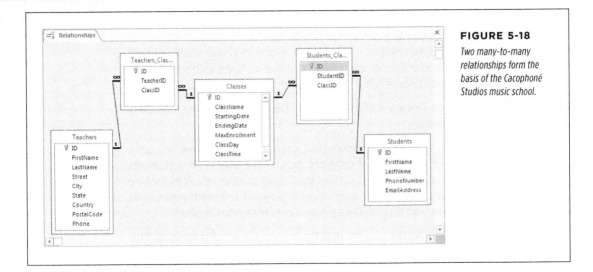

FIGURE 5-18

Two many-to-many relationships form the basis of the Cacophoné Studios music school.

> **NOTE** Each record in the Students_Classes table represents a student enrollment in a class. You may want to add some additional fields to Students_Classes to track information like the enrollment date, an enrollment discount you might have offered for early booking, and so on.

GETTING MORE DETAILED

Cacophoné Studios is off to the right start, but there's a lot more they still need to think about. First of all, each time they offer a class, they need to create a separate record in the Classes table. This method makes sense, but it causes a potential problem. That's because when a class (like Electro-Acoustic Gamelan) ends, it's usually offered again in a new session, with new students. Although this is a whole new class, it has some information in common with the previous class, like the description, fee, course requirements, and so on.

To deal with this requirement, you need to create another table, named ClassDescriptions. The ClassDescriptions record should have all the descriptive information for a class. The Classes record represents a single, scheduled session of a particular class. That way, the school can offer the same class multiple times without confusion.

To make this design work, each record in Classes links to a single record in ClassDescriptions. There's a one-to-many relationship between ClassDescriptions (the parent table) and Classes (the child table), as shown in *Figure 5-19*.

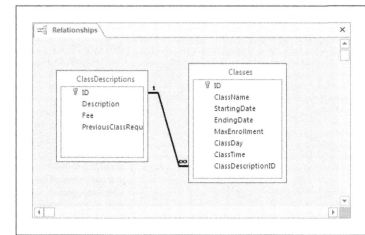

FIGURE 5-19

Thanks to the ClassDescriptions table, you can use the same description for several sessions of the same class, thereby avoiding redundant data.

Cacophoné Studios also needs to think about the sticky financial side of things. Each time they put a student in a class, they need to collect a set fee. Each time they assign a teacher to a class, they need to pay up.

Two tables can fill in these details: TeacherPayments and StudentCharges. Obviously, these tables need relationships—but maybe not the ones you expect. You may assume that you should link the StudentCharges record directly to the records in the Students table. That linking makes sense, because you need to know which student owes money. However, it's also important to keep track of what the money is for—namely, the class that the student is paying for. In other words, every record in StudentCharges needs to link to both the Students and the Classes table.

But there's an easier approach. You can save some effort by linking the StudentCharges table directly to the Students_Classes table. Remember, each record in Students_Classes has the student and class information for one enrollment. Every time you add a record in Students_Classes, you need to add a corresponding charge in StudentCharges. One record in the Students_Classes table should link to exactly one record in the StudentCharges table. A similar relationship exists between the Teachers_Classes and TeacherPayments tables. *Figure 5-20* shows the whole shebang (not including the ClassDescriptions table shown in *Figure 5-19*).

TIP Remember, to create a one-to-one relationship, you need to use a primary key or an index that doesn't allow duplicates (page 134). In this example, you need to add a no-duplicates index to the Student_ClassesID field in the StudentCharges table and to the Teacher_ClassesID field in the Teacher-Payments table. These indexes make sure that students get charged only once for each class they take and that teachers get only a single payment for each class they teach.

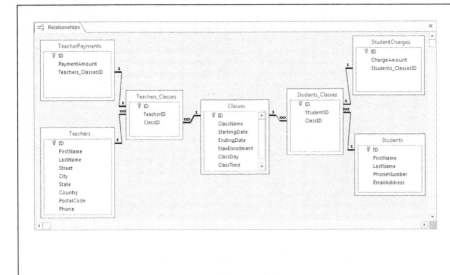

FIGURE 5-20

Every assigned class results in a payment in the TeacherPayments table (top left). Every enrollment results in a charge in StudentCharges (top right). Although this picture is a bit intimidating at first glance, you should be able to work your way through all the tables and relationships one by one. When building a database, it's easiest to start with a few tables, and then keep adding on.

Printing Your Relationship

Why is the File→Print command disabled when I'm looking at the Relationships tab?

Once you've created your relationships, you might want to have a printed copy at your fingertips. You can't print the contents of the Relationships tab directly, but you *can* convert the tab data into a *report*, which is a specialized database object that lets you create a printout whenever you want. (You'll learn how to create reports in Part Three.)

To create a report for your relationships, first arrange all the tables to your liking in the Relationships tab. Then, choose Relationship Tools | Design→Tools→Relationship Report. A preview window appears, which looks more or less the same as the current contents of the Relationships tab. You can then choose File→Print to send it to the printer.

When you close the relationship report, Access asks you if you want to save it permanently in your database. Usually, you won't bother, because you can easily regenerate the report whenever you need it. However, if you have a complex database and you want to print several different diagrams (each showing a different group of relationships), you may decide to save your relationship report for later use. You'll learn more about reports in Chapter 10.

This database has quickly become quite sophisticated. And Cacophoné Studios probably isn't done yet. (For example, it'll more than likely want a table to track student payments.) As with most realistic databases, you can keep adding on new tables and relationships endlessly.

The Chocolate Store

A *sales* database that stores the products, customers, and orders for a company that sells something is one of the most common databases. In fact, this pattern turns up so often that it's worth looking at a quick example. As you'll see, a few basic principles apply to every sales-driven business, whether the business is selling collectible books or discount pharmaceuticals.

In this example, you'll meet Boutique Fudge, a mail-order company that sells decadent treats to a large audience of chocolate-crazed customers. Their daring chefs are always innovating, and they need a better way to manage their ever-growing catalog of chocolate goodness. They also need a way to keep track of customers and the orders they make.

▩ THE PRODUCT CATALOG AND CUSTOMER LIST

Even though you don't know much about Boutique Fudge, you can already think of a few key tables that it'll need. To put anything up for sale, they should have the following tables:

- **Products** lists the sinful chocolate delicacies they have for sale. This table records the name, description, and price of each item available. A few optional details also make sense—for example, why not keep track of the current stock using two numeric fields (UnitsInStock and UnitsOnOrder) and a Yes/No field (named Discontinued) to identify products that aren't available any longer?

NOTE   In many databases, you can't delete old information. A company like Boutique Fudge can't simply delete old products from their catalogs, because these products might be linked to old orders. Also, it makes sense to keep historical information to allow data analysis. (Boutique Fudge could use a query to uncover the top-selling products in 1999 and could then check if declining cocoa levels are linked to sales dropping.) For this reason, you need tricks like the Discontinued field. When you list the products for sale, you can leave out all the discontinued ones, using the filtering skills you picked up on page 107.

- **ProductCategories** organizes products into a few descriptive groups. That way, customers can browse just the products in the category they want (whether it's Beverages, Candies, Chocolate, or Personalized Choco-wear).

- **Customers** holds the list of chocoholics who have signed up to make an order. You need all the customary information here, like customer names, shipping information, and billing information.

TIP   Many companies let customers supply multiple shipping addresses and credit cards. If you allow this flexibility, you'll need (surprise) more tables. You could create a table of CustomerCreditCards. Every record in Customers could then link to one or more records in CustomerCreditCards. Boutique Fudge takes the easy way out and stores a customer credit card and address directly in the Customers table.

So far, there's only one relationship at work: a one-to-many relationship between ProductCategories and Products. *Figure 5-21* shows this design.

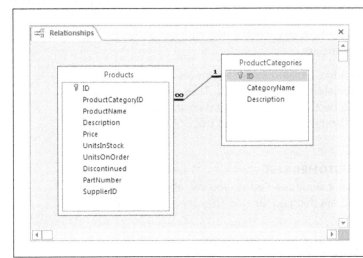

FIGURE 5-21

As shown here, a one-to-many relationship connects the ProductCategories table to the Products table. That means a product (like Chocolate Jasmine Tea) can be placed in only one category (like Beverages), but a single category can hold many products.

▧ ORDERING PRODUCTS

It doesn't matter how fancy your sales database is—if it doesn't have a way for customers to *order* the items they're interested in, Boutique Fudge will run out of money fast.

Database newbies often make the mistake of assuming that they can use one table to store order information. In truth, you need two tables:

- **Orders** records each order a customer places. It links to the customer who made the order and adds information like the date the order was placed.

- **OrderDetails** lists the individual items in an order. Each record in the OrderDetails table includes the ID of the product that was ordered, the number of units ordered, and the price at which they were ordered.

Because the average order includes more than one item, a single record in the Orders table is usually linked to multiple records in the OrderDetails table (as shown in *Figure 5-22*). This setup may sound a bit awkward (because it means you'll need to create a batch of new records for just one order), but the process doesn't have to be that difficult. Access has two features that help out: the subdatasheet feature you've already seen (*Figure 5-23*) and the forms feature (Chapter 12).

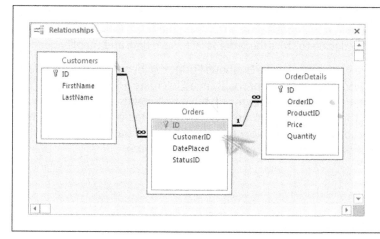

FIGURE 5-22

Every order can hold an unlimited number of order items. This ability makes Boutique Fudge happy.

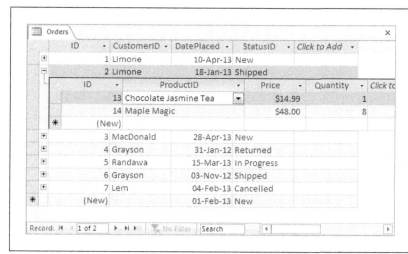

FIGURE 5-23

Thanks to the subdatasheet feature, you can add an order record and the linked order items in the same place.

Notice in *Figure 5-22* that the OrderDetails table stores the price of each ordered item. This system may seem to violate the redundant data rule. After all, the product prices are always available in the Products table. However, product prices change, and companies offer discounts. For those reasons, it's absolutely essential that you keep track of the price of an item when it was ordered. Otherwise, you'll have to guess how much each customer owes you.

NOTE   Database nerds call this sort of information *point-in-time data*, because it varies over time.

You should also notice that the Orders table doesn't store the total cost of the order. That's because the total cost is simply the sum of all the ordered items. If you stored a total cost, you'd open up the possibility of inconsistent data—in other words, you've got a problem if the order total you store doesn't match the cost of all the items. (This is a situation where database pros often bend the rules. Despite the potential problems, they may decide to store the order total to save time and simplify queries.)

You still have more work to do before Boutique Fudge can become a true database-driven company. For example, you'll probably need to create a Shipments table that tracks orders that it's mailed and a Payments table that makes sure customers pay up. Conceptually, there's nothing new here, but the more tables you add, the more complex your databases become. Now that you know the basics of relationships and good table design, you can stay cool under the pressure.

Manipulating Data with Queries

Queries That Select Records

I n a typical database, with thousands or millions of records, you may find it quite a chore finding the information you need. In Chapter 3, you learned how to go on the hunt using the tools of the datasheet, including filtering, searching, and sorting. At first glance, these tools seem like the perfect solution for digging up bits of hard-to-find information. However, there's a problem: The datasheet features are *temporary*.

To understand the problem, imagine you're creating an Access database for a mail-order food company named Boutique Fudge. Using datasheet filtering, sorting, and column hiding, you can pare down the Orders table so it shows only the most expensive orders placed in the past month. (This information is perfect for targeting big spenders or crafting a hot marketing campaign.) Next, you can apply a different set of settings to find out which customers order more than five pounds of fudge every Sunday. (You could use this information for more detailed market research, or just pass it along to the Department of Health.) But every time you apply new datasheet settings, you lose your previous settings. If you want to jump back and forth from one view to another, you need to painstakingly reapply all your settings. If you've spent some time crafting the perfect view of your data, this process adds up to a lot of unnecessary extra work.

The solution to this problem is to use *queries*: readymade search routines that you store in your database. Even though the Boutique Fudge company has only one Orders table, it may have dozens (or more) queries, each with different sorting and filtering options. If you want to find the most expensive orders, you don't need to apply the filtering, sorting, and column hiding settings by hand—instead, you can just fire up the MostExpensiveOrdersLastMonth query, which pulls out just the information you need. Similarly, if you want to find the fudge-aholics, you can run the LargeRepeatFudgeOrders query.

Queries are a staple of database design. In this chapter, you'll learn all you need to design and fine-tune basic queries.

Query Basics

As the name suggests, queries are a way to ask *questions* about your data, like which products net the most cash, where do most customers live, and who ordered the monogrammed toothbrush? Access saves each query in your database, like it saves any other database object. Once you've saved a query, you can run it anytime you want to take a look at the live data that meets your criteria.

A query's central ability is its amazing ability to reuse your hard work. Queries also introduce some new features that you don't have with the datasheet alone:

- **Queries can combine related tables**. This feature is insanely useful because it lets you craft searches that take related data into account. In the Boutique Fudge example, you can use this feature to create queries that find orders with specific product items or orders made by customers living in specific cities. Both these searches need relationships, because they branch out past the Orders table to take in information from other tables (like Products and Customers). You'll see how this works on page 227.

- **Queries can perform calculations**. The Products table in the Boutique Fudge database lists price information, along with the quantity in stock. A query can multiply these details, and then add a column that lists the calculated value of the product you have on hand. You'll try this trick in Chapter 7 (page 237).

- **Queries can perform summaries**. To analyze large chunks of data, you can group together rows with similar information. You can group all the orders by customer to find out who is spending the most. Or you can group orders by products, to have a quick line-by-line list that compares the sales of Thermo-Nutcular Fudge against Vanilla Bean Dream. You'll learn this technique in Chapter 8 (page 266).

- **Queries can automatically apply changes**. If you want to find all the orders made by a specific person and reduce the cost of each one by 10 percent, a query can apply the entire batch of changes in one step. This action requires a different type of query, an *action query*, which you'll consider in Chapter 9.

In this chapter, you'll consider the simplest and most common type of query: the *select query*, which retrieves a subset of information from a table. Once you've retrieved this information, you can print or edit it using a datasheet, the same way you work with with a table.

▩ Creating Queries

Access gives you three ways to create a query:

- **The query wizard** gives you a quick-and-dirty way to build a simple query. However, this option also gives you the least control.

TIP If you decide to use the query wizard to create your query, then you'll probably want to refine your query later on using Design view.

- **Design view** offers the most common approach to query building. It provides a handy graphical tool that you can use to perfect any query.

- **SQL view** gives you a behind-the-scenes look at the actual query *command*, which is a piece of text (ranging from one line to more than a dozen) that tells Access exactly what to do. The SQL view is where many Access experts hang out—and though it seems intimidating at first glance, it's actually not that difficult to decipher (as you'll see on page 219).

Creating a Query in Design View

The best starting point for query creation is the Design view. The following steps show you how it works. (To try this yourself, you can use the BoutiqueFudge.accdb database that's included with the downloadable samples for this chapter.) The final result—a query that gets the results that fall in the first quarter of 2013—is shown in *Figure 6-6*.

Here's what you need to do:

1. **Choose Create→Queries→Query Design.**

   A new design window appears, where you can craft your query. But before you get started, Access pops open the Show Table window, where you can choose the tables that you want to work with (*Figure 6-1*).

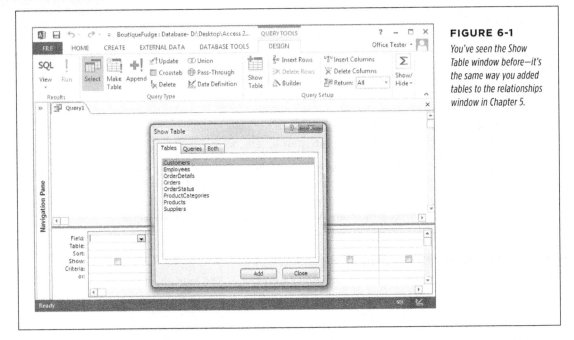

FIGURE 6-1

You've seen the Show Table window before—it's the same way you added tables to the relationships window in Chapter 5.

2. **Select the table that has the data you want, and then click Add (or just double-click the table).**

   In the Boutique Fudge example, you need the Orders table.

   Access adds a box that represents the table to the design window. You can repeat this step to add several related tables, but for now stick with just one.

3. **Click Close.**

   The Show Table dialog box disappears, giving you access to the Design view for the query.

4. **Select the fields you want to include in your query.**

   To select a field, double-click it in the table box (*Figure 6-2*). Take care not to add the same field more than once, or that column shows up twice in the results. If you're using the Boutique Fudge example, make sure you choose at least the ID, DatePlaced, and CustomerID fields.

   You can double-click the asterisk (*) to choose to include *all* the columns from a table. However, in most cases, it's better to add each column separately. Not only does this help you more easily see at a glance what's in your query, but it also lets you choose the column order and use the field for sorting and filtering.

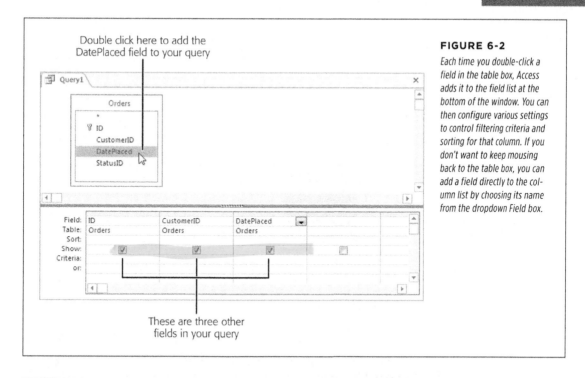

Double click here to add the
DatePlaced field to your query

These are three other
fields in your query

FIGURE 6-2

Each time you double-click a field in the table box, Access adds it to the field list at the bottom of the window. You can then configure various settings to control filtering criteria and sorting for that column. If you don't want to keep mousing back to the table box, you can add a field directly to the column list by choosing its name from the dropdown Field box.

TIP A good query includes only the fields you absolutely need. Keeping your query lean ensures it's easier to focus on the important information (and easier to fit your printout on a page).

5. **Arrange the fields from left to right in the order you want them to appear in the query results.**

   When you run the query, the columns appear in the same order as they're listed in the column list in Design view. (Ordinarily, this system means the columns appear from left to right in the order you added them.) If you want to change the order, all you need to do is drag (as shown in *Figure 6-3*).

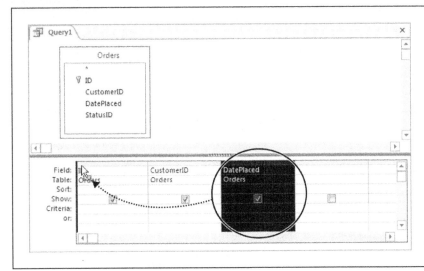

FIGURE 6-3

To reorder your columns, click the column header (the thin gray button at the top of the column), release the mouse button, and then drag the column to its new position. This technique is similar to the technique you use to arrange columns in the datasheet. In this example, the DatePlaced field is being moved to the far left side.

6. **If you want to hide one or more columns, clear the Show checkbox for those columns.**

   Ordinarily, Access shows every column you've added to the column list. However, in some situations you want to work with a column in your query, but not actually display its data. Usually, it's because you want to use the column values for sorting or filtering.

7. **Choose a sort order.**

   If you don't supply a sort order, you'll get the records right from the database in whatever order they happen to be. This convention usually (but not always) means the oldest records appear first, at the top of the table. To sort your table explicitly, choose the field you want to use to sort the results, and then, in the corresponding Sort box, choose a sorting option. In the current example, the table is sorted by date in descending order, so that the most recent orders are first in the list (*Figure 6-4*).

TIP You can sort based on several fields. The only trick is that your columns need to be ordered so that the first sorting criterion appears first (leftmost) in the column list. Use the column-rearranging trick from step 5 to make sure you've got it right.

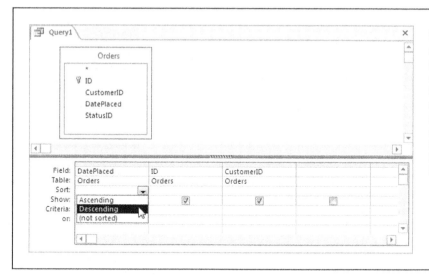

FIGURE 6-4

Choose Ascending if you want to sort a text field from A–Z, a numeric field from lowest to highest, or a date field from oldest to most recent. Choose Descending to use the reverse order. Page 104 has more information about sorting and how it applies to different data types.

8. **Set your filtering criteria.**

   Filtering (page 107) is a tool that lets you focus on the records that interest you and ignore all the rest. Filtering cuts a large swath of data down to the information you need, and it's the heart of many a query. (You'll learn much more about building a filter expression in the next section.)

   Once you have the filter expression you need, place it in the Criteria box for the appropriate field (*Figure 6-5*). In the current example, you can put this filter expression in the Criteria box for the DatePlaced field to get the orders placed in the first three months of the year:

   ```
   >=#1/1/2013# And <=#3/31/2013#
   ```

   You aren't limited to a single filter—in fact, you can add a separate filter expression to each field. If you want to use a field for filtering but don't want to display it in the results, then clear the Show checkbox for that field.

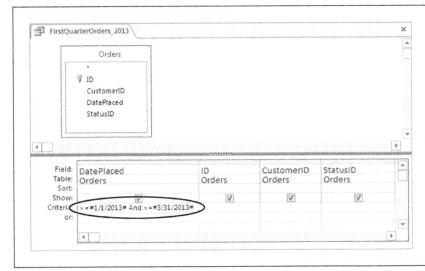

FIGURE 6-5

Here's a filter that finds orders made in a date range (from January 1 to March 31, in the year 2013). Notice that when you use an actual hard-coded date as part of a condition (like January 1, 2013 in this example), Access brackets the date with # symbols. For a refresher about date syntax, refer to page 150.

TIP Not comfortable with the >= and <= symbols? You can rewrite the filter in this example using the Between keyword, like this:

    Between #1/1/2013# And #3/31/2013#

The end result is the same—Access gets the order records from the first three months.

9. **Choose Query Tools | Design→Results→Run.**

    Now that you've finished the query, you're ready to put it into action. When you run the query, you'll see the results presented in a datasheet (complete with lookups on linked fields), just like when you edit a table. *Figure 6-6* shows the result of the query on the Orders table.

    You can switch back to Design view by right-clicking the tab title and then choosing Design View.

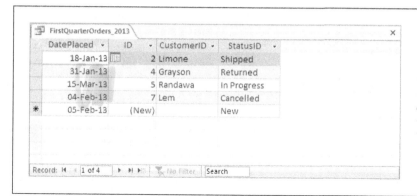

FIGURE 6-6

*Here are the results of a query
that shows orders placed within
a specific date range. You can use
the datasheet window to review or
print your results, or you can edit
information just as you would in a
table datasheet.*

NOTE The datasheet for your query acquires any formatting you applied to the datasheet of the underlying table. If you applied a hot-pink background and cursive font to the datasheet for the Orders table, the same settings apply to any queries that use the Orders table. However, you can change the datasheet formatting for your query just as you would with a table (see page 98).

10. **Save the query.**

You can save your query anytime by using the keyboard shortcut Ctrl+S. If you don't, Access automatically prompts you to save your query when you close the query tab (or your entire database). Of course, you don't *need* to save your query. Sometimes you might create a query for a specific, one-time-only task. If you don't plan to reuse the query, then there's no point in cluttering up your database with extra objects.

The first time you save your query, Access asks for a name. Use the same naming rules that you follow for tables—refrain from using spaces or special characters, and capitalize the first letter in each word. A good query describes the view of data that it presents. One good choice for the example shown in *Figure 6-6* is FirstQuarterOrders_2013.

TIP Remember, when you save a query, you aren't saving the query *results*—you're just saving the query *design*, with all its settings. That way, you can run the query anytime to get the live results that match your criteria.

Once you've created a query, you'll see it in your database's navigation pane (*Figure 6-7*).

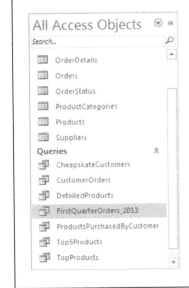

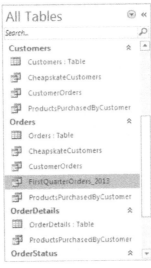

FIGURE 6-7

Ordinarily, the navigation pane is set to use Object Type viewing mode (left), which puts all tables in a group named Tables and all queries in a group named Queries. However, if you click the down-pointing arrow in the top-right corner of the navigation pane, you'll see a menu with more viewing options. Choose Tables and Related Views, and each query will appear under the table that it uses (right). If a query uses more than one table, the same query appears in more than one group in the navigation pane. For more information about the different viewing modes of the navigation pane, see page 460.

> **TIP** You can get this completed example, along with all the queries shown in this chapter, from the Missing CD page at *www.missingmanuals.com/cds/access2013mm*. Most of the queries, including FirstQuarterOrders_2013, are in the Boutique Fudge database.

You can launch the query anytime by double-clicking it. Suppose you've created a query named TopProducts that grabs all the expensive products in the Products table (using the filter criteria >50 on the Price field). Every time you need to review, print, or edit information about expensive products, you run the TopProducts query. To fine-tune the query settings, right-click the query in the navigation pane, and then choose Design View.

Access lets you open your table and any queries that use it at the same time; they all appear in separate tabs. However, you can't modify the design of your table until you close all the queries that use it.

If you add new records to a table while a query is open, the new records don't automatically appear in the query. Instead, you'll need to run your query again. The quickest way is to choose Home→Records→Refresh→Refresh All. You can also close your query and open it again, or switch to Design view and then back to Datasheet view. Access runs your query every time it opens the Datasheet view.

> **TIP** Remember, a query is a *view* of some of the data in your table. If you edit some of the data in your query results, Access will change the corresponding records in the underlying table.

▓ BUILDING FILTER EXPRESSIONS

The secret to a good query is getting the information you want, and nothing more. To tell Access what records it should get (and which ones it should ignore), you need a *filter expression*.

The filter expression defines the records you're interested in. If you want to find all the orders that were placed by a customer with the ID 1032, you could use this filter expression:

```
=1032
```

To put this filter expression into action, you need to put it in the Criteria box under the CustomerID field.

Don't Get Confused by Lookups

Lookups change the way values appear on the datasheet. If you add a lookup on the CustomerID field in the Orders table, you don't see a cryptic number like 1032. Instead, you see some descriptive information, like the name *Hancock, John*.

However, when you write your filter expression, you need to remember what information is actually stored in the field. So the CustomerID filter expression *=1032* works fine, but *="Hancock, John"* doesn't, because the name information is actually stored separately. (It's in the Customers table, not in the Orders table.)

Sometimes, you really *do* want to create a filter expression that uses linked information. You may want to find records in the Orders table using a customer name instead of a customer ID, because you don't have the ID value handy. In this situation, you have two choices:

- You can look up the ID value you need in the Customers table before you start. Then, you can use that value when you build your query for the Orders table.

- You can use a *join query* to get the name information from the Customers table, and display it alongside the rest of your order details. You'll learn how to perform this trick on page 227.

Technically, you could just write *1032* instead of *=1032*, but it's better to stick to the second form, because that's the pattern you'll use for more advanced filter expressions. It starts with the *operator* (in this case, the equal sign) that defines how Access should compare the information, followed by the *value* (in this case, 1032) you want to use to make the comparison.

NOTE If you're using a multi-value field (page 188), Access includes the record in the query results if *any* value matches your filter. Imagine a Classes table that includes a multi-value InstructorID field (indicating that more than one teacher can team up to teach the same class). If you write the filter expression *=1032* for the InstructorID field, Access includes any record where instructor 1032 teaches, whether or not other teachers are also assigned to the class.

Filter expressions are also called *filter conditions*—in fact, the two terms are interchangeable. This makes sense, because every filter sets out a *condition* that a record must match to be included in your results.

If filters seem uncannily familiar, there's a reason. Filters have exactly the same syntax as the validation rules you used to protect a table from bad data (page 146). The only difference is the way Access interprets the condition. A validation rule like *<50 And >10* tells Access a value shouldn't be allowed unless it falls in the desired range (10 to 50). But if you pop the same rule into a filter condition, it tells Access you aren't interested in seeing the record unless it fits the range. Thanks to this similarity, you can use all the validation rules you saw earlier (starting on page 149) as filter conditions.

> **TIP** In Chapter 7, you'll learn how to beef up filter conditions with Access functions.

■ GETTING THE TOP RECORDS

If you're matching text, you need to include quotation marks around your value. Otherwise, Access wonders where the text starts and stops.

```
="Harrington Red"
```

Instead of using an exact match, you can use a range. Add this filter expression to the OrderTotal field to find all the orders worth between $10 and $50:

```
<50 And >10
```

This filter expression actually contains two conditions (less than 50 and greater than 10), which are yoked together by the powerful *And* keyword. Alternatively, you can use the *Or* keyword if you want to see results that meet any one of the conditions you've included. (You can see examples of both on page 153. In Chapter 7, you'll consider some more powerful tools for crafting filter expressions.)

Date expressions are particularly useful. Just remember to bracket any hard-coded dates with the # character. If you add this filter condition to the DatePlaced field, it finds all the orders that were placed in 2013:

```
<#1/1/2014# And >#12/31/2012#
```

This expression works by requiring that dates are earlier than January 1, 2014, but later than December 31, 2012.

> **NOTE** With a little more work, you could craft a filter expression that gets the orders from the first 3 months of the *current* year, no matter what year it is. This trick requires the use of the functions Access provides for dates. You'll see how to use them on page 256.

In some cases, filters are a bit more work than they should be. Suppose you want to see the 10 most expensive products. Using a filter condition, you can easily get the products that have prices above a certain threshold. Using sorting, you can arrange the results so the most expensive items turn up at the top. However, you can't as easily tell Access to get just 10 records and then stop.

In this situation, the query Design view has a shortcut that can help you. Here's how it works:

1. **Open your query in Design view (or create a new query, and add the fields you want to use).**

   This example uses the Products table, and includes the ProductName and Price fields.

2. **Sort your table so that the records you're most interested in are at the top.**

   If you want to find the most expensive products, add a descending sort (page 104) on the Price field.

3. **In the Query Tools | Design→Query Setup→Return box, choose a different option (*Figure 6-8*).**

   The standard option is All, which gets all the matching records. However, you can choose 5, 25, or 100 to get the top 5, 25, or 100 matching records, respectively. Or, you can use a percentage value like 25 percent to get the top quarter of matching records.

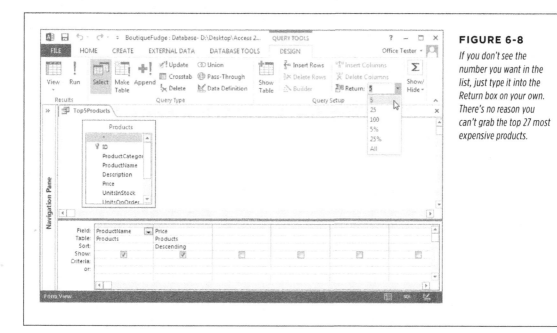

FIGURE 6-8

If you don't see the number you want in the list, just type it into the Return box on your own. There's no reason you can't grab the top 27 most expensive products.

NOTE For the Query Tools | Design→Query Setup→Return box to work, you must choose the right sort order. To understand why, you need to know a little more about how this feature works. If you tell Access to get just five records, it actually performs the normal query, gets all the records, and arranges them according to your sort order. It then throws everything away except for the first five records in the list. If you've sorted your list so that the most expensive products are first (as in this example), you're left with the top five budget-busting products in your results.

4. **Run your query to see the results (*Figure 6-9*).**

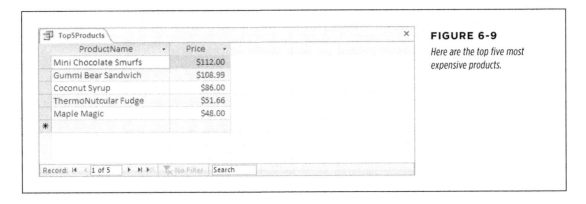

FIGURE 6-9

Here are the top five most expensive products.

How Indexes Speed Up Searches

In Chapter 4, you learned about table indexes, and how to create them. (An *index* is a list of all the values in one field, in sorted order. Next to each value is a pointer to the full record in the table.)

Indexes have two purposes. First, they can prevent duplicate values (page 134). Second, they can help Access perform searches more speedily. Access can often hunt through an index faster than it can scan an entire table. Not only is the index physically smaller (because it has the value from only one field), but it's also sorted, so Access can skip to the right place more quickly.

To understand the difference, suppose you ask Access to find the Bavarian Tart record in the Products table. If you have an index for the ProductName field, Access can scan the B section until it finds the right entry, and then jump to the full details. If you don't have an index, Access is forced to search the entire table, record by record. The table isn't in any sorted order, so there's no telling how long it'll take before Access stumbles across the right record.

At first glance, indexes sound tremendously useful, and you'll be tempted to create them for all your table fields. But indexes have drawbacks. The more indexes you add, the more work Access needs to do when inserting and updating records. Each index also takes up some space. In fact, indexes are a waste of resources unless you *know* they'll improve search performance.

Here are some reasons to consider using an index to improve performance:

- **Your database is huge.** If you have only a few hundred records, Access can almost always scan the entire table faster than it can use an index, due to the way that hard drives work. Even if you have thousands of records, Access can often load the whole shebang into your computer's memory, so it doesn't have to wait for the hard drive to respond, and all your queries are blisteringly fast.

- **Your search is slow.** You have no reason to enhance a query if it's already working at top speed. Most Access fans can search giant databases day after day without ever having to wait.

- **The field you want to index is used in a search.** Don't index a field unless you're using it for filtering. If you often search for a single, specific customer by looking up the last name, consider adding an index on the LastName field.

- **The field you want to index is unique (or close to it).** It makes sense to add an index to the ProductName field in the Products table, because very few products (if any) share the same name. On the other hand, it doesn't make sense to index the City field in the Customers table, because many customers live in the same city. As a result, an index on the City field would be inefficient, and Access probably wouldn't bother to use it at all.

Creating a Simple Query with the Query Wizard

Design view is usually the best place to start constructing queries, but it's not the only option. You can use the query wizard to give you an initial boost, and then refine your query in Design view.

The query wizard works by asking you a series of questions, and then creating the query that fits the bill. Unlike many of the other wizards in Access and other Office applications, the query wizard is relatively feeble. It's a good starting point for query newbies, but not for an end-to-end performer.

Here's how you can put the Query Wizard to work:

1. **Choose Create→Queries→Query Wizard.**

   Access gives you a choice of several different wizards (*Figure 6-10*).

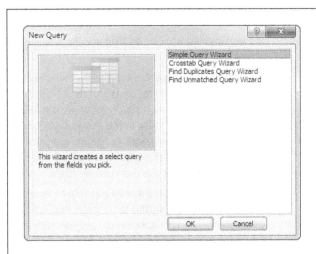

FIGURE 6-10

In the first step of the query wizard, you choose from a small set of basic query types.

2. **Choose a query type. The Simple Query Wizard is the best starting point for now.**

   The query wizard includes a few common kinds of queries. With the exception of the crosstab query, there's nothing really unique about any of these choices. You'll learn to create them all by using Design view:

   - **Simple Query Wizard** gets you started with an ordinary query, which displays a subset of data from a table. This query is the kind you created in the previous section.

   - **Crosstab Query Wizard** generates a crosstab query, which lets you sum-marize large amounts of data using different calculations. You'll build one of your own on page 270.

   - **Find Duplicates Query Wizard** is similar to the Simple Query Wizard, except it adds a filter expression that shows only records that share dupli-cated values. If you forgot to set a primary key or to create a unique index for your table, this option can help you clean up the mess.

   - **Find Unmatched Query Wizard** is similar to the Simple Query Wizard, ex-cept it adds a filter expression that finds unlinked records in related tables. You could use this to find an order that isn't associated with any particular customer. You'll learn how to find unmatched records on page 232.

3. **Click OK.**

   The first step of the query wizard appears.

4. **In the Tables/Queries box, choose the table that has the data you want. Then, add the fields you want to see in the query results, as shown in *Figure 6-11*.**

For the best control, add the fields one at a time. Add them in the order you want them to appear from left to right in the query results.

You can add fields from more than one table. To do so, start by choosing one of the tables, add the fields you want, and then choose the second table and repeat the process. This process really makes sense only if the tables are related. You'll learn more on page 227.

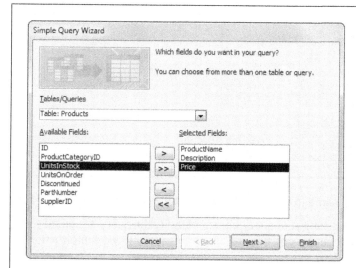

FIGURE 6-11

To add a field, select it in the Available Fields list, and then click the > arrow button (or just double-click the field). You can add all fields at once by clicking the >> arrow button, and you can remove fields by selecting them in the Selected Fields list and then clicking <. In this example, three fields are included in the query.

5. **Click Next.**

If your query includes a numeric field, the query wizard gives you the choice of creating a summary query that arranges rows into groups and that calculates information like totals and averages. You'll learn about summary queries in Chapter 8. For now, if you get this choice, choose Detail and then click Next.

The final step of the query wizard appears (*Figure 6-12*).

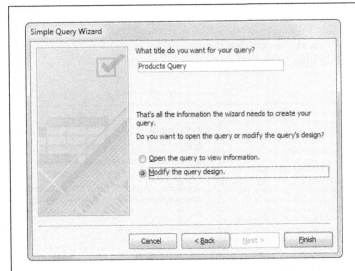

FIGURE 6-12

In the last step, you choose the name for your query, and decide whether you want to see the results right away or refine it further in Design view.

6. **Supply a query name in the "What title do you want for your query?" box.**

   If you want to fine-tune your query, choose "Modify the query design." If you're happy with what you've got, choose "Open the query to view information" to run the query.

   One reason you may want to open your query in Design view is to add filter conditions (page 211) to pick out specific rows. Unfortunately, you can't set filter conditions in the query wizard.

7. **Click Finish.**

   Your query opens in Design view or Datasheet view, depending on the choice you made in step 6. You can run it by choosing Query Tools | Design→Results→Run.

Queries on Queries

The examples in this chapter assume you're creating a query based on a table in your database. But keen eyes may have spotted a different choice—namely, you can create a query that selects results from another query. If you're creating a query in the design window, you simply need to use the Queries tab of the Show Table window (instead of the Tables tab). If you're creating a query with the wizard, all your queries appear in the Tables/Queries list in the first step, along with your tables.

You most often build a query on another query when you want to reuse your hard work and simplify complex queries.

For example, imagine you want to create a query for Boutique Fudge that gets the customers who've placed an order in the last month and retrieves all their customer information. Based on that query, you may want to build a more specialized summary query (page 266) that arranges the customers into groups based on their city and counts how many recent purchasers you have in each location. You could create a single query that does both these steps. But by splitting this logic into two pieces, you can easily reuse the first query (recent customers) to create many more related queries.

Understanding the SQL View

Behind the scenes, every query is actually a text command written in a specialized language called *SQL* (Structured Query Language). SQL is a staple of the database world, and it's supported in all major database products, albeit with minor variations and idiosyncrasies.

> **NOTE** Database gurus still argue about whether SQL is pronounced "Es-Cue-El" (which is historically correct) or "Sequel" (which is how it's used in the product name "Microsoft SQL Server"). In this book, we assume you'll use the more hip "Sequel."

As you craft a query in the design window (or using the query wizard), Access generates a matching SQL command. When you save your query, Access simply stores the text of this command in your database. That text is all Access needs to run the query later on.

Most of the time, you won't spend much time contemplating the SQL that lurks under your queries' surfaces. However, in some cases you may want to take a closer look. Here are some examples:

- You want to perform an action that's supported by SQL but isn't available in the query designer. Of course, you'll need to know more than a little about SQL to edit your command. Later in this chapter, you'll see how to use SQL view to create a union query that combines the results from two similar tables.

- You want to learn SQL. That's a good skill to have if you're planning a career as a database administrator, but it's not really necessary if you're sticking with Access.

- You want to transplant a command into another type of database. Say you're moving databases from Access to a high-powered Oracle database. This job is ambitious, and you'll find that while you can move your data to its new home, you can't move other database objects like queries. Instead, you need to take a closer look at the underlying SQL, which you can use to reconstruct the query in the new database.

- You're just plain curious. Looking at the SQL for your queries clears up a lot of the mystery behind how Access works.

- You're a SQL coding genius, and the query designer slows you down.

To take a look at the SQL command for a query, right-click the tab title, and then choose SQL view. *Figure 6-13* shows what you see.

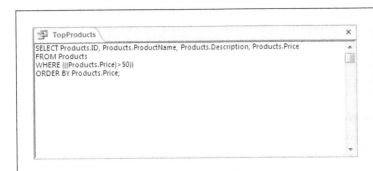

FIGURE 6-13

Here's the SQL command for the TopProducts query, which finds products that cost more than $50. If you're intimidated, you can jump back to another view at any time by right-clicking the tab title, and then choosing Design View or Datasheet View.

▣ ANALYZING A QUERY

Although SQL looks complex at first glance, all queries boil down to essentially the same ingredients. Consider the query for finding high-priced orders, which looks like this (with each line numbered for easy reference):

```
1 SELECT Products.ID, Products.ProductName, Products.Price
2 FROM Products
3 WHERE (((Products.Price)>50))
4 ORDER BY Products.Price;
```

> **NOTE** Sometimes, Access adds square brackets around field names. That means you might see *Products.[ID]* instead of *Products.ID*. Both variations are equivalent. However, you need the square brackets if your field name includes characters that have a specialized meaning in the SQL language, like the space. For example, if you have field called Product Name, the query must refer to it as *Products.[Product Name]* rather than *Product. Product Name*. Access always adds the square brackets when you need them, and it often adds them even when you don't.

Here's a breakdown of the first two lines:

- **Line 1** starts with the word *SELECT*, which indicates it's a query that selects records (like all the queries you've seen in this chapter).

After the word *SELECT* is a comma-separated list of fields that you want to see. Each field is written out in the long format *TableName.FieldName*, just in case you decide to create a query that uses more than one table.

- **Line 2** starts with the word *FROM*, which indicates the table (or tables) that you're searching. In this case, the Products table has the records you need.

These two lines represent a complete functioning query. However, you'll often have more lines that apply filtering settings and sorting:

- **Line 3** starts with the word *WHERE*, which indicates the start of your filter conditions. In this case, there's only one—a requirement that the product price be over $50. If you've defined more than one criteria on different fields, you see them all here, joined together using the AND operator.

> **NOTE** Access goes a little crazy with parentheses in the filter conditions. You could rewrite *WHERE (((Products. Price)>50))* more simply as *WHERE Products.Price>50*. Access uses the parentheses because they make it easier to sort out complex queries with multiple conditions.

- **Line 4** starts with the words "ORDER BY," which define the sorting order. In this case, records are sorted from lowest to highest using the value in the Price field. In the case of a descending sort, you'd see the abbreviation "DESC" after the field name. If you're sorting on multiple fields, you see a comma-separated field list.

  The command ends with a final semicolon (;). Access doesn't need this detail, but it's a SQL-world convention.

The lesson is that every query you build is shaped out of a few common ingredients, represented by the SELECT, FROM, WHERE, and ORDER BY sections.

Access keeps all the different views of a query synchronized. If you make a change to the SQL text and then switch back to the Design view, you then see the newly modified version of the query (unless you've made a mistake, in which case Access delivers an error message).

To try it out, you can modify the SQL text so it selects an extra column and sorts on two fields, so products with the same price are arranged alphabetically (the new parts are highlighted in bold):

```
SELECT Products.ID, Products.ProductName, Products.Price,Products.Description
FROM Products
WHERE (((Products.Price)>100))
ORDER BY Products.Price,Products.ProductName;
```

Right-click the tab title, and then choose Design View to see how these changes appear in the query designer.

CREATING A UNION QUERY

The query designer doesn't recognize some rare SQL tricks. You can use them only by editing the SQL command in SQL view, and once you've made the change, you can't look at your query in Design view any longer (unless you remove the unsupported change later on).

A *union query* merges the results from more than one table and then presents them in a single datasheet. This kind of query doesn't fully work in the query designer, but that's no reason you can't use it.

Essentially, a union query is composed of two (or more) separate select queries. The trick is that the results from each select query must have the same structure. That means you need to retrieve similar columns from each table, in the same order. Assuming you can meet this standard, all you need to do is add the word "UNION" between the two queries.

Here's a union query that presents a list of names drawn from two tables—Customers and Employees:

```
SELECT Customers.FirstName, Customers.LastName
FROM Customers
UNION
SELECT Employees.FirstName, Employees.LastName
FROM Employees
```

This query works even though the structure of the Customers and Employees tables are different. The important part is that the query results from both tables—in this case, the FirstName and LastName fields—match up.

NOTE You can create a union query even if the column names differ. In this example, that means that the query would still work if the columns in the Employees table were F_Name and L_Name. Access simply uses the column names from the first query when it displays the results in the datasheet.

In this example, when you view the query results, you see a list of customer names followed by a list of employee names, although you can't necessarily tell where one table leaves off and the other begins. You also can't edit any of the data—union queries are strictly for reviewing information, not changing it. Access doesn't let you edit union queries in the query designer. If you right-click the tab title and then choose Design View, you wind up in SQL view instead.

NOTE   If there are any duplicates in the results, union queries show just one copy. You can change this behavior by replacing UNION with UNION ALL. In the previous example, this step causes a person who's both an employee and a customer to show up twice in the combined results.

Access puts union queries in the Unrelated Objects section of the navigation pane and uses a different icon for them than for normal queries (*Figure 6-14*).

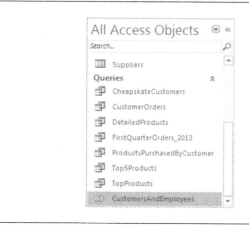

FIGURE 6-14

Union queries, like the CustomersAndEmployees query shown here at the bottom of the list, have a different icon in the navigation pane. The two joined circles indicate that more than one set of results are being shown together.

Union queries are a good way to link together similar tables that have been separated for reasons of performance, security, or distribution. (See the box on page 186 for the different reasons you might split a single set of data into different tables.) Union queries *aren't* a good way to work with parent-child relationships. For this task you need *join* queries, which are described in the next section.

Think Twice Before Redesigning Your Tables

Access is surprisingly savvy at keeping track of which queries use particular tables. This trait becomes important when you crack open a table in Design mode to change something about its structure.

Suppose you rename the Orders table to Sales, and the DatePlaced field to OrderDate. The next time you run the FirstQuarterOrders_2013 query (*Figure 6-6*), you find that—remarkably—it still works. Access knows that the FirstQuarterOrders_2013 query *depends* on the Orders table. When you change the names in the table, it adjusts the query accordingly.

Access includes a nifty tool that can look at any database object you choose, and tell you what other database objects depend on it. You can use this tool to figure out what queries, forms, and reports use the Orders table before you change it. To use this feature, follow these steps:

1. In the navigation pane, select the database object that you want to examine.

2. Choose Database Tools→Relationships→Object Dependencies. The Object Dependencies box appears on the Access window's right side. (Choose the same command again when you want to hide it.)

3. In the Object Dependencies box, choose either "Objects that depend on me" (to see other objects that use this object) or "Objects that I depend on" (to see all the objects this object uses).

4. At the top of the Object Dependencies box, click the Refresh link. The Object Dependencies box lists all the appropriate objects, divided into categories by type (*Figure 6-15*).

Access can't spot all dependencies, like when you need to delve into the SQL view to create a query that you can't build in Design view. If you create a union query (as in the previous example), Access isn't smart enough to figure out which tables your query depends on. If you redesign those tables, you'll get an error the next time you run your query, saying that Access can't find the correct field or table. (To fix the error, you need to open your query in SQL view again, and change the field and table names to their new values.)

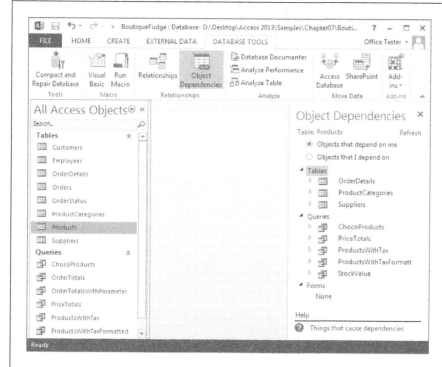

FIGURE 6-15

Here, the Object Dependencies box analyzes the Products table. It shows three tables that link to Products, and four queries that use the Products table. You can dig deeper into any object by clicking the plus (+) box next to its name. (Click the + next to TopProducts to check if any other database objects use that query.) The Ignored Objects section is at the bottom of the list. The CustomersAndEmployees union query shows up here, and it tells you that Access has no idea what it depends on.

Queries and Related Tables

In Chapter 5, you learned how to split data into fundamental pieces and store it in distinct, well-organized tables. This sort of design's only problem is that it's more difficult to get the full picture when you have related data stored in separate places. Fortunately, Access has the perfect solution—you can bring the tables back together for display using a *join*.

A join is a query operation that pulls columns from two tables and fuses them together in one grid of results. You use joins to amplify child tables by adding information from the parent table. Here are some examples:

- In the bobblehead database, you can show a list of bobblehead dolls (drawn from the child table Dolls) along with the manufacturer information for each doll (from the parent table Manufacturers).

- In the Cacophoné music school database, you can get a list of available classes, with instructor information.

- In the Boutique Fudge database, you can get a list of orders, complete with the details for the customer who placed the order.

NOTE You've already learned how to create lookup tables to show just a bit of information from a linked table. A lookup can show the name of a product category in place of the ID number in the ProductID field. However, a join query is far more powerful. It can grab oodles of information from the linked table—far more than you could fit in a single field.

Figure 6-16 shows how a table join works.

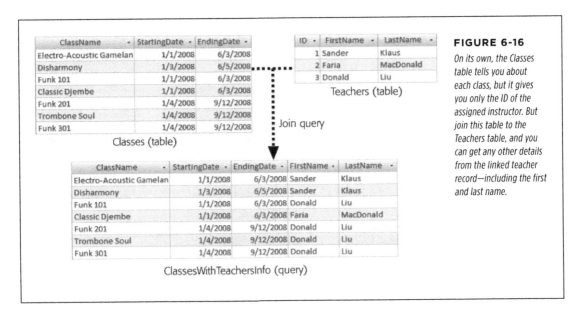

FIGURE 6-16

On its own, the Classes table tells you about each class, but it gives you only the ID of the assigned instructor. But join this table to the Teachers table, and you can get any other details from the linked teacher record—including the first and last name.

Relationships vs. Joins

It's important to understand the differences between a relationship and a query join:

- **Relationship.** A permanent link between two tables, which is stored in your database. When creating a relationship in the database, you have the option of switching on *referential integrity*, a set of rules that prevents inconsistent data in related tables (page 173).

- **Join.** A query feature that lets you combine related data from two tables into one set of results. The join doesn't

affect how you enter or edit that information in the underlying tables.

If you have a relationship in place, Access assumes you want to use a join to link those tables together in a query, which only makes sense.

Joining Tables in a Query

Access makes it remarkably easy to join two tables. The first step is adding both tables to your query, using the Show Table window. If you're creating a new query in Design view, the Show Table window appears right away. If you're working with a query you've already created, make sure you're in Design view, right-click the window, and then choose Show Table.

TIP You can add extra tables to a query without using the Show Table window. All you need to do is drag the table from the navigation pane and drop it on the query design surface.

If you've already defined a relationship between the two tables (using the Relationships window, as described on page 167, or by creating a lookup, as described on page 180), Access uses that relationship to automatically create a query join. You'll see a line on the diagram that connects the appropriate fields, as shown in *Figure 6-17*.

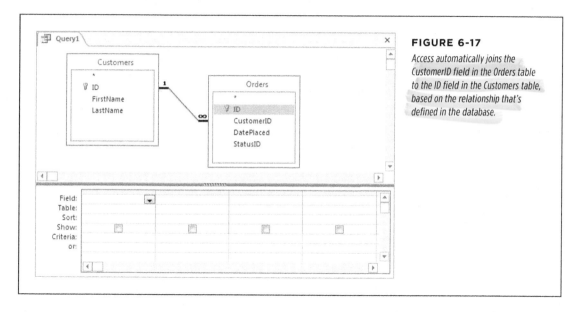

FIGURE 6-17

Access automatically joins the CustomerID field in the Orders table to the ID field in the Customers table, based on the relationship that's defined in the database.

If you add two unrelated tables, Access tries to help you out by guessing a relationship. If it spots a field with the same data type and the same name in both tables, it adds a join on this field. This action often isn't what you want—for example, many tables share a common ID field. Also, if you're following the database design rules from "Six Principles of Database Design" on page 89, your linked fields have slightly different names in each table, like ID and CustomerID. If you run into a problem where Access assumes a relationship that doesn't exist, just remove the relationship before adding the join you really want.

If you *haven't* already defined a relationship between the two related tables, you probably should, before you create your query (see Chapter 5 for full instructions). But if for some reason you've decided not to create the relationship (perhaps the database design was set in stone by another, less-savvy Access designer), you can manually define the join in the query window. To do so, just drag the linked field in one table to the matching field in the other table. You can also remove a join by right-clicking the line between the tables, and then choosing Delete.

Once you have your two tables in the query design window and you've defined the join, you're ready to choose the fields you want. You can pick fields from both tables. You can also add filter conditions and supply a sort order, as you would with any other query. *Figure 6-18* shows an example of a query that uses a join, and *Figure 6-19* shows that same query in action.

> **TIP** When you have two linked tables, it's easy to forget what you're showing. If you join the Orders and Customers tables, and then select fields from each, what do you end up with: a list of customers or a list of orders? Easy—you get a list of orders, complete with customer information. Queries with linked tables always act on the *child* table and bring in additional information from the parent.

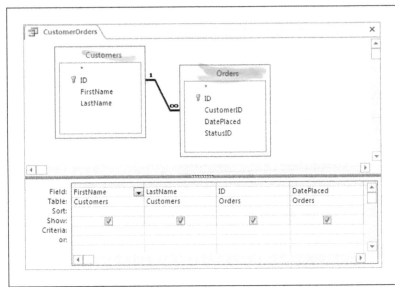

FIGURE 6-18

This query shows information from the Orders and Customers tables. It doesn't matter whether the first field is from the Orders or Customers table—either way, you're creating a list of orders with added customer information. Notice how the Table box (under the Field box) shows which table each field comes from.

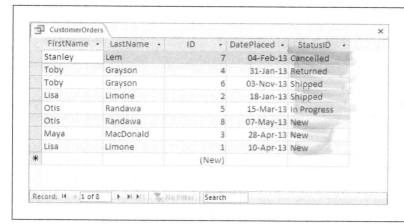

FIGURE 6-19

You can easily see at a glance who ordered what. The ID column is the order ID (although you could display the IDs from both the Customers and Orders tables).

NOTE When you perform a join, you see repeated information. If you join the Customers and Orders tables, you see the first and last name of a shopaholic customer appear next to several orders. However, this doesn't violate the database rule against duplicate data. Even though the customer details *appear* in more than one place in the query results, they're *stored* only once in the Customers table.

Remember, when you link a parent and child table with a join query, you're really performing a query that gets all the records from the child table and then adds extra information from the parent table. For example, you can use a join query to get a list of orders (from the child table) and supplement each record with information about the customer that made the order. No matter how you create the join, you won't ever get a list of customers with order information tacked on. That wouldn't make sense, because every customer can make multiple orders.

Joins are one of the most useful features in any query writer's toolkit. They let you display one table that has all the information you need.

NOTE When using more than one table, there's always a risk that two tables have a field with the same name. This possibility isn't a problem if you don't plan to show these fields in your query, but it can cause confusion if you do. One way to distinguish between the two fields is to rename one of them in the query datasheet. You'll learn how to perform this trick with a calculated field on page 237.

Modifying Information Using a Join Query

You need to be careful when modifying the data in a query that uses a join. You'll never have a problem if you want to modify the details from the child table. In the example in *Figure 6-19*, it's easy enough to change the DatePlaced or StatusID fields to change the order record.

However, consider what happens if you change one of the values in the *parent* table, like the customer's first or last name. Obviously, the same customer information may appear several times in the query. (For example, the query in *Figure 6-19* shows two orders by a customer named Toby.) If you modify the customer name in one place, then Access automatically changes the information in the Customers table, and then refreshes the

entire query. So, if you change "Toby" to "Tony" in *Figure 6-19*, Access refreshes the second and third rows of the datasheet.

A potential problem occurs if you want to change the *link* between the order record and the customer record. You may want to edit an order that's assigned to Toby so that the database says Lisa made the order. However, you *can't* make this change by editing the FirstName and LastName fields in the query. (If you do, you'll simply wind up changing Toby's record in the Customers table.) Instead, you need to change the CustomerID field in the Orders table so that it points to the right person. In the query shown in *Figure 6-19*, the CustomerID field isn't included, so there's no way to change the link.

Outer Joins

The queries you saw in the previous example use what database nerds call an *inner join*. Inner joins show only linked records—in other words, records that appear in both tables. If you perform a query on the Customers and Orders tables, you don't see customers that haven't placed an order. You also don't see orders that aren't linked to any particular customer (the CustomerID value's blank) or aren't linked to a valid record (they contain a CustomerID value that doesn't match up to any record in the Customers table).

Outer joins are more accommodating—these joins include all the same results you'd see in an inner join, *plus* the leftover unlinked records from one of the two tables (it's your choice which one). Obviously, these unlinked records show up in the query results with some blank values, which correspond to the missing information that the other table would supply.

Suppose you perform an outer join between the Orders and Customers tables, and then configure it so that all the order records are shown. Any orders that aren't linked to a customer record have blank values in all the customer-related fields (like FirstName and LastName). In this example, there are two unlinked orders at the end of the listing:

FIRST NAME	LAST NAME	ID	DATE PLACED	STATUS ID
Stanley	Lem	7	13-Jun-2013	Cancelled
Toby	Grayson	4	03-Nov-2012	Returned

FIRST NAME	LAST NAME	ID	DATE PLACED	STATUS ID
Toby	Grayson	6	03-Nov-2012	Shipped
		18	01-Jan-2011	In Progress
		19	01-Jan-2011	In Progress

In this particular example, it doesn't make sense for orders that aren't linked to a customer to exist. In fact, it probably indicates an order that was entered incorrectly. However, if you suspect a problem, an outer join can help you track down the problem.

TIP You can prevent orphaned order records altogether by making CustomerID a required value (page 130) and enforcing referential integrity (page 170).

You can also perform an outer join between the Orders and Customers tables that shows all the *customer* records. In this case, at the end of the query results, you'll see every unlinked customer record, with the corresponding order fields left blank:

FIRST NAME	LAST NAME	ID	DATE PLACED	STATUS ID
Stanley	Lem	7	13-Jun-2013	Cancelled
Toby	Grayson	4	03-Nov-2012	Returned
Toby	Grayson	6	03-Nov-2012	Shipped
Ben	Samatara			
Goosey	Mason			
Tabasoum	Khan			

In this case, the outer join query picks up three stragglers.

So how do you add an outer join to your query? You start with an inner join (which Access usually adds automatically), and then *convert* it to an outer join. To do so, just right-click the join line that links the two tables in the design window, and then choose Join Properties (or just double-click the line). The Join Properties window (*Figure 6-20*) appears and lets you change the type of join you're using.

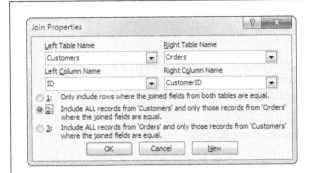

FIGURE 6-20

The first option, "Only include rows where the joined fields from both tables are equal," performs the standard inner join. The other two options let you create an outer join that incorporates all the unlinked rows from one of the two tables.

■ FINDING UNMATCHED RECORDS

Inner joins are by far the most common joins. However, outer joins let you create at least one valuable type of query: a query that can track down unmatched records.

You've already seen how an outer join lets you see a list of all your orders, *plus* the customers that haven't made any orders. That combination isn't terribly useful. But with a little fine-tuning, you can filter out the real customers and create a list with only those people who haven't bought anything. The marketing department is already salivating over this technique, which could help them target potential customers for a first-time-buyer promotion.

To craft this query, you start with the outer-join query that includes all the customer records. Then, you simply add one more ingredient: a filter condition that matches records that don't have an order ID. Technically, these are considered *null* (empty) values.

Here's the filter condition you need, which you must place in the Criteria box for the ID field of the Orders table:

```
Is Null
```

Now, when Access performs the query, it includes only the customer records that aren't linked to anything in the Orders table. *Figure 6-21* shows the query in Design view.

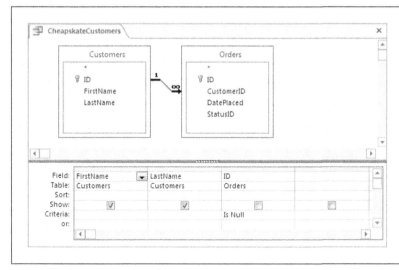

FIGURE 6-21

This query combines an outer join with a filter condition that matches only unlinked customer records. Notice the Show checkbox isn't checked. That's because the ID field is used for a filter condition, but there's no point in displaying it in the results datasheet.

Multiple Joins

Just as you're getting comfortable with inner and outer joins, Access has another feature to throw your way. Many queries don't stop at a single join. Instead, they use three, four, or more to bring multiple related tables into the mix.

Although this sounds complicated at first, it really isn't. Multiple joins are simply ways of bringing more related information into your query. Each join works the same in a multiple-join situation as it does when you use it on its own. To use multiple joins, just add all the tables you want from the Show Table window, make sure the join lines appear, and then choose the fields you want. Access is almost always intelligent enough to figure out what you're trying to do.

Figure 6-22 shows an example where a child table has two parents that can both contribute some extra information.

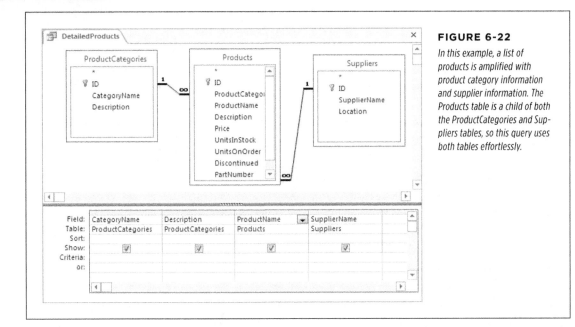

FIGURE 6-22

In this example, a list of products is amplified with product category information and supplier information. The Products table is a child of both the ProductCategories and Suppliers tables, so this query uses both tables effortlessly.

Sometimes, the information you want is more than one table away. Consider the OrderDetails table Boutique Fudge uses to list each item in a customer's order. On its own, the OrderDetails table doesn't provide a link to the customer who ordered the item, but it does provide a link to the related order record. (See page 196 for a discussion of this design.) If you want to get the information about who ordered each item, you need to add the OrderDetails, Orders, and Customers tables to your query, as shown in *Figure 6-23*.

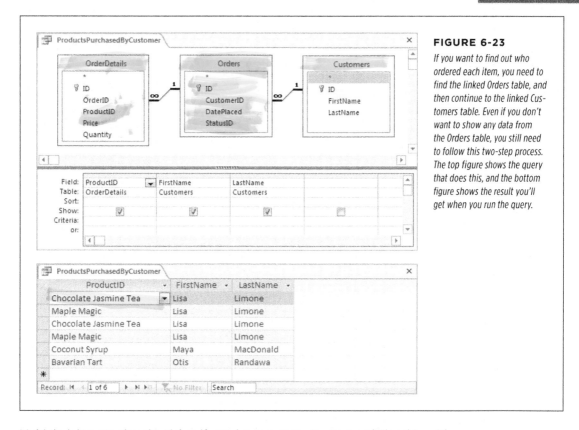

FIGURE 6-23

*If you want to find out who
ordered each item, you need to
find the linked Orders table, and
then continue to the linked Customers table. Even if you don't
want to show any data from
the Orders table, you still need
to follow this two-step process.
The top figure shows the query
that does this, and the bottom
figure shows the result you'll
get when you run the query.*

Multiple joins are also the ticket if you have a many-to-many relationship with a junction table (page 186), like the one between teachers and classes. As you'll remember from Chapter 5 (page 191), the Cacophoné Studios music school uses an intermediary table to track teacher class assignment. If you want to get a list of classes, complete with instructor names, you need to create a query with three tables: Classes, Teachers, and Teachers_Classes (see *Figure 6-24*).

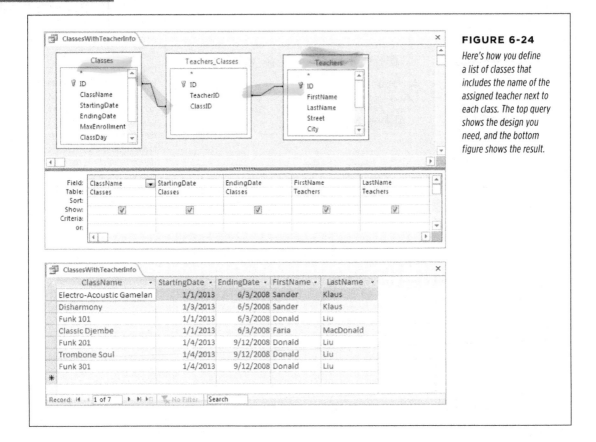

FIGURE 6-24

Here's how you define a list of classes that includes the name of the assigned teacher next to each class. The top query shows the design you need, and the bottom figure shows the result.

Essential Query Tricks

E very Access expert stocks his or her database with a few (or a few dozen) useful queries that simplify day-to-day tasks. In the previous chapter, you learned how to create queries that chew through avalanches of information and present exactly what you need to see. But as Access masters know, there's much more power lurking just beneath the surface of the query design window.

In this chapter, you'll delve into some query magic that's sure to impress your boss, coworkers, and romantic partners. You'll learn how to carry out calculations in a query with numbers and dates. You'll also learn how to write super-intelligent filter expressions and how to create dynamic queries that ask for information every time you run them. These techniques are indispensable to the repertoire of any true query fanatic.

▇ Calculated Fields

When you started designing tables, you learned that it's a database crime to add information that's based on the data in another field or in another table. An example of this mistake is creating a Products table that has both a Price and a PriceWithTax field. The fact that the PriceWithTax field is calculated based on the Price field is a problem. Storing both is a redundant waste of space. Even worse, if the tax rate changes, you're left with a lot of records to update and the potential for inconsistent information (like a with-tax price that's lower than a no-tax price). And don't even ask what happens if you need to add a separate TaxRate table that lists different tax rates for different locations.

Even though you know not to create fields like PriceWithTax, sometimes you *will* want to see calculated information in Access. Before Boutique Fudge prints a product list for one of its least-loved retailers, it likes to apply a 10 percent price markup. To do this, it needs a way to adjust the price information before printing the data. If the retailer spots the lower price without the markup, they're sure to demand it.

Queries provide the perfect solution for these kinds of problems, because they include an all-purpose way to mathematically manipulate information. The trick is to add a *calculated field*: a field that's defined in your query, but doesn't actually exist in the table. Instead, Access calculates the value of a calculated field based on one or more other fields in your table. The values in the calculated field are never stored anywhere—instead, Access generates them each time you run the query.

Defining a Calculated Field

To create a calculated field, you need to supply two details: a name for the field, and an *expression* that tells Access what calculation it must perform. Calculated fields are defined using this two-part form:

```
CalculatedFieldName: Expression
```

For example, here's how you can define the PriceWithTax calculated field:

```
PriceWithTax: [Price] * 1.10
```

Essentially, this expression tells Access to take the value from the Price field, and then multiply it by 1.10 (which is equivalent to raising the price by 10 percent). Access repeats this calculation for each record in the query results. For this expression to work, the Price field *must* exist in the table that the query is using. However, you don't need to show the Price field separately in the query results.

You can also refer to the Price field using its *full name*, which is made up of the table name, followed by a period, followed by the field name, as shown here:

```
PriceWithTax: [Products].[Price] * 1.10
```

This syntax is sometimes necessary if your query involves more than one table (using a query join, as described on page 227), and the same field appears in both tables. In this situation, you must use the full name to avoid ambiguity. (If you don't, Access gives you an error message when you try to run the query.)

NOTE Old-time Access users sometimes replace the period with an exclamation mark, as in *[Products]![Price]*, which is equivalent.

To add the PriceWithTax calculated field to a query, you need to use Design view. First, find the column where you want to insert your field. (Usually, you'll just tack it onto the end in the first blank column, although you can drag the other fields around to make space.) Next, type the full definition for the field into the Field box (see *Figure 7-1*).

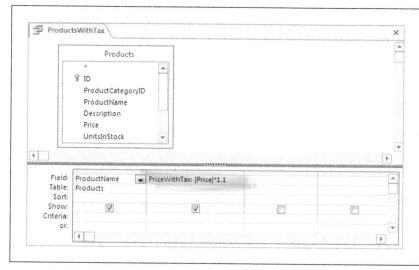

FIGURE 7-1

This query shows two fields straight from the database (ID and Name), and adds the calculated PriceWithTax field. The ordinary Price field, which Access uses to calculate PriceWithTax, isn't shown at all.

Now you're ready to run the query. When you do, the calculated information appears alongside your other columns (*Figure 7-2*). If you don't like the fact that your calculated information appears in a slightly messier format—with more decimal places and no currency symbol—you can fix it by using the rounding (page 245) and formatting (page 250) features discussed later in this chapter.

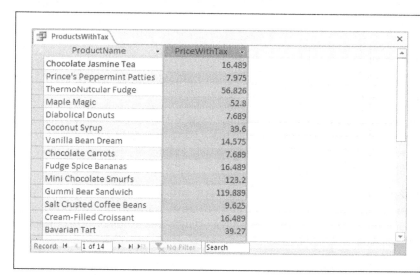

FIGURE 7-2

The query results now show a PriceWithTax field, with the result of the 10 percent markup. The neat part is that this calculated information is now available instantaneously, even though it isn't stored in the database. Try to beat that with a pocket calculator.

Calculated fields do have one limitation—since the information isn't stored in your table, you can't edit it. If you want to make a price change, you'll need to edit the underlying Price field—trying to change PriceWithTax would leave Access thoroughly confused.

NOTE An expression works on a single record at a time. If you want to combine the information in separate records to calculate totals and averages, you need to use the grouping features described on page 266.

Query Synchronization

Here's an interesting trick to try. Run the ProductsWithTax query and leave it open, displaying its results. Now, open the Products table that has the actual data, and then change the price of any product, and move to another record to save your changes. Switch back to the ProductsWithTax query. Has the PriceWithTax value changed?

If you can't stand the suspense, fear not—the PriceWithTax is automatically refreshed to reflect the new price. Access automatically keeps query views synchronized with the live data in your table. When you change a record, Access notices—and it instantly refreshes the query window.

It's worth noting a few exceptions to this rule:

- Access doesn't notice if you insert a new record after you launch a query—to get that to appear in your query results, you need to refresh the results.

- If you change a record so it no longer appears in your query, it doesn't automatically disappear from view. If you have a query showing all products over $100, and you cut the price of one down to $50, it still appears in your query result list (with the new price) until you refresh the results.

- Similarly, if you change a record that currently appears in your query so it no longer fits one of your filter criteria, it doesn't disappear from view until you rerun the query.

- If multiple people are editing the database on different computers (as described in Chapter 19), you don't see other people's changes right away.

To get the latest results, you can refresh individual records or the entire query. To refresh a single record, choose Home→Records→Refresh→Refresh. To rerun the query and refresh everything, choose Home→Records →Refresh→Refresh All. This action also shows any new records and hides any that have been changed so that they no longer satisfy your filter conditions.

Before going any further, it's worth reviewing the rules of calculated fields. Here are some pointers:

- **Always choose a unique name**. An expression like Price: [Price] * 1.10 creates a *circular reference*, because the name of the field you're using is the same as the name of the field you're trying to create. Access doesn't allow this sleight of hand.

- **Build expressions out of fields, numbers, and math operations**. The most common calculated fields take one or more existing fields or hard-coded numbers and combine them using familiar math symbols like addition (+), subtraction (-), multiplication (*), or division (/).

- **Expect to see square brackets**. The expression PriceWithTax: [Price] * 1.10 is equivalent to PriceWithTax: Price * 1.10 (the only difference is the square brackets around the field name Price). Technically, you need the brackets only if your field name contains spaces or special characters. However, when you type in expressions that don't use brackets in the query Design view, Access automatically adds them, just to be on the safe side.

GEM IN THE ROUGH

Renaming a Field in a Query

Tired of seeing long field names in your query results? Based on what you've just learned about expressions, you can painlessly rename a field in your query results. All you need is a calculated field.

The trick is to create a calculated field that matches one of the existing fields (using an expression) and supplies a new name. Technically, you aren't performing any calculation here, but it

still works. Here's an example of a calculated field that renames DateCustomerPlacedPurchaseOrder to OrderDate:

    OrderDate: DateCustomerPlacedPurchaseOrder

The new name (in this example, OrderDate) is known as an *alias*.

When using this technique, remember not to include the original field (in this case, DateCustomerPlacedPurchaseOrder) in your query. The calculated field (OrderDate) already shows the information you want.

Simple Math with Numeric Fields

Many calculated fields rely entirely on ordinary high school math. Table 7-1 gives a quick overview of your basic options for combining numbers.

TABLE 7-1 *Arithmetic Operators*

OPERATOR	NAME	EXAMPLE	RESULT
+	Addition	1+1	2
–	Subtraction	1–1	0
*	Multiplication	2*2	4
^	Exponentiation	2^3	8
/	Division	5/2	2.5
\	Integer division (returns the lowest whole number and discards the remainder)	5\2	2
Mod	Modulus (returns the remainder left after division)	5 Mod 2	1

You're free to use as many fields and operators as you need to create your expression. Consider a Products table with a UnitsInStock field that records the number of units in your warehouse. To determine the value of what you have on hand for a given product, you can write this expression that uses two fields:

    ValueInStock: [UnitsInStock] * [Price]

TIP When performing a mathematical operation with a field, you'll run into trouble if the field contains a blank value. To correct the problem, you need the Nz( ) function, which is described on page 259.

▓ DATE FIELDS

You can also use the addition and subtraction operators with date fields. (You can use multiplication, division, and everything else, but it doesn't have any realistic meaning.)

Using addition, you can add an ordinary number to a date field. This number moves the date forward by that many days. Here's an example that adds 2 weeks of head-room to a company deadline:

```
ExtendedDeadline: [DueDate] + 14
```

If you use this calculation with the date January 10, 2013, the new date becomes January 24, 2013.

Using subtraction, you can find the number of days between any two dates. Here's how you calculate how long it was between the time an order was placed and when it was shipped:

```
ShippingLag: [ShipDate] - [OrderDate]
```

If the ship date occurred 12 days after the order date, you'd see a value of 12.

TIP Date fields can include time information. In calculations, the time information is represented as the fractional part of the value. If you subtract two dates and wind up with the number 12.25, that represents 12 days and 6 hours (because 6 hours is 25 percent of a full day).

Remember, if you want to include *literal* dates in your queries (specific dates you supply), you need to bracket them with the # character and use Month/Day/Year format. Here's an example that uses that approach to count the number of days between the date students were expected to submit an assignment (March 20, 2013) and the date they actually did:

```
LateDays: [DateSubmitted] - #03/20/2013#
```

A positive value indicates that the value in DateSubmitted is larger (more recent) than the deadline date—in other words, the student was late. A value of 4 indicates a student that's 4 days off the mark, while –4 indicates a student that handed the work in 4 days ahead of schedule.

▓ ORDER OF OPERATIONS

If you have a long string of calculations, Access follows the standard rules for *order of operations*: mathematician-speak for deciding which calculation to perform first when there's more than one calculation in an expression. So if you have a lengthy expression, Access doesn't just carry on from left to right. Instead, it evaluates the expression piece by piece in this order:

1. Parentheses (Access always performs any calculations within parentheses first)

2. Exponents

3. Division and multiplication

4. Addition and subtraction

Suppose you want to take the UnitsInStock and the UnitsOnOrder fields into consideration to determine the value of all the product you have available and on the way. To see the order of operation rules in action, try this expression:

```
TotalValue: [UnitsInStock] + [UnitsOnOrder] * [Price]
```

The problem here is that Access multiplies UnitsOnOrder and Price together, and *then* adds it to the UnitsInStock. To correct this oversight, you need parentheses, like so:

```
TotalValue: ([UnitsInStock] + [UnitsOnOrder]) * [Price]
```

Now the UnitsInStock and UnitsOnOrder fields are totaled together, and then multiplied with the Price to get a grand total.

TIP Need some more space to write a really long expression? You can widen any column in the query designer to see more at once, but you'll still have trouble with complex calculations. Better to click in the Field box, and then press Shift+F2. This action pops open a window named Zoom, which shows the full content in a large text box, wrapped over as many lines as necessary. When you've finished reviewing or editing your expression, click OK to close the Zoom box and keep any changes you've made, or click Cancel to discard them. (Another option is to use the Expression Builder, which also gives you a bigger space for editing long formulas, and is discussed on page 246.)

Expressions with Text

Although calculated fields usually deal with numeric information, they don't always. You have genuinely useful ways to manipulate text as well.

If you have text information, you obviously can't use mathematical operations like addition and subtraction. However, you can join text together. You can, for instance, link several fields of address information together and show them all in one field, conserving space (and possibly making it easier to export the information to another program).

To join text, you use the ampersand (&) operator. For example, here's how to create a FullName field that draws information from the FirstName and LastName fields:

```
FullName: [FirstName] & [LastName]
```

This expression looks reasonable enough, but it's actually got a flaw. Since you haven't added any spaces, the first and last name end up crammed together, like this: *BenJenks*. A better approach is to join together *three* pieces of text: the first name, a space, and the last name. Here's the revised expression:

```
FullName: [FirstName] & " " & [LastName]
```

This produces values like *Ben Jenks*. You can also swap the order and add a comma, if you prefer to have the last name first (like *Jenks, Ben*) for better sorting:

```
FullName: [LastName] & ", " & [FirstName]
```

You can even use the ampersand to tack text alongside numeric values. If you want the slightly useless text "The price is" to appear before each price value, use this calculated field:

```
Price: "The price is: " & [Price]
```

Query Functions

By now, it may have2 crossed your mind that you can manipulate numbers and text in even more ambitious ways—ways that go beyond what the basic operators let you do. You may want to round off numbers or capitalize text. Access does include a feature that lets you take your expressions to the next level, and it's called *functions*.

A function is a built-in algorithm that takes some data that you supply, performs a calculation, and then returns a result. The difference between functions and the mathematical operators you've already seen is the fact that functions can perform far more complex operations. Access has a catalog with dozens of different functions, many of which perform feats you wouldn't have a hope of accomplishing on your own.

Functions come in handy in all sorts of interesting places in Access. You can use them in:

- **Calculated fields**. To add information to your query results
- **Filter conditions**. To determine what records you see in a query
- **Visual Basic code**. The all-purpose extensibility system for Access that you'll tackle in Part Five

As you explore the world of functions, you'll find that many are well suited to calculated fields but not filter conditions. In the following sections, you'll see exactly where each function makes most sense.

NOTE Functions are a built-in part of the Access version of SQL (page 219), which is the language it uses to perform data operations.

Using a Function

Whether you're using the simplest or the most complicated function, the *syntax*—the rules for using a function in an expression—is the same. To use a function, simply enter the function name, followed by parentheses. Then, inside the parentheses, put all the information the function needs in order to perform its calculations (if any).

For a good example, consider the handy Round() function, which takes a fractional number and then tidies up any unwanted decimal places. Round() is a good way to clean up displayed values in a calculated field. You'll see why Round() is useful if you create an expression like this, which discounts prices by 5 percent:

```
SalePrice: [Price] * 0.95
```

Run a price like $43.97 through this expression, and you wind up with 41.7715 on the other side—which doesn't look that great on a sales tag. The Round() function comes in handy here. Just feed it the unrounded number and the number of decimal places you want to keep:

```
SalePrice: Round([Price] * 0.95, 2)
```

Technically, the Round() function requires two pieces of information, or *arguments*. The first is the number you want to round (in this case, it's the result of the calculation Price * 0.95), and the second is the number of digits that you want to retain to the right of the decimal place (2). The result: the calculation rounded to two decimal places, or 41.77.

> **NOTE** Most functions, like Round(), require two or three arguments. However, some functions can accept many more, while a few don't need any arguments at all.

FREQUENTLY ASKED QUESTION

Banker's Rounding

Access doesn't seem to round numbes correctly. What's going on?

It may surprise you that Access rounds the number 21.985 to 21.98. If you were taught to always round up the number 5, you probably expect 21.99 instead. That is known as *arithmetic rounding*. However, Access doesn't use arithmetic rounding—instead, it chooses *banker's rounding*, which is better in some situations.

The difference between arithmetic rounding and banker's rounding is how they treat the number 5. Since 21.985 lies exactly halfway between 21.98 and 21.99, it isn't easy to decide what to do with it. If you always round 5 up, you'll introduce a bias in totals and averages. Because you round up more often than you round down, any total or average that you calculate ends up just a smidge higher than it should be.

Banker's rounding addresses this by rounding 5 up sometimes and down other times, depending on whether it's paired with an even or odd number. 21.985 is rounded down to 21.98, but 21.995 is rounded up to 22. This way isn't the only way to fight rounding bias (you could decide randomly when to round and when not to), but it's a commonly accepted practice in accounting and statistics.

■ NESTED FUNCTIONS

You can use more than one function in a single calculated field or filter condition. The trick is *nesting*: nerdspeak for putting one function inside another. For example, Access provides an absolute-value function named Abs() that converts negative numbers to positive numbers (and leaves positive numbers unchanged). Here's an example that divides two fields and makes sure the result is positive:

```
Speed: Abs([DistanceTraveled] / [TimeTaken])
```

If you want to round this result, you place the entire expression inside the parentheses for the Round() function, like so:

```
Speed: Round(Abs([DistanceTraveled] / [TimeTaken]), 2)
```

When evaluating an expression with nested functions, Access evaluates the innermost function first. Here, it calculates the absolute value, and then rounds the result. In this example, you could swap the order of these steps without changing the result:

```
Speed: Abs(Round([DistanceTraveled] / [TimeTaken], 2))
```

In many other situations, the order you use is important, and different nesting produces a different result.

Nested functions can get ugly fast. Even in a relatively simple example like the speed calculation, it's difficult to tell what's going on without working through the calculation piece by piece. And if you misplace a bracket, the whole calculation can be thrown off. When you need to nest functions, it's a good idea to build them up bit-by-bit, and run the query each time you add another function into the mix, rather than try to type the whole shebang at once.

The Expression Builder

Functions are a great innovation, but Access just might have too much of a good thing. Access provides a catalog of dozens of different functions tailored for different tasks, some of which are intended for specialized mathematical or statistical operations.

NOTE This book doesn't cover every Access function. (If it did, you'd be fighting to stay awake.) However, in the following sections, you'll see the most useful functions for working with numbers, text, and dates. To discover even more functions, use the Expression Builder. Or, if you prefer to do your learning online, check out the pithy resource *www.techonthenet.com/access/functions*.

To quickly find the functions you want, Access provides a tool called the Expression Builder. To launch the Expression Builder, follow these steps:

1. **Open a query in Design view.**

2. **Right-click the box where you want to insert your expression, and then choose Build.**

   If you're creating a calculated field, you need to right-click the Field box. If you're creating a filter condition, you need to right-click the Criteria box.

   Once you choose Build, the Expression Builder appears, showing any content that's currently in the box (*Figure 7-3*).

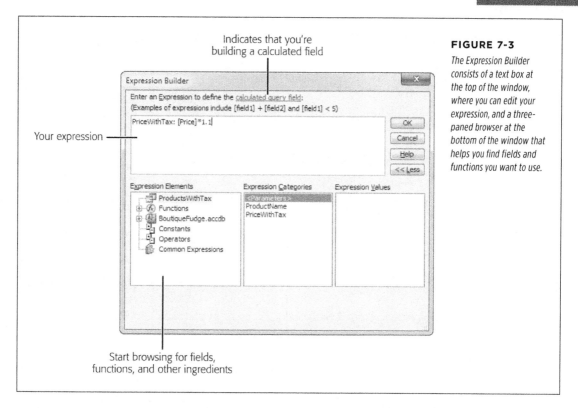

Indicates that you're
building a calculated field

Your expression

Start browsing for fields,
functions, and other ingredients

FIGURE 7-3

*The Expression Builder
consists of a text box at
the top of the window,
where you can edit your
expression, and a three-
paned browser at the
bottom of the window that
helps you find fields and
functions you want to use.*

3. Add or edit the expression.

The Expression Builder includes two shortcuts that you'll want to try. You can
insert a name without typing it by hand (*Figure 7-4*), and you can find a function by browsing (*Figure 7-5*).

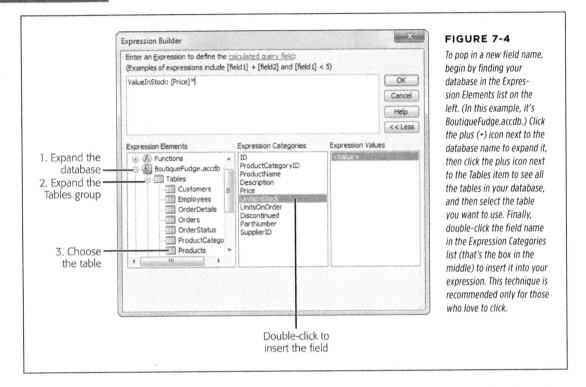

1. Expand the
   database

2. Expand the
   Tables group

3. Choose
   the table

Double-click to
insert the field

FIGURE 7-4

To pop in a new field name, begin by finding your database in the Expression Elements list on the left. (In this example, it's BoutiqueFudge.accdb.) Click the plus (+) icon next to the database name to expand it, then click the plus icon next to the Tables item to see all the tables in your database, and then select the table you want to use. Finally, double-click the field name in the Expression Categories list (that's the box in the middle) to insert it into your expression. This technique is recommended only for those who love to click.

The Expression Builder is an all-purpose tool to create expressions for calculated fields and filter conditions. Some options make sense only in one context. The logical operators like the equals (=) symbol and the And, Or, Not, and Like operators are useful for setting criteria for filtering, but don't serve any purpose in calculated fields.

When you insert field names in the Expression builder, they're written in a slightly lengthier format that always includes the table name. You'll see [Products]![Price] instead of just [Price]. Don't worry—both mean the same thing to Access.

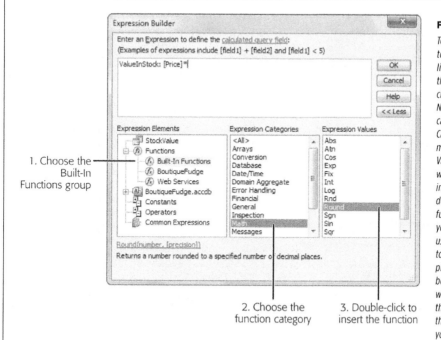

FIGURE 7-5

To find a function, head to Expression Elements list (on the left), expand the Functions item, and choose Built-In Functions. Next, choose a function category in the Expression Categories list (in the middle). The Expression Values list (on the right) will show all the functions in that category. You can double-click one of these functions to insert it into your expression. When you use the Expression Builder to add a function, it adds placeholders (like <number> and <precision>) where you need to supply the arguments. Replace this text with the values you want to use.

1. Choose the Built-In Functions group

2. Choose the function category

3. Double-click to insert the function

4. **Click OK.**

Access copies your new expression back into the Field box or Criteria box.

Most Access experts find that the Expression Builder is too clunky to be worth the trouble. But even though the Expression Builder may not be the most effective way to write an expression, it's a great way to learn about new and mysterious functions, thanks to its built-in function reference. If you find a function that sounds promising but you need more information, select it in the list and then click Help. Access opens a web browser and shows you a brief reference summary that explains the purpose of the function and the arguments you need to supply, as shown in *Figure 7-6*.

NOTE There's one quirk to watch out for. At the time of this writing, Access fails to find the function reference if it's configured to look for help details online. If you get a message stating "This page is unavailable" when you try to use the function reference, look in the bottom-right corner of the help window, click the text "Connected to Office.com," and choose "Show content only from this computer." Then close the help window and click the Help button again to get the information you're after.

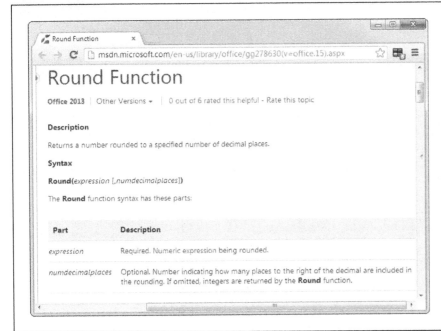

FIGURE 7-6

The reference for the Round() function spells out what it does, and explains the two parameters. One parameter—the number of decimal places—is wrapped in square brackets, which means it's an optional value. Leave it out, and Access rounds to the nearest whole number. You'll also notice a table of contents on the left that lets you browse to any other Access function and read its description.

Formatting Numbers

Format() is one interesting mathematical function that transforms numbers into text. Format() is interesting because the text it creates can be formatted in several different ways, which lets you control exactly how your numbers are presented.

To understand the difference, think back to the expression you used earlier for discounting product prices:

```
SalePrice: [Price] * 0.95
```

Even if the Price field has the Currency data type, the calculated values in the Sale-Price field appear as ordinary numbers (without the currency sign, thousands separator, and so on). So you see 43.2 when you might prefer $43.20.

You can remedy this problem by using the Format() function to apply a currency format:

```
SalePrice: Format([Price] / 0.95, "Currency")
```

Now the calculated values include the currency sign. Even better, since currencies are displayed with just two decimal places, you no longer need to clean up fractional values with the Round() function.

The trick to using the Format() function is knowing what text to supply for the second argument in order to get the result you want. Table 7-2 spells out your options.

TABLE 7-2 *Formatting Options*

FORMAT	DESCRIPTION	EXAMPLE
Currency	Displays a number with two decimal places, thousand separators, and the currency sign.	$1,433.20
Fixed	Displays a number with two decimal places.	1433.20
Standard	Displays a number with two decimal places and the thousands separator.	1,433.20
Percent	Displays a percent value (a number multiplied by 100 with a percent sign). Displays two digits to the right of the decimal place.	143320.00%
Scientific	Displays a number in scientific notation, with two decimal places.	1.43E+03
Yes/No	Displays No if the number is 0 and Yes if the number is anything else. You can also use the similar format types True/False and On/Off.	Yes

POWER USERS' CLINIC

More Advanced Number Formats

True perfectionists won't be happy with the format options in Table 7-2. Instead, they'll want complete control over the number of decimal places. One option is to use the FormatCurrency(), FormatPercent(), and FormatNumber() functions (depending on whether you want the resulting text to use currency format, percent format, or to be displayed as an ordinary number). When using these functions, you pass the value that you want to format as the first argument, and

the number of decimal places you want to keep in the second argument.

For even more control, you can define a custom number format that spells out exactly what you want, and use that with the Format() function. You won't learn about custom number formats in this book, but you can get more information on this feature in *Excel 2013: The Missing Manual* or in Access Help (*Figure 7-6*).

More Mathematical Functions

The mathematical functions in Access don't get much respect, because people don't need them terribly often. You've already seen Round() and Format()—the most useful of the bunch—but from time to time Access mavens still turn to a few others in calculated fields. They're listed in Table 7-3.

TABLE 7-3 *Functions for Numeric Data*

FUNCTION	DESCRIPTION	EXAMPLE	RESULT
Sqr()	Gets the square root.	Sqr(9)	3
Abs()	Gets the absolute value (negative numbers become positive).	Abs(-6)	6
Round()	Rounds a number to the specified number of decimal places.	Round(8.89, 1)	8.9
Fix()	Gets the integer portion of the number, chopping off any decimal places.	Fix(8.89)	8
Int()	The same as Fix(), but negative numbers are rounded down instead of up.	Int(-8.89)	-9
Rnd()	Generates a fractional random number between 0 and 1.	Int ((6) * Rnd() + 1)	A random integer from 1 to 6
Val()	Converts numeric data in a text field into a bonafide number, so that you can use it in a calculation. Stops as soon as it finds a nonnumeric character, and returns 0 if it can't find any numbers.	Val("315 Crossland St")	315
Format()	Turns a number into a formatted string, based on the options you chose.	Format(243.6, "Currency")	$243.60

Use Random Numbers for a Random Sort

People rarely use the Rnd() function—after all, who needs to fill a column with made-up information? However, enterprising Access gurus have come up with one intriguing use for Rnd(). They use it to sort a table so that all the records appear in a random order.

This first step is to add a calculated field that holds the random number. To do so, you use a field expression such as Random: Rnd(ID). This example assumes that your table has a unique numeric field named ID. By passing a different number to the Rnd() function each time you call it, you force Access to reinitialize the random number generator. If you skip this step and simply call Rnd() with no arguments, Access tries to

optimize the query. It calls Rnd() just one time and reuses that single random number for each record, which is no help at all.

When you run a query like this one, you'll see that each record gets a random number between 0 and 1 (like 0.7045, 0.2344, and so on). This number is displayed next to each record, in the Random field.

Now, switch back to Design view, and then clear the Show checkbox so that the Random field doesn't appear in the datasheet. Next, choose Ascending or Descending (it really doesn't matter) in the Sort box, and then rerun the query. Voilà! Every time you use this query, the records appear in a different order, according to the random numbers that Access generates on the fly.

Text Functions

So far, all the functions you've seen have worked with numeric data. However, there's still a lot you can do with text. Overall, you can manipulate text in three ways:

- **Join text**. You can do things like combining several fields together into one field. This technique doesn't require a function—instead, you can use the & operator described on page 243.

- **Extract part of a text value**. You may want just the first word in a title or the first 100 characters in a description.

- **Change the capitalization**. You may want to show lowercase text in capitals, and vice versa.

Table 7-4 shows the most common functions people use with text.

TABLE 7-4 *Functions for Text*

FUNCTION	DESCRIPTION	EXAMPLE	RESULT
UCase()	Capitalizes text.	UCase("Hi There")	HI THERE
LCase()	Puts text in lowercase.	LCase("Hi There")	hi there
Left()	Takes the number of characters you indicate from the left side.	Left("Hi There", 2)	Hi

FUNCTION	DESCRIPTION	EXAMPLE	RESULT
`Right()`	Takes the number of characters you indicate from the right side.	`Right("Hi There", 5)`	There
`Mid()`	Takes a portion of the string starting at the position you indicate, and with the length you indicate.	`Mid("Hi There", 4, 2)`	Th
`Trim()`	Removes blank spaces from either side (or use `LTrim()` and `RTrim()` to trim spaces off just the left or right side).	`Trim(" Hi There ")`	Hi There
`Len()`	Counts the number of characters in a text value.	`Len("Hi There")`	8

Using these functions, you can create a calculated field that shows a portion of a long text value or that changes its capitalization. However, how you can use these functions in a filter expression may not be as obvious. You could create a filter condition that matches part of a text field, instead of the whole thing. Here's an example of a filter condition that selects records that start with *Choco*:

```
Left([ProductName], 5) = "Choco"
```

Figure 7-7 shows how you enter this filter condition.

The `Len()` function is a bit of an oddity. It examines a text value and returns numeric information (in this case, the number of characters in the value, including all spaces, letters, numbers, and special characters). The `Len()` function isn't too useful in a simple calculated expression, because you'll rarely be interested in the number of letters in a text value. However, it does let you write some interesting filter conditions, including this one that grabs records with a Description of less than 15 characters (which probably could use some extra information):

```
Len(Description) < 15
```

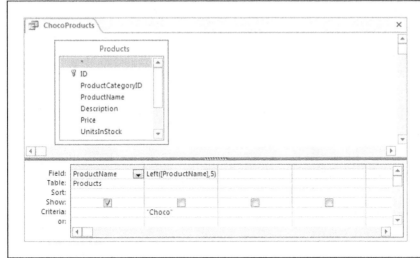

FIGURE 7-7

You can use the Left(),
Right(), *and* Mid() *functions in much the same way as
you use the Like operator (page
151) to help you match bits and
pieces of long text values.*

How to Extract the First Word from a Text Value

The string manipulation functions are designed with characters in mind. They can count letters, but they don't have any
understanding of words and sentences.

One way you can get around this limitation is to use the unusual
InStr() function, which searches for one or more characters
inside a text value. (The name InStr() is short for "in string,"
because you're looking for specific characters inside a text
string.) To search for the characters "he" in the text string "Hi
There," you'd use InStr() like this:

```
InStr("Hi There", "he")
```

The result is 5, because the text "he" begins in the fifth
character position. If Access can't find a match, InStr()
returns a result of 0. If there are multiple matches, InStr()
gets the first.

On its own, InStr() isn't terribly useful for filter conditions or
calculated fields. However, you can use it in combination with
other functions, like Mid() and Left(), to snip out a part of
a string near another letter. You could use InStr() to search
for the first space, and take all the text *before* that space. In
this way, you end up extracting an entire word.

Here's a slightly mind-bending calculated field that gets the
first word from a ProductName field, using nested functions
(page 245). (It's split over two lines here to fit the page. When
you type it in, you'll put the entire expression on one line.)

```
FirstWordProduct: Left([ProductName],
    InStr([ProductName], " ") - 1)
```

This expression translates as "find the position of the first
space, subtract one, and take that many characters from the
left of the text." Run this on a field with the value *Banana
Cream Fudge*, and you'll wind up with the truncated text
Banana, which makes for an impressive party trick. (Sadly,
this expression falters if it encounters a value that doesn't
contain a space, in which case the InStr() function returns
-1, confusing the Left() function and generating an error.
You could avoid this problem too by adding yet another nested
function to your expression, like the IIf() function that
chooses between two values based on a condition. But at this
point you're probably better off writing a custom function with
Visual Basic code, as described in Chapter 18.)

Date Functions

You've already seen how you can use simple addition and subtraction with dates (page 242). However, you can accomplish a whole lot more with some of Access's date functions.

Without a doubt, everyone's favorite date functions are Now() and Date(), which you first saw in Chapter 4 (page 150). These functions grab the current date and time, or just the current date. You can use these functions to create queries that work with the current year's worth of orders.

Here's a filter condition that uses Date() to select projects that are past due:

```
=<Date()
```

Add this to the Criteria box for the DueDate field, and you'll see only those records that have a DueDate that falls on or before today.

WORD TO THE WISE

Calculations with Dates and Times

When using date functions, you always need to be mindful of dates that include time information. (Remember, all date values can include time information. However, you tell Access whether to show the time component of a date, and you let people enter it by choosing the right format for your date field, as explained on page 73. Most of the time, you'll use a format that hides any time information.)

Here's the issue: The Date() function returns the current date with a time value of 0. In other words, if the current date is July 4, 2013, the Date() function gives you the very first second of July 4, 2013—the moment when the clock hit 12:00 a.m. (midnight).

If you aren't storing time values, this issue isn't important, because all your dates have a time value of 0. But consider what happens if you use the General Date format for your DueDate, which lets you enter both date and time information. Now the

=<Date() filter expression has a slightly different meaning—it tells Access to match all the fields that were due on or before the *first second* of the current day. This filter expression doesn't match a record with a due date of 4:00 p.m. today.

In this situation, you probably want to change the filter expression to this:

```
<(Date()+1)
```

Date()+1 is tomorrow. In other words, this filter matches any records that have a due date that falls before the first second of tomorrow.

Incidentally, Access also has a function named Now() that gets the current date *and* time. So this filter expression matches any records that were due at the current time (of the current day) or any time and any day before that:

```
=<Now()
```

Date logic becomes even more powerful when paired with the DatePart() function, which extracts part of the information in a date. DatePart() can determine the month number or year, letting you ignore other details (like the day number and the time). Using DatePart() and Date(), you can easily write a filter condition like this one, which selects all the orders placed in the current month:

```
DatePart("m", [DatePlaced])=DatePart("m", Date())
 And DatePart("yyyy", [DatePlaced])=DatePart("yyyy", Date())
```

This rather lengthy expression is actually a combination of two conditions joined by the *And* keyword. The first condition compares the month of the current date with that of the date stored in the DatePlaced field:

```
DatePart("m", [DatePlaced])=DatePart("m", Date())
```

This expression establishes that they're the same calendar month, but you also need to make sure it's the same year:

```
DatePart("yyyy", [DatePlaced])=DatePart("yyyy", Date())
```

The trick to using DatePart() (and several other date functions) is understanding the concept of *date components*. As you can see, using the text *m* with the DatePart() functions gets the month number, and using the text *yyyy* extracts a four-digit year. Table 7-5 shows all your options.

TABLE 7-5 *Date Component*

COMPONENT	DESCRIPTION	VALUE FOR FEBRUARY 20, 2013, 1:30 PM
yyyy	Year, in four-digit format	2013
q	Quarter, from 1 to 4	1
m	Month, from 1 to 12	2
y	Day of year, from 1 to 365 (usually)	51
d	Day, from 1 to 31	20
w	Day of week, from 1 to 7	4
ww	Week of the year, from 1 to 52	8
h	Hour, from 1 to 24	13
n	Minute, from 1 to 60	30
s	Second, from 1 to 60	0

You use the date components with several date functions, including DatePart(), DateAdd(), and DateDiff(). For example, the DateAdd() function lets you perform more complex date arithmetic that adds entire weeks, months, or years to a date. (By comparison, just using the plus sign, as you learned to do on page 242, always adds a number of *days* to a date.) Table 7-6 describes DateAdd() and several other useful date-related functions.

TABLE 7-6 *Functions for Dates*

FUNCTION	DESCRIPTION	EXAMPLE	RESULT
Date()	Gets the current date.	Date()	1/20/2013
Now()	Gets the current date and time.	Now()	1/20/2013 10:16:26 PM

FUNCTION	DESCRIPTION	EXAMPLE	RESULT
DatePart()	Extracts a part of a date (like the year, month, or day number).	DatePart("d", #1/20/2013#)	20
DateSerial()	Converts a year, month, and day into an Access date value.	DateSerial(2013, 5, 4)	5/4/2013
DateAdd()	Offsets a date by a given interval. This is similar to date addition, but you can add intervals that are bigger than days.	DateAdd ("yyyy", 2, #22/11/2012#)	22/11/2014
DateDiff()	Measures an interval between two dates. This is similar to date subtraction, but you don't need to get the answer in days.	DateDiff("ww", #10/15/2012#, #1/11/2013#)	12
MonthName()	Gets the name that corresponds to a month number (from 1 to 12).	MonthName(1)	January
WeekdayName()	Gets the name that corresponds to a weekday number (from 1 to 7).	WeekdayName(1)	Sunday
Format()	Converts a date into formatted text (using any of the date formats described on page 73).	Format (#27/04/2013#, "Long Date")	April 27, 2013

NOTE Access has other date functions that provide part of the functionality of DatePart(). One example is Month(), which extracts the month number from a date. Other duplicate functions include Year(), Day(), Hour(), Minute(), and Second(). These functions don't add any advantages, but you may see them used in other people's queries to get an equivalent result.

Dealing with Blank Values (Nulls)

Databases have two types of fields: required and optional. Ordinarily, fields are optional (as discussed on page 130), which means a sloppy person can leave a lot of blank values. These blank values are called *nulls*, and you need to handle them carefully.

If you want to write a filter condition that catches null values, simply type this text into the Criteria box:

```
Is Null
```

This condition matches any fields that are left blank. Use this on the CustomerID field in the Orders table to find any orders that aren't linked to a customer. Or ignore unlinked records by reversing the condition, like so:

```
Is Not Null
```

Sometimes, you don't want to specifically search for (or ignore) null values. Instead, you want to swap those values with something more meaningful to the task at hand. Fortunately, there's an oddly named tool for just this task: the Nz() function.

The Nz() function takes two arguments. The first is a value (usually a query field) that may contain a *null* value. The second parameter is the value that you want to show in the query results if Access finds a null value. Here's an example that uses Nz() to convert null values in the Quantity field to 0:

```
Nz([Quantity], 0)
```

Converting to 0 is actually the standard behavior of Nz(), so you can leave off the second parameter if that's what you want:

```
Nz([Quantity])
```

At this point, you may not be terribly impressed at the prospect of changing blank values in your datasheet into zeroes. But this function is a lifesaver if you need to create calculated fields that work with values that could be null. Consider this innocent-seeming example:

```
OrderItemCost: [Quantity] * [Price]
```

This expression runs into trouble if Quantity is null. Nulls have a strange way of spreading, somewhat like an invasive fungus. If you have a null anywhere in a calculation, the result of that calculation is automatically null. In this example, that means the OrderItemCost for that record becomes null. Even worse, if the OrderItemCost enters into another calculation or a subtotal, that too becomes null. Before you know it, your valuable query data turns into a ream of empty cells.

To correct this problem, use the Nz() function to clean up any potential nulls in optional fields:

```
OrderItemCost: Nz([Quantity]) * Nz([Price])
```

Finally, you can use Nz() to supply a different value altogether. In a text field, you may choose to enter something more descriptive. Here's an example that displays the text "[Not Entered]" next to any record that doesn't include name information:

```
Name: Nz([LastName], "[Not Entered]")
```

■ Query Parameters

Query parameters are the Access database's secret weapon. Query parameters let you create supremely flexible queries by intentionally leaving out one (or more) pieces of information. Every time you run the query, Access prompts you to supply the missing values. These missing values are the query *parameters*.

Usually, you use query parameters in filter conditions. Suppose you want to view the customers who live in a specific state. You could create a whole range of different queries, like NewYorkCustomers, CaliforniaCustomers, OhioCustomers, and so on. If you're really interested in only a few states, this approach makes sense. But if you want to work with every one, it's better to create a single query that uses a parameter for the state information. When you run the query, you fill in the state you want to use at that particular moment.

To create a query that uses parameters, follow these steps:

1. **Create a new query by choosing Create→Queries→Query Design.**

2. **From the Show Table window, add the tables you want to use, and then click Close.**

   This example uses the Customers table.

3. **Choose Query Tools | Design→Show/Hide→Parameters.**

   The Query Parameters window appears.

4. **Choose a name and data type for your parameter (*Figure 7-8*).**

   You can use any name you want (but don't choose a name that's already in use for a field in your query). The data type should match the field on which you're using the parameter. You set the data type by choosing one of the options in the drop-down list. Common choices are Text, Integer, Currency, and Date/Time.

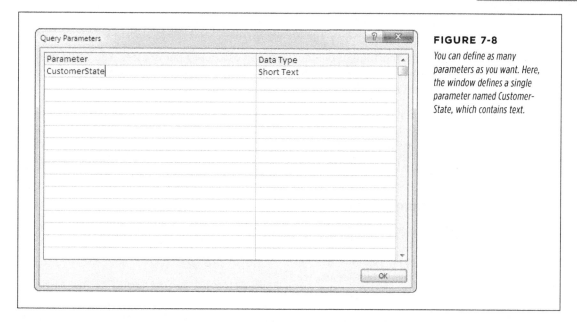

FIGURE 7-8

You can define as many parameters as you want. Here, the window defines a single parameter named Customer-State, which contains text.

5. **Click OK to close the Query Parameters window.**

Now you can use the parameter by name, in the same way that you'd refer to a field in your query. For example, you can add the following filter condition to the Criteria box for the State field:

[CustomerState]

Make sure you keep the square brackets so Access knows you're not trying to enter a piece of text.

When you run this query, Access pops open the Enter Parameter Value window, asking for a value (*Figure 7-9*). Enter the state you're interested in, and then click OK. Access uses your value for the filter on the State field.

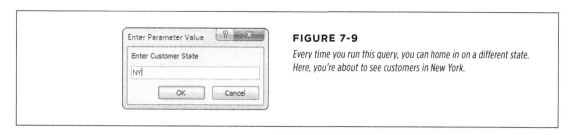

FIGURE 7-9

Every time you run this query, you can home in on a different state. Here, you're about to see customers in New York.

TIP Even though you can, it's best not to use more than one query parameter in the same query. When you run a query, Access shows a separate Enter Parameter Value window for each value. If you have a handful of parameters, you need to click your way through an annoying number of windows.

There's no shortage of practical ways to use query parameters. You could adapt a yearly sales query to use whatever year you choose. You could work similar magic to create a single query to show sales from any month.

However, you shouldn't use query parameters to help you out with day-to-day data entry tasks (like updating a single customer record). Forms, which you'll begin building in Part Four, give you a more powerful way to browse and edit information.

GEM IN THE ROUGH

More Helpful Parameter Names

If you're concerned that the person using your database won't understand the Enter Parameter Value window, you can sneak in some extra guidance by altering your parameter name. For example, instead of naming a parameter CustomerState, you can name it "Enter Customer State" or even "Type in the two-letter Customer State (like NY)." Access doesn't care what you use for your parameter name, but it will dutifully copy the text into the Enter Parameter Value window (*Figure 7-9*).

Of course, the longer you make the field name, the more unwieldy it is as a filter condition. No matter what your parameter name is, you need to type the exact match into the Criteria box, wrapped in square brackets. This isn't so bad:

    [Enter Customer State]

But this long-winded parameter name all but invites a typo:

    [Type in the two-letter Customer State
    (like NY)]

If you need to add even more information to the Enter Parameter Value window, you're better off designing your own forms. You'll see how in Part Four.

Queries That Summarize Data

ccess is ready and willing to store *all* the details in your database. But sometimes you don't need to know everything—instead you just want the big
picture. You need a way to take your raw data, which may include hundreds
or thousands of records, and *summarize* it in some meaningful way.

In this chapter, you'll look at two ways to analyze large volumes of information.
First you'll use totals queries to boil columns of numbers down to neatly grouped
subtotals. Next, you'll learn about crosstab queries, which use extra columns to
pack summary information into extremely tight tables. Both features provide the
same data-summarizing service, but they *present* the data in a slightly different way.

NOTE If you've used previous versions of Access, you might remember that it included two more data
analysis tools: pivot tables and pivot charts. Access 2013 drops these features. If you need them, you'll find more
powerful versions of both in Excel 2013. The only catch is that you'll need to use Excel's data connection features
to let it get to your Access data.

Totals Queries

All the queries you've used so far work with individual records. If you select 143
records from an Orders table, you see 143 records in your results. You can also
group your records to arrive at totals and subtotals. That way, you can review large
quantities of information much more easily, and make grand, sweeping conclusions.

Some examples of useful summarizing queries include:

- Counting all the students in each class

- Counting the number of orders placed by each customer

- Totaling the amount of money spent on a single product

- Totaling the amount of money a customer owes or has paid

- Calculating the average order placed by each customer

- Finding the highest- or lowest-priced order that a customer has placed

These operations—counting, summing, averaging, and finding the maximum and minimum value—are the basic options in a *totals query*. A totals query is a different sort of query that's designed to chew through a large number of records and spit out neat totals.

To create a totals query, follow these steps:

1. **Create a new query by choosing Create→Queries→Query Design.**

2. **Add the tables you want to use from the Show Table window, and then click Close.**

   The following example uses the Products table from the Boutique Fudge database.

3. **Add the fields you want to use.**

   This example uses the Price field, but with a twist: The Price field is added three separate times. That's because the query will show the result of three different calculations.

4. **Choose Query Tools | Design→Show/Hide→Totals.**

   Access adds a Total box for each field, just under the Table box.

5. **For each field, choose an option from the Total box. This option determines whether the field is used in a calculation or used for grouping.**

   A totals query is slightly different from a garden-variety query. Every field must fall into one of these categories:

   - **It's used in a summary calculation (like averaging, counting, and so on).** You pick the type of calculation you want to perform using the Total box. Table 8-1 describes all the options in the Total box.

   - **It's used for grouping.** Ordinarily, a totals query lumps everything together in one grand total. But you can subdivide the results into smaller subtotals, as described in the next section.

   - **It's used for filtering.** In this case, in the Total box, you need to choose Where. (Database nerds may remember that Where is the keyword used to define criteria in SQL, as described on page 220.) You also need to clear the checkmark in the Show box, because Access doesn't have a way to show individual values in a totals summary.

TIP If you try to add a field to a totals query that isn't used for a calculation, isn't used for grouping, and isn't hidden, you'll receive an error when you try to run the query.

In this example (*Figure 8-1*), the Price field uses three different summarizing options: Max, Min, and Avg.

TABLE 8-1 *Options for Summarizing Data*

CHOICE IN THE TOTAL BOX	DESCRIPTION
Group By	Subgroups records based on the values in this field.
Sum	Adds together the values in this field.
Avg	Averages the values in this field.
Min	Retains the smallest value in this field.
Max	Retains the largest value in this field.
Count	Counts the number of records (no matter which field you use).
First	Retains the first value in this field.
Last	Retains the last value in this field.

NOTE Table 8-1 leaves out two options that are tailor-made for statisticians—StDev and Var—which calculate the standard deviation and variance of a set of numbers.

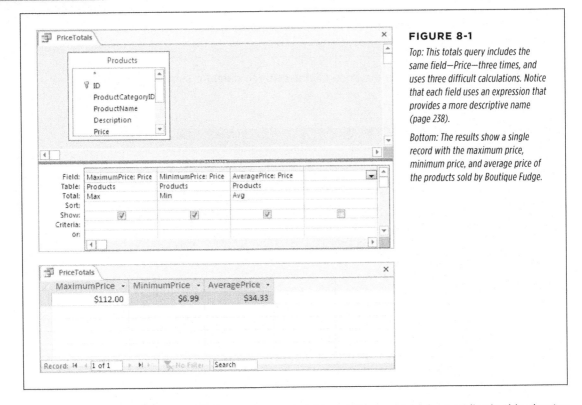

FIGURE 8-1

Top: This totals query includes the same field—Price—three times, and uses three difficult calculations. Notice that each field uses an expression that provides a more descriptive name (page 238).

Bottom: The results show a single record with the maximum price, minimum price, and average price of the products sold by Boutique Fudge.

You can use all the same query-writing skills you picked up earlier in this chapter when designing a totals query. If you want to summarize only the products in a specific category, you can use a filter expression like this in the CategoryID field:

=3

This expression matches records that have a CategoryID of 3 (which means they're in the Candies category).

> **TIP** If you want to perform a filter on a field that you aren't using for a calculation or grouping, make sure that in the Total box, you choose Where, and in the Show box, you clear the checkmark.

Grouping in a Totals Query

The simplest possible totals query adds all the records you select into a single row of results, as shown in *Figure 8-1*. A more advanced totals query uses grouping to calculate *subtotals*.

The trick to using grouping properly is remembering that the field you use should have many duplicate values. For example, it's a good idea to group customers based on the state in which they live. Because a given state has many customers, you'll end up with meaningful subtotals. However, it's a bad idea to group them based on their Social Security numbers, because you'll end up with just as many groups as you have customers. *Figure 8-2* shows an example of a totals query that uses grouping.

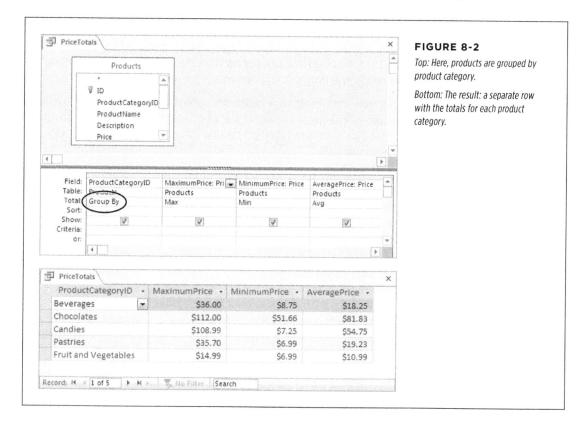

FIGURE 8-2

Top: Here, products are grouped by product category.

Bottom: The result: a separate row with the totals for each product category.

You can use *multiple* levels of grouping in a totals query by adding more than one field with the Total box set to Group By. However, the results might not be exactly what you expect. Suppose you group a long list of sales records by product and by customer. You'll end up with a separate group for every customer-and-product combination. Here's part of the results for a query like this that groups records from the OrderDetails table in the Boutique Fudge database and then sorts them by CustomerID:

CUSTOMER ID	PRODUCT ID	TOTAL SALES
10	108	$432.12
10	134	$16.79
10	210	$53.30

CUSTOMER ID	PRODUCT ID	TOTAL SALES
14	144	$18.99
18	112	$107.04
18	210	$12.02

This table tells you that customer #10 has spent a total of $432.12 dollars on product #108 across all orders. Customer #10 also spent a total of $16.79 on product #134, $53.30 on product #210, and so on. (You could take the same information and sort it by ProductID to look at the total sales of each product to different customers. You still get the same information, but you can analyze it in a different way.)

This is the result you want—sort of. It lacks nice subtotals. It would be nice to know how much customer #10 spent on each type of product *and* how much customer #10 spent in total. But thanks to the rigid tabular structure of the totals query, this result just isn't possible.

If you want to look at this subgrouped information with subtotals, you have two choices. You can use a crosstab query (page 270). Or, if you're really interested in printing your information, you can generate a report that includes multiple levels of grouping and subtotals, as described in Part Three.

Joins in a Totals Query

Summary queries are insanely useful when you combine them with table joins to get related information out of more than one table. In the Boutique Fudge database, the OrderDetails table stores the individual items in each order. You can group this information (as shown in the previous section) to find top-selling products or customers. However, you see only the customer and product ID values, which isn't very helpful.

> **NOTE** If you have a lookup defined on the ProductID field and CustomerID field, you *will* see the descriptive information from the lookup (like the product name or customer name). This information helps a bit, but you may still want to pull extra information—like the customer's address, the product description, and so on—out of the linked table.

If you throw a join or two into the mix, you can pull in related information from linked tables (like Customers, Products, and Orders) and add it to your results. *Figure 8-3* shows an example that groups the OrderDetails table by OrderID to find the total cost of each order. It then sorts the results by CustomerID.

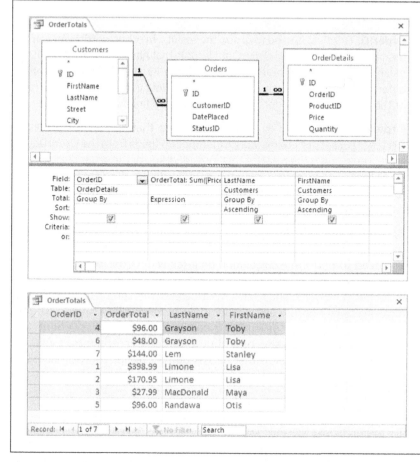

FIGURE 8-3

Top: This totals query gets more advanced by drawing from three related tables—Customers, Orders, and OrderDetails—to show a list of order totals, organized by customer. The query ignores orders less than $25. You could also add a filter expression on the DatePlaced field to find out how much customers spent so far this year, how much they spent last year, how much they spent last week, and so on.

Bottom: The results are grouped by OrderID and sorted by LastName and FirstName, which preserves a good level of detail.

You already know enough to build the query shown in *Figure 8-3*. Here's what you need to do:

1. **Create a new query by choosing Create→Queries→Query Design.**

2. **Add the tables you want to use from the Show Table window, and then click Close.**

   The example in *Figure 8-3* uses the Customers, Orders, and OrderDetails tables. As you add these tables, Access fills in the join lines in between, based on the relationships defined in your database.

3. **Choose Query Tools | Design→Show/Hide→Totals.**

   This command adds the Total box for each field.

4. **Add the fields you want to use, and then, in the Total box, choose the appropriate grouping or summarizing option for each one.**

You can choose your fields from any of the linked tables. This example uses several fields:

- **OrderID.** This field is used to group the results. In other words, you want to total all the records in the OrderDetails table that have the same OrderID. To make this work, in the Total box, choose Group By. (Incidentally, it makes no difference whether you choose the OrderID field in the OrderDetails table or the ID field in the Orders table—they're both linked.)

- **OrderTotal.** This field is a calculated field that uses the expression [Price]*[Quantity] to multiply together two fields from the OrderDetails table. The result is the total for that individual line of the order. Access adds up all these line totals to create the grand order total, so set the Total box to Sum. In addition, the OrderTotal field includes the filter expression >=25, which hides any orders that have a combined value of less than $25.

- **LastName and FirstName.** These fields identify the customer who made the order. However, there's a trick here. To show any field in a totals query, you need to perform a calculation on it (as with OrderTotal) or use it for grouping (as with OrderID). That means you must set the Total box to Group By for both LastName and FirstName. However, this setting doesn't actually have an effect, because every order is *always* placed by a single customer. (In other words, you'll never find a bunch of records in the OrderDetails table that are for the same order but for different customers. It just isn't possible.) The end result is that Access doesn't perform any grouping on the LastName and FirstName fields. Instead, they're simply displayed next to every order.

NOTE This grouping trick is a little weird, but it's a common technique in totals queries. Just remember, Access creates the smallest groups it can. If you want to group by customers only (so you can see how much everyone spends), you simply need to remove the OrderID grouping and group on CustomerID instead. Or, if you want to total all the sales of a particular product, remove all the customer information, group on ProductID, and then add any extra fields you want to see from the Products table (like ProductName and Description).

5. **You can now run your query.**

▓ Crosstab Queries

A *crosstab query* is a powerful summary tool that examines huge amounts of data and uses it to calculate information like subtotals and averages. If this sounds familiar, it's because you've already seen totals queries pull off a similar feat.

As with totals queries, crosstab queries use two key ingredients: grouping and summary functions. The grouping is used to organize the rows into small sets. The summary function is used to calculate a single piece of information for each group.

Behind the scenes, crosstab queries and totals queries work in almost exactly the same way. Both take large numbers of records and boil them down to totals, averages, minimums, maximums, and so on. However, there are two important differences.

First, crosstab queries always use two levels of grouping. For example, a typical totals query may group order records by product, so you can see the top sellers and how much cash they bring in. But a crosstab query can analyze sales figures by country *and* product category. Using this type of analysis, you can quickly see what product categories do well in particular countries.

The other difference between totals queries and crosstab queries is the way Access organizes the results. A totals query creates a separate row for each different group. For example, if you're analyzing sales by country and product category, a totals query gives you a row for each country and category combination, as shown in *Figure 8-4*, top. A crosstab query works a little differently; it takes the same information and packs it into separate columns, creating a denser view (*Figure 8-4*, bottom).

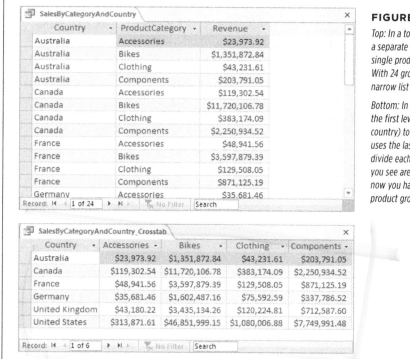

FIGURE 8-4

Top: In a totals query, each group resides on a separate row, representing the sales of a single product category in a single country. With 24 groups in all, this makes for a long, narrow list of results.

Bottom: In a crosstab query, Access uses the first level of grouping (in this case, the country) to divide the data into rows and uses the last level (the product category) to divide each row into columns. The numbers you see are the same as in the top figure, but now you have just six rows, each with four product groups.

At the bottom, *Figure 8-4* shows you what things look like with two levels of grouping: countries and products. But if you want, your crosstab queries can use more than two levels of grouping. (More levels are helpful when you want to perform really detailed analysis—for example, to find out what product categories do well in specific countries, states, and cities.) In this case, the *last* grouping level is used to split the row into columns. Every other level is used to subdivide your results into more rows. If you create a crosstab query that groups sales by product category, product name, and country, you see the result shown in *Figure 8-5*.

> **NOTE** Remember, if you use more than two levels of grouping, the last level of grouping (the one used to create the columns) shouldn't be related to any other level. However, the other levels can be related. The example in *Figure 8-5* works because it follows this rule (grouping by category, product, and then country). The same data grouped differently (for example, by category, country, product) doesn't work nearly as well.

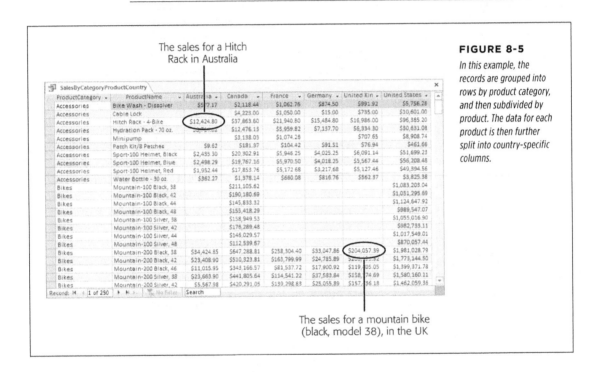

The sales for a Hitch
Rack in Australia

The sales for a mountain bike
(black, model 38), in the UK

FIGURE 8-5

In this example, the records are grouped into rows by product category, and then subdivided by product. The data for each product is then further split into country-specific columns.

> **NOTE** To try out crosstab queries, you need data—and lots of it. The sample databases used in earlier chapters just don't have enough raw data. Instead, the examples in this chapter use some of the tables from Microsoft's huge AdventureWorks sample database, which has the product catalog and sales data for a fictional bicycle manufacturer. Surf over to the Missing CD page for this book (at *www.missingmanuals.com/cds/access2013mm*) to download everything you need.

Summary Smackdown: Totals Query vs. Crosstab Query

Which is better: the totals query or the crosstab query?

It all depends on the type of information you want to analyze and how it's structured. Here are some guidelines to help you decide which option is right for your data:

- **If you want to group according to one field only, use a totals query**. Crosstab queries always have at least two levels of grouping.

- **If you want to perform more than one type of calculation (for example, averages *and* totals, or minimums *and* maximums), use a totals query**. Because of their compact format, crosstab queries can show only a single calculated value for each group. Totals queries can show as many calculated values as you want, because each one is placed in a separate column.

- **If you want to compare one group against another, use a crosstab query**. This is where crosstab queries really shine. They put subgroups on a single row so you can see trends at a glance. To see an example, look at *Figure 8-4*. In the crosstab query, it's easy to spot that accessories bring in the least amount of money, no matter what country you're looking at. In the totals query, your eyes need to jump back and forth between different categories and countries to make the same comparison.

- **If your grouping criteria results in a large number of groups, consider using a totals query**. A crosstab query is hard to read if it has too many columns. Another option is to use filtering (page 211) to cut down the number of different groups.

- **If you're using two *unrelated* levels of grouping, consider the crosstab query**. For example, product category and customer country are two totally separate criteria. You have no way to know whether some countries favor certain categories until you dig into the numbers. This type of organization is an ideal candidate for the dense grid of the crosstab query. On the other hand, product category and product name *are* related. Every product falls into a set category, and no product turns up in more than one category. If you use this type of grouping in a crosstab query, you wind up with a lot of wasted space, as you can see in *Figure 8-6*.

In many cases, you may want to try both approaches—creating a totals query and a crosstab query—and then compare them to see which representation you prefer.

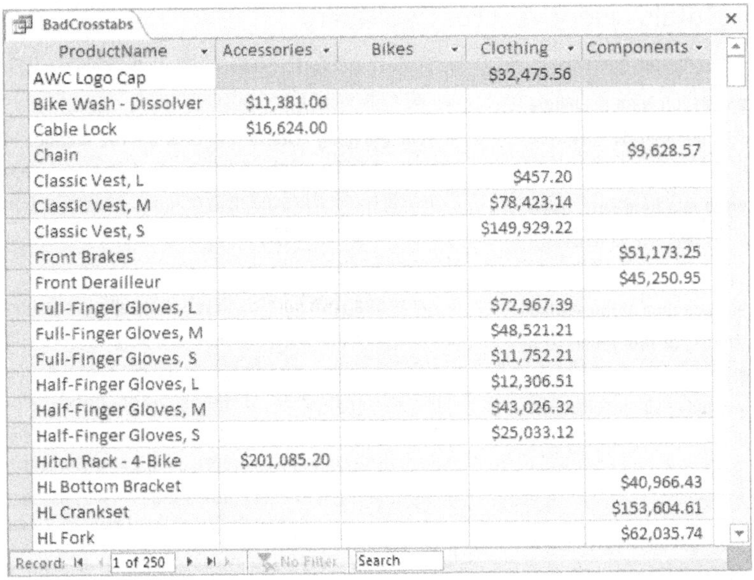

BadCrosstabs

ProductName	Accessories	Bikes	Clothing	Components
AWC Logo Cap			$32,475.56	
Bike Wash - Dissolver	$11,381.06			
Cable Lock	$16,624.00			
Chain				$9,628.57
Classic Vest, L			$457.20	
Classic Vest, M			$78,423.14	
Classic Vest, S			$149,929.22	
Front Brakes				$51,173.25
Front Derailleur				$45,250.95
Full-Finger Gloves, L			$72,967.39	
Full-Finger Gloves, M			$48,521.21	
Full-Finger Gloves, S			$11,752.21	
Half-Finger Gloves, L			$12,306.51	
Half-Finger Gloves, M			$43,026.32	
Half-Finger Gloves, S			$25,033.12	
Hitch Rack - 4-Bike	$201,085.20			
HL Bottom Bracket				$40,966.43
HL Crankset				$153,604.61
HL Fork				$62,035.74

Record: 1 of 250 No Filter Search

FIGURE 8-6

Consider yourself warned: Don't group by using related fields in a crosstab query. In this example, rows are grouped by product name, and columns are grouped by product category. The problem is that every product is in a single category, so each row has data in just one column—the row for that product's category. To solve this problem and to create a better summary, you could use three levels of grouping, as shown in Figure 8-5.

WORD TO THE WISE

Create a Join Query for Better Grouping

When you use any type of query that involves grouping, you often need to pull information from several different tables. For example, if you're considering a table with sales records, you probably want to pull in additional details about the products sold, the customers who bought them, the location where they were purchased, and so on. Most of the time, this involves bringing together information from several related tables.

The easiest way to prepare for a summary query (like a crosstab query) is to create *another* query that has all the information you need. This new query will use joins (page 227) to combine all the tables that have the information you need. You can then use this query to build your summary. This technique is particularly useful with crosstab queries, because the Crosstab Query Wizard is able to use only one table or query. It can't join tables together on its own.

The AdventureWorks database uses a query named OrderedItems, which forms the basis for all the crosstab queries that you've seen so far. The OrderedItems query gets all the individual items that have been purchased in every order that's ever been made (from the SalesOrderDetails table). Then it uses joins to get additional information from the SalesOrderHeader table (which represents the entire order), the Customers table, the Products table, the Store table, and the ShipMethod table. You need to make several jumps to get to the customer address information, which lets you profile how sales stack up in different cities, states, and countries. (You can study this query by downloading the AdventureWorks database from the Missing CD page at *www.missingmanuals.com/cds/access2013mm.*)

Creating a Crosstab Query with the Wizard

Access gives you two ways to create a crosstab query: You can use the Crosstab Query Wizard, or you can build it by hand. Most Access fans prefer to use the Crosstab Query Wizard to get started and then further refine their query in Design view to add other details, like filtering.

In this chapter, you'll cook up a crosstab query both ways, but you'll start with the Crosstab Query Wizard. Here's how you can use it to create a crosstab query for the AdventureWorks database:

1. **If you want to bring together information from linked tables, start by creating a join query.**

   In this example, you'll use the already created OrderedItems join query that draws on a wealth of information about the ordered items, the corresponding products, the customers, the geographic location where they live, and so on. For more information about building a join query of your own, see page 227.

   If you decide that you can get everything you need from a single table, you can skip this step.

2. **Choose Create→Queries→Query Wizard.**

   Here's where the wizard magic begins. A New Query window appears, with a list of the different types of queries the wizard can create.

3. **Choose Crosstab Query Wizard, and then click OK.**

   The first step of the wizard prompts you to pick a table or query (*Figure 8-7*). Make your selection by clicking one of the buttons in the View box.

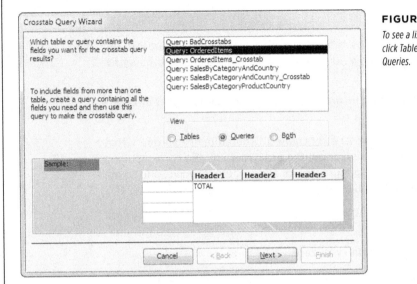

FIGURE 8-7

To see a list of tables in your database, click Tables. To see the queries, click Queries.

4. **Select your table from the list, or click Queries and choose a query. Then, click Next.**

In this example, you need to pick the Queries option, and then choose the OrderedItems query.

The next step asks you to supply the grouping criteria that will be used to combine your data into rows (*Figure 8-8*).

If you're creating a simple two-level crosstab query, you pick one criterion for rows and one for columns (in the next step). However, it's possible to pick up to *three* levels of grouping for rows. This approach works best if the different levels are related. For example, you can choose to group rows by customer country, subgroup each country by city, and subgroup each city by customer ID. See *Figure 8-5* for an example of a nicely subgrouped crosstab query.

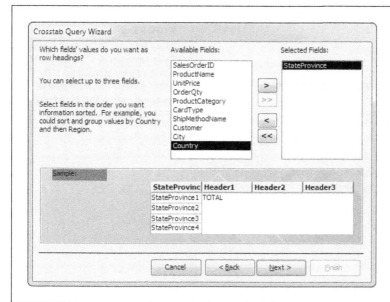

FIGURE 8-8

To use a field as a row heading, select it in the Available Fields list, and then click the funny > button to move it to the Selected Fields list.

5. **Add the fields you want to use to the Selected Fields list, and then click Next.**

In the OrderedItems example, rows are grouped by the StateProvince field. You can easily change your grouping in the query design window after you try out your query. For example, if you wanted, you could switch the StateProvince field to the Country field.

The next step asks you to supply the grouping criteria used to split your rows into columns (*Figure 8-9*). This time, you can choose only one field.

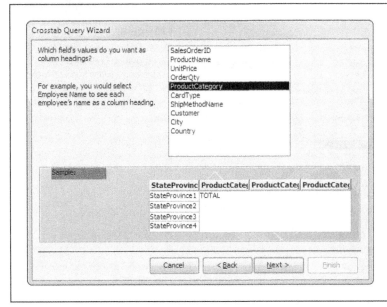

FIGURE 8-9

*As you move through the wizard, Access
shows a mini-preview of the structure of
your in-progress crosstab query at the
bottom of the window. In this example,
rows are grouped by StateProvince and
columns by ProductCategory.*

6. **Choose the field you want to use for column grouping, and then click Next.**

   In this example, it's the ProductCategory field.

Picking the Right Groups

Trying to decide which field to use for row grouping and which one to use for column grouping? If these two fields are unrelated (and they should be), it makes sense to use the field that creates the fewest groups for column grouping. That's because tables with lots of rows and few columns are easier to read (and print) than tables with lots of columns and few rows.

For example, if you're grouping by product name and country, it's a safe bet that you'll wind up with more product groups than country groups. (For example, you may have customers in eight different countries but a product catalog with 480 items.) So use the product grouping for rows, and the country grouping for columns.

7. **Choose the field you want to use for your calculation, and then choose a summary function (*Figure 8-10*).**

   For example, you can choose to find the lowest-priced sale, the order with the highest number of units sold, the average item price, and so on. In this example, you're using the OrderQty field to count the number of items sold.

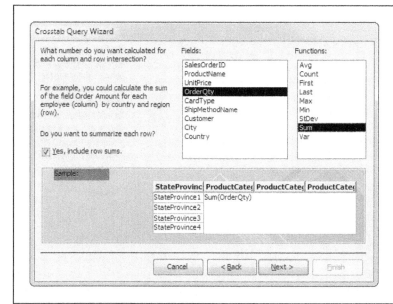

FIGURE 8-10

In this example, the Sum function totals up the OrderQty value from each record. For example, this query tells you that you've sold a total of 53 items from the Bike category to customers in Alabama. If you want to count how many orders your customers have made (instead of how many items you've shipped), you'd need a slightly different query—in this case, you'd use the Count function to count the number of distinct SalesOrderID values.

8. **If you want to show a subtotal for each row, turn on the "Yes, include row sums" checkbox.**

The row subtotal is shown in the very first column. For example, if you activate this option with the states and categories query, the total sales for each state are shown in the first column, followed by a category-by-category breakdown (*Figure 8-11*).

9. **Click Next.**

The final step asks you to supply the query name. You can then choose to run the query and view its results, or continue editing it in Design view. If you need to apply filtering, head over to Design view. Otherwise, it's time to see the fruits of your labor.

10. **Click Finish.**

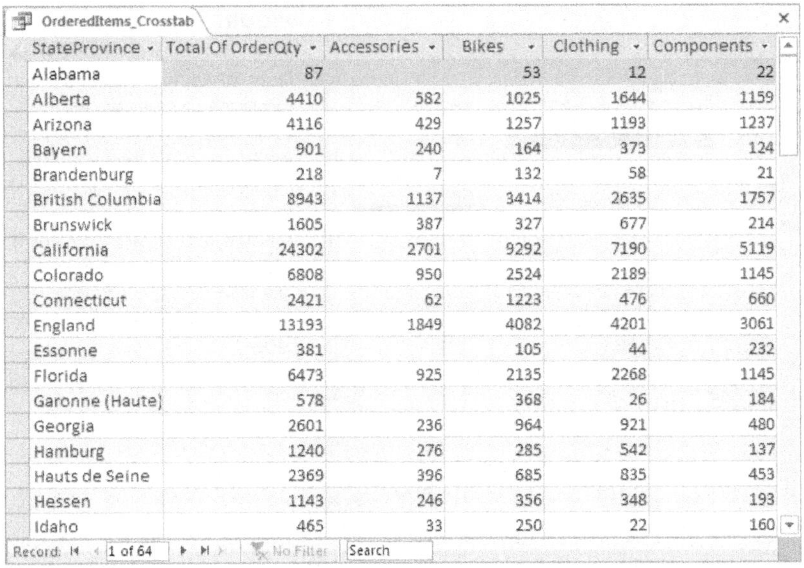

OrderedItems_Crosstab

StateProvince	Total Of OrderQty	Accessories	Bikes	Clothing	Components
Alabama	87		53	12	22
Alberta	4410	582	1025	1644	1159
Arizona	4116	429	1257	1193	1237
Bayern	901	240	164	373	124
Brandenburg	218	7	132	58	21
British Columbia	8943	1137	3414	2635	1757
Brunswick	1605	387	327	677	214
California	24302	2701	9292	7190	5119
Colorado	6808	950	2524	2189	1145
Connecticut	2421	62	1223	476	660
England	13193	1849	4082	4201	3061
Essonne	381		105	44	232
Florida	6473	925	2135	2268	1145
Garonne (Haute)	578		368	26	184
Georgia	2601	236	964	921	480
Hamburg	1240	276	285	542	137
Hauts de Seine	2369	396	685	835	453
Hessen	1143	246	356	348	193
Idaho	465	33	250	22	160

Record: 1 of 64 No Filter Search

FIGURE 8-11

The final crosstab query highlights the relationship between states and the types of products their inhabitants buy. (At the far left is the total for each state or province across all product categories.) Who knew Californians prefer bikes to clothing?

Creating a Crosstab Query from Scratch

As with any query, you can fine-tune a crosstab query in Design view. You can also create a new crosstab query from scratch by following these steps:

1. **Choose Create→Queries→Query Design.**

   Access creates a new, blank query and opens it in Design view.

2. **Add the table or query you want to use from the Show Table window, and then click Close.**

   If you're using the AdventureWorks database, the easiest option is to choose the Queries tab of the Show Table box, and then to add the OrderedItems query.

TIP Alternatively, you can close the Show Table window, and just drag the tables you want from the navigation pane onto the query design surface.

3. **Choose Query Tools | Design Query Type→Crosstab.**

   Access converts your query into a crosstab query. Crosstab queries look like totals queries, with one difference. In the field list at the bottom of the window, you find an extra property named Crosstab (*Figure 8-12*).

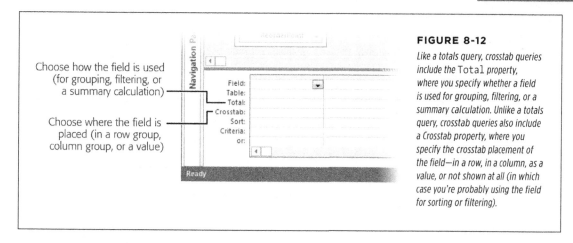

FIGURE 8-12

Like a totals query, crosstab queries include the Total *property, where you specify whether a field is used for grouping, filtering, or a summary calculation. Unlike a totals query, crosstab queries also include a* Crosstab *property, where you specify the crosstab placement of the field—in a row, in a column, as a value, or not shown at all (in which case you're probably using the field for sorting or filtering).*

Choose how the field is used (for grouping, filtering, or a summary calculation)

Choose where the field is placed (in a row group, column group, or a value)

4. **Choose the fields you want to use in your crosstab query.**

   Every field in a crosstab query plays one of the following roles:

   - **It's used for row grouping.** In this case, set the Total property to Group By and the Crosstab property to Row Heading.

     Although the Crosstab Query Wizard limits you to three fields for row grouping, you can add as many as you want in Design view. Make sure you arrange them in the order you want them applied. For example, if you have two row-grouping fields, the field on the left is used first for grouping, and then the groups are subdivided using the next field.

   - **It's used for column grouping.** In this case, set the Total property to Group By and the Crosstab property to Column Heading.

     You must use exactly one field for this purpose. Remember, column grouping is applied after your row grouping.

   - **It's displayed as a value in the table.** In this case, set the Total property to the summary function you want to use (like Sum, Count, Avg, and so on), and then set the Crosstab property to Value.

     You must use exactly one field for this purpose. However, you can use an expression that performs a calculation based on more than one field. For example, the crosstab queries shown in *Figure 8-4* and *Figure 8-5* use the expression Revenue: [UnitPrice]*[OrderQty] to calculate the total revenue for each line item in an order.

TIP You may remember that the Crosstab Query Wizard gives you the option of showing the total for each row in a separate column. *Figure 8-13* shows how to create the same effect on your own.

- **It's used for filtering.** In this case, set the Total property to Where, and set the Crosstab property to "(not shown)." Then, fill in your filter criteria in the Criteria slot. (See page 211 for a review of filter expressions.)

NOTE Unfortunately, you can't use filtering or sorting on the calculated field. That means that if you're creating a query that totals sales numbers, you can't filter out just the rows with high sales totals.

Figure 8-13 shows the query definition for the query you built with the wizard in the previous section (*Figure 8-11*).

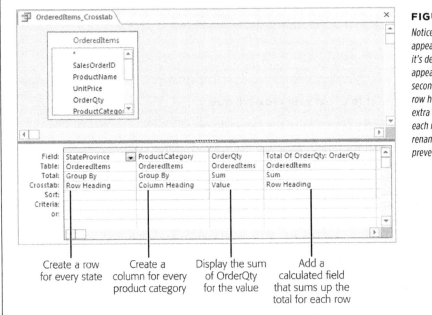

FIGURE 8-13

Notice that the OrderQty field appears twice. The first time, it's defined as the value that appears in the table grid. The second time, it's defined as a row heading, which creates an extra column with the total for each row. The extra column is renamed to Total Of OrderQty to prevent confusion.

Create a row for every state

Create a column for every product category

Display the sum of OrderQty for the value

Add a calculated field that sums up the total for each row

Queries That Change Tables

Q ueries are most famously known for their ability to show small subsets of huge amounts of information. This type of query is called a *select query*, and it's the variety you learned about in the previous two chapters.

Many Access fans don't realize that queries have another identity. Not only can you use them to search for information, but you can also use them to *change* data. Queries that take this more drastic step—whether it's deleting, updating, or adding records—are known collectively as *action queries*.

Understanding Action Queries

Action queries aren't quite as useful as select queries, because they tend to be less flexible. You create an ideal query once and reuse it over and over. Select queries fit the bill, because you'll often want to review the same sort of information (last week's orders, top-selling products, class sizes, and so on). But action queries are trickier, because they make *permanent* changes.

In most cases, a change is a one-time-only affair, so you don't have any reason to hang onto an action query that just applies the same change again. And even if you do need to modify some details regularly (like product prices or warehouse stocking levels), the actual values you set aren't the same each time. As a result, you can't create an action query that can apply your change in an automated fashion.

But before you skip this chapter for greener pastures, it's important to consider some cases where action queries are surprisingly handy. Action queries shine if you have:

- **Batch tasks that you want to repeatedly apply**. Some tasks *can* be repeated exactly. You may need to copy a large number of records from one table to another, delete a batch of old information, or update a status field across a group of records. If you need to perform this kind of task over and over again, action queries are a perfect timesaver.

- **Complex or tedious tasks that affect a large number of records**. Every once in a while, a table needs a minor realignment. You may decide that it's time to increase selling prices by 15 percent, or you may discover that all orders linked to customer 403 really should point to customer 404. These are one-off tasks, but they affect a large number of records. To polish them off, you'd need to spend some serious time in the datasheet. Or you can craft a new action query that makes the change more efficiently. When you're done, you decide whether to delete the action query or to save it in case you want to modify and reuse your work later.

- **Tasks that depend on a single piece of information, which you supply every time you run the query**. You can create an action query that also uses parameters, which let you supply critical values every time you run the query. (Query parameters are explained on page 260.) Using query parameters, you can change a relatively inflexible query (like one that deletes a specific record) to a more flexible one (like one that deletes any record you choose).

Testing Action Queries (Carefully)

In the wrong hands, action queries are nothing but a high-tech way to shoot yourself in the foot. They commit changes (usually to multiple records), and once you've applied the changes, you can't reverse them. Some database fans avoid action queries completely.

If you do decide to use action queries (and there are plenty of handy tricks you can accomplish with them), you need to take precautions. Most importantly, before you use an action query, make a database backup. This step is especially crucial when you're creating a new action query, because it may not always generate the result you expect. To make a backup, you can copy your .accdb database file (just as you would any other file; one way is to right-click it, and then select Copy). If you don't want to mess with Windows Explorer, you can create a backup without leaving Access. Just choose File→Save As to enter Backstage view, look in the Advanced section of the Save Database As list, and then choose Back Up Database (page 40).

> **TIP** It's always easier to make a backup than to clean up in the wake of changes left by a rampaging action query.

Backups are great for disaster recovery, but it's still a good idea to avoid making a mistake in the first place. One safe approach is to start by creating a select query. You can then make sure your query is selecting the correct records before taking the next step and converting it into an action query (by choosing one of the action query types in the Query Tools | Design→Query Type section of the ribbon).

The Action Query Family

Access has four types of action queries:

- **An update query** changes the values in one or more records.

- **An append query** selects one or more records, and then adds them to an existing table.

- **A make-table query** selects one or more records, and then creates a new table for them.

- **A delete query** deletes one or more records.

In the following sections, you'll try out all of these queries.

▇ Update Queries

An update query searches for some records and then modifies them. Usually, you'll limit your modifications to a single field, but Access lets you change as many fields as you want. You also have a fair bit of flexibility in *how* you apply the update. The simplest option is to stuff an entirely new value into a field. You could create a query that moves all the products in one category into another by entering a new value in the CategoryID field. Alternatively, you could take the current values in a field and change them, using an *expression* (a specialized database formula that can perform a variety of different calculations). You could increase all your product prices by 10 percent, or add a week to the due date of every outstanding project.

> **TIP** If you have a relatively straightforward, one-time-only update to make, you may prefer to use the datasheet's find-and-replace feature (page 112). This approach gives you the chance to review the matches and choose whether to apply the change for each value.

The example that follows uses the Products and ProductsCategories tables from the Boutique Fudge database (which is described on page 195). The query updates all the products in the Beverages category, increasing their prices by 10 percent. You can try this example for yourself by downloading the examples for this chapter from the Missing CD page at *www.missingmanuals.com/cds/access2013mm*.

Creating an Update Query

Here's how you can create the update query:

1. **Create a new query by choosing Create→Queries→Query Design.**

   The Show Table window appears.

2. **Add each table you want to include in your query by selecting it and then clicking Add (just as you did when creating a select query). Click Close when you're finished.**

Usually, an update query uses a single table. However, if you need information from more than one related table, add them all. Adding multiple tables creates a join (page 227). Joins work the same in an action query as they do in a select query—they pull information from a parent table, and display it alongside the records from the child table.

In this example, you need the Products and ProductCategories tables.

3. **Change your query to an update query by choosing Query Tools | Design→Query Type→Update.**

The column list at the bottom of the window changes to reflect your new type of query. The Sort and Show boxes disappear (because they have no meaning in the world of update queries), and a new Update To box appears for every field that's included in the query.

4. **Add the field (or fields) you want to use for filtering, and then set the Criteria box for each one.**

Your filter conditions determine what records Access selects. Since this query is an update query, the records you select are the records you'll end up changing.

In this example, you need to use the CategoryID field or CategoryName field. If you use the CategoryID field, you need to supply the ID value for your category. If you use the CategoryName field, you can match records by using the descriptive name.

To add a field, double-click it in the Table box, just as you would with a select query. Then set the Criteria to the value you want to match, as in *Figure 9-1*. If you want to apply an update to all the records in a table, you don't need to set any filter criteria.

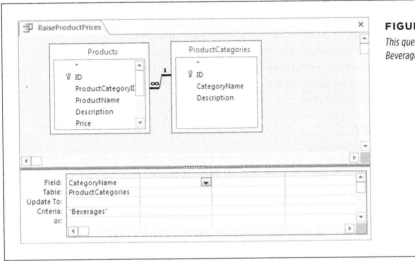

FIGURE 9-1

This query matches products in the Beverages category.

5. **Add the field (or fields) you want to change.**

   In this example, you need to add the Price field so you can modify the product prices.

6. **In the Update To box, supply the new value that your query will apply to each field.**

   You have two options for updating a field. You can apply a fixed value by typing it into the Update To box. If you take this approach, Access updates every record you select with the exact same value.

   You can also use an expression that takes one or more existing field values and uses them to calculate a new value. You can use all the operations and functions described in Chapter 7 to manipulate text, numbers, and dates. You can, for instance, use the following expression on the Price field to ratchet up product prices by 10 percent:

   [Price]*1.10

TIP You can also use one or more parameters (page 260) in your update expression. That way, Access prompts the person running the query to supply critical information (like the percentage to use for changing the price).

---

7. **Add any other fields that you want to inspect to confirm that you're selecting the correct records.**

   Before you run your query and apply your changes, you perform a preview that displays all the rows your update query will select (and thus, all the records it'll change when you run it). To confirm that your query is grabbing the right records, you may need to see some other identifying information in the datasheet grid, like the ProductName.

   However, there's one bit of bureaucratic trickery you need to perform to make this preview work. Access ignores fields that you don't plan to update. So if you want to make sure the ProductName field appears in the datasheet preview, you need to supply something in the Update To box. In this case, use the value [ProductName]. This step tells Access to update the ProductName field with the current value of the ProductName field. In other words, Access doesn't actually change anything, but it shows the ProductName field in the datasheet preview.

   Figure 9-2 shows the finished update query.

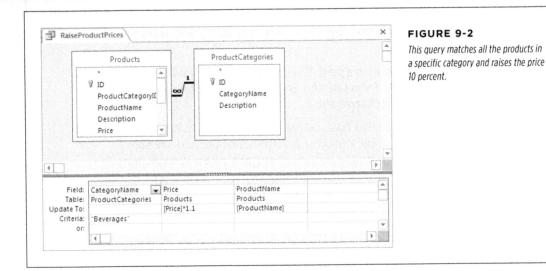

FIGURE 9-2

This query matches all the products in a specific category and raises the price 10 percent.

8. **Right-click the query's tab title, and choose Datasheet View to see the rows that your query affects (*Figure 9-3*).**

This step lets you preview the rows you're about to change, before you actually pull the trigger. In the datasheet, you see all the records that match your query's filters—in other words, all the records you'll change when you run the query. However, you won't see the changes you want to make.

FIGURE 9-3

Here's the datasheet preview. It shows all the products in the Beverages category, with the current prices. When you run this query, these are the records that are changed.

NOTE In a basic select query, viewing the datasheet and running the query are equivalent actions. In an action query, viewing the datasheet shows you the rows that'll be affected, but doesn't actually change them. Running the query performs the modification, but doesn't show you the changed records.

9. **Now switch back to Design view (right-click the tab title, and then choose Design View).** If you're confident you've got your query right, choose Query Tools | Design→Results→Run to run your update query and have Access apply your changes.

Remember, it's always a good idea to back up your database (page 40) before you take this step.

When you run an action query, Access warns you about the change it's about to make (*Figure 9-4*). Click Yes to make the change.

Sadly, Access doesn't show you the updated records—in fact, it doesn't show you anything. If you're wondering what happened, you may want to review the records you just changed. One way to do this is to show the preview for your update query again (by right-clicking the tab title, and then choosing Datasheet View). This method works as long as you haven't changed the records in such a way that they no longer match your filtering conditions. (If you have, you'll need to create a new query or browse the table to double-check your data.)

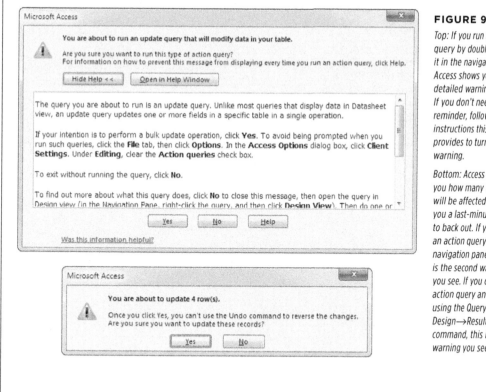

FIGURE 9-4

Top: If you run an action query by double-clicking it in the navigation pane, Access shows you this detailed warning message. If you don't need this reminder, follow the instructions this window provides to turn off the warning.

Bottom: Access always tells you how many records will be affected and gives you a last-minute chance to back out. If you run an action query from the navigation pane, this is the second warning you see. If you open an action query and run it using the Query Tools | Design→Results→Run command, this is the only warning you see.

10. **If you want to save your query, press Ctrl+S and supply a name for your query.**

Consider using a query name that clearly indicates that this is an action query. You may want to use a name like UpdateProductPrices. Action queries show up with an exclamation-mark icon in the navigation bar. Each type of action query has a slightly different icon—for update queries, you'll see a pencil with an exclamation mark beside it (*Figure 9-5*).

If you don't plan to use your query again, consider deleting it. Deleting it prevents you (or someone else) from accidentally rerunning the query and applying changes you don't want.

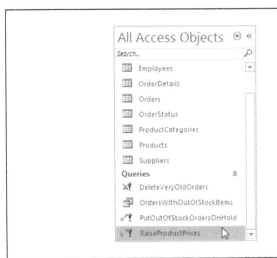

FIGURE 9-5

Remember, every time you double-click a query in the navigation pane, you run it. If the query you click is an action query, like the one highlighted here, you may have just updated or deleted some important data. (To open an action query without running it, right-click it, and then choose Design View instead.)

When Access Blocks Your Update

Consider this bit of Access existential philosophy: What happens if you click Run, and nothing happens? There's no warning, no message box, and no error to explain what went wrong. All you get is a cryptic message in the status bar at the bottom of the Access window, which blandly advises you, "The action or event has been blocked by Disabled Mode." What does it all mean?

Access is a truly paranoid program. It's just not ready to let you perform some actions unless you explicitly say it's OK. As you already learned, when you open a new database, Access shows a message bar with a security warning. It's up to you what you do about that security warning. You can click the X in the top-right corner to hide the message bar altogether. In this case, your database remains in a slightly disabled state.

You can still create, modify, and delete database objects on your own. However, you can't run any code or action queries.

Alternatively, you can click the Enable button in the message bar to bring your database back to life, and give it full support for code and action queries. And if the message bar isn't visible anymore, choose File→Info to switch to Backstage view, click the Enable Content button, and then choose Enable All Content. Either way, you've just turned your database into a trusted database, which means Access won't need your permission the next time you open it. To learn more about trusted databases, or to see how you can trust a database *temporarily*, refer to the discussion on page 512.

■ Append Queries

An append query selects records from a table and then inserts them into another table. (Technically speaking, *appending* is the process of adding records to the end of a table.)

You may create an append query for a number of reasons, but usually you do it to transfer records from one table to another. You may want to use an append query to transfer records from one database to another. This technique is handy if you have duplicate tables in different databases (perhaps because different people need to use the database on different computers).

TIP Once you've finished copying records to a new table, you may want to follow up with a delete query (page 297) to remove the old versions.

Append queries also make sense if you're working with a super-sensitive database. In this case, you might enter new records in a temporary table so someone else can look them over. When the inspection is finished, you can then use an append query to transfer the records to the real table.

Append queries are a bit stricter than other types of action queries. To transfer the records, you need to make sure the two tables line up. Here are some guidelines:

- **Data types must match**. The fields you select (from the source table) and the fields you're heading toward (in the target table) must have matching data types. However, the names don't need to match. You can configure your query so that information drawn from a field named FirstName is placed into a field named F_Name, provided they're both text fields.

> **NOTE** Ideally, each source field has the same data type as the corresponding destination field. However, that's not a requirement, as long as your source data can be *converted* into the destination data types. In other words, there's no problem taking the value from a number field and inserting it into a text field, because any numeric value can be converted into ordinary text. But the reverse operation—copying values from a text field into a number field—is riskier. If the text field contains a value that Access can't convert into a number, the query fails.

- **You can ignore some fields**. If the source has fields that aren't in the destination table, just don't include them in your query. If the destination table has fields that aren't in the source, Access leaves them blank, or uses the default values (page 133). However, if you leave out a required field (one that has the Required field property set to Yes, as explained on page 130), you'll get an error.

- **Access enforces all the normal rules for adding a record**. You can't do things like insert data that violates a validation rule (page 146), and you can't insert duplicate values into a field that has a primary key or a unique index (page 134).

- **If the destination table has an AutoNumber field, don't supply a value for that field**. Access automatically generates one for each record you insert.

> **NOTE** You can't copy AutoNumber values in an append query. If you use AutoNumber fields for your ID fields, the new, copied records have different ID numbers from the originals.

Access gives you another choice that's similar to the append query: the *make-table query*, which is the same in all ways but one. The make-table query *creates* the destination table, and then copies the records to it.

Creating an Append (or Make-Table) Query

The following steps show you how to create an append or make-table query. You'll transfer records from the Contacts table in the Marketing.accdb database to the PotentialClients table in the Sales.accdb database. (You can find both these databases on the Missing CD page at *www.missingmanuals.com/cds/access2013mm*.)

1. **Open the source database.**

   In this example, the Marketing.accdb database has the contact information.

2. **Create a new query by choosing Create→Queries→Query Design.**

   The Show Table window appears.

3. **Using the Show Table window, add the source table that has the records you want to copy. Then click Close to close it.**

   This example uses the Contacts table.

4. **Change your query to an append query by choosing Query Tools | Design→ Query Type→Append (or choose Query Tools | Design→Query Type→Make Table to convert it to a make-table query).**

The destination table (the PotentialClients table in the Sales.accdb database) already exists. For that reason, you use an append query instead of a make-table query.

When you change your query to an append or make-table query, Access asks you to supply the destination table (the place where you'll copy the records), as shown in *Figure 9-6.*

FIGURE 9-6

Access wants to know where you plan to transfer the records you're copying. You can choose a table from the handy drop-down list. If you're copying data from one database to another, choose the Another Database option, click the Browse button to specify the database file, and then click OK.

5. **If you want to transfer the records to another database, choose Another Database, and then click Browse. Browse to your database file, and then click OK to select it.**

You're transferring records to the Sales.accdb database.

Especially if you plan to keep using this new query, be sure to keep the destination database in the same spot. If you move the destination file to another location (or rename it), Access can't find it when you run the query and gives you an error.

6. **In the Table Name box, enter the name of the table to which you want to transfer the records.**

If you're creating an append query, the table you choose must already exist somewhere—either in the database file or in another one you have on hand. You can pick it out of the Table Name drop-down list.

If you're creating a make-table query, you need to type in the name for a brand-new table. Access creates this table when you run the query.

Here, you're transferring records to the PotentialClients table.

7. **Click OK to close the Append or Make Table window.**

8. **Now, add the field (or fields) you want to copy from the source table.**

Remember, you don't have to copy *all* the fields. In this example, all you need is the FirstName and LastName fields.

9. **If you're creating an append query, fill in the names of the destination fields in the Append To boxes.**

   In this example, set the Append To box for the FirstName field to F_Name. That way, Access copies the information from the FirstName field in the source table to the F_Name field in the destination table (*Figure 9-7*). Similarly, set LastName so it appends to L_Name.

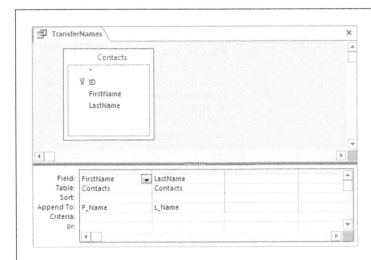

FIGURE 9-7

This append query transfers the information from the Contacts table in the Marketing database to the PotentialClients list in the Sales database. Since both these tables use ID fields with the AutoNumber data type, the ID numbers in the copied records are different from the ID numbers in the original records. (If this isn't the behavior you want, you need to copy the AutoNumber ID from the Contacts table to a normal numeric column in the PotentialClients table—one that doesn't use the AutoNumber feature.)

10. **If you want to copy only some of the records in the source table, set the filter conditions you need.**

    Like everywhere else in Access, these filters determine what records are copied from the source table. To set a filter condition, just fill in the Criteria box for the appropriate field.

    If you add a filtering field to an append query but don't want to copy the field's value to the target table, don't put anything in its Append To box.

    If you add a filtering field to a make-table query but don't want to copy the field's value to the target table, turn off that field's Show checkbox.

11. **Right-click the tab title, and then choose Datasheet View to see the rows that your query affects.**

    This step lets you preview the rows you're about to copy.

12. **If you're confident you've got things right, switch back to Design view, and then choose Query Tools | Design→Results→Run to transfer your records.**

Access warns you about the change it's about to make. Click Yes to copy the records. Access doesn't show you the copies—you need to track those down by browsing the destination table's datasheet.

At this point, you have the same records in two places—the source table and the destination table. You may want to follow up with a delete query to clean out the original versions. If so, the best approach is to convert the current append query into a delete query by choosing Query Tools | Design→Query Type→Delete. That way, your query keeps the same filters, which ensures it won't accidentally delete records you didn't copy.

13. **If you want to save your query, press Ctrl+S and supply a name for your query.**

    If you don't plan to use your query again, consider deleting it.

Getting AutoNumbers to Start at Values Other Than 1

Access gurus also use append queries in one of the trickiest Access workarounds: changing a table so its AutoNumber field doesn't start at 1.

As you learned in Chapter 2, Access always generates AutoNumber values beginning with the number 1. (The only exceptions are if you're using random numbers or replication IDs, two rare choices that are described on page 84.) However, for plenty of reasons you might not want Access to work this way. A company like Boutique Fudge might want its customer numbers to start at 1,000, its product numbers to start at 5,000, or its orders to start at 10,000. Numbering schemes like these often make for easier bookkeeping. They let you keep a consistent number of digits in your AutoNumber values, they help you distinguish between the IDs in different tables, and they help you avoid the embarrassment of telling a customer she just placed order number 1.

Thankfully, there *is* a way (albeit slightly awkward) to cheat the system and force Access to start at whatever number you want. Basically, you use an append query to do something you can't do on your own: directly insert a record with a specific AutoNumber value. Once you create that record, Access keeps incrementing values starting from the new number you inserted. So if you append a record with the AutoNumber value 999, Access gives the next record a value of 1000, and so on.

Here's how it all goes down:

1. **Create a new table (Create→Tables→Table Design).**

   You're going to keep this table around only for a few minutes.

2. **Add one field. Give this field the same name as the AutoNumber field in the table you're trying to change.**

   Usually, this name is just ID.

3. **Set the field to use the Number data type (not AutoNumber), and make sure its Field Size property is set to Long Integer (the standard choice).**

4. **Right-click the table title, and then choose Datasheet View.**

   Save the table when Access prompts you, but don't worry about the name—*Table1* is fine. When Access asks you if you want a primary key, just click No.

5. **In Datasheet view, enter a value in the Number field of the temporary table that's 1 less than the starting value you want for the AutoNumber field.**

   If you want the AutoNumber field to start at 100, enter 99 in the Number field. Close the table.

6. **Create a new query (Create→Queries→Query Design).**

   In the Show Table window that appears, pick the temporary table you created (like Table1), and then click Close.

7. **Choose Query Tools | Design→Query Type→Append to change this query into an append query.**

   When Access asks you what table to append to, choose the table that has the AutoNumber value you're trying to modify.

8. **Double-click the field you added to your table (like ID).**

   Access sets the Append To box to the same name, which is what you want.

9. **Choose Query Tools | Design→Results→Run to run the query.**

   Click Yes when Access warns you that it's about to add a record.

10. **Open the table you just updated, and then delete the newly inserted record.**

    From this point onward, the AutoNumber values will keep incrementing from that number.

11. **Delete the temporary table you created in step 1, because you don't need it anymore.**

    Similarly, don't opt to save your query when you close it.

If your table has strict validation rules—for example, one or more fields have the Required field property set to Yes—Access won't let you insert the new record using the append query. However, the technique described here still works, due a quirk in the behavior of Access's autonumbering system. Read the box on the next page to find out why.

Why Access Skips Numbers in an AutoNumber Field

Every time Access attempts to insert a record into a table that uses an AutoNumber field, Access reserves a new, unique number for that record. For example, if the last AutoNumber value in your table is 6 and you start to insert a new record, Access grabs the AutoNumber value 7 and reserves it for your new record.

Here's where things get interesting. Even if the insert fails, Access moves on to the next value in the AutoNumber sequence. So if Access fails to insert a new record with an AutoNumber value of 7 (either because of an error or because you canceled an edit), the next record you insert gets the AutoNumber value 8. This leaves a harmless gap in your AutoNumber sequence, because you'll never have a record with the number 7.

The same quirk works with the append query trick described on page 295. Even if the append query fails to insert its record

(for example, because you've left out a required field), Access still reserves the AutoNumber value you specified. The next time you insert a record, Access jumps to the AutoNumber value you want. (Best of all, you don't need to worry about deleting the inserted record. Because the insert failed, there's no extra record.)

Don't be put off by, or attempt to remove, the gaps in a table's AutoNumber sequence. The best advice is to simply ignore missing values, and remember that an AutoNumber field isn't meant to record any real, concrete information. However, if there is a rare, compelling reason to renumber your records, you can create an append query that copies your records to a new table. Make sure the destination table has a new AutoNumber field, and copy every field from the source table except the original AutoNumber values.

Delete Queries

Delete queries are the simplest—and most dangerous—of the action queries. A delete query works much like a normal select query. You specify a set of filter conditions, and then Access finds the matching records in the table. But the delete query doesn't just display the records—instead, it erases them from the database.

> **NOTE** Think twice before you delete anything. You just might need old information for reporting and analysis. Page 36 explains why.

Delete queries are great for clearing out a huge number of records at once after you've finished transferring them to another table. In the append-query example described earlier (page 292), you probably want a way to remove the original records once you've copied them to the new table. A delete query fits the bill perfectly. In the following section, you'll build the query you need.

Creating a Delete Query

To create a delete query, follow these steps:

1. **Create a new query by choosing Create→Queries→Query Design.**

2. **When the Show Table window appears, add the table that has the records you want to delete. Then click Close.**

3. **Change your query to a delete query by choosing Query Tools | Design→ Query Type→Delete.**

The Sort and Show boxes disappear from the column list, and the Delete box appears.

4. **Add the fields you want to use for filtering, and then set your filter conditions.**

Your filter conditions determine what records are deleted, so make sure you define them carefully. If you don't include any filter conditions—gulp—Access will delete all the records when you run the query.

5. **Add any other fields that you want to inspect to confirm you're getting the correct records in the datasheet preview.**

It's critical that you verify that you're removing only the records you want to delete. Delete queries have a nifty feature that can help you identify each record before you perform the actual delete operation. To use it, double-click the asterisk (*) in the table field list. The Delete box automatically sets itself to From, which indicates this information isn't being used as part of a filter condition—instead, it's just there to show the list of to-be-deleted records in your previews (*Figure 9-8*).

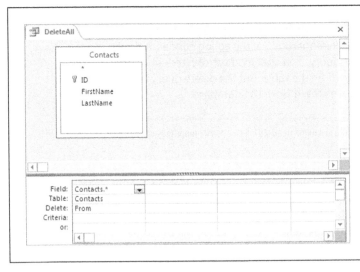

FIGURE 9-8

This window shows the DeleteAll query, which you can find in the Marketing.accdb database at www.missingmanuals.com/cds/access2013mm. This query clears out everything from the Contacts table, allowing you to start fresh after you run the TransferNames query to copy the contacts to the Sales.accdb database.

6. **Right-click the tab title, and then choose Datasheet View to see the rows that'll be affected by your query.**

This step lets you preview the rows that you're about to delete. If you used the asterisk (*), you'll see the full information for each record.

7. **If you're confident you've got things right, switch back to Design view, and then choose Query Tools | Design→Results→Run to remove the records.**

   Access warns you about the change it's about to make. Click Yes to delete the records for good.

8. **If you want to save your query, press Ctrl+S and supply a name for your query.**

   If you don't plan to use your delete query again, consider not saving it. It's a dangerous tool to have lying around.

GEM IN THE ROUGH

Hiding a Query

If you want to keep a delete query around for later use, but you've decided it's just too dangerous, Access does give you a safer option. You can hide the query, so that it doesn't appear in the navigation pane. That way, you won't inadvertently use it. Those who use it will need to hunt it down.

To hide a query, right-click it in the navigation pane, and then choose "Hide in this Group." The query quietly disappears from view.

The only way to get a hidden database object back is to right-click the title of the navigation pane (which says something like "All Tables"), and then choose Navigation Options. Then you can switch on the Show Hidden Objects setting. When this setting is active, you see hidden objects in the navigation pane, but they're displayed in a lighter gray color. To return an object to normal, fully visible status, right-click it, and then choose "Unhide in this Group."

Be careful you don't overuse hiding. If you do, you'll just encourage others to switch on the Show Hidden Objects option, which makes all the queries visible and usable.

If you're still not comfortable leaving a dangerous query in your database, consider placing the action query in an entirely separate database file—and don't let other people use that file. Page 642 has more information about splitting databases into multiple files.

Deleting Linked Records

Sometimes, you may need to delete records that are linked to other records in other tables. For example, imagine you create a query that finds and deletes old order records from the Orders table, as shown in *Figure 9-9*.

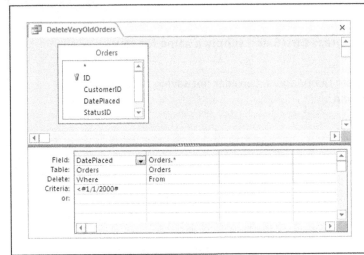

FIGURE 9-9

This query removes old order records. The first field in the query defines the filter condition: orders with a DatePlaced before the year 2000. The second field (*) lets you see all the fields in the preview, so you can carefully review the data you're removing. However, you can't delete orders if they have linked child records in the OrderDetails table.

This example seems straightforward, but it has a potential problem. That is, each record in the Orders table is linked to one or more records in the OrderDetails table, since each order consists of one or more ordered items. Try to delete an order, and you'll run afoul of the first commandment of referential integrity: Thou Shalt Not Delete a Parent Record That Has Linked Children. And if you run this delete query, Access politely explains the problem and refuses to make the change.

Fortunately, there are two good solutions:

- **Turn on cascading deletes for the relationship (page 174).** That way, when you delete a record from the Orders table, Access automatically wipes out the linked records from the OrderDetails table, and you can use the delete query in *Figure 9-9* as written. However, this change isn't constrained to your query—it affects everyone who deletes orders, no matter how they do their work. If you aren't comfortable removing this safeguard, you'll need to use a different approach.

- **Use two queries.** This option works as long as you always delete the child records *first*. In this example, that means deleting the old records from the OrderDetails table and *then* deleting the corresponding records from the Orders table. To figure out which OrderDetails records are linked to old orders, your delete query needs to use a join, like the one shown in *Figure 9-10*.

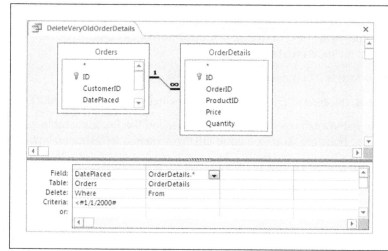

FIGURE 9-10

This query deletes all the records from the OrderDetails table that are connected to an old order. You'll need to follow this query up with the one shown in Figure 9-9 to remove the old records in the Orders table, too.

◼ Tutorial: Flagging Out-of-Stock Orders

Boutique Fudge has a challenge. It makes all its products in small batches, and products frequently sell out. For example, if its supply of imported durian dries up, so too does its world-famous Mocha Malaysian Milk Chocolate.

However, eager shoppers keep ordering products that aren't in stock. Eventually they'll get the goods, but an order for an out-of-stock product might linger, lonely and forgotten, in the database for weeks. Boutique Fudge could prevent a lot of customer confusion (not to mention hunger) by tracking down the folks who've ordered out-of-stock items and warning them about the wait.

The database designers at Boutique Fudge have thought about this problem and have decided they want a field in the Orders table that lets them mark orders that are waiting due to out-of-stock ingredients. They decide to use a Yes/No field (page 78) named OnHold. That way, when the warehouse workers are filling an order, they can save time by ignoring all the orders on hold. And the customer service department can track down the customers who placed these orders and explain the problem.

So far, there's nothing new in this example. But here's the trick: Boutique Fudge wants to *automate* the process of setting the OnHold field. It wants to be able to run a query that can look at the UnitsInStock field in the Products table and then set the OnHold field for any in-progress orders that include an out-of-stock item. Now that you've mastered action queries, you're ready to consider this mind-bending puzzle.

As with many problems in Access, you can solve this challenge by attacking it one piece at a time. Here, you'll solve the problem by creating two separate queries:

- A select query that finds orders containing out-of-stock products

- An action query that updates the OnHold field for the out-of-stock items

Finding Out-of-Stock Items

The first step is finding all the orders that include out-of-stock items. To do this, you need a query that includes two tables:

- **Products**, because it contains the fields with the stock levels

- **OrderDetails**, because it tells you which orders include a specific product

In this case, the OrderDetails table is the child table, and the Products table is the parent. (See "The Chocolate Store" on page 195 if you need a refresher on how the Boutique Fudge database is structured.) As a result, when you perform this query, you're really getting a list of OrderDetails records, supplemented with the product information.

Once you've created a query with the right tables, you need to add the appropriate fields:

- **UnitsInStock** (from the Products table). This field tells you if the product is out of stock. To find just the out-of-stock order items, set the Criteria box to 0.

- **OrderID** (from the OrderDetails) table. This field identifies the orders that are affected.

There's still one problem. When you run this query, you may see the same order ID appear multiple times. That's because you're retrieving a list of out-of-stock order *items*, and several out-of-stock items might be in the same order. (You certainly don't want customer service calling shoppers multiple times, telling them their orders are delayed, right?) The easiest way to fix this problem is to tell Access to ignore duplicates in your query by following these steps:

1. **Choose Query Tools | Design→Show/Hide→Property Sheet.**

   A Property Sheet box appears on the right side of the Access window, with low-level query settings.

2. **Click somewhere on the empty space on the query design surface (like just beside one of the table boxes).**

   The Property Sheet box should say "Selection Type: Query Properties" at the top.

3. **In the Property Sheet box, change the Unique Values setting from No to Yes (*Figure 9-11*).**

   Now each order ID appears only once in the query results.

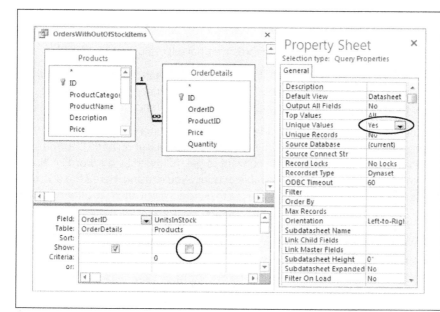

FIGURE 9-11

The completed query. This query (named OrdersWith-OutOfStockItems) generates a list of out-of-stock product IDs. Notice that it uses the UnitsInStock field for filtering, but it doesn't include it in the results (the Show box, circled, isn't turned on). To avoid having the same OrderID appear more than once (if it contains more than one out-of-stock item), the Unique Values query property (also circled) is set to Yes.

Putting the Orders on Hold

Next, you need to perform an update query that modifies all the problematic orders in the Orders table. Clearly, this a job for an update query.

You might think the best solution is to transform the current OrdersWithOutOfStockItems query into an update query. You've got the right idea, but there's one flaw: although you can add the Orders table to the OrdersWithOutOfStockItems query, Access won't let you change the OnHold field. That's because Access gets confused by all the joins—it doesn't understand how you can be searching for product records (to find out what's out of stock) *and* updating order records, all in the same query.

The solution is to build an update query that *uses* the OrdersWithOutOfStock query to find the records it should change. Obviously, the update query must be based on the Orders table, and it needs to include two fields:

- **ID**. You use this field to find the order records you want to update.

- **OnHold**. You update this field to Yes to place the order on hold.

You already know enough to create the update query, add both these fields, and fill in the Update To box for the OnHold field (with the value Yes). However, the tricky part is finding just the right records. Clearly, you need to find orders that have one of the ID values you pinpointed in the OrdersWithOutOfStockItems query. But how can you use that query inside your update query?

To pull this off, you need a couple of new tricks in your filter expression. First, you need to use the In keyword, which checks to see if a value falls somewhere within a list of values. Here's an example of the In keyword at work:

```
In (14,15,18)
```

This filter expression matches any records that have ID values of 14, 15, or 18.

Obviously, it's way too much work to type in all the ID values by hand. It makes more sense to reuse the work you did when you created the OrdersWithOutOfStockItems. To make this process happen, you need to use another fancy move: a *subquery*.

A subquery is a query that's embedded inside another query. When you write your subquery, you need to use the SQL syntax you learned about on page 219. You start with the word SELECT, list the fields you want to get, followed by the word FROM, and finish things off with the name of the table or query you're using. Here's the SQL for a select query that gets all the order IDs from the OrdersWithOutOfStockItems query:

```
SELECT OrderID FROM OrdersWithOutOfStockItems
```

Now that you have both the ingredients you need, you just need to fuse them together into one super-elegant filter expression. Here's the final product:

```
In (SELECT OrderID FROM OrdersWithOutOfStockItems)
```

You place this filter expression in the ID field. It gets all the IDs for problematic orders using the OrdersWithOutOfStockItems query, and then compares that against the full list of records in the Orders table. The completed action query is shown in *Figure 9-12*.

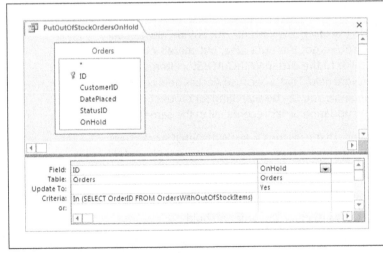

FIGURE 9-12

This update query (PutOutOfStock OrdersOnHold) ensures that Boutique Fudge will have happy customers for years to come. It selects the orders that have out-of-stock items and then applies the change to the OnHold field. Now you just need to make sure that the customer service reps are polite.

If you create a query like this one, you'll probably want to include another query that does the reverse, and puts on-hold queries back into action, provided that stock is available. Based on what you've learned in this section, you shouldn't have any problem crafting the query you need.

Printing Reports

Creating Reports

There are many reasons to create a hard copy of your lovingly maintained Access data. With a good printout, you can:

- Carry your information without lugging your computer around. For example, you can take an inventory list while you go shopping.

- Show your information to non-Access users. For example, you can hand out product catalogs, order forms, and class lists to other people.

- Review details outside the office. For example, you can search for mistakes while you're on the commuter train home.

- Impress your boss. After all, it's difficult to argue with 286 pages of raw data.

In Chapter 3 you learned how to print the raw data that's in a table, straight from the datasheet. This technique is handy, but it provides relatively few features. You don't have the flexibility to deal with large blocks of information, you can't fine-tune the formatting of different fields, and you don't have tools like grouping and summarizing that can make the information easier to understand. As you've probably already guessed, Access provides another printing feature that fills in these gaps. It's called reports, and it lets you create a fine-tuned blueprint that tells Access exactly how it should prepare your data for the printer.

Reports are specialized database objects, much like tables and queries. As a result, you can prepare as many reports as you need, and keep them on hand indefinitely. Life isn't as easy if you stick to the datasheet alone. For example, if you're using the bobblehead database, you may want to print a list of bobblehead dolls with the doll's name and manufacturer information for your inventory list, and a separate list with prices for your budgeting process. To switch back and forth between these two types of printouts using the datasheet, you have to manually rearrange and hide columns every time. Reports don't suffer from this problem, because each report is saved as a separate database object. So if you want to print your inventory list, you simply run the DollInventory report. If you want the budgeting details, you fire up the DollPrices report.

> **NOTE** This philosophy is the same one that you saw with queries in Chapter 6. Rather than get locked into one set of sorting and filtering options, reports let you cook up every combination you could ever want, and then store each one as a separate database object.

To see one reason why reports are insanely better than ordinary datasheet printouts, compare *Figure 10-1* (which shows a datasheet printout) and *Figure 10-2* (which puts the same data into a simple report). Notice how the datasheet printout has both wasted space and missing information.

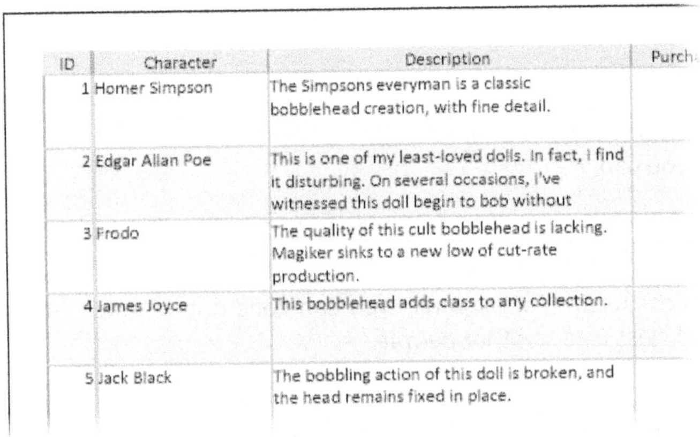

ID	Character	Description	Purch
1	Homer Simpson	The Simpsons everyman is a classic bobblehead creation, with fine detail.	
2	Edgar Allan Poe	This is one of my least-loved dolls. In fact, I find it disturbing. On several occasions, I've witnessed this doll begin to bob without	
3	Frodo	The quality of this cult bobblehead is lacking. Magiker sinks to a new low of cut-rate production.	
4	James Joyce	This bobblehead adds class to any collection.	
5	Jack Black	The bobbling action of this doll is broken, and the head remains fixed in place.	

FIGURE 10-1

Ordinary printouts are notoriously bad at dealing with large amounts of data in a single column. Consider the Description field in this Dolls table. Every record has the same-sized box for its description, which fits three short lines. If the information is larger than the available space (as it is for the Edgar Allan Poe doll), it's chopped off at the end. If the information is smaller (as with the James Joyce doll), you have some wasted white space to look at.

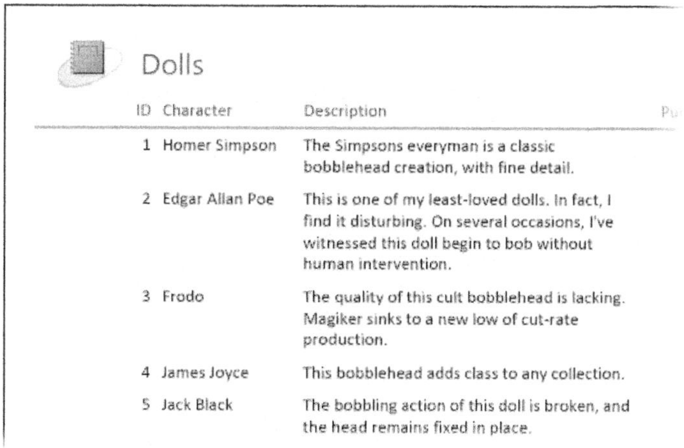

FIGURE 10-2

Dolls

ID	Character	Description	Pu
1	Homer Simpson	The Simpsons everyman is a classic bobblehead creation, with fine detail.	
2	Edgar Allan Poe	This is one of my least-loved dolls. In fact, I find it disturbing. On several occasions, I've witnessed this doll begin to bob without human intervention.	
3	Frodo	The quality of this cult bobblehead is lacking. Magiker sinks to a new low of cut-rate production.	
4	James Joyce	This bobblehead adds class to any collection.	
5	Jack Black	The bobbling action of this doll is broken, and the head remains fixed in place.	

In a typical report, you size the column widths, but the height of each row depends on the amount of information in the record. That means each row is just large enough to show all the text in the Description field. Best of all, you don't need to apply any special settings to get this behavior. Reports do it automatically.

Report Basics

You can take more than one path to create a report. Experienced report writers (like you, once you've finished this chapter) can build a report from scratch using Layout view or Design view. Report newbies (like you, right now) can create a simple report with a single click. But either way, your report-generating path starts when you click one of the buttons in the Create→Reports section of the toolbar.

Creating a One-Click Report

The simplest way of all to create a report is to select a table in the navigation pane and choose Create→Reports→Report. This command creates a tabular report with a separate column for each of your table's fields. The columns are arranged from left to right in the same order as in the table. (It doesn't matter whether you've rearranged the columns in the datasheet.) However, any columns you've hidden in the datasheet (page 102) are left out of the report. At the top, Access adds a stand-in logo (it looks like a notebook), a title, and the date and time the report was last generated. Page numbers are at the bottom.

Doing the Heavy Lifting with a Query

The most obvious way to build a report is to base it on an existing table. However, you can also create a report on top of a *query*. This approach lets you use some heavy-duty filtering or sorting on your records before they reach the report. It also makes sense if you want to create a report that uses information from more than one table.

For example, imagine you decide you want to create a product list that includes additional details from another table (like the category description from the ProductCategories table). Although you can create this report from scratch, it often makes

more sense to structure your data with a query first. That way, you can reuse the query for different purposes (like editing), and you can change it anytime.

In this example, the first step is to create a query that joins the Categories and Products table (page 227). Then, you save this query, select it in the navigation pane, and choose Create→Reports→Report to create a report that's based on the query. You can then follow the normal steps to perfect your report.

The one-click report generating approach gets you started in a hurry, but it's not as convenient as it sounds. Most tables have quite a few fields, and an automatically generated report includes them *all*. The resulting report is often so wide that it stretches right off the edge of the page (*Figure 10-3*). You can remove and resize columns after you create the report to solve the problem, but you'll also need to move the page number and resize the report in Design view (page 347). With all that trouble, it's usually easier to create a blank report and then add the columns you want. You'll learn how in the next section.

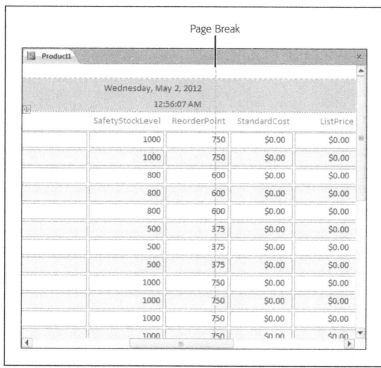

Page Break

FIGURE 10-3

Access adds a dotted line on the right side of your report to indicate the edge of the page. If your report goes over the edge of one page, it ends up on another page—in other words, Access creates a printout that's two pages wide. At best, this is somewhat confusing. At worst, you'll be forced to assemble a jigsaw of printed pages to read a single row of your report. Generally, it's better to make sure all your fields fit the width of the page.

Building a Report in Layout View

Using layout view to create a report is a great technique—it's practical without being overly complicated. If you want to try creating a report of your own, open the Boutique Fudge database (included with the downloadable content for this chapter) or a database of your creation, and follow these steps:

1. **Choose Create→Reports→Blank Report.**

   A new tab appears. This is the surface where you'll design your report.

2. **Pick your table in the Field List.**

   To add fields to a report, you need the help of the Field List pane (see *Figure 10-4*). Access shows the Field List pane automatically when you create a blank report, but if you've accidentally closed it, you can bring it back by choosing Report Layout Tools | Design→Tools→Add Existing Fields.

   At first, Access doesn't know what to display in the Field List pane because it doesn't know what table you want to use. It's up to you to choose one. Click "Show all tables," find your table in the list, and then click the tiny icon next to it (the square with the plus sign in it) to expand the table and reveal all the fields it contains (*Figure 10-4*). This example uses the Products table from the Boutique Fudge database.

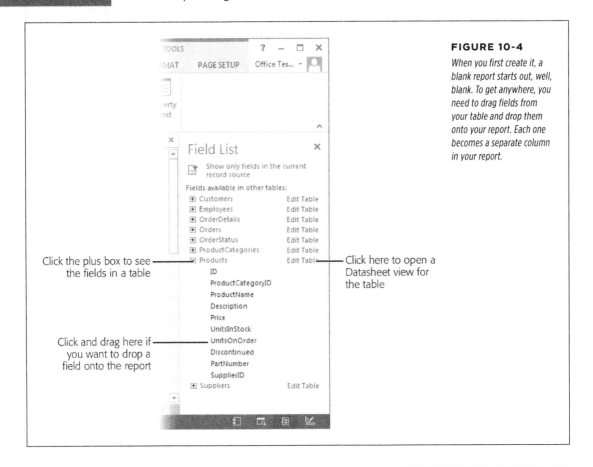

Click the plus box to see the fields in a table

Click and drag here if you want to drop a field onto the report

Click here to open a Datasheet view for the table

FIGURE 10-4

When you first create it, a blank report starts out, well, blank. To get anywhere, you need to drag fields from your table and drop them onto your report. Each one becomes a separate column in your report.

NOTE Often, your report fields will come from a single table. But you can also add fields with related information from a linked table. For example, when creating a report for the Products table, you could add fields from the ProductCategories table to show information about the category that each product is in.

3. **Add your columns to the report.**

   To add a column, click the field in the Field List, drag it over to your report, and let it go in the appropriate position (*Figure 10-5*).

   When you add a new field, Access uses the field name for the column heading, which isn't always what you want. Maybe you'd prefer *Product Name* (with a space) to *ProductName*. Or maybe you'd like to shorten *ProductCategoryID* to just *Category*. After all, the report shows the name instead of the numeric category ID, because the ProductCategoryID field uses a lookup (page 180). Fortunately, renaming the column headers is easy. Just double-click one to switch it into Edit mode. You can then edit the existing text or replace it altogether.

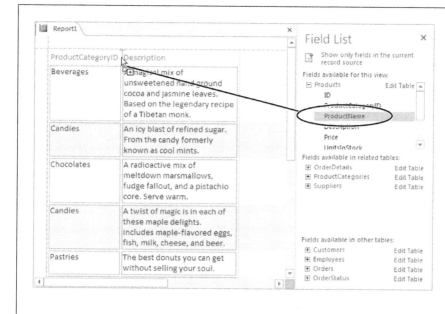

FIGURE 10-5

In this example, the report has two fields so far, and you're in the process of adding a third. As you drag, Access shows a small yellow I-beam to indicate where the new column will go. (To rearrange your columns after you've added them, follow the instructions on page 320.) If you watch closely, you see the Field List change the moment you add your first field. It separates itself into three sections, putting the table you're using at the top, tables that are linked by relationships in the middle, and unrelated tables at the bottom.

TIP The average computer monitor can show a lot of columns at once, and if you run out of space, there's always that nifty scrolling feature to help you out. But ordinary paper isn't that accommodating. If you create a report with way too many fields, you'll find that it stretches right off the right side of the page (*Figure 10-6*). One option is to rotate the page sideways into landscape orientation (page 321). But if you really need to shrink a report, the best starting point is to remove unnecessary columns. To remove a column, right-click it and choose Delete Column. The columns on the right side then move left into the newly freed space.

---

4. **Resize the columns smaller or larger until you have the balance you want.**

   To resize a column, first click the column header to select it. (A solid yellow line will appear around the column.) Next, move the mouse to the right side of the column header, so it changes into the two-way resize pointer. Finally, drag the column border to the left (to make it smaller) or to the right (to make it larger). *Figure 10-6* shows this process in action.

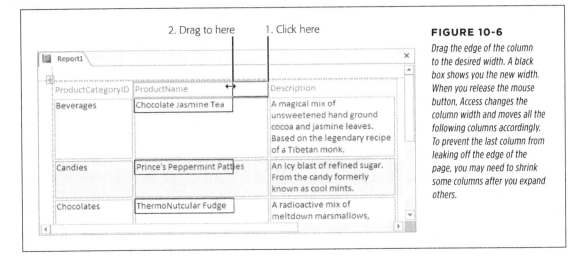

FIGURE 10-6

Drag the edge of the column to the desired width. A black box shows you the new width. When you release the mouse button, Access changes the column width and moves all the following columns accordingly. To prevent the last column from leaking off the edge of the page, you may need to shrink some columns after you expand others.

5. **Add any other elements you want, like a title, a logo, page numbers, and the date.**

   To add any of these ingredients, head to the Report Layout Tools | Design→Header/Footer section of the ribbon (see *Figure 10-7*):

   - **The title** is the large-text caption that appears at the top of the first report page.

   - **The logo** is a tiny picture that usually sits in the top-left corner of a report, next to the title.

   - **Page numbers** indicate the current page (and, optionally, the total number of pages) in a printout. But in Layout view, Access treats the report as though all the data occupies one page, so you need to scroll to the end to see this element.

   - **The date information** indicates the day and time that the report was run. Ordinarily, it appears in the header section, to the right of the title. Once you print a report, the date information tells you how recent (and therefore how relevant) your information is.

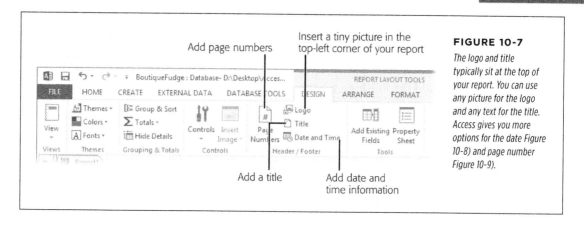

Add page numbers

Insert a tiny picture in the
top-left corner of your report

Add a title

Add date and
time information

FIGURE 10-7

*The logo and title
typically sit at the top of
your report. You can use
any picture for the logo
and any text for the title.
Access gives you more
options for the date Figure
10-8) and page number
Figure 10-9).*

FIGURE 10-8

*When adding date information, you can choose whether to include the
date, the time, or both. You also pick the format. Once you've added
the date information, you can change the font, borders, and colors, as
with any other report element.*

FIGURE 10-9

*With page numbers, you can choose the format, the position, and the
alignment. The position determines whether the page numbers appear
above or below the report data. Although you can drag the page
numbers around after you add them, Access will shift the report data
to make room, based on your choice.*

6. **Optionally, you can tweak the formatting by changing fonts, colors, and borders.**

   The quickest way to change the formatting of your report is to select the appropriate part (by clicking) and then use the buttons in the Report Layout Tools | Format→Font section of the ribbon. Using this technique, you can change how titles, column headers, and data appear. Page 330 has more on this technique.

7. **Add the finishing touches.**

   Now's the time to change the headings, add a logo, tweak the borders, or apply page numbers. You'll learn how to adjust these details starting on page 330.

8. **Optionally, choose File→Print→Print to print the report now.**

   You can also adjust the print settings in Print Preview mode (choose File→Print→Print Preview).

9. **Save your report to use later.**

   You can save your report at any time by pressing Ctrl+S. If you close the report tab without saving it, Access prompts you to make the save. Either way, you need to supply a name for your report.

It's possible to create reports that have the same names as tables or other database objects. For example, you could create a Products report that shows information about the Products table. However, in practice it's usually better to pick a more specific report name (like ProductsByCategory, ProductListForDealers, and Top-50Products). The report shown in *Figure 10-2* and elsewhere in this chapter is named ProductCatalog.

Adding Pictures to Reports

Can I store pictures in a table and show them in a report?

Many tables include embedded pictures, using the Attachment data type. You can use this technique to store employee photos, product pictures, or supplier logos. Depending on the type of picture, you may then want to include them in your printouts.

It's possible to show your pictures in a report (and even print them), provided you meet the following requirements:

- **Your picture is stored in an** *attachment field.* (See page 80 for more information about the Attachment data type.)

- **Your picture is stored in a standard picture format** (think .bmp, .jpg, .gif, .tif, .wmf, and so on). If you have another type of file in an attachment field, you just see the icon of the related application (like Microsoft Word for a .doc file) in your report.

- **Your picture is the first attachment**. If you have more than one attachment, when you select the row in the report,

tiny arrow buttons appear above it that you can use to move from one attachment to another. But it's way too much work to do this with all your records before you print a report.

The Dolls table in the bobblehead database Products table fits the bill, which lets you create a report like the one shown in *Figure 10-10.*

Alternatively, you can show the file name or the file type of an attachment in a report. To do this, you need to use the Field List pane. For example, if you have an attachment field named Picture, it appears with a + button next to it in the Field List pane. Click the + button, and you'll see the three Picture-related details you can display in a report: Picture.FileData (the attachment content itself, which is the image), Picture.FileName (the name of the file), and Picture.FileType (the type of file). If you want to show these details, just drag them onto your report.

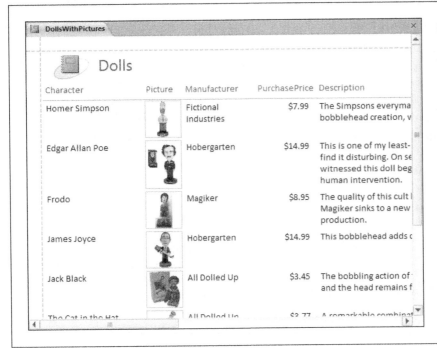

FIGURE 10-10

You can see this in the sample Bobblehead database examples for this chapter. (They're available on the Missing CD page at www.missingmanuals.com/cds/access2013mm.) The report is named DollsWith-Pictures.

The Many Views of a Report

Just as with tables and queries, you can use several different views to change a report. When you create a report by using the quick creation technique described earlier, you begin in Layout view, which is an ideal starting place for report builders. But depending on the task at hand, you may choose to switch to another view. You have four viewing options:

- **Layout View**. Shows what the report will look like when printed, complete with the real data from the underlying table. You can use this view to format and rearrange the basic building blocks of the report.

- **Report View**. Looks almost the same as Layout view, but doesn't let you make changes. If you double-click a report in the navigation pane, Access opens it in Report view so you can see the data it contains without accidentally changing its design. One common reason to use Report view is to copy portions of your report to the Clipboard, so you can paste them into other programs (like Microsoft Word). *Figure 10-11* shows how that works.

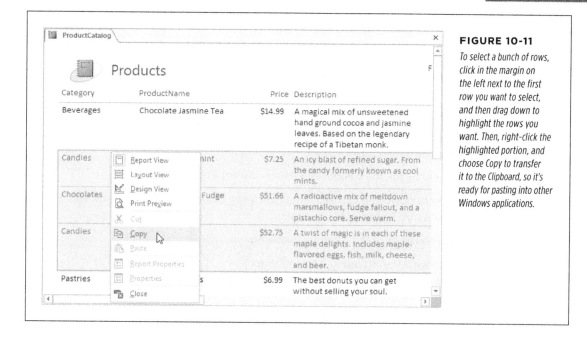

FIGURE 10-11

To select a bunch of rows, click in the margin on the left next to the first row you want to select, and then drag down to highlight the rows you want. Then, right-click the highlighted portion, and choose Copy to transfer it to the Clipboard, so it's ready for pasting into other Windows applications.

TIP If you want to transfer the entire content of a report, you should consider the export features described on page 323.

- **Print Preview**. Shows a live preview of your report, just like Layout view and Report view do. The difference is that the preview is paginated (divided into print pages), so you can figure out how many pages your printout needs and where the page breaks fall. You can also change print settings (like page orientation) and export the complete report.

- **Design View**. Shows a template view where you can define the different sections of your report. It's not nearly as intuitive as Layout view, but it does give you complete, unrestrained flexibility to customize your report. Access experts often begin creating a report in Layout view and then add more exotic effects in Design view. You'll learn more about Design view in Chapter 11.

NOTE Design view is a throwback to old versions of Access, which didn't include the more intuitive Layout view and Report view options. It's still useful for some tasks, but it's no longer the central station for shaping and formatting a report.

You can switch from one view to another by right-clicking the report tab title, and then choosing the appropriate view from the pop-up menu. (Or, you can use the

Home→Views→View menu or the view buttons in the bottom-right corner of the Access window. It's just a matter of personal preference.)

After you've closed your report, you can reopen it in the view of your choice. Just right-click the report in the navigation pane, and then choose the appropriate view. Or double-click the report in the navigation pane to open it in Report view.

Rearranging a Report

Few reports stay the same forever. Whether you want to give your report a quick tune-up or a radical overhaul, it's easy enough to do by flipping back into Layout view.

Before you do anything, it's important to understand how to select a whole column (see *Figure 10-12*). You can use two techniques:

- Right-click the column and choose Select Entire Column.

- Hold down the Ctrl key. Then, click the column header, and any value in the column. This selects both parts.

Once you've selected a column, you can:

- Move it (by dragging it to new place).

- Remove it (by pressing Delete).

- Resize it (by clicking and dragging the right edge to either side).

TIP If you're a keyboard lover, you can move or resize a column without taking your fingers off the keyboard. Select the column, and then press Shift with the left or right arrow key to narrow or widen the column. Use Alt+left arrow or Alt+right arrow to move the column one spot to the left or right, so it swaps positions with its nearby neighbor.

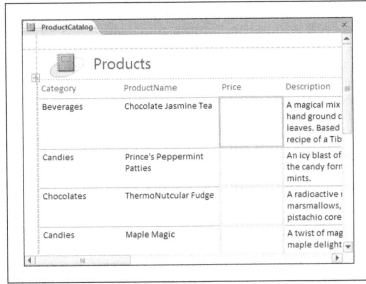

FIGURE 10-12

A common mistake when deleting columns is to click a column and then press Delete. Unfortunately, this deletes either the column header or the entire column except the header (as shown with the Price column here), depending on where you click. As a result, Access isn't able to rearrange the report to fill in the empty space. If you have this problem, click Undo and try again, using the column selection technique described above. Or, just finish the job by right-clicking the column and choosing Delete Column.

You can also move, remove, or resize other report elements, like the title, logo, and page numbers. Just click once to select the object you want, at which point a thick yellow border appears around it. It's then ready for you to drag it, resize it, or dispatch it with a quick press of the Delete key.

Printing, Previewing, and Exporting a Report

Once you've created the perfect report, it's time to share it with rest of the world. Most commonly, you'll choose to print it.

Printing a report is easy—simply select the report in the navigation pane (it doesn't even need to be open), and choose File→Print→Print. But before you inadvertently fire off an 87-page customer list in jumbo 24-point font, it's a good idea to preview the end result. Access makes it easy with its integrated Print Preview feature.

Previewing a Report

To get a preview of what your printed report will look like, select it in the navigation pane and choose File→Print→Print Preview. Or, if the report is already open, you can right-click the report tab title and choose Print Preview.

Print Preview mode doesn't let you make any changes or select any part of the report. You're limited to zooming in and out, and moving from page to page (see *Figure 10-13*). When you're finished looking at your print preview, choose Print Preview→Close Preview→Close Print Preview. Or, right-click the tab title of the preview window and choose a different report view.

In Print Preview mode, the ribbon changes dramatically. The tabs you've grown to know and love disappear, and Access replaces them with a single tab named Print Preview. (This is the same Print Preview tab you saw when you previewed a datasheet printout in Chapter 3.) You can use all the same techniques that you learned on page 124 to move around the preview, see multiple pages at once (which lets you study where page breaks occur), and change the page margins and paper orientation.

For example, the Portrait and Landscape buttons let you quickly switch between the standard portrait orientation (which places the short edge at the top of the page) and landscape (which rotates the page, placing the long edge at the top). Portrait fits more rows, while landscape fits more columns. Generally, portrait is best, provided it can fit all your columns. If portrait mode doesn't fit all your columns, you can try using landscape orientation, a smaller font size, narrower margins, or a larger size of paper.

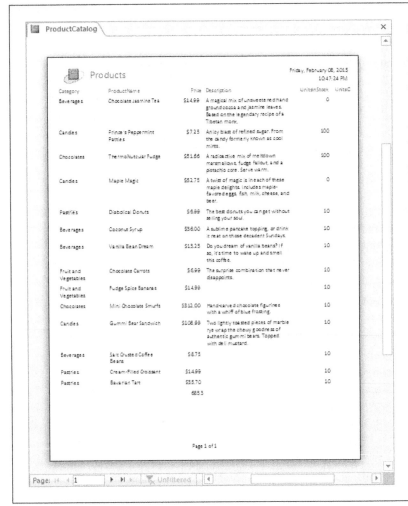

FIGURE 10-13

To zoom in, click once with the mouse. Click again to zoom back out to the full page view. You can also use the page navigation buttons at the bottom of the window to move from one page to the next, and the zoom slider (not shown) for more precise zooming. But the most useful commands appear in the ribbon, and let you tweak the print settings and export your report results to another type of file.

NOTE Reports always use your standard paper size (which is usually 8.5 x 11 inches, or letter size) when you first create them. However, if you change the size, the new size setting is stored with the report. That means the next time you open your report, it still has the customized paper size. The same applies for the paper orientation setting.

Access has two extra options that aren't provided in a normal datasheet print preview:

- **Print data only**. Click the Print Preview→Page Size→Print Data Only checkbox to produce a streamlined printout that leaves out details like column headers and titles. This option is rarely useful, because the resulting printout is harder to read.

- **Print multiple columns**. Click Print Preview→Page Layout→Columns to fit more report data on a page. This option works only if your report is much narrower than the page width. For example, if your report is less than half the width of the page, you can double-up by using two columns. You'll need half the number of pages. On page 360, you'll see how the Label Wizard uses a multicolumn report to pack mailing labels on a page.

> **TIP** You can change several of the page layout settings (like margins and paper orientation) without heading to the print preview. You'll find the same buttons in the Report Layout Tools | Page Setup tab of the ribbon, which appears whenever you have your report open in Layout view.

Export Formats

The Print Preview tab is a bit of an oddity, because it includes a few commands that don't have anything to do with printing your report. The commands in the Print Preview→Data section let you take a snapshot of the current report data, and then *export* the snapshot into some other type of file so you can view it outside of Access or work with it in another program. This technique is a great one to use if you want to share some data with other people (read: impress the boss).

Although Access supports many different export formats, you'll use just a few of them with reports. (The others are more useful when you're exporting pure data from a table or query, as explained in Chapter 23.) The useful formats for exporting reports include:

- **PDF or XPS**. This option lets you preserve your exact report formatting (so your report can be printed), and it lets people who don't have Access (and possibly don't even have Windows) view your report. It's one of the most popular export options. For more information about the PDF and XPS formats, see the box on page 324.

- **Word**. This option transforms your report into a document you can open in Microsoft Word. However, the format Access uses is a bit clumsy. (It separates each column with tabs and each line with a hard return, which makes it difficult to rearrange the data after the fact in Word.) A nicer export feature would put the report data into a Word table, which would make it far easier to work with.

- **HTML Document**. This option transforms your report into a rich HTML document, suitable for posting on the Web or just opening straight from your hard drive. The advantage of the HTML format is that all you need to view it is a Web browser (and who doesn't have one of those?). The only drawback is that the formatting, layout, and pagination of your report won't be preserved exactly, which is a disadvantage if someone wants to print the exported report.

NOTE When you export a report, Access does its best to honor your page setup. For example, if your report takes 12 printed pages and you export it to Word, Access distributes the contents in exactly the same way over a 12-page Word document. If you export the same report to HTML, Access creates a separate HTML file for each page of the report (like ProductCatalog1.html, ProductCatalog2.html, and so on). It also adds navigation links at the bottom of each page, so you can jump to the next, previous, first, or last page when viewing the report in a browser.

Learning to Love PDFs

You've probably heard about PDF, Adobe's popular format for sharing formatted, print-ready documents. PDFs are used to pass around product manuals, brochures, and all sorts of electronic documents. Unlike a document format such as .xlsx, PDF files are designed to be viewed and printed, but not edited.

The best part about PDFs is that they can be viewed on just about any type of computer and operating system using the free Adobe Reader. You can download Adobe Reader at *http://get.adobe.com/reader*, but you probably don't need to. Most computers already have Adobe Reader installed, because it comes bundled with so many different programs (usually so you can view their electronic documentation). It's also used widely on the Web.

PDF isn't the only kid on the block. Microsoft's Windows operating system includes an electronic paper format called XPS (XML Paper Specification). However, the PDF standard is dramatically more popular and widespread, so it's the one to stick with.

Exporting a Report to a PDF

Exporting a report to a PDF is slightly different than exporting it to any other format, due to the fact that PDF and XPS exporting ability started out as a separate plug-in (in the dark ages of Access 2007). Now, this functionality is incorporated into Access, and you can create a PDF (or XPS) anytime by following these steps:

1. **Switch to Print Preview mode.**

   If your report is open, right-click the report tab title, and then choose Print Preview. Otherwise, select the report in the navigation pane and choose File→Print→Print Preview.

2. **Click Print Preview→Data→PDF or XPS.**

   The "Publish as PDF or XPS" window appears (*Figure 10-14*).

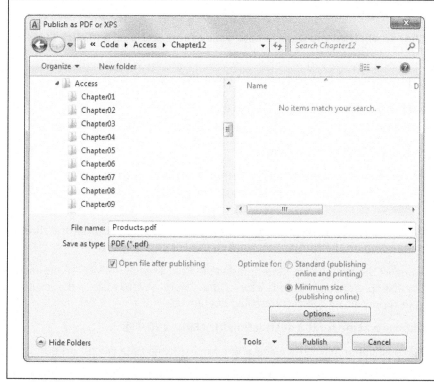

FIGURE 10-14

The "Publish as PDF or XPS" window has some extra options crammed into the bottom. You can turn on the "Open file after publishing" checkbox to tell Access to open the PDF or XPS file after the publishing process is complete, so you can check the result.

3. **Choose your file name, file type, and quality.**

   The most important details are the file name and the file type (either PDF or XPS). Enter this information first.

   You can export PDF files with different resolution and quality settings, which mostly affect reports that have pictures. Normally, you use higher-quality settings if you're planning to print your PDF file, since printers use higher resolutions than computer monitors. You have some control over PDF quality using the "Optimize for" options. If you're planning to email the PDF so people can *view* your report onscreen, choose "Minimum size (publishing online)." On the other hand, if the people reading your PDF might print it, choose "Standard (publishing online and printing)" instead. You'll export a slightly larger file that will make for a better printout.

   Finally, if you want to publish only a portion of your report as a PDF file, click the Options button to open a window with yet a few more settings. You can opt to publish a fixed number of pages rather than the full report.

4. **Click Publish to perform the export.**

If you have the "Open file after publishing" checkbox turned on, Access launches your PDF viewer after it creates the file. Or, if you're exporting an XPS file, Access opens the exported file in the XPS Viewer.

5. **Choose whether you want to save your export settings, and click Close.**

By saving your export settings, you can quickly export the same report later on. You can read how to do that on page 807.

Exporting a Report to a Different Format

If you want to export a report to any format *but* PDF or XPS, follow these steps:

1. **Switch to Print Preview mode.**

If your report is open, right-click the report tab title, and then choose Print Preview. Otherwise, select it in the navigation pane and choose File→Print→Print Preview.

2. **Click one of the buttons in the Print Preview→Data section of the ribbon, depending on the format you want to use for your export.**

Some of the options are stored under the Print Preview→Data→More menu. For example, choose Print Preview→Data→More→Word to copy the results of your report into a Word-compatible document.

3. **Choose a name for the destination file (*Figure 10-15*).**

The destination file is the place where the exported data will be stored.

4. **If you wish to open your exported file in the related program, check the setting "Open the destination file after the export operation is complete."**

Say you're exporting a Word document and you choose this option; Access will export the data, launch Word, and load the document. This is a good way to make sure your export operation worked as expected. This option works only if you have the program you need on your computer.

5. **Click OK to perform the export.**

Ignore the other two checkboxes, which are grayed out. They apply only to export operations that work with other database objects.

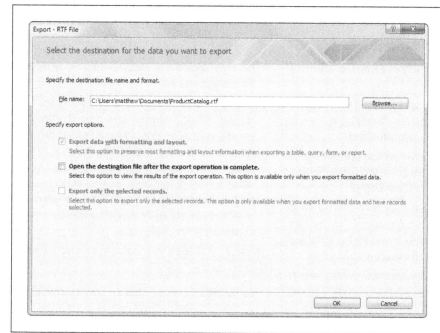

FIGURE 10-15

Access assumes you want a name that matches your report (for example, ProductCatalog.rtf if the ProductCatalog report is exported to a rich text document that can be opened in Word). However, you can change the file name to whatever you want.

NOTE Remember, exporting a report is like printing a report. Your exported file contains the data that existed at that moment in time. If you decide a week later that you need more recent data, you need to export your report again.

6. **Choose whether you want to save your export settings, and click Close.**

   By saving your export settings, you can quickly repeat your export operation later on. For example, if you export to a Word document and save the export settings, you can export the report data tomorrow, next week, or a year in the future. This feature is described on page 807.

TIP You don't need to open your report in order to export it. Instead, you can use all the commands you need straight from the navigation pane. Just right-click the report name, and then choose Export to show a menu of all your export options, from PDF files to HTML pages. You'll also see a few options that don't appear in the Export tab of the ribbon, including options for exporting the report to older, almost forgotten database and spreadsheet products like dBase, Paradox, and Lotus 1-2-3.

FREQUENTLY ASKED QUESTION

Different Ways to Export Data

Is it better to export the results of a report, or the entire contents of a table?

There are several ways to transport data out of Access. You can take data directly from a table, or you can export the results of a query or a report. So which approach is best?

Generally, the easiest option is to get data straight from the appropriate table (as described in Chapter 23). However, in a few cases it makes more sense to use a report:

- You want to use the unique arrangement of columns that you've defined in a report. (For example, you may not want the full Products table—instead, the ProductCatalog report lays out exactly what you need.)

- You want to use the filtering, sorting, or grouping settings that you've applied to a report. (You'll learn about these features in Chapter 11.)

- You want to take advantage of the formatting you've applied to a report. Depending on what exporting option you use, you may be able to keep formatting details like fonts. If you export to a PDF file, XPS file, or HTML document, all the formatting remains in place. If you export to an Office application like Word or Excel, only some of the formatting is retained. But if you export a table or a query, you get the data only, and it's up to you to make it look nice all over again.

In Chapter 23, you'll take a closer look at how to export tables and query results.

Formatting a Report

So far, you've learned to create simple reports that show all the information you want in a compact table. The only problem with these reports is that they all look the same. If you're working in a cubicle farm for a multinational insurance company, this drab sameness is probably a good thing. But those who still have a pulse may want to jazz up their reports with borders, exotic fonts, and a dash of color.

Applying a Theme

The quickest way to apply formatting is to use one of the prebuilt themes (shown in *Figure 10-16*) from the Report Layout Tools | Design→Themes→Themes list. Each theme applies a combination of fonts and colors. Themes let you transform the entire look of your report in one step, but they don't give you the fine-grained control to apply exactly the details you want.

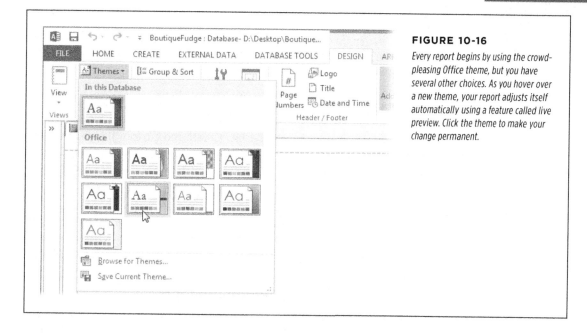

FIGURE 10-16

Every report begins by using the crowd-pleasing Office theme, but you have several other choices. As you hover over a new theme, your report adjusts itself automatically using a feature called live preview. Click the theme to make your change permanent.

NOTE   Remember, to format a report, it needs to be in Layout view or Design view. If you double-click a report in the navigation pane, it opens in Report view. Right-click the tab title, and then choose Layout View to switch over.

You can do a few interesting things with themes:

- **Apply just part of a theme**. The Access designers might cringe, but you can combine the fonts from one theme with the colors of another. Just pick the fonts from the Design→Themes→Fonts list and pick the colors from the Report Layout Tools | Design→Themes→Colors list.

- **Apply the same theme to every report in your database**. Find the theme in the Report Layout Tools | Design→Themes→Themes list. Right-click it, and choose Apply Theme to All Matching Objects. You can also right-click a theme and choose "Make This Theme the Database Default" to ensure that new reports get the same formatting.

- **Create custom theme**. When you set up a custom theme, you can consistently use the same combination of fonts and colors in different reports. Start by picking your favorite font combination (choose Report Layout Tools | Design→Themes→Fonts→Create New Theme Fonts). Then, pick your favorite set of colors (choose Report Layout Tools | Design→Themes→Colors→Create New Theme Colors). Now your font combination will appear in the Fonts list, and your color combination will appear in the Colors list, so you can apply it to other reports in the database.

NOTE The Themes feature isn't bad, but it would be far more useful if themes grouped together more settings. For example, an Access theme really should include borders, alternating row formatting, a separate font for the column headers, and so on. (Themes don't have these abilities because they're an Office-wide feature that isn't specifically tailored to Access.)

- **Export a theme and share it between databases**. If you want to reuse your theme in other databases (or share it with friends), you can save your custom fonts and colors as a .thmx Theme file. Create the custom theme, and then choose Report Layout Tools | Design→Themes→Themes→Save Current Theme. To apply your custom theme later on, just choose Report Layout Tools | Design→Themes→Themes→Browse for Themes, and browse to your .thmx file.

TIP Since Access shares its theming system with Word, Excel, and PowerPoint, you can create a .thmx file in Access, and then use it to set document colors and fonts in other Office applications. That way, you can create memos in Word, presentations in PowerPoint, and reports in Excel that all share the same hot colors and fonts.

Formatting Columns and Column Headers

Themes are a great way to get a bunch of formatting done in a hurry. However, sometimes you want to use more of a personal touch and format the different parts of your report by hand.

To apply more targeted formatting, you need to follow a two-step approach. First, select the portion of the report you want to format. Second, click a command in the Report Layout Tools | Format→Font section of the ribbon (*Figure 10-17*).

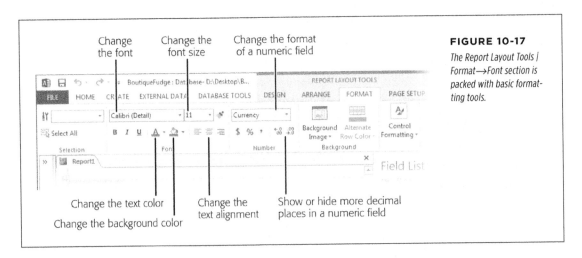

FIGURE 10-17

The Report Layout Tools | Format→Font section is packed with basic formatting tools.

The Report Layout Tools | Format→Font section lets you adjust all the following details:

- The font and font size (11-point Calibri is the easy-on-the-eyes standard.)
- The text alignment (left, right, or center)
- The text color and background color

Although you can format the title, date, or page number sections of the report, you'll spend most of your time formatting the column headers and the column values. Here are some quick pointers that describe how to select the right part of your report so you can format it:

- To select a column header, click it.
- To select the column *values*, click any one of the values in the column.
- To select both the header and the values, click the column header, and then Ctrl-click a value in the column. Or, just right-click the column and choose Select Entire Column.
- To select a group of columns at once, click a value in the first one and then Ctrl-click the other columns and (optionally) the column headers that you want to format.
- To select the entire grid of report values (including the column headers), click the four-way-arrow icon, as shown in *Figure 10-18*.

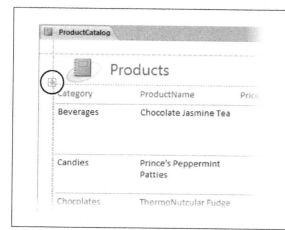

FIGURE 10-18

To select the entire table, click anywhere inside the table of report data, and then click the four-way arrow icon that appears next to the top-left corner of your report table.

You can't format the individual values in a column. That means, for example, that you can format the ProductName column to look different from the Price column, but you can't format Chocolate Jasmine Tea differently from Prince's Peppermint Patties. This limitation makes sense—after all, you could have thousands of records, and keeping track of the formatting of each one would be way too much work for Access.

TIP You have a way around this shortcoming. You can use conditional formatting (page 336) to tell Access when it should kick in some extra formatting based on the value in a cell.

GEM IN THE ROUGH

Format Painter

The Format Painter is an often-overlooked tool that copies formatting from one spot in your report to another. The neat bit is that the format painter copies all the formatting details in one go, including color, font, and border settings.

The Format Painter is most useful in document-oriented applications like Word or Excel. However, the Format Painter is occasionally handy in an Access report. For example, if you've just finished perfecting the formatting for one column and you want to apply the same settings to another, the Format Painter can make short work of the job.

Here's how to use the Format Painter:

1. Click to select the area that has the formatting you want to copy.

   For example, this may be a value in a formatted column.

2. Choose Report Layout Tools | Format→Font→Format Painter.

3. The Format Painter icon looks like a paintbrush.

4. Click the area where you want to apply the copied formatting.

   For example, this could be another column.

That's it: Access copies your formatting from the first column to the second.

■ FORMATTING NUMERIC FIELDS

You can use the Report Layout Tools | Format→Number section of the ribbon to adjust numeric fields (like the Price field in the ProductCatalog report). You'll find a drop-down list that lets you pick various options for formatting numbers:

- **General Number** gives a basic, no-frills number. Access gives each value the number of decimal digits it needs.

- **Currency** makes sure each number has two decimal points and gets the currency symbol that's configured for your computer (based on its geographic locale). Large numbers get thousands-separator commas to separate the digits, as in $1,111.99.

- **Euro** is similar to Currency, except it shows the currency symbol for the euro.

- **Fixed** gives each number the same number of decimal places. (Initially it's two, but you can use the Increase Decimals and Decrease Decimals buttons, shown in *Figure 10-17*, to change this.) Large numbers don't get commas.

- **Standard** is the same as fixed, except large numbers do get the thousands separator comma (as in 1,111.99).

- **Percent** assumes each number is a fractional value that represents a percentage, where 1.0 is 100 percent. So if you have the number 48, Access changes this to 4800.00 percent. (You can change the number of decimal places with the Increase Decimals and Decrease Decimals buttons.)

- **Scientific** displays each number using *scientific notation*, so 48 becomes 4.80E+01 (which is a fancy way of saying 4.8 multiplied by 10^1 gives you the number that's stored in the field). Scientific notation is used to show numbers that have vastly different scales with a similar number of digits. You can change the number of decimal places using the Increase Decimals and Decrease Decimals buttons.

You can also change the number of digits that are displayed to the right of the decimal point by clicking the Increase Decimals and Decrease Decimals buttons in the Report Layout Tools | Format→Number section of the ribbon.

■ ALTERNATING ROW FORMATTING

Here's a simple but powerful formatting trick: Add a shaded background to every second row. Alternating row formatting gives a bit of polish to the plainest report, but it also serves a practical purpose. In dense reports, the shaded bands make it easier for readers to distinguish each row and follow a row from one column to the next.

To apply an alternating row format, you need to click immediately to the left of any row. At that point, the entire row becomes selected, and the Report Layout Tools | Format→Background→Alternate Row Color button is turned on. You can click it, and then choose a color.

Remember to click just to the left of any row. If you click one of the values in the row, the Alternate Row Color button won't be turned on, and you won't be able to change the alternating fill color.

■ GRIDLINES

Every simple report uses a table to lay out its content. However, it's your choice whether you want to make that table obvious, with clearly defined gridlines, or keep it sleek and lightweight. Most of the examples in this chapter have been gridline-free, which makes sure that printouts look fresh and modern. However, if your report holds a dense thicket of numbers and text, a few gridlines can make it more readable.

It's up to you whether you want to add gridlines everywhere to keep data carefully regimented in separate cells or just add gridlines judiciously to highlight important columns. Either way, you follow the same basic process:

1. **Select the part of the report on which you want to apply (or change) gridlines.**

   The simplest option is to apply gridlines to the entire table (*Figure 10-19*). Alternatively, you can select individual columns, groups of columns, and column headers, and change just their gridlines. Page 331 describes how to select different parts of a report.

TIP Gridlines are useful with dense reports where the data may otherwise appear to run together into a jumbled mess. Access gurus know that less is more. Using just a few gridlines is often better than adding them between every column and row.

---

2. **Choose one of the gridline options from the Report Layout Tools |
   Arrange→Table→Gridlines list (*Figure 10-19*).**

   The commands in the Gridlines section of the ribbon let you apply gridlines in
   the most common patterns: everywhere, between columns only, between rows
   only, around the outside of your data, and so on.

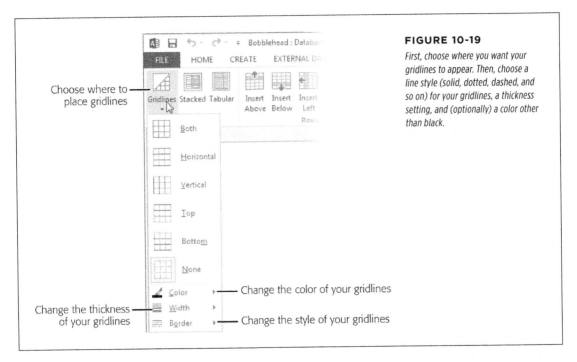

FIGURE 10-19

*First, choose where you want your
gridlines to appear. Then, choose a
line style (solid, dotted, dashed, and
so on) for your gridlines, a thickness
setting, and (optionally) a color other
than black.*

3. **Use the other buttons in the Report Layout Tools | Arrange→Gridlines menu
   to change the thickness, color, and style of your gridlines.**

   Light-colored gridlines are an expert Access trick—they cleanly separate content
   but don't distract report readers from the actual content.

■ BORDERS

Along with report gridlines, you can also use a similar set of border options. The difference between gridlines and borders is that gridlines apply to the table of report
data, while borders can be attached to any ingredient in your report.

As with all types of formatting, you begin by selecting the portion of your report
that you want to change. Then, head to the Report Layout Tools | Format→Control
Formatting→Shape Outline menu. As with gridlines, you can pick a line thickness,
color, and style.

When you first create a report, your report has no gridlines but uses borders around each value. To get rid of these borders, select the entire report (*Figure 10-18*) and choose Report Layout Tools | Format→Control Formatting→Shape Outline→Line Type→Transparent (which is the first option in the list).

The border options don't make much sense when you use them on column values, because you'll end up with a box around each value. Borders are more useful around other report elements, like the report title.

■ MARGIN AND PADDING

If you use the border feature, you might also want to tweak the space that appears around each cell in the report. Access provides two related settings for this purpose. The *margin* is the space between the content and the border around it. The *padding* is the space between the border and the edge of the cell. *Figure 10-20* shows the difference.

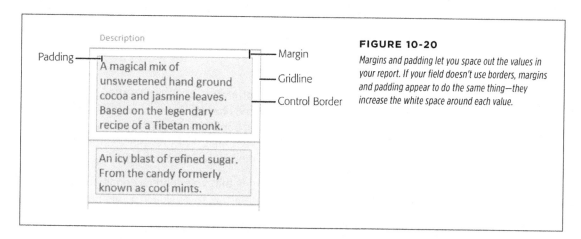

FIGURE 10-20

Margins and padding let you space out the values in your report. If your field doesn't use borders, margins and padding appear to do the same thing—they increase the white space around each value.

To change the margin and the padding space, head to the Report Layout Tools | Arrange→Position section of the ribbon. Click Control Margins to choose from a small set of margin presets (None, Narrow, Medium, and Wide), or click Control Padding to choose one of the same options for padding. If you want to set the exact amount of margin or padding spacing, or you want to use different spacing on different sides of a cell, you need to set the margin and property settings in the Property Sheet (page 365).

Some controls don't take well to large margins. If you increase the margin space of a text box, you may find that the white margin space starts to cut off the bottom of your text. This is an annoying, but easily avoidable, Access quirk. (To avoid it, just use more modest margins.)

■ BACKGROUND IMAGE

One of the most exotic effects you can apply to any report is a background image—a picture that appears behind your report data on every page. To select a background, choose Report Layout Tools | Format→Background Image→Browse. Choose an image file on your hard drive, and click Open to add it to your form.

NOTE Access adds every picture you use to the Report Layout Tools | Format→Background Image→Background list, so you can apply it again to another report or form in the same database.

Usually, a background image looks perfectly awful in a report. But if you're set on using this feature, you should follow three tips to make it look better:

- Use a very light-colored picture if your report data uses dark lettering, or a very dark picture if your report data uses light lettering. Without strong visual contrast, your background picture will make your report illegible.

- Make sure you remove all borders and gridlines from your report.

- Give the report a transparent background so nothing will interfere with your picture. To do this, select the whole table and go to the Report Layout Tools | Format→Font section of the ribbon. Then, click the drop-down arrow next to the Background Color button (it looks like a paint can) and choose Transparent.

Conditional Formatting

The average report packs in a lot of information. Some information is more important than other data. For example, you may have good reasons for wanting to spot out-of-stock products, orders over $100, bobbleheads you've purchased in the last year, or wedding guests who haven't sent gifts. With *conditional formatting*, you can emphasize these pieces of information with different formatting.

The idea behind conditional formatting is that you define a condition that, if true, prompts Access to apply additional formatting to a value in a column.

To apply conditional formatting, follow these steps:

1. **Select a value in the column where you want to apply the conditional formatting.**

   For example, if you want to highlight products that top $100, click one of the values in the Price column. It doesn't matter what value you select—a conditional formatting rule applies to every value in the column.

2. **Choose Report Layout Tools | Format→Control Format→Conditional Formatting.**

   If the Conditional Formatting button is turned off, you probably don't have the right part of the report selected. For example, if you select a column header instead of a column value, you can't apply conditional formatting.

   When you click Conditional Formatting, the Conditional Formatting Rules Manager window appears. You can use this window to create multiple conditions for a column, but one is often enough.

3. **Click New Rule to create a new conditional formatting rule.**

The New Formatting Rule window appears. At the top is the rule type. The default rule type, "Check values in the current record or use an expression" is the one to use. The second rule type, "Compare to other records," is used to create data bars. You'll learn about them in the following section.

4. **Set the condition that Access should evaluate.**

To configure your rule, you use the series of boxes under the caption "Format only cells where the."

The first drop-down list box lets you choose whether you want to evaluate the actual data in the field ("Field Value Is") or a calculation that uses that data ("Expression Is"). The simplest and most common option is to base your condition on the field value.

Using the second drop-down list box, choose the type of comparison you want to perform. You can choose to test whether the cell value equals a set number, is greater or less than a set number, or lies within some range of values.

Finally, enter the information that Access should use for the comparison. For example, if you choose to perform a less-than comparison, type in the value that Access should compare against. If you choose to test whether a cell is between certain values, enter both values in this range.

Figure 10-21 shows a rule that tests for high product prices in the Price field.

NOTE All "between" comparisons are inclusive. For example, if you set the condition "between 1 and 10," the condition is true for the numbers 1, 10, and anything in between. On the other hand, if Access comes across the value 0.99, it won't apply the conditional formatting.

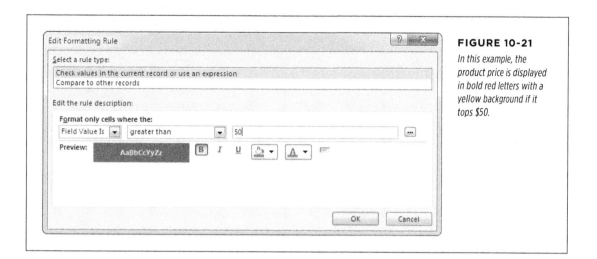

FIGURE 10-21

In this example, the product price is displayed in bold red letters with a yellow background if it tops $50.

5. **Set the formatting that Access should apply if the condition is true.**

To configure the rule's formatting, you use the buttons in the "Preview" section. This formatting can apply bold, italic, or underlining to the text. It can also change the color of the text or the background fill. However, you can't change the font or font size conditionally.

Underneath your condition, you'll see a preview of the formatting choices you make.

6. **Click OK to add your conditional rule.**

Your rule appears in the Conditional Formatting Rules Manager window.

If you want to preview your conditional formatting, click Apply. If your formatting isn't exactly what you want, select the conditional formatting rule and click Edit Rule.

7. **If you want to add a second or third condition, click New Rule, and then return to step 3.**

For example, you could use blue lettering to flag prices over $50 and red lettering if the price exceeds $100. If you have more than one condition that overlaps, Access will apply only the first one that matches. (You can change the order of rules by selecting one and clicking the up or down arrow button. You can remove a rule altogether by selecting it and clicking Delete Rule.)

> **TIP** To prevent confusion, you should structure your conditions carefully so they don't overlap. For example, use one condition that matches values between 100 and 499 and another that grabs values of 500 or more.

8. **Click OK.**

As soon as you click OK, Access evaluates the condition for every value in the column and adjusts the formatting as needed. *Figure 10-22* shows the final report.

Data Bars

Data bars make it easier for you to spot important data and make quick comparisons. They place a shaded bar in the background of every cell in a column, as shown in *Figure 10-23*. The trick is that the data bar's length varies depending on the content in the cell. Larger values generate longer data bars, while smaller values get smaller data bars.

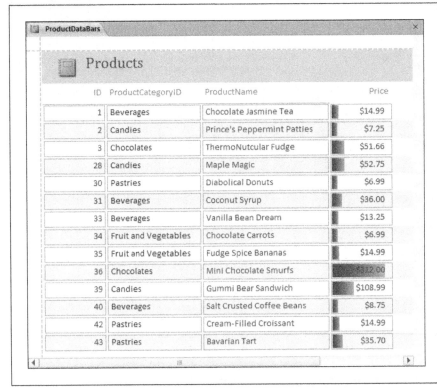

FIGURE 10-23

Here, data bars let you to quickly pick out the priciest products. For example, there's no doubt that the Mini Chocolate Smurfs break the bank. Data bars can also help you find the top-selling stores in a sales report or the worst eating excesses in a calorie-counting log. (If you've seen this trick before, it was probably in Excel.)

Access lets you use data bars only if your report gets its data directly from a table or query object in your database. Although this requirement seems straightforward enough, if you create a blank report by dragging fields from the Field List pane, Access actually builds a query on the fly and uses *that* for your report's data source. Ordinarily, this fact is a behind-the-scenes detail that you don't need to worry about. But if you want to use data bars, you need to dig a little deeper to straighten things out.

The easiest fix is to change your report to use the right data source, which is the table or query that has the fields that you display in your report. Here's how:

1. **If your report uses fields from more than one table, begin by creating a join query that gets all the data you want (page 227).**

   If your report uses the fields from a single table, you don't need to create a query, because you can use the corresponding table as your data source.

2. **Open your report in Layout view.**

If the Property Sheet pane isn't visible on the right side of the window, choose Report Layout Tools | Design→Tools→Property Sheet.

3. **In the list at the top of the Property Sheet, select Report. Just underneath, click the Data tab, and on that tab, click the first setting, Record Source.**

   A drop-down arrow appears on the right side of the box.

4. **Click the drop-down arrow to see a list of all the tables and queries in your database. Choose the table you're using from the list.**

   Or, if you created a specially designed query in step 1, choose that instead.

Even though this change makes no obvious difference to your report, it's now ready to use data bars. To add them to your report, follow these steps:

1. **Select a value in the column where you want to apply the conditional formatting and choose report Layout Tools | Format→Control Format→Conditional Formatting.**

   The Conditional Formatting Rules Manager window appears.

2. **Click New Rule, and change the rule type to "Compare to other records."**

   You see a group of data bar settings.

3. **If you want to see just the bar, turn on the "Show Bar only" checkbox.**

   If you show just the bar, Access hides the actual numeric value in the cell. This option makes it easier to see the data bars, but removes the specific data that you probably want. Only use this setting if you're using data bars to get an overall feel for a certain field. (Alternatively, you can add the same column to your report twice, and use one to show the number and the other to show the data bars.)

4. **Choose how Access calculates the shortest and longest bars.**

   Ordinarily, Access finds the largest value and makes that the largest data bar, so it fills almost the entire cell. Access fills every other cell proportionately. That means a cell with a value that's half the maximum gets a data bar that fills just under half the cell, and a cell with a value of 0 has the tiniest data bar of them all.

   In some cases, this isn't the best scale choice—for example, if most of your values fall into a small range, but a few values are dramatically higher or lower than the rest. These values will skew the scale and make it hard to see the variance between the other values. In this situation, you can set maximum or minimum bar lengths (either as a specific value or a percentage) to limit your scale. For example, if you set the Type of the longest bar to Number (instead of "Highest value"), and you set the Value to 50, the scale stops at 50. All values larger than 50 get the longest possible data bar, and smaller values are sized proportionately.

5. **Set the bar color.**

All Access data bars use a slight gradient fill, but you pick the starting color. For example, if you use red, the bar fades from the original shade of red to a lighter color as it stretches from one side of the cell to the other.

6. **Click OK to add your rule.**

Your rule appears in the Conditional Formatting Rules Manager window.

If Access displays an error message stating that "Data bars are supported only for tables and named queries," your report has the wrong data source. To change the data source so your report supports data bars, follow the earlier set of steps on page 340.

7. **Click Apply to preview your data bars or OK to make them permanent.**

You can return the Conditional Formatting Rules Manager window to edit or remove the data bars at any time.

■ Filtering and Sorting a Report

Reports offer much the same filtering and sorting features that you learned to use with the datasheet in Chapter 3. In addition, you have options for grouping and subtotals, which you'll explore in Chapter 11.

Filtering a Report

The ProductCatalog report presents all the records from the Products table. However, reports often need to filter out just an important subset of information. For example, you may want to analyze the sales of products in a specific category or the orders made by customers in a specific city. In the case of the ProductCatalog, it's logical to leave out discontinued items. After all, there's no reason for Boutique Fudge to advertise items it no longer sells.

You can pare down the results that are included in a report in two ways. You've already learned about one option: creating a query that extracts the results you want, and then using that query to build your report. This option is a good choice if you already have a query that fits the bill or you plan to use this subset of data for several purposes (reports, editing, other queries, and so on).

Another choice is to apply the filtering through report *settings*. The advantage of this technique is that you can change the filter settings quickly and repeatedly. If you plan to use the same report to print several different subsets of data, this approach is best. For example, you could filter out the products in one category, print them, and then adjust the filtering to select products in a different category, which you could also print.

Report filtering works the same way datasheet filtering does. You have two options:

- If you want to quickly build a filter condition based on an existing value, right-click that value, as shown in *Figure 10-24*. For example, in the CategoryName field, you can right-click the value "Beverages." The menu that pops up includes several filtering options based on the current value. Depending on the option you choose, you can include records in the Beverages category, records in different categories, records that have a category name that includes "Beverages" (like "Alcoholic Beverages"), and so on.

- If you need more flexibility to create the filter expression you want, right-click any value in a column, and then look for the filter submenu. The exact name of the menu depends on the data type. For example, if you right-click the CategoryName field, you see a submenu named Text Filters. If you right-click the Price field, you see a submenu named Number Filters. These submenus include a range of filtering options that let you set specific ranges. For all the exquisite details and help creating a variety of filter expressions, refer to the instructions on page 107.

You can apply filters to multiple columns at once. To remove a filter, right-click the column, and then choose Clear Filter.

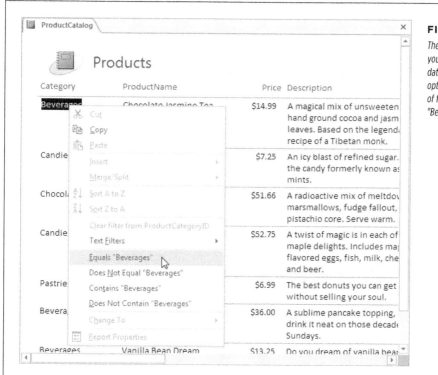

FIGURE 10-24

The quick filtering options you see vary based on the data type. Here, the filtering options let you set a variety of filters based on the term "Beverages."

Sorting a Report

Ordinarily, a report has the same order as the underlying data source. If you've built your report on a query, the order is determined by the sort order you used in the query. If you've built your report on a table, the records have no particular order at all, although they'll typically appear in the order you added them.

Either way, you can apply formatting directly in your report, in much the same way that you can with the datasheet (page 98). Simply right-click the appropriate column header, and then look for the sorting options. The sort commands depend on the data type—for example, you can order text fields alphabetically, dates chronologically, and numeric fields in ascending or descending order.

NOTE You can sort using only one field at a time. If you want to apply a more complex sort that uses more than one column (for example, a sort that separates products into alphabetical categories and then orders each category by price), you need to build a query for your report.

Designing Advanced Reports

In the previous chapter, you learned to create simple reports—nicely formatted printouts that arrange information inside a single table. Simple reports are a great way to create a hard copy that has more polish than a datasheet printout. As you learned in the previous chapter, simple reports give you the fine-grained formatting you need to highlight important columns and values, and they handle long text fields gracefully, without wasting space or chopping off part of the data.

Simple reports are a great Access tool, but they're still, well, *simple*. Their structure is their main limitation. No matter how you format or arrange your data in a simple report, Access always presents it as a table. In the real world, you may want your printed data to take other forms. You may want to transform your data into customer invoices, class attendance lists, or mailing labels. All these reports perform the same task—they take the data in a table, and then arrange it on the printed page—but you can't create any of them with a plain-vanilla report and its simple tabular structure.

In this chapter, you'll see how to create a variety of more specialized reports that take the concepts you learned in the last chapter, and extend them with a few new tricks. Along the way, you'll take a look at Design view, you'll learn how to add pictures and shapes and tell Access where to break pages in long printouts. You'll also see how to use grouping to analyze data and calculate subtotals.

Improving Reports in Design View

Design view is the secret to setting your reports free. As you learned in the previous chapter, Design view is another way of looking at your report. Unlike in Layout view, in Design you don't see any report data. Instead, you see a blueprint that tells

Access *how* to create the report. Using this blueprint, you can do things that just aren't possible in any other view.

Consider the simple report with the list of products that you created in the previous chapter. If you switch to Design view, you see what makes this report tick (*Figure 11-1*). To get to Design view, right-click the tab title, and then choose Design view.

Goes at the top of each page

Goes at the top of the report

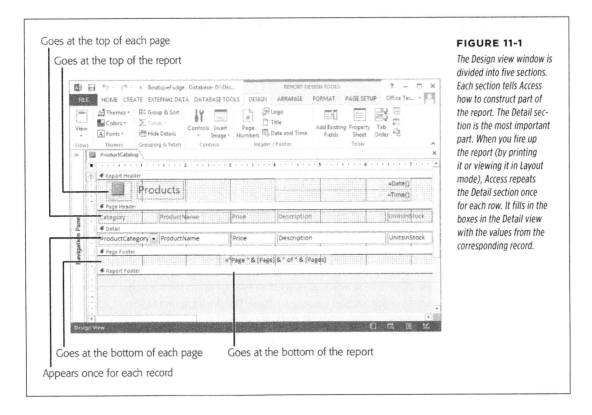

FIGURE 11-1

The Design view window is divided into five sections. Each section tells Access how to construct part of the report. The Detail section is the most important part. When you fire up the report (by printing it or viewing it in Layout mode), Access repeats the Detail section once for each row. It fills in the boxes in the Detail view with the values from the corresponding record.

Goes at the bottom of each page   Goes at the bottom of the report

Appears once for each record

NOTE   The odd grid of lines and dots you see in Design view is intended to help you line up different parts of your report when you aren't using a layout table. As you'll see, it's often important to place report elements in precise positions when using Design view.

The Design View Sections

The secret to mastering Design view is understanding its five different sections. Although you can leave some sections blank, every report includes them in exactly the same order:

- **Report Header**. Appears once at the beginning of your report, on the first page. This section is where you add titles, logos, and your own personal byline.

- **Page Header**. Appears just under the report header on the first page, and at the top of each subsequent page. It's the place to add page numbers, and you can also use it for column headers in simple, tabular reports like the product catalog.

- **Detail**. Appears once immediately after the page header, and it's the heart of all reports. The trick is that the Detail section is repeated once for each record in your report. In a simple tabular report, this section represents a single row.

- **Page Footer**. Appears at the bottom of each page. If you don't use the page header for page numbers, this section provides your other option.

- **Report Footer**. Appears once at the very end of the report. You can use it to print summary information, copyright statements, the date of printing, and so on.

The content in these sections looks a fair bit different from what you see in other views, because Design view doesn't show the live data. Instead, it includes place-holders where Access inserts the necessary information each time it runs the report. When you run the product report, for example, Access grabs the values from the ProductCategoryID, ProductName, Price, and Description fields and then shuffles them into the matching boxes.

You'll need a bit of time before you're comfortable manipulating the content in Design view. First, you need to learn that you can adjust each section's size. This ability makes sense, because different reports allocate different amounts of space to each region. *Figure 11-2* shows how this works.

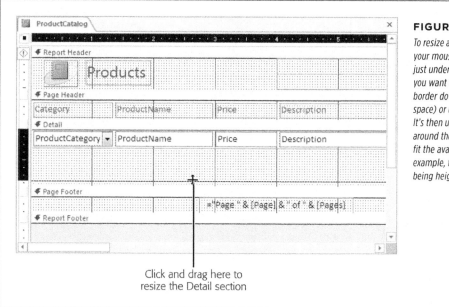

Click and drag here to
resize the Detail section

FIGURE 11-2

To resize a section, move your mouse to the border just underneath the section you want to change. Drag the border down (to add more space) or up (to remove space). It's then up to you to shuffle around the content inside to fit the available space. In this example, the Detail section is being heightened.

TIP If you don't want to use a section, you can resize it almost out of existence. Look at the report footer section in *Figure 11-1*. It's there, but vanishingly small, because this report doesn't use the footer. Alternatively, you can delete the header and footer section. Just right-click the report surface (in Design view), and then choose Page Header/Footer to remove the page header and page footer sections, or Report Header/Footer to remove the report header and footer sections. Click these commands again to make these sections reappear, but without any content (you need to fill that in yourself).

Understanding Controls

Design view gives you a different perspective for your report. Access represents everything in your report with *controls*: graphical widgets that have text, pictures, and formatting. Each control is a distinct element. You can change what it looks like, or you can drag it to a different position (although you may need to pull it out of its layout table first, as described on page 349).

Figure 11-3 points out the controls in the product catalog report. You don't see all the controls, because not all the columns fit into view at once.

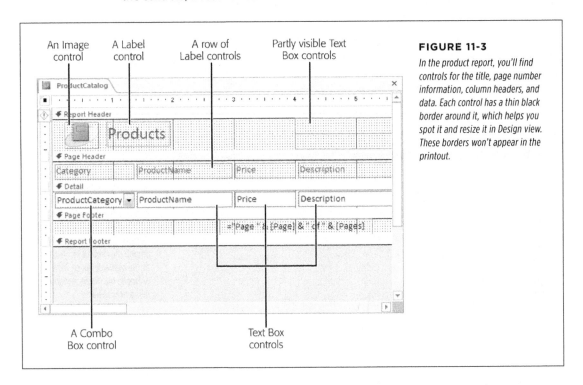

An Image control · A Label control · A row of Label controls · Partly visible Text Box controls

A Combo Box control · Text Box controls

FIGURE 11-3

In the product report, you'll find controls for the title, page number information, column headers, and data. Each control has a thin black border around it, which helps you spot it and resize it in Design view. These borders won't appear in the printout.

NOTE Something may strike you as a little odd in *Figure 11-3*. Namely, several text box controls look more like label controls. As you'll learn later in this chapter, reports use label controls for text that never changes and use text box controls for text that does (based on the current date, the current record, the current page, and so on).

To get a little more comfortable in Design view, play around with a simple report. (If you don't have a report handy, you can download the Boutique Fudge database with the examples for this chapter; see the Missing CD page at *www.missingmanuals.com/cds/access2013mm*.) Here are some tasks to try out:

- Drag the controls in the report header and page footer sections from one place to another.

- Change the size of a control in the report header or page footer section by dragging the black border that appears around it.

- Rearrange the columns by dragging the column headers around the page header section, or by dragging the fields around the Detail section. When you move a column, Access automatically arranges the other columns around it. Access works the same way when you rearrange the columns in Layout view.

- Select a control, and then change its formatting by using the ribbon's Report Design Tools | Format→Font section. This method works with the elements in the page header and footer sections as well as the column headers and individual fields.

When you're finished making a change, right-click the tab title, and then choose another view (like Report view, Layout view, or Print Preview) to see what your printed report will look like. When you close your report, Access prompts you to save the changes you've made.

You should be able to do everything you did to customize a report in Layout view by using Design view. Of course, Layout view is easier to use for most of these tasks. But as you'll see in the following section, Design view gives you more freedom to break out of the typical report table and arrange your data however you want.

Moving Fields Out of a Layout

In a simple report, Access groups all the fields into something called a *layout*. The layout is actually a specialized container that lets you easily work with groups of fields. It provides several indispensable conveniences that you saw in Chapter 10:

- When you move a column to a new position, Access rearranges all the other columns accordingly.

- When you widen a column, Access bumps all the following columns out of the way. Similarly, when you shrink a column, the following columns move to fill the extra space.

Without a layout, you couldn't move your columns around as quickly. Every time you wanted to make a change in one column, you'd need to painstakingly reposition every other column. In a report with several dozen fields, this process adds up to a major headache.

Although layouts are small miracles of convenience, they're also a bit of a straitjacket if you want to arrange your data differently. Suppose you want to take the product catalog report and make it look less like an inventory list and more like a retail publication, as shown in *Figure 11-4*. You can't do this with a layout, because your fields are always locked into a tight tabular structure. You can only get this result if you take your fields out of their layout table, and then arrange them by hand.

> **NOTE** Don't get confused between *layouts* and *Layout view*. A layout is a container that arranges a bunch of controls. Layout view is a way to look at your report and change various aspects of it. You can use Layout view even if you don't use any layout containers.

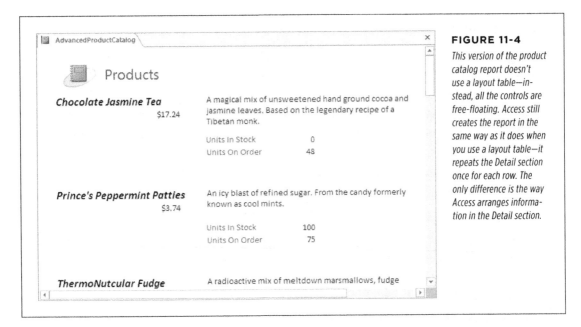

FIGURE 11-4

This version of the product catalog report doesn't use a layout table—instead, all the controls are free-floating. Access still creates the report in the same way as it does when you use a layout table—it repeats the Detail section once for each row. The only difference is the way Access arranges information in the Detail section.

In the following steps, you'll learn how to transform the layout-based product catalog into the table-free version shown in *Figure 11-4*. You'll begin in Layout view, where you can remove the fields from their layout. Then you'll switch into Design view to customize the arrangement of your fields. (Word of advice: Once you know your way around Design view, you'll probably get the job done quicker by creating a new, layout-free report from scratch in Design view, as described on page 354.)

1. **Switch to Layout view (right-click the tab title and then choose Layout View).**

   You can remove fields in Design view, but the results aren't as pleasant. When you remove a field from a layout in Layout view, Access automatically bumps it aside and gives it a little space of its own. But when you remove a field in Design view, Access leaves it in its original position. You end up with controls that are bunched up on top of each other, which makes them very difficult to arrange.

2. **Select the entire table.**

   It's neater and easier to remove all of a layout's fields at once than to remove them one by one. To liberate the entire report at once, click any value in your report; a tiny four-way-arrow icon appears next to the top-left corner of your layout table. Click that icon to select the entire table.

3. **Right-click the now-selected table and choose Layout→Remove Layout.**

   The Layout submenu provides three choices:

   - **Tabular** puts fields into a column-based arrangement, which is what you already have.

   - **Stacked** puts fields one on top of the other, which takes up more space but is nicer for certain types of data (for example, tables with just a few fields that contain a lot of text).

   - **Remove Layout**, the final option, puts the control in your hand, letting you create any arrangement you can imagine.

4. **Right-click the tab title, and then choose Design view.**

   You could arrange your fields in Layout view, but most people find this tricky because Layout view shows several records at a time. Instead, you'll probably have an easier time arranging them by using the section templates in Design view.

5. **Make the Detail section larger by dragging down the bottom edge (as shown in *Figure 11-2*).**

   In a simple report, you need exactly one row to fit your record. But when you create a custom arrangement, you almost always need more space.

6. **Drag the text box control for each field to the right place in the Detail section, and then resize it to the right size.**

   It may take some rearranging before you finally get all the boxes in the right places. Since the information isn't in a layout table anymore, Access doesn't automatically move information out of the way. Instead, you need to arrange everything by hand and make sure no two fields overlap.

7. **In the Page Header section, select a column header for one of the fields in the Detail section. Either press Delete to remove it, or drag it down into the Detail section.**

   It makes no sense to include a column header at the top of a page when your field isn't a part of the table any longer. If the data is fairly self-explanatory, you don't need a caption at all. However, you could also drag the column header into the Detail section, and place it next to the corresponding data, so it acts like a caption. The report in *Figure 11-4* keeps the captions for the UnitsInStock and UnitsOnOrder fields.

8. **If you haven't already, select each field, and then apply the formatting you want.**

   You can format the data in Design view in much the same way you do in Layout view. Just select the field, and then use the ribbon's Report Design Tools |

Format→Font section. Hold down Shift if you want to select (and then format) several controls at a time.

When you're finished, switch to Layout view or Report view to see the result of your changes. *Figure 11-5* shows the final arrangement for the revamped product catalog report shown in *Figure 11-4*.

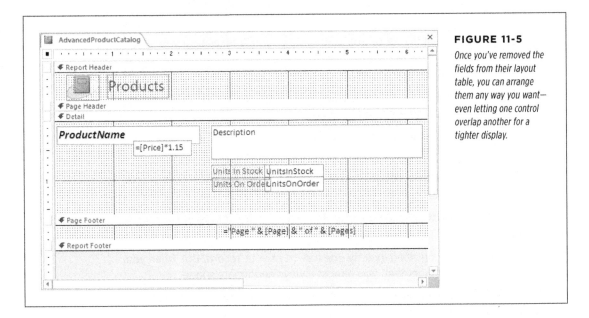

FIGURE 11-5

Once you've removed the fields from their layout table, you can arrange them any way you want— even letting one control overlap another for a tighter display.

Adding More Controls

In the previous example, you used your knowledge of controls to unshackle the fields in your report. However, text boxes with field values aren't the only type of control you can use. Access reports also support labels, pictures, buttons, and other graphical gizmos that can jazz up the dullest report. Some of the reasons you may add more controls include:

- To add more text information, like subtitles, disclaimers, explanatory notes, the company name, and so on

- To draw separating lines between regions in the Detail section

- To draw additional borders around important content

- To pop a logo into the header or footer (The automatic logos you learned about on page 314 are limited to the report header.)

You can easily add a few more controls to your report. Just find the right button on the ribbon. When your report is in Design view, you'll find one-stop shopping in the Report Design Tools | Design tab, as shown in *Figure 11-6*.

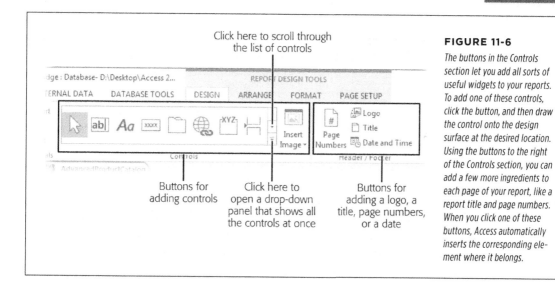

FIGURE 11-6

The buttons in the Controls section let you add all sorts of useful widgets to your reports. To add one of these controls, click the button, and then draw the control onto the design surface at the desired location. Using the buttons to the right of the Controls section, you can add a few more ingredients to each page of your report, like a report title and page numbers. When you click one of these buttons, Access automatically inserts the corresponding element where it belongs.

Some of these controls—like text boxes, checkboxes, and other editing controls—are really intended for use in forms and aren't much use in a report. Others, like buttons and hyperlinks, can trigger useful actions when combined with a dash of macro code (as you'll see in Chapter 15). But right now, you'll want to use only a few controls:

- **The label control** holds small or large amounts of fixed text. For example, all the column headers with the field names are labels.

- **The text box control** holds a dynamic expression—in other words, text that can change.

- **The image control** holds a picture.

- **The line control** lets you draw vertical, horizontal, and even diagonal lines. It's handy when you want to separate content graphically, and borders alone don't give you the effect you want.

- **The rectangle control** lets you draw formatted rectangles around other controls to help content stand out.

- **The page break control** lets you split the Detail section into separate pages—exactly where you want. It's useful when there's a large amount of information in the Detail section, or when you're printing forms that need to wind up on separate pages (like invoices for different customers).

NOTE Although Access has controls for pictures, rectangles, and lines, it doesn't have the Clip Art features you find in other Office applications. So don't look around for fancy shapes and word art—you won't find them.

Once you've picked the control you want, you can add it your report, as shown in *Figure 11-7*.

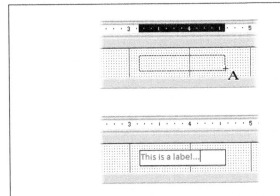

FIGURE 11-7

Top: To add a control to your report, click it in the toolbar. Then, drag the design surface until the rectangle covers the area where you want to place the control.

Bottom: When you release the mouse button, the control appears in the rectangle. Of course, you can move or resize the control after the fact to get it just right. If you're adding a label (as shown here), you need to follow up by typing in your text.

If you're adding a label, you'll want to set the text that appears inside. Once you add the label, the cursor appears inside so you can enter some text. If you want to edit the text in a label later on, click once to select the label, and then pause until the mouse pointer changes into a text pointer (known to techies as an I-beam). Then, click again in the label to start editing its text.

NOTE When you add a new label, Access may pop up an exclamation-mark icon. If you hover over the exclamation mark, you see a warning that tells you your label isn't linked to any other control (like a text box with the value of a field). Don't worry; if you're just adding a basic title or some unchanging bit of text, this situation is exactly what you want.

If you're adding a rectangle, you probably want to set both the line color and the background fill color (using the Shape Outline and Shape Fill buttons in the Report Design Tools | Format→Control Formatting section). If you put two controls in the same place, then Access stacks the control that you added most recently on top of the control you added first. To move a control into the background, select it, and then choose Report Design Tools | Arrange→Sizing & Ordering→Send to Back.

You can also give some controls (especially text boxes and labels) a transparent background, so the content underneath them shows through. To try it out, select the control and choose Report Design Tools | Format→Control Formatting→Shape Fill→Transparent.

Creating a Report from Scratch (in Design View)

So far, you've tried your hand at modifying a simple report by using Design view. But if you don't want to use a layout table, then it's easier to start out in Design view and build your report there. When you build a report in Design view, Access doesn't automatically add your fields to a layout, as it does in Layout view.

To create a report in Design view, you simply need to create a new, blank report, and then add all the controls you need to the appropriate sections. The following steps walk you through the process:

1. **Choose Create→Reports→Report Design.**

   This action creates a new, blank report, and then opens it in Design view.

2. **Choose Report Design Tools | Design→Tools→Add Existing Fields.**

   The Field List pane appears at the right of the window.

3. **In the Field List pane, click the "Show all tables" link.**

   Access lists all the tables that are in your database in the Field List pane.

4. **Expand the table you want to use by clicking the plus sign (+) next to it.**

   Now Access shows all the fields that are in that table.

5. **Drag the fields you want to show in your report from the Field List into the Detail section.**

   Each time you drop a field onto your report, Access adds two controls: a label that shows the field name and a text box that displays the field data (see *Figure 11-8*).

> **NOTE** Access needs to use the text box control instead of the label control to display field values, because the label control is limited to fixed, unchanging text. Only the text box can get live values from a field.

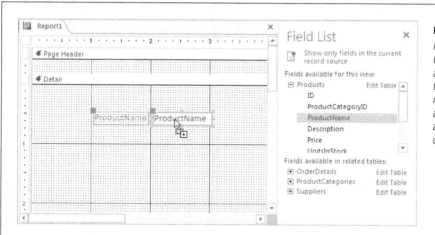

FIGURE 11-8

Here the ProductName field has been added to a new report. As you add the fields you want, you'll need to spend considerable time moving them around the design surface until the report looks right.

6. **Move the field to the right place, and then resize it to the right size.**

   Resizing is a bit tricky at first, because you're working with two linked controls. If you drag either piece, the other moves along with it. *Figure 11-9* shows how to move just the caption or just the field value.

If you don't want the label at all, just select it, and then press Delete.

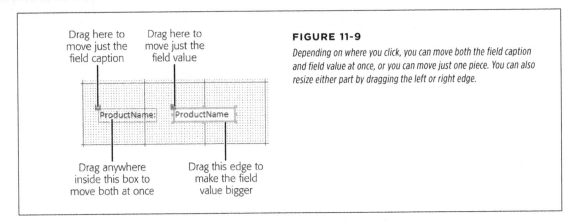

Drag here to
move just the
field caption

Drag here to
move just the
field value

FIGURE 11-9

Depending on where you click, you can move both the field caption and field value at once, or you can move just one piece. You can also resize either part by dragging the left or right edge.

ProductName:

ProductName

Drag anywhere
inside this box to
move both at once

Drag this edge to
make the field
value bigger

7. **Add additional content (like page numbers or miscellaneous text and pictures).**

   The Report Design Tools | Design→Controls section lets you insert a wide range of different controls (page 352). The Report Design Tools | Design→Header/ Footer section lets you add image and text content that repeats at the top or bottom of every page (page 314).

8. **Apply any formatting you want to your controls.**

   The Report Design Tools | Format→Font section has the commands you need to change the typeface, text size, and colors, while the Report Design Tools | Format→Control Formatting section has the commands needed to add borders around a control or to change the background color.

   You can format field values and field captions separately—just make sure you select the right part before you click the formatting command.

TIP You can use conditional formatting to make certain values stand out, just like you did in Layout view (page 336).

---

9. **If you want to use a report header or footer, right-click a blank space on the design surface, and then choose Report Header/Footer.**

   This action makes the report header and report footer sections appear. You can then add controls to these sections. If you decide you don't need the report header and footer, right-click the design surface and choose Report Header/ Footer again.

   You can also delete the page header and footer sections by right-clicking the design surface, and then choosing Page Header/Footer.

NOTE Headers and footers always come in pairs. For example, if you include the page header, you get the page footer, too. Even if you leave a footer blank, it still takes some extra space in your printout. To reclaim unused space, resize the footer by clicking the bottom border and dragging it up.

10. **Resize the Detail section so it doesn't have extra space at the bottom.**

    The Detail section starts out being quite large. If you don't shrink it to fit your content, you'll end up with a considerable amount of blank space between each record in your report.

11. **Save your report.**

    You can save your report at any time by choosing File→Save, or you can close your report, at which point Access prompts you to save it.

The Report Wizard

Creating a report in Design view is a labor of love. Adding and arranging the controls you need takes time. Since the average Access fanatic is about as patient as a caffeine junkie in New York City traffic, Microsoft decided to add a shortcut for quickly generating different types of reports. That shortcut is the *Report Wizard*.

NOTE The Report Wizard lets you more easily create a report that doesn't use a layout, provided you like the preset options it gives you for arranging controls. If you want to create a simple report that uses a layout (as you did in Chapter 10), you don't have to use the Report Wizard—you can create the report you need in one step (page 309).

The Report Wizard asks a few basic questions, and then creates the corresponding report. You can then tweak it to your heart's content in Design view. Here's how it works:

1. **Choose Create→Reports→Report Wizard.**

   The Report Wizard's first step appears.

2. **From the drop-down list, choose the table you want to use.**

   In the Available Fields list, the wizard shows all the fields in your table.

   You'll probably recognize this window, because it's exactly the same as the one you use to start building a query with the Query Wizard.

3. **Add the fields you want to include, as shown in *Figure 11-10*. When you're finished, click Next.**

   You can choose fields from more than one table, provided these tables are related.

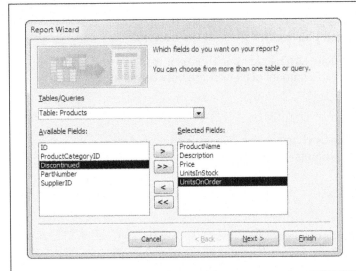

FIGURE 11-10

To add a field, select it, and then click the > button to move it from the Available Fields list to the Selected Fields list. Click >> to add all the fields in one shot.

4. **If your report uses the fields from just one table, skip ahead to the next step. If your report uses fields from more than one related table, you need to answer an additional question about how you want to organize your data. One you've chosen, click Next.**

   You can organize your report by using the parent table or the child table. For example, if you've created a report that combines data from the Product and ProductCategory tables, you can organize your report by ProductCategory (the parent) or Product (the child). Here's the difference:

   - **By the parent table** creates a report that uses grouping. For example, you can use this approach to create a list of products grouped by product category. Don't choose this option yet; you'll learn more about grouping on page 372.

   - **By the child table** creates a standard report that looks like one big table. For example, it creates a list of products with the product category fields added next to every row. Right now, this simple option is a good choice. Later on, you'll learn how you can add grouping to save some space.

5. **The next step asks you if you want to add any grouping. For now, click Next to create a report without grouping.**

   You'll learn how to use grouping in a report on page 372.

6. **Choose the field (or fields) you want to use to sort your report results and then click Next.**

You can sort your results by a combination of four fields, but usually one is enough to get them in the order you want.

7. **Choose a layout option for your report (*Figure 11-11*).**

   Your layout options include:

   - **Columnar** puts each field on a separate row, one after the other. The name is a little misleading—essentially your report has two columns. The first column holds the field caption, and the second column shows the field data. Both columns are in the Detail section.

   - **Tabular** uses invisible layout tables that you explored in Chapter 10. Access transforms each field into a separate column. The field labels are in the Page Header section, while the field data is the Detail section.

   - **Justified** packs the information into the smallest space possible. One row could include several fields. The name "justified" refers to the fact that the data fills the entire width of the page with no spaces. Where one fields ends, the next begins. All the report content is crammed into the Detail section.

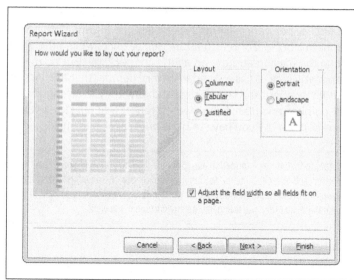

FIGURE 11-11

The layout option tells Access how it should organize your fields in the Detail section.

8. **If you want to turn the page on its side, then choose Landscape orientation, and then click Next.**

   Landscape orientation lets you fit wide tables or large amounts of information, but it includes fewer rows per page.

9. **Enter the name for your report.**

   When the Report wizard finishes, it immediately saves your report.

10. **Choose "Preview the report" if you want to look at the finished product in Print Preview mode, or "Modify the report's design" if you want to change it in Design view first. Then, click Finish.**

Access saves your report, and then opens it in Print Preview mode or Design mode, depending on your choice.

As you can see, the Report wizard really isn't that flexible. It supports only a few types of layouts, and it doesn't let you tailor how Access arranges different fields. However, it may give you a good starting point (and even if it doesn't, it's a worthwhile way to explore report layout in Design view).

■ The Label Wizard

If you have a table with address information (like customer homes, business locations, or suspected UFO sites), Access has another wizard to offer you. The *Label Wizard* pulls address information out of any table you want and uses it to print handy mailing labels.

To make this work, you just need to buy a few sheets of label paper from your favorite office supply store. Label paper varies—some types pack the information in very tightly, so you can print out dozens of return addresses at once, while others use larger labels for putting the mailing address on a letter or package. But no matter what type of label paper you pick, it has a standard *Avery number* that tells Access everything it needs to know about the labels' size, and how they're arranged. You give Access the Avery number, and then it can create a report that puts the address information in the correct place. All you have to do is print, peel, and stick.

> **NOTE** If you have a database that stores information about people, you may have thought about using Access reports to build form letters and other documents. Getting Access to cooperate isn't all that easy. Instead, you'll do better using a real word-processing program like Word. Word includes a *mail merge* feature that can extract data from an Access database, and then use it to generate any document you want.

To create a batch of labels, here's what you need to do:

1. **In the navigation pane, select the table with the address information.**

It doesn't actually need to be address information. If you want to print employee nametags or product stickers, or you just have an insatiable urge to label mysterious items around the house, you can place that data on your labels instead.

> **TIP** If you need to create labels using the information in more than one table, you'll need to create a join query (page 227), and then select that before you launch the Label Wizard.

2. **Choose Create→Reports→Labels.**

The Label Wizard starts. The first step asks you to pick the type of label paper you're using (*Figure 11-12*).

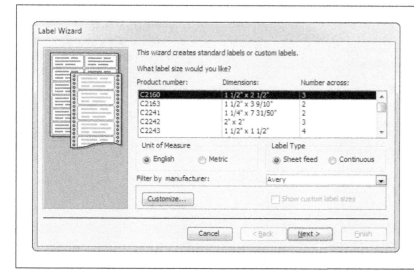

FIGURE 11-12

This example uses the common C2160 type of label, which arranges labels in three columns per page.

3. **If your label paper is one long roll (as opposed to individual sheets), choose Continuous instead of "Sheet feed."**

   Unless you have a printer from the dark ages of computer printing, you're unlikely to use this option.

4. **Find the label that has the same product number as your label paper. Double-check that the dimensions Access shows make sense.**

   Normally, the product number is the Avery number, which is what most people use. (You should have no trouble finding the Avery number on the front of a package of label paper.) However, if your label paper uses a different numbering system, then pick the company that made the paper from the "Filter by manufacturer" list.

TIP If you're creating strange nonstandard labels of your own devising, click the Customize box to show the New Label Size window, and then click New to show the New Label window. Then you can fill in the exact measurements for each part of your label.

---

5. **Click Next.**

   The next step of the wizard asks you to choose the formatting for your label text (*Figure 11-13*).

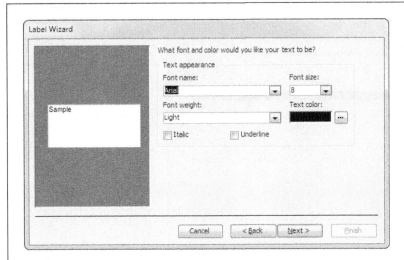

FIGURE 11-13

*Access shows a Preview box
with some text so you won't
inadvertently make a dangerously
oversized label.*

6. **Pick the font, text size, and the font color you want and then click Next.**

    Of course, you can change these details in Design view after the fact, but it's
    better to get them right from the beginning. Usually, you should keep the font
    size that Access recommends—this size fits a good four to six lines of text in
    your label (depending on the label type).

    In the next step, you get to pick the fields that Access should place on the label.

7. **To add the first line to your table, find the fields you need in the "Available
    fields" list and then double-click them.**

    Add the fields in the order you want them to appear (FirstName, LastName,
    Street, City, and so on). As you pick fields, Access inserts a special placeholder
    in the "Prototype label" box. It adds the code {FirstName} to show you where
    it'll place the value from the FirstName field.

    It's up to you to add the spacing you want between these fields. (Usually, you
    just want spaces and commas.) *Figure 11-14* shows how.

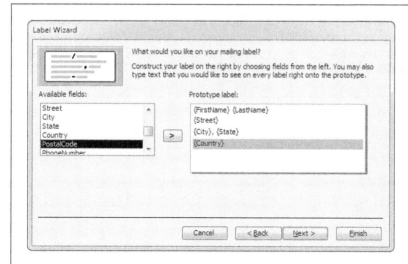

FIGURE 11-14

To space out the information in your label, click between two fields you want to separate in the "Prototype label" box. Then, press the space bar to add a space. You can also add plain text wherever you want (like the word "To:" or a comma).

8. **In the "Prototype label" box, click the second line. Now, repeat step 7 to add fields to this line.**

   Repeat this step until you've added all the fields you need, each on the appropriate line.

9. **Click Next.**

   The final step of the wizard appears. Here's where you pick the sort order, choose a report name, and create your report.

10. **Optionally, pick a field to use to sort the labels, and then click Next.**

    The sort order may or may not be important to you. (It could help you match a label up with a letter, if the letters are also in the same sorted order. But it doesn't make a difference if you're preparing a mass mailing that's the same for every person.)

    Often, people don't use sorting but *do* use filtering (page 342) to get just some labels (like all the customers living in a specific city).

    If you use sorting, Access will arrange your labels from left to right, and then down the page.

11. **Enter your report's name.**

    When the Label Wizard finishes, it immediately saves your report.

12. **Choose "See the labels as they will look printed" if you want to look at the finished product in Print Preview mode, or "Modify the label design" if you want to change it in Design view first. Then, click Finish.**

Access saves your report, and then opens it in Print Preview mode (*Figure 11-15*) or Design mode, depending on your choice. If you open it in Design mode, then you can add extra touches. (You could place a company logo in the corner of the address, and so on.)

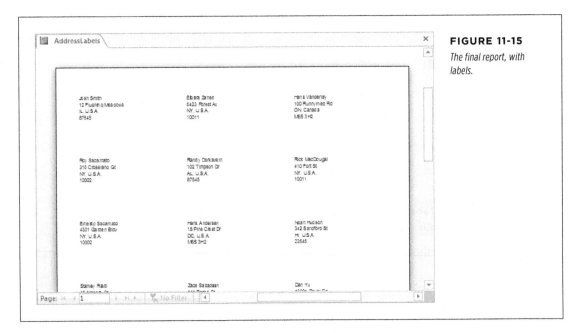

FIGURE 11-15

The final report, with labels.

The label report is really just an ordinary Access report, like the kind you've learned about throughout this chapter. The Detail section contains a template that defines how Access places the fields for a single label, and that template is copied across the form.

The only difference between label reports and ordinary reports is that label reports use multiple columns. That way, the Detail section (which represents the label) can be copied from right to left across the width of the page, and then down the page. This method gives you a tightly packed grid of labels. (Usually, the Detail section is copied in one direction only: down the page.)

You can create your own report that also uses multiple columns to put records in a grid. You simply need to open your report in Design view, make sure your Detail section is very narrow, and then choose Report Design Tools | Page Setup→Page Layout→Columns. This pops open a window where you can set the number of columns, and the space between them. You can also choose whether Access lays out your records from top to bottom and then left to right, or from left to right and then top to bottom. Either way, check the Print Preview to make sure everything fits nicely on the page.

Fine-Tuning Reports with Properties

As you've already learned, you can most easily tweak your report's controls with the ribbon buttons. However, although the ribbon is packed full of useful features, it doesn't have everything. Behind the scenes, each control has a host of low-level settings, known as *properties*. Many of these settings are obscure, and people rarely use them. Some are known only to a small number of antisocial Access junkies. But a few are genuinely useful, because they provide features that you can't reach anywhere else in Access. To hunt down and change these settings, you need the Property Sheet.

NOTE   The Properties window is occasionally useful for report writing, but it becomes much more important when you tackle forms in Part Four and add code in Part Five.

To show the Property Sheet in Design view, choose Report Design Tools | Design→ Tools→Property Sheet. The Property Sheet appears at the window's right side (*Figure 11-16*).

The Property Sheet lets you fine-tune a single report item at a time. You choose the item by selecting it on the design surface or by choosing it from the drop-down list at the top of the Property Sheet. If you want to tweak a specific control, it's usually easier to click to select it on the design surface. The drop-down list is sorted alphabetically by name, and Access doesn't always use the most intuitive names. Sometimes the names match the underlying field (like ProductCategoryID), and sometimes they don't (like Text3).

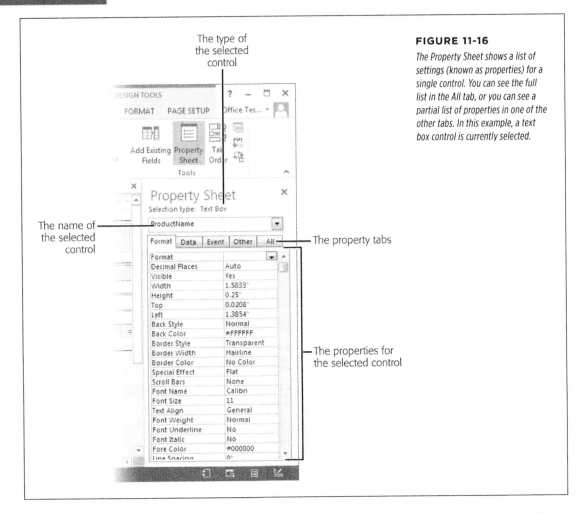

The type of
the selected
control

The name of
the selected
control

The property tabs

The properties for
the selected control

FIGURE 11-16

The Property Sheet shows a list of settings (known as properties) for a single control. You can see the full list in the All tab, or you can see a partial list of properties in one of the other tabs. In this example, a text box control is currently selected.

Most controls have a similar set of properties. To help get around this intimidating long list, the Property Sheet divides it into the following tabs:

- **Format** contains the options you'll change most often, including the font, color, borders, and margins.

- **Data** identifies where the control gets its information. For the controls in the Detail section, this tab identifies the linked field's name. Usually, you don't need to change these settings on your own.

- **Event** lets you attach Visual Basic code that springs into action when something specific happens. You'll learn much more about code in Part Five.

- **Other** includes the Name property, which defines the control name, and a few miscellaneous properties that are more relevant with forms.

- **All** shows the whole shebang.

> **TIP** To get a quick one-sentence description of a mysterious property, click to select it in the Property Sheet, and then, at the bottom of the Access window, look for the descriptive text that appears in the status bar.

Interestingly, controls aren't the only thing you can change in the Property Sheet. You can also adjust report settings (at the top of the Property Sheet, choose Report in the drop-down list), which identify where the data comes from and how you can view or edit the report. And you can tweak settings that are specific to a particular section (like ReportHeader, ReportFooter, PageHeaderSection, PageFooterSection, and Detail), which include page break details and additional formatting.

Of course, it's one thing to know that there are a bunch of settings you can change, and another thing entirely to know what settings are worth tweaking. The Property Sheet is cluttered with a lot of properties that aren't worth your time. In the next section, you'll consider a table (Table 11-1) that lists the most useful properties in reports.

Modifying Common Properties

If you're still a little overwhelmed by the Property Sheet, try the following steps. They walk you through the process of making a change:

1. **Select a control on the design surface.**

   Its properties appear in the Property Sheet.

2. **Click the Format tab, and then scroll down the list until you find the Back Color setting.**

   The Back Color setting determines the color that appears for the control background, behind the text.

3. **Click the Back Color box. An ellipsis (...) button appears in the box. Click it.**

   A small window of color choices pops open. Access divides colors into two sections: theme colors, which vary based on the theme you choose for your report (page 328), and standard colors, which never change.

   If you don't want to use one of the theme colors or standard colors, click More Colors at the bottom of the color window. A Colors window opens, where you can build a custom color by specifying the exact portion of red, green, and blue you want in it (using numbers from 0 to 255).

4. **Choose a color.**

   The new color appears immediately.

You can also use this technique to set the background for an entire *section* of the report. From the drop-down list in the Property Sheet, just choose a section like ReportHeader or Detail, and then follow these steps.

NOTE If you change the background color of a report section, make sure you also change it for all the controls on that part of the report, or they'll have white boxes around them. You can select all the controls you want to change at once by dragging a selection box around them, or you can just hold down Shift, and then click each one. Then, head to the Property Sheet to make your batch change.

In this example, you could change the background color more easily using the ribbon. However, you can change many properties in the Property Sheet that have no equivalent in the ribbon. Table 11-1 lists a few useful examples, all of which you find in the Format tab.

TABLE 11-1 *Useful Control Properties (In the Format Tab)*

SELECTED ITEM	PROPERTY	DESCRIPTION
Text box	Can Grow	If you set Can Grow to Yes, Access expands the field vertically to fit its content. Can Grow is switched on for all fields when you create a simple tabular report, but it's not necessarily on for other types of reports that you generate with the Report wizard. When it's not switched on, Access chops down long content to fit the available space.
Text box	Hide Duplicates	If you set Hide Duplicates to Yes and several adjacent rows have the same value, Access shows the field value in the first row only. Access leaves the column blank in the following rows. This feature works best if your field has lots of repeated values, and you've sorted the report using this field so duplicate values are grouped together. For example, you might use Hide Duplicates for a Category field in a list of products, so you see each category name just once.
Report	Default View	Determines what view your report starts in when you open it by double-clicking its name in the navigation pane. Ordinarily, you start in Report view.
Report	Page Header and Page Footer	The standard setting, All Pages, places the header and footer on every page. Alternatively, you can choose to leave out the page header or page footer on pages that include the report header or report footer.

SELECTED ITEM	PROPERTY	DESCRIPTION
PageHeadeSection, PageFooterSection, ReportHeader, ReportFooter, and Text box	Display When	Ordinarily, these sections appear onscreen and in the final printout. Alternatively, you can choose to include them in either the onscreen representation or the printout, but not both.
Detail	Force New Page	Ordinarily, this property is set to None, and Access packs in as much information as possible before moving to the next page. Alternatively, you can use Before Section to start each record on a new page. The other Force New Page options are intended for use with grouping (page 372).
Detail	Keep Together	If set to Yes, Access never splits the Detail section over a page break in a printout. If there isn't enough room for a complete record left on a page, Access skips straight to the next page and resumes printing the next year.

Expressions

Earlier in this chapter, you learned how to add a label and set its text. But if you look at the controls on a typical report, you'll quickly notice that they don't all use ordinary text. Consider the date or page number information (which appears in the top-right corner of a simple report). Both these details appear in ordinary label controls, but the text looks distinctly different. It starts with an equal (=) sign, which indicates the presence of an *expression*.

Expressions let text boxes and other controls show dynamic values. No one wants to type in a specific date in a report, because you'd be forced to update it every time you want to make a printout. Instead, you use an expression like =Date(), which tells Access to grab the current date from the computer clock and display that.

Expressions aren't new. You learned about them with queries on page 238. However, until now you probably didn't realize that they're equally at home in reports. You can add your own expressions to a report to display dynamic data, or perform calculations based on other fields.

Suppose you want to improve the wedding list by combining the first and last names into a compact one-line display. As you learned on page 238, the & symbol is the ticket for fusing together pieces of text. Here's the expression you need:

```
=FirstName & " " & LastName
```

NOTE Refer to Chapter 7 (starting on page 238) for an overview of expressions, the different types of calculations you can perform, and the different functions you can use with them.

You can't enter an expression into a label control, because a label is limited to fixed, unchanging text. Instead, you need to use the text box control. (Access also uses the text box control to display most fields.)

Once you've added the text box to the design surface, click to select it. The mouse pointer changes into the text pointer. Click again to edit the text, and then enter your expression exactly, remembering to start with the equal sign (*Figure 11-17*).

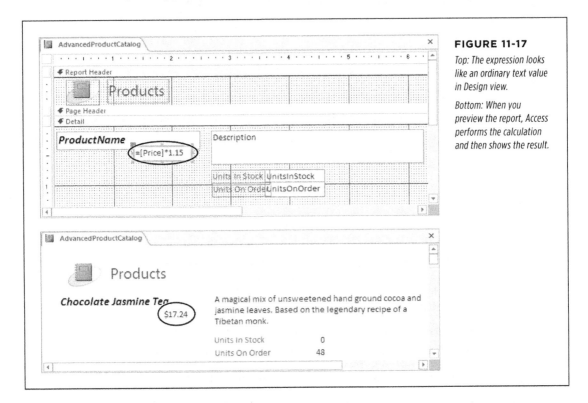

FIGURE 11-17

Top: The expression looks like an ordinary text value in Design view.

Bottom: When you preview the report, Access performs the calculation and then shows the result.

Normally, when there's numeric information in a report, Access uses the number formatting that's defined for your table. However, when you're using a calculated expression, Access shows the result as an ordinary number, even if you want two decimal places and a currency symbol. To fix the formatting, select the text box that contains the expression, and choose the format you want (like Currency) from the Report Design Tools | Format→Number→Format list. (You can also change the format by using the Format property in the Property Sheet.)

Expression Errors

Why does my expression display #Error *when I preview it?*

The #Error code indicates, unsurprisingly, that something isn't quite right with your expression. Access tries to evaluate it, runs into trouble, and shows the error message instead.

You can often get a good indication of the problem by switching back to Design view, and then looking at the offending text box control. Usually, you'll see a green triangle in the control's top-left corner to highlight the problem. Select it, and an error icon appears immediately to the left. You can hover over the error icon to see a description of the problem, and click it to see a short menu of possible fixes that you can apply and error-checking options that can tell Access to ignore this problem in the future.

Access error messages are notoriously unclear, so even when you find the error icon and get the details, you may still be in the dark about the real problem. To get you on the right track, consider this short list of common problems:

- You didn't start your expression with an equal sign.
- You misspelled the field name, or you referred to a field that isn't in the underlying table or query.
- You included a mismatched set of parentheses.
- Your text box has the same name as one of the fields you're trying to use. If you have the expression =UnitsInStock+UnitsOnOrder and your text box control is named UnitsInStock, Access becomes confused. To resolve this, rename the text box by changing the Name property of the text box to something else (like UnitsInStockCalculation), using the Property Sheet. (The Name property appears at the top of the All tab.)

Grouping

Grouping is an indispensable tool for making sense of large volumes of data by arranging them into smaller groups. You can then perform calculations on each individual group. Consider a list of orders in the Boutique Fudge database. Depending on how you want to group your data, you can consider whether chocolate milk outsells chocolate beer, whether customers in New York crave more cocoa than those in Alabama, and so on.

You have three ways to use grouping to analyze information in a report:

- **Use grouping with a query**. In this case, your report doesn't include any details. Instead, it features calculated sums, averages, maximums, or minimums form the underlying query. You don't need any fancy reporting mojo to pull this off—just create a totals query with grouping (as described on page 263), and then use that query to build a report.

- **Use report grouping**. This way, you can organize large volumes of information into subgroups. You still see all the details, but you can use subtotals and other calculations. You can also add multiple grouping levels to pull out buried trends.

- **Use subreports**. This way has the same effect as report grouping. The only difference is that you create your report in two distinct pieces.

Report Grouping

To create groups, switch to Layout view or Design view. Then, find the field you want to use for grouping. For example, if you want to group a product list by product category, you need to group on the ProductCategoryID field. (Or, if you've added a related field to your report from the ProductCategories table, like CategoryName, you can use that instead—it's the same thing.)

To apply your grouping, right-click the field you want to use for grouping and then select Group On. Access sorts your results by that field, and then groups them. *Figure 11-18* and *Figure 11-19* show two reports that group products by category.

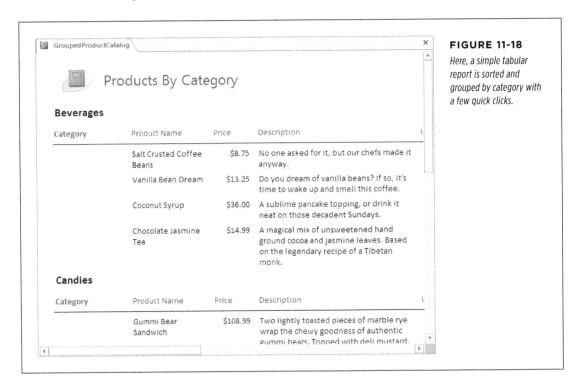

FIGURE 11-18

Here, a simple tabular report is sorted and grouped by category with a few quick clicks.

Grouping works by adding more sections to your report. If you group using the ProductCategoryID field, your report gains a new section named ProductCategoryID Header, which Access places just above the Detail section (see *Figure 11-20*). This group header includes information about the grouping—in this case, the product category. The Detail section has the data for each record that's placed in the group.

NOTE As you'll see later, you can actually add multiple levels of grouping. When you do, Access adds one group header for each level.

When you use grouping, it may not make sense to keep your column headers in the page header section. That's because every group header interrupts your table. Often, you're better off placing the column headers at the bottom of the group header, so they appear at the beginning of every group (not at the top of every page). *Figure 11-18* uses this approach. (*Figure 11-19* doesn't need to, because it doesn't use any headers at all.) Unfortunately, to use this more attractive arrangement, you need to remove your fields from their automatic layout (page 349).

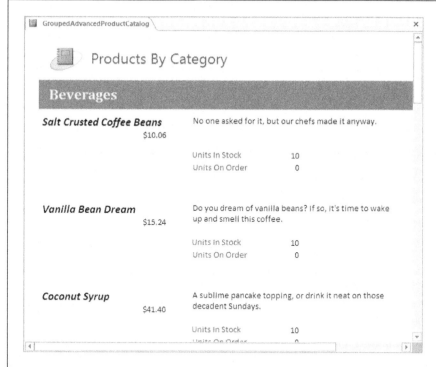

FIGURE 11-19

Grouping works equally well with reports that have complex, non-tabular layouts. However, you could have a slightly harder time seeing where the groups begin and end, so consider giving the category section a different background color (using the Back Color property described on page 367) to make it stand out, as in this example. Or, you can use the line control to create a divider at the top of each category. Figure 11-20 shows this report in Design view.

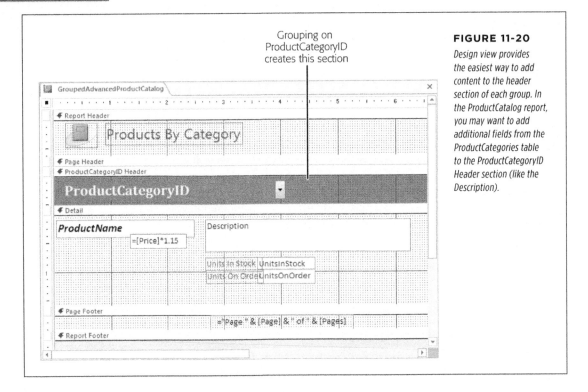

Grouping on
ProductCategoryID
creates this section

FIGURE 11-20

Design view provides the easiest way to add content to the header section of each group. In the ProductCatalog report, you may want to add additional fields from the ProductCategories table to the ProductCategoryID Header section (like the Description).

Fine-Tuning with the "Group, Sort, and Total" Pane

Once you have your grouping in place, you have many more options:

- You can add an extra layer of sorting that sorts each subgroup.

- You can perform summary calculations for each group.

- You can force page breaks to occur at the start of each new group.

You can most easily add any of these features with the "Group, Sort, and Total" pane. To show it in Design view, choose Report Design Tools | Design→Grouping & Totals→Group & Sort. Or, in Layout view, choose Report Layout Tools | Design→Grouping & Totals→Group & Sort.

The "Group, Sort, and Total" pane appears at the bottom of the window. *Figure 11-21* shows what you'll see if you examine the products-by-category report from *Figure 11-19*.

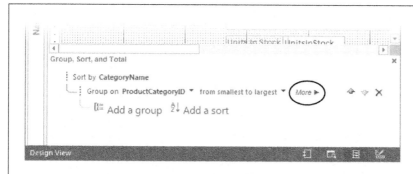

FIGURE 11-21

This report has one level of sorting (alphabetically by CategoryName) and one level of grouping (byProductCategoryID). To see more options for any given level, select it and then click More (circled).Figure 11-22 shows the grouping settings you can change.

The following sections describe your options in the "Group, Sort, and Total" pane:

■ SORT BY

Chooses the field that's used for sorting. In *Figure 11-22*, fields are sorted by CategoryName, and then grouped by ProductCategoryID.

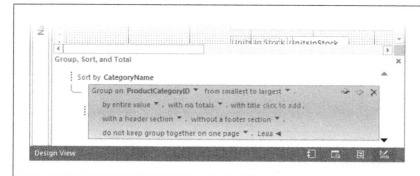

FIGURE 11-22

The "Group, Sort, and Total" pane gives you a quick way to set up subtotals, headers and footers, and page break options for each level of grouping you use.

■ GROUP ON

Chooses the field that's used for grouping. This option lets you switch up your grouping in a flash.

■ WITH A ON TOP / FROM SMALLEST TO LARGEST

Changes the sort order. The exact wording depends on the data type, but you can sort alphabetically for text, numerically for numbers, or chronologically for dates.

■ BY ENTIRE VALUE

Tells Access to create a separate group for every different value in the grouped field. If you're grouping by ProductCategoryID, this option ensures that Access places each category in a distinct group. In some situations, this approach creates too many groups, making it difficult to perform any analysis (and wasting reams of paper). In cases like that, you need a way to create larger groups that include more records. If you're grouping products by price, or orders by date, then you may prefer to group a range of values, as shown in *Figure 11-23*.

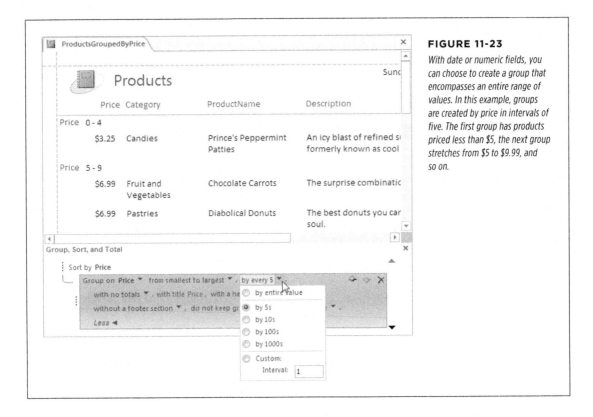

FIGURE 11-23

With date or numeric fields, you can choose to create a group that encompasses an entire range of values. In this example, groups are created by price in intervals of five. The first group has products priced less than $5, the next group stretches from $5 to $9.99, and so on.

WITH ... TOTALED

Subtotals is the most popular grouping feature. Subtotals let you compare how different groups stack up to one another. The "Group, Sort, and Total" pane lets you perform calculations using any numeric fields for your subtotals (*Figure 11-24*).

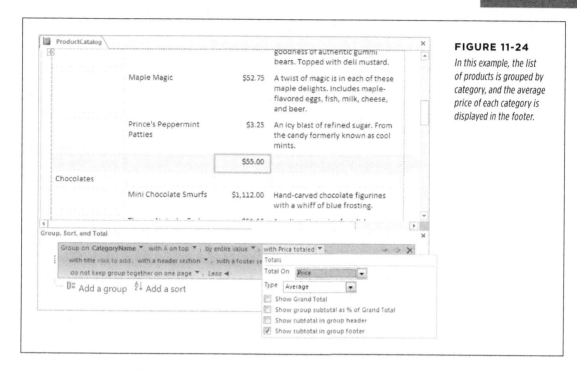

FIGURE 11-24

In this example, the list of products is grouped by category, and the average price of each category is displayed in the footer.

Depending on what you're trying to accomplish, you can count values, add them, calculate averages, or determine maximum and minimum values in a group. You can place this information into a header that appears at the beginning of each group or into a footer that follows at the end. Finally, you can top your report off with a final grand total that adds up all the subgroups.

■ WITH TITLE

Click this section to add a fixed title that appears in the category header, at the beginning of each category section. Of course, you can add a title on your own by inserting a label in Design view, but this option provides a convenient shortcut.

■ WITH A HEADER SECTION / WITH A FOOTER SECTION

You can apply a header at the beginning of each group, and a footer at the end. Once you add these sections, you can place any content you want in them by using Design view. You'll use them most often to display information about the entire group, show subtotals, or draw separating lines with the line control (page 353).

■ KEEP GROUP TOGETHER ON ONE PAGE

This setting helps you prevent orphaned category headers. In the product catalog example, this option makes sure you don't wind up with a group title like Beverages at the bottom of a page, and all the matching products on the following page.

Ordinarily, Access doesn't prevent awkward page breaks. Instead, it simply tries to fill each page. If this isn't what you want, then you have two other choices. You can choose to make sure the entire group is always placed on the same page (assuming it's less than one page long), or you can choose to make sure the header and *at least* one record are kept together on the same page.

One option the "Group, Sort, and Total" pane *doesn't* offer you is forcing a new page break at the beginning of each group. To accomplish this, you need to switch to Design view, select the group header section, and then, in the Format section Property Sheet, look for the Force New Page setting. Set it to Before Section to force a page break at the beginning of each new section, or After Section to force the page break at the end of the section. (You don't see a difference between these two settings unless you're using a report header and footer. If you have a report header and you use Before Section, you end up with a page break between the report header and the first section.)

> **NOTE** You don't see Force New Page setting's effect in Layout view, Report view, or Design view. It appears only when you use the Print Preview feature, or when you actually print your report.

In many scenarios, you'll want a group to start on a new page. This stipulation makes sense when printing the class list shown in *Figure 11-25*. In this case, the Force New Page setting lets you avoid putting two attendance lists on the same page.

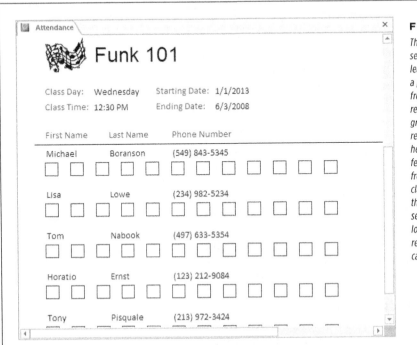

FIGURE 11-25

This class attendance list uses several of the tricks you've learned in this chapter to create a printout that's a world away from a typical report. The report displays a list of students grouped by class. There's no report header, but the group header for each class adds a few key pieces of information from the Classes table. Each class group starts on a new page thanks to the Force New Page settings, and each student is followed by a row of hand-drawn rectangle controls where you can tick off the attendance.

Multiple Groups

Your reports aren't limited to a single group. In fact, you can add as many levels of sorting and grouping as you want, to slice and dice your data into smaller, more tightly focused subgroups.

To add another level of grouping, just right-click the field you want to use, and then click Group On. This adds it to the list in the "Group, Sort, and Total" pane. (You can also add additional levels of sorting by right-clicking a field, and then choosing a sort command. If you began by sorting and grouping your products into categories, you could sort each category by product name.)

When you have more than one group in the "Group, Sort, and Total" pane, it's important to make sure they're applied in the right order. For example, if you want to create a list of all the items that each customer has ordered, you need to group first by order (to group together all the items in each order) and *then* by customer (to assemble all the orders made by each customer). If you group first by customer and then by order, you'll get a nonsensical report that attempts to subdivide each order into customer-specific groups. And unless your business lets customers join together to make orders, this arrangement is meaningless.

To change the order of your groups, select one of the grouping levels in the "Group, Sort, and Total" pane and then click the up or down arrow button to move it (*Figure 11-26*). To remove a grouping level altogether, select it and then press Delete.

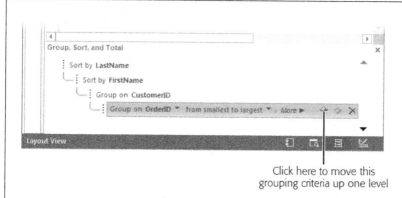

FIGURE 11-26

Access applies groups in a top-to-bottom order. So in this example, the results are grouped by CustomerID, and then by OrderID, which is what you want. The result is a list of orders for each customer Figure 11-27).

Click here to move this grouping criteria up one level

The OrderID header   The CustomerID header

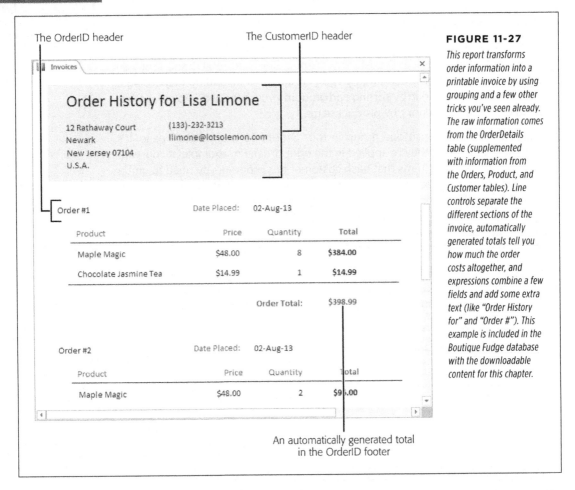

FIGURE 11-27

This report transforms order information into a printable invoice by using grouping and a few other tricks you've seen already. The raw information comes from the OrderDetails table (supplemented with information from the Orders, Product, and Customer tables). Line controls separate the different sections of the invoice, automatically generated totals tell you how much the order costs altogether, and expressions combine a few fields and add some extra text (like "Order History for" and "Order #"). This example is included in the Boutique Fudge database with the downloadable content for this chapter.

An automatically generated total
in the OrderID footer

Each group you add can have a header and footer section and its own set of totals. You add these ingredients by using the "Group, Sort, and Total" pane—just select the appropriate grouping level, click More, and then change the various options, as described in the previous section.

When you have more than one level of grouping, you can hide some of your information so you see just the totals. In Layout view, simply choose Report Layout Tools | Format→Grouping & Totals→Hide Details. If you use this technique on the example in *Figure 11-27*, Access hides the line-by-line order details, and all you'll see is the total for each order.

TIP The invoice example creates a report that prints invoices for all the orders in your database. However, you can use filtering (page 342) to filter down the results to a specific order or customer.

Building a User Interface with Forms

Creating Simple Forms

So far, you've learned how to create tables that house your data, queries that search it, and reports that prepare it for printing. You've also created action queries that automate big updates. But your actual database users (whether that's you or someone else) will spend most of their time on an entirely different job: daily database upkeep.

Database upkeep includes reviewing, editing, and inserting information. Real databases go through this process continuously. In a typical day, the staff at Cacophoné Studios adds new students, the customer service department at Boutique Fudge places new orders, and the Gothic Wedding planners tweak the seating arrangements. Bobbleheads are bought, addresses are changed, purchases are logged, test scores are recorded, and your data grows and evolves.

You can perform your daily upkeep, using the datasheet (Chapter 3), but that isn't the easiest approach. Although the datasheet packs a lot of information into a small space, it's often awkward to use, and it's intimidating to Access newcomers. The solution is *forms*: specialized database objects that make it easier for anyone to review and edit the information in a table.

> **NOTE** Remember, if you're using Access in a business environment, different people probably use your database. You may create it, but others need to be able to use it to perform a variety of tasks—usually data entry and searches. These other folks may not be as Access-savvy as you are.

■ Creating Forms

Forms get their name from paper forms that people use to record information when a computer isn't handy. Depending on your situation, you may create an Access form that resembles a paper form that your company or organization uses. If you're working at a bank, you can create an Access form that lays out information in the same basic arrangement as a paper-based customer application form. This arrangement makes it easy to copy information from the paper into your database. However, most of the time the forms you design won't have a real-world equivalent. You'll create them from scratch, and use them to make data entry easier.

To understand why forms are an indispensable part of almost all databases, it helps to first consider the datasheet's shortcomings. Here are some areas where forms beat the datasheet:

- **Better arrangements**. In the datasheet, each field occupies a single column. This arrangement works well for tables with few fields, but leads to endless side-to-side scrolling in larger tables. In a form, you can make sure the data you need is always in sight. You can also use color, lines, and pictures to help separate different chunks of content.

- **Extra information**. You can pack a form with any text you want, which means you can add clues that help newbies understand the data they need to supply. You can also add calculated details—for example, you can calculate and display the total purchases made by a customer without forcing someone to fire up a separate query.

- **Table relationships**. Many tasks involve adding records to more than one related table. If a new customer places an order in the Boutique Fudge database, you need to create a new record in the Customers and Orders tables, along with one or more records in the OrderDetails table. A form lets you do all this work in one place (rather than forcing you to open two or three datasheets).

- **Buttons and other widgets**. Forms support *controls*—buttons, links, lists, and other fancy pieces of user interface matter you can add to your form. The person using your database can then click a button to fire off a related task (like opening another form or printing a report).

Properly designed forms are what the geeks call a database's *front end*. In a database that uses forms, you can edit data, perform searches, and take care all of your day-to-day tasks without ever touching a datasheet.

Building a Simple Form

As with reports, Access gives you an easy and a more advanced way to construct a form. The easy way creates a readymade form based on a table or query. Keen eyes will notice that this process unfolds in more or less the same way as when you automatically generate a simple report.

Here's how it works:

1. **In the navigation pane, select the table or query you want to use to generate the form.**

   Try the Products table from the Boutique Fudge database.

2. **Choose Create→Forms→Form.**

   A new tab appears, with your form in Layout view. The simple form shows one record at a time, with each field on a separate line (*Figure 12-1*).

   When you first create a form, Access arranges the fields from top to bottom in the same order in which they're defined in the table. It doesn't make any difference if you've rearranged the columns in the datasheet. However, Access leaves any columns you've hidden in the datasheet (page 102) out of the form.

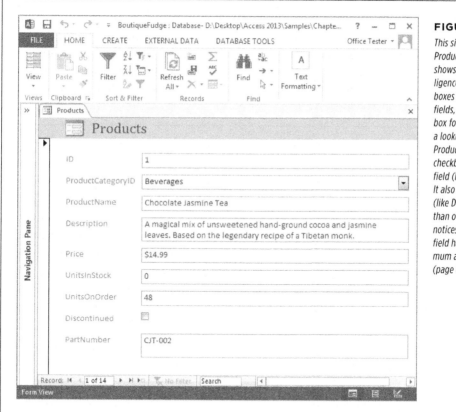

FIGURE 12-1

This simple form for the Products table already shows a fair bit of intelligence. Access uses text boxes for all the text fields, a drop-down list box for fields that have a lookup (in this case, ProductCategoryID), and a checkbox for any Yes/No field (like Discontinued). It also makes some boxes (like Description) larger than others, because it notices that the underlying field has a larger maximum allowable length (page 65).

Form Facts

A number of factors influence Access and affect the way it creates a simple form for a table. Here are the most important:

- **Field size.** Access sizes text boxes based on the amount of data it expects the field to contain. If you don't reduce the Field Size property of your fields (page 65), your form will end up with huge text boxes that waste valuable space. To reclaim the extra room, you have to resize the text boxes by hand.

- **Linked tables.** If you create a form for a parent table that's linked to a child table, you end up with a special type of form that shows related records. For example, if you create a form for the Categories table (a parent of the Products table), your form shows all the category fields, as you would expect, and a grid that lists the linked product records in each category. You'll take a closer look at using

forms with linked tables in Chapter 13.

- **Field count.** If your table has lots of information, Access may decide to create more than one column in your form (*Figure 12-2*). Interestingly, this decision actually depends on two details: the number of fields in your table *and* the current size of the Access window. So if you've resized the Access window to a relatively small stature, you're more likely to get additional columns.

Once the form layout is set, it stays the same unless you take control and start moving things around. For example, if you change the Field Size of a field after you generate a form, the size of the existing text box remains unchanged. Similarly, if you generate a form while the Access window is small, you get several scrunched-up columns of fields. These columns don't change if you make the Access window bigger.

FIGURE 12-2

In this form for the Customers table, Access can't fit all the fields using the ordinary one-field-per-line arrangement. Instead, it adds a second column.

3. **Arrange the fields in the order you want by dragging them around.**

Although a simple form doesn't look like the simple reports you learned about back in Chapter 10, you can actually work with it in much the same way. One of the easiest ways to tailor your form is to drag fields from one place to another (*Figure 12-3*).

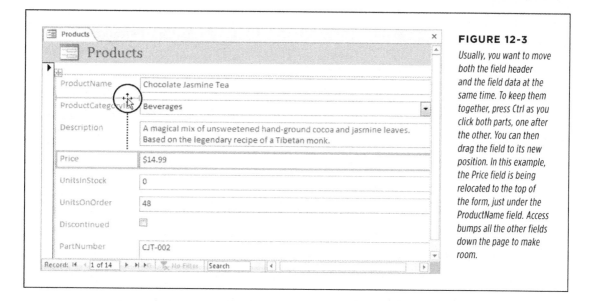

FIGURE 12-3

Usually, you want to move both the field header and the field data at the same time. To keep them together, press Ctrl as you click both parts, one after the other. You can then drag the field to its new position. In this example, the Price field is being relocated to the top of the form, just under the ProductName field. Access bumps all the other fields down the page to make room.

TIP You can add or remove fields in a form in the same way you do with a report. If the Field List pane isn't open, then choose Form Layout Tools | Design→Tools→Add Existing Fields. Then, drag the field you want from the Field List pane onto the form. To remove a field, click to select it on the form, and then press Delete. However, keep in mind that people often use forms to add records, and if you want to preserve that ability, you need to make sure your form includes all the required fields for the table.

4. **Change the widths of your columns.**

   When you create a new form in Layout view, Access makes all the fields quite wide. Usually, you'll want to shrink them down to make your form more compact. It's also hard to read long lines of text, so you can show large amounts of information better in a narrower, taller text box.

   To do so, just click to select the appropriate field; a yellow rectangle appears around it. Then, drag one of the edges. *Figure 12-4* shows this process in action.

NOTE You may like to make a number of changes that you can't accomplish just by dragging, such as adding a new column or giving each field a different width. To make changes like these, you need to understand layouts, which are covered on page 401.

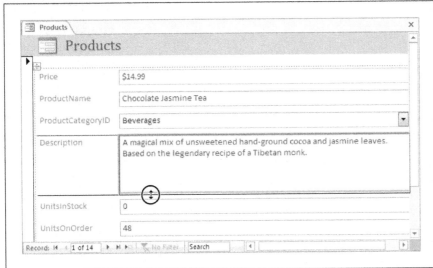

FIGURE 12-4

Here, the Description field is being heightened to fit more lines of text at a time. You can also make a field wider or narrower, but there's a catch—when you do so, it affects the entire column. In this form for the Products table, every field always has the same width. (You'll learn how to get around this limitation later on page 407.)

5. **Optionally, you can double-click a field header to edit its text.**

   This option lets you change ProductCategoryID to just Category.

6. **Optionally, you can tweak the formatting to make the form more attractive, by changing fonts and colors.**

   You can most quickly change the formatting of your form by selecting the appropriate part (by clicking), and then using the buttons in the ribbon's Form Layout Tools | Format→Font section. You can also use the Form Layout Tools | Format→Number section to adjust the way Access shows numeric values. You learned about all your formatting options in Chapter 11 when you built basic reports. You can also use themes to quickly change the font of every control on your form, and the color of the title region. Just choose from the Form Layout Tools | Design→Themes section.

   Often, you'll want to format specific fields differently to make important information stand out. You can also format the title, header section, and form background. *Figure 12-5* shows an example of judicious field formatting.

   TIP To select more than one part of a form at once, hold down Ctrl while you click. This trick lets you apply the same formatting to several places at once.

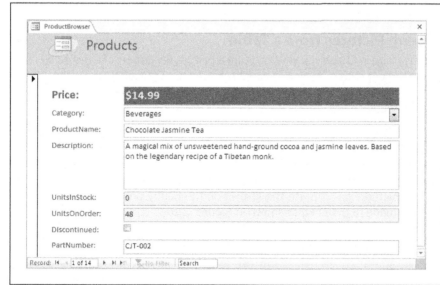

FIGURE 12-5
You can select the field header (Price, for example) and the box with the field value separately, which means you can give these components different formatting. This form gives a shaded background fill to the Price, UnitsIn-Stock, and UnitsOnOrder fields. It also gives a larger font size to the Price field and Price header, so this information stands out.

7. **Save your form.**

   You can save your form at any time by choosing File→Save. Or, if you close the form without saving it, Access prompts you to save it at that time.

Using AutoNumber Fields in Forms

As you already know, the best way to uniquely identify each record in a table is with an AutoNumber field (page 83). When you insert a record into a table that has an AutoNumber field, Access automatically fills in a value for that field. All the tables you'll see in this book include a field named ID that uses the AutoNumber data type.

Only Access can set an AutoNumber field. For that reason, you may not want to show it in your forms. (If you decide not to show it, just select it in Layout view and then press Delete.) However, there are some reasons that you might actually want to keep the AutoNumber field on display:

- **You use the AutoNumber field on some type of paperwork**. Cacophoné Studios puts each student's ID number on their registration papers. When you need to look up the student record later on, it's easier to use the ID number than search by name.

- **You use the AutoNumber field as a tracking value or confirmation number**. After you enter a new order record in the Boutique Fudge database, you can record the order record's ID number. The next time you have a question about the order (has it shipped?), you can use the ID number to look it up.

Depending on how you use the ID number, you may choose to place it at the bottom of the form rather than in its usual position at the top. That approach avoids confusion. (It's less likely that people will try to type in their own ID numbers when they create new records.)

Showing Pictures from a Table

As you learned in Chapter 2, you can store a picture file as part of a record by using the Attachment data type. Forms handle attachments gracefully using the *Attachment control*. The Attachment control has one truly useful perk—it shows picture content directly on your form.

Here's how it works. If your attachment field stores a picture, that picture appears in the Attachment control box so you can admire it right on your form. This behavior is a great improvement over the datasheet, which forces you to open the picture file in another program to check it out. Even better, if the attachment field stores more than one picture, you can use the arrows on the handy pop-up minibar to move from one image to the next, as shown in *Figure 12-6*.

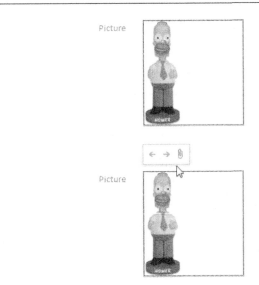

FIGURE 12-6

Top: Here, the Picture field shows a bobblehead doll's picture. Access sizes the picture to fit the Attachment control box (without unnaturally stretching or skewing the picture).

Bottom: When you select the Picture field, you see a minibar with additional options appear right above the image. The arrows let you step through all the attached files for this record. The paper-clip icon opens the Attachments window, where you can add or remove attachments, or open them in a different program. (The Attachments window is described on page 82.)

As you know, attachment fields can store any type of file. If you're not storing a picture, the Attachment control isn't nearly as useful. All you see is an icon for the program that owns that file type. If your attachment field contains a Word document, you see a Word icon. If it contains a text document, you see a Notepad icon, and so on. If your attachment fields don't include pictures, you may as well resize the box for the Attachment control so that it's just large enough to display the file type icon. There's no reason to make it any bigger, because the rest of the space will be wasted.

■ Using Forms

Now that you've created your first form, it's time to take it for a test spin. All forms have three different viewing modes:

- **Layout view**. This is the view you've been using so far. It lets you see what your form looks like (with live data), rearrange fields, and apply formatting.

- **Design view**. While Layout view provides the simplest way to refine your form, Design view gives you complete power to fine-tune it. In Design view, you don't see the live data. Instead, you see a blueprint that tells Access how to construct your form. You'll start using Design view later in this chapter.

- **Form view**. Both Layout view and Design view are there to help you create and refine your form. But once you've perfected it, it's time to stop designing your form and start *using* it to browse your table, review the information it contains, make changes, and add new records.

> **NOTE**   When you open a form by double-clicking it in the navigation pane, it opens in Form view. If you don't want this view, right-click your form in the navigation pane, and choose Layout View or Design View to start out in a different view.

To try out the form you created, switch it to Form view if you're not already there. Just right-click the tab title, and choose Form View.

In Form view, you can perform all the same tasks you performed in the datasheet when you worked with a table. With a simple form, the key difference is that you see only one record at a time.

Most people find forms much more intuitive than the datasheet grid. The following sections give a quick overview of how you can use Form view to perform some common tasks.

Different People, Different Forms

In many situations, you'll want to create more than one form for the same table. That way, you can design forms to help with specific tasks.

At Boutique Fudge headquarters, a single person is in charge of setting prices. This individual (known as the Price Fudger) reviews the product list every day and tweaks the prices based on the current inventory. To do this, the Price Fudger needs just three pieces of information for each product: the field values for ProductName, Price, and UnitsInStock. To streamline this process, you can create a form that includes just these details.

To make this form really practical, you can add some features that you haven't seen yet, but which are described later in this chapter. You can do things such as prevent changes in all the fields except Price to guard against accidental changes, you can pack several records onto the form for a quick, at-a-glance

price setting, and you can filter the product list down to leave out discontinued items. These steps make the form better suited to the task at hand. And if you really want to impress your fellow Access fans, you can throw in the macro and code features described in Part Five to create buttons that perform a task (like jacking up a price by 10 percent) *automatically*.

It's up to you how many forms you want to create. Some people try to create as few forms as possible and make them flexible enough to work for a variety of different tasks. Other people create dozens of specialized forms that can save time. In a large company like Boutique Fudge, each department (like sales, shipping, customer service, and so on) will probably use its own tailored form. Every form guides employees to do exactly what they need to do (and stops them from doing what they shouldn't).

Finding and Editing a Record

Rare is the record that never changes. Depending on the type of data you're storing, most of your work in Form view may consist of hunting down a specific record and making modifications. You may need to ratchet up the price of a product, change the address details of an itinerant customer, or reschedule a class.

Before you can make any of these changes, you need to find the right record. In Form view, you have four ways to get to the record you need. The first three of these methods use the navigation controls that appear at the bottom of the form window.

- **By navigating**. If your table is relatively small, the fastest way to get going is to click the arrow buttons to move from one record to the next. Page 104 has a button-by-button breakdown.

- **By position**. If you know exactly where your record is, then you can type in the number that represents the position (for example, *100* for the 100th record), and then press Enter. If you don't get exactly where you want, then you can also use the navigation buttons to move to a nearby record.

- **By searching**. The quick search feature finds a record with a specific piece of text (or numeric value) in one of its fields. To use quick search, type the text you want to find in the search box, as shown in *Figure 12-7*. If you want a search that examines a specific field or gives you additional options, use the Home→Find→Find command, which is described on page 112.

- **By filtering**. Using filtering, you can narrow down the displayed records to a small set. Filtering's best-kept secret is that you can use a feature called *filter by form* to quickly hunt down a single record. You'll see how that works on page 397.

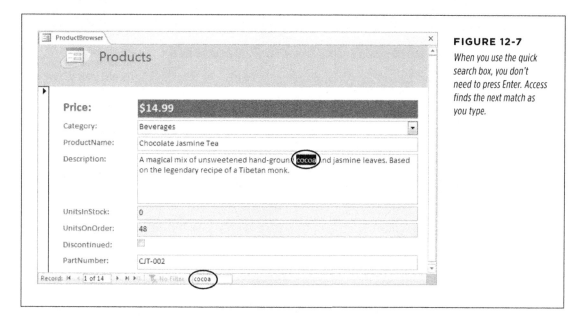

FIGURE 12-7

When you use the quick search box, you don't need to press Enter. Access finds the next match as you type.

Once you've found the record you want to change, you can edit it in the same way you would in the datasheet. If you make a change that breaks a rule (like typing the text *Exasperated Bananas* in a date field), you get the familiar error messages.

Access commits any change you make as soon as you move to another record or field. To back out of a change, press Esc before you move on. When you do, the original value reappears in the cell, and Access tosses out your changes. And if you do commit a change by accident, you can use the Undo button in the Quick Access toolbar (above the ribbon), or press Ctrl+Z, to reverse it.

Adding a Record

As you already know, you add a new record in Datasheet view by scrolling to the very bottom of the table, and typing just underneath the last row. In Form view, the concept is similar—scroll to the very end of your table, just past the last record.

You'll know you've reached the magic ready-to-add-a-record spot when all the fields in your form are blank (*Figure 12-8*). To save yourself the scrolling trip, use the New Record button at the bottom of the form.

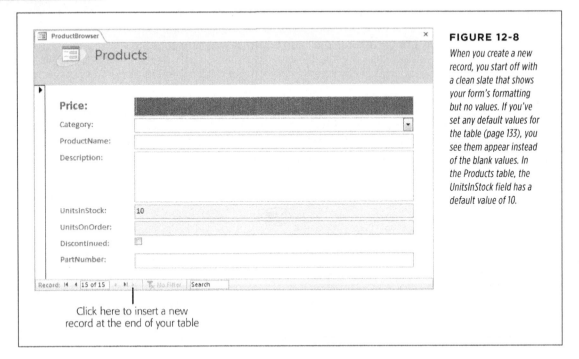

FIGURE 12-8

When you create a new record, you start off with a clean slate that shows your form's formatting but no values. If you've set any default values for the table (page 133), you see them appear instead of the blank values. In the Products table, the UnitsInStock field has a default value of 10.

Click here to insert a new record at the end of your table

If you've decided that you don't want to add a new record after all, press Esc twice. The first time you press Esc, Access wipes out the value in the current field. The second time, Access removes all the other values you entered. Now that your form has been restored to its original emptiness, you can safely scroll off to another record.

If you scroll away from your new record while there's still some data left in it, Access creates the new record and adds it to the table. You can't reverse this action. If you want to get rid of a newly created record, you need to delete it, as described in the next section.

Deleting a Record

When you find a record that shouldn't exist, you can wipe it out in seconds. The easiest way to delete the current record is to choose Home→Records→Delete. But you have another option. You can select the whole record by clicking the margin on the form window's left side. Then you can liquidate it by pressing Delete.

No matter what approach you use, Access asks you for confirmation before it removes a record. You can't recover deleted records, so tread carefully.

Printing Records

Here's a little-known secret about forms: You can use them to create a quick printout. To do so, open your form, and then choose File→Print→Print. The familiar Print window appears, where you can choose your printer and the number of copies you want.

When you print a form, Access prints *all* the records, one after the other. If you want to print just the current record, then, in the Print window, choose the Selected Records option before you click OK.

You can also use File→Print→Print Preview to check out the result before you send it to the printer (*Figure 12-9*). Click Print Preview→Close Preview→Close Print Preview to return to your form.

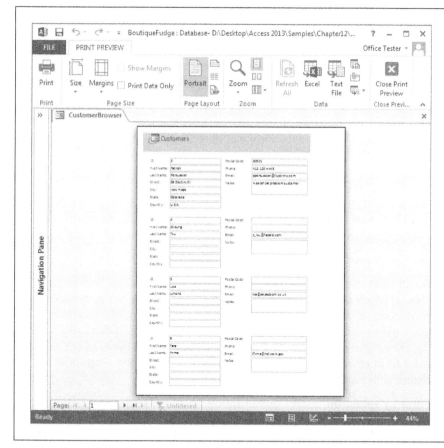

FIGURE 12-9

This preview shows what you'll get if you print the CustomerBrowser form. The printout closely matches the form, with the same formatting and layout. When Access first creates the form, it gives it the same width as an ordinary sheet of paper. When you print the form, Access crams as many records—four in this case—as it can fit on each page.

Although you might be tempted to use forms as a convenient way to create snazzy printouts, you'll always get more features and better control if you use reports.

■ Sorting and Filtering in a Form

Sorting and filtering are two indispensable features that Access gives you with Form view. Learning how to use them could hardly be easier—in fact, you already learned everything you need to know when you tackled the datasheet in Chapter 3. The creators of Access took great care to ensure that filtering and sorting work the same in forms as they do in the datasheet. You use the same commands, on the same part of the ribbon, to put them into action.

Sorting a Form

As you've probably realized by now, forms show your data in raw, unsorted order. So records appear in the order you created them. (The only exception is if you create a form that gets its data from a query, and that query uses sorting.)

Fortunately, sorting is easy. In fact, you can sort the records that are shown in a form in exactly the same way you sort records in a datasheet. Choose the field you want to use for sorting, right-click it, and then choose one of the sorting options. In a text-based field, you'll see the sorting choices "Sort A to Z" (for an alphabetical sort) and "Sort Z to A" (for a reverse-alphabetical sort). You can also use the Ascending and Descending buttons on the ribbon's Home→Sort & Filter section.

For more information about your sorting options (including how to sort by multiple fields), see page 104.

Filtering a Form

Filtering is a feature that lets you cut down the total number of records so you see only those that interest you. Filtering can pick out active customers, in-stock products, expensive orders, and other groups of records based on specific criteria.

In a form, you have the following filtering choices:

- **Quick filter** shows you a list of all the values for a particular field and lets you choose which ones you want to hide. It's easy to use, but potentially time-consuming. If you want to hide numeric values that fall into a certain range, you'll get the job done much faster with the "filter by condition" approach (as described later). To show the list of quick filter values, move to the field you want to filter, and then click Home→Sort & Filter→Filter. Page 108 has full details about quick filters.

- **Filter by selection** applies a filter based on an existing value. First, find the value in one of the records, right-click it, and then choose a filter option. You can right-click a price value of $25, and choose "Greater Than or Equal to 25" to hide low-cost items. For more information, see page 109.

- **Filter by condition** lets you define the exact criteria you want to use to filter records. You don't need to base it on an existing value. To add this sort of filter, right-click the field and then look for a submenu with filtering options. This menu item is named according to the data, so text fields include a Text Filters option, number fields have a Number Filters option, and so on. You can learn more about this type of filter on page 111.

- **Advanced filters** are filters that you design using a window that looks just like the query designer. The advantage of advanced filters is that you can apply filters on more than one field in a single step. To create a set of advanced filters, choose Home→Sort & Filter→Advanced→Advanced Filter/Sort.

> **NOTE** If you insert a new record that doesn't match the currently active filter conditions, your new record disappears from sight as soon as you add it. To get it back, remove the filter settings by using the ribbon: Select the Home tab, click the Advanced button in the Sort & Filter group, and then choose Clear All Filters. Or, use the Toggle Filter button to temporarily suspend your filter settings (and click Toggle Filter later to get them back).

Using the "Filter by Form" Feature

One other filtering technique works with forms: *Filter by Form*. Essentially, "Filter by Form" transforms your form into a full-fledged search form. Using this search form, you supply one or more criteria. Then you apply the filter to see the matching record (or records).

Although you can use "Filter by Form" with the datasheet, it really shines with forms. "Filter by Form" is particularly useful for searching out a single hard-to-find record. (If you want to use filtering to pull out a whole group of records, one of the other filtering options is generally easier.)

Here's how to use the "Filter by Form" feature:

1. **Choose Home→Sort & Filter→Advanced→Filter by Form.**

   Access changes your form to Search mode. In Search mode, your form looks exactly the same, except all the fields are blank.

   If you've already used the "Filter by Form" feature and you're returning to change the filter settings, then you should start by clearing the previous set of filters. To do so, right-click a blank spot on the form surface, and then choose Clear Grid.

2. **Move to the field you want to use for filtering.**

   A drop-down arrow appears in the field.

3. **Click the drop-down arrow, and then choose the value you want to include in your results.**

   The drop-down list shows all the values from the different records in the table (*Figure 12-10*). When you choose one, it appears in the field box in quotation marks.

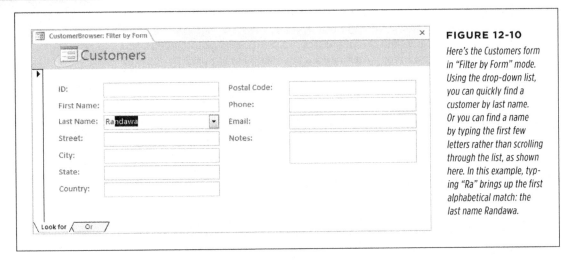

FIGURE 12-10

Here's the Customers form in "Filter by Form" mode. Using the drop-down list, you can quickly find a customer by last name. Or you can find a name by typing the first few letters rather than scrolling through the list, as shown here. In this example, typing "Ra" brings up the first alphabetical match: the last name Randawa.

4. **If you want to apply a filter to more than one field, return to step 2.**

   Use multiple filter conditions if a single filter condition may result in more matches than you want. If you don't remember a customer's last name, you could apply a FirstName filter. But if that customer has a common first name, you may also want to apply a filter on another field, like City.

   If you don't want to use exact matches, you can write in more complex filters by using an expression. Use <10 to find numeric values under 10, and *Like Jon** to find text values like "Jones," "Jonathon," and "Jonson." Filtering is particularly useful with date fields. Page 211 has the full scoop on filtering expressions.

5. **If you want to perform more than one filtering operation and combine the results, click the Or tab and fill out more filter settings (*Figure 12-11*).**

   If you fill out your first search form so that it matches the LastName "Gorfinkel," and the second search form to match the FirstName "Jehosophat," your results will include all the records that have the last name Gorfinkel and all those that have the first name Jehosophat. However, if you put both those filter conditions on the same search form, your matches include only people named Jehosophat Gorfinkel.

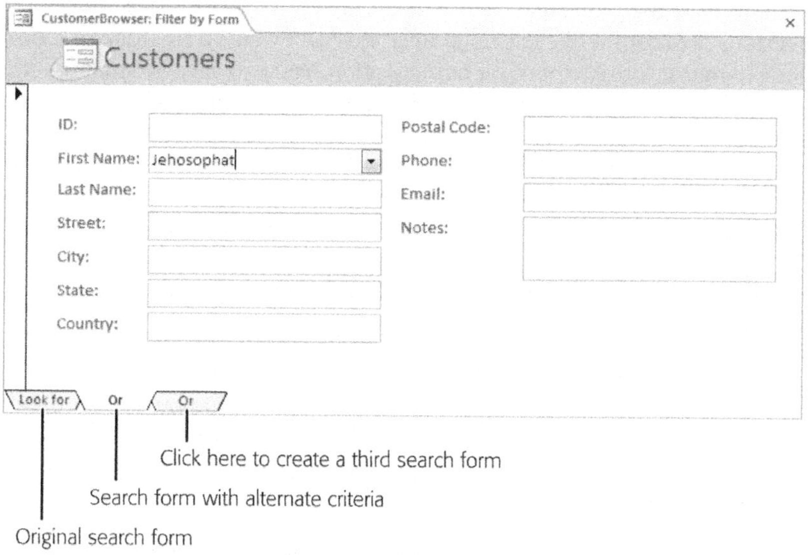

FIGURE 12-11

The Or tab appears at the bottom of the form. When you click the Or tab, a second copy of your search form appears, where you can fill out additional filter conditions. Each time you click the Or tab, another Or tab appears. You can repeat this process to fill in a dozen search forms at once, but there's rarely any reason to go to such lengths.

6. **Right-click a blank spot on the form surface, and then choose Apply Filter/ Sort.**

   Access switches back to your normal form and then applies the filter settings. At the bottom of the form, between the navigation buttons and the search box, you see the word "Filtered" appear to let you know that you aren't seeing all the records.

   If you decide not to apply the filter settings, just close the search form. Access switches back to your normal form, but doesn't apply any filtering.

> **TIP** To remove your filter settings but keep them handy for later use, choose Home→Sort & Filter→Toggle Filter. To reapply the filter settings later on, click Toggle Filter a second time. Access stores the most recent filter settings with your form, so they're always available.

Saving Filters for the Future

One of form filtering's limitations is that Access remembers only your most recent set of filters. If you've perfected a complex filter expression that you want to reuse later, there's no way to save it. As soon as you apply a different filter, you'll lose all your hard work.

Fortunately, you have several solutions to this dilemma. One is to create a whole new query that performs the filtering and then use that query in a whole new form. This way, you can use your filter criteria to perform a specific task, and also customize the way the form works or the way it displays its data.

On the other hand, if you don't plan to use your filtering settings very often, but just want to have them on hand for the next time you need them (or if you need to store dozens of different filter settings, and you don't want to be stuck with dozens of nearly identical forms), there's a better option. You can save your filter settings as a query. Then, when you want them back, you can load them up and apply them to your form.

Here's how to pull off this trick:

1. **Apply your filters.**

   Use any of the techniques described on page 396.

2. **Choose Home→Sort & Filter→Advanced→Advanced Filter/Sort.**

   This command opens a query window. This query uses the same data source (table or query) as your form, and it applies your filtering by using the Criteria box under the appropriate field. You don't need to make any changes in the query window because Access automatically fills in the Criteria box (or boxes) based on the current filter settings.

3. **Choose Home→Sort & Filter→Advanced→Save as Query. Supply a name for the query and then click OK.**

   Although you can use this query like a normal query, you probably won't. To prevent confusion, use a different type of name, like CustomerBrowser_Filter, that clearly indicates this query is designed for form filtering.

The next time you want to retrieve your filter settings and reapply them, open your form and follow these steps:

1. **Choose Home→Sort & Filter→Advanced→Advanced Filter/Sort.**

   This action shows the query window.

2. **Choose Home→Sort & Filter→Advanced→Load From Query.**

   Access shows all the queries that use the same table and don't involve joins.

3. **Pick the filter query you created earlier, and then click OK.**

   The filter settings for that query appear in the query window.

4. **Right-click anywhere on the blank space in the query window, and then choose Apply Filter/Sort to put your filter settings into effect.**

> **TIP** You can use this trick to apply the same filter expression to *different* forms, as long as these forms include the fields you want to filter. In other words, you can use the filter settings that you created for the CustomerBrowser form to filter another form that shows a list of customers, but not a form that shows products.

◼ Creating Fancy Forms

So far, all the forms you've been creating look fairly similar: All the fields get chan-neled into one or more columns of tightly packed information. In many cases, that system works perfectly fine. But sometimes you want to let your inner form designer come out and play.

You've already seen this idea with reports in Chapter 11. Once you break a report out of its layout table, you can create a printout that looks more like a retail product catalog than like a drab table of information. The same principle is at work with forms—once you decide to leave the simple world of Simple Forms, you can create forms that are a lot more original. You can create forms that use white space to break up dense groupings of information; forms that add graphical frills like pictures, lines, and rectangles; forms that pack information more tightly or more loosely; forms that resemble the paper documents they're based on; and so on.

Manipulating Layouts

Like reports, forms use a helpful feature called a *layout*: a formatting container that Access uses behind the scenes to arrange a group of controls. If you widen one field in a layout, all the other fields in it are widened as well. If you move a layout, all the controls move along with it. And if you rearrange a layout, all the controls maintain a consistent amount of spacing.

> **NOTE** Remember, *controls* are the ingredients you can add to a form or report. Controls include things like labels, pictures, and text boxes. You use some controls to display fixed content (like your form title), while others have dynamic content (like the field values from the current record).

Starting on page 407, you'll learn how to get absolute control over your forms by pulling them out of their layouts. Access pros do this all the time, and there's no more powerful approach. However, there are two reasons that you might not want to jump into Design view:

- If all you want is a relatively straightforward data entry form, Design view might be overkill. It takes more work to create an arrangement of fields in Design view than it does in Layout view, and it's more work to modify and maintain your form as your database evolves.

- If you have plans to get your forms online, Layout view is your only option. Access's web database feature (as described in Chapter 20) puts limits on the things you can do with database objects. One feature it doesn't support is layout-free forms. So if you want to design forms that can run on the Web, you need to know how to get the most out of layouts.

Rest assured, if you decide to stick with Access's layout feature, you can still cus-tomize your forms. In fact, crafty form designers know a few tricks to keep using layouts but still make more free-flowing forms. The secret is understanding that a layout is really an invisible table. In a simple form, that table corresponds exactly with the structure of your fields. In this case, the layout is formed out of a fairly standard combination of columns and rows, and each field header or field value takes a single slot in that table. However, you can shape the table into something different in the following ways:

- **Adding extra columns**. Lets you place your fields in discrete groups in different columns.

- **Adding blank columns, rows, or individual cells**. Lets you add extra spacing just where you want it.

- **Splitting and merging cells**. These options let you break out of the rigid grid of a table by subdividing individual cells or grouping adjacent cells together. You can use these options to give more space to some fields than to others.

You perform all of these tasks in Layout view, using the buttons in the Form Layout Tools | Arrange section of the ribbon. The following sections demonstrate how to use these commands to create more nuanced layouts.

■ INSERTING COLUMNS AND ROWS

The form in *Figure 12-12* demonstrates several enhancements over a bare-bones layout. It uses multiple columns to separate fields, and blank rows and columns to add space. Although Layout view doesn't give you as much flexibility as Design view, you can still use it to do a surprising amount of customization.

If you want to try creating this form for yourself, follow these steps:

1. **Start by creating a simple form for the Dolls table in the Bobblehead sample database.**

   Use the standard process: select the Dolls table and choose Create→Forms→Form. Initially, Access generates a form that has just one column.

2. **Add the extra columns.**

   To add a new column in the simple Dolls form, click any field value and choose Form Layout Tools | Arrange→Rows & Columns→Insert Right. Click Insert Right three times to add three columns: one for blank space, one for the fields' captions, and one for the field values.

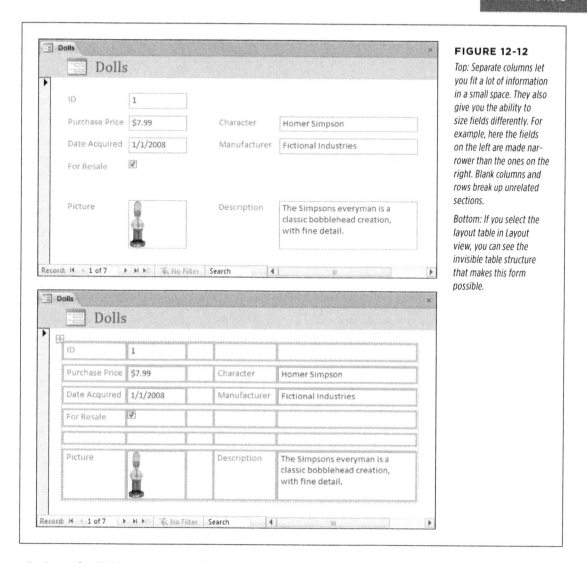

FIGURE 12-12

*Top: Separate columns let
you fit a lot of information
in a small space. They also
give you the ability to
size fields differently. For
example, here the fields
on the left are made nar-
rower than the ones on the
right. Blank columns and
rows break up unrelated
sections.*

*Bottom: If you select the
layout table in Layout
view, you can see the
invisible table structure
that makes this form
possible.*

3. **Drag the fields into the newly created columns.**

   Although you can drag the field header and the field value separately, you can
   get things done faster if you select them both at once. Just click the header
   and press Ctrl as you click the value. Then, drag your mouse to the cell where
   the field header should go (*Figure 12-13*).

TIP If you're really crafty, you can even drag several fields at once. Just pretend you're dragging the top-left cell from your selection to a new place, and the other cells will follow into the rows below and the columns on the right.

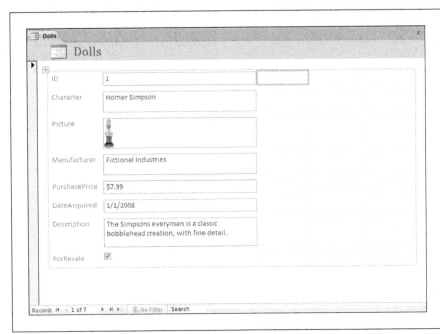

FIGURE 12-13

Access uses dotted lines to show blank cells. Here, you see three blank columns that have been added to the right. The next step is to drag some fields to these cells.

4. **Delete any blank cells that you don't want.**

   In this case, it makes sense to remove the rows that held the fields that you've now dragged to the new column. To delete a cell, click it and press Delete, or Ctrl-click to select several at once, so you can clear them out in one fell swoop.

5. **Resize your columns.**

   Once your data is in place, you need to size your columns to balance out the two field groups and the blank space in between.

6. **Add any extra blank rows you need.**

   For example, to add the blank row between ForResale and Picture, just click the ForSale field and choose Form Layout Tools | Arrange→Rows & Columns→Insert Below.

▩ SPLITTING AND MERGING CELLS

The previous example split a simple form into multiple columns. This gives you the flexibility to resize these columns separately (for example, making the Character field larger than the PurchasePrice field). However, all the values that fall in the same column (like Character, Manufacturer, and Description) are forced to have the same width. Similarly, fields that fall on the same row (like Picture and Description) automatically have the same height. That's just the nature of a table.

To get around this limitation, you can subdivide individual cells so they have extra rows and columns. Or, you can perform the same task in reverse, and group separate cells into a bigger section. With these techniques, you can create forms like the one shown in *Figure 12-14*.

Here's how to create this form:

1. **Start with the form from the previous example.**

   Although you could create a new form from scratch (select the Dolls table and choose Create→Forms→Form), you'll get the job done quicker by starting with the form from the previous example, which already has some of the extra cells you need.

   To create your form, begin by dragging the fields to their new locations. Along the way, split and merge cells to get the right table structure.

2. **Merge cells together if you need to get more space.**

   For example, in the form shown in *Figure 12-14*, several columns are merged at the bottom of the form to create a wide cell for the Description field. To create this effect, Ctrl-click as many adjacent cells as you need. Then, to combine them, choose Form Layout Tools | Arrange→Merge/Split→Merge. You can then drag a field with a large value into the newly merged cell you've created. In this example, that's the Description field.

3. **Split cells if you need to get extra slots to pack information more closely together.**

   For example, in the form shown in *Figure 12-14*, the Picture field is only half the width of the Manufacturer and Character fields. In this example, the half-size Picture field makes sure Access doesn't draw a big border around a small image. However, you can also use the extra space next to it to wedge in more fields.

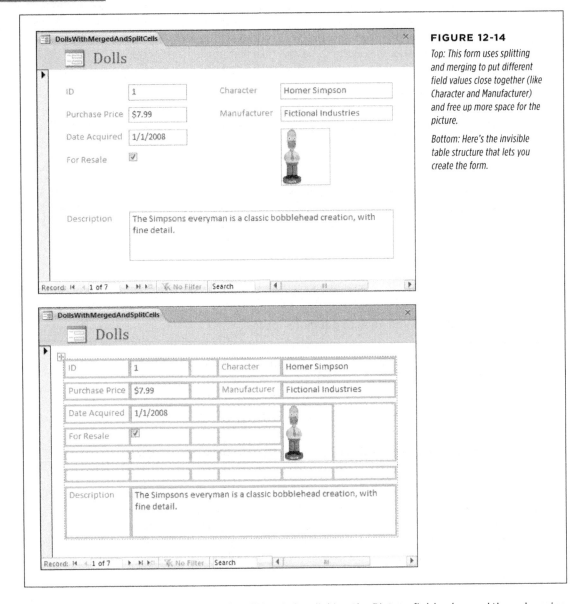

FIGURE 12-14

*Top: This form uses splitting
and merging to put different
field values close together (like
Character and Manufacturer)
and free up more space for the
picture.*

*Bottom: Here's the invisible
table structure that lets you
create the form.*

To add the blank cell, begin by clicking the Picture field value and then choosing
Form Layout Tools | Arrange→Merge/Split→Split Horizontally. The cell changes
into two side-by-side cells, with the picture on the left. You can then choose the
blank cell on the right and further subdivide it (for example, you can split it into
multiple vertical cells if you want to place more fields in this space).

4. **Clean up your form.**

In this case, that means removing the "Picture" caption and the blank rows that were left behind, and resizing your columns. You may also decide to edit field captions (if so, select each caption by double-clicking) to add spaces or to use clearer names.

Liberating Controls from Layouts

If you want to be able to arrange your controls with exact precision, then you need to start by removing them from the layout. (And, as with reports, it takes a fair amount of time to place each control by hand and still make sure things looks nice.)

Before you pull a control out of its layout, make sure you're in Layout view or Design view (by right-clicking the tab title, and then choosing Layout View or Design View). Layout view is a bit nicer to look at, but Design view makes it a bit easier to move your fields. When you drag a field header (like the label that contains the word "ProductName") in Design view, the linked control that shows the field value moves along with it. In Layout view, you need to move both pieces separately, which makes for twice as much work. (Incidentally, you *can* drag the captions and field boxes separately in Design view too, if you understand where to click. Page 356 explains.)

To actually remove a field from its layout, right-click the field you want to reposition, and then choose Layout→Remove. Finally, drag the field to its new location. *Figure 12-15* shows an example of a form that doesn't use layouts for any of its controls.

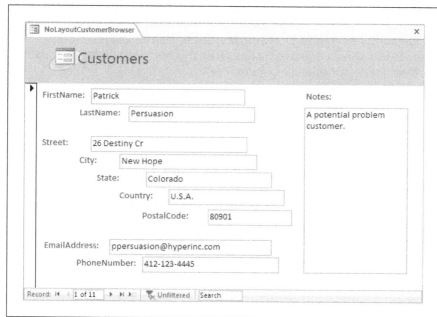

FIGURE 12-15

The weird staggered effect shown here wouldn't be possible with the rigid table-based structure of a layout. But you pay a price for this design (and it's not just eyestrain). If you ever modify the table and need to update the form, you'll have more work to rearrange the fields, since there's no layout behind the scenes holding them all together.

Using Tabular Layouts

Layouts can organize controls in two different ways: in stacked groups (where each field is in a separate row) and in tables (where each field is placed in a separate column). Usually, stacked group layouts are more useful for forms, while tabular layouts make sense for densely packed reports. However, you may occasionally choose to use a tabular layout in a form. You'd do this most often when you want to show more than one record at a time; it's often easier to fit more onscreen when you pack fields into columns.

To change an ordinary form (with a stacked layout) so that it uses a tabular layout, follow these steps:

1. **Open the form in Layout view. Select all the fields on your form by Ctrl-clicking them one at a time.**

   To save some time, look for the four-way-arrow icon that appears at the table's top-left corner when you select something inside it. You can click this icon to select the whole layout in one shot.

2. **Right-click your selection, and then choose Layout→Tabular.**

   When creating a tabular layout, Access puts each field caption in the form's header area and the corresponding field value underneath. You'll need to perform some drag-and-drop fiddling to get all the fields in the right order, and to make them the right sizes.

This process is a bit awkward. Fortunately, there's a shortcut. If you know you want to use a tabular layout, you can create one from the beginning. Instead of choosing Create→Forms→Form to create your form, choose Create→Forms→More Forms→Multiple Items. Doing so creates a form that uses a tabular layout *and* shows more than one record at a time (*Figure 12-16*).

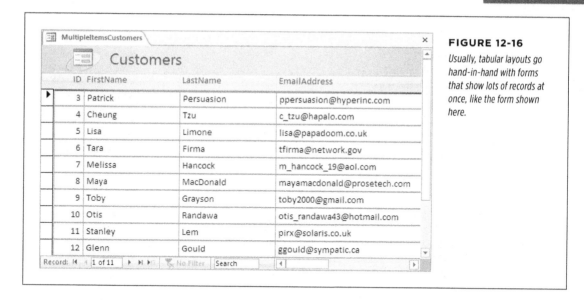

FIGURE 12-16

Usually, tabular layouts go hand-in-hand with forms that show lots of records at once, like the form shown here.

Showing Multiple Records in any Form

You can show more than one record in a form even if you don't use a tabular layout. In fact, as long as your form is fairly compact, it's easy. Here's how:

1. **Arrange your form so that it's as compact as possible.**

   When showing multiple records, they're placed one above the other, as shown in *Figure 12-17*. So the shorter you make your form, the more records you can see at once. On the other hand, it doesn't matter how wide or narrow your form is (so long as everything fits on your screen at once).

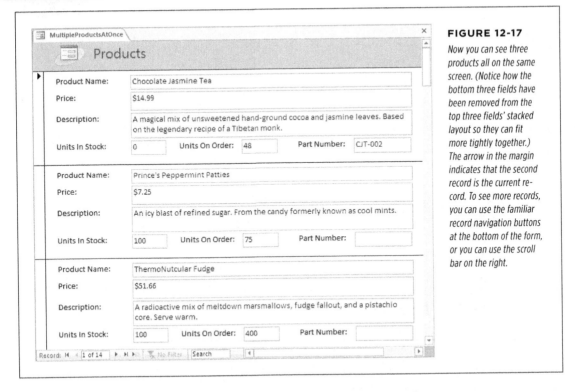

FIGURE 12-17

Now you can see three products all on the same screen. (Notice how the bottom three fields have been removed from the top three fields' stacked layout so they can fit more tightly together.) The arrow in the margin indicates that the second record is the current record. To see more records, you can use the familiar record navigation buttons at the bottom of the form, or you can use the scroll bar on the right.

2. **Switch to Design view, if you're not there already.**

   As always, you can switch to Design view by right-clicking the tab title and then choosing Design View.

3. **Resize your form so there's no blank space, as shown in *Figure 12-18*.**

   As you rearrange your controls, you'll free up space at the bottom of your form. However, it's up to you to reclaim this space by shrinking the overall form. If you try to shrink a form but it remains stubbornly locked in place, there's probably a control on the form that extends into that space. You need to shrink the control first and then the form.

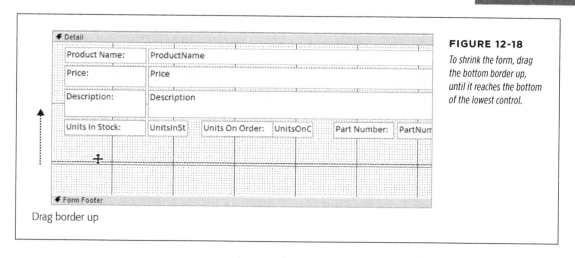

FIGURE 12-18

*To shrink the form, drag
the bottom border up,
until it reaches the bottom
of the lowest control.*

Drag border up

NOTE   To fit more than one record into view at once, the form window needs to be larger than the actual
form.

---

4. **If the Property Sheet isn't visible, choose Form→Design→Tools |
Design→Tools→Property Sheet.**

   As you learned in Chapter 11, the Property Sheet lets you tweak the settings
   for controls and other items. In this case, the setting you need to change isn't
   available in the ribbon. Instead, it's buried in the Property Sheet.

5. **In the Property Sheet list box, choose Form.**

   This action shows settings that apply to the entire form, not just a single control.

6. **Click the Format tab, and then find the Default View setting.**

   The Default View setting appears near the top of the list. It lets you control how
   the form appears when you first open it.

7. **Choose Continuous Form.**

   The most common options are Single Form (which shows a single record of
   information), and Continuous Form (which shows multiple records, one after
   the other). You can also choose a non-Form view, like Datasheet (the boring
   spreadsheet-like tables you learned about in Chapter 3), PivotTable, or Pivot-
   Chart. Finally, you can use Split Form for a view that combines the datasheet
   with your custom form. You'll learn more about this option in the next section.

8. **Optionally, set the Dividing Lines property to Yes to show a thin horizontal
   line between each record.**

Now, when you switch back to Form view, you'll see several records at once, provided they fit into the window.

Split Forms

Both single-record view and multiple-record view have their advantages. With single-record view, you have plenty of room to examine one record, and you don't get distracted by onscreen clutter. With multiple-record view, you can compare the current record to other nearby records.

Access has a type of form that lets you get the best of both worlds: *split forms*. Split forms combine two views of your data in one form. The idea is that you can use the datasheet to scroll through all your records, and use the form to view or edit a record—but all in the same window. *Figure 12-19* shows an example.

NOTE Usually, you'll use the datasheet to move to the record you want to edit and the form to review or edit it, but that's not the only possible setup. You can change records in the datasheet, and you can navigate using the navigation buttons at the bottom of the form.

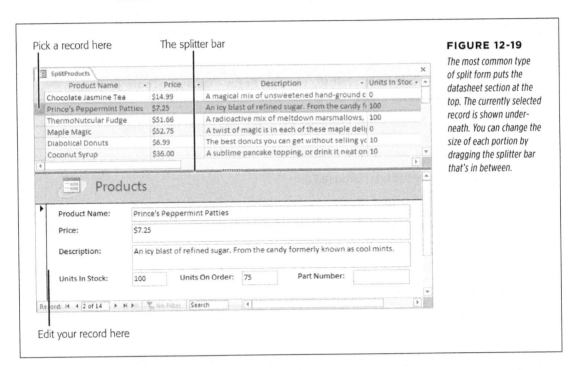

Pick a record here   The splitter bar

Edit your record here

FIGURE 12-19

The most common type of split form puts the datasheet section at the top. The currently selected record is shown underneath. You can change the size of each portion by dragging the splitter bar that's in between.

It's easy to create a split form—choose Create→Forms→More Forms→Split Form. However, you need to know a little bit more if you want to convert an existing form into a split form, or if you want to change how Access presents the two sections of a split form.

The secret lies in changing the form settings by using the Property Sheet. Here's how:

1. **Switch your form to Design view.**

2. **If the Property Sheet isn't already visible, then show it by choosing Form Design Tools | Design→Tools→Property Sheet.**

3. **In the Property Sheet drop-down list, choose Form.**

4. **Choose the Format tab, which includes all the settings that relate to split forms.**

5. **Find the Default View, and then set this to Split Form. Now you get the two-part window shown in *Figure 12-19*.**

Several more settings let you control how split forms work. Table 12-1 has the details.

TABLE 12-1 *Form Properties for Split Forms*

PROPERTY	DESCRIPTION
Split Form Orientation	Using this setting, you can place the datasheet portion of the window at the top (the standard choice), at the bottom, on the left, or on the right.
Split Form Size	Sets how large the datasheet portion of the window appears. You'll need to experiment with different numbers to find what works. Most people prefer to size the split window by hand in Form view.
Split Form Splitter Bar	If you change this setting to No, there won't be a splitter bar in between the two portions of the window. You (or the person using the form) can't change the space allocated to each portion by dragging the splitter bar. Instead, you'll be stuck with the size that's specified in the Split Form Size setting.
Save Splitter Bar Position	If you change this setting to Yes, every time you move the splitter bar, the datasheet size is recorded in the Split Form Size setting. The next time you open the form, the splitter bar is positioned where it was most recently. If you change this setting to No, Access doesn't save your position changes. The splitter bar reverts to its original position, as set in the Split Form Size property.
Split Form Datasheet	Change this setting to Read Only if you want to prevent people from changing data in the datasheet section of the window. (They can still use the datasheet to navigate from one record to another.) Doing so is one way to prevent errors caused by accidental key presses. If you want to prevent edits altogether, use the Allow Edits, Allow Deletions, and Allow Additions settings described in Table 12-2.

PROPERTY	DESCRIPTION
Split Form Printing	Tells Access whether to use the Datasheet view (Datasheet Only) or the Form view (Form Only) to create a printout. The standard setting is Form Only, which means Access organizes the information in your printout to fit your form's layout.

More Useful Form Properties

So far, you've used the Property Sheet to change the view of your form, letting an ordinary form show multiple items or a split view. However, the Property Sheet is packed with many more settings. Some are useful; others you'll almost never touch. Table 12-2 lists a few more settings that may come in handy.

TABLE 12-2 *Useful Form Properties*

PROPERTY	TAB	DESCRIPTION
Record Source	Data	Where the data comes from. This property is usually the name of a table or query in the database. However, you can also build a new query that's just for this form, and doesn't appear anywhere else in your database. (To do that, click in this box, then click the ellipsis (...) button to load the query designer.) if you're technically inclined, you can type a new SQL command (page 220) directly into this field.
Filter	Data	The filter expression that's used to limit results. You can set this field by hand, or build a filter expression by using the ribbon, as described on page 396.
Filter On Load	Data	If set to Yes, the filter expression is applied as soon as you open the form. If No, the filter expression is stored, but not applied until you choose Home→Sort & Filter→Advanced→Apply Filter/Sort.
Order By	Data	The sorting expression you use to order results. You can set this field by hand, or set the sort order by using the ribbon, as described on page 396.
Order By On Load	Data	If set to Yes, Access applies the sort order as soon as you open the form. If No, the sort order is stored but not applied. That option isn't particularly useful—unless you open the Property Sheet again and set Order By On Load back to Yes, the stored sort order won't ever come into effect.
Allow Filters	Data	If set to No, you can't use any of the filtering commands described in this chapter. Instead, you'll always see all the records.

PROPERTY	TAB	DESCRIPTION
Caption	Format	The text that appears in the tab title (or in the window caption, if you're using overlapping windows instead of tabbed documents). If you leave this blank, Access uses the form's name as the caption.
Allow [...] View	Format	These settings let you turn off a particular view. For example, if you set Allow Layout View to No, you don't see the option for switching your form to Layout view.
Allow Edits	Data	If set to No, you can't change any data in the form. However, you can still add a new record with all-new data. The standard option is Yes.
Allow Deletions	Data	If set to No, you can't delete any record while using this form. The standard option is Yes.
Allow Additions	Data	If set to No, you can't insert a new record with this form. The standard option is Yes.
Data Entry	Data	If set to Yes, this form can *only* be used to add new records. When you switch to Form view, you don't see any of the existing records. Instead, you see a blank slate where you can add a new record. As you add new records, they remain visible—at least until you close the form and reopen it.
Record Selectors	Format	If set to No, your form doesn't include the margin on the left. This margin has two roles. First, it shows an arrow next to the current record (which is useful in forms that show several records at a time). Second, if you click the margin, you can select the entire record (after which you can quickly delete it with the Delete key).
Navigation Buttons	Format	If set to No, your form doesn't include the handy navigation controls at the bottom that let you jump from record to record. You're most likely to use this option if you're designing a form with a radically different appearance and you don't want any of the Access staples, or if you're creating your own navigation buttons that use VBA code.

NOTE Some form properties apply only in the rare case that you're using free-floating windows (page 49). In this situation, you can choose whether the window is automatically centered (Auto Center), whether it can be resized (Border Style), whether it includes minimize and maximize icons (Min Max Buttons), and so on. These properties have no effect if your database is using the more standard tabbed windows.

The Access Form Family

Access forms manage to please just about everyone. If you're in a hurry, you can create a readymade form with a basic layout and add a dash of formatting. Or, if you're feeling a creative buzz coming on, you can pull your fields out of the standard layouts and place them absolutely anywhere. In other words, forms are flexible—time-pressed business types get the convenience they need, while serious artistes get the creative control they demand.

Here's a roundup of all your form choices:

- **A simple form** shows one record at a time in a basic stacked layout. To create a simple form, select a table and choose Create→Forms→Form. Or choose Create→ Forms→Blank Form to start from scratch in Layout view.

- **A layout-less form** lets you place controls anywhere you want on a form. It's up to you whether you want to show a single record at once, or several records at a time. When creating a layout-less form, you need to do all the work. You can get started by choosing Create→Forms→Form Design.

- **A tabular form** shows records in a tabular layout. Usually, tabular forms show several records at once (which gives the appearance of a table). To quickly create one of these

babies, choose Create→Forms→More Forms→Multiple Items.

- **A datasheet form** looks exactly like the Datasheet view you get with a table. This form isn't as powerful as other form types, but it's still useful if you want a customized datasheet-like view of your data. You can create a datasheet form that shows fewer columns, uses filtering to hide certain records, prevents record insertions, uses different formatting, and so on. To create a datasheet form, choose Create→Forms→More Forms→Datasheet.

- **A split form** combines two types of form in one window. One portion of the window shows the current record in a simple form. The other portion of the window shows a datasheet with several records. To create a split form, choose Create→Forms→More Forms→Split Form.

- **A modal dialog** is a special type of form. Rather than show data from a table, the modal dialog asks you a question. The idea is that you can pop it up at some critical moment as part of an automated task. To create a modal form, you choose Create→Forms→More Forms→Modal Dialog. To use a modal form, you'll need to mix in some VBA code. You'll see an example that uses a modal form on page 627.

■ The Form Wizard

By now, you've learned how to create a number of common forms. Access gives you one other way to build a form: using the Form Wizard. The Form Wizard has an uncanny similarity to the Report Wizard you used in Chapter 11. It asks you a series of questions and then builds a form to match. However, the questions are fairly rudimentary, and the form it builds is little more than a good starting point for further customization.

Here's how to put the Form Wizard through its paces:

1. **Choose Create→Forms→Form Wizard.**

   The first step of the Form Wizard appears.

2. **From the drop-down list, choose the table you want to use.**

In the Available Fields list, the wizard shows all the fields that are in your table.

3. **Add the fields you want to include, as shown in _Figure 12-20_. When you're finished, click Next.**

You can choose fields from more than one table, provided these tables are related.

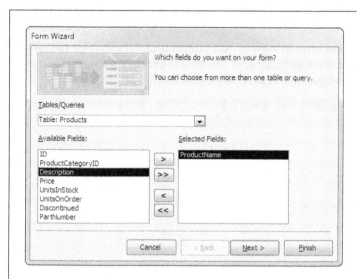

FIGURE 12-20

To add a field, select it, and then click the > button to move it from the Available Fields list to the Selected Fields list. To add all the fields, click >>.

4. **Choose a layout option for your form.**

Your layout options include:

- **Columnar** creates a form with a stacked layout. It's similar to clicking Create→Forms→Form in the ribbon.

- **Tabular** creates a form with a tabular layout. It's similar to clicking Create→ Forms→More Forms→Multiple Items in the ribbon.

- **Datasheet** creates a datasheet form. It's similar to selecting Create→ Forms→More Forms→Datasheet in the ribbon.

- **Justified** creates a form that doesn't use any set layout. Instead, it packs controls closely together, combining several fields on a single line if they're small enough to fit. A justified form is the only kind of form you can't create directly from the ribbon by using another command. It's similar to the layout-less forms you designed on page 407.

NOTE Justified forms are difficult to modify later. For example, if you need to add a field into the middle of a layout form, you're stuck with the painstaking task of moving many more fields out of the way to new positions. Often it's easier to recreate the form from scratch using the wizard.

5. **Click Next.**

   The final step of the Form Wwizard appears.

6. **Enter a name for your form.**

   When the Form Wizard finishes, it immediately saves your form, using this name.

7. **Choose "Open the form to view or edit information" if you want to start using your form to work with data, or "Modify the form's design" if you want to adjust it in Design view first. Then, click Finish.**

   Access saves your form and opens it in Form view or Design view, depending on your choice.

Designing Advanced Forms

As you learned in the previous chapter, forms can streamline day-to-day tasks and even give your database a sharp, distinctive look. To be a master database builder, you need to be able to craft top-notch forms.

In this chapter, you'll take form building to the next level with a whole new arsenal of techniques. First, you'll learn how to create a form in the no-holds-barred Design view, where you can tweak and polish every square inch of your form. Then, you'll take a tour of Access's different controls, and jazz up your form with links, tabbed panels, and buttons. You'll also learn how to work with linked tables by creating special types of forms called *subforms* that work in harmony with other forms.

■ Customizing Forms in Design View

In the previous chapter, you learned how to quickly create different forms using the ribbon's buttons and the Form wizard. But serious form gurus take a different approach—they build a form by hand. You go about this task in two ways:

- **Create a form in Layout view**. Choose Create→Forms→Blank Form. Then, drag the fields you want from the Field List pane onto your form (*Figure 13-1*). You learned everything you need to pull this off in Chapter 12. You can quickly create a standard form with a stacked or tabular layout, but it doesn't give you any extra frills.

- **Create a form in Design view**. Choose Create→Forms→Form Design. Now you'll start with a blank form in the design window. You can drag fields onto your form from the Field List pane (just as you do in Layout view), and you can add a wide variety of more specialized controls from the ribbon.

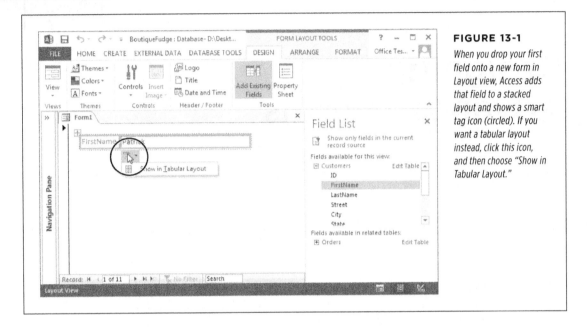

FIGURE 13-1

When you drop your first field onto a new form in Layout view, Access adds that field to a stacked layout and shows a smart tag icon (circled). If you want a tabular layout instead, click this icon, and then choose "Show in Tabular Layout."

NOTE If you don't see the Field List pane, choose Design→Tools→Add Existing Fields (while in Design view or Layout view).

Of course, while you're working with a form, you can easily jump back and forth between the two views. (Just right-click the tab title and choose the view you want, or click the view buttons at the window's bottom-right corner.) You can add fields to your form using either view. However, when you add fields in Layout view, Access automatically positions them in a layout. When you add fields in Design view, they start out layout-free. Access assumes that people who use Design view want more control over how their fields are placed.

There's another, more important difference between Layout view and Design view. In Design view, you have access to a greater selection of controls. These controls make the difference between the cookie-cutter forms Access creates automatically, and forms that exhibit your own style.

Form Sections: The Different Parts of Your Form

In Chapter 11, you learned that a report is divided into separate sections (like a report header, a details section, a report footer, and so on), each of which appears in a specific place. The same is true for forms. However, newly created forms start life with only one section: the Details section, which defines the content for each record.

If you want to add a title or logo at the top of your form, or some sort of summary information or message at the bottom, you'll want to include a header and footer section. To add these elements to your form, right-click anywhere on the form's surface, and then choose Page Header/Footer.

When working with form sections, remember to keep them small (as shown in *Figure 13-2*). Each form section should be just large enough to fit the content you're displaying. An oversized form with a lot of blank space looks unprofessional. Also, you'll end up with unnecessary scroll bars on your form's sides.

TIP You can't make a form smaller than the controls it contains. If Access doesn't let you resize a form, then something, somewhere, is still too big. (If all else fails, check that you don't have a large box in the form header or form footer sections.)

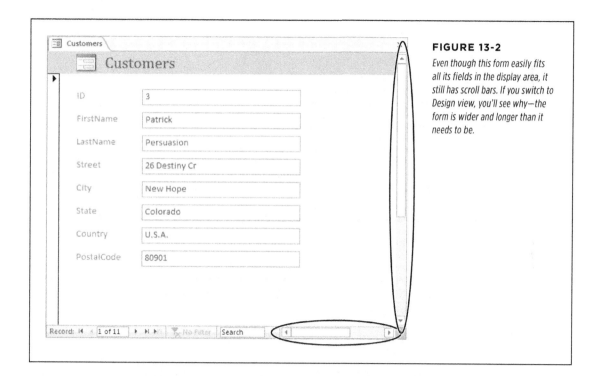

FIGURE 13-2

Even though this form easily fits all its fields in the display area, it still has scroll bars. If you switch to Design view, you'll see why—the form is wider and longer than it needs to be.

NOTE If your database is set to use overlapping windows instead of tabs (page 49), you'll see a slightly different problem—your form windows are unnecessarily large. In fact, they may not even fit in the main Access window, in which case Access chops off the edges.

Adding Controls to Your Form

You first learned about controls—graphical widgets like labels and text boxes—when you created advanced reports in Chapter 11. Access gives you the same ability to use controls with forms. In fact, you use the same ribbon section to add them. However, many of the controls that didn't make much sense with reports really shine with forms.

NOTE Behind the scenes, everything on a form is actually a control. Each time you add a field, you end up with two linked controls: a label that displays the field name, and a text box that holds the field value.

One of the simplest and most useful controls is the humble label. Using the label, you can add formatted text anywhere on your form. You could choose to use labels to highlight additional instructions, as shown in *Figure 13-3*.

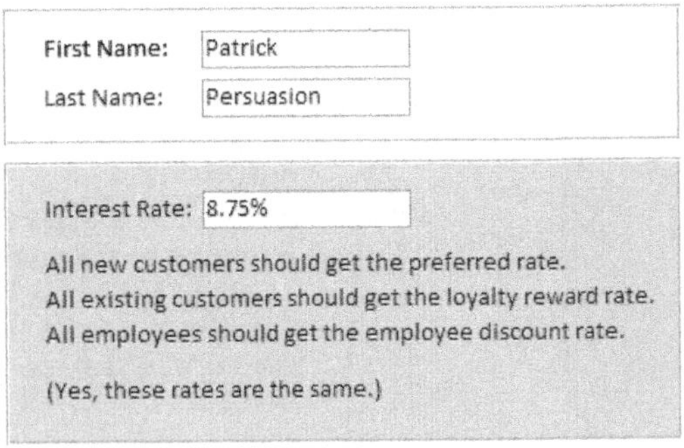

First Name: Patrick
Last Name: Persuasion

Interest Rate: 8.75%

All new customers should get the preferred rate.
All existing customers should get the loyalty reward rate.
All employees should get the employee discount rate.

(Yes, these rates are the same.)

FIGURE 13-3

Use labels to add helpful instructions (or cheeky commentary) to your forms. Line and rectangle controls add a little polish.

To add a control, follow these steps:

1. **Head to the ribbon's Form Design Tools | Design→Controls section.**

   The Controls section has one-stop shopping for all the controls you can use.

TIP It's equally valid to insert many controls in Layout view, using the ribbon's Form Layout Tools | Design→Controls section. These tools are particularly handy if you want to add a control into a layout table, so you don't need to fiddle with its exact position and size. However, the Controls section in Layout view leaves out quite a few controls in an attempt to make Layout view seem simpler to use than Design view. For that reason, this book assumes you mostly add your controls in Design view.

2. **Optionally, switch on the Use Control Wizards button.**

   Some types of controls, like buttons and lists, come equipped with helpful wizards. As soon as you drop one on your form, the wizard pops up to help you perfect it. Ordinarily, wizards are switched on. However, control experts who know exactly what they want may find that the wizards just slow them down.

   To see the Use Controls Wizards button, head to the Form Design Tools | Design→Controls section of the ribbon, and click the drop-down arrow to the right of the control gallery. When the Use Control Wizards button is *not* high-lighted, the Control wizards leave you alone.

3. **Click the icon for the control you want.**

   On most people's screens, Access can't fit the control name on the ribbon's control button. (Thirty-inch monitor owners, congratulate yourselves and skip to the next paragraph.) Hover over each control icon for a moment, and Access displays the control name in a tooltip.

   Once you click your icon, it remains highlighted. Your mouse cursor changes to a cross with a small picture of the control superimposed. That change is your indication that your control is ready and waiting for you to drop it onto the form.

TIP If this is your first time experimenting with controls, why not try the label—it's easy to master, and genuinely useful.

---

4. **To place your control on the form, drag the mouse cursor to draw the control on the form.**

   If you don't get it right the first time, you can always drag a control to a new position, or drag its borders to resize it.

   If you decide that you don't want to add the control you picked, then just press Esc, or click the arrow at the far left of the control gallery. Either way, your mouse pointer returns to normal, and you can now click the form to select an existing control.

5. **If your control has a Control wizard and you choose to use Control Wizards (see step 2), the wizard appears now.**

   Answer all the questions to configure your control, or just press Esc to skip out of the wizard, and do all the configuration on your own.

6. **If you're adding a label, supply some text for the control.**

   After you drop a label onto your form, Access waits for you to type in some text (which is set in the Caption property). If you don't type anything for your label, Access assumes you don't really want the label, and just gets rid of it.

Bound Controls

A *bound* control is a control that displays the value in a database field. (It's called a bound control because it's "bound"—tightly linked—to the appropriate field in your table.) The most familiar example is the text box, but other bound controls include the checkbox, the list box, and so on.

When you add a bound control, you need to specify the linked field so Access knows what to display. You can most easily add a bound control by dragging a field from the Field List pane and letting Access create the control for you. However, there's no reason you can't choose to create a bound control by hand.

Begin by dropping the right control type (like a text box) onto your form. Then, select the Data tab and look for the Control Source setting. This setting is where you fill in the corresponding field. For example, a text box with a Control Source set to

ProductName displays the contents of the ProductName field on your form.

Of course, this procedure works only if the form's data source—the table *or* query on which you're building the form—has the field you want to use. To change a form's data source, select Form in the Property Sheet, click the Data tab, and then look for the Record Source property. The Record Source property has the name of the linked table or query or a SQL select command (page 220) that gets the records you need. To choose a different table or query, type in its name. Or, click the ellipsis button in the Record Source box to open a query window that lets you pick and choose exactly the fields you want to use, from as many linked tables as necessary, with the exact filtering and sorting options you want.

7. **If the Property Sheet isn't already visible (at the right side of the window), click Form Design Tools | Design→Tools→Property Sheet to show it.**

   To configure the control's many settings, or properties, you need to use the Property Sheet.

8. **Change the appropriate settings in the Property Sheet.**

   If you've added a bound control (see the box above), select the Data tab, and then set the Control Source field to the name of the field you want to display.

TIP If you have a label control that doesn't fit all the text you've entered, you can bump its size up in one step. Just right-click the control, and then choose Size→To Fit. Access resizes the label so it's just large enough to fit all its content. Don't try this with other controls like text boxes—it won't work.

---

9. **Optionally, give your control a better name by setting the Name property (in the Other tab).**

   If you've just created a new label, Access bestows a name like "Label46." If you want to honor your control with something more becoming, just change the text in the Name property. You'll have an easier time finding your control in the drop-down list in the Property Sheet next time you want to change it.

10. **Format your control.**

Although you can adjust many formatting details via the Property Sheet, the ribbon is much easier to use. Use the Form Design Tools | Format→Font section for basic font and color formatting, and use the Form Design Tools | Format→Control Formatting section to add a stylized border around your control.

GEM IN THE ROUGH

Reusing Your Favorite Border Settings

If you head to the Form Design Tools | Design→Controls section of the ribbon and click the drop-down arrow on the right side of the control gallery, you'll see an often overlooked button named Set Control Defaults. This button lets you reuse border settings over and over again. That way, if you come up with a nifty border for one control, you can quickly apply it to others.

Here's how it works. Suppose you create a label and use the buttons in the Form Design Tools | Format→Control Formatting section to apply a carefully formatted border around it, with just the right thickness (hairline), color (fuchsia), and line style (dotted). You can reuse these settings by selecting the newly created label control and then clicking Set Control Defaults. Now, the next time you add a label to this form, it'll automatically have the same border settings. However, these settings don't affect the labels you add to other forms.

The Set Control Defaults command works on a per-control basis, so you can store different border settings for labels, pictures, text boxes, and so on. Although it's an interesting frill, many Access experts prefer to use a different technique to apply the same formatting to several controls: they select them all at once, and then choose the border options.

The Control Gallery: A Quick Tour

Later in this chapter, you'll consider how to create some popular form designs with controls. But first, it's worth taking a quick overview of all the controls on the ribbon so you can see exactly what's available (and what isn't). Table 13-1 introduces you to every member of the control family.

TABLE 13-1 *Form Controls*

CONTROL	DESCRIPTION
Text Box	Displays the value of a field from a record. You can also use a text box to show the result of an expression, as described on page 369.
Label	Displays fixed text. Perfect for captions, notes, and helpful instructions.
Button	Performs an action (when the user clicks it). For example, you could add a new record or show a different form. Page 450 explains how to configure a button's action.
Toggle Button	Shows a button that can be in two different states: normal and pressed. You switch it from one state to the other by clicking it. The toggle button is a rarely used oddity, but you can substitute it for the check box to display the value of a Yes/No field. In this case, the button is depressed if the field value is Yes.
Combo Box	Displays a list that pops into view when you click the drop-down arrow. This list can be a list of values you supply, or it can be drawn from another table. Access automatically uses a combo box for lookup fields or linked tables.

CONTROL	DESCRIPTION
List Box	Displays a large box with a list of items. This list can be a list of values you supply, or it can be drawn from another table. You can use list boxes and combo boxes interchangeably—the key difference is the fact that list boxes take more space, and combo boxes let you type in your own values that aren't in the list.
Check Box	Displays the value of a Yes/No field. If it's Yes, the check box has a checkmark.
Attachment	Shows the first file in an attachment field. If this file is a picture, the picture is displayed directly on the form. Otherwise, all you see is a small icon that indicates the file type. If the attachment field holds more than one file, you can step through each one by using the arrows in the minibar (which appears when you click this field), as described on page 390.
Image	Displays a picture that you supply. Perfect for logos and eye candy that set your form apart. Set the Size Mode property to determine whether your picture is chopped down to fit its box (Clip), stretched to fit (Stretch), or resized without changing the shape (Zoom, which is the standard setting). You can even use the Picture Tiling property to repeat a picture over a larger surface. To keep your pictures (and database files) small, use compact .jpg files rather than bloated .bmp files.
Hyperlink	Displays a fixed hyperlink—blue underlined text that, when clicked, transports the clicker to a specific web page. Page 443 shows how it works.
Web Browser	Places a web page window right inside your form. You can use this area to show an external website or some database content, as demonstrated on page 445.
Navigation Control	Lets you use web-style navigation tabs, which sit in a strip at the side or top of your form. You'll use this feature on page 479.
Line and Rectangle	The line and rectangle controls are just decoration. Skillful designers use them to separate sections and highlight important information.
Tab Control	Displays several tabs of information. You can see the content in one tab at a time—you click to pick which tab you want. This Windows staple lets you pack more information into a smaller space. Page 442 shows an example.
Option Group and Option Button	The option group is a rectangular container that holds one or more option buttons. The form user can select just one of these option buttons at a time.
Subform	Displays a form inside a form. Usually, a subform shows linked records from a related table. You'll see how this works on page 455.
Chart	Creates a basic chart, using the Chart Wizard that's included with Office. Alas, charts aren't very well integrated into Access. If you want to provide a graphical view of your data, you're better off using a pivot chart (see Chapter 9) or just exporting your raw data to Excel, which is much more capable.

CONTROL	DESCRIPTION
Unbound Object Frame	Shows content, which is known as an *object*, from another program using a somewhat old-fashioned standard called OLE. You can use this control to do things like embed a spreadsheet, audio file, or Word document within your form. Most folks resist the urge, because the results tend to be awkward and confusing.
Bound Object Frame	Similar to the unbound object frame, but this control retrieves the object you want to display from a field in the current record. This feature seems nifty, but the quirky and outdated OLE standard causes more trouble than it's worth. If you want this sort of feature, you're far better off using an attachment field with an attachment control (page 390), which is designed to solve these problems.
Page Break	Indicates where a page break should fall. This control has an effect only when you use your form to create a printout. Usually, you should steer clear of this control in forms and use it exclusively in reports, which are tailor-made for printing.

Arranging Controls on Your Form

By now, you're probably comfortable working with controls in Design view. Here's a quick refresher if your memory needs a little jumpstart:

- **Create a control**. Use the ribbon to pick the control you want, and then draw it in the right place.

- **Move a control**. Just drag it. You can also move several controls at once, as explained in *Figure 13-4*.

- **Resize a control**. Drag the edges of the rectangle that surrounds it. If you have a linked label-and-text-box combination (which Access creates when you add a field), be careful to click the right part. *Figure 11-9* (page 356) shows where to click to move just the caption, just the field value box, or both.

- **Modify a control**. Select it, and then, in the Property Sheet, find the setting you want to change.

- **Delete a control**. Select it, and then press Delete to wipe it out forever.

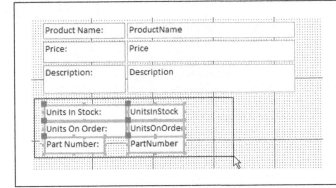

FIGURE 13-4

To move multiple controls at once, start by clicking somewhere on the form surface. Drag a selection box around all the controls you want to move, as shown here. Then, once all the controls are highlighted, drag any one of them. All the controls move as a unit. (You could also hold down Shift, and click each control one by one.)

If your controls aren't contained in a layout, it can be difficult to get them neatly arranged. To help, Access supplies some shortcuts that can line up rogue controls and iron out minor variances. The following sections provide a few useful tips for using these features.

Breaking Free from the Grid

When you place or move a control in Design view, Access always lines it up with the nearest part of the grid. (The grid lines are represented by all those dots that appear underneath your controls in Design view.) Access does this lining up because it makes it easier to create a consistent form. If controls were completely free-floating, it would be difficult to line up two controls next to each other. Even if you don't have shaky hands, it's hard to control the mouse that precisely!

However, in some situations, you may want to nudge a control just between the grid dots. Usually, it's because your form includes pictures, and you're trying to create a snazzy effect.

In such cases, Access lets you free yourself from the grid. Just choose Form Design Tools | Arrange→Sizing & Ordering→Size/

Space→Snap to Grid. Ordinarily, this button is highlighted to indicate that controls are always lined up with the grid. To turn it off, click it. You can turn it back on when you're finished by clicking it again.

Incidentally, if you find that the grid dots are distracting, you can hide them by choosing Form Design Tools | Arrange→Sizing & Ordering→Size/Space→Grid. And if you decide that you do want your controls to line back up with the grid, just select them all, right-click the selection, and then choose Align→To Grid. Access bumps each control over to the nearest grid line. Use Size→To Grid to make sure their heights and widths also fit the grid.

ALIGNING CONTROLS

If you have a group of controls that needs to be neatened up, select them all (by drawing a selection box, as shown in *Figure 13-4*), right-click the selection, and then choose an option in the Align submenu. Use the ever-popular "left" option to line all the controls up along their left edges. You can also line up controls on the right (see *Figure 13-5*), top, or bottom edges.

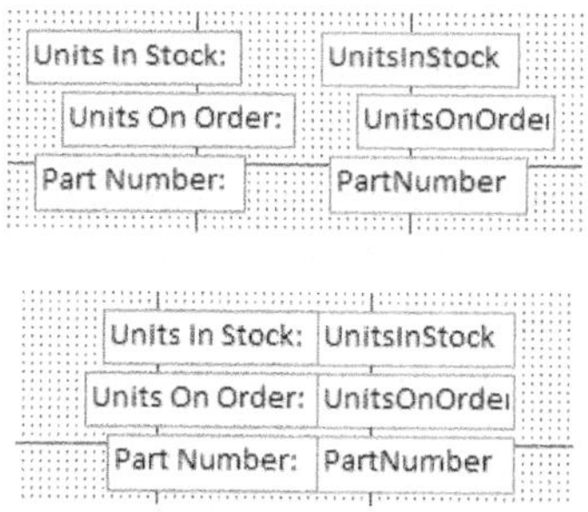

FIGURE 13-5

Top: These controls look messy.

Bottom: Even though the controls aren't in a layout, you can line them up properly using the Align options. Here, someone used the Align→Right command to pull them together against the right edge.

NOTE Many of the commands you'll learn about in the following sections for alignment, sizing, positioning, and anchoring, exist in two places. You can get them from the Form Design Tools | Arrange tab of the ribbon or by right-clicking a selection of one or more controls and looking in the pop-up menu. The menu approach is often faster, but the ribbon approach is sometimes more convenient for setting complex formatting.

▉ SIZING CONTROLS

If you have controls of different sizes, you can tell Access to make them all the same size. Select them all, right-click the selection, and then choose an option from the Size menu. Use To Widest to make all the controls as wide as the widest one of the bunch (see *Figure 13-6*). Alternatively, you can shrink controls by choosing To Narrowest, or change their heights with To Tallest and To Shortest.

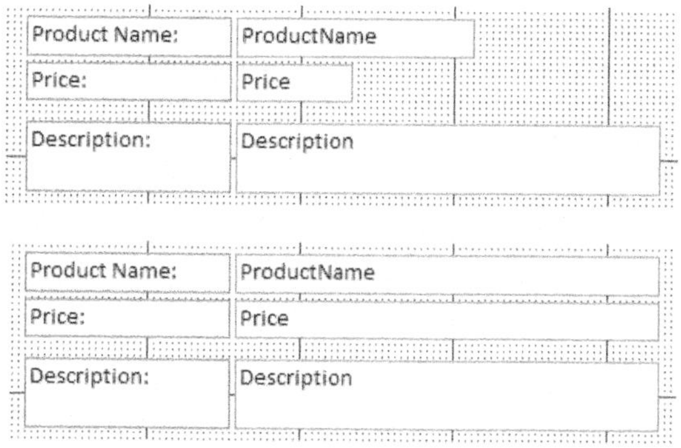

FIGURE 13-6

The To Widest command makes all these text boxes (top) the same width (bottom), which creates a cleaner and more visually pleasing form.

▉ SPACING CONTROLS

If you have controls that are scattered unevenly over the form, you can reposition them so that a consistent amount of space appears between them. To do so, select all the controls, and then head to the ribbon's Form Design Tools | Arrange→Sizing & Ordering→Size/Space menu. Under the Spacing heading, you'll find several commands to adjust the spacing between controls:

- **Equal Horizontal** spaces out controls so they're an even distance apart (from side to side). The control on the far left and the control on the far right keep their positions, while the controls in between are spread out evenly.

- **Equal Vertical** spaces out controls so they're an even distance apart (from top to bottom). The control on the top and the control on the bottom remain in position, while the others are spread out between.

- **Increase Horizontal** and **Increase Vertical** add a bit more space between all the controls you've selected.

- **Decrease Horizontal** and **Decrease Vertical** remove a bit of space between all the controls you've selected.

■ CONTROLS THAT OVERLAP

If you have overlapping controls, you may want to decide which one is placed on top and which one on the bottom. To do so, select one of the controls, right-click it, and choose Position→Bring to Front (to move the control to the top) or Position→Send to Back (to banish it to the background).

It goes without saying that most forms don't have overlapping controls. The exception is if you're aiming for a unique graphical effect, or if you're trying to use a rectangle to frame a bunch of controls (in which case the rectangle needs to sit behind the other controls or have a transparent background).

Anchoring: Automatically Resizing Controls

Ordinarily, your controls have a fixed, unchanging size. This characteristic lets you precisely arrange a large number of controls next to each other. However, fixed-size controls also have a downside. If you resize the Access window to make it very large, the controls can't use the extra space. Conversely, if you make the Access window very small, you're sure to cut off part of your form. In other words, fixed-size controls make for easy design, but they're inflexible.

Most people don't worry too much about these limitations. They design their forms to fit comfortably on an average-sized screen. However, if you have one or more fields that display a large amount of data—like a Long Text field that's chock-full of text—you might want to get a bit more ambitious.

Access includes a feature called *anchoring*, that lets you create controls that can grow to fill extra space when the Access window is resized. Anchoring is a little tricky to get right, but if you have huge text fields, it's worth the trouble.

Essentially, anchoring lets you attach a control to the sides of the form. As a result, when the form changes size, the control is dragged to a new position or resized. *Figure 13-7* shows an ordinary form that uses standard anchoring settings. Nothing happens when this form is resized.

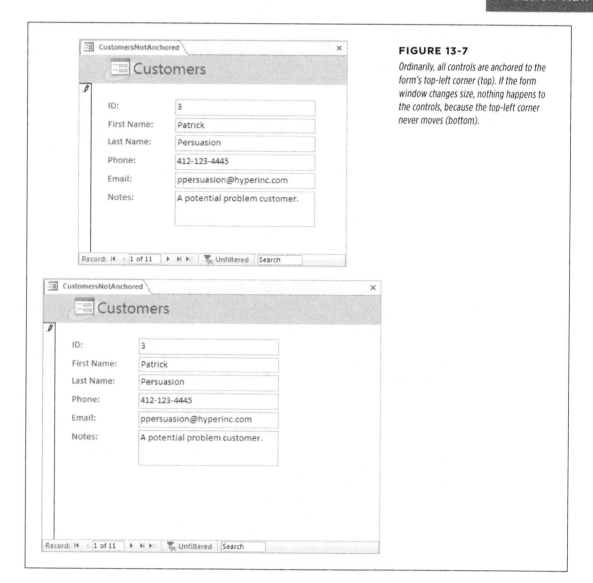

FIGURE 13-7

Ordinarily, all controls are anchored to the form's top-left corner (top). If the form window changes size, nothing happens to the controls, because the top-left corner never moves (bottom).

If you anchor a control to a form's right side, it's a different story. As the form is resized wider, the control hugs the right side, moving to a new position. Similarly, if you attach a control to the bottom of the window and make it taller, the control keeps close to the bottom, no matter how small or large the window becomes. The really exciting bit is what happens when you anchor a control to opposite sides. In this case, its position doesn't change, but its *size* does. If you anchor a control to a form's left and right sides, the control widens as the form widens. (This makes sense for a title at the top of your form with center-aligned text.) *Figure 13-8* shows how life changes when you anchor your control to different sides.

> **NOTE** The amount of space between the control and the anchored side always remains the same.

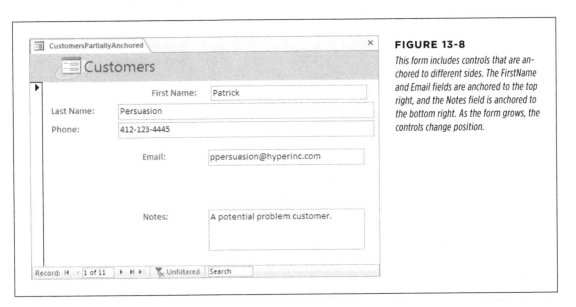

FIGURE 13-8

This form includes controls that are anchored to different sides. The FirstName and Email fields are anchored to the top right, and the Notes field is anchored to the bottom right. As the form grows, the controls change position.

Theoretically, you can use anchoring to create all kinds of bizarre effects. You could anchor controls to all different sides of the form, so they move and overlap as the form changes size, scrambling the form in complete confusion. More realistically, people use anchoring to achieve two effects, which are demonstrated in the following two sections.

▓ MAKING CONTROLS AS WIDE AS THE FORM

Ordinarily, you size a text box, and its size never changes. But with anchoring, you can make controls stretch wider or narrower to match your Access window's size. And as long as you don't put any other controls in the way, you don't have a problem with overlapping controls.

Just follow these steps:

1. **First, make sure your form doesn't have extra blank space. In Design view, shrink the width of the Details section so it's just wide enough to fit your controls.**

    If you leave extra blank space, it's harder to see anchoring at work. Flip back to *Figure 13-2* for a quick review of how to size forms properly.

2. **Choose the controls that you want to expand along with the window's size.**

    If you have the form shown in *Figure 13-7*, you may choose all the text boxes. Hold down the Shift key while you click to select them all.

Figure 13-9 shows the final result you're after.

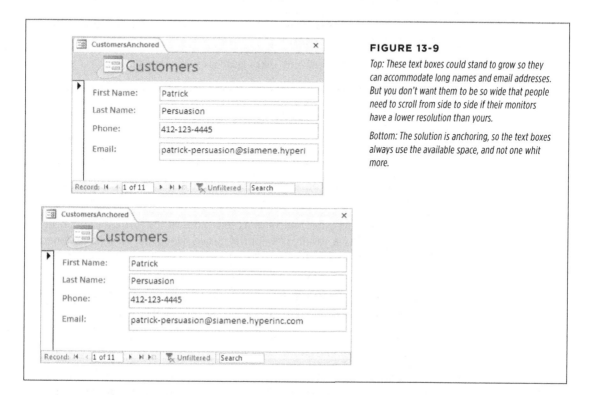

FIGURE 13-9

Top: These text boxes could stand to grow so they can accommodate long names and email addresses. But you don't want them to be so wide that people need to scroll from side to side if their monitors have a lower resolution than yours.

Bottom: The solution is anchoring, so the text boxes always use the available space, and not one whit more.

3. **Choose Form Design Tools | Arrange→Position→Anchoring→Stretch Across Top. (If you prefer to adjust your anchoring settings in Layout view, then choose Form Design Tools | Arrange→Position→Anchoring→Stretch Across Top.)**

This action anchors your control to three sides of the form: the top, left, and right. The top anchoring just makes sure the control stays at the same vertical position if the form window grows taller or shorter. The anchoring to the left and right sides ensures that the text box grows as the form widens, and shrinks as it narrows.

■ MAKING A SINGLE CONTROL AS LARGE AS POSSIBLE

In the previous example, you saw how to use anchoring to make a control grow horizontally. You can also use anchoring to make a control grow vertically, but there's a catch. In most forms, you have several controls placed one on top of the other. If you're not careful, when a control gets taller, it starts blotting out the control underneath it.

The solution is to make sure that only one control on the form can grow vertically. This control (probably a large field that's stuffed with text) then expands to consume all the extra space. All the controls above this control must be anchored to the top of the form. All the controls underneath it must be docked to the bottom so they stay out of the way.

Here's how to put this model into practice:

1. **In Design view, shrink the width of the Details section so it's just wide enough to fit your controls.**

   As with all types of anchoring, extra space is your enemy.

2. **Select the control that you want to grow vertically to get the extra space.**

   Consider the form in *Figure 13-10*, which shows customers. In this case, it's the Notes field that has the most text and would benefit most from the extra space. Even if you anchor the Notes field to both sides, you'll still get only a bit of extra space. Better to use whatever blank space you can get at the bottom of the form.

3. **Choose Form Design Tools | Arrange→Position→Anchoring→Stretch Down and Across.**

   This action anchors your control to all four sides of the form: the top, bottom, left, and right. As a result, the control grows when the form is widened or heightened. If you want the control to grow vertically but not horizontally, you choose Anchoring→Stretch Down instead.

4. **Select the first control under the control that grows vertically. Choose Form Design Tools | Arrange→Position→Anchoring→Bottom Left.**

   This action anchors the control to the left and bottom sides. That way, as the form is heightened, the control drops down to make space for the one above.

   You could also use the Stretch Across Bottom option. In this case, the control is still anchored to the bottom, but it grows horizontally to fit the width of the form.

> **NOTE** In the previous example, you didn't need to anchor the labels in front of every field, because they stayed fixed in place. However, in this example, you do need to use Bottom Left anchoring for all the labels that appear underneath the control that stretches vertically. (Otherwise, this label doesn't line up with its value box.) You never use one of the stretch anchoring options with a label, because you don't want your label to change size.

5. **Repeat step 4 for each control underneath.**

   If you forget a control, you see a telltale sign. When you resize the form window smaller, some controls overlap because the different anchoring settings don't agree.

   Assuming you anchor everything correctly, you get the result that's shown in *Figure 13-10*.

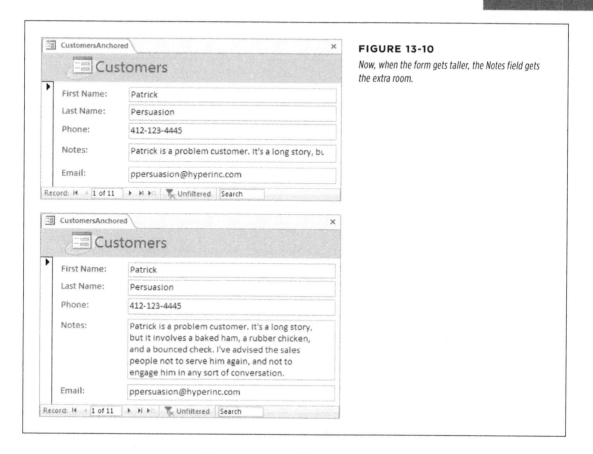

FIGURE 13-10

Now, when the form gets taller, the Notes field gets the extra room.

Tab Order: Making Keyboard Navigation Easier

When you're using a form to edit a record, you need to skip from one field to another. You can jump anywhere you want by using your mouse, but hard-core keyboard jockeys don't want to waste time raising their fingers from the keys. Here's where the Tab key comes into the picture.

You probably already know that the Tab key lets you move from one control to another in any Windows application. The Tab key also works in the datasheet, letting you skip from one column to the next. So it should come as no surprise that the Tab key also works in your forms.

The first time you press Tab in a form, you may be in for an embarrassing surprise. If you've spent a fair bit of time fiddling with your controls and rearranging them, the Tab key doesn't necessarily take you to the control you expect. *Figure 13-11* illustrates the problem.

NOTE The Tab key always works correctly if you're using a tabular or stacked layout, because Access keeps it up-to-date as you move the controls around. It's only when you've taken your controls *out of* a layout that you'll see the problem described here.

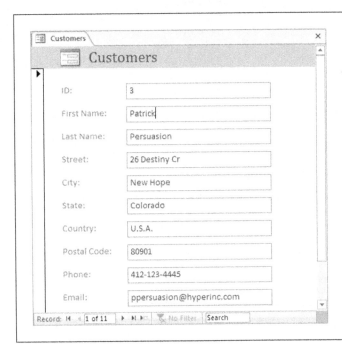

FIGURE 13-11

You'd expect that you could press the Tab key here to jump from the FirstName field to the LastName field. But try it and you wind up in the Country field instead, halfway down the form.

Getting a form straightened out so that the Tab key moves from one control to the next in an orderly fashion is called setting the *tab order.* Essentially, every control that supports tabbing has three important properties (which you can find in the Other tab in the Property Sheet). These properties are:

- **Tab Stop** determines whether a control supports tabbing. If set to Yes, you can tab to this control. If you change this setting to No, then it doesn't matter how much tabbing you do—you'll never get here. When you first add a control, this property is always set to Yes.

- **Auto Tab** has an effect only if the control is using an input mask (see page 138). If you set Auto Tab to Yes, as soon as you type the last character into the mask, you're automatically tabbed to the next control. This feature is handy for really fast data entry, but it's annoying if you make a mistake, because you're tabbed out of the control before you can fix it.

- **Tab Index** controls the tab order—in other words, where you go each time you press Tab. When you first open a form, you start at the control that has a tab index of 0. When you press Tab, you then move to the control with the next highest tab index (like 1). This process continues until you reach the control with the highest tab index. Press Tab again, and you'll get to the first control on the next record.

> **NOTE** The only controls that have these properties are controls that can accept *focus*—in other words, controls you can click and interact with. Obviously, text boxes, checkboxes, and buttons support tabbing. However, labels and pictures don't, because there's no way to interact with these items.

Every time you add a new control, Access gives it a new, higher tab index. Even if you drop a new control at the top of the form, Access puts it at the end of the tab order. To fix this problem, you could select each control in Design view, and then change the Tab Index setting by hand. However, a much less time-consuming alternative lets you set the tab order for the entire form in one go. Here's how it works:

1. **Right-click a blank spot on the form design surface, and then choose Tab Order.**

   The Tab Order window appears. It lists all the controls on your form that support tabbing, from lowest to highest Tab Index.

2. **In the Selection list, choose the section of your form you want to work with. It's almost always the Details section.**

   The Tab Order window lets you set the tab order separately for each section of your form. If your form includes a header and footer, you can choose to work with the header, footer, or Details section. However, it's very rare to find a form that has controls to support tabbing outside the Details section.

3. **If you want to let Access take a crack at setting the correct tab order, click Auto Order.**

   When you click Auto Order, Access sets the tab order based on the controls' position. The order goes from left to right, and then from top to bottom. Most of the time, the Auto Order feature gets you the correct tab order (or at least gets you closer to it). However, it doesn't work as well if you have a multicolumn layout and you want to tab through the controls one column at a time.

4. **To move a single control to a new position in the tab order, drag it.**

   This step is a bit tricky. *Figure 13-12* shows how it works.

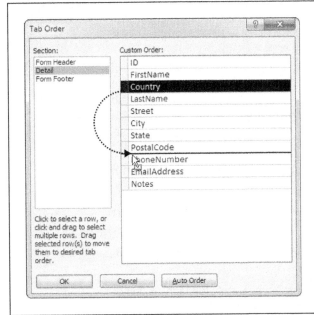

FIGURE 13-12

To reposition a control in the tab order, begin by clicking the gray margin that's just to the left of the control. The entire row is selected. Next, drag the control to a new position on the list. In this example, the Country field is being moved down the tab order.

5. **Click OK when you've got the tab order perfected.**

> **TIP** The tab order goes both ways. You can move one step forward in the tab order by pressing Tab, and you can move one step backward by pressing Shift+Tab.

▨ Taking Control of Controls

So far, you've seen how to create a form from scratch and how to add all the controls you want. However, you haven't used this newfound power to do anything special. Sure, you've picked up the ability to add extra labels, lines, and rectangles. But that kind of eye candy pales in comparison to the truly helpful features Access lets you add to your forms. Want to prevent people from entering buggy data? Check. Want to add web-style hyperlinks? No problem. The list of what you can do to soup up your forms' abilities is almost endless. The following sections show you the most popular ways to take charge of the controls on a form.

Locking Down Fields

In a database, almost every piece of information is subject to change. However, that doesn't mean people should have free range over every field.

Suppose Boutique Fudge creates a form named CurrentOrders that lets people in the warehouse review outstanding customer orders, sorted by date. The warehouse personnel need to review each order, pack it up, and then ship it out. The only change they need to make is to update the order status (to indicate when it's been sent out), or to add a record to the shipment log. Other details, like the order date, the order contents, and the customer who's receiving the order, should be off limits. The warehouse people have no reason to change any of this information.

Forms are powerful tools in scenarios like this, because they let you prevent changes in certain fields. That way, there's no chance that a misplaced keystroke can wipe out a legitimate piece of information.

Every bound control (a control that displays a field from your table) provides the following two properties that you can use to control editing. You can change these properties by using the Property Sheet in Design view.

- **Locked** determines whether you can make changes in a field. If Locked is set to Yes, you can't edit the field value. However, you can still select the text in a text box, and then copy it.

- **Enabled** lets you deactivate a control altogether. If Enabled is set to No, the control appears with dimmed (gray) text. Although you can still see the field value in a disabled control, you can't interact with it in any way. If it's a text box, you can't even select and copy the text it contains.

NOTE If you want to prevent edits altogether, consider using the Allow Edits, Allow Deletions, and Allow Additions form properties instead, which are described on page 415.

Prevent Errors with Validation

In Chapter 4, you learned how to prevent errors from creeping into your tables by using validation rules, default values, and input masks. This bulletproofing is an essential part of database design.

However, validation rules don't help in some situations because the rules apply sometimes, but not always. You don't want the salespeople at Boutique Fudge to enter a new order with an old date. Clearly, that's a mistake—a new order should receive today's date. To try and stamp out the problem, a clever database designer like yourself may use the following validation rule on the OrderDate field:

```
<=Date()
```

However, a few weeks later you discover that the catering department neglected to enter the information about *their* orders on time. For recordkeeping purposes, these orders need to indicate when the order was originally placed. So you need to remove your well-intentioned validation rule before you can enter these records.

It turns out situations like these abound in real life. Fortunately, there's a way to handle this scenario without giving up on validation. The trick is to place the validation in the controls on the form. That way, different forms can use different validation rules. If you want to make completely unrestricted changes, you can edit the data directly by using the datasheet for the table.

If you plan to move the validation out of your tables and into your forms, you'll be interested in the following control properties, which you can tweak in the Property Sheet:

- **Validation Rule** sets an expression that the value must meet to be considered valid. For example, the expression *<=Date()* compares the current field value to the date returned by the Date() function (which is today's date). The entry is allowed only if it's today's date or before. You can find many more examples of validation expressions starting on page 149.

- **Validation Text** sets the error message that appears if you attempt to enter a value that violates the validation rule. This custom text replaces Access's generic error message—"The value you entered does not meet the validation rule defined for the field or control"—which doesn't make much sense to real people.

- **Input Mask** sets a pattern that both guides and restricts people's input. Input masks are a good way to deal with fixed-length text values like phone numbers, postal codes, and social security numbers. Page 138 has more about how input masks work and how to create them.

- **Default Value** sets the value that appears in a field when you create a new record. (You're free, of course, to change the default value if it's not what you want.) You'll find it particularly useful to set default values at the form level, because defaults often apply to a specific task rather than to the entire table.

> **NOTE** You can set a default value for the same field at the table level *and* the form level. If you do, the form's default value takes over.

Performing Calculations with Expressions

An expression is a formula that manipulates some information, like numbers, dates, or text, and displays the final result (see *Figure 13-13*). Often, expressions perform calculations with field values. You've used expressions before to crunch the numbers in queries (Chapter 7) and reports (Chapter 10), and now you'll put them to work in your forms.

To create an expression, follow these steps:

1. **Add a text box control to your form (from the ribbon's Form Design Tools | Design→Controls section).**

   You need to use the text box, because it can show dynamic values like expressions. A label can show only a fixed piece of text, so it's no help.

2. **In the Property Sheet, choose the Data tab. Place your expression in the Control Source setting.**

   Remember, expressions start with the equal sign. The expression =Price*1.15 calculates the price with tax for a product by multiplying the value in the Price field by 1.15.

3. **Optionally, set Enabled to No to hammer home the point that this value can't be edited.**

   When you create a control that uses an expression, Access doesn't let you edit the calculated value. It's just as if you set the Locked property to Yes. However, some people may still *try* to change this value. If you think this scenario is a problem, set Enabled to No so that the control appears dimmed and nobody can tab to it. This setting also means that you can't copy the value in the text box.

4. **Optionally, apply formatting.**

   You can adjust fonts and colors by using the ribbon's Form Design Tools | Format→Font section. You can configure the way Access shows numeric values by using the Form Design Tools | Format→Number section.

Organizing with Tab Controls

One of the control world's unsung heroes is the *tab control*, which lets you present large amounts of content in a limited space. The tab control's trick is the way it lets you organize this content into separate *pages*. You can see only one page at a time, and you choose which one by clicking the corresponding tab (see *Figure 13-14*).

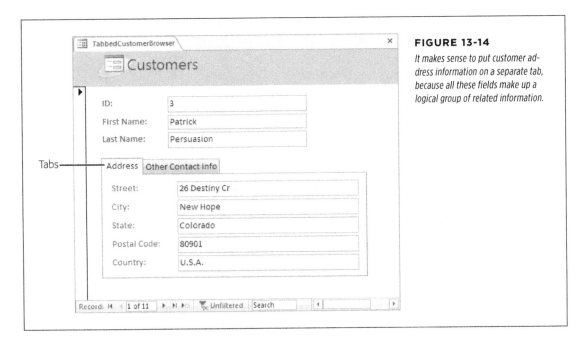

FIGURE 13-14

It makes sense to put customer address information on a separate tab, because all these fields make up a logical group of related information.

The tab control isn't all good news. Its main drawback is that you need to use extra clicks to get from one tab to another. For that reason, the tab control isn't a great choice in forms that you've set up to create new records. In those instances, it's better to streamline the new-record creation process and have all the controls on one page, so you can move through them quickly. A tab control makes most sense in forms that are primarily designed for editing or reviewing data. If this data can be subdivided into logical groups, and if editing tasks often involve just one group, then the tab control is a good choice.

To use a tab control, follow these steps:

1. **In the ribbon's Form Design Tools | Design→Controls section, click the Tab Control.**

2. **Draw the tab control onto your form in the place you want it.**

You'll want to make it fairly large, so it can accommodate the content you'll place inside.

3. **Add all the tab pages you need.**

Every new tab control starts with two pages. You can move from page to page by clicking the correct tab.

To create a new page, right-click any tab and choose Insert Page. To remove an existing page, right-click it and choose Delete Page.

4. **Give the tabs good names.**

The tabs that Access creates start out with pointless names like Page19 and Page20. To change the name, select the page, and change the Caption setting in the Property Sheet. The page that displays customer address fields could have the caption "Address Information."

To rearrange your pages, right-click the tab control, and then choose Page Order. Access opens a Page Order window with a list of tabs. To change the order of a tab, select it, and then click Move Up or Move Down.

NOTE If you create more pages than can comfortably fit in your tab control, Access adds a strange scroll bar in the top-right corner that lets you scroll through the tabs. To avoid this oddity, resize your tab control so that it's wide enough to fit every tab, or avoid using long tab names.

5. **Place controls on the different pages.**

You can drag controls from the rest of your form onto a page, or you can add new controls from the ribbon. Either way, remember to select the tab you want first, and then add the controls you need. Even in Design view, you can see only one page of a tab control at a time.

TIP If your controls are in a layout, you can't drag them into a tab. Instead, select them, right-click your selection, and then choose Cut. Next, right-click inside the tab page where you want to place them, and then choose Paste.

Going Places with Links

Links are the less powerful cousin of buttons. Whereas command buttons (page 450) can perform almost any action, links are limited to exactly two tasks:

- Launching your default browser and navigating to a specific site.

- Opening a file (like a Word document) in the program that owns it.

To create a link, follow these steps:

1. **In the ribbon's Form Design Tools | Design→Controls section, click the Hyperlink.**

The Insert Hyperlink window appears (see *Figure 13-15*). Using this window, you can supply the text for the link and the destination where the link transports people when clicked.

2. **Click the Existing File or Web Page option on the window's left side.**

   You can also use the "Object in This Database" option to create a link that opens another database object, like a form. However, command buttons are better suited to this task.

   Alternatively, you can choose E-mail Address to create a link to an email address. When you click this link, your default email program launches and creates a new message with the starter text you supply.

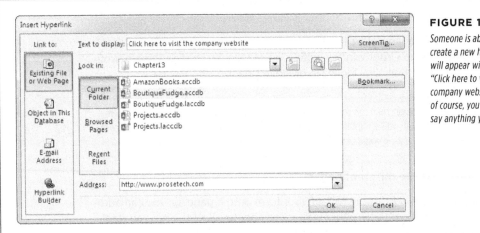

FIGURE 13-15

Someone is about to create a new hyperlink. It will appear with the text "Click here to visit the company website" (which, of course, you can edit to say anything you want).

3. **In the "Text to display" text box, enter whatever you would like the link to say.**

   Common choices for the text include the actual web address (like *www.my-company.com*) or a descriptive message (like "Click here to go to my company's website").

4. **If you want to set a custom tooltip for this hyperlink, click the ScreenTip button. Type in your message, and then click OK.**

   As you no doubt already know, a tooltip is a little yellow message-bearing window that opens above a hyperlink when your mouse pointer hovers over the link. If you don't specify a custom tooltip, Access shows the full path or URL (web address) instead.

5. **If you want to add a link to a document, browse to the appropriate file, and then select it. If you want to add a link to a web page, type the URL into the Address text box.**

If you're adding a link to a document, Access sets the address to the full file path, as in *C:\Documents\Resume.doc*. You can type this path in, and if your network supports it, you can use UNC (Universal Naming Convention) paths that point to a file on another computer using the name of the computer, as in *\\SalesComputer\Documents\CompanyPolicy.doc*.

> **NOTE** You're free to link to files on your computer or those that are stored on network drives. Just remember that when you click the link, Access looks in the exact location you've specified. If you move the target file to a new location, or you open the database on another computer, Access can't find the linked file.

6. **Click OK to insert the hyperlink.**

    The new hyperlink appears on your form. You can then drag it wherever you want.

    To use a hyperlink, just click it. You'll notice that the mouse pointer changes to a pointing hand as soon as you move over the hyperlink.

Showing Web Pages with the Web Browser

Access includes a Web Browser control that lets you embed a web browser window in a form. This way, you can display web pages that are in some way related to your record data.

There are two scenarios where the Web Browser control makes sense:

- You have a record that includes a web link (otherwise known as a URL). For example, a Businesses table might include a field named CompanyWebSite. When you view a business record in a form, you can use the Web Browser control to show that website.

- You have a record that includes some data that can be incorporated into a web link. For example, you might have a product code that can be fused into a URL to send a browser to a product catalog page on your company's website. *Figure 13-16* shows an example.

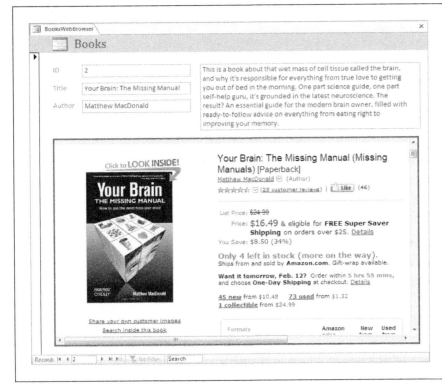

FIGURE 13-16

The Books table includes a field named Ama-zon_ASIN, which stores an Amazon identification number. (For books with ten-digit ISBN numbers, the ASIN and the ISBN are the same.) When you view a book record in the BookDisplay form, the Web Browser uses the ASIN value to display the book's Amazon product page, which includes up-to-date reviews and a sales ranking. You can find this example in the AmazonBooks database with the samples on the Missing CD page (www.missingmanuals.com/cds/access13mm).

Here's how to use the Web Browser control to build an example like the one shown in *Figure 13-16*:

1. **In the ribbon's Form Design Tools | Design→Controls section, click the Web Browser Control and drag it onto your form.**

   Assuming you have Control Wizards switched on (page 422), the Insert Hyperlink window appears. Using this somewhat awkward window, build the URL you want to use with the Web Browser. You have to assemble the web address out of several distinct pieces, each of which is classified differently. But if you understand the basics of expressions, it's far easier to press Esc (or click Cancel) and configure the Web Browser on your own, as described in the next step.

2. **Using the Property Sheet, choose the Data tab and set the Control Source property with an expression that builds the web address.**

   A URL is nothing more than a long piece of text. As you've already learned, any expression can join pieces of text together using an & symbol (which is known as the *concatenation operator*). With this in mind, it's easy to build an expression that creates the URL you need.

Consider the example shown in *Figure 13-16*. Amazon URLs can be written in several different forms, but one of the most common is this:

```
http://amazon.com/o/ASIN/ASIN-VALUE-HERE
```

So, if a book has an ASIN of 1449382371, you can reach its Amazon product page by typing this URL into a browser:

```
http://amazon.com/o/ASIN/1449382371
```

Now, assuming the ASIN is stored in a field named Amazon_ASIN, you can build the right URL for any record by using this straightforward expression:

```
="http://amazon.com/o/ASIN/" & [Amazon_ASIN]
```

And that's what you need to type into the Control Source property.

3. **Switch to Form view and try it out.**

   As you move from one record to the next, the matching Amazon page loads up in the web browser window.

NOTE When you set the Web Browser URL, you set its starting point. The person using the form can click hyperlinks to navigate somewhere else. However, the Web Browser control doesn't include an address bar, so the person can't type a URL to just anywhere.

Navigating with Lists

There are two list controls in Access forms: the *list box* and the *combo box*. The difference is that the list box shows several items at once (depending on how large you make it). The combo box shows just one item—to see the list, you need to click the drop-down arrow.

Access gives you two ways to use list controls:

- **You can use them to edit a field**. Access automatically creates a combo box control when there's a lookup defined for the field. This combo box works the same as a lookup list in the datasheet.

- **You can use them to navigate to the record you want**. In this case, the list shows the field value for every record in the table. When you choose one of the values, Access jumps to the corresponding record.

Using lists for navigation is a true Access power trick. If you often look for a record by using the same criteria (like if you hunt down products by name or employees by Social Security number), this technique is much faster than using the navigation buttons or filtering the records.

Here's how to add a navigation list for an existing form:

1. **Make sure the Control Wizard feature is turned on.**

If you're not sure, check that the Form Design Tools | Design→Controls→Use Control Wizards button is highlighted.

2. **In the ribbon's Form Design Tools | Design→Controls section, click List Box or Combo Box.**

Both these controls work exactly the same when you're using them for navigation. The only difference is that the List Box takes more space. If you decide to use it, place it at the side of the form. People usually choose the Combo Box (*Figure 13-17*).

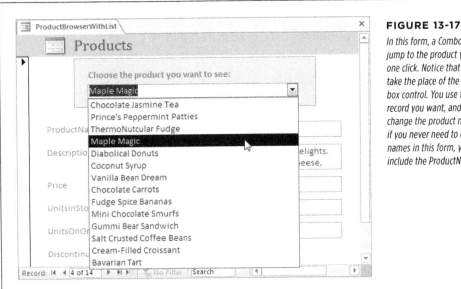

FIGURE 13-17

In this form, a Combo Box lets you jump to the product you want with one click. Notice that this list doesn't take the place of the ProductName text box control. You use the list to find the record you want, and the text box to change the product name. Of course, if you never need to change product names in this form, you don't need to include the ProductName text box.

3. **Draw the control on the form.**

As soon as you finish, a wizard appears to help you set up the list (*Figure 13-18*). This process works in a similar way to the Lookup Wizard you used to set up table relationships (page 180).

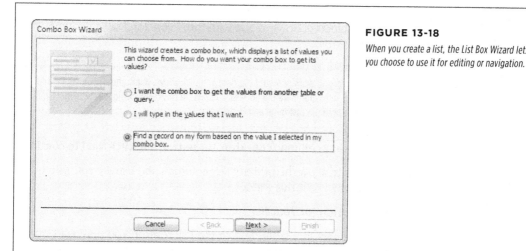

FIGURE 13-18

When you create a list, the List Box Wizard lets you choose to use it for editing or navigation.

4. **Choose "Find a record on my form," and then click Next.**

   If you don't see the "Find a record on my form" option, there are two possible problems:

   You have a new, completely blank form. This form isn't set up to display any records, so you can't use a list to hunt one down.

   The other, more likely snafu, is that the data source of your form isn't a table or query object. This situation occurs if you start with a blank form and then build it up with fields from the Field List pane. Access writes a query statement on the fly and uses that query as the form's data source. Ordinarily, this sleight of hand isn't a problem, except it confuses the List Box and Combo Box wizards. The fix is to change the form's data source so it points directly to the table that has the data: Open the Property Sheet, choose Form in the list at the top, click the Data tab, and then set the Record Source underneath to the correct table. Then, return to step 3.

   However, there's a potential complication. If you've built your form using fields from related tables, no single table will do. Instead, you need a query. You could create one by hand, save it, and then pick it in the Record Source list. But there's an easier option. Click in the Record Source box and then click the ellipsis (...) button to open the ad hoc query that Access has already created for your form. Then, save it as a separate query object in your database (choose Query Tools | Design→Close→Save As). Now you can pick the query from the Record Source list and return to step 3 to add the List Box control.

5. **Choose the field you want to use for the lookup, and then click Next.**

The example in *Figure 13-17* uses the ProductName field. Technically, the list always works the same way—it finds items based on their unique primary key value (page 88). The list you're creating actually has two columns. The first column stores the primary key, and the second column shows the value that's in the field you selected. However, on your form, you don't see the primary key, because it's hidden.

> **NOTE** This technique doesn't work as well if the field you pick allows duplicates. If you create a list that uses the LastName field, you may spot more than one MacDonald. In this case, consider adding more than one field to your lookup list (like both the LastName and FirstName).

6. **Leave the "Hide key column" checkbox turned on, and click Next to continue.**

   If you don't plan to show the primary key column—and usually you won't—just click Next to breeze past this window.

7. **Enter a text caption for your list.**

   This caption appears in a label next to the list control. You may want to use something like "Click the product you want to see." You can move or delete the label after the fact.

8. **Click Finish to create the list.**

   Now you can try out your list. Right-click the tab title, and choose Form View to switch back to the form. Then, choose an entry from the list to jump straight to the appropriate record.

> **NOTE** List-based navigation has one quirk. If you change the value that appears in the list, Access doesn't update the list until you move to another record. In the previous example, this property means that if you rename a product, the old name appears in the list until you move on.

Performing Actions with Command Buttons

The last control you'll consider is one of the most powerful. Command buttons let you trigger just about any action, like opening a new form, printing a report, or polishing off last year's taxes. (All right, some tasks are more difficult than others, but if you're willing to hunker down with some Visual Basic code, almost anything is possible.)

When you add a button to a form, Access launches the useful Command Button Wizard, where you can choose the action you want from a list of readymade choices. The Command Button Wizard then helps you build a macro (see Chapter 15) that does whatever you requested.

The choices in the Command Button Wizard provide a good menu of possibilities. Some Access fans find that they can do almost everything they want to do by just using buttons and the wizard. Other people eventually want to do something more original, in which case they need to create their own macros or write custom code (tasks you'll tackle in Part Five).

The following steps lead you through the Command Button Wizard:

1. **In the ribbon's Form Design Tools | Design→Controls section, click the Button.**

2. **Draw the button onto your form.**

   When you finish, the Control wizard starts, and gets right down to business. The first questions it asks is what action you want to perform (see *Figure 13-19*).

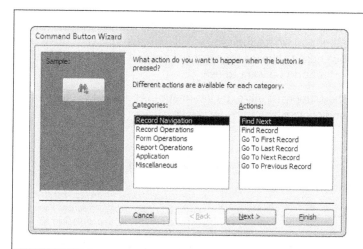

FIGURE 13-19

You can instruct your form to carry out six categories of actions. Once you select a category (in the list on the left), you see a list of actions in that category (in the list on the right).

3. **Choose the action you want to perform.**

   Most actions are self-explanatory. Here are some of the highlights:

   • In the Record Navigation category, you can use commands like Go To First Record, Go To Last Record, Go To Next Record, and Go To Previous Record to create your own navigation buttons. If you do, set the form's Navigation Buttons property to No to hide the standard buttons.

   • In the Record Operations category, you can create a new blank record (Add New Record) or do something with the current one (like Delete Record, Duplicate Record, and Print Record). You can even choose to commit changes right away before you navigate to the next record (Save Record), or undo the last change (Undo Record).

   • In the Form Operations category, you can close the current form (Close Form) or print it (Print Current Form). You can also open another form (Open Form), which is one of the most used button actions because it helps you move from task to task.

   • In the Report Operations category, you can work with other reports using commands like Open Report, Preview Report, and Print Report. These

actions help you make the jump from reviewing data (in a form) to printing it (in a report).

- In the Application category, you're limited to one action—the self-explanatory
Quit Application.

- In the Miscellaneous category, you'll find options to run a separate query
(Run Query) or fire off a macro (Run Macro). You'll learn how to create
macros in Chapter 15.

4. **Click Next.**

   The next step depends on what action you selected. Some actions require extra
   information. If you chose to show a form or print a report, Access prompts you
   to pick the form or report you want to use.

   Once you've finished supplying any extra information, Access asks you to supply
   the button text and choose a picture (*Figure 13-20*).

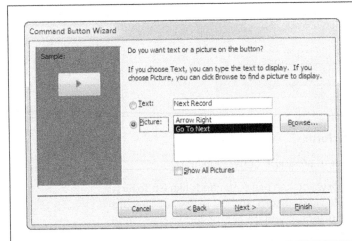

FIGURE 13-20

*Pictures are tempting, but the ones Access
includes are decidedly old-fashioned. Most Access
fans decide to create picture-less buttons. If you
want to include a picture, turn on the Show All
Pictures checkbox to see everything Access has to
offer (even pictures that may not make sense for
your current action), or use the Browse button to
add your own picture.*

NOTE Any bitmap (.bmp file) works for your button picture, so long as it's small enough to fit. Icons, .jpeg,
and .gif files are also acceptable.

5. **Enter some text and choose a picture. Then, click Next.**

   You can change these details after the fact by modifying the Caption and Picture
   properties (which appear in the Format tab).

6. **Supply a name for the button.**

   The name is what appears in the Property Sheet list. Better names make your
   button easier to find. And if you write code that works with your buttons

(Chapter 17), better names make for code that people can more easily read and understand.

7. **Click Finish.**

To try out your button, switch to Form view, and then give it a click.

8. **Optionally, use the commands in the Form Design Tools | Format→Control Formatting section of the ribbon to give your button a slick new style.**

Buttons have a unique ability. With a few mouse clicks you can replace the drab look of a vanilla button with a fancy style that incorporates visual effects (like a bevel edge, shadow, glow, or outline). The fastest way to transform your button is to select it and pick a fancy style from the Form Design Tools | Format→Control Formatting→Quick Styles menu. *Figure 13-21* shows several stylized buttons.

The quick styles change several formatting characteristics at once, but you can also refine your button with more targeted changes using the Shape Fill, Shape Outline, and Shape Effects menus, which are also found in the Form Design Tools | Format→Control Formatting section of the ribbon.

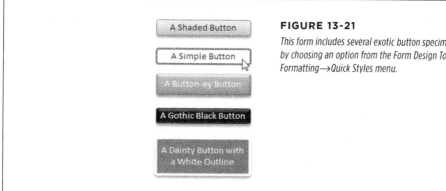

FIGURE 13-21

This form includes several exotic button specimens that you can create by choosing an option from the Form Design Tools | Format→Control Formatting→Quick Styles menu.

Forms and Linked Tables

As you learned in Chapter 5, few tables are truly independent. Most are linked to others in a web of relationships. Forms can take advantage of these relationships to show linked information. You can use a single form to view (and edit) information about customers and their orders. Or, you can look at products and product categories. This freedom just isn't possible in the Datasheet view.

NOTE Enterprising Access developers use *join queries* (page 227) to show information from more than one table. However, you can't edit the linked information in a join query. In a properly designed form, you don't have this limitation—you can change the information in both the parent and child records.

Table Relationships and Simple Forms

Access is intelligent enough to notice relationships when you create a new form for a parent table. To see what this ability means in practice, select a table that's the parent of another table. You can use the ProductCategories table in the Boutique Fudge database, because every category is a parent record that's linked to one or more child records in the Products table. (You can also use the Customers table, because customers are linked to orders, or the Orders table, because orders are linked to order items. To try this, use the Boutique Fudge database that's included with the downloadable content for this chapter.)

Figure 13-22 shows what happens if you select the ProductCategories table and then choose Create→Forms→Form. (Don't create a split form or a multi-item form. Access ignores relationships when you create these form types.) Access creates a form that displays the records you expect (the categories) and the linked records in the child table (in this case, the products).

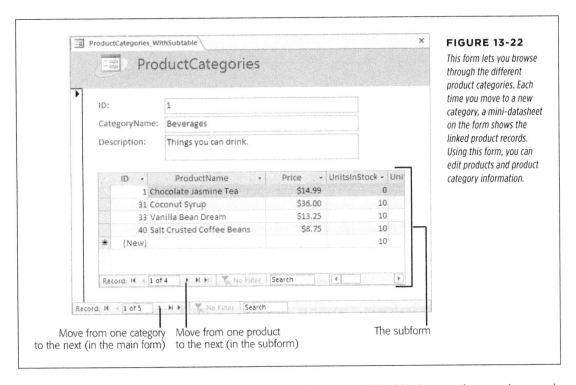

FIGURE 13-22

This form lets you browse through the different product categories. Each time you move to a new category, a mini-datasheet on the form shows the linked product records. Using this form, you can edit products and product category information.

If your table is the parent of more than one child table, Access shows only records from one table. It chooses the first relationship it finds. If this relationship isn't the one you want, don't worry—it's easy to change it once you understand how the subform control works. The next section has the inside scoop.

The Subform Control

Access shows linked records using the subform control. You can add the subform control to any form to show linked records. It's available in the ribbon's Form Design Tools | Design→Controls section with all the other controls. If you add it by hand, Access prompts you to pick the table you want to show.

Three properties determine what the subform control shows. First, the Source Object property identifies the object in the database that has the related records. You can choose an existing table, query, or form.

The next two properties—Link Master Fields and Link Child Fields—let you define the way the two tables are related. The master field is the field in the form, and the child field is the field in the source object. In the product category example, the master field's ID (in the ProductCategories table) and the child field's ProductCategoryID (in the Products table) are linked. Once this link is defined, Access knows how to filter the subform. It looks at the master field and displays only records that have the same value in their child fields. In *Figure 13-22*, Access shows only the products in the current category.

Usually, the master field corresponds to the parent table, and the child field is in the child table. However, you can reverse this relationship. You could create a form of products that includes a subform that shows each product's matching category. When you use this approach, the subform includes only a single record (because only one parent is linked to any child).

Now that you understand how the subform control works, you can add it to your forms with wild abandon. There's no reason you can't add several subforms to show a whole collection of related data at once. If you're creating a form for the Customers table, you could display two subforms—one for the orders made by that customer, and one for the payments. You just need two subform controls with different data sources.

> **TIP** When your form includes a subform, consider using the anchoring features described on page 430 so the subform grows to fit the available space when the form is resized.

Creating Customized Subforms

When you set the Source Object property to a table or query, Access always displays the linked records in a mini-datasheet. If you're intent on customizing every last piece of your form, you may not want that behavior. Interestingly, Access lets you control exactly how linked records are shown, if you do a little more work.

The trick is to set the Source Object to the form that you want to show in the subform control. Then, the form appears in its default view mode, which is whatever that form's Default View property is set to. You can show linked records in a tabular or stacked form. *Figure 13-23* shows an example.

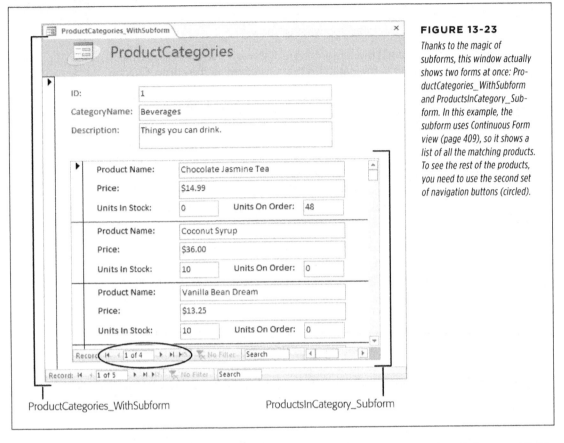

FIGURE 13-23

Thanks to the magic of subforms, this window actually shows two forms at once: ProductCategories_WithSubform and ProductsInCategory_Subform. In this example, the subform uses Continuous Form view (page 409), so it shows a list of all the matching products. To see the rest of the products, you need to use the second set of navigation buttons (circled).

Depending on the effect you're trying to achieve, you may already have a suitable form lying around ready to use. If you're designing a form for the ProductCategories table, you can use the form you created for the Products table in a subform control. However, you'll often want to use a completely separate form so you can customize it. In the Products table example, you may want to show products differently in the subform than they appear in their own dedicated form. After all, there's less space available when you use the subform control, so you may choose a more compact format and leave out the report header altogether.

> **TIP** If you choose to create a dedicated form to use with a subform control, consider indicating that in the name. The name "ProductsInCategory Subform" suggests a form that's designed for use as a subform.

Sometimes, try as you might, there's no way to fit everything in the small subform area of a form. In this case, you have two options: Try to rearrange your subform to make it more compact, or use two separate forms. Page 485 in Chapter 14 shows how you can use navigation and filtering to show related records in a separate form.

Building a Navigation System

Throughout the last 13 chapters, you've assembled all the pieces for a first-rate database. But without a good way to bring them all together, they're just that—a pile of unorganized pieces.

The best Access databases include some way for people to jump from one part of the database to another. The goal is to make the database more convenient and easier to use. Rather than forcing you to hunt through the navigation pane for the right object, these databases start with some sort of menu form and let you work your way from one task to another by clicking handy buttons. This sort of design is particularly great for people who aren't familiar with Access's kinks and quirks. If the navigation system is built right, these people don't need to know a lick about Access—they can start entering data without learning anything new.

You already know most of what you need to create a first-rate navigation system. Now you need a new perspective on databases—namely, that they can (and should) behave more like ordinary Windows programs, and less like intimidating forts of data. In this chapter, you'll learn different ways to add user-friendly navigation tools to a database. You'll learn how to show related information in separate forms, make a form appear when you first start the database, and create navigation forms (that is, forms that direct people to other forms). But first, you'll start by taking a closer look at the navigation pane to learn how you can control navigation without creating anything new.

Mastering the Navigation Pane

Chapter 1 introduced the navigation pane, and you've used it ever since to breeze around the database. However, the navigation pane starts to get congested as your database grows. Depending on your monitor size, once you hit about 20 database objects, they don't fit into view all at once. As a result, you need to scroll from top to bottom to find what you need, which can be a major pain in the wrist.

One way you can combat this confusion is by designing your own menu forms that let you move around the database. But before you jump to that solution, it's worth considering some of the features built right into the navigation pane. These features may solve the problem with less work.

Configuring the Navigation List

For starters, consider using filtering to cut down the amount of information shown in the navigation pane. You might have a database with three dozen objects, only ten of which you use regularly. In this case, there's no reason to show the objects you don't use.

Essentially, Access lets you make two decisions with the navigation pane:

- You can choose the way objects are arranged in the navigation pane. This process is known as *categorizing* your database objects.

- You can choose which objects are hidden from view. This process is known as *filtering* your database objects.

The confusing part is that you make both these choices using the same menu. To open this menu, click the drop-down arrow in the navigation pane's title region. *Figure 14-1* explains how it works.

You can choose to categorize the navigation pane in five ways:

- **Object Type** groups database objects based on the type of object. This method clearly distinguishes tables from forms, reports, and other sorts of objects, imposing order on the unruliest database. This viewing mode also works particularly well if you don't remember the exact name of the object you want. For example, if you know you need to print a report that shows a list of classes, you can head straight to the Reports group.

  When you use Object Type, the filtering list lets you see just a single type of object. If you've created forms for every task you need, select Forms to see your forms and hide everything else.

- **Tables and Related Views** groups database objects based on the table they use. If you've created two forms, three queries, and a report for a Students table, you'll see all these objects together in one group (under the heading "Students"). The challenge with this option is that you can have a hard time telling the difference between the different types of database objects, particularly if you use similar names. You need to look carefully at the icon to determine whether a given item is a form, a report, or something else.

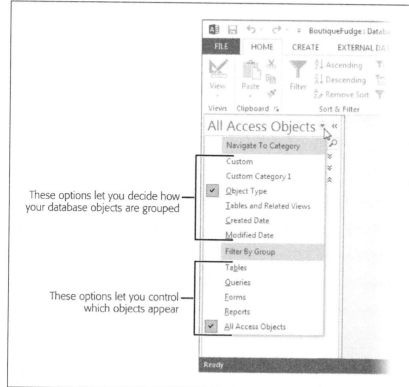

These options let you decide how your database objects are grouped

These options let you control which objects appear

FIGURE 14-1

When you're ready to tell Access how to arrange objects in the navigation pane, make your selection in the menu's top portion (named Navigate To Category). The current choice—Object Type—groups tables, queries, forms, and reports into separate sections. To decide which objects appear, make a selection in the menu's bottom portion (named Filter By Group).

NOTE Many database objects use more than one table. If you create a query that uses a join (page 227) to show products with category information, then your query uses both the Products and Product-Categories tables. In "Tables and Related Views" mode, you see this query in two places—under the Products heading *and* under the ProductCategories heading.

When you use "Tables and Related Views," the menu's Filter By Group section includes every table in your database. If you choose a specific table, you see only the objects that are related to that table. You can also choose Unrelated Objects to see any objects that don't fit into one of the table-specific categories, like code files.

- **Created Date** groups database objects based on the time they were created. Access creates a group for Today, groups for the recent days of the week (Monday, Sunday, and so on), and groups for longer intervals (Last Week, Two Weeks Ago, and so on). You probably won't use this view mode regularly, because as time passes, the objects move from one group to another. However, it's a good way to hunt down recent work.

When you use Created Date, the filtering options let you pick out just those object that were created today, yesterday, last week, last month, and so on (as shown in *Figure 14-2*). If you remember when you created an important form or report, but don't know its name, this ability can save serious time.

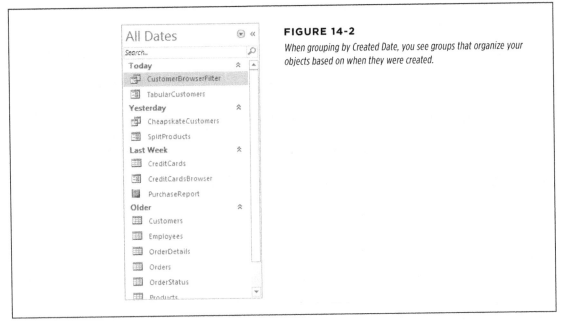

FIGURE 14-2

When grouping by Created Date, you see groups that organize your objects based on when they were created.

- **Modified Date** works like the Created Date option, except it lets you pick out database objects that have been changed recently. This option is handy if you want to ignore tables and other objects that you rarely use.

  When you use Modified Date, you get all the same filtering options you do with Created Date.

- **Custom** lets you choose exactly what database objects are shown and which ones are hidden. This choice is good if you have certain commonly used objects, and others that you want to tuck out of sight. You'll try out custom groups on page 467.

> **TIP** You can quickly apply filtering. Right-click a group heading, and then choose Show Only [GroupName]. To show just tables when grouping by Object Type, right-click the Tables group, and then choose Show Only Tables. To remove the filtering, right-click the navigation pane again, and then choose Show All Groups.

When you apply filtering in the navigation pane, Access completely hides whatever you don't want to see. But as you probably already know, Access gives you another option. You can click the collapse arrows next to a specific section to shrink it so that only the section title is visible (*Figure 14-3*). You can then pop it back into display when you need it.

FIGURE 14-3

Click the collapse arrows to quickly hide the objects in a particular section. In this example, the Queries group is collapsed neatly out of the way.

Sort and View Options in the Navigation Pane

The navigation pane has many carefully buried settings you can configure. For example, if you don't like the way items are ordered in each group, you have several sorting options. To see them all, right-click the navigation pane's title bar, and then choose the Sort By submenu.

As you'll see, you can apply an ascending or descending sort according to any of the following criteria:

- **Name** sorts according to the database object's name.

- **Type** sorts according to the object type (form, report,

table, and so on). This option has no effect if you're already grouping by object type.

- **Created Date** and **Modified Date** sort so that older or newer objects appear first.

You can also change what the navigation pane looks like by right-clicking the navigation pane's title, and then choosing an option from the View By menu. *Figure 14-4* compares the different settings.

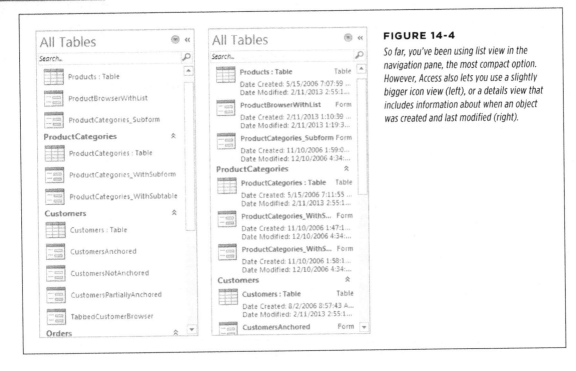

FIGURE 14-4

So far, you've been using list view in the navigation pane, the most compact option. However, Access also lets you use a slightly bigger icon view (left), or a details view that includes information about when an object was created and last modified (right).

Better Filtering

The filtering system has one limitation—it lets you choose only one category at a time. If you've chosen "Tables and Related Views," you can filter the list down to the objects that are related to a single table. However, you can't choose to include two (or more) table groups. Similarly, if you choose Object Type, you can show all the forms or all the reports in your database, but you can't show forms *and* reports without including everything else (although the collapsing trick shown in *Figure 14-3* helps to reclaim most of the space).

You can use an easy way around this restriction. To get more control over filtering, follow these steps:

1. **Right-click the navigation pane's title bar, and then choose Navigation Options.**

   The Navigation Options window appears (*Figure 14-5*).

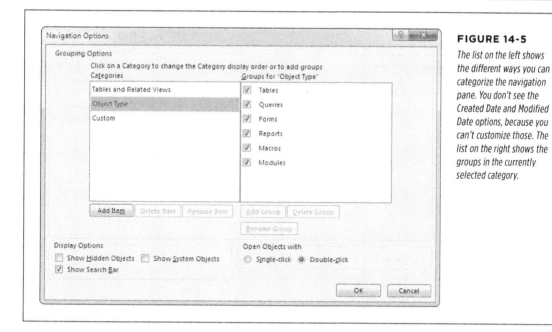

FIGURE 14-5

The list on the left shows the different ways you can categorize the navigation pane. You don't see the Created Date and Modified Date options, because you can't customize those. The list on the right shows the groups in the currently selected category.

2. **Choose the category you want to customize—either "Tables and Related Views" or Object Type.**

   The list on the right shows all the groups in that category.

3. **If you don't want a category to appear in the navigation list, clear the checkmark next to it.**

   If you want your navigation pane to show only reports and forms, choose the Object Type category, and then clear the checkmark next to Tables, Queries, Macros, and Modules.

4. **If you're customizing the "Tables and Related Views" category, you can also change the order of the groups, as shown in *Figure 14-6*.**

   The only item you can't move is Unrelated Objects, which always appears at the bottom. And you can't change the order of the groups in the Object Type category at all.

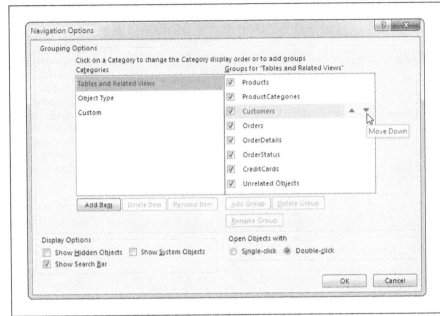

FIGURE 14-6

To move a group, just select it. An up-and-down-arrow icon appears in the item, as shown here. You can click these arrows to move the group up or down.

5. **Click OK to close the window.**

> **NOTE** Many databases get a whole lot clearer the moment you hide the extra objects. If you've outfitted your database with a full complement of forms and reports, these objects may be all you need to see. So why not go ahead and hide the lower-level tables, queries, and code?

Hiding Objects

Hiding the groups you don't want to see is all well and good—but what if there's a single object you want to tuck out of sight? Maybe you want to make sure other people who use your database aren't distracted by a few potentially risky action queries (Chapter 8) that they really shouldn't use. No problem. Just right-click the query in the navigation pane, and then choose "Hide in this Group."

> **NOTE** When you hide an object, it's hidden in the current view mode, in the current group. (Remember, in "Tables and Related Views" mode, some objects may appear in more than one group.) If you want to hide an object everywhere, you need to track it down in each group, and hide it there.

To reveal a hidden object, you first need to configure the navigation pane so that it shows hidden objects. To do so, right-click the title bar, choose Navigation Options, add a checkmark in the Show Hidden Objects box, and then click OK. Now, hidden objects appear in the navigation pane, but they're slightly faded so you can distinguish them from the other non-hidden objects. To unhide an object, right-click it, and then choose "Unhide in this Group."

All of these approaches—filtering, custom groups, hidden objects—are designed to make your database easier to use. These approaches don't provide any security. (A person who really wants to use a database object can just change the navigation settings to get to it.)

NOTE On page 642, you'll learn how to divide a database into separate files, which gives you the best way to keep some database objects out of the wrong hands. However, no matter what you do, Access is *not* bulletproof. Access is designed to be intuitive, capable, and easy to use. Unlike server-side databases like SQL Server, it's not designed to lock out bad guys if they get hold of your database files.

Using Custom Groups

Ordinary people don't think in terms of tables and database objects. Instead, they think about the *tasks* they need to accomplish. But none of the readymade grouping options fit this approach. Fortunately, you can build your own groups that do. Here's how:

1. **Click the drop-down arrow in the navigation pane's title bar, and then choose Custom.**

   In a new database, you start out with two groups in the Custom view. The first, Custom Group 1, is empty. The second, Unassigned Objects, contains all the objects in your database.

2. **Create the groups for your objects.**

   You can create a new group and move an object into it in one step. To do so, right-click the object you want to relocate (in the Unassigned Objects section), and then choose Add To Group→New Group. Enter the group name, and then press Enter. *Figure 14-7* shows the results.

   Repeat this step to create all the groups you need. If you want to move an object into an existing group, right-click it, choose Add To Group, and then pick the corresponding group name.

TIP For speedier work, just drag and drop your objects into the right groups.

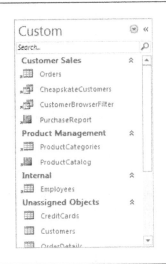

FIGURE 14-7

It's often a good idea to create groups that reflect specific types of tasks, as in this database. You'll notice that in Custom view, the items have slightly different icons, with a superimposed arrow in the bottom-left corner. This feature is Access's attempt to highlight the fact that they are shortcuts to your database objects, and their arrangement doesn't reflect any intrinsic property of the objects themselves.

3. **Optionally, you can also rename, remove, and reorder your groups now.**

   The easiest way to do this is to use the Navigation Options window. Right-click the navigation pane's title, and then choose Navigation Options. When the Naivgation Options window appears, you can carry out the following tasks:

   - Select a group, and then click Rename Group to apply a new name.

   - Remove your group—just select it, and then click Delete Group.

   - Add a group, by clicking Add Group. It starts with no objects.

   - Rearrange your groups. Just click one, and then use the arrow icons that appear to move it up or down.

   - Move your custom category to a different place in the list, which affects how the menu appears when you click the drop-down arrow in the navigation pane.

   - Hide a group (temporarily, or for the long term). Just remove the checkmark next to the group.

   The only thing you can't do with groups in the Navigation Options window is change the objects that each group contains. (To change them, you need to drag your objects around the navigation pane, as described in step 2.)

   You can also change the name of the view that *contains* all your groups. Initially, this category is named Custom, but you can change it to something more descriptive by selecting it in the Navigation Options window, and then clicking the Rename Item button. And if you're more ambitious, you can create more than one top-level custom view mode. Click Add Item to add a new one, and Delete Item to remove it. *Figure 14-8* shows an example with several custom categories.

4. **Click OK when you're finished making your changes.**

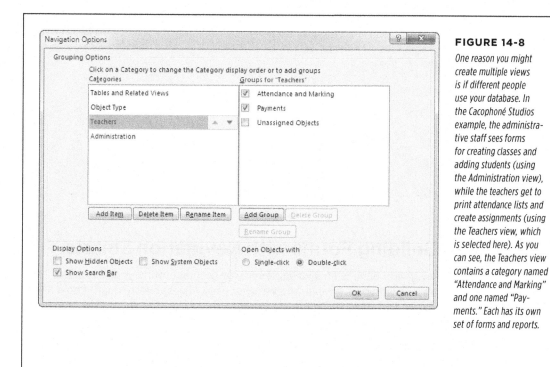

FIGURE 14-8

One reason you might create multiple views is if different people use your database. In the Cacophoné Studios example, the administrative staff sees forms for creating classes and adding students (using the Administration view), while the teachers get to print attendance lists and create assignments (using the Teachers view, which is selected here). As you can see, the Teachers view contains a category named "Attendance and Marking" and one named "Payments." Each has its own set of forms and reports.

Searching the Navigation List

If you just can't bear to have anything out of your sight, you may need to put up with a cumbersomely long list of objects in the navigation pane. However, Access still provides you with one convenient feature that can save you hours of scrolling.

It's the *search box*, and it lets you jump to an object almost instantaneously, provided you know its name.

To show the search box, follow these steps:

1. **Right-click the navigation bar's title, and then choose Navigation Options.**

2. **In the Navigation Options window, choose Show Search Bar.**

3. **Click OK.**

The search box appears at the top of the list in the navigation pane. As you type, Access filters the list so it includes only matching objects (*Figure 14-9*).

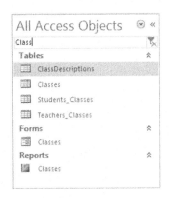

FIGURE 14-9

The search box matches objects that contain the text you type. So if you type Class, you'll see objects like Classes and Students_Classes.

Building Forms with Navigation Smarts

The navigation pane is an invaluable tool for getting around your database, but it doesn't suit everyone. People who've never used Access before might find it a little perplexing, and there's nothing stopping someone from changing the navigation options (and opening objects they shouldn't).

To get more control and to add a friendly veneer, many Access experts build navigation features into their forms (and occasionally their reports). After all, a form gives you virtually unlimited possibilities for customization. You can add a paragraph of text, throw in a hot pink background and a company logo, and reduce confusing options to a few fat, friendly buttons.

If you do decide to use forms for navigation, your first decision is what kind of form to build. Access gives you a wide range of options, and you'll explore them in the following sections.

Custom Menu Forms

A *menu form* has just one purpose—to transport people to other forms (usually, when they click a button). A typical menu form doesn't display any information—it simply provides a stack of buttons that lead to different places. It serves as both a starting place and the central hub of activity for your database.

Building a custom menu form is one of the simplest and most effective ways to provide navigation for your database. You simply create a series of buttons and configure each one to show the appropriate form (as described on page 450). You can even place a background picture on your form, or add an effect to make your buttons stand out. *Figure 14-10* shows an example.

FIGURE 14-10

This custom menu is just an ordinary form with a lot of navigation buttons. The advantage to crafting your own custom menu form is that you can make everything just the way you like it. The disadvantage is that you need to maintain it. For example, every time you add a new form to your database, you need to add a button to your menu to use it.

This menu form presents a clean blank surface along with an image control that shows a snazzy graphic. It also includes several ordinary button controls that were created with the Command Button Wizard (page 450). Each button's Back Style property is set to Transparent, to give it a more modern flat look. The Cursor On Hover property is set to "Hyperlink hand" so that the mouse pointer changes to a pointing hand when you move over a button, which lets you know that you can click there.

Another approach is to use a picture as the background for the whole form and to put other controls on top of the background. To do this, you need to set these properties on the form: Picture (the picture file you want to show), Picture Tiling (whether the image should be repeated to fill the available space), Picture Alignment (use Top Left so that it starts from the form's top-left corner), and Picture Size Mode (use Clip, so the picture isn't stretched, resized, or otherwise mangled). All the controls you place on top of a form with a background picture should have their Back Style property set to Transparent so that the picture shows through.

NOTE Before you invest a lot of effort building your own menu forms, check out Access's navigation form feature later in this chapter (page 479). It's a simple menu-making approach that may be just the ticket if you can make do with a little less flexibility.

NOSTALGIA CORNER

Switchboard Forms

Previous versions of Access promoted a menu-building feature called switchboard forms. The idea was simple: You run through a short wizard, and Access creates a menu form for you, complete with a stack of buttons. Interestingly, Access stores all the data for a switchboard form in the database, which means you can change the menu options by simply editing a table.

Unfortunately, switchboard forms also have a long list of shortcomings. They're limited to eight forms per page. They support a multiple pages feature, but it's almost as annoying as the touchtone menus on automated voicemail systems that force you to go through level after level of options. And worst of all, the switchboard forms Access creates are scandalously ugly.

Access 2013 still includes the switchboard generator, but it's no longer on the ribbon. Instead, Microsoft recommends you create your own menu form, or use the navigation form feature (page 479). But if you feel a wave of nostalgia coming on, you can give the old Switchboard Wizard a whirl. To access it, you need to customize the ribbon, as described in the Appendix. Just choose the "Commands Not in the Ribbon" option, look for the command named Switchboard Manager, and add it back to the ribbon. But don't be surprised if the result is tackier than the pants Uncle Stan wears to his New Year's Eve disco party.

Designating a Startup Form

Since a custom menu form is the gateway to your Access database, it's a good starting point for folks who are going to use your database. You can tell Access to open any form automatically when someone first opens your database. Here's how:

1. **Choose File→Options.**

   The Access Options window appears.

2. **In the list on the left, click Current Database.**

   The settings for the current database appear.

3. **Under the Application Options heading, look for the Display Form box. Choose your custom menu form in the list.**

   Now, whenever you open the database, Access launches your form immediately.

   Optionally, if your custom menu completely eliminates the need for the navigation pane, look under the Navigation heading, and clear the checkbox next to the Display Navigation Pane setting.

Compound Forms

Alternatively, you could forget about designing a way to jump from form to form, and instead create a form that brings everything you need into one place. This trick, called a *compound form*, uses the subform control you learned about on page 455.

In Chapter 13, you learned how the subform control lets you show related data (like a list of products for the current product category). However, the subform also makes sense if you want to show several *unrelated* tables in one place. Just leave the Link Master Fields and Link Child Fields properties of the subform empty—that way the subform shows all the records without filtering. *Figure 14-11* shows an example.

> **TIP** You can use a shortcut to create a compound form. First, choose Create→Forms→Form Design to create a blank new form. Find a form you want to use in the subform, and then drag it from the navigation pane to your new form's design surface. Access creates a subform control that shows that form. You can also drag a table onto your form, in which case Access creates a subform for that table (and asks you to pick a name for it).

FIGURE 14-11

This compound form is an all-in-one dashboard for adding and reviewing products and reviewing the customer list. The prebuilt templates that Access includes (page 27) often use compound forms to put several related editing tasks in one place.

When creating a compound form like the one in *Figure 14-11*, you should set the form's Navigation Buttons property to false (because the real navigation buttons are in the subforms, not the main form). You can also set the Record Selectors property to No to prevent the record selection margin from appearing at the left.

If you're using "Tables and Related Views" mode in the navigation pane, a compound form usually appears in the Unrelated Objects area. That's because the form itself doesn't use any tables. Instead, it contains subforms, and these subforms use the various tables you're displaying.

Showing All Your Forms in a List

You may find one last trick useful when building a navigation hub. Rather than create a button for each form you want to use, you can create a list control that has them all. When the person using the database picks a form from the list, Access jumps to that form. This approach works well if you have a large number of forms, which would irredeemably clutter the button-only approach.

> **TIP** This technique works as well for reports as it does for forms.

The first step is to put the form names in a list box. Access gives you three ways to do this:

- **Type the names in by hand**. Just drop a combo box control onto your form. When the wizard starts, choose "I will type in the values that I want," and then enter the form names in the appropriate order.

> **NOTE** Page 447 has more about the List Wizard. Just remember, at the end of the wizard, you need to choose "Remember the value for later use." Your list is used for navigation, not record editing.

- **Pull the names out of a custom table you create**. Create a new table, and then fill it with the names of the forms you want to show in the list. Then, when you create the combo box, choose "I want to look up the values in a table or query," and then specify your custom table.

- **Pull the names out of the system table**. For a really nifty trick, you can get the full list of forms straight from your database. The trick is to use one of the hidden *system tables*. These system tables are tables that Access uses to keep track of database objects. Every Access database has these tables, but tucked out of sight.

The first two options are straightforward. The third option is more impressive, but it takes a little more work. Ordinarily, the system tables are hidden from sight. You can pop them into view (see *Figure 14-12*) by choosing Show System Objects from the Navigation Options window. Showing the system tables isn't a good choice for the long term, because any change you make in these tables could damage your database and confuse Access.

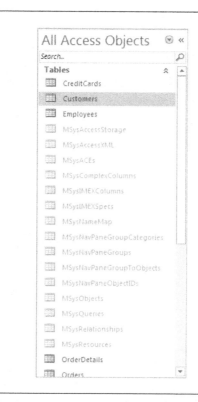

FIGURE 14-12

Here, the navigation pane shows a bunch of system tables, which are ordinarily hidden. You can open them to take a look, but you'll have a hard time making sense of the (mostly numeric) data they contain.

Even if you don't show the system tables, you can still use them. The most interesting system table is MSysObjects, which lists all the objects in your database. You can get a list of all the forms in your database by querying this table with an SQL command (see page 220 for a refresher on how queries use SQL). The Name field provides the database objects' name. The Type field contains a numeric code that identifies the type of object. Table 14-1 lists the types in which you may be interested.

TABLE 14-1 *Useful Type Codes*

OBJECT	TYPE
Table	1
Query	5
Form	–32768
Report	–32764

Based on this information, you can get a list of forms by retrieving the Name field, and then filtering out those records with a Type value of –32768.

You can most easily build this bit of logic into your list control by adding your list to the form and skipping out of the wizard (press Esc when it starts). Then, you can configure the control using the Property Sheet. In the Data tab, find the Row Source property, and then enter the following SQL statement, which performs the query you need:

```
SELECT Name FROM MSysObjects WHERE MSysObjects.Type=-32768
```

You now have a list that shows all the forms in the database. You can substitute the number –32764 for –32768 to get reports instead; *Figure 14-13* shows the results.

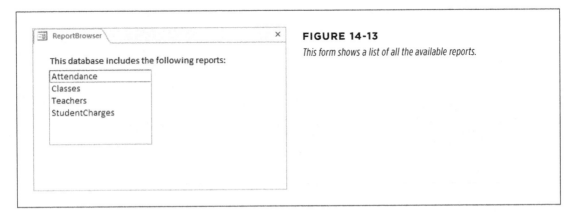

FIGURE 14-13

This form shows a list of all the available reports.

So far, you've seen only half of the solution you need. You've learned how to get the list into the right control, but at the moment nothing happens when you *use* the control. You really need a way to jump to the selected form or report.

It turns out that this solution is a bit more advanced than the examples you've seen so far. To make it work, you need to customize a macro. (A *macro* is a list of one or more instructions stored as a database object so you can use it anytime.)

As you learned in Chapter 13, when you create a command button, the Button wizard asks you a few questions, and then builds the macro you need. However, the Button wizard is woefully underpowered. For instance, while it can create a macro that navigates to a specific form, it can't create a macro that can go to any form. But with just a little more work, you can create a simple macro with the wizard, and then fix it up to really suit your needs. Here's how:

1. **Drop the button onto your form.**

   Place it next to the combo box control. The Button wizard launches.

2. **Choose the Report Operations category and the Open Report action, and then click Next.**

   Or, if you're showing a list of forms, choose the Form Operations category and the Open Form action.

3. **Pick any report (or form), and then click Next.**

   It doesn't matter what you choose here, because you'll change this part later.

4. **Complete the wizard.**

   Make sure you give your button a suitable caption, like "Go," "Open Form," or "Show Report."

   Once the wizard is finished, it's time to take a closer look at the button in the Property Sheet.

5. **In the Property Sheet, select your newly created button, and then switch to the Event tab.**

   Events are occurrences that can trigger your macros. For example, every button has an OnClick event that takes place when you click the button.

6. **Find the OnClick property, and then click inside the property box, where it says "[Embedded Macro]."**

   An ellipsis (…) appears at the corner of the box.

7. **Click the ellipsis to edit the macro.**

   A macro-editing window appears. It shows a single action (named either Open-Report or OpenForm, depending on what you chose in step 2). Click to select this action. Each configurable piece of information turns into a text box (*Figure 14-14*).

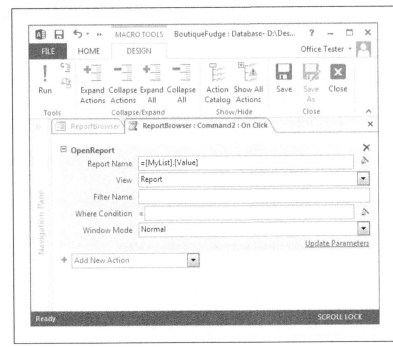

FIGURE 14-14

You'll learn much more about this window in Chapter 15. For now, all you need to know is that this macro has a single action, named OpenReport. *The Report Name text box is the one we're interested in, because it tells Access which report to open.*

8. **In the Report Name (or Form Name) text box, type the expression** =MyList. Value.

    This expression finds your combo box and pulls out the currently selected value. It assumes your combo box is named MyList. If not, change the expression accordingly. (If you don't remember the name of your list control, click to select it, and then look at what name appears in the drop-down list at the top of the Property Sheet.)

9. **Close the macro window, and then choose Yes to save your changes when prompted.**

    You return to the form design window.

10. **Switch to Form view, and then try out your new list mojo.**

    You should be able to select a form in the list, and then click the button to open the form you chose.

Navigation Forms

If you're tired of building navigation forms on your own, you'll be happy to learn about Access's *navigation forms*. This feature lets you create a form that has a tab-based menu built right into it. *Figure 14-15* shows an example.

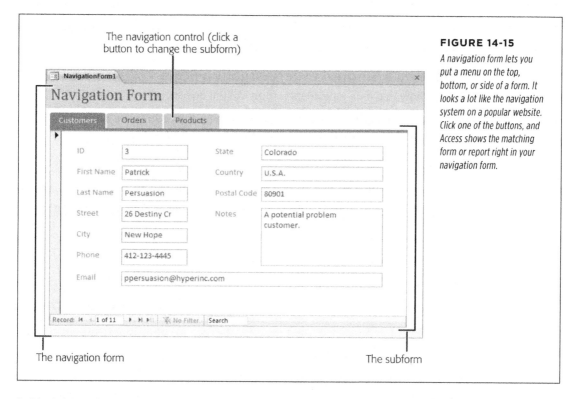

The navigation control (click a button to change the subform)

The navigation form

The subform

FIGURE 14-15

A navigation form lets you put a menu on the top, bottom, or side of a form. It looks a lot like the navigation system on a popular website. Click one of the buttons, and Access shows the matching form or report right in your navigation form.

Behind the scenes, navigation forms use some of the same techniques you've already learned about. For example, when you choose a new form from the menu, the navigation form brings it into view using a subform. But the best part is that you can create a fairly complex navigation form just by dragging and dropping your forms into the navigation menu. In a few short minutes, you can build a complete menu for your database.

As great as they are, navigation forms have two limitations:

- **You can't completely change the way they look**. Even though you can make the individual navigation buttons look different with colors and shape effects, they're always arranged the same basic way—as a strip along one of the sides of your form.

- **They force you to work on one form at a time**. Whenever you click a navigation button, the current subform is closed and a new subform is loaded. But in certain editing situations, you might want to have two forms open at once, so you can edit two different records at the same time. One way to accomplish this is to create buttons that open forms in separate tabs (as you'll see on page 485). You can then move back and forth between the tabs at will. Another option is to include both forms as subforms in a single superform (a technique that's demonstrated on page 472). Either way, these techniques don't neatly fit into navigation forms.

If you can live with these restrictions, navigation forms are a great way to give your database an attractive navigation system with minimal work.

Creating a Single-Level Navigation Form

Here's how to create a navigation form like the one shown in *Figure 14-15*.

1. **To create your navigation form, pick one of the top three options from the Create→Forms→Navigation menu (see *Figure 14-16*).**

   Access gives you six different navigation forms to choose from, which vary in two ways. First, there's the location of the navigation menu—the most common choices are on the top or side. Second, the menu can be either a simple single-level menu or a more complex two-level menu. (You'll learn about two-level menus in the next section.)

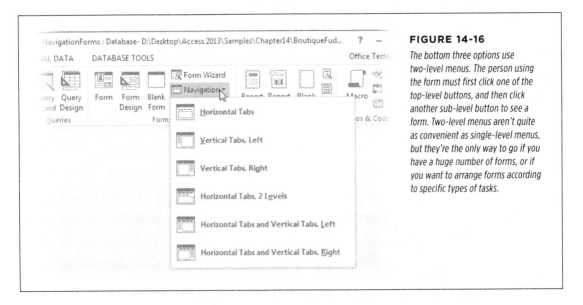

FIGURE 14-16

The bottom three options use two-level menus. The person using the form must first click one of the top-level buttons, and then click another sub-level button to see a form. Two-level menus aren't quite as convenient as single-level menus, but they're the only way to go if you have a huge number of forms, or if you want to arrange forms according to specific types of tasks.

When your navigation form first appears, you'll see a linked combination of two controls: a large, blank subform, and a navigation control (a thin strip of buttons) off to one side. These two pieces are connected by a layout table.

NOTE Unlike many other form design tasks, navigation menus are easier to create in Layout view than in Design view. That's because the drag-and-drop feature that lets you quickly fill your navigation menu with forms needs Access's layout feature to make sure each button gets put in the right place.

2. **To add a navigation button for one of your forms, click the form in Access's navigation pane, and drag it onto the navigation control (*Figure 14-17*).**

   When you release the form onto the navigation control, Access adds a new navigation button for it.

TIP There's no need to limit yourself to forms. You can just as easily drag reports onto a navigation control.

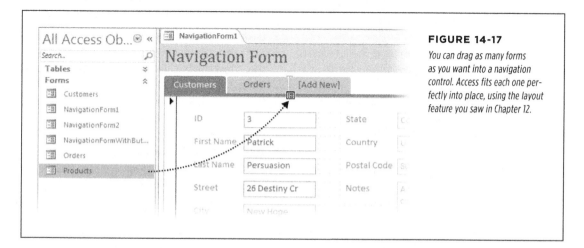

FIGURE 14-17

You can drag as many forms as you want into a navigation control. Access fits each one perfectly into place, using the layout feature you saw in Chapter 12.

3. **If you want to change the navigation button caption, double-click the caption and type the new name.**

   For example, you might prefer the button for TaxReportsYearEnd to read "View Tax Reports." You can also drag the right or bottom edge of the new navigation button to make it larger, so you can fit more text.

4. **Repeat steps 2 and 3 until you've added all the forms you want.**

   To remove a form that you don't want, click it once and then press Delete.

   When you've finished, you can switch to Design view and try out your form. A simple click of a button takes you to the matching form—and best of all, you didn't need to write any code or work your way through any wizards.

Making Navigation Forms Shine

The standard-issue Access navigation form is pleasant, but a little plain. Fortunately, you can use a number of easy tricks to make your navigation forms stand out. Here are the best:

- **Adjust the headers**. In a freshly created navigation form, you see two headers at once—the header of the navigation form, and the header of the form you're viewing in the navigation control. You can declutter your navigation form by removing one (or both) of these headers. The example in *Figure 14-17* has the header cut from the Customer form inside the navigation control. You don't need that header anyway, since the currently selected navigation button indicates the current form. In *Figure 14-18*, the header is removed from the navigation form instead. After all, the navigation form's header doesn't really provide any information about the content you're currently looking at.

- **Apply anchoring**. As you learned on page 430, anchoring lets specific controls grow to fill the available space in a form. Because the navigation subform will be called on to show forms of different sizes, it's a perfect candidate for anchoring. To apply anchoring, select the navigation subform (*not* the combination of subform and navigation buttons). The easiest way is to look for a control with a name like NavigationSubform in the Property Sheet list. Then make a selection from the Form Layout Tools | Arrange→Position→Anchoring menu. Two common choices are Stretch Down and "Stretch Down and Across."

- **Check the padding on the navigation control**. When you create a navigation form with buttons on the left or right side, Access inserts a little gap between your buttons and the navigation subform. You can remove this gap by selecting the strip of navigation controls and choosing Form Layout Tools | Arrange→Position→Control Padding→None.

- **Add a splash with fancy buttons**. Your buttons can be shaped, colored, and outfitted with a small set of special effects. You'll learn how on page 484.

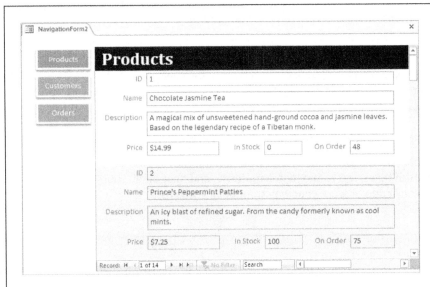

FIGURE 14-18

This navigation form uses several tricks to improve its appearance. It has no header, the navigation buttons are artfully styled, and the navigation subform uses anchoring so it expands to fill the available space. You can find this example, along with all the navigation forms in this chapter, on the Missing CD page (www.missingmanuals.com/cds/access13mm).

Creating a Two-Level Navigation Form

Creating a two-level menu is almost as easy as creating a simple single-level menu. Here's how to do it:

1. **To create your navigation form, pick one of the bottom three options from the Create→Forms→Navigation menu.**

   Your navigation form gets a linked combination of three controls: a large, blank subform, and two navigation controls.

   The navigation control at the top is the top-level menu. The navigation control underneath or off to the side is the submenu. The person using your navigation form will choose a category from the top-level menu, and then pick one of the forms listed in the submenu.

NOTE You can think of it as a collection of one-level menus. Each one-level menu has a single caption and a group of forms. The form user chooses which menu appears by clicking the appropriate button in the top-level menu.

---

2. **Begin by adding a heading for your top-level menu. Click "[Add New] text in the top level" and type in a new caption.**

   You might create headings for different tasks (like Sales, Stock Management, and Reporting) or for different form users (like Sales Department, Warehouse, and Admin). *Figure 14-19* shows an example.

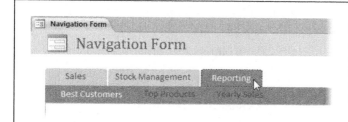

FIGURE 14-19

Here the top-level menu is on top, and the submenu is underneath. When you click a different top-level heading, you see a different submenu. In this case, clicking Reporting brings up a list of reports you can run.

3. **To add the submenu for this heading, drag a form from the navigation pane onto the submenu.**

   When you release the form onto the navigation control, Access adds a new navigation button for it.

4. **Repeat step 3 to add more forms to this group. Or, repeat step 3 to add a new top-level category.**

   If you want to change a submenu, just click the top-level heading to select it (at which point the corresponding submenu appears). You can then add new forms or remove existing ones.

Fine-Tuning Your Navigation Buttons

Ordinary navigation buttons don't look *bad*, but with a little more effort you can replace them with something a bit more stylish.

Your first option is to add a picture to a navigation button, which can either replace your text or sit alongside it (*Figure 14-20*). Before you do so, open the Property Sheet by choosing Form Layout Tools | Design→Tools→Property Sheet. Then, select a button and set the following properties:

- **Picture**. Click in this box and then click the ellipsis (...) to pick your picture file. Make sure you use a small picture (a tiny icon-sized image is best), otherwise you'll obliterate the button caption text.

- **Picture Caption Arrangement**. This determines how your picture and text share the button space. Choose No Picture Caption to display the picture only. The other options set where the text should go, which means that Left puts the text on the left side of the picture, Top puts it above the picture, and so on. Depending on your arrangement, you may need to enlarge the button, which you can do easily by dragging its edge.

Your second option is to alter the button's appearance by using the formatting commands in the Form Layout Tools | Format→Control Formatting section of the ribbon, just as with ordinary buttons. Here's a quick review:

- **Shape Fill**. Changes the color of your button, even giving it a smoothly blended gradient.

- **Shape Outline**. Changes the thickness, color, and style (for example, dashed or solid) or the border around the edge of your button.

- **Shape Effects**. Adds a shadow, glow, blurred edge, or beveled edge to your button.

- **Quick Styles**. Gives you a choice of snazzy, readymade button designs that change the fill, outline, and effect all at once. *Figure 14-18* features an example with stylized buttons.

- **Change Shape**. You may not have noticed it, but the navigation buttons automatically use a slightly different shape than normal buttons, with a gently rounded top edge that makes them look more like tabs.

  Access's designers added the Change Shape feature so you can give your buttons this distinctive shape, too. If you don't want the standard tab titles, you have a few other choices to choose from, including circles, ordinary rectangles, tabs with even more rounding on the top edge, and rectangles with a chip off the top-right corner (*Figure 14-20*).

FIGURE 14-20

Here, tiny icons make it obvious which form is for viewing data, and which is for editing it.

Linking to Related Data

A menu or navigation form providing a bird's-eye view of your database. However, your work doesn't end here. A well-designed navigation system lets you move easily from one form to the next, so you can move efficiently through your entire database.

The secret to form-to-form navigation is thinking about your *workflow* (that is, the order in which you move between tasks when working on your database). Suppose you're a furniture company selling hand-painted coffee tables. What happens when you receive a new order? Probably, you start by creating or selecting the customer (in one form), and then you add the order information for that customer (in another form). The menu doesn't need to go directly to the order form. Instead, you should start with a customer form. That form should provide a button (or some other control) that lets you move on to the order form.

You need to go through a similar thought process to create forms for, say, the customer service department. In their case, they need a way to pick a customer and to see, at a glance, the billing and payment details, the order information, and the shipping records. The best solution in this scenario could be to create a compound form that pulls everything together.

Getting from one form to another is easy. All you need is the right button. The following two sections walk you through two common examples.

Showing Linked Records in Separate Forms

In Chapter 13, you learned how a subform control can show linked records in one place (page 455). However, subforms don't always give you enough room to work. Depending on the way you work and the sheer volume of information you're facing, you may prefer to show the related records in a different place. You could add a button to your form that pops open another form with the linked records. The trick to making this work is using filtering in the second form so that it shows only the related records. *Figure 14-21* and *Figure 14-22* show an example with the Cacophoné Studios database.

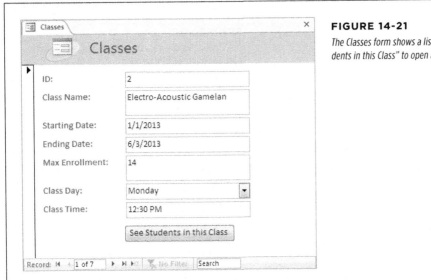

FIGURE 14-21

The Classes form shows a list of classes. Click "See Students in this Class" to open a second form Figure 14-22).

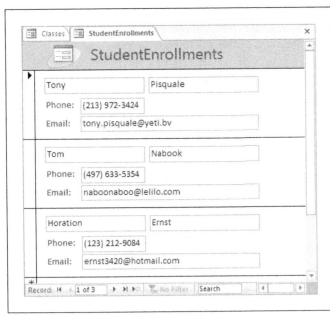

FIGURE 14-22

The StudentEnrollments form homes in on the students in just one class.

You can create the two forms that appear in *Figure 14-21* and *Figure 14-22* without much effort. The tricky bit is creating the "See Students in this Class" button.

Here's what you need to do to wire up a button that opens another form to show related records:

1. **Open the parent form in Design view (or Layout view).**

   Here, you start with the Classes form.

2. **Find the control gallery in the ribbon. Then click the Button icon, and draw the button onto your form.**

   In Design view, you can find all the controls in the Form Design Tools | Design→Controls section. In Layout view, they're in the Form Layout Tools | Design→Controls section.

   Once you add the button to your form, the Button wizard springs into action.

3. **Choose the Form Operations category, choose Open Form, and then click Next.**

   The next step in the wizard shows all the forms in your database.

4. **Choose the child form that has the related records, and then click Next.**

   In this case, choose the StudentEnrollments form.

5. **Choose "Open the form and find specific data to display," and then click Next.**

   The next step appears, with a list of fields in both forms (*Figure 14-23*). It's now up to you to tell Access how to filter the second form based on the first.

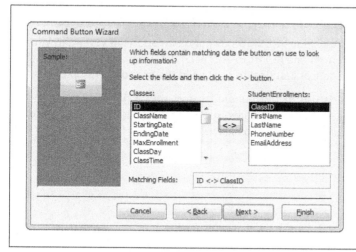

FIGURE 14-23

On the left is a list of fields from the table that the original form uses (in this case, Classes), and on the right is a separate list of fields from the table that the new form uses (StudentEnrollments). It's up to you to tell Access how these two tables are related.

6. **In the list on the left, choose the unique identifying field from the first table.**

   In this case, it's the ID field from the Classes table.

7. **In the list on the right, choose the matching field from the second table.**

   It's the ClassID field from the StudentEnrollments table.

8. **Click the two-way arrow button.**

   The two fields appear in the Matching Fields box. In the Cacophoné Studios example, you'll see the text "ID <-> ClassID." This tells Access to show an enroll-ment record only if the ClassID value in the StudentEnrollments form matches the ID value in the Classes form. In other words, you're getting the student enrollments for the current class.

9. **Click Next.**

   From this point on, the Button Wizard shows the standard steps you learned about earlier (page 450).

10. **Supply a name for the button, and then click Finish.**

    To try your link, switch to Form view and then click your link. When you click the "See Students in this Class" button and the StudentEnrollments form appears, your filtering takes effect.

> **NOTE** Nothing stops someone from *removing* your filtering by using the ribbon's Home→Sort & Filter→Toggle Filter command (or clicking the Filtered button that appears at the bottom of the form, next to the navigation buttons). If you don't want to allow this flexibility, you can configure the StudentEnrollments form so it doesn't let anyone change its filtering settings. To do so, open the form in Design view, select the Form item in the Property Sheet list, and then change the Allow Filters property from Yes to No.

Showing More Detailed Reports with Links

You can use a similar technique to allow navigation in reports. If you want, you can create a way to jump from one report to another, related report. In fact, the macro you need to create is almost identical to the one in the previous example.

Usually, Access experts use this technique to start with a general report and let people click their way to a more detailed report that highlights part of the data. *Figure 14-24* and *Figure 14-25* show an example.

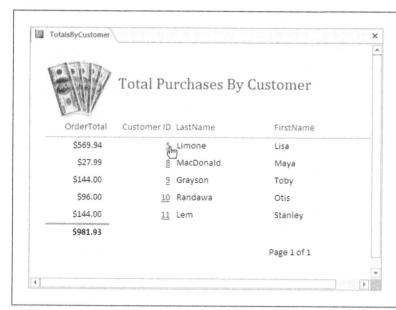

FIGURE 14-24

The first report (TotalsByCustomer) shows all the customers and their total orders. Click a single customer, and then Access launches the more detailed report shown in Figure 14-25.

FIGURE 14-25

Here's the CustomerPurchases report that profiles the selected individual's spending habits. A string-building expression ="Products Purchased By" & [FirstName] & " " & [LastName] *puts the current customer's name into the title.*

NOTE Reports are designed to be printed. For that reason, big gray buttons look a little out of place. Your other option—linking—as shown in this example, is much more common because it shows the data you need to print and adds interactivity at the same time.

To create this navigation, you need to begin by creating a text box that looks like a hyperlink. (You can't use the bonafide hyperlink control, because it displays only fixed, unchanging text. Instead, you need a way to display a field's content as a link—in this example, the customer ID.) You can then create a macro that, when the text field is clicked, springs into action to move you to the new report. This macro's job is to open the detailed report that you want, and then apply filtering so that only the related records appear.

You can easily format the text box. You can select any control, and then change its color, font, and so on, using the commands in the ribbon. However, you don't even need to perform this work. That's because every text box has an odd property named Is Hyperlink—set this to Yes, and the text box morphs into a blue underlined piece of text, which is just what you want.

Once that's out of the way, it's time to add the macro you need. You can use the following steps with the Boutique Fudge database (included with the download-able content for this chapter) to add the link to the TotalsByCustomer report (which opens the CustomerPurchases report).

NOTE A macro is a list of actions that you want Access to perform. In the next chapter, you'll explore macros in depth. For now, you'll learn just enough to create the navigation feature you need.

1. **Open the report you want to use in Design view (or Layout view).**

   In this example, everything starts at the TotalsByCustomer form.

2. **If the Property Sheet isn't visible, then choose Report Design Tools | Design→Tools→Property Sheet.**

   In Layout view, the tab title is different, so the full command is actually Report Layout Tools | Design→Tools→Property Sheet.

3. **Decide what field you want to use to create the link and then select it.**

   Usually, you'll want to use the unique ID value that links two tables together. Here, you use the ID field that stores the customer ID. If you haven't already, you should format this field to look like a link using the Is Hyperlink property.

   Now it's time to create and attach your macro.

4. **In the Property Sheet, switch to the Event tab, and then click the On Click box. Click the ellipsis (...) button.**

   The Choose Builder window appears and asks you how you want to create the code that runs when the link is clicked.

5. **Choose Macro Builder and then click OK.**

   The macro-editing window appears. Initially, it's blank except for a single drop-down list with the text "Add New Action."

6. **In the Add New Action list, click the drop-down arrow and choose** Open-Report.

   You can also use OpenForm to launch a form (for editing) when the report link is clicked.

   Once you choose an action, a bunch of text boxes with related settings appears. Access also moves the Add New Action list down so it's under your newly added action.

7. **Click in the Report Name box, and type the name of the report you want to use.**

   In this example, that's CustomerPurchases.

8. **Click in the Where Condition box, and type in your filter expression.**

   This filter expression needs to select the linked records. In the current example, your filter needs to select order records that match the current customer ID.

   Your expression needs to pick the right field in the report you're opening (the CustomerID field in the CustomerPurchases report), and then match it to the field where you clicked the link (the ID field in the TotalsByCustomers report). Here's the expression you need:

   ```
   [CustomerID]=[Reports]![TotalsByCustomer]![ID]
   ```

   The syntax [Reports]![TotalsByCustomer]![ID] is just a fancy way to tell Access to go looking for the ID value it needs on a currently open report named TotalsByCustomer. Once it finds that value, Access uses it to filter the new report that you're opening (the CustomerPurchases report) so it only shows records that have a matching value in the CustomerID field. In other words, you're telling Access to show the purchases made by this customer only.

9. **Close the macro window, and then choose Yes to save your changes when prompted.**

   You return to the report design window.

10. **Switch to Report view and then try out your link.**

    Now you can click the link to drill down to the more detailed report.

As always, you can try this example for yourself by using the sample databases for this chapter.

NOTE As written, this example has one minor problem. To see it, leave the CustomerPurchases report open, go back to the TotalsByCustomer report, and click a different customer link. Access won't refresh the CustomerPurchases report. To get around this problem, just close the CustomerPurchases report before you pick a new customer. Or, get your macro to call the CloseWindow action before it calls the OpenReport action, which quietly and seamlessly corrects this quirk. (Download the sample code to take a look for yourself.)

Programming Access

Automating Tasks with Macros

The secret to a long and happy relationship with Access is learning how to make it work the way *you* want. As you've already seen, true Access fanatics don't use the ordinary datasheet to enter information. Instead, they create their *own* customized data entry forms. Similarly, Access fans don't print their data by using basic yawn-inspiring tables. Instead, they create richly formatted reports that are just right for presenting *their* data. And Access pros definitely don't struggle through the same tedious series of steps to accomplish a common task—instead, they create macros that make Access do the work for them.

A *macro* is a miniature program that you create and store in your database. Macros can range from the exceedingly simple (like a command that shows a form) to the mind-bendingly complex (like a conditional macro that checks how much raw meat you have in stock, and automatically prints an order in triplicate if your fridge is empty).

In this chapter, you'll learn how to create basic macros. Then, you'll learn how to make them smarter. By the end of the next chapter, you'll have completed your macro exploration, and you'll be able to put together macros that can fire themselves up when needed, perform an entire sequence of steps, and even make decisions.

Macros vs. Code

In the past, macros have had a bit of a mixed reputation. Some Access gurus avoided them, preferring to use more powerful Visual Basic (VB) programming language (which you'll pick up in Chapter 17). Microsoft contributed to the confusion by suggesting that macros were an old-school technique, and not the best option for forward-thinking developers.

These days, macros have a more respectable reputation. Although macros don't have anywhere near the power of raw VB code, they're simple, clean, and convenient in a way that VB code can never be. They also have a couple of advantages.

One advantage that macros have over VB code is *security*. Because Access knows what every macro does, it can vouch that most macros are safe. (For example, Access knows that an OpenForm macro action can be used only to open a form, so it doesn't need to worry that it could delete your files, spam your friends, or reformat your hard drive.) On the other hand, Access isn't as trusting with VB code. As a result, it's liable to lock out your code-powered features, even if they're no more threatening than two bunnies cuddling on a pillow. You'll take a closer look at the security story on page 510.

Macros are also important if you decide to build a web database (Chapter 20), because web databases don't support Visual Basic code. (Web databases don't support the full range of macro commands either, but they don't support *any* VB.)

Even if you're planning to give macros a pass and become a black-belt Visual Basic coder, you should still start your Access programming career by learning about macros. That's because many of the concepts you'll pick up—how macros plug into forms, how conditional logic works, and so on—also apply to VB code.

◼ Macro Essentials

Although you may not realize it, you've already used macros. In Chapter 14, you created buttons that could perform useful tasks, like opening another form or navigating to a specific record. To create these actions, you used the Command Button Wizard, which asks a few simple questions, and then generates a made-to-measure macro.

Although the Command Button Wizard is easy to use, it's not all that flexible. Now, you're ready to get more power by building your own macros by hand.

Creating a Macro

In the following example, you'll start slow, with a simple macro that opens a table, and then heads straight to the last row. Here's how to create it:

1. **Choose Create→Macros & Code→Macro.**

   A new window appears for you to create your macro. Unofficially, this window is known as the *macro builder*.

   Every macro is made up of a sequence of one or more steps, or *actions*. To create a macro, you supply this list of actions, putting each one in a separate row (see *Figure 15-1*). Initially, this list is empty, and your macro doesn't do anything at all.

The first action

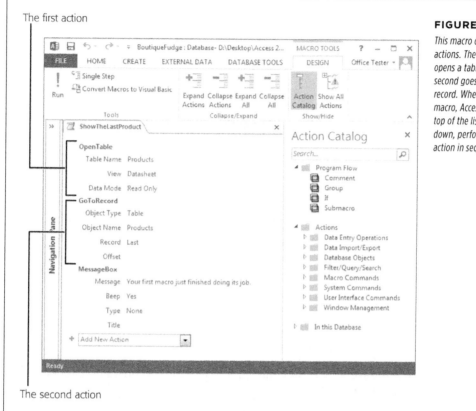

FIGURE 15-1

This macro consists of two actions. The first action opens a table, and the second goes to a specific record. When you run the macro, Access starts at the top of the list and moves down, performing each action in sequence.

The second action

2. **Choose your first action in the Add New Action list.**

Access has a predefined list of actions you can use to cook up a macro. When you add an action, you simply choose it from this list, as shown in *Figure 15-2*. For this example, begin by choosing the OpenTable action.

NOTE For the most part, the Add New Action list is alphabetical. However, Access makes an exception with a few special macro actions that it places right at the top of the list. They include Comment, for adding descriptive information (page 502); Group, for organizing sections of a macro (page 505); If, for creating conditional logic (page 536); and Submacro, for embedding several complete macros in a single macro object (page 524).

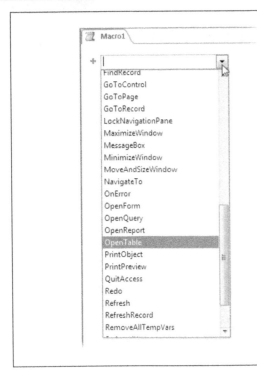

FIGURE 15-2

Click the drop-down arrow to see all the actions you can use. Right now, you're working with only the actions that Access considers safe for all databases. A little later (on page 510) you'll consider how you can use a few actions that Access considers risky business.

3. **Fill in the arguments for your action, using the text boxes that appear under it (see *Figure 15-3*).**

   Most actions need some information from you in order to carry out their business. An OpenTable action doesn't have much meaning unless you tell Access exactly what table you want it to open. These extra bits of information are called *arguments*.

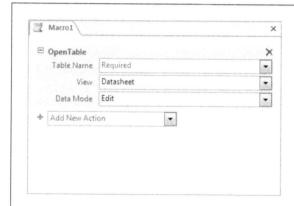

FIGURE 15-3

When you select an action in the list, all the arguments appear in text boxes under the action name. As this example shows, the OpenTable action has three arguments: Table Name, View, *and* Data Mode. *You can type directly in a text box to set the argument value or, for some values, you can click the drop-down arrow at the right side of the text box to show a list of options. For example, if you click the drop-down arrow in the Table Name text box, you get a list of all the tables in your database.*

The OpenTable action has three arguments:

- **Table Name** is the table you want to open. You can choose it from a drop-down list of tables. For this example, you can use any table that isn't empty.

- **View** lets you pick the view mode that's used. You can choose ordinary Datasheet to enter information, Design to change the table structure, or Print Preview to get ready to print the data. (Ignore the PivotTable and PivotChart choices; these correspond to features that have been removed in Access 2013.) For this example, choose Datasheet. (Of course, once the table is open, you can still switch to a different view by right-clicking the tab title or by using the View button on the ribbon.)

- **Data Mode** determines what types of changes are allowed. You can use the standard option, Edit, to allow all changes, Read Only to allow none, or Add to allow only record insertions. In this example, choose Read Only.

NOTE You've already seen how custom macros have more power than the Command Builder Wizard. When using the Command Builder Wizard, you can open forms and reports, but not ordinary tables, and you can't control the view mode or the allowed types of edits. Macros don't face these limitations.

4. **Repeat steps 2 to 3 to add another action.**

Every time you add an action, the Add New Action list moves down, so it sits right after the last action in your macro. To add a new action there, you simply pick a new action from the list.

You can add a practically unlimited number of actions to a macro. (For Access trivia buffs, macros top out at 999 actions.) When you run your macro, Access performs your actions in order, from top to bottom.

To complete this example, add a GoToRecord action. This action moves through the table you just opened to get to the record you want.

Using arguments, you'll need to point out the correct object (set the Object Type to Table, and the Object Name to whatever table you picked in step 3). Then, you can use the Record and Offset arguments to specify exactly where you want to end up. Using the Record argument, you can choose to head to the previous row (Previous), the next row (Next), the new row placeholder at the bottom of the table (New), a specific row (Go To), the first row (First), or—as in this example—the last row (Last). If you choose Go To, then you can use the Offset argument to point out a specific position—like setting it to 5 to jump to the fifth record.

> **NOTE** Some macro actions depend on previous macro actions. GoToRecord is a prime example—it assumes you opened a table, form, or query that has the record you want to see. If you use GoToRecord without having a suitable object open, you get an error message when you run the macro.

And just for fun, why not add one more macro action? Try the MessageBox action, which displays a message of your choosing in a small message window. You set the message in the Message argument. Try something like "Your first macro just finished doing its job." You can also add an optional title (using the Title argument), warning beep (by setting the Beep argument to Yes), and predefined icon (using the Type argument).

5. **Press Ctrl+S to save your macro, and then provide a macro name.**

   You could name the macro in this example *ShowTheLastProduct*. If you don't save the macro explicitly, Access politely asks you to when you close the macro window, or when you run your macro for the first time.

   Macros appear in the navigation pane. If you're grouping objects by type, you'll see that macros get their own type (named, rather predictably, Macros). If you're using the "Tables and Related Views" grouping, Access adds macros to an extra group at the bottom named Unrelated Objects.

> **NOTE** When you use the Command Builder Wizard, you're also creating a macro. However, this macro doesn't appear in the navigation pane, because it's locked into a specific form. This type of macro is known as an *embedded macro*, because it's embedded inside a form object. You'll learn how to edit embedded macros on page 533.

Running a Macro

Now that your macro is finished, you're ready to try it out. Access gives you four ways to run a macro:

- **You can run it directly**. Just find the macro you want in the navigation pane, and then double-click it. (This method works only if the macro isn't already open.) Or, if the macro is open, choose Macro Tools | Design→Tools→Run.

TIP If you've filtered the navigation pane (page 460) so that macros don't appear, you can still run your macros. Just select Database Tools→Macro→Run Macro. You'll then get the chance to pick your macro out of a list.

- **You can trigger it by using a keystroke**. You can, for instance, set up a macro that opens your end-of-month financial report whenever you press Ctrl+F. You'll learn how on page 526.

- **You can run it automatically when the database is first opened**. You could create a macro that always starts you out by running your favorite query and showing you the results. You'll try this on page 527.

- **You can attach it to a form**. You could set your macro to spring into action automatically when a button is clicked or new data is entered. This way is the most common way to use macros, and the way the Command Builder Wizard works. You'll explore this technique on page 532.

In this chapter, you'll get a chance to try all these techniques. But right now, keep to the simplest option, and run the macro you created in the previous section by using the Macro Tools | Design→Tools→Run command. *Figure 15-4* shows the result.

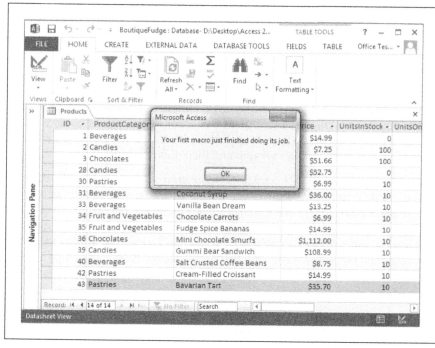

FIGURE 15-4

Here's the result of running the ShowTheLastProduct macro. Access opens the Products table (in Read-Only mode, so no changes are allowed), moves to the last, most recent record, and then shows a message informing you that the macro is finished.

Editing a Macro

As you've just seen, building a simple macro is easy. You simply pick your actions one by one out of the Add New Action list. For each action, you fill in the related arguments, using the handy text boxes.

Changing a macro is just as easy, and a few tricks can help you become a macro master. But before you can do anything, you need to open your macro in Design view. To do so, right-click it in the navigation pane and choose Design View. You arrive back at the macro window you used to create the macro in the first place.

Here's what you can do to make changes to your macro:

- **Change action arguments**. This part is easy. Just click to select an action, and all the text boxes appear again, so you can change as many values as you want.

- **Reorder actions**. Click any part of an action (except inside a text box), and then drag the action to its new position. Access automatically bumps other actions out of the way. Alternatively, you can click it, and then use the up and down arrow keys on the keyboard. (And if you're looking for yet another way to slide actions around, try using the green up and down arrow icons, which appear in the top-right corner of the action box when the action is selected.)

- **Add a new action**. You already know about the Add New Action list, which sits at the bottom of every macro, waiting for you to choose another action. However, there's another way to find the action you want—using the Action Catalog, which sits at the right of the Access window. For more information, read the next section.

- **Remove an action**. Select the action and press the Delete key. Or select the action and click the X icon in the top-right corner of the action box. Either way, make sure you really want to remove the action, because Access doesn't ask you twice, and the Undo feature can't bring it back. (If you do make a mistake, close your macro without saving it, and then open it anew.)

- **Add comments**. Although a long, complex macro may make perfect sense to you, it might not be so clear to someone else who needs to change it (or to yourself, if you return to make changes many months later). To help keep things clear, good macro writers always add comments—simple text descriptions that Access ignores. To add a comment, choose the Comment action from the Add New Action list, which is the very first entry (*Figure 15-5*). Or, use this no-click shortcut: type // into the Add New Action box, followed by the text of your comment, and press Enter.

> **TIP** Don't use comments to explain something that's already obvious based on the action arguments. For example, "This opens the Orders table" isn't a helpful description, because anyone looking at an OpenTable action can quickly figure out what table it opens. Instead, use comments to explain the *significance* of a step in a more complex operation. For example, "Opens the Orders table so you can delete expired orders" is better, because it fills in some details about what you're trying to accomplish. Right now, you don't need comments, but later on, when you create submacros and use conditions, you'll see how they become useful.

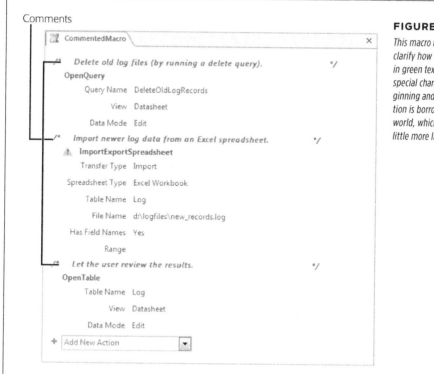

Comments

FIGURE 15-5

This macro uses three comments to clarify how it works. Comments appear in green text and bracketed with the special character sequence /* at the beginning and */ at the end. This convention is borrowed from the programming world, which helps make macros look a little more like real code.

Finding Actions in the Action Catalog

There's nothing wrong with the Add New Action list. In fact, it's a pretty convenient way to add new actions to a macro, if you already know what you want. But if you don't know the name of the action you need, an alphabetical list isn't a great help. That's where the Action Catalog comes in.

The Action Catalog is a pane on the right side of the macro designer, listing all of the possible actions you can use. (If you inadvertently close the Action Catalog, you can open it again by choosing Macro Tools | Design→Show/Hide→Action Catalog.) The difference between the Action Catalog and the Add New Action list is that the Action Catalog organizes actions into easy-to-understand groups (*Figure 15-6*).

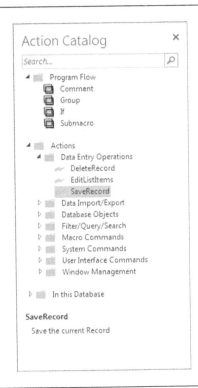

FIGURE 15-6

If you're not sure what action you need, you can browse the categories in the Action Catalog. To expand a category, simply click the arrow next to it. When you select an action, a mini-description appears in the box at the bottom of the Action Catalog. At the top of the Action Catalog are special macro language actions, which include comments and conditional logic. At the bottom is an "In this Database" category, which lists the other macro objects in your database. Drag one of these onto your macro, and Access inserts a RunMacro action that triggers the corresponding macro.

For example, the Data Entry Operations group includes actions that delete and save records, and the Filter/Query/Search group includes actions that open queries, apply filters, hunt for records, and trigger a refresh. To add an action from the Action Catalog, just find the right entry and drag it onto your macro. Unlike the Add New Action list, the Action Catalog doesn't force you to place your new actions at the end of the macro. To save time, you can drop the new action between any existing actions.

The Action Catalog can also help out if you only roughly know the name of the action you want. At the top of the Action Catalog is a search box. Type a word from an action's name, press Enter, and Access filters the Action Catalog so it shows only the actions that contain your search term. Access compares your search text to the action name *and* the action description. For example, typing *import* matches actions like *Import*ExportSpreadsheet, RunSaved*Import*Export, and Beep (because beep refers to "*import*ant visual changes" in its description).

Collapsing, Expanding, and Grouping Macro Actions

When you start writing longer, more complex macros, you may find that the macro designer gets cluttered with an overwhelming number of details. To make your life easier, you can temporarily hide some of this information.

The easiest technique is to *collapse* any macro actions that you're not interested in, by simply clicking the +/- button that appears to the left of the action name (*Figure 15-7*). Click it again to expand the action back into view. Alternatively, keyboard lovers can use the left arrow key to collapse the currently selected action and the right arrow key to expand it.

> **TIP** To get some instant perspective, you can collapse *every* action in your macro by choosing Macro Tools | Design→Collapse/Expand→Collapse Actions. You can then expand just the ones you're interested in, or expand them all with Macro Tools | Design→Collapse/Expand→Expand Actions.

FIGURE 15-7

When a macro action is collapsed, it occupies just a single line, and all its arguments are listed in a compressed format on that line. If you hover over a collapsed action, the arguments appear in a pop-up (as with the MessageBox action show here).

In some cases, you may want to subdivide a single macro in sections. For example, if you have a macro that updates a record and sends an email, you want to place the appropriate actions in two sections (the first section, which takes care of the update, and the second one, which takes care of the emailing). That way, you can concentrate on tweaking the portion of the macro that interests you while collapsing the other sections out of sight.

To accomplish this, you need to use a *group* action. The concept is simple—you place actions in a group, and you can then expand or collapse that entire group of actions to a single line (*Figure 15-8*).

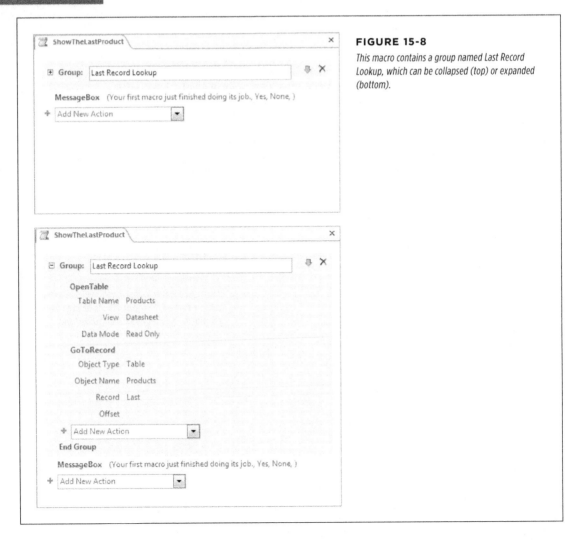

FIGURE 15-8

This macro contains a group named Last Record Lookup, which can be collapsed (top) or expanded (bottom).

Here's how to create a group of your own:

1. **In the Add New Action list, choose Group. It's the second entry.**

   Alternatively, you can drag the Program Flow→Group action from the Action catalog. Either way, Access inserts a new empty group.

2. **Give your group a name.**

   While the action is selected, type a descriptive name in the Group text box. The name is for your reference only, so use whatever seems appropriate.

Every group starts with the group name (at the top) and ends with the text "End Group." In between, you place the actions that are a part of the group.

3. **Add actions to your group.**

Usually, you drag the actions you want from elsewhere in your macro into the macro group. However, you can also add new actions to a group by dragging them from the Action Catalog or by choosing them from the Add New Action list that appears inside the group.

Once your group is fully stocked, you can collapse it—and all of its actions—in one fell swoop. In the Macro Tools | Design→Collapse/Expand section of the ribbon, the Collapse Actions command collapses all your actions, but none of your groups. Collapse All collapses all your actions *and* all your groups. Similarly, Expand Actions leaves groups untouched, while Expand All expands every group and action you've got.

As with collapsed actions, you can hover your cursor over a group to temporarily expand it and review its contents.

TIP Here's a nifty trick that creates a new group and puts some existing actions into it, all at once. Click the first action that you want to place in the new group. Then, Shift-click the last action. (Access highlights all the actions in between, too.) Then, right click any part of this selection and choose Make Group Block.

Solving Macro Problems

Not all macros run without a hitch. If you've made a mistake—maybe your macro tries to open an object that doesn't exist, or tries to use an argument that doesn't make sense—you get a detailed error message, as shown in *Figure 15-9*.

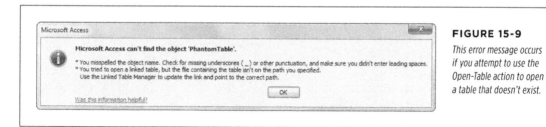

FIGURE 15-9

This error message occurs if you attempt to use the Open-Table action to open a table that doesn't exist.

Although macro error messages are quite descriptive, they don't always give you enough information to pinpoint the problem. For example, the error message shown in *Figure 15-9* has more than one possible cause—it could result from a failed OpenTable action (as it does in this example), or a failed ImportExportText or ImportExportSpreadsheet action. And even if you know it's OpenTable that's to blame, that information won't help you if you call OpenTable more than once in the same macro.

To diagnose problems like these, you need to find the problem by using a programming technique called *debugging*. Debugging lets you put your macro under the microscope and see exactly what's happening. The type of debugging that Access gives you with macros is called *single-step debugging*, because it lets you test your macro one action at a time. That way, you know exactly when the error occurs.

To use single-step debugging, follow these steps:

1. **Open your macro in Design view.**

   All new macros begin in Design view. If you want to test a macro you created earlier, find it in the navigation pane, right-click it, and then choose Design View.

2. **Choose Macro Tools | Design→Tools→Single Step.**

   Single Step is a toggle button, which means it appears highlighted when it's selected. After you click Single Step, it should be highlighted. (If not, single-step debugging was already switched on, and you just turned it off. Click Single Step again to switch it back on.)

3. **Choose Macro Tools | Design→Tools→Run.**

   Your macro begins to run. But now there's a difference. Before each action, Access shows you the relevant information in the Macro Single Step window. *Figure 15-10* shows you how it works.

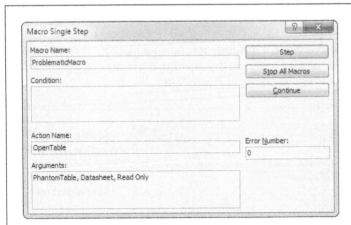

FIGURE 15-10

This window tells you that you're running a macro named ProblematicMacro. The next step is to perform an OpenTable *action, with the argument values shown in the Arguments box. (Pay no heed to the Condition box, because you haven't yet learned how to craft conditional macros.)*

4. **Click Step, Continue, or Stop All Macros, depending on what you want to do next.**

   - **Step** performs the action. If the action completes successfully, then Access pauses the macro again, and then shows you the Macro Single Step window with information about the next action. That's why this process is called single-stepping—it lets you perform a single step at a time. If you click Step and the action fails, then you see the error information, as shown in *Figure 15-11*.

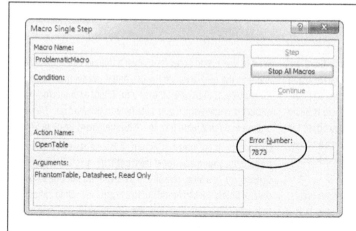

FIGURE 15-11

When an error occurs, you can't go any further. The Macro Single Step window shows the Access error number for your problem (which is useful if you need to search for help in Microsoft's online knowledge base), but it doesn't let you keep going. You must click Stop All Macros, fix the problem, and then try again.

- **Continue** switches off Single Step mode and runs the rest of the macro without interruption. If an error occurs, it fails with an error message, just like before.

- **Stop All Macros** stops the macro before it performs any more actions. The "all" in Stop All Macros indicates that if there's more than one macro running at once, Access aborts them all. You could create a macro that calls another macro. If you stop processing during this sequence of events, both macros give up.

NOTE The Single Step setting affects all macros, including any you created with the Command Builder Wizard. So remember to switch it off when you're done testing your macro. Otherwise, the Macro Single Step window appears when you're using macros that work perfectly fine.

Dealing with Macro Errors

You'll face two types of errors with macros. First, there are the errors you make when you design your macro. Using single-step debugging, you can track these down and fix them. Second, there are errors that occur when the macro is being used in the wrong context. Perhaps the data you need isn't in the current record, or the form you're trying to use isn't open. You can't avoid this sort of error by changing the macro, but you can tell Access what to do about it.

Ordinarily, Access halts your macro as soon as an error occurs. If you want to take a different approach, start your macro with the OnError action. The OnError action chooses one of three error-handling options, depending on the Go To argument. Set it to Fail, and you get the standard behavior.

Set it to Next, and Access skips over a trouble-causing action and runs the next action in the list. And if you set it to Macro Name, Access jumps down the list until it finds a submacro with a specific name (which you specify with the Macro Name argument). You'll learn how to create submacros on page 524.

OnError is an unusual action, because its effects last throughout your macro (or at least until the next time you use OnError). In a long, complex macro, you can call OnError several times. But be careful not to use error-handling options that may cause additional problems. In many macros, one action depends on the next, so it's best to halt the entire macro at the first sign of trouble.

Macros and Security

In recent years, the people at Microsoft have become paranoid about security. They've clamped down in Office programs like Access in a bid to lock out evil virus writers. And although these changes make Access a safer place to be, they also make it a bit inconvenient to use certain types of macros.

Unsafe Macro Actions

Access distinguishes between two types of macros: those that are always harmless, no matter how they're used, and those that have the potential for abuse. The OpenTable action is harmless. It could open a table you don't want to see, but it can't cause any real mischief. On the other hand, the PrintOut action isn't as innocent. In the wrong hands, it could send 400 copies of your data to the printer in 80-point font. Similarly, DeleteObject could wreak real havoc in your database, and RunApplication definitely isn't safe—it could launch the latest spyware or install a computer virus.

When you create a macro, the drop-down list of actions shows only actions that are 100 percent harmless. These actions are known as *safe* actions. Of course, you can have valid reasons to use potentially *unsafe* macros. Maybe you really *do* want to print a report, delete an object, or run another program. In that case, you need to use potentially *unsafe* macro actions—ones that Access doesn't trust quite so readily.

NOTE As long as you're the one in control of your database, you know it doesn't contain devious code and other trickery. There's no good reason to stay away from potentially unsafe macro actions. However, if someone's just sent you a database in an email message, or if you've downloaded a database from the Web, you may not be so sure. For that reason, Access automatically disables the unsafe macros in a database, unless you tell it otherwise.

To see the full list of macro actions, including those that Access considers unsafe, create a new macro (or open an existing one), and then choose Macro Tools | Design→Show/Hide→Show All Actions. Now the drop-down list of actions includes several more possibilities. When you choose an unsafe action while building a macro, Access lets you know with a warning icon (*Figure 15-12*).

NOTE Access has no concept of what actions may be more or less dangerous. Instead, it simply distinguishes between safe and unsafe.

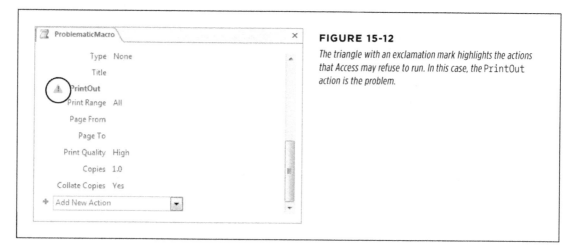

FIGURE 15-12

The triangle with an exclamation mark highlights the actions that Access may refuse to run. In this case, the PrintOut *action is the problem.*

If you open an untrusted database, Access quietly disables unsafe macro actions. If you try to run one, you'll get an error message that describes the problem. The only solution is to tell Access to trust the database (either temporarily or permanently), as described in the next section.

The Actions that Access Doesn't Trust

Here's the lineup of the most common unsafe actions:

- **Deleting an object**. Clearly, a dangerous move.

- **Printing an object**. Because who knows how much paper you'll need?

- **Copying an object**. A devious attacker could use this to create a macro that fills up your database.

- **Saving an object**. This action may seem fairly innocent, but it could easily be combined with other actions to create a macro that changes a database object, and then saves a tampered version.

- **Copying your database file**. This action could overwrite a copy that you've already made, or replace another important file. Exporting data is considered just as risky.

- **Maximizing, minimizing, or moving a window**. Perhaps Microsoft was being a little too conservative when it decided not to trust these actions, which let you reposition forms and other windows. In any case, people don't use these actions too often in modern versions of Access, because they don't apply to tabbed windows, only the less commonly used free-floating windows page 49).

- **Running SQL**. As you learned on page 220, SQL is the language that underlies Access queries. You can use raw SQL commands to perform just about any task in your database, from deleting a dozen records to creating a new table.

- **Running VB code**. Although this action doesn't appear with an exclamation icon, Access treats all VB code as unsafe. You'll learn more in Chapter 17.

- **Sending arbitrary keystrokes**. The SendKeys action lets you send a stream of keystrokes to the currently active window. You can do just about anything, and that's the problem. Respectable Access users avoid SendKeys anyway, because it's a bit buggy. (Weird problems occur if you click with the mouse while the macro runs, and end up directing the keystrokes to a different window from the one you intended.)

Some actions may be considered unsafe, depending on what arguments you use with them:

- **Quitting Access**. Access lets you perform a normal Quit action, which prompts the person using the database to save changes, discard them, or cancel the exit request. However, you can configure the Quit action to close immediately *without* prompting you to save anything (or to close immediately, and save all outstanding changes). If you use either of these options, Access treats the action as unsafe.

- **Sending an email**. This action is considered unsafe if you don't let the macro user confirm or cancel the message before it's sent.

Trusted Databases

As you first learned in Chapter 1, Access can be a bit paranoid. The first time it meets a new database, it decides not to trust the database, even if the database is one you created. You know that Access doesn't trust the current database when it shows the security warning shown in *Figure 15-13*. This message warns you that Access has switched off any potentially risky parts of your database, including unsafe macro actions.

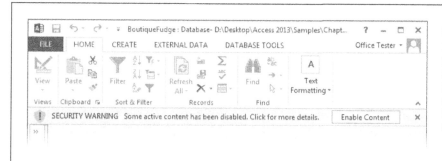

FIGURE 15-13

The message bar gives you an ominous alert. To tell Access to trust this database and switch the unsafe macros back on in this database, click Enable Content.

The trusted database system is simple at heart. Every time you choose to trust a database, Access stores the information about that database in the *Windows registry*—the massive catalog of settings on every Windows computer). The next time you open the same database, Access looks in the registry and sees that you already trust it. As a result, once you've clicked Enable Content, your database will work happily ever after.

However, there are a few exceptions. Access stops trusting your database (and displays the message bar again) if you rename the database file, move it to another folder, or move it to another computer, because in these situations Access can't be sure that it's the same database. Similarly, Access won't trust your database if you log into your computer as another user, and you can't fool Access by replacing a trusted database with another file that has the same name. (This sneaky strategy fails because Access stores other details about the database file, like its size and creation date. If these don't match, Access knows something's up.)

The Enable Content button doesn't work the same way when you open a database from a network drive. When you click Enable Content in this situation, Access trusts the database for the current session only. It doesn't designate the database file as a trusted database. Instead, it shows an additional warning message (*Figure 15-14*) that gives you the choice. If you're certain you want to trust this database permanently, click Yes. If you want to enable the database for this session only, click No. All the code and macros will then work, but Access will disable them again the next time you open the database.

FIGURE 15-14

Network databases represent a different type of risk. Because they aren't stored on your computer, it's possible that someone else might modify the database file after you decide to trust it. If you're worried about this scenario, click No to enable the database but refrain from designating the file as a trusted database. If you're not so paranoid, and you're opening the file from a personal or company network, you're probably safe to click Yes.

You can also give temporary trust to a database that's stored on your hard drive, but it's a lot less common and requires a little more work. The following section shows you how.

Temporary Trust

Usually, the trusted database system is exactly what you want. Potentially dangerous files are locked up until you check them out and click Enable Content. After that point, they're family, and Access lets them run any macro action they want. However, it's possible that you might decide to temporarily trust a database—in other words, trust it for the current session only.

In that case, don't click the Enable Content button. Instead, follow these steps:

1. **Click File→Info.**

   This switches you to Backstage view.

2. **Click the big Enable Content button and choose Advanced Options.**

   A new window appears, with two options: to keep the database disabled or to trust it just this once.

3. **Choose "Enable content for this session" and click OK.**

   Now the database can run all its code and macros—at least until the next time you close and reopen it.

The Trust Center

If you want more control over Access's security settings, you need to visit Access's Trust Center. It gives you several options to make it even easier to work with databases that contain code and macros:

- You can lower the Access security settings so that unsafe macros are allowed. This approach isn't recommended, because it allows any code in your database.

If you accidentally open a database that contains troublemaking code, you have no protection.

- You can tell Access to trust the database files in certain folders on your computer (or on other computers). This way is the most convenient way to go.

- You can tell Access to trust databases that have been created by a *trusted publisher*. This option is the most secure, but to set it up, you need to pay another company to get a security certificate. For that reason, only big companies with money to burn use this option.

All these actions take place in the Trust Center window (*Figure 15-15*). To get to it, follow these steps:

1. **Choose File→Options.**

2. **In the list on the left, choose Trust Center.**

3. **Click the Trust Center Settings button.**

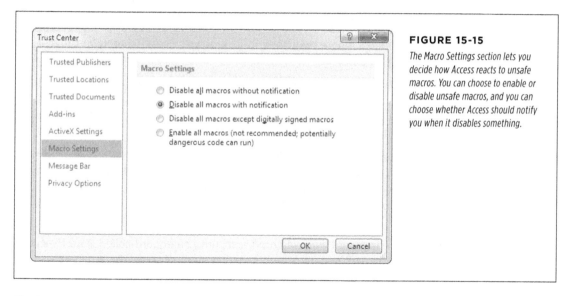

FIGURE 15-15

The Macro Settings section lets you decide how Access reacts to unsafe macros. You can choose to enable or disable unsafe macros, and you can choose whether Access should notify you when it disables something.

The Trust Center has several sections:

- **Trusted Publishers** lets you tell Access to trust databases that are *digitally signed* by certain people. To use this feature, your company needs to buy a digital certificate from a company like VeriSign (*www.verisign.com*). Then, when you open a signed database, Access contacts the company that issued the certificate, and checks that it's valid. If it is, everything is kosher, the database is trusted, and all unsafe macros are allowed. Digital certificates are outside the scope of this book.

NOTE If you dig around long enough, you'll discover that Microsoft has a tool (named *makecert.exe*) for generating your own digital certificates. However, this tool is for testing purposes only, because the certificates it generates don't work on anyone else's computer. Beware—some Access books and websites may lead you astray.

- **Trusted Locations** lets you pick out the places on your hard drive where you store your databases. That way, Access knows to trust your database files, but not anyone else's. You'll learn how to set up a trusted location in the following section.

- **Trusted Documents** lets you switch off the trusted database feature altogether, or switch it off for network databases only. You can also remove the current list of trusted databases (in other words, you can "untrust" everything you've trusted so far) by clicking the Clear button. However, Access doesn't provide a list of the documents you trust.

- **Add-ins** lets you adjust whether Access add-ins (miniprograms that extend the features in Access) should be supported even if they weren't created by a supported publisher. Ordinarily, all add-ins are allowed. (After all, if you don't trust a specific add-in, don't install it!) People use this setting only in corporate environments where they need to lock down Access severely to prevent any chance of a problem.

- **ActiveX Settings** lets you adjust how Access treats ActiveX controls. ActiveX controls are graphical widgets (like super-fancy buttons) that developers create (or buy), and then plop into databases and other documents. These days, people don't often use ActiveX controls.

- **Macro Settings** lets you configure how Access deals with macros. You can make it more rigorous (so that no macros are allowed, unless they're from a trusted publisher), or less rigorous (so that all macros are allowed, no matter what they might do). By far the best choice is to leave this option at the standard setting: "Disable all macros with notification."

- **DEP Settings** lets you switch off a security safeguard called Data Execution Prevention. This feature prevents certain types of computer attacks that work by inserting malicious code into your computer's memory, and then tricking your computer into running that code. It's possible, but extremely unlikely, that some old Access add-ins may not work when DEP is switched on. But otherwise, there's no reason to turn off DEP.

- **Message Bar** lets you set whether Access shows the message bar when it blocks unsafe macros in an untrusted database.

- **Privacy Options** lets you tweak a few options that aren't related to macros at all. You can choose whether Access checks the Web for updated Help content, and whether it sends troubleshooting information to Microsoft when a problem occurs (so that Microsoft can spot bugs and learn how to improve Access in the future). If you're paranoid about Internet spies, you may want to disable some of these options. Most of the time, these settings are only for conspiracy theorists.

Setting Up a Trusted Location

Wouldn't it be nice to have a way to distinguish between your databases, which contain perfectly harmless code, and other databases? Access makes this easy. It lets you designate a specific folder on your hard drive as a trusted location. If you open a database in this location, Access automatically trusts it and allows unsafe macros.

NOTE Of course, it's still up to you to make sure that you don't put potentially dangerous databases in the trusted location. If you do, then you won't have any protection when you open it. However, this compromise is reasonable, because most Access fans are already in the habit of putting their databases in a separate folder.

Here's how you can set up a new trusted location:

1. **Open the Trust Center window.**

   If you're not there already, follow the steps on page 515.

2. **Choose the Trusted Locations section.**

   You see a window that lists all the trusted locations (*Figure 15-16*). Initially, you just see one trusted location: the ACCWIZ folder that Access uses to store its wizard.

3. **Make sure the "Disable all Trusted Locations" option isn't set.**

   If it is, you need to switch it off before you can use the trusted locations feature.

4. **If you want to trust a folder on your company or home network, choose "Allow Trusted Locations on my network."**

   This setting is a bit riskier, because a network location is out of your control. A hacker could sneak a virus-laden database into that location without your noticing. However, if you're reasonably certain that the network is secure (and the other people who use the folder aren't likely to download databases from the Web and place them there), you don't need to worry.

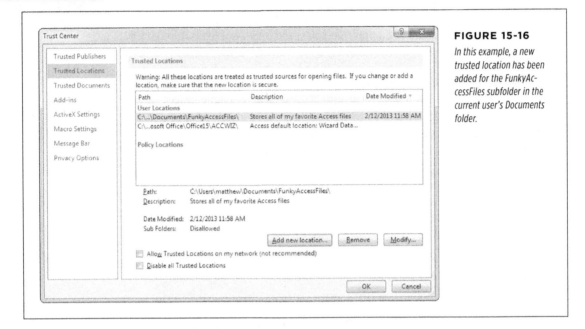

FIGURE 15-16

In this example, a new trusted location has been added for the FunkyAccessFiles subfolder in the current user's Documents folder.

5. **Click "Add new location."**

   Access asks you to fill in a few pieces of information (*Figure 15-17*).

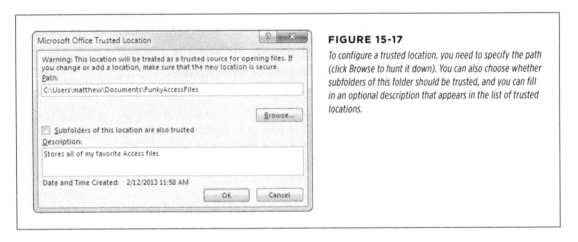

FIGURE 15-17

To configure a trusted location, you need to specify the path (click Browse to hunt it down). You can also choose whether subfolders of this folder should be trusted, and you can fill in an optional description that appears in the list of trusted locations.

6. **Click OK to add the location to the list.**

   You can configure the location or remove it at any time by selecting it in the list, and then using the clear-as-a-bell Remove and Modify buttons.

Three Macro Recipes

So far, you've created a basic macro, tried it out, and thought deeply about macro security. It's about time you got a payoff for all your work and considered a few practical ways to use macros.

The full list of macro actions contains many actions that aren't that interesting or are useful only in very specific scenarios. The following sections highlight a few of the more useful macro commands. You can check them out in the downloadable content for this chapter, or try the shake-and-bake recipes in your own database.

Find a Record

The FindRecord action works just like the Datasheet Find feature you saw on page 112. You fill in all the search information by using arguments.

Let's say you want to search the Diet field in the AnimalTypes table, looking for the word "hay." Here are the actions you may use:

- **OpenForm** to open the form that you'll use to display the matching record (in this case, AnimalTypes). You can substitute OpenTable to search using a datasheet.

- **GoToControl** to move to the field you want to search (in this case, Diet). If you're planning to perform a search that spans every field, then you can skip this step.

- **FindRecord** to find the text. It's up to you whether you want to start searching at the first record or the current one, as in this example. You can also choose whether you'll search for the text anywhere inside the field, or require the whole field value to match the search text exactly.

Once you put together the complete macro, you'll get something like this:

ACTION	IMPORTANT ARGUMENTS*	DESCRIPTION
1. OpenForm	Form Name: AnimalTypes	Opens the form. If it's already open, this switches to the existing window.
2. GoToControl	Control Name: Diet	Jumps to the Diet field.
3. FindRecord	Find What: ="hay" Match: Any Part of Field Only Current Field: Yes Find First: No	Finds the specified text anywhere in the Diet field, starting at the current record.

You can use the default values for all other arguments.

NOTE You may have noticed that the Find What argument of the FindRecord action starts with an equal sign. That's because it accepts an *expression*. In this example, the expression is nothing more than a fixed piece of text, which is wrapped in quotation marks. However, you could substitute a more complex expression that uses operators, functions, and other advanced techniques.

The neat thing about this macro is that you can use it several times in a row to look for more occurrences of the text. If the AnimalTypes form is already open, then this macro just carries on to the next match.

> **TIP** For even more flexibility, you could create a macro that uses *only* the FindRecord action. That way, you could search for specific text in any field in any form or table. Of course, if you try to run such a macro and you don't have any forms or tables open, FindRecord can't do anything, and you get an error.

Print a Report

Do you need a helpful macro that automatically spits out a frequently used report? Access gives you several options. Here are two:

- If you want to use the standard print settings, you can print any report by using the OpenReport action, and setting the View argument to Print.

- If you want to customize the print quality, number of copies, and starting and stopping page, you need to use a three-step approach. Start with OpenReport, use PrintOut to send it off, and then wind up with CloseWindow to tidy up.

> **NOTE** Make sure the Macro Tools | Design→Show/Hide→Show All Actions option is switched on before you create your macro, or you won't see the PrintOut action. And don't try either of these techniques with an untrusted database, because Access won't run your macro.

The following sequence of actions demonstrates the second approach. This macro prints two copies of a list of so-called customers who haven't actually ordered a single thing, using the CheapskateCustomers report:

ACTION	IMPORTANT ARGUMENTS*	DESCRIPTION
1. OpenReport	Report Name: CheapskateCustomers	Opens the report (but as you'll see, it's only around for a couple of seconds).
2. PrintOut	Copies: 2	You can use other arguments to print just a range of pages or change the quality. However, you can't pick the printer.
3. CloseWindow	Object Type: Report Object Name: CheapskateCustomers	There's no need to keep this report open, now that the printout is sent off.

* You can use the default values for all other arguments.

As soon as Access performs the PrintOut action, the pages start streaming out of the default printer on your computer. You don't get a chance to confirm or cancel the operation. For even more fun, you can extend this macro with more steps so it prints several reports at once.

TIP There's one more option. You can open a table or a report with the View argument set to Print Preview. This option doesn't actually send the data to your printer, but it gets you one step closer. This option is best if you want a final chance to choose a printer, make sure the data is correct, and check that the report isn't ridiculously long. It also works in untrusted databases.

Email Your Data

One of the hidden gems of the Access macro language is EMailDatabaseObject—an all-purpose action for sending email messages. The EMailDatabaseObject action uses a standard called MAPI (Messaging Application Programming Interface), which means it lets you use just about any Windows email program to send your message. However, EMailDatabaseObject doesn't work with web-based mail services like Hotmail or Yahoo! Mail.

EMailDatabaseObject is surprisingly versatile. You can use it in three ways:

- **To email a database object to another person**. The database object is converted to another format you choose, like an Excel spreadsheet, an HTML web page, or even a print-read PDF file. You specify the object you want to send, using the Object Type and Object Name arguments.

- **To email the current database object**. This way gives you an infinitely flexible macro that can send off whatever data you're currently looking at. The only limitation is that you need to know what type of object you're planning to send, whether it's a full table, a query that highlights important information, or a report with grouping and subtotals. Just set the Object Type argument accordingly, and leave Object Name blank.

- **To send an ordinary email message**. To send a message, you simply leave both the Object Type and Object Name arguments blank. You can fill in the message using the Message Text property. This method is a handy way to let someone know when you've added some new data or finished a hefty editing job.

NOTE EMailDatabaseObject can send only a single database object at a time. If you want to send several database objects, you need to use EMailDatabaseObject several times. To send three reports, you need three email messages, with three attached files. In some cases, you may be able to get around this requirement by creating a clever query that fuses together all the information you want to send into one set of results. (For example, see union queries on page 222.)

The nicest thing about EMailDatabaseObject is that you can use it in an untrusted database, provided you follow one rule: Set the Edit Message argument to Yes. That way, when the macro runs, you get a final chance to review the message, change any text, and cancel it if you're unhappy. But if you set Edit Message to No, the EMailDatabaseObject action fires the message off without giving you a chance to step in. That behavior is considered risky, so Access doesn't allow it in an untrusted database.

The following macro converts two queries with sales information into Excel spreadsheets. It then mails them to the head honchos.

ACTION	IMPORTANT ARGUMENTS*	DESCRIPTION
1. EMailDatabaseObject	Object Type: Query Object Name: MonthlySalesTotals Output Format: Excel Workbook (.xlsx) To: *headhoncho@acme.com* Subject: *Monthly Update* Message Text: *Here are the most recent sales figures, straight from our macro-fied Access database. You'll get the customer totals in a separate email.* Edit Message: Yes	Sends an email message to *headhoncho@acme.com*, with the data from the MonthlySalesTotals query converted to an Excel workbook. The message subject and message text are set by the Subject and Message Text arguments. You have a chance to tweak them before the message is sent. *Figure 15-18* shows this action.
2. EMailDatabaseObject	Object Type: Query Object Name: CustomerSalesTotals Output Format: Excel Workbook (.xlsx) To: *headhoncho@acme.com* Subject: *Monthly Update* Message Text: *Here are the totals by customer.* Edit Message: Yes	Sends an email message to *headhoncho@ acme.com*, with the data from the CustomerSalesTotals query.

* You can use the default values for all other arguments.

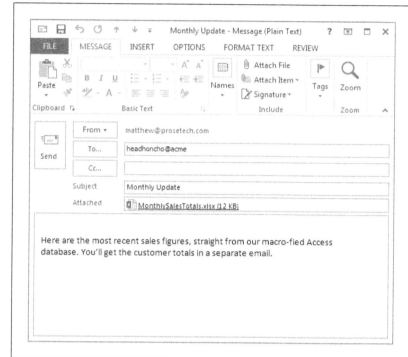

FIGURE 15-18

When the Edit Message property is set to Yes, you get a final chance to review (and change) the message before it's sent.

If you're crafty, you can mail huge numbers of people at once. The most straightforward option is to supply a whole list of addresses for the To, Cc, or Bcc argument, separating each one with a semicolon (;). For an even better approach, use a mailing list. This technique may vary depending on your mail software, but in Outlook and Outlook Express, it's easy—just put the name of the mailing list in the To field. If you've created a mailing list named FairweatherFriends, just type the word FairweatherFriends for the To argument.

> **TIP** Running out of room to edit your message? Press Shift+F2 while you're editing the Message Text property to pop up a much larger Zoom window, where you can see several lines of text at once.

Managing Macros

As you build more and more snazzy macros, you'll need some way to keep them all organized and to make sure the macros you need are at your fingertips when you need them. Access gives you a few tools to help, including submacros, which combine related macros into one object for easier storage, and macro shortcut keys, which let you trigger the right macro exactly when you need it.

Submacros

The average macro is only three to five actions long. However, the average data-base that uses macros quickly accumulates dozens of them. Managing these tiny programs can become quite a headache, especially when you need to remember what each macro does.

To help manage your macros, you can use the *submacro* feature. Technically, a sub-macro is a small, named bundle of actions. The nifty part about submacros is that you can put as many submacros as you want into a single macro object. (It's sort of like the way you organize computer files by grouping them together in folders.) Using submacros, you can keep related functionality close together, so you have an easier time finding the macro you need when it's time to edit it. However, the individual submacros remain separate, and when you run one submacro it doesn't trigger the others.

> **NOTE** Access masters use submacros to group together macros that they use on the same form, macros that work with the same table, or macros that perform a similar type of task (like printing or record editing).

To try out submacros, begin by opening an existing macro object (or creating a new one). Then, choose Submacro from the Add New Action list. Or, drag the Program Flow→Submacro action from the Action Catalog and drop it onto your macro. Either way, you'll create a new, blank submacro like the one shown in *Figure 15-19*.

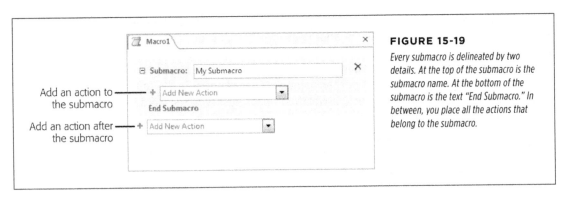

FIGURE 15-19

Every submacro is delineated by two details. At the top of the submacro is the submacro name. At the bottom of the submacro is the text "End Submacro." In between, you place all the actions that belong to the submacro.

Once you've added a submacro, you need to give it a name, using the Submacro text box. Then, you can fill it with actions. To add an action in a submacro, use the Add New Action list that appears inside the submacro. Or, if your action already exists outside the submacro, just drag that action into the submacro using the mouse. This process is very similar to the way you created macro groups on page 505. You can even take a bunch of existing actions (select them while pressing Shift) and turn them into an instant submacro (right-click the selection and choose Make Submacro Block).

Eventually, you'll want to create more submacros that contain different actions, and you'll end up with something like the macro shown in *Figure 15-20*.

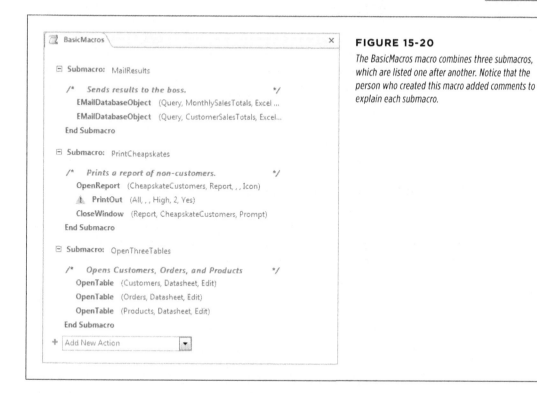

FIGURE 15-20

The BasicMacros macro combines three submacros, which are listed one after another. Notice that the person who created this macro added comments to explain each submacro.

TIP If you want to focus on a specific submacro, you can collapse the other submacros out of sight. Just click the +/– box that appears at the top-left of the submacro. When the submacro is collapsed, all you'll see is the submacro name. To expand a submacro that's collapsed, click the +/– box again.

Every submacro has a two-part name. The first part is the name of the macro object, and the second part is the submacro name. For example, the PrintCheapskates submacro in the BasicMacros macro, which is shown in *Figure 15-20*, has the full name BasicMacros.PrintCheapskates. You need to use the full name when you want to run the macro.

One limitation to submacros is that you can't use them from the navigation pane. If you right-click a macro group in the navigation pane and then choose Run, Access runs only the first submacro in the macro object. To run a different submacro, you need to choose Database Tools→Macro→Run Macro. You can then type in the correct two-part name or pick it from a list (as shown in *Figure 15-21*).

NOTE   If this sounds like too much work, don't worry. Most macros aren't launched through the navigation pane, but linked to a form, in which case the two-part name doesn't require any extra work. But if you have a macro that you do want to run from the navigation pane, grouped macros obviously aren't the way to go.

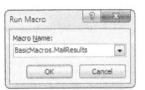

FIGURE 15-21

In this example, Access is poised to run the MailResults submacro from the BasicMacros macro object.

Assigning a Macro to a Keystroke

Occasionally, you'll create a macro that's just so handy you want it at your fingertips at all times. You can make this happen by assigning your macro to a key combination. Then, instead of heading to the navigation pane, you press something like Ctrl+M, and your macro springs into action right away.

NOTE   Keys are valuable. Only assign a macro to a key combination if you know that you'll use that macro often, and with many different forms or tables.

Oddly enough, the way you assign key combinations in Access is by creating *another* macro. This macro must be named AutoKeys, and its sole purpose in life is to assign keystrokes to other macros. Technically, the AutoKeys macro contains one or more macro groups, and each group is mapped to a different key combination.

So how does AutoKeys work? It's all in the group name. When you add an action to the AutoKeys macro, you give it a specially coded group name that's really a keystroke combination. If you name the macro group ^M, Access knows to trigger it when you press Ctrl+M on the keyboard. *Figure 15-22* shows a few macro examples.

In *Figure 15-22*, notice that each macro group runs a separately stored macro object using the RunMacro action. This design isn't necessary (you could add all the actions for each macro group right inside the AutoKeys macro), but it improves organization. It also gives you better flexibility, because you can choose to use a different set of macros with the same key combinations without removing the macro from the AutoKeys group.

The only trick to using the AutoKeys macro group is knowing how to name your macro so Access uses the key combination you want. Access lets you use letters and numbers, in combination with the Ctrl and Shift keys. (The Alt key is off-limits, because it lets you choose commands on the ribbon, as described on page 9.) Additionally, you can use the function keys (F1 through F12), and the Insert and Delete keys, also in conjunction with Ctrl and Shift.

Here's how you name your macros:

- **^ means Ctrl**. So ^M means Ctrl+M.

- **+ means Shift**. So ^+M means Ctrl+Shift+M.

- **{F1} means the F1 key**. So +*{F1}* means Shift+F1. You can use all the other function keys in the same way.

- **{INS} means Insert and {DEL} means Delete**. So *^{INS}* is Ctrl+Insert.

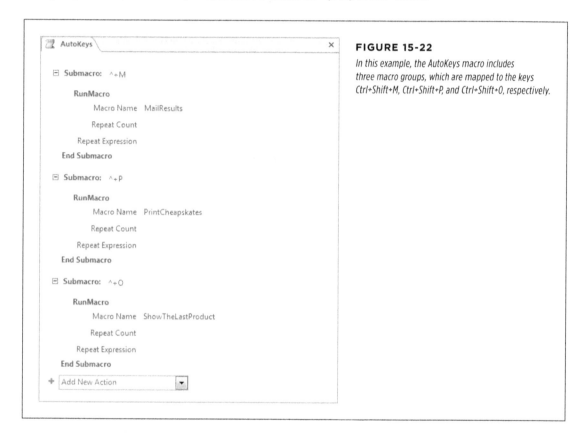

FIGURE 15-22

In this example, the AutoKeys macro includes three macro groups, which are mapped to the keys Ctrl+Shift+M, Ctrl+Shift+P, and Ctrl+Shift+O, respectively.

TIP Before you assign a macro to a key combination, you should check that the keystroke doesn't already do anything useful. Your macro overrides any built-in Access commands. One example is Ctrl+S, which saves the current object. To help reduce the chance of keystroke collisions, you can use keystrokes that involve the Shift key, which are less commonly used.

Configuring a Startup Macro

Every once in a while, you'll create a macro that's so important you want to call it into action as soon as you open a database. Perhaps this macro opens a few important forms and reports, imports data from another file, or runs a cleanup query.

No matter what the reason, Access makes it easy to launch a startup macro. All you need to do is name your macro AutoExec.

Access also gives you a way to sidestep the AutoExec macro. If you hold down the Shift key while a database is first loading, Access doesn't run the AutoExec macro (and it doesn't show any startup form you may have configured, as described on page 472). However, don't rely on this dodge, because it's all too easy to forget to hold Shift down at the right time.

NOTE Remember, if your macro contains unsafe actions and your database isn't trusted, Access doesn't run it. If you open an untrusted database and choose to trust the database using the message bar, Access reloads the database, at which point it runs the AutoExec macro again.

Connecting Macros to Forms and Tables

I f all you do with macros is launch them from the navigation pane, you're missing out on the real fun. Macros become far more powerful when you attach them to forms and tables and use Access events to run them automatically when something important happens. For example, you can use events to run an email-sending macro when someone clicks a button, or to trigger a data-checking macro when someone edits a field.

In this chapter, you'll start by learning how you can plug your macros into forms and controls and trigger them with Access events. It's time well spent, because you'll use almost the same approach to hook up Visual Basic code in Chapter 17. Next, you'll see how to build smarter macros that evaluate conditions and make decisions. Finally, you'll connect a macro to a table, so Access runs the macro when a specific type of editing action takes place.

■ Macro-Powered Forms

The slickest macros work with the forms in your database. Using this combination, you can create macros that fire automatically when something happens (like when a button is clicked or a record is changed). You can also build much more flexible macros that don't have fixed argument values—instead, they can read the data they need from the text boxes on a form.

In the following sections, you'll learn how to help macros and forms come together.

Understanding Events

So far, you've been running macros the hard way: by finding the ones you want in the navigation pane, and then launching them by hand. But in a well-oiled database, macros seldom play an up-front role. Instead, they hide behind the scenes until they're sparked into action. You could create a macro that's triggered when you click a button, open a form, or make a change in a text box. These triggers are known as *events*.

A form has three types of events:

- **Control events**. These events are the most useful. They happen when you do something with a control. For example, when you click a button, it fires an On Click event. (This is a great time to perform just about any action.) When you change a value in a text box, you get an On Change event. (This is a good time to check that the text makes sense by using your crafty validation code.) You'll notice that most event names start with the word "On."

> **NOTE** Many controls have the same events. If you have two text boxes and a button on your form, they all have an On Click event. However, Access isn't confused, because it keeps track of what event happens, and what control it happens *to*.

- **Section events**. As you learned earlier, forms are divided into sections so you can separate the header and footer content from the rest of the record. Each section has a few of its own events, which fire when you move the mouse around (On Mouse Move), or click somewhere on a blank space (On Click). These events tend to be less useful for macro programmers.

- **Form events**. A long list of more general events relate to the form. This list includes events that fire when the form is first opened (On Open) and when it's closed (On Close), when you move from one record to the next (On Current), and when you complete a data operation like an update (After Update).

To see the list of events for a form's different parts, follow these steps:

1. **Open your form in Design mode.**

   If the Property Sheet isn't visible, show it by choosing Form Design Tools | Design→Tools→Property Sheet.

2. **Select the item that has the events you want to examine.**

   You can select an individual control, a section, or a form. If you have trouble clicking on the design surface to select the item you want, just choose it by name from the drop-down list at the top of the Property Sheet.

3. **In the Property Sheet, choose the Event tab.**

   Now you'll see the list of events that are provided by the control, as shown in *Figure 16-1*.

FIGURE 16-1

Here are the events for a typical text box. When you click one of the Event boxes, a one-line description of the event appears in the status bar at the window's bottom-left section. As you can see, right now all the Event boxes are empty, which means there aren't any attached macros.

The biggest challenge in using events is figuring out which ones to employ. If you take a few seconds exploring the events on your form, you'll find dozens of events, many that are rarely used or ridiculously specialized. That's where Table 16-1 fits in—it highlights some of the most useful events for macro programming.

TABLE 16-1 *Useful Events for Macro Programming*

CONTROL	EVENT	DESCRIPTION
All Controls	On Enter	Occurs when you move to a control for the first time (either by pressing a key like Tab or by clicking with the mouse).
	On Mouse Move	Occurs when you move the mouse over the control.
Any Editable Control	On Change	Occurs when you modify the value in a control.
Button	On Click	Occurs when you click a button. Other controls have click events too, but most people are in the habit of clicking buttons to get things done.
Combo Box	On Not In List	Occurs when you type in an entry that's not in the list.

CONTROL	EVENT	DESCRIPTION
Form	On Load	Occurs when the form is first opened (and you can initialize it).
	On Close	Occurs when the form is closed. You can cancel this event if you want the form to stay open.
	On Current	Occurs when you move to a record (including when you open the form, and then move to the first record).
	On Dirty	Occurs when you make the first change in a record. It's now in Edit mode.
	On Undo	Occurs when you back out of Edit mode and cancel your changes (usually, by pressing Esc).
	Before Insert, Before Update, Before Del Confirm	Occurs when you're in the process of applying an insert, update, or delete. You can cancel this event if you don't like what you see (for example, if you find invalid data).
	After Insert, After Update, After Del Confirm	Occurs after the operation is complete. You can't cancel it any longer, but you may want to react to the change to perform another task or update the information you're showing.

NOTE The update, insert, and delete confirmation events (the last two rows in the table) also apply to any editable control. A text box also uses the Before Update and After Update events to indicate when its value has changed. In Chapter 18 (page 622), you'll see an example that uses this event to react immediately when a specific field is changed (rather than wait until the entire record is updated).

If you browse the Property Sheet's Event tab, you'll find many more events, including ones that let you react when someone presses a key, clicks somewhere with the mouse, or moves from one control to the next. You don't need to worry about all these options right now. Once you've learned how to respond to an event with a macro, you'll be able to deal with just about *any* event.

Attaching a Macro to an Event

Now that you've seen the events that forms and controls offer, it's time to try hooking up a macro. The basic sequence of steps is easy:

1. **Create and save a macro, as described on page 496.**

2. **Open your form in Design mode, and make sure the Property Sheet is visible.**

3. **Select a control, a section, or the entire form.**

4. **In the Property Sheet, choose the Events tab, and then find the event you want to use.**

5. **In the Event box, click the drop-down arrow, and then choose the macro you want to use.**

Figure 16-2 shows an example.

Embedded Macros

I created a macro with the Command Button Wizard. How can I edit it?

When you drop a button onto a form, Access fires up the Button wizard, which creates a macro for you (page 450). The macros that the Command Button Wizard creates are *embedded* macros, which means they're stored inside the form object. This system has some advantages (for example, you can transfer your form from one database to another without losing the associated macros). It also has a downside—namely, you can't edit or run the macro independently.

Fortunately, you can still modify your embedded macros (or just take a look at them if you're curious). The trick is to use the Property Sheet. Here's how:

1. Select the control that uses the macro (in this case, a button).

2. Find the event that has the attached macro. In the case of the button, it's the On Click event. You'll see the text "[Embedded Macro]" in the Event box, rather than a macro name.

3. Click once inside the Event box. The ellipsis (...) button appears next to it.

4. Click the ellipsis button to edit the embedded macro in the familiar macro builder.

Reading Arguments from a Form

In Chapter 15, you saw macros that could search for records, print reports, and email data. In all these cases, the macro arguments were fixed values—in other words, you type them in exactly, and they never change. On page 519, you saw a macro that searched for the text "hay." Convenient as this macro is, you can't reuse it to search for anything else. If you want to dig up different text, you need to create a whole new macro.

To make more flexible macros, you can use an *expression* instead of a fixed value. You've already used expressions extensively in the past (see page 238 for examples with queries, page 369 with reports, and page 440 with forms), so you won't have any problem building basic expressions that combine text, add numbers, and use Access functions. But when you're creating a macro, the most useful expressions are those that can pull a value out of a form. All you need to know is the control's name.

To see how this process works, you can revise the filtering example shown earlier and create a search form like the one shown in *Figure 16-3*.

FIGURE 16-3

Instead of searching for the word "hay," this example finds any text you want. The trick? You supply the search text in a text box at the top of the form.

To create this example, you need to start by adding the text box you need for searching. Here's how:

1. **Open the form in Design mode.**

2. **Select Form Design Tools | Design→Controls→Text Box, and then draw the text box onto the form.**

3. **Once it's there, select it, and then, in the Property Sheet, choose the Other tab.**

4. **At the top of the Other tab, change the** Name **property to something more descriptive, like** *SearchText.*

> **NOTE** You don't always have to create a new control. Macros can read the value in any control on your form, including those that are linked to the database record. However, in this example, you need a way to supply some text that isn't part of a record, so it makes sense to add another text box for that purpose.

Next, it's time to build the macro. You no longer need the OpenForm action (which you used in the original macro), because you can assume that Access will launch this macro from the already open AnimalTypes form. So the first action you need is GoToControl, with the Control Name argument set to Diet.

The second action is FindRecord. However, instead of setting the Find What argument to a fixed piece of text (="hay"), you point it to the SearchText control by using the control name (=SearchText). If any spaces or special characters are in the control name, make sure you wrap the name in square brackets (=[SearchText]).

> **TIP** If you're referring to a field or control on the current form, all you need to do is use the field or control name. However, sometimes you may want to refer to a control on another form. In this case, you need a wacky-looking syntax that indicates the form name and the control name. If you want to refer to a control named SearchText on a form named SearchForm, you'd write =Forms!SearchForm!SearchText.

Once you've polished off the macro, the last step is adding a button to the Ani-malTypes form to trigger it. Here's how:

1. **Select Form Tools | Design→Controls→Button, and then draw the button onto the form.**

2. **Press the Esc key to cancel the Button wizard.**

3. **In the Property Sheet, choose the Events tab.**

4. **Click the drop-down arrow in the On Click box, and then, from the list, choose the macro you've just created.**

5. **Now choose the Format tab, and, in the Caption field, enter the word *Search*. This descriptive text appears on the button.**

This step completes the example. To try it out, switch to Form view, type something in the SearchText text box, and then click the Search button. You'll skip ahead to the next matching record.

Changing Form Properties

Not only can you read form values, but you can also *change* them. The trick is a macro action called SetValue. SetValue is a remarkably powerful action, because it can change any property of a control. You can use it to change the text in a control, hide it, change its formatting, and so on. (For more about different control proper-ties you may want to use, see Chapter 13.) The only catch is that Access considers SetValue to be an unsafe action. You won't see it unless you choose Macro Tools | Design→Show/Hide→Show All Actions, and Access won't let you use it in an un-trusted database (page 510).

SetValue has only two arguments. The first argument, Item, identifies what you want to change. You can modify a form, section, field, or control. The second argument, Expression, sets the new value. You can use a fixed value, or you can read the value you want from another control using an expression.

If you want to create a macro that clears the search text from the SearchText text box, you could add a SetValue action, and set the Item property to SearchText and the Expression property to " " (which represents a bit of text with nothing in it).

NOTE This example assumes you're using SetValue on the current form (for example, by clicking a button named Clear). If you're running the macro from the navigation pane, you'll need to change SearchText to the full name Forms!AnimalTypes!SearchText so it clearly tells Access which form you're using.

If you like SetValue, you may be interested in the related SetProperty action. The SetProperty action changes one of a control's properties. (You choose what property you want to change with the Property argument.) You can use SetProperty to change a control's color, position, or captioning. However, the most common way to use SetProperty is to modify the Enabled property (to lock down controls that shouldn't be editable) or the Visible property (to hide controls that aren't relevant). You can set both properties to True or False.

SetProperty's nicest quality is that Access always considers it a safe action. The only drawback is that Access doesn't let you set the Text property of a control, because then you could use it to modify a table.

◼ Conditional Macros

The macros you've seen so far run all their actions from start to finish. If that seems a little boring, well, it is. But your macros don't need to stay that way. You can let them make decisions and perform conditional actions.

To create a conditional macro, you need to use the If action. You can pick the If action from the Add New Action list (where it's the third item), or you can drag it from the Program Flow section of the Action Catalog. *Figure 16-4* shows an example.

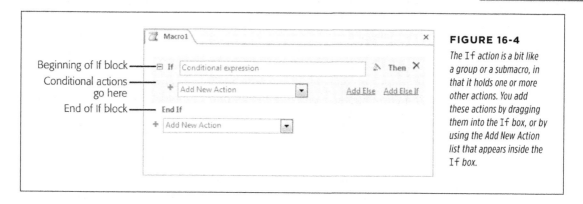

FIGURE 16-4

The If action is a bit like a group or a submacro, in that it holds one or more other actions. You add these actions by dragging them into the If box, or by using the Add New Action list that appears inside the If box.

Beginning of If block — If [Conditional expression]   Then ✕
Conditional actions go here — + Add New Action
End of If block — End If
+ Add New Action

TIP To save some serious time, you can take a bundle of existing actions and wrap it in a new If block, with no dragging required. Simply press Shift as you select the actions you want to make conditional. Then, right-click any part of this selection and choose Make If Block.

The If action requires a single argument, which is a *condition*. A condition is a little like an expression, except it always produces one of two results: True or False. Access examines the condition and uses it to decide whether to run the actions inside the If box. (This is known as *evaluating the condition* in programmer-speak.) Here's how it works:

- If the condition turns out to be True, Access runs the actions in the If box.

- If the condition turns out to be False, Access skips over the actions in the If box and continues with the next action after the If box.

Presto—you have a way to make an action run only when you need it.

Building a Condition

This discussion raises one excellent question—namely, how do you build a condition? The simplest types of conditions compare two different values. Here's an example:

    [ProductName] = "Baloney"

This condition compares the current value of the ProductName field with the word *Baloney*. If ProductName currently contains that text (and only that text), this condition is True. If ProductName contains anything else, the condition is False.

TIP Sometimes you wind up with exactly the opposite of the condition you want. In a pinch, you can always reverse a condition by putting the word Not at the beginning. Not [ProductName]="Baloney" is True only if the current item *isn't* everyone's favorite meat product.

The equal sign (=) is one of the staples of conditional logic, but it's not your only option. You can also use the greater than (>) and less than (<) symbols, and the "not equal to" (<>) operator. (You learned to use these operators with validation expressions on page 149.) Here's an expression that checks if a numeric field is above a certain value:

```
[Price] > 49.99
```

For even more fun, you can throw your favorite Access functions into the mix. (Chapter 4 and Chapter 7 describe plenty of useful functions.) Here's a condition that checks the length of a field, and then evaluates to True if the field is less than three characters:

```
Len([FirstName]) < 3
```

Instead of using the operators you've seen so far to create your own conditions, you can use a function that gives you a True or False result. Programming nerds call a result that can be True, False, and nothing in between a Boolean value, after the British uber-mathematician George Boole.

Access has quite a few functions that return Boolean values, but the all-star most valuable one is named IsNull(). As you learned earlier (see page 132), *null* fields are fields that don't have any information in them. IsNull() checks if a given field or control is empty. Here's how you can use it to pick up a missing last name:

```
IsNull([LastName])
```

This condition evaluates to True if there's no value in the current LastName field.

This technique is a basic building block of validation logic (as you'll see in the next section). You can use IsNull() to spot missing information, and then warn the person using your macro that he's left out something important.

Finally, the last trick you may want to try with conditions is combining more than one to make still more powerful super-conditions. You have two keywords that can help you join conditions: And and Or.

And enforces two conditions at once, making your condition that much more stringent. The following condition evaluates to True only if *both* the FirstName and the LastName fields are greater than three characters apiece:

```
Len([FirstName]) > 3 And Len([LastName]) > 3
```

Or gives you two alternate ways to satisfy a condition. The following condition evaluates to True if the FirstName or the LastName field is empty. It evaluates to False only if both fields have text in them.

```
IsNull([FirstName]) Or IsNull([LastName])
```

With all these building blocks—conditional operators, functions, and the Not, And, and Or keywords—you can build conditions galore. In the next section, you'll see an example that puts conditions to work.

Validating Data with Conditions

Many Access gurus use macros to prevent bad edits and other suspicious data operations (like insertions and deletions). Now that you understand how to write conditions, you can easily create this sort of validation logic.

The first step is to react to the right events—mainly, the Before Insert, Before Update, and Before Del Confirm events of a form. When these events occur, you can perform your conditional logic to check for error conditions. If you see something you don't like, use the CancelEvent action to stop the process altogether (and thus cancel the insert, update, or delete operation).

> **NOTE** As you learned in Chapter 4, Access has several tools that can help safeguard the data in your table, including input masks, validation rules, and lookups. You should always try to use these features before you resort to macro code. However, other situations require macro logic. One common example is if you want to enforce validation for a particular *task*, which happens in a specific form. If you try to validate at table level, it will apply to all forms, and it will even restrict direct edits in the datasheet, which isn't what you want.

Suppose you want to create a simple condition that stops certain record updates. Consider the form shown in *Figure 16-5*.

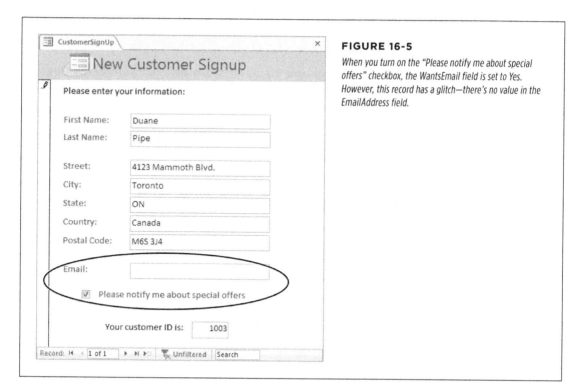

FIGURE 16-5

When you turn on the "Please notify me about special offers" checkbox, the WantsEmail field is set to Yes. However, this record has a glitch—there's no value in the EmailAddress field.

In this example, a missing email address causes severe headaches. You could solve the problem by changing EmailAddress into a required field (page 130), but what you really want is something a little more sophisticated. When WantsEmail is Yes, the EmailAddress field shouldn't be empty. A conditional macro can implement exactly this sort of logic with the If action.

Here's the condition your If action needs:

```
[WantsEmail]=Yes And IsNull([EmailAddress])
```

This condition evaluates to True if WantsEmail is Yes and EmailAddress is blank. When that happens, it's time to cancel the update by using the CancelEvent action.

CancelEvent doesn't use any arguments—it simply halts the process currently underway. CancelEvent works with any event that starts with the word "Before," which indicates the actual operation is just about to take place, but hasn't happened yet.

> **TIP** There's another option. You could use the SetValue action to fix up invalid values. But it's usually better to cancel the change and let the person who's making the update try to fix the problem.

When you cancel an event, it doesn't roll back the process altogether. Instead, it stops you from *finishing* the operation. If you modify a record and then try to move to another record, the Before Update event fires. If a macro cancels the Before Update event, Access doesn't let you move on—instead, you're locked in place. However, the current record stays in Edit mode, with all the same edited values. It's up to you to fix the problem or press Esc to cancel the update attempt altogether.

The conditional CancelEvent action is the heart of many validation macros. However, you still need one more finishing touch: an error message. Otherwise, the person who's making the update or insert won't have any idea what's wrong. She's likely to think that Access has gone completely off its rocker.

To show the error message, you can use the MessageBox action. Obviously, you want to show the error message only if the error has actually occurred, so both the CancelEvent and the MessageBox actions need to be conditional.

Figure 16-6 shows the completed StopMissingEmail macro, and *Figure 16-7* shows the macro in action.

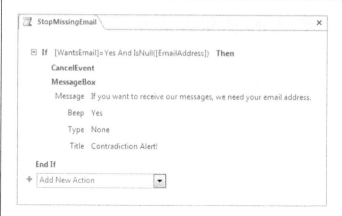

FIGURE 16-6

This macro consists of two conditional actions. To lock out bad data, attach this macro to both the BeforeUpdate *and the* BeforeInsert *events.*

FIGURE 16-7

Here, the macro detects the missing email address and explains the problem.

More Complex Conditional Macros

As conditional macros get longer and more complex, they can become a little awkward to manage. You may have several conditions on the go at once, each requiring separate actions. If some conditions are true, you may want to skip other conditions entirely. Or, you may want to stop running the macro.

To see a typical example of the challenges you'll face, it's worth revisiting the Stop-MissingEmail macro you saw in the previous section. But this time you'll add a new wrinkle. Instead of canceling the update or insert, your macro will ask for confirmation that this really is what you want to do, as shown in *Figure 16-8*.

FIGURE 16-8

Now it's up to you to decide whether to apply this apparently contradictory update: signing up for email updates, but not providing an email address. (Maybe you really do want regular emails, but you need to come back later to add the right email address.)

Creating a confirmation message is easy enough. You can do it all with this odd-looking condition:

```
MsgBox("Is this really what you want to do?", 4) = 7
```

The first part of this condition uses the MsgBox() function to show a message box. The number "4" tells Access that the message box should include a Yes button and a No button. The MsgBox() function returns a result of 6 if you click Yes, and 7 if you click No, so this condition is True only if you click No to cancel the change.

> **NOTE** You could easily confuse the MsgBox() function with the MessageBox macro action. The two are closely related. However, it's the MsgBox() function that makes this example work, because you can trigger it from inside a condition.

To sum up, you need a macro that checks for invalid data and, if it exists, shows a confirmation message box. This macro is a bit trickier than the previous example, because two conditions are at work—one that tests the data and one that lets the user decide whether to commit an apparently invalid edit.

To handle this sort of situation, you need nested If actions. Here's how the setup works:

1. Your first If action checks if the data is valid.

2. If it isn't, your second, nested If action shows the message box that asks if Access should apply the edit anyway.

3. If the user clicks No, the macro uses the CancelEvent action to stop the edit.

Figure 16-9 shows the complete AskAboutMissingEmail macro.

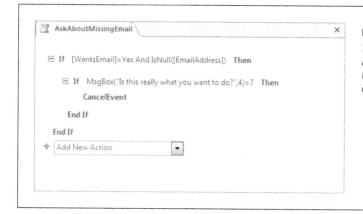

FIGURE 16-9

The AskAboutMissingEmail macro needs two If actions—one to check for invalid data, and one to cancel the update if someone clicks No in the confirmation message box.

This macro does the trick perfectly well. But sometimes, in extraordinarily long macros, the nested-If-action approach can get a little confusing. The problem is that if you have one If action nested in another If action, which is, in turn, nested in another If action, and so on, you can easily lose your place and forget what conditions are in effect at any given point in your macro.

In this case, you may be able to simplify your macro with a judicious use of the StopMacro and RunMacro actions. StopMacro ends the current macro immediately, which makes it a handy way to skip out of a macro if you know the following actions don't apply. RunMacro launches another macro, which makes it a good way to run a separate task when a specific condition is met.

Using StopMacro, you can create an alternate version of the AskAboutMissingEmail macro. Here's how it works:

1. Your first If action checks if the data is valid.

2. If it is, you don't need to take any more steps, so run the StopMacro action.

3. Your second If action shows the message box that asks if Access should apply the update.

4. If the user clicks No, the macro uses the CancelEvent action to stop the edit.

This example still has two If actions, but they aren't nested, which reduces the macro's complexity. Avoiding nested If actions makes sense if you have a lot of actions to perform and more conditions to check after the initial data test. *Figure 16-10* shows this version.

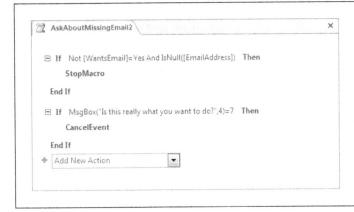

FIGURE 16-10

The revised AskAboutMissingEmail macro uses the same number of If actions, but in a different arrangement. The first one stops the macro if the data checks out, and the second one cancels the update if someone clicks No in the message box.

In this example, the macro is still quite simple, and the StopMacro action doesn't add any real benefit. However, you can use either approach, depending on what makes most sense to you.

Data Macros

So far, you've seen how to make a macro run when a specific event occurs in a form. However, you can also make a macro run when an event occurs in a *table*. This feature gives you a way to make smarter tables that log changes, synchronize values, and refuse to accept bad data.

Macros that respond to table events are called *data macros*, and they follow different rules than the macros you've seen so far. Although you create data macros by using the same macro designer, you'll notice that data macros support a different set of actions. For example, data macros can't do anything user-interface related (like show a message box or open a form), and they can't perform risky actions (like running an application, deleting a database object, or starting a printout). In fact, pretty much the only things data macros can do are create a record, edit a record, and send an email. There's good reason for this design—it means data macros are light, efficient, and fast.

Data macros are analogous to a concept called *triggers* that's featured in server-based databases like SQL Server. There's a reason for that, too. Microsoft's ultimate goal is to make data macros portable—in other words, to make sure that data macros can stick with your database even if you transfer it to another platform, like SQL Server. However, Access doesn't provide that feature yet. It may be included in a future version of Access or provided by other companies through an Access plug-in.

Table Events

To understand how data macros work and where they make sense, you need to know what events a table provides. After all, tables don't have controls like forms. Instead, tables use a small number of events to signal when certain editing actions take place. These events are detailed in Table 16-2.

TABLE 16-2 *Table Event*

DESCRIPTION	DESCRIPTION
Before Change	Occurs just before Access commits an edit or inserts a new record. If you need to distinguish between the two, you can create conditions that use the IsInsert property, which is True for inserts and False for updates.
Before Delete	Occurs just before Access removes a record from a table (and after the user has confirmed the action).
After Insert	Occurs after Access has finished inserting a new record.
After Update	Occurs after Access has finished updating a record after an edit.
After Delete	Occurs after Access has removed a deleted record from the table.

The "Before" events are the simplest. They're ideal for performing validation that restricts record deletions and locks out bad data. When you create a macro for a Before event, you'll find that the macro designer allows an extremely limited set of commands. That's because the Before events are designed for speed, and the last thing you need slowing down your database is a clunky data macro.

The "After" events let you use more commands and work with a greater variety of tasks. Almost always, these tasks involve editing or inserting data—whether it's in the current record, or in a completely different table. You can also use the After events to send an email notification, although this is a risky move. If you're not careful, you could end up firing off dozens of unnecessary emails in response to routine edits.

To create a data macro, first open the corresponding table. If the table is in Datasheet view, you'll find the buttons for creating data macros in the Table Tools | Table→Before Events and Table Tools | Table→After Events section of the ribbon. You can also create data macros in Design view (choose Table Tools | Design→Field, Record & Table Events→Create Data Macros), but that's not quite as convenient. If you use Datasheet view, you can test your macros immediately after you create them by editing the table.

The best way to understand how you can use data macros is to build a few. In the following sections, you'll see several classic examples that you can adapt for your own databases.

Validation with Before Events

Earlier in this chapter, you used the StopMissingEmail macro (page 541) to prevent inconsistent information. If someone attempts to set a customer's WantsEmail field to Yes while leaving the EmailAddress field blank, the StopMissingEmail macro stops them cold.

However, the StopMissingEmail macro is bound to a form. As a result, it's still possible to dodge the macro's restriction and create an email-requesting customer record with no email address—all you need to do is ignore the form and edit the Customers table in Datasheet view.

Data macros close this back door. They let you bake that validation logic right into your table, so it always applies. If you use a data macro, it doesn't matter whether you edit the table through the Datasheet view, a form, a query, or even some custom Visual Basic code. In every case, the table events occur and the data macros do their work.

FREQUENTLY ASKED QUESTION

Crafting a Validation Strategy

Where's the best place to put my validation logic?

When you first hear about the data macro feature, you may think it sounds like the ultimate tool for data validation. The truth, however, is more subtle. Sometimes it makes sense to perform validation at the table level, but other times form validation makes more sense. It depends on what you're trying to accomplish.

Consider the customer email example. When someone enters a new customer record in a form, you want to catch missing email addresses. However, in special cases it *is* acceptable to have a customer record with WantsEmail set to Yes and EmailAddress left blank. Perhaps you need to remove the email address from a current user because you know it's no longer valid and you don't want anyone to use it inadvertently, but you don't yet have a replacement. Or, perhaps you're copying customer information from an old table of regular-mail subscribers, and

you want to flag them as potential email recipients and fill in their email addresses later. These situations might seem a bit farfetched, but they demonstrate that it's perfectly reasonable to treat validation as a part of a particular *task* (like entering new customers in a form) rather than a part of your actual *data* (like the underlying Customers table). Doing so gives you more flexibility to use different validation rules with different forms and lets you bypass the validation for low-level tasks or when it isn't appropriate.

No matter what you decide, remember that data macro validation is designed for situations when Access's other validation tools aren't enough. If you can get the result you want using validation rules (page 146), it makes no sense to bring a more complex data macro into the picture. On the other hand, if you need to do something a validation rule can't—like make a change to another field or get information from another table—then data macros are an invaluable tool.

Here's how to create a data macro that prevents a blank value for EmailAddress when WantsEmail is Yes:

1. **Open your table in Datasheet view.**

   In this case, that's the Customers table. As explained earlier, you can also add a data macro in Design view, but Datasheet view is the most convenient place to test the end result.

2. **Choose Table Tools | Table→Before Events→Before Change.**

   Because you want the ability to cancel an edit before it takes place, you need to use the Before Change event, not the After Insert or After Update event. When you click the Before Change button, the macro designer appears.

3. **Add the actions you need.**

   In this example, you can build the macro you need with just two actions (*Figure 16-11*).

   First, the If action tests to see if the rules are being broken. You can use the same condition you used earlier with the form-based validation example: [WantsEmail]=Yes And IsNull([EmailAddress].

   Second, the RaiseError action cancels the change and provides an error message. This strategy is a bit different from the method you used with the form-based example, since data macros don't include a CancelEvent action. When using RaiseError, you must supply two arguments: an error number (which is for the logging feature described on page 553) and an error description (which is what the person using your database sees).

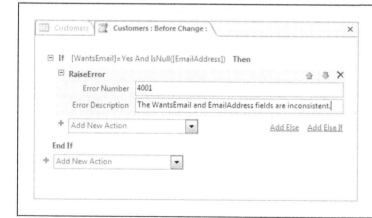

FIGURE 16-11

This data macro needs just two actions to do its work. First, a condition spots a mistake, and second, the RaiseError action notifies your database user and stops the edit from going any further.

4. **Close your data macro and save it.**

   You've got several ways to do that, including clicking the Close button in the ribbon or right-clicking the tab title and choosing Close. Either way, Access asks if you want to save your work, and you should click Yes.

5. **Try out your data macro.**

In this case, it's easy. Remove the email address from a customer that's requested email, and Access stops you in your tracks, keeps the record in Edit mode, and shows the RaiseError message that you set (*Figure 16-12*).

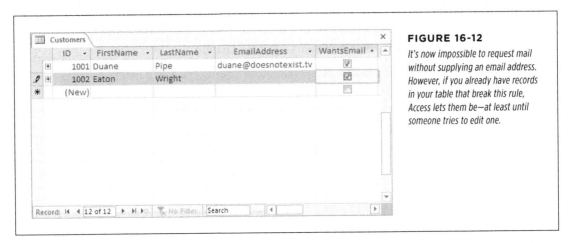

FIGURE 16-12

It's now impossible to request mail without supplying an email address. However, if you already have records in your table that break this rule, Access lets them be—at least until someone tries to edit one.

If you want to edit a data macro, choose the same command as when you created it (for example, Table Tools | Table→Before Events→Before Change for a data macro that's attached to the Before Change event). You can tell that you have a data macro for a specific event because the corresponding button appears highlighted in the ribbon.

The easiest way to remove a macro is to choose Table Tools | Table→Named Macros→Named Macro→Rename/Delete Macro to show the Data Macro Manager window (*Figure 16-13*).

In this example, the validation macro simply refuses changes that break the rules. However, there's another way to treat bad values in a data macro—you can fix them yourself. For example, you can create a macro that automatically sets WantsEmail to No if the EmailAddress field is blank. To do so, replace the RaiseError action with the SetField action. SetField takes two arguments: Name, which specifies the field you want to change, and Value, which sets the new value. *Figure 16-14* shows the completed macro.

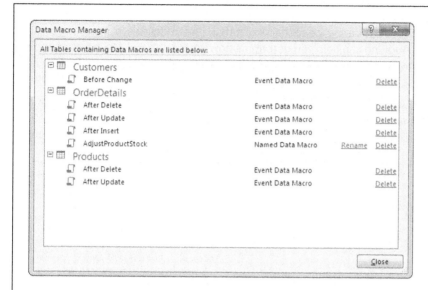

FIGURE 16-13

The Data Macro Manager lists all the data macros in your database, organized according to the table where they live. Next to each macro is a Delete link that you can click to banish it forever.

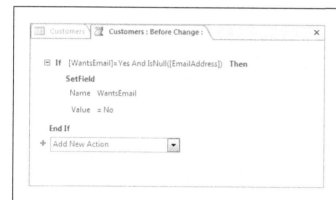

FIGURE 16-14

This version of the Before Change macro quietly fixes inconsistent data, rather than displaying an error message.

WARNING Correcting errors can be a dangerous technique. After all, your "fix" might make the problem worse by overwriting an important value or committing a change your database user doesn't really want. So use common sense and stick with small touch-ups.

Keeping a Change Log

The After events give you a great way to *audit* a table. Relax—this kind of auditing has nothing to do with taxes. When you audit a table, you track the editing actions that affect that table and record them in another table. For example, you can use auditing to create a log of every record that's been deleted from your customer catalog. Auditing can help you determine how your database is being used and can keep an eye out for problems or suspicious patterns of activity. And if you ever need to reverse a change later on, the details in an audit table can help you track it down.

The following macro uses the After Update event to keep track of price changes. Every time someone edits a record in the Products table and changes the Price field, it adds a record to the Products_Audit table. See *Figure 16-15* for an example.

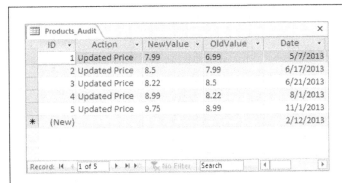

FIGURE 16-15

This table shows that a single product has had its price changed five times. For each price change, the Products_Audit table records the initial price, the edited price, and the date the change was made. To find out which product is being modified, you need to look up the ProductID in the Products table or create a join query (page 227).

> **TIP** Audit tables like Products_Audit are usually hidden. (Page 466 explains how.) But remember, audit tables are just one tool to verify consistency, and a malicious user can tamper with them as well.

You can build the auditing macro in much the same way you built the data macro for the Before Change event. Only now, you need to click your way to the slightly different command Table Tools | Table→After Events→After Update.

When a change happens, your macro needs to insert a new record in the Products_Audit table. But before you get started, you need to decide what sort of information you want to track. In this example, the macro logs price changes, but ignores everything else.

Access gives data macros a new function called Updated(), which lets you determine whether a specific field has been changed. When using the Updated() function, you supply a single argument: the field name, wrapped in quotes. The function returns a result of True if that field has been changed, or False if it hasn't. Here's how you can use the Updated() function to test if the most recent edit changed the product's price:

```
Updated("Price")
```

Don't forget to put the field name in quotation marks when using the Updated() function. Otherwise, you'll end up using the *value* in the field, rather than the *name* of the field, which isn't what you want.

In this example, you need to use Updated("Price") as the condition for an If action. Inside the If block, you place the actions that the macro will perform if the price has changed. In this case, that's the CreateRecord action, which inserts a new record in the Products_Audit table, as shown in *Figure 16-16*.

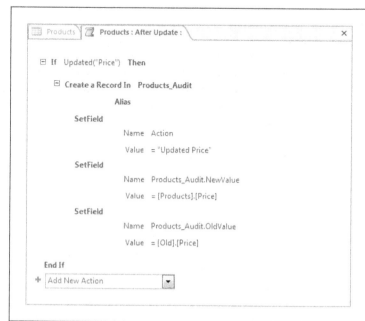

FIGURE 16-16

"After" macros support a small set of actions for creating, deleting, and editing records— CreateRecord, EditRecord, *and* DeleteRecord. *The current example uses the* CreateRecord *action to create a new record in the Products_Audit table, followed by three* SetField *actions to enter the field values.*

If you change a product price while the Products_Audit table is open, you need to refresh the table (choose Home→Records→Refresh All) to see the newly added record.

The CreateRecord action simply creates the record. It's up to you to fill the fields with the right values. You set each field separately using a SetField action. In this example, the SetField action fills the Action field (with a text description of the change), the NewValue field (with the changed price), and the OldValue field (with the original price).

You can get the new price from the Price field. But you need one more trick to get the old price that existed *before* the edit. Access provides all the original record values in a temporary object called Old. To get the old price, you use Old.Price, as shown in *Figure 16-16*.

A common macro mistake is using the wrong *nesting*. (A nested action is an action that's placed inside another action box.) In the current example, the SetValue actions are nested inside the CreateRecord action, which makes it clear that you're setting values in the new record. Similarly, the CreateRecord action is nested inside the If block. If you're not paying close attention, it's easy to slip up—for example, by putting a SetValue action *after* the CreateRecord action instead of *inside* the CreateRecord action. If you make this sort of mistake, your data macro won't work, and you'll probably need the debugging techniques described on page 553 to figure out what's wrong.

Currently, this example logs price changes and nothing else. But you can, if you wish, enhance the macro to check other fields for changes. All you do is add more If blocks after the first If block. Each If action can use the Updated() function to check a different field for changes, and then create a new Products_Audit record with the appropriate values. This design also means that a single edit operation can result in the creation of multiple Products_Audit records—one for each edited value. In a frequently modified database, audit tables can quickly balloon in size. To make sure your database stays manageable, you'll probably want to back up the audit information and clear the audit table regularly (say, weekly).

Using Two-Part Field Names

There are two ways to refer to a field. You can use just the field name (as in Price). Or, you can use the full name, which includes the table and field name, separated by a period (as in Products. Price). It's tempting to use the shorter names, but when you do, Access naturally assumes you're referring to a field in the *current table*, which isn't always the case.

In the product auditing example (*Figure 16-16*), the current table starts out being the Products table. However, when the macro performs the CreateRecord action, the current table *changes* to the Products_Audit table. As a result, when you grab the current price from the Products table, you need to write Products.Price. If you write just Price, Access assumes you're referring to an imaginary Products_Audit.Price field, which causes an error that will silently derail your macro. (To figure out what went wrong, you need to check the log table, as described on page 553.)

Even experienced macro programmers make this sort of mistake. For that reason, it's a good idea to always use two-part names. That means replacing NewValue with Products_Audit. NewValue and OldValue with Products_Audit.OldValue. It's a bit more to type, but it prevents pointing Access to the wrong table.

If you're faced with a long, unwieldy table name, you can clean up your macro by using an *alias*, which is the name you want to temporarily use to refer to a table. The alias can even be as short as a single character. To set up an alias, look for the Alias argument that's provided with actions like EditRecord, LookupRecord, ForEachRecord, and CreateRecord (*Figure 16-17*).

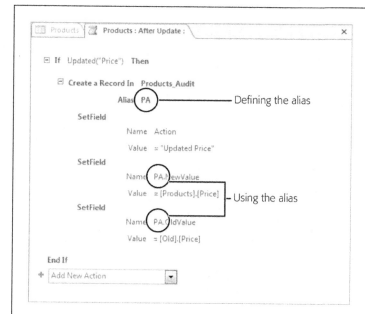

FIGURE 16-17

In this example, the CreateRecord *action creates a new record and sets an alias of PA for the Products_Audit table. The rest of the macro can use that alias—for example, to refer to the table in the* SetValue *action.*

Debugging Data Macros

When a Before event triggers a data macro, and that macro meets a problem, a message box fills you in on what went wrong. As you saw on page 547, you can use this behavior to your advantage by using the RaiseError action, which simultaneously stops the edit and informs the database user.

But After events don't work the same way. When an After event triggers a macro that hits a problem, the macro quietly stops running. Conceptually, this makes sense. When a Before event happens, the record is still being edited. But when an After event occurs, the edit is over.

This behavior makes it difficult to diagnose problems. When an error happens, the only indication you get is a small scrap of status bar text in the bottom-right corner of the Access window, which says "New Application Errors." And unlike ordinary macros, data macros don't have a single-step debugging feature that lets you walk through them one action at a time, so you can't pin down the error that way either.

Fortunately, Access has another tool—a hidden table named USysApplicationLog—that can help you rein in misbehaving macros. When an error occurs in an After macro, Access adds a new record to USysApplicationLog. That new record describes the key details—the error description, when the error occurred, and what action the macro was doing at the time. The only problem is that it's up to you to seek out the USysApplicationLog to get these details.

Here's a simple test that works with the product auditing example described in the previous section. You can try it out with the DataMacros database that's included with the samples for this chapter at *www.missingmanuals.com/cds/access2013mm*.

1. **In the navigation pane, right-click the Products_Audit table and choose Design.**

   The table opens in Design view.

2. **Double-click the Products table to open it. Now change the price of any record, and move to the next record to commit the edit.**

   Although the edit succeeds, the data macro fails, and Access doesn't add a record to the Products_Audit table.

3. **To track down the problem, choose File→Info→View Application Log Table.**

   Access opens the USysApplicationLog table.

> **TIP** If the problem is recent, you can use a shortcut to open the USysApplicationLog table. Look for the "New Application Errors" text in the bottom-right corner of the status bar, and click it.

4. **Scroll to the bottom row to see the most recent error.**

   In this case, the Description field makes the issue clear (*Figure 16-18*). While the Products_Audit table is open in Design view, it's locked and you can't edit it. As a result, the data macro can't insert a new record. When a macro hits a problem like this, it gives up and doesn't try to perform any other actions, unless you've changed this behavior with the OnError action (page 510).

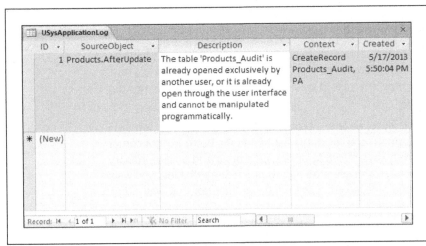

FIGURE 16-18

In the USysApplicationLog table, the SourceObject field tells you where the problem occurred (in a macro for the Products. AfterUpdate event). The Description field gives you the details, the Context field tells you what action failed, and the Created field records when it all went down.

When testing complex macros, you might want to write your own messages to the USysApplicationLog table. Access has an action for just this purpose, called LogEvent. It takes a single argument, Description, which sets the text that appears in the USysApplicationLog record. LogEvent comes in handy if you have a macro that fails, but you're not exactly sure where it goes off the rails. In this situation, you can use LogEvent at several different points in your macro. You can then check the USysApplicationLog table to find out exactly how far your macro made it before failing.

> **TIP** You can tell the difference between notifications and errors by checking the Category field in the USysApplicationLog table. The Category is User if you've logged a record with LogEvent, or Execution if the macro reported a critical error.

FREQUENTLY ASKED QUESTION

Using Data Macros for Summaries

I want to use a data macro to keep up-to-date summary information, like a TotalAmountSpent field in a Customers record. Is this a bad idea?

Usually, yes.

Access's best summary-generating tool is the query. Using a query, you can calculate up-to-date totals whenever you need them, with no chance of inconsistencies. But like every database rule, it has exceptions. Sometimes database whizzes accept the risks and use data macros to store summary information when they need hardcore optimization. For example, the tradeoff just might be worth it if:

- It takes a very long time to calculate the summary information (because it involves millions of records, for example).

- The people using the database retrieve the summary information frequently (so your database is forced to perform the same time-consuming calculations over and over again).

The bottom line is that storing calculated data is a tradeoff. The drawback is the risk of inconsistent data (in other words, summaries that aren't perfectly accurate). The benefit is better performance in challenging situations where Access queries just can't keep up.

An Advanced Data Macro: Synchronizing Data

You've already seen how you can use data macros for validation and auditing. The third scenario where you might use them is to *synchronize* data. For example, you might choose to automatically adjust the product stock numbers when a customer makes an order (*Figure 16-19*). Or, you might keep a running sales total. (This last option is a risky prospect. See the box on this page before you even consider this approach.)

To create the interaction shown in *Figure 16-19*, you need to react to the After Insert event in the OrderDetails table to reduce the corresponding stock number. That much is obvious. But what if an order is changed after it's been placed? In this case, it makes sense to use an After Update data macro to tweak the stock numbers up or down to reflect the change. And what if an erroneous order is placed and then deleted? To fix this problem, you need an After Delete data macro to return the stock numbers to their original values.

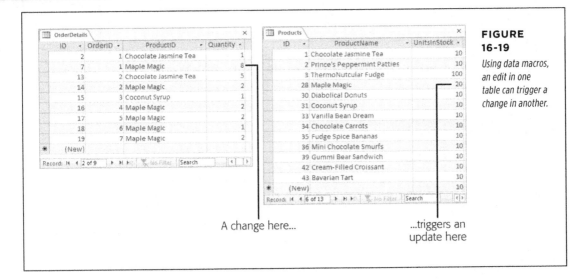

A change here...

...triggers an
update here

FIGURE
16-19

*Using data macros,
an edit in one
table can trigger a
change in another.*

In other words, you need no less than *three* data macros with maddeningly similar logic to accomplish the seemingly simple task of maintaining up-to-date stock numbers. But you can simplify this design by placing some of your code in a *named macro*—one that's stored with your table but doesn't react to any table event. Instead, it's up to you to call the named macro into action from another macro, when you need it. By placing some common logic in your named macro, you can reuse it whenever you need it, and avoid writing the same thing 12 times.

Here's how to create a named macro:

1. **Open the table where you want to place the macro, in Datasheet view.**

   This example puts the named macro in the OrderDetails table. That's because the data macros that use it are also in the OrderDetails table.

   > **NOTE** You could just as easily decide that the named macro makes sense in the Products table, because it updates a product record. It's really just a question of how you want to organize your database. Your data macros can call your named macro no matter where you put it.

2. **Choose Table Tools | Table→Named Macros→Named Macro→Create Named Macro.**

   The macro designer appears. However, this time the window has a difference. At the top is a section for defining parameters.

3. **Add your parameters (*Figure 16-20*).**

To make a named macro truly reusable, you need to use parameters—bits of information are passed to the named macro from another macro. In the case of the UpdateStock macro, you need to create two parameters:

- The ProductID parameter identifies the product that you want to update.

- The StockChange parameter is the number you want to add to the UnitsIn-Stock field (if positive) or subtract (if negative).

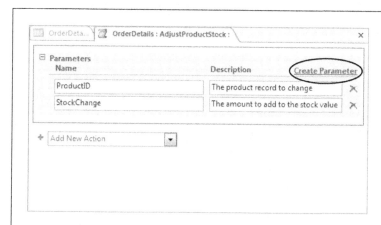

FIGURE 16-20

To create a new parameter, click the Create Parameter link in the top-right section of the macro designer, and give the parameter a short name and an optional description.

4. **Add the macro actions.**

In this case, the macro begins by performing the LookupRecord action to retrieve the record from the Products table with the matching ID. It then starts editing it with the EditRecord action and uses a single SetField action to adjust the UnitsInStock field (by adding the value from the StockChange parameter). *Figure 16-21* shows the completed macro.

5. **Close your macro. When Access prompts you, save your macro and give it a name.**

In this example, the macro is named *AdjustProductStock*. You use the name later when you call the named macro.

If you want to edit your macro later, choose Table Tools | Table→Named Macros→Named Macro→Edit Named Macro, and pick your macro from the list. To rename or delete it, choose Table Tools | Table→Named Macros→Named Macro→Rename/Delete Macro, which opens the Data Macro Manager window you saw earlier (*Figure 16-13*), with all the data macros (named and unnamed) in your database.

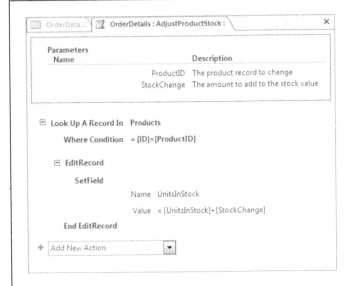

FIGURE 16-21

Now that it's completed, this named macro finds the product you specify and adjusts the stock number. Once again, proper nesting is critical. To make this macro work properly, you must place the EditRecord *action inside the* LookupRecord *action, and the* SetField *action inside the* EditRecord *action.*

Next, you need to create data macros for the After Update, After Insert, and After Delete events of the OrderDetails table. But the hard work is already taken care of by your named macro. As a result, each data macro has the simple task of calling AdjustProductStock, and passing it the stock change.

To call AdjustProductStock from another macro, you use the RunDataMacro action. It takes a single argument, Macro Name, which identifies the macro you want to run using its two-part name. The first part of the name is the table where the macro is defined, and the second part is the name you gave it when you saved it. With this naming scheme, you can call a named macro in any table from a data macro (or even from a regular macro). In this example, the two-part macro name is OrderDetails. AdjustProductStock.

Figure 16-22 shows the three data macros that update stock numbers when someone inserts, updates, or deletes an OrderDetails record. To try out these data macros, download the sample DataMacros database from the Missing CD page (*www.missingmanuals.com/cds/access2013mm*).

```
RunDataMacro
   Macro Name   OrderDetails.AdjustProductStock
Parameters

      ProductID    = [OrderDetails].[ProductID]
   StockChange   = -[OrderDetails].[Quantity]
```

```
RunDataMacro
   Macro Name   OrderDetails.AdjustProductStock
Parameters

      ProductID    = [Old].[ProductID]
   StockChange   = [Old].[Quantity]
```

```
RunDataMacro
   Macro Name   OrderDetails.AdjustProductStock
Parameters

      ProductID    = [OrderDetails].[ProductID]
   StockChange   = [Old].[Quantity]-[OrderDetails].[Quantity]
```

FIGURE 16-22

The After Insert macro (top) subtracts the quantity from stock by calling AdjustProductStock with the RunDataMacro action. The After Delete macro (middle) adds it back. (Notice how you need to use the temporary Old object to get values from the deleted record.) Finally, the After Update macro (bottom) calculates the difference between the old order quantity and the new order quantity.

NOTE A table can have just one data macro for each table event. But what if you want to create an After macro that does more than one thing? First, think seriously about whether you're overcomplicating your database (and your life). But if you're sure that's what you need, you can just pack all the actions you need into a single macro. Or, for better organization, put each task in a separate named macro, and call each named macro with the RunDataMacro action.

UP TO SPEED

The Drawbacks of Synchronization with Data Macros

Sadly, using data macros to synchronize data is an idea that sounds great in theory, but often causes headaches in real life. Here are some of the problems it can cause:

- **Inconsistent data.** As you learned earlier, a data macro can fail. It can't update a table that's locked (for example, one that's currently in Design view). In this situation, the edit that triggered the macro will still succeed, but the synchronized data won't be updated. In the product stock example, that means the stock numbers could remain artificially high after a purchase.

- **Complexity.** There's more than one way to edit a table, and

you need to take all possible changes into account. That means one data macro usually isn't enough. You'll often need to create (and test) a macro for every After event.

- **Inflexibility.** Once you've created a data macro, it's always in effect, so there's a chance it could run when it doesn't really apply. For example, you might want to enter an old order record (for bookkeeping purposes), without triggering your data macro and changing the current stock numbers. But once a data macro is in place, there's no way to temporarily turn it off. Instead, you need to remove it altogether.

Automating Tasks with Visual Basic

M acros are plenty of fun, but they can do only so much. If you can't find a readymade macro action that does the job you want, you can't use a macro. No such limit applies in the world of Visual Basic code, where you can do just about anything (if you spend enough late-night hours at the computer keyboard).

Here are some examples of tasks you can accomplish with code, but not with macros:

- Modify a whole batch of records at once.

- Deal intelligently with errors so Access doesn't pop up a cryptic message.

- Perform complex calculations. You can calculate an order confirmation code using a secret algorithm, or transform a line of text into Pig Latin.

- Interact with other programs on your computer. For example, you can copy some data out of a table and into a Word document.

- Write even more sophisticated validation routines that lock out bad data.

The goal of this chapter (and the next) isn't to make you a full-time code jockey. If that's your ambition, you can continue on to read entire books about programming Access. Instead, this chapter aims to teach you just enough to get the low-hanging fruit of Access programming. In other words, you'll pick up enough VB smarts to use the popular and practical code tricks discussed in the next chapter. You'll also build a great foundation for future exploration.

NOTE   The version of Visual Basic that Access and other Office applications use is called *VBA*, which stands for *Visual Basic for Applications*.

The Visual Basic Editor

Although Visual Basic code is stored in your database, you need to use a different tool to view and edit it. This tool is called the Visual Basic editor.

The Visual Basic editor works in concert with Access, but it appears in a separate window. To get to the Visual Basic editor, in the Access ribbon, choose Database Tools→Macro→Visual Basic. Access launches the standalone window shown in *Figure 17-1*, complete with an old-fashioned menu and toolbar.

> **NOTE** You can lose the Visual Basic editor at any time. If you don't, Access shuts it down when you exit.

The Project window   The current database

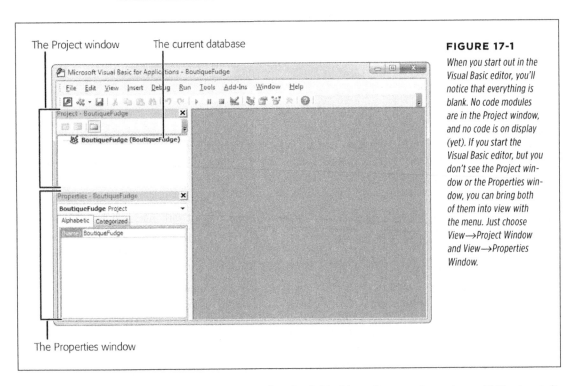

FIGURE 17-1

When you start out in the Visual Basic editor, you'll notice that everything is blank. No code modules are in the Project window, and no code is on display (yet). If you start the Visual Basic editor, but you don't see the Project window or the Properties window, you can bring both of them into view with the menu. Just choose View→Project Window and View→Properties Window.

The Properties window

The Visual Basic editor window is divided into three main regions. At the top left, the Project window shows all the *modules* in your database. (Each module is a container for one or more code routines.) Initially, the Project window is almost empty, because you haven't created any code yet. In *Figure 17-1*, the Project window has a single item (named "BoutiqueFudge" to correspond with the current database). However, this project doesn't contain any modules with code.

> **NOTE** Depending on the recent tasks you've undertaken in Access, you may see an oddly named *acwztool* project in the Projects window. This project is an Access add-in that powers most of the wizards you use in Access. Don't try to browse any of the code in this project—Access doesn't let you.

Just under the Project window is the Properties window, which shows settings that you can change for the currently selected item in the Project window. Everything else is empty space that's used to display your code files, once you create them.

In the following sections, you'll learn the most straightforward way to create a piece of code for your database. Here's an overview of what you'll do:

1. **First, you'll create a brand-new module, which is the container where you place your code.**

2. **Then, you'll write the simplest possible code routine inside your module.**

3. **Finally, you'll run your code to see it in action.**

And when you've finished all this, you'll consider how code can plug into the forms and reports that are already in your database. (This is where things really start rocking.)

Adding a New Module

Usually, you'll build code routines that connect to forms and spring into action when specific events (page 530) take place. However, in this chapter you'll start a bit slower by creating a standalone code routine that runs only when you tell it to.

The first step is to add a new module for your code. In the Visual Basic editor's menu, choose Insert→Module. *Figure 17-2* shows what you'll see.

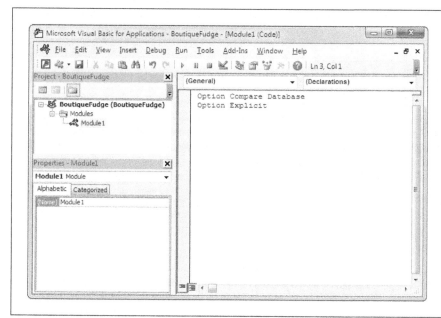

FIGURE 17-2

Once your project has at least one module, the Project window shows a Modules group. Access gives new modules boring names like Module1, Module2, and so on. To choose something better, select the module in the Project window, and then, in the Properties window just underneath, change the "(Name)" property. DataCleanupCode makes a good module name.

When you add a new module, the Visual Basic editor automatically opens a code window that shows the contents of that module. (If your database has more than one module, you can open the one you want by double-clicking it in the Project window.)

In *Figure 17-2*, the code window is *maximized*, so it fills all the available space in the Visual Basic editor. The first time a code window appears, it may not start out this way. Instead, it may show up as a smaller floating window inside the Visual Basic editor. To maximize your code-writing space, double-click the title bar of the floating code window, which expands it to full size. (Unless you really do want to see more than one code file at a time, in separate floating windows, but that's usually not worth the hassle.)

Initially, a brand-new module has just one line of code, which looks like this:

```
Option Compare Database
```

This line is an instruction that tells Visual Basic how to handle operations that compare pieces of text. Ordinarily, Visual Basic has its own rules about how to deal with text, but this statement tells it to use the Access settings instead.

The Access settings depend on the *locale* of the current database (like whether your version of Windows is using U.S. English or Japanese kanji script). Most English-speaking people use *case-insensitive* comparisons. That means *fudge* is considered the same as *fUdGe*, which is the same way Access treats text when you write queries.

Before you write code that actually does anything, you should add one more instruction to the top of your code file. Just before (or after) the `Option Compare Database` instruction, add this:

```
Option Explicit
```

This instruction tells Visual Basic to use stricter error checking, which catches common typos when using variables (page 592).

TIP You can tell Visual Basic to add the Option Explicit line automatically to all new code files. To do so, select Tools→Options, check the Require Variable Declaration option, and then click OK. Access experts *always* use this setting.

As with other Access database objects, when you close the Visual Basic editor, Access prompts you to save any newly created modules. If you don't want to wait that long, choose File→Save [DatabaseName] where DatabaseName is the name of your database file.

NOTE Once you've saved your module, you can see it in the Access window's navigation pane. If you're using the Tables and Related Views mode, your module appears in the Unrelated Objects category. If you're using the Object Type mode, it appears in a separate Module category. If you double-click a module in the navigation pane, Access opens it in the Visual Basic editor.

Writing the Simplest Possible Code Routine

Inside every module (except the empty ones) are one or more Visual Basic *subroutines*. A subroutine is a named unit of code that performs a distinct task. In the VB language, subroutines start with the word Sub followed by the name of the subroutine. Subroutines end with the statement End Sub. Here's an example subroutine that's rather unimaginatively named MyCodeRoutine:

```
Sub MyCodeRoutine()
    ' Your code goes here.
End Sub
```

This small snippet of VB code illustrates two important principles. First, it shows you how to start and end any subroutine (by using the Sub and End Sub statements). This code also shows you how to create a *comment*. Comments are special statements that Access completely ignores. Comments are notes to yourself (like explaining in plain English what the following line of code actually does). To create a comment, you just place an apostrophe (') at the beginning of the line.

NOTE The Visual Basic editor displays all comments using green text so you can clearly see the difference between comments and code.

Right now, MyCodeRoutine doesn't actually do anything. To give it more smarts, you add code statements between the Sub and End Sub. The following exceedingly simple code routine shows a message box:

```
Sub MyCodeRoutine()
    ' The following statement shows a message box.
    MsgBox "Witness the power of my code."
End Sub
```

This code works because the Visual Basic language includes a command named MsgBox. (See the box "The Visual Basic Language Reference" on page 566 for advice on how to master all the commands you have at your disposal.) You use the MsgBox command to pop up a basic message box with a message of your choosing. The message itself is a piece of text (or *string* in programmer parlance), and like all text values in VB, it needs to be wrapped in quotation marks so Access knows where it starts and where it ends. (As you may remember, Access forces you to obey the same rules when you use text in an expression.)

Once you've typed this in (go ahead—try it!), you're ready to *run* your code routine. To do so, place the cursor anywhere inside the subroutine so the Visual Basic editor knows what code you're interested in. Now, on the Visual Basic toolbar, click the Run button (which looks like the play button on a VCR control), or, from the menu, choose Run→Run Sub/UserForm. *Figure 17-3* shows the result.

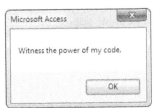

FIGURE 17-3

Your first code routine isn't terribly useful, but it does prove that you know enough to write a line of code and run it.

Access runs the code in a subroutine one line at a time, from start to finish. When you show a MsgBox, your code pauses until you click the OK button in the message box, when it finishes the subroutine.

NOTE Remember, Access considers VB code potentially dangerous, so it doesn't run it in an untrusted database. In other words, if you see a message bar with a security warning, you need to click Enable Content to trust your database. Page 512 has the full story.

GEM IN THE ROUGH

The Visual Basic Language Reference

Visual Basic is stuffed full of magical commands like MsgBox. You'll explore many of them in this chapter and the next, but for the full scoop on the language, you need to visit Microsoft's VBA language reference site at *http://tinyurl.com/VBA-lang.*

Once you're there, click "Visual Basic language reference" in the table of contents to delve deeper. Then, click Functions to see a list of Visual Basic commands, including MsgBox. Finally, click any function to see a detailed reference page about it.

The Visual Basic language reference has topics that describe the VB language itself. These fundamentals apply to Visual Basic in any Office program. You can also find detailed reference information about the programming commands and techniques that Access supports at *http://tinyurl.com/accessVBA.*

The Visual Basic reference is a great way to learn more Access programming—once you know a few fundamentals. If you dive into it too soon, you'll probably find that the explanations are about as clear as split-pea soup. But by the time you've finished working through the code examples in this book, you'll be ready to use it to learn more.

■ Putting Code in a Form

Running a code routine directly is a bit awkward. At least when you run a macro directly, you can launch it from the navigation pane or use a handy button in the ribbon. Neither option is available with VB code. Instead, you need to open the Visual Basic editor, choose the right module, scroll to the right subroutine, and then click Run. No one actually takes this approach, because it's just too tedious.

Fortunately, there's a better approach. You can place code in a form, and then set it to run automatically when something important happens. The following sections explain how.

Responding to a Form Event

Instead of running code routines straight from the editor, Access fans wire them up to form events, just as you can with macros. Here's how you can try this out:

1. **Open a form in Design mode.**

   The fastest way is to right-click a form in the navigation pane, and then choose Design View.

2. **Add a new button.**

   To do so, choose Forms Tools | Design→Controls→Button, and then draw the button onto your form.

3. **When the Button wizard begins, press Esc to cancel it.**

   You don't need to create a macro for your button. Instead, this button will be powered by pure VB code.

4. **If the Property Sheet isn't currently visible, choose Forms Tools | Design→Tools→Property Sheet.**

5. **In the Property Sheet, choose the Other tab, and then set the** Name **property to give the button a good name.**

   Access uses the button name to name the subroutine for your button. It's much easier to remember what `CommitOrder_Click` does than `Command42_Click`. Now is also a good time to set the text that's shown on the button (the `Caption` property) if you haven't already done so.

6. **In the Property Sheet, choose the Event tab, and then select the button's On Click event.**

   When you click inside an Event box, a drop-down arrow appears in it.

7. **In the On Click Event box, click the ellipsis (...).**

   The Choose Builder window appears.

8. **Select Code Builder and click OK.**

   You've just told Access that you're supplying VB code for this event, rather than a macro.

   Once you click OK, Access opens the Visual Basic editor and creates a code routine for your button. If you've already created the code routine, Access switches to your existing code so you can edit it.

The first time you add code to a form, Access creates a new module for that form. This module is named after the form and placed in a special group in the Project window named Microsoft Office Access Class Objects (see *Figure 17-4*). If you add more code to the same form, whether it's connected to the same control or to another one, Access inserts the code routine in the existing module for that form.

NOTE Form modules don't appear in the navigation pane. If you want to edit them, you have to open the Visual Basic editor yourself, and then, in the Project window, double-click the module. Or you can open the corresponding form, select the appropriate event, and use the ellipsis (...) button to jump straight to the code routine that interests you.

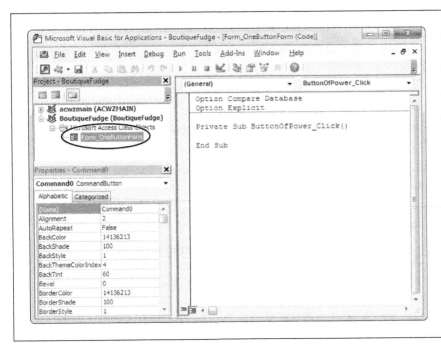

FIGURE 17-4

The module for a form is always named Form_ [FormName]. *Here's the module you'll see for a form named* OneButtonForm.

When you follow these steps, Access doesn't just create a new module; it also inserts a new, empty subroutine for your event. Assuming your button was named ButtonOfPower, you'll see code that looks like this:

```
Private Sub ButtonOfPower_Click()
End Sub
```

This subroutine looks similar to the subroutine you created earlier, but with two differences:

- **It starts with the word Private**. This word ensures that other modules can't use this subroutine. Instead, it's accessible only to the form where your button is placed. (If you don't specify Private, you get the default accessibility, which is Public, and your code routine is available to all. Most of the time, it doesn't matter which one you use, but Private is considered tidier.)

- **It has a name in the format [ControlName]_[EventName]**. For example, the subroutine shown above responds to the On Click event of a button named ButtonOfPower.

NOTE Wait a second—isn't it the On Click event? Just to keep you on your toes, Visual Basic uses a slightly different naming convention for events than the Access form designer does. It ignores the word "On" and leaves out any spaces, which means that On Click becomes just Click. It's best not to worry about the naming discrepancy. Instead, let Access create the right subroutine names for you.

To try out your subroutine, you need to add some code. So far, you've learned only one code command, so try using that to show a message:

```
Private Sub ButtonOfPower_Click()
    MsgBox "You clicked the ButtonOfPower."
End Sub
```

Now switch back to the form and click your button. You should see the message shown in *Figure 17-5*, which indicates that your code caught the event and responded successfully.

TIP You don't need to save your module when you make changes. Instead, you can freely jump back and forth between your code window and the form you're using in the Access window to test every change you make.

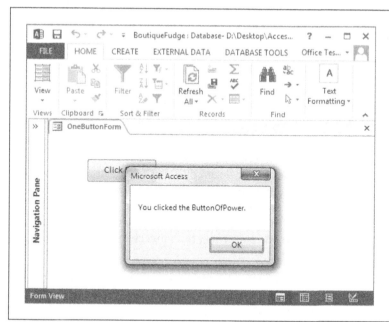

FIGURE 17-5

Events make code run automatically. In this case, if you click the ButtonOf-Power *control, Access instantly shows a message.*

If you delete the `ButtonOfPower` control later on, Access doesn't remove your code. Instead, it stays there, inactive. This behavior is good if there's something really useful in that code that you might want to use somewhere else later on. (In this case, a little cutting and pasting can help you out.) But if it's just a bunch of old code, use the Visual Basic editor to delete the subroutine as soon as you get the chance.

How Code Connects to Events

It's all in the name—the subroutine name, that is. When you open a form that has a matching code module, Access looks for code routines with specific names. If it finds a subroutine named `MyButton_Click`, it checks first for a control named `MyButton`, and then it verifies that this control has an event named `Click`. If both details check out, this code routine becomes an *event handler*, which is fancy programmer-speak that means your code is linked to the event. When the event happens (for example, when the button is clicked), Access runs the code in your subroutine.

If Access finds a subroutine named `MyButton_Click` and the form doesn't have a control named `MyButton`, don't panic. Access simply assumes you've created a subroutine for your own use. Since this subroutine isn't an event handler, Access doesn't run it automatically in response to an event.

However, your code can still call upon it when needed, as described in the next section.

This system introduces two opportunities to trip yourself up. First, don't change the name of an event handler on your own—if you do, you'll break the connection between your form and your code, and the event handler won't run when the event takes place. (In other words, you click the button, but nothing happens.) Second, don't change the name of your control by using the Property Sheet on the form, because that *also* breaks the connection. Or, if you really must fix up a bad name, just make sure you change the name of the subroutine to match the new control name.

In both these cases (renaming the subroutine and renaming the control), Access doesn't warn you about the possible effect. So keep these guidelines in mind to prevent unwanted surprises.

Calling the Code in a Module

Based on what you've learned so far, you may wonder why you would ever bother to create an ordinary module by hand. After all, there's no convenient way to run the code, and you can't connect it to a control event in a form.

Ordinary modules become useful if you create a fantastically useful piece of code that you want to use in several different places. You could design the perfect search routine and use it in two, three, or four dozen different forms. And you could cut and paste the code into each subroutine that needs it. Except that duplicate code is always a Bad Idea (just like duplicate data). Why? Consider what happens if you need to fix a problem or add an improvement. With duplicate code, you'll be forced to hunt down each copy of the code and repeat the same change. That's a sure way to waste your holiday weekends.

The solution is to take your useful, reusable code routine, and place it in a module. You can then call that code routine wherever you need it—and you can edit it just once when you need to update or fix it. To call a code routine in another module, you simply type in the name of the subroutine. Here's an example:

```
Private Sub ButtonOfPower_Click()
```

```
        MyCodeRoutine
    End Sub
```

Here's a play-by-play account of what happens when you use this code:

1. You click the ButtonOfPower button.

2. Access finds the ButtonOfPower_Click code and then runs it.

3. The code runs another routine, the MyCodeRoutine subroutine in your module. This code shows the message box you saw earlier (page 569).

4. After MyCodeRoutine completes, Access runs the rest of the code in ButtonOfPower_Click. In this example, there aren't any code statements, so the process ends here.

You can break a single task into as many subroutines as you want. You can also call subroutines that call other subroutines, which call still more subroutines, and so on. Access doesn't care. All it's interested in are the actual code statements.

This trick works only with *public* subroutines. As you saw earlier, MyCodeRoutine doesn't start with the word Private or Public, so Access considers it public. But if you add the word Private at the beginning, before the word Sub, then MyCodeRoutine becomes private, and your form code won't be able to call it. (The only way to call a private subroutine is from another subroutine in the same module.)

Event handlers are different. When you create a subroutine that responds to an event (like ButtonOfPower_Click), Access adds the word Private, making it off limits to other forms and modules. This makes sense, because there's no good reason for a piece of code on one form to call the event-handling routine on another form. In fact, that would make for seriously messy code.

> **TIP** The secret to stress-free programming is code reuse. If you want to use a piece of code in several places in the same form (for example, in response to different button clicks), create a new subroutine in that form, and put your code there. If you want to reuse a piece of code in several different forms, create a new subroutine in a separate module.

Reading and Writing the Fields on a Form

As you learned in Chapter 16, the most exciting macros are those that take charge of your forms and controls. In VB code, this task is spectacularly easy. You just need to know the names of all the controls you want to work with.

Suppose you're creating a (somewhat dangerous) code routine that clears a text box. You plan to use this routine to reset the text in the Description field. Here's the line of code that does the job:

```
    Description = ""
```

This line is a simple Visual Basic *assignment statement* (a line of code that modifies a piece of data), and it all revolves around the equal sign (=). When Access runs this line of code, it takes the content on the right-hand side of the equal sign (in this case, an empty set of quotation marks that represents no text), and it stuffs that content into the receptacle on the left-hand side (in this case, the Description field). The end result is that the current content in the Description field is wiped out.

> **NOTE** You can also use the familiar square brackets so that it's written [Description] rather than Description in your code. The brackets are optional, unless you've been reckless enough to break the good field-naming rules you learned about on page 90. If you have a text box name with a space in it, you always need to wrap the name in square brackets.

Of course, you can also substitute a specific piece of text:

```
Description = "Type something here, please"
```

The effect of running this code is the same as if you were to type in the new text yourself (except it happens a whole lot faster). As you know, when you modify any field, you place the current record into Edit mode. As soon as you move to another record or close the form, Access commits your edit and saves your new values in the database.

You can do only so much with fixed text values. After all, when you use a fixed piece of text, you need to decide at the outset exactly what you want to use. By the time you actually click a button and trigger your code, you may want something different. For that reason, programmers rarely use fixed values in this way. Instead, they use more complex *expressions*, which are a lot like the Access expressions you used for query calculations and validation rules.

With text, you can use the & operator to create a large piece of text out of several smaller pieces. Here's an example that takes the current description and adds a sentence at the end that identifies the product by name:

```
Description = Description & " This is a description for " & ProductName & "."
```

If the description starts off as "Enjoy delectable waves of fudge.", it may end up being "Enjoy delectable waves of fudge. This is a description for Fudge Tsunami."

More commonly, expressions manipulate numeric or date values. Here's the code for an Increase Price button that ratchets up a price by 10 percent every time you click the button (and best of all, you can click it as many times as you like):

```
Private Sub IncreasePrice_Click
    Price = Price * 1.10
End Sub
```

For a review of the different operators you can use with expressions to perform different types of calculations (like addition, multiplication, division, and so on), go back to page 241.

> **NOTE** Visual Basic treats Yes/No fields (page 78) as True/False fields. The end result is the same, but the syntax you use is just a bit different. To set the value of a Yes/No field, you use one of two built-in Visual Basic keywords: `True` or `False`.

GEM IN THE ROUGH

Splitting Long Lines of Code

If you're dealing with overly long lines of code, it's a good time to use Visual Basic's *line continuation character*, which is a fancy name for the underscore (_). End any line with a space and the underscore, and you can continue your code straightaway on the next line:

```
Description = Description & _
  " This is a description for " & _
  ProductName & "."
```

If you're going to use this trick, it helps to indent every line except the first one so you can see at a glance that they're part of one code statement.

Understanding Objects

You can actually do a whole lot more with the controls on your form. Rather than just changing their content, you can also change their color, font, position, visibility, and many other details. The secret to unlocking the magic is to realize that all controls are programming *objects*.

In the programming world, an object is nothing more than a convenient way to group together some related features. The Description field isn't just a single value, it's an entire text box *object*, and that means it has all sorts of built-in features. If you understand how text box objects work, you have a way to get to these other features.

> **NOTE** Access invites some confusion because it uses the word *object* in two different ways. Throughout this book, you've referred to all the ingredients of your database (things like tables, queries, and forms) as *database objects*. Programmers use the word "object" in a stricter sense to refer to a programming construct that brings together related features (and that's how this chapter uses the term).

You can interact with objects in three ways:

- **Properties**. Properties are pieces of information about an object. You change properties to modify the object or how it behaves. A text box object has a `FontSize` property that controls its text size.

- **Methods**. Methods are actions you can perform with an object. For instance, every form has a `Requery` method that lets you rerun the query that gets its data.

- **Events**. Events are notifications that an object sends out, which you can respond to with your code. You can react to button clicks by using the button control's `On Click` event.

The following sections take a closer look at these three object ingredients.

Properties

Properties aren't anything new. After all, you've spent considerable time tweaking them with the Property Sheet to get just the right formatting and behavior. However, properties show a whole different side when you change them by using your code. With code, you can modify properties *dynamically* in response to various actions (like clicking a button or editing the text in a text box). This technique opens up a world of new possibilities.

The secret to accessing the built-in features of an object is the lowly period (.), which programming nerds call the *dot operator*. Suppose you want to modify the background color of the Description text box. You can do this job by setting the BackColor property of the corresponding text box object. Here's how it's done:

```
Description.BackColor = vbYellow
```

This line of code takes the Description object and then uses the dot operator to pick out its BackColor property. The BackColor is then set with the help of a specially created keyword called vbYellow. As you saw with events, the name of a property in code doesn't always match the name of the property in the Property Sheet. In code, property names never include spaces.

You can use this line of code in any subroutine in a form module, as long as that form really and truly has a text box control named Description.

> **NOTE** Access colors are set using cryptic numbers. VB simplifies life for the most common colors by giving you predefined names to use, which start with the letters *vb*. These names are just shorthand ways to refer to the corresponding color numbers. Behind the scenes, vbYellow is really the number 65535. (If you search the Visual Basic Help for "vbYellow," you'll find the full list of eight color constants. You'll also learn how to get more color choices on page 584.)

If you don't include the dot, you end up using the *default property*. For the text box object, the default property is Value, which represents the content of the field. That's why you can write code like this, which doesn't include the dot operator:

```
Description = "A very fine product, indeed."
```

So now that you know that all the controls on your forms are objects with a whole range of useful details that you can change, the important question is: How do you know what properties there are, and how do you find the ones you want? Several guidelines can help you out:

- **Identical controls have identical properties**. Even though every text box on your form is represented by a distinct text box object, each object has exactly the same properties. Obviously, the property *values* will differ, but you can rest assured that if you find a BackColor property in one text box, you'll find a BackColor property in every other one as well.

- **Similar controls have similar properties**. All controls have a BackColor property, whether it's a text box, button, or a lowly label. Even the objects that represent parts of the form (like Detail, FormHeader, and FormFooter) provide a BackColor property for setting background colors. This bit of standardization lets you reuse what you learn with one control on another control.

- **You can look it up in the Property Sheet**. The property names you use in code usually correspond to the property names you see in the Property Sheet. One difference is that the names you use in code never have spaces, so the Back Color property in the Property Sheet becomes the BackColor property in code.

- **You can find it with Visual Basic IntelliSense**. The Visual Basic editor offers a great feature that can help you find the property you want. As soon as you type the period after the name of an object, it pops up a list with all the properties and methods you can use for that object (*Figure 17-6*).

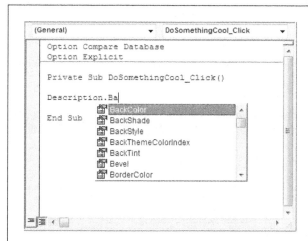

FIGURE 17-6

When you type an object name, and then enter the period, Visual Basic pops up a list of choices. If you type a few letters, Visual Basic moves to the matching part of the list. If you see the property you want, you can insert it or by clicking it or pressing the space bar.

NOTE The IntelliSense list actually contains two types of elements: properties (which are separate characteristics that are associated with an object) and methods (which are actions you can perform on an object). Properties are used more often, and they're marked with an icon that looks like a hand holding a card (*Figure 17-6*). Methods have an icon that looks like a flying green eraser. You'll learn how to use methods on page 578.

Talking About Me

Sometimes Access coders use the word Me in front of field names and control names. So instead of write this:

```
Description = ""
```

They write this:

```
Me.Description = ""
```

Technically, Me is a programming object that represents the current form. So the reference Me.Description tells Access to use the Description field on the current form. It's the same as writing just Description.

You might wonder why anyone would type more to achieve the same thing. The reason is because of Visual Basic's handy IntelliSense. When you type Me followed by a period, the Visual Basic editor pops open a long list of every ingredient on the current form. And if you start typing the first few letters of Description, you'll see the Description field appear as one of the suggestions, which you can then accept by pressing the space bar (just like in *Figure 17-6*). So while using Me makes no difference to the way code *works*, it does help some programmers type their code more quickly.

Table 17-1 lists some control properties that you may want to manipulate with Visual Basic code.

TABLE 17-1 *Useful Control Properties*

PROPERTY	TYPE OF DATA	DESCRIPTION
Value	Depends	Stores a control's value. Usually, each control is linked to a field, so the Value property lets you read or change a value from the current record. Depending on the field's data type, the property could be text, a number, a True/False value, and so on.
Locked	True or False	Determines whether a control value can be changed. If you set this property to False, it locks the control so the person using the form can't edit the field (although the user can still select the content inside and press Ctrl+C to copy it to the clipboard).
Enabled	True or False	Similar to Locked, except the content in a disabled control can't be selected. Controls that are disabled look a little different from enabled controls—typically, they have a grayed out or "dimmed" appearance.
Visible	True or False	Determines whether the person using a form can see a control. If you set this property to False, the control disappears from the form. This property is a handy way to hide fields that don't apply. If a customer lives in Zambia, you can hide the State box.

PROPERTY	TYPE OF DATA	DESCRIPTION
ForeColor and BackColor	A number	Determines the color that's used for text (the foreground color) and the color that's shown behind the text (the background color).
Left and Top	A number	Determines the position of a control on a form. The Left property provides the distance between the left edge of the form and the left edge of the control. The Top property gives the distance between the top of the form and the top edge of the control. Both values are in twips (see the box on page 578).
Width and Height	A number	Determines the size of a control, in twips (page 578).
FontName and FontSize	A text string and a number (respectively)	Determines the font that's used to show the text in a control. FontName is the name of the font (like "Arial"), and FontSize is the point size (like 10).
FontBold and FontItalic	True or False	Determines whether text should be bolded or italicized.
Picture*	A text string	Lets you show a background picture on part of a form, or a tab, image, or button. You supply a path that points to a picture file.
Text*	A text string	Provides the current text inside a text box. In most cases, this property gives you the same information as the Value property. However, if someone has edited the text but hasn't yet moved to another control, these properties differ. In this situation, Value is the text that's stored in the table, and Text is the newly edited information that hasn't been applied yet.
Caption*	A text string	Sets the text for a label or button control, or the title of a form. This property is important when you create labels that aren't linked to fields in a table. You could use a label to display a status message.
ItemsSelected*	A collection object	Provides a collection, which is a special type of object that contains zero or more subobjects. This collection holds the values of all the items currently selected in the list. The ItemsSelected property is useful only if you've created a list that supports multiple selections. Otherwise, use the Value property.

*These properties are more specialized, and they don't apply to most controls.

What's in a Twip

The Left, Top, Width, and Height properties use units of measurement called *twips*. A single twip translates into 1/20 of a point. In turn, a point is a typographic convention, defined as 1/72 of an inch. In an ideal world, all this would add up to make one twip equal 1/1440 of an inch, and you'd know exactly how big everything is on an Access form. However, the story isn't quite that simple, because different screen densities mean that one inch, as measured on a laptop screen, isn't the same as one inch on the average desktop monitor.

The bottom line is this: once, long ago, twips were meant to save confusion by linking measurements to actual physical dimensions. However, the rest of the Windows operating system didn't cooperate, and now twips are just another arbitrary unit system. The best way to use twips is to not think about them very much. Instead, treat a measurement in twips the same as any other number. So if you have a button that's 1.125 twips wide, and it's still too narrow, try a Width of 1.5—but don't waste time thinking about what that number is supposed to represent in the real world.

Methods

Methods let you perform *actions* with an object. In many cases, calling a method does more than set a property. In fact, a single method may launch a complex operation that affects many properties. The Requery method tells your form to get the latest data from the database, and then to refresh all its controls.

> **NOTE** When you use controls, you'll spend most of the time working with properties. In fact, controls have a whole lot of properties, but just a few odd methods.

To use a method, you type the object name, followed by a period, followed by the method name. However, you don't use the equal sign because you aren't *setting* the method. You're just *calling* it into action.

Here's an example that refreshes the current record on a form (for example, to pick up the changes someone else has just made) by using the Refresh method:

```
Form.Refresh
```

In some cases, a method requires some extra information. If this is the case, you'll know, because Visual Basic's IntelliSense lets you know as you write your code (see *Figure 17-7*).

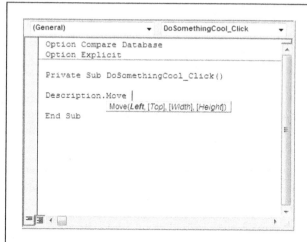

FIGURE 17-7

The rarely used Move method lets you reposition and resize a control in one blow. Once you type the name of this method, the Visual Basic editor shows you the four values you can supply. In this example, only the first value (Left) is required— the others are placed in square brackets, which means you can leave them out.

If you need to supply extra information for a method, you must add a space after the method name, followed by the appropriate value. If you need to supply several values, you separate each one with a comma. Here's an example that moves a control to the top-left corner of a form:

```
Description.Move 0, 0
```

Table 17-2 lists the most important control methods.

TABLE 17-2 *Useful Control Methods*

METHOD	DESCRIPTION
SetFocus	Moves the cursor into the control so that it becomes the currently active control. This technique is useful when you're performing validation. If you notice an error in a field, you can send the person back to the control that has the error.
Undo	Reverse any recent (uncommitted) changes in a control. You can also call this method on a form to abandon all changes and revert back to the original values. If the form isn't currently in Edit mode, this method does nothing.
Recalc*	Recalculates any expressions in the controls of a form.
Refresh*	Gets the latest values for this record from the table, and then refreshes the form accordingly. This method is useful if you've just triggered another task that may have modified the record, or if you're using a multiuser database (see Chapter 19), where several people might be changing a record at once.

METHOD	DESCRIPTION
Requery*	Reruns the query that's used to get the data for the form, and then shows that data, starting at the first record. This method is like Refresh, but instead of affecting the current record, it refreshes them all. You can also use this method on a lookup list to refresh its contents.

* These methods apply only to form objects, not individual controls.

Events

As you know, events are the notifications that objects use to tell your code something important has just happened. You've already mastered events, and you've used them in this chapter to react to button clicks. For a list of the most common control events, refer to page 531.

One topic that you haven't considered yet is how events can provide extra bits of information. As you may have already noticed, every subroutine includes a pair of parentheses. Here's a second look:

```
Private Sub ButtonOfPower_Click()
```

In the examples you've seen so far, those parentheses don't contain anything at all. However, they exist for a reason. Some events provide your code with additional event information, and this information is sandwiched between the two parentheses.

Consider the On Key Press event of a text box, which occurs every time someone types a character. It provides a special numeric code that represents the key that was pressed. (Programmers call this the *ASCII code.*)

If you add a subroutine to respond to the On Key Press event, Access generates code like this:

```
Private Sub MyTextBox_KeyPress(KeyAscii As Integer)
End Sub
```

This code means that the On Key Press event is providing your code with another piece of information. It's an integer (whole number) named KeyAscii, and you can use it in your own code. Here's an example that simply shows the key code in a message box:

```
Private Sub MyTextBox_KeyPress(KeyAscii As Integer)
    MsgBox "Your pressed the key with the code: " & KeyAscii
End Sub
```

Some events provide several pieces of information. In these cases, you'll spot a whole list between the parentheses. Each piece of information is separated by a comma and called a *parameter*.

NOTE Technically, parameters are a type of *variable*. Variables are handy containers that store some information. This information can *vary*, which is what gives the term its name. You'll learn more about using variables on page 592.

Here's an example for the On Mouse Move event (which occurs when you move the mouse pointer over the control). The opening declaration for the subroutine is so long that it had to be split over two lines by using the underscore:

```
Private Sub SomeControl_MouseMove(Button As Integer, _
    Shift As Integer, X As Single, Y As Single)
End Sub
```

In this case, you get four pieces of information. The Button parameter indicates which mouse buttons are currently pressed. The Shift parameter indicates whether the Shift, Ctrl, and Alt keys were held down while the mouse was moved. Finally, the X and Y parameters indicate where the mouse pointer is (its coordinates). You'll notice that the Private Sub line that declares the subroutine is split over two lines by using the underscore.

■ Using Objects

Now that you've learned the basics of Visual Basic, you're probably itching to get to work with some practical code. The following sections present two examples that put control objects to work.

> **TIP** If you're eager to explore even more objects, Microsoft's online developer reference is an invaluable resource. For an object-by-object reference, visit *http://tinyurl.com/access-obj*. For broader information that covers virtually everything you need to know about programming Access with VBA, visit *http://tinyurl.com/accessVBA*.

Indicating That a Record Has Changed

Record editing is a two-stage process. First, you change one or more field values, which places the record into Edit mode. Then, you close the form or move to another record, which *commits* your change. Or you press Esc, which cancels your changes, and then reverts to the original values.

If you're using the Record Selection bar (meaning the Record Selectors property of the form is set to Yes in the Property Sheet, which is the standard setting), Access indicates when you're in Edit mode by changing the tiny arrow in the form's top-left corner to a tiny pencil icon. This icon is a helpful indicator that something has changed on your form and that you need to decide whether to go through with the update. However, Access newbies and pros alike can easily miss the tiny pencil icon. That's why some people prefer to make the change much more obvious by showing a message on the form, or by changing the background color.

The following example demonstrates this technique. *Figure 17-8* shows the result.

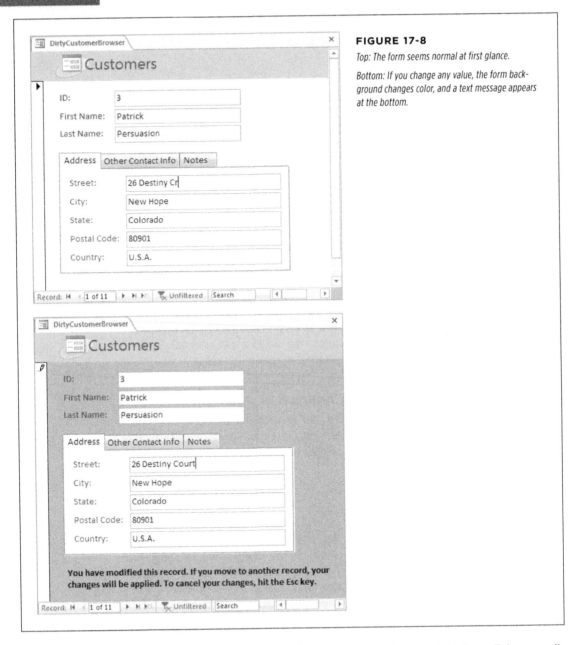

FIGURE 17-8

Top: The form seems normal at first glance.

Bottom: If you change any value, the form background changes color, and a text message appears at the bottom.

To create this example, you need to start by building the right form. Take an ordinary form, and then add a label to the form footer (see page 421). Give the label a respectable name, like InfoMessage, by changing the Name in the Property Sheet. Now you're ready to write some code.

NOTE Control names are important. You use the control name to refer to the control object in your code. And when you're reading a piece of code, no one—not even you—knows what Label44 means.

Before you add the code to your form, you need to determine two things:

- **Where does the code go?** You need to identify the event that should trigger your code. Once you've answered this question, you can create the right subroutine.

- **What does your code need to do?** You need to decide what objects you're using and what properties you're modifying. Once you've figured this part out, you can write the code in your subroutine.

In this example, you need to respond to the On Dirty event of the form. This event occurs when the record is changed in any way, and the form switches into Edit mode. (Deeply repressed programmers say this moment is when the form "becomes dirty.") If several values are modified, the On Dirty event fires only for the first change. After that, the form is already in Edit mode, and already "dirty."

NOTE Each individual control also has its own On Dirty event, which fires the first time someone changes a particular control. Don't pay any attention to these events. Instead, you want to use the On Dirty event of the form, so you catch *all* possible changes.

Here's the subroutine you need to react to the On Dirty event of your form:

```
Private Sub Form_Dirty(Cancel As Integer)
End Sub
```

NOTE This subroutine looks a little different from the previous ones you've seen because it includes a Cancel parameter that provides cancellation support. Don't worry about this feature right now—you'll learn all about it on page 597.

You can type this into an existing form module by hand (as long as you use exactly the same name for your subroutine), or you can add it using the Property Sheet (just select the Form in the Property Sheet list, find the On Dirty event, choose Event Procedure from the list, and then click the ellipsis button).

Now comes the fun part—writing the code. First, you need a statement that changes the form's background color. Although the form object doesn't provide a BackColor property, the objects that represent the individual parts of the form (Details, Form-Footer, and FormHeader) do. So you can use code like this:

```
Detail.BackColor = vbRed
```

You also need to fill in a message in the label. You can stitch together the text you need using the familiar & operator. You'll need a fairly long code statement to do the trick, so you'll also want to use the underscore to split the statement over multiple lines. Here's the code that does the trick:

```
InfoMessage.Caption = "You have modified this record. " & _
    "If you move to another record, your changes will be applied. " & _
    "To cancel your changes, hit the Esc key."
```

Place these two code statements into the Form_Dirty subroutine, and you're ready to go.

Getting the Color You Want

If you set colors only by using keywords like vbRed, vb-White, and vbYellow, you're missing out. There's a whole world of pastel shades and vibrant hues just waiting to be welcomed into your Visual Basic code. Unfortunately, you can't use keywords to set these colors. Instead, you need to use a numeric color code.

Most of the time, you won't know the right color code to use. However, you can solve this problem using the handy RGB function, which is a part of the Visual Basic language (just like the MsgBox function you used earlier). RGB takes three separate numbers, which represent the red, green, and blue components of color, and transforms them into a color code you can use to set the ForeColor or BackColor property. Here's an example that uses this technique to apply a shade of light salmon:

```
Detail.BackColor = RGB(266, 160, 122)
```

This statement works in two stages. First, Access runs the RGB function to create your color code. Then, it stuffs the color code into the BackColor property.

You might wonder what advantage the RGB function provides, since it forces you to come up with three separate numbers. In fact, the RGB color notation is a common standard that's used on the Web and in most Windows applications. You can even find a color by using the color picker in Access, and then determine the right RGB components by following these steps:

1. Open a form in Design mode.

2. Select a control, and then, in the Property Sheet, click in the ForeColor or BackColor box.

3. Click the ellipsis (...) button in the color box to open the quick color picker, which shows some common and recently used color choices.

4. Choose More Colors to open the full color picker.

5. Click the Custom tab.

6. Choose a color, as shown in *Figure 17-9*.

7. Make note of the RGB values. You can use these values in your code.

8. Click Cancel to return to Access.

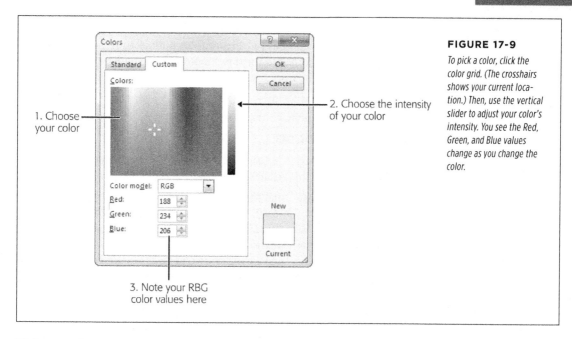

1. Choose your color

2. Choose the intensity of your color

3. Note your RBG color values here

Right now, the form has a flaw. When you make your first change, the label appears and the background color changes, just as it should. However, once you commit that change by moving to another record, the color and message remain. This result is obviously not what you want.

To fix this problem, you need to react to another event: the form's After Update event. This event takes place after Access has successfully applied the change. Here's the code you need to return the form back to its normal appearance:

```
Private Sub Form_AfterUpdate()
    Detail.BackColor = vbWhite
    InfoMessage.Caption = ""
End Sub
```

NOTE You don't want to use the Before Update event, because it takes place just before the change is committed. At this point, you have no way of knowing if Access will spot some invalid data, show an error message, and prevent the update (in which case the red background color should remain).

The example still isn't quite complete. Besides committing a change, someone can also press Esc to cancel it. You need to respond to this possibility as well, and to use the same code to return the form to normal. In this case, you use the form's On Undo event:

```
Private Sub Form_Undo(Cancel As Integer)
    Detail.BackColor = vbWhite
    InfoMessage.Caption = ""
End Sub
```

This step completes the example. To see all three subroutines together and try them out, download the sample database for this chapter (from the Missing CD page at *www.missingmanuals.com/cds/access2013mm*).

Continuous Forms and Unbound Controls

I changed the Default View property of my form to Continuous Form, and my code has gone wonky. What happened?

The Continuous Form view (page 409) is a handy way to see multiple records at once in your form. However, it has some significant limitations when it comes to code. You'll see these limitations when you add *unbound* controls—controls that aren't linked to any field in the database. In the previous example, the InfoMessage is an example of an unbound control. Your code uses it to show text whenever you want. It doesn't interact with a field value in a table.

Here's the problem: When you use an unbound control, you get exactly one copy to play with. If you combine an unbound control with a continuous form, you get an M. C. Escher style paradox—namely, there's only one control in existence, but this control appears in several places at once (next to each record).

This phenomenon isn't such a problem until you decide to modify your unbound control. Since there's really just one unbound control, when you modify it in one place, it's changed wherever it appears. In the example you just looked at, when you start editing a record, the editing message appears next to every record, even though you're actually modifying only one record.

Unfortunately, this scenario simply reflects an Access design limitation. The best workaround is to avoid using continuous forms if you need to use an unbound control.

Creating a Mouseover Effect

A *mouseover effect* is an action that takes place when you move the mouse over some region of a form. You could do things like highlight the control underneath by changing its formatting or content. Web designers often use mouseover effects to create fancy buttons that glow or light up when you hover over them.

You can easily create a mouseover effect in Access. You simply need to respond to the On Mouse Move event. You can use the form's On Mouse Move event if you want to watch the mouse move all over. More typically, you can use the On Mouse Move event for specific controls, which lets you detect when the mouse moves over those controls. The form in *Figure 17-10* uses a mouseover effect.

FIGURE 17-10

Top: The form as it first appears.

Bottom: When you move the mouse over the Don't Click Me button, the image at the side changes from a happy face to a frowning face. Move anywhere else, and the happy face returns.

As usual, to create this, you need to start by adding the extra controls you need, like the Don't Click Me button (which we'll name DoNotClickButton) and the image (named Face).

Once those details are in place, you need to create two subroutines. The first responds to the On Mouse Move event of the button. It swaps in the new image when you move over the button:

```
Private Sub DoNotClickButton_MouseMove(Button As Integer, _
  Shift As Integer, X As Single, Y As Single)

    Face.Picture = "c:\Images\UnHappy.jpg"
End Sub
```

This code assumes that you've placed the picture file (named UnHappy.jpg) in a folder named *c:\Images*.

As with all your code, you can type this into an existing form module by hand or, more conveniently, you can use the Property Sheet to create it.

NOTE The On Mouse Move event happens frequently. As you move the mouse from one side of the form to the other, you trigger it dozens of times. For that reason, you should make sure that the code that you use in response to that event is fast, or it could make your whole form feel sluggish.

The second subroutine responds to the On Mouse Move event of the form's Detail section, which happens when you move out of the button and over the blank space around it. This subroutine switches the image back to its original happy face:

```
Private Sub Detail_MouseMove(Button As Integer, _
 Shift As Integer, X As Single, Y As Single)

    Face.Picture = "c:\Images\Happy.jpg"
End Sub
```

The way this example is currently written has one weakness. Right now, it relies on the UnHappy.jpg and Happy.jpg files being in specific locations on the hard drive. This detail is hard to guarantee—after all, who's to say you won't move them somewhere else or try to open the database on another computer?

A better solution is to place the images in the same folder as the database file. You can point Access to that location by using code like this:

```
Face.Picture = CurrentProject.Path & "\Happy.jpg"
```

This code works using a special object that's always available in any code you write: the CurrentProject object, which provides information about your current database and the objects it contains. CurrentProject has a Path property, which gives you the location of the current database as a text string.

With this code in place, you can confidently copy your database anywhere, as long as you make sure the image files are placed in the same folder.

Linking Records to Images

In Chapter 2, you learned how you can store images in a table by using an attachment field. However, this technique isn't always suitable, particularly if your image files need to be modified or used outside Access, or if they're extremely large. In these cases, you might prefer to store the file *name* for your image.

You can still show the image inside an Access form. This trick is easy—just follow these steps:

1. Add a new image control to the form, but don't link this control to any field. Instead, you'll show the right picture using code.

2. Create an event handler for the form's On Current event, which you trigger every time you move to a record.

3. In the event handler, set the Picture property of the image control to the picture you want to show. If your table has a field named ImageFileName and an image control named Img, you'd write code like this:

```
Img.Picture = CurrentProject.Path & _
    "\Images\" & ImageFileName
```

This example assumes that all the picture files are stored in an Images subfolder inside the folder that contains your database file. When the form first loads (and every time you move to a different record), this code runs and places the appropriate picture in the picture control.

If you use this code, you should also use error handling (page 609). Error handling is important since you can't be certain that the pictures haven't been moved or removed—and if they have, you want to handle the problem gracefully.

Writing Smarter Code

I n Chapter 17, you dove headfirst into the world of Visual Basic code, writing routines that could show messages, respond to events, and modify forms. Along the way, you learned a fair bit about the Visual Basic language and the object-based system that gives VB its mojo.

There's still more to explore. In this chapter, you'll learn how to use VB code to solve some of the most common problems Access experts face. You'll focus on improving the Boutique Fudge database, which you've worked with throughout this book. However, the solutions you'll use are so useful that you'll want to incorporate them into your own databases.

But first, before you tackle these more advanced examples, you'll start by brushing up on the Visual Basic language, learning how to defang errors, and taking a closer look at objects. These topics complete the Visual Basic picture and prepare you to become a true Access programmer.

■ Exploring the VB Language

Although you now know enough to react to events and change control properties, there's still a lot to learn about the Visual Basic language itself. In the following sections, you'll learn how to use variables, conditional logic, and loops to write more powerful code. Finally, you'll see how to use these features to build a more complex code routine that checks for invalid credit card numbers.

Storing Information in Variables

Every programming language includes the concept of *variables*, which are temporary storage containers where you can keep track of important information.

Suppose you want to swap the content in two fields. On the surface, this operation seems fairly straightforward. All you need to do is take the text from one text box, place it in the other, and then insert the second box's text in the first box. Here's a first crack at a solution:

```
TextBoxOne.Value = TextBoxTwo.Value
TextBoxTwo.Value = TextBoxOne.Value
```

To make this code work, you need to put it in the right subroutine. In this example, the code runs when someone clicks a button in a form. You can create the subroutine you want for the On Click event using the Property Sheet. (See page 567 for a refresher.)

Sadly, this code is doomed from the start. *Figure 18-1* illustrates the problem.

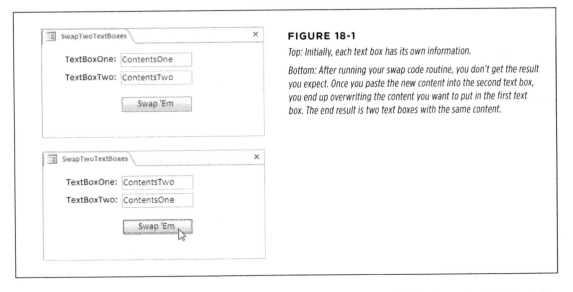

FIGURE 18-1

Top: Initially, each text box has its own information.

Bottom: After running your swap code routine, you don't get the result you expect. Once you paste the new content into the second text box, you end up overwriting the content you want to put in the first text box. The end result is two text boxes with the same content.

The easiest way around this problem is to use a variable to keep track of the information you need. To create a variable in VB, you use the oddly named Dim keyword (short for *dimension*, which is programmer jargon for "create a new variable"). After using Dim, you enter the variable's name.

Here's how you'd create a variable named TextContent:

```
Dim TextContent
```

Once you've created the variable, you're free to put information in it and to take information out. To perform both these operations, you use the familiar equal sign, just as you would with properties.

Here's an example that stores some text in a variable:

```
TextContent = "Test text"
```

The following code puts all these concepts together. It uses a variable to swap the content of two text boxes.

```
Dim TextContent
' Copy the text from the first text box for later use.
TextContent = TextBoxOne.Value

' Change the text in the first text box.
TextBoxOne.Value = TextBoxTwo.Value

' Change the text in the second text box, using the variable.
TextBoxTwo.Value = TextContent
```

Mistyping a variable's name is a serious mistake. For example, if you write TextContents instead of TextContent, Access will quietly create a new variable named TextContents, while ignoring the data you actually want in TextContent. This issue can cause plenty of mysterious glitches in your VB code. Fortunately, the solution is simple. Just add Option Explicit on a separate line at the top of every code file (right after Option Compare Database). This tells Access to complain whenever you use a variable name that you haven't defined with Dim. So if you type TextContents, Access catches the error and forces you to fix it right away, before it causes your code to start acting unpredictably.

To make your life even easier, tell the Visual Basic edit to add Option Explicit to every new code file. To do that, choose select Tools→Options in the Visual Basic window, check the Require Variable Declaration option, and click OK.

Using Smarter Variables

The example on this page shows the simplest way to create a variable in VB code. It creates a variable that's known as a *variant*, which means it can store any type of content, including text, numbers, True/False values, and so on. Advanced VB programmers often prefer to be stricter and explicitly identify the data type for each variable they create. That way, nobody can accidentally store text in a variable that's intended for numeric content, and vice versa.

To create a variable that has a locked-in data type, you add the As keyword to your declaration. Here's how you create a TextContent variable for storing text only:

```
Dim TextContent As String
```

And here's a variable that stores a large integer:

```
Dim NumberContent As Long
```

This approach is good coding style, and it can help you catch certain types of mistakes. However, to use this approach, you need to be familiar with the various Visual Basic data types. The most commonly used ones are String, Date, Boolean (a True or False value), Long (an integer that can be very small or very big), Single (a number that can include digits to the right of the decimal point), and Currency (a numeric data type that's ideal for storing financial amounts).

You can find a reference of all the data types in Microsoft's online VB reference at *http://tinyurl.com/vba-data-types*.

Making Decisions

Conditional logic, another programming staple, is code that runs only if a certain condition is true. There's no limit to the number of ways you can use conditional logic. You may want to prevent an update if newly entered data doesn't check out. Or you may want to configure the controls on a form differently, depending on its data. You can do all this, and more, using conditional logic.

All conditional logic starts with a *condition*: a simple expression that can turn out to be true or false (programmers call this process *evaluating* to true or false). Your code can then make a decision to execute different logic depending on the condition's outcome. To build a condition, you need to compare a variable or property by using a logical operator like = (equal to), < (less than), > (greater than), and <> (not equal to). For example, Price = 10 is a condition. It can be true (if the Price field contains the number 10), or false (if Price contains something else). You've already used conditions to create validation rules (page 149), to filter records in a query (page 238), and to build smarter macros (page 534). Visual Basic conditions follow a very similar set of rules.

On its own, a condition can't do anything. However, when used in conjunction with other code, it can become tremendously powerful. Once you've created a suitable condition, you can put it inside a special structure called the *If* block. The If block evaluates a condition and runs a section of code if the condition is true. If the condition isn't true, Access completely ignores the code.

Here's an If block that checks whether the Price field's value is greater than 100. If it is, Access displays a message:

```
If Price > 100 Then
    MsgBox "I hope you budgeted for this."
End If
```

Note that the If block always starts with If and ends with End If. Inside the If block, you can put as much code as you want. This is the conditional code—it runs only if the condition is true.

An If block can also evaluate several different conditions. Here's an example that calculates the fully taxed price of a product, and then displays that in a label. The trick is that the tax rate depends on another field (the Country), which is where the conditional logic comes into play.

```
' Store the tax rate you want to use in this variable.
Dim TaxRate

If Country = "U.S.A." Then
    ' Taxes are charged for U.S. customers (7%).
    TaxRate = 1.07
ElseIf Country = "Canada" Then
    ' Even more taxes are charged for Canadian customers (14%).
    TaxRate = 1.14
Else
    ' Everyone else gets off with no tax.
    TaxRate = 1
End If

' Display the final total in a label.
TotalWithTax.Caption = Price * TaxRate
```

Only one segment of code runs in an If block. In this example, Access works its way through the block, testing each condition until one matches. As soon as it finds a match, it runs the conditional block of code, jumps down to the closing End If, and then continues with any other code that's in the subroutine. If no condition matches, Access runs the code in the final Else clause (if you've added it). *Figure 18-2* shows this code in action.

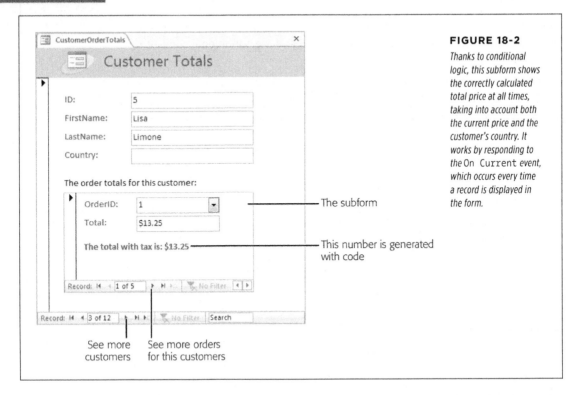

FIGURE 18-2

Thanks to conditional logic, this subform shows the correctly calculated total price at all times, taking into account both the current price and the customer's country. It works by responding to the On Current event, which occurs every time a record is displayed in the form.

These examples only scratch the surface of what careful conditional logic can do. You can use *And* and *Or* keywords to combine conditions, put one conditional block inside another, and much more.

In Chapter 16, you saw an example that performed a specific type of validation with customer records (page 539). This validation worked using two fields: WantsEmail and EmailAddress. If the WantsEmail field was set to Yes, the EmailAddress field couldn't be empty. However, if WantsEmail was set to No, a blank EmailAddress was completely acceptable. You can implement the identical validation logic by using VB code, but there's a twist—it uses *two* If blocks (a line-by-line explanation follows the code):

```
1 Private Sub Form_BeforeUpdate(Cancel As Integer)
       ' Check if this person wants the email.
2      If WantsEmail = True Then

          ' Make sure the EmailAddress isn't blank or null.
3         If EmailAddress = "" Or IsNull(EmailAddress) Then
             ' This is considered invalid.
             ' Cancel the change and show a message.
```

```
4              MsgBox "You can't be notified without an email address."
5              Cancel = True
6         End If

7      End If
8 End Sub
```

Here's how it works:

- **Line 1** declares a code routine that handles the Before Update event of the form. Notice that this event handler gets one piece of information—a true or false value named Cancel, which you can set to stop the update.

- **Line 2** starts an If block that checks if the WantsEmail checkbox has a check-mark in it.

- **Line 3** performs a second check. It's a bit more complex because there are two things that can cause the conditional code to run. It runs if the email address is a blank value (which happens if someone enters an email address and then deletes it) or if the email address is *null* (which means that an email was never entered in the first place; see page 132 for a discussion of null values).

- **Line 4** shows an explanatory error message. Remember, the code gets to this spot only if both the If blocks evaluate to true. If either check turns out false (the WantsEmail checkbox isn't turned on, or the EmailAddress is supplied), Access breezes right on past.

NOTE Technically, you could combine both these If blocks into a single If block by writing a more complex condition that checks for everything at once. However, getting this right (and understanding what you've written later on) is more difficult. Veteran programmers know that it's always better to write code clearly, even if that makes the code a little more verbose.

- **Line 5** *cancels* the update using the Cancel parameter that the On Before Update event provides. That way, the change doesn't go ahead, and the record remains in Edit mode.

- **Lines 6–8** finish up by closing both If blocks, and ending the subroutine.

Access has many events you can cancel, like On Before Update. Look for the Cancel parameter between the parentheses after the subroutine name. If it's there, you can set it to True to stop the action that's about to occur.

Repeating Actions with a Loop

A *loop* is a tool that lets you repeat an operation as many times as you want. Visual Basic has several types of loops you can use. The most popular are the Do/Loop block and the For/Next block, both of which you'll see in this section.

Here's an example Do/Loop block that's sure to infuriate people:

```
Do
    MsgBox "Ever ever get that nagging deja vu feeling?"
Loop
```

When Access enters this block of code, it starts by displaying the message box and pausing your code. Once you click OK, the code continues until Access reaches the final Loop statement at the bottom of the loop. At this point, Access automatically jumps back to the beginning (the Do statement) and repeats your code, showing a second message box. However, there's one problem—this process continues forever! If you make the mistake of running this piece of code, your database will lock up indefinitely (until you press the emergency-stop key combination, Ctrl+Break).

To avoid this situation, you should build all loops with an *exit condition*, a condition that signals when the loop should end. Here's a rewritten version of the same loop that stops after it's shown a message five times:

```
' Keep track of how many times you've looped.
Dim NumberOfTimes

' Start the count at 0.
NumberOfTimes = 0

Do
    MsgBox "Ever ever get that nagging deja vu feeling?"

    ' Up the count by 1.
    NumberOfTimes = NumberOfTimes + 1
Loop Until NumberOfTimes = 5
```

The important bit is the final clause at the end of the loop block, Until NumberOfTimes = 5. This clause defines a condition, and as soon as it's true (the NumberOfTimes variable reaches 5) and Access reaches the end of the loop, it jumps out and continues running the rest of your subroutine.

If you have this type of code, where you're looping a fixed number of times, you may be interested in the For/Next loop. The For/Next loop is exactly the same as the Do/Next loop, except that it has a built-in counter, which it increments for you.

Here's how you could rewrite the previous example in a more compact form with a For/Next loop:

```
Dim NumberOfTimes

For NumberOfTimes = 1 To 5
    MsgBox "Ever ever get that nagging deja vu feeling?"
Next
```

The important part is NumberOfTimes = 1 To 5, which tells Access to start NumberOfTimes at 1, to increment it by 1 at the beginning of each pass through the loop, and to stop after the fifth pass.

The Do/Loop block works well when you need to move through a collection of data. You can use the loop to keep going until you run out of information, even though you don't know how much information there is when you first start the loop. You'll see an example of this technique at the end of this chapter (page 632), when you perform a batch update on your database by using code.

On the other hand, the For/Next loop shines when you can determine at the outset exactly how many times you want to repeat a loop. You'll see an example where this is true later in this chapter (page 601), when you test credit card numbers.

Creating Custom Functions

You've already learned how to create your subroutines. But you haven't yet seen how to create their big brother, *functions*.

Like a subroutine, a function is a self-contained piece of code that can hold as many or as few statements as you want. And as with subroutines, you add functions to modules. In fact, any number of subroutines and functions can exist side by side in a module.

```
Function DoSomething()
    ' Function code goes here.
End Function
```

The key difference between functions and subroutines is that a function produces a final *result*. In other words, functions give you a piece of information that you may need.

You set the result by writing a line of code that assigns the result value to the function name. (Essentially, you pretend that the function name is a variable where you can stuff some data.) Here's an example:

```
Function GetMyFavoriteColor()
    GetMyFavoriteColor = "Magenta"
End Function
```

This function is named GetMyFavoriteColor. The result is the text string "Magenta".

Calling a function is slightly different than calling a subroutine. To call a subroutine, you use the module name, followed by a period, followed by the subroutine name. You can use the same technique with a function, as shown here:

```
MyModule.GetMyFavoriteColor
```

However, there's a problem. This step triggers the GetMyFavoriteColor function, causing its code to run, but it tosses away the result (the string with the text "Magenta").

If you're interested in the result, you can call your function as part of an assignment statement. The following code creates a variable, uses it to store the result, and then displays the result in a message box:

```
' Create a variable to store the result in.
Dim Color

' Call the function and hold on to the result in the variable.
Color = MyModule.GetMyFavoriteColor

' Show the result in a message box.
MsgBox "Your favorite color is " & Color
```

If you're really clever, you can shorten this code to a single line and avoid using the Color variable altogether:

```
MsgBox "Your favorite color is " & MyModule.GetMyFavoriteColor
```

The GetMyFavoriteColor function is particularly simple because it doesn't use any arguments. But you can get a little fancier. Consider the following custom function, which takes two arguments—Length and Width—and calculates the total area by multiplying them together:

```
Function Area(Length, Width)
    Area = Length * Width
End Function
```

The two parameters are defined in the parentheses after the function name. You can add as many parameters as you want, as long as you separate each one with a comma.

Here's how you call this function and show the result. In this example, fixed numbers are used for the Length and Width parameters. However, you can substitute a field name, variable, or property that you want to use instead with the Area function instead.

```
MsgBox "The area of a 4x4 rectangle is " & Area(4, 4)
```

This displays the message "The area of a 4x4 rectangle is 16."

Neither the GetMyFavoriteColor nor Area function shows you anything particularly impressive. But in the next section of this chapter, you'll build a much more powerful custom function that tests credit card numbers.

Using a Custom Function in a Query

Once you've created a function, you can use it anywhere in your database to build queries and validation rules. The only requirements are that your function must be in a custom module that you've added (not a form module), and it can't include the word `Private` in the declaration. If your function meets these rules, you can call upon it just as easily as you can call on a built-in Access function.

You could create a query with a calculated field like this (assuming the query includes two fields named `LengthOfRoom` and `WidthOfRoom`, respectively):

```
RoomArea: Area(LengthOfRoom, WidthOfRoom)
```

Or, you could build a table validation rule like this:

```
Area(LengthOfRoom, WidthOfRoom) < 1000
```

See Chapter 7 for some more ideas about using functions in calculated fields and Chapter 4 for more information about validation rules. And if you want to see this specific example in action, check out the MyHouse database that's included with the samples for this chapter.

Putting It All Together: A Function for Testing Credit Cards

Now that you've made your way around the Visual Basic language, it's time to wrap up with an example that demonstrates everything you've learned about VB (and a little bit more).

In this example, you'll consider a custom function called `ValidateCard` that examines a credit card number. The `ValidateCard` function returns one of two results: `True` (which means the card number is valid) and `False` (which means it's not).

It's important to understand that a *valid* credit card number is simply a number that meets all the not-so-secret rules of credit card numbering (the box on page 602 tells you more). This number may be attached to a real credit card, or it may not. The `ValidateCard` function is just smart enough to catch inadvertent errors and not-so-bright computer hackers. Truly sneaky people can find programs that let them generate potentially valid credit card numbers.

The Luhn Algorithm

The ValidateCard function uses the *Luhn algorithm*, which was developed by an IBM scientist in the 1960s. The Luhn algorithm works because credit card companies follow its rules. In other words, they issue only numbers that are considered valid according to the Luhn algorithm.

For a complete explanation of the Luhn algorithm, check out *http://tinyurl.com/luhn-algorithm*. Here's the "Reader's Digest" version of what it does:

1. Starting at the end of the credit card number, double the value of every second digit. Leave the even-numbered digits alone. For example, 1111 becomes 2121.

2. If this doubling process produces a number larger than 9, add the two digits in that number together. For example, 1166 becomes 2136. The second-to-last number 6 was

doubled (to 12) and the digits (1 and 2) were totaled (to make 3).

3. Add all these digits together. If you're currently left with 2136, then calculate 2+1+3+6 (which makes 12).

4. If the total ends in 0 (or, put another way, if the total is divisible evenly by 10), the number is valid. Otherwise it's not.

The Luhn algorithm checks to see if the number you've supplied is a possible credit card number. However, the Luhn algorithm can do only so much. It can't catch a credit card number that's technically valid but not actually hooked up to an account (and it obviously can't determine whether someone's credit card account is in good standing and has the required purchasing limit).

Here's the full code for the ValidateCard function. Each code statement is numbered so you can break it down one piece at a time (a line-by-line explanation follows the code):

```
1 Function ValidateCard(CardNumber As String)

    ' This is the running total (created using Luhn's algorithm).
2    Dim SumOfDigits
3    SumOfDigits = 0

    ' This keeps track of whether you're at an odd or even position.
    ' You start on an odd number position (1).
4    Dim OddNumbered
5    OddNumbered = True

6    Dim i
7    For i = Len(CardNumber) To 1 Step -1
8        Dim CurrentNumber
9        CurrentNumber = Mid(CardNumber, i, 1)
```

```
10          If OddNumbered = False Then
                ' Double the digit.
11              CurrentNumber = CurrentNumber * 2
12              If CurrentNumber >= 10 Then
                    ' If this number is two digits, add them together.
                    ' This is the wacky part, because you need to use
                    ' string conversion functions.
13                  Dim NumText As String
14                  NumText = CurrentNumber
15                  CurrentNumber = Val(Left(NumText, 1)) + _
16                      Val(Right(NumText, 1))
17              End If
18          End If

            ' Add the number to the running total.
19          SumOfDigits = SumOfDigits + CurrentNumber

            ' Switch from odd to even or even to odd.
            ' This line of code changes True to False or
            ' False to True
20          OddNumbered = Not OddNumbered
21      Next

        ' If the sum is divisible by 10, it's a valid number.
22      If SumOfDigits Mod 10 = 0 Then
23          ValidateCard = True
24      Else
25          ValidateCard = False
26      End If

27 End Function
```

Here's how it works:

- **Line 1** declares the function. Notice that the function takes one parameter, which is the text with the credit card number. This parameter is explicitly identified as a string with the As String clause. This way, you avoid errors where someone might try to pass in an actual number.

- **Lines 2–3** create the variable that stores the running total during the whole process.

- **Lines 4–5** create the variable that keeps track of whether you're on an odd-numbered position or an even-numbered position. Remember, all second numbers must be doubled.

- **Lines 6–7** start a For/Next loop. This loop looks a little different from the ones you saw earlier, because it has the Step -1 clause at the end. This clause tells the loop to subtract 1 from the counter after every pass (rather than adding 1, which is the standard behavior). You can work your way from the end of the number to the front.

> **NOTE** The For/Next loop uses another trick. The lower limit is set by using the Len function (page 254), which gets the length of a piece of text. In other words, if the credit card is 11 digits, this code runs 11 times (once for each digit).

- **Lines 8–9** grab the number at the current position, as indicated by the loop counter. The Mid function lets you snip out a single digit. (You learned about the Mid function on page 254.)

- **Line 10** checks if you're on a second number.

- **Lines 11–17** run only if you're on a second number. In this case, the number needs to be doubled (line 11). If the doubled number has two digits, these digits must then be combined (lines 13–15).

- **Line 19** adds the current number to the running total. If you were in an even-numbered position, the number hasn't been changed. If you were in an odd-numbered position, it's been doubled and combined.

- **Line 20** makes sure that if you just processed an even-numbered position, you're switched to an odd-numbered position (and vice versa).

- **Line 21** returns to line 6 and repeats the loop for the next digit in the credit card number.

- **Lines 22–26** check the final total. If it's divisible by 10, it's valid. To find out, this code uses the Mod operator, which performs division, and then gets the remainder. (If there's no remainder when you divide a number by 10, you know it divided evenly without a problem.)

It may take some time to work through the function and figure out exactly what's going on, but in the end it's all about VB basics like conditions, loops, and variables. If you really want to study this example, you can watch it in action, using the debugging techniques that are covered on page 606.

Once you've finished creating a function like ValidateCard, you can call it to test whether a credit card checks out. Here's an example that reacts when credit card information is entered into a text box named CardNumber:

```
Private Sub CardNumber_BeforeUpdate(Cancel As Integer)

    If ValidateCard(CardNumber) Then
        MsgBox "Your card is valid."
    Else
        MsgBox "Your card is invalid. " & _
```

```
            "Did you forget a number, or are you trying to cheat us?"
        Cancel = True
    End If

  End Sub
```

To try it out, run this code and supply one of your credit card numbers in the Card-Number field, as shown in *Figure 18-3*. Or send your credit card numbers to the author so he can conduct his own extensive testing.

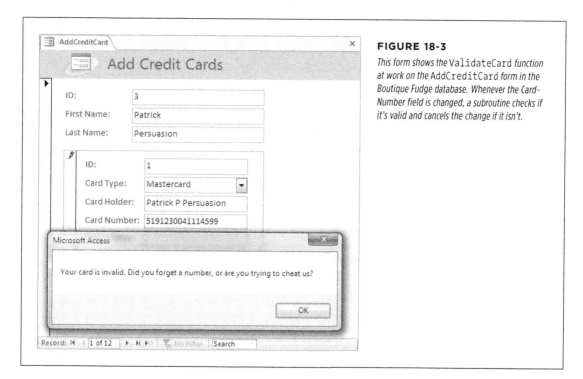

FIGURE 18-3

This form shows the ValidateCard function at work on the AddCreditCard form in the Boutique Fudge database. Whenever the Card-Number field is changed, a subroutine checks if it's valid and cancels the change if it isn't.

Dealing with Trouble

It would be nice to pretend that Access always sails through your code without the slightest hiccup. But the truth is, errors *do* occur, and they occur often. This fact shouldn't frighten you. After all, one of the reasons you're using Visual Basic code instead of ordinary macros is so that you can detect and respond to errors gracefully.

You'll face two types of errors with your code:

- **Mistakes.** These errors are coding errors that you introduce accidentally. Usually, you catch these while testing your database. (If you're lucky, the Visual

Basic editor spots the problem as soon as you type it in and then warns you with a message.)

- **Unexpected limitations**. These errors arise under specific circumstances that you may not have anticipated. Say you create two forms: Order, and Order_Subform. Order_Subform is designed to be used as a subform in Order, and it includes code that accesses the controls in Order. However, if someone opens Order_Subform directly, the Order form isn't available, and this code fails.

As a conscientious programmer, it's your job to correct all your mistakes and deal with unforeseen limitations in the best possible way. Visual Basic gives you two tools to help out. You can use *debugging* to diagnose bizarre problems and fix them, and you can use *error-handling code* to catch unexpected problems and to alert other people.

Debugging

Debugging is a nifty feature that lets you walk through your code, watch what it does, and spot errors. Code debugging is similar to macro debugging (page 507) in that it lets you run your logic one statement at a time. However, code debugging is much more powerful, because it lets you make your way through complex routines, loops, and conditional statements. It even lets you see what's currently stored in your variables.

NOTE Debugging's real benefit is that it helps you test your *assumptions*. Every programmer has assumptions about how a piece of code works. However, if code did exactly what you expected, you wouldn't ever have an error. With debugging, you can find the exact point where code does something that you don't expect—when a calculation provides a strange result, a conditional statement sends you the wrong way, a loop is repeated one time too many, and so on. Then you can correct the mistake.

The easiest way to perform debugging is to set a *breakpoint*—a special marker that tells Access where you want to start debugging. When Access reaches a line of code that has a breakpoint, it pauses your code. Access then lets you step through the code at your own pace, one line at a time.

Here's how to use a breakpoint:

1. **Find the first line in your code that you want to debug.**

   If you want to debug an entire routine, start with the opening Sub or Function statement. If you want to look at a specific section of your code, go there.

2. **Click the margin on the left to place a breakpoint on this line (*Figure 18-4*).**

   Each breakpoint is a signal that tells Access you want to start debugging *here*.

   Some lines can't accommodate a breakpoint: for example, lines that don't contain executable code, line blank spaces, comments, and variable declarations. Everything else is fair game.

NOTE   When you close your database and open it later, all your breakpoints disappear.

DEALING WITH
TROUBLE

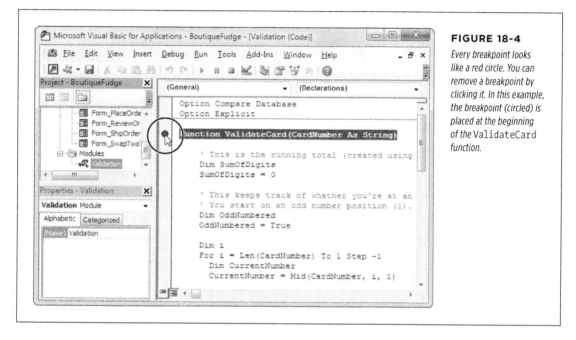

FIGURE 18-4

Every breakpoint looks like a red circle. You can remove a breakpoint by clicking it. In this example, the breakpoint (circled) is placed at the beginning of the ValidateCard *function.*

3. **Trigger your code.**

   You can get your code to run in the normal way. If you're debugging an event handler for a button click, open the appropriate form, and then click the button.

   When Access reaches your breakpoint, it pauses and switches into *Break mode*. Everything in your application is put on hold.

Once you're in Break mode, you have several options:

- **You can single-step through your code**. That means you run one statement at a time, pausing after each statement. To try this, press the F8 key. This action runs the current statement (which is highlighted with the yellow arrow), moves to the next executable statement, and then pauses again (*Figure 18-5*). You can continue for as long as you want, pressing F8 to run each line of code.

NOTE   Single-step debugging lets you follow how your code works. If you try it with the ValidateCard function shown earlier, you'll see how Access moves through the loop several times, and how it branches into different conditional sections depending on whether it's processing a number in an odd or even position.

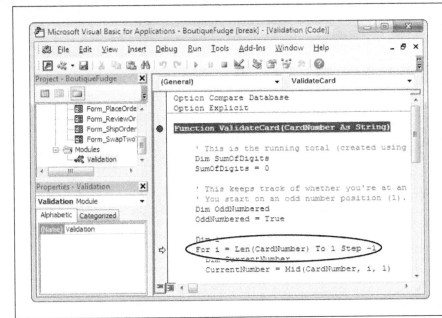

FIGURE 18-5

In this example, the breakpoint stopped the code at the beginning of the ValidationCard function. Then, the person debugging this code pressed F8 a few times to move on through the code. Right now, the code is paused at the beginning of the For/Next loop (circled).

- **You can stop running your code**. Click the Stop button (it looks like a square) in the Visual Basic toolbar to shut down your code.

- **You can make changes**. If you find what's wrong, you can edit your code, and then keep running with the new changes. Of course, certain types of edits force Access to stop debugging. If you make one of these changes, you see a message box that warns you that "This action will reset your project." If you click OK, Access stops your code just as if you had clicked the Visual Basic toolbar's Stop button.

- **You can see what's stored inside a variable**. To do so, just hover over the variable name somewhere in your code (*Figure 18-6*).

- **You can resume normal execution**. If you've found the source of your problem and you don't want to keep debugging, just press F5 (or click the Visual Basic toolbar's Play button). Access runs the current line and then continues on its merry way (at least until it meets another breakpoint).

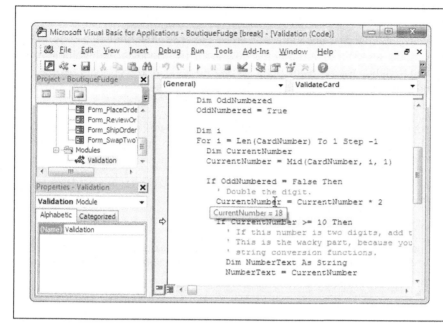

FIGURE 18-6

*By hovering over the
CurrentNumber
variable, you can see that
it's currently storing the
number 18. You can hover
over variables on any line
in your code, not just the
current line. However,
you'll see only the current
contents of the variable. If
you press F8 to single-step
through your code, you
can watch a value change
as you perform operations.*

TIP   You can pull off a wacky trick with the yellow arrow. You can use it to run code in a completely different place. Just drag the yellow arrow to the line you want to run next, and then press F5 to switch out of Debug mode, and resume running your code normally.

The Visual Basic editor has many more debugging tools. However, breakpoints are really all you need to start exploring what's taking place under the hood when you run your code.

Error Handling

Some errors occur through no fault of your own. Perhaps you're trying to perform a task with information someone else gave you, and that information just isn't valid. Imagine what happens if someone calls ValidateCard and passes in a credit card number that contains letters and punctuation!

Although this sort of error can occur as a result of somebody else's carelessness, it's up to you to deal with it in the best way possible. You need to explain the problem with a helpful message box, and end the current task (or jump ahead to the next step). You can take care of this job with error-handling code.

Ordinarily, when Access encounters an error, it jumps to the offending code, enters Break mode, and shows you an error message. This behavior is helpful if you're planning to debug the problem, but it's a bit traumatic for the ordinary people who may be using your database. Not only have they never seen code before, they're in danger of changing it and introducing a new problem.

Instead, you need a way to deal with the error the way *you* want, using code. Visual Basic has a special statement that tells Access how to deal with errors. It's the On Error statement.

The On Error statement gives you several options. You can tell Access to skip over any errors and try to run the next line of code like this:

```
On Error Resume Next
```

This option is almost always a bad idea. If one error has occurred, more are likely to follow. At worst, this could cause your program to do something you don't intend it to do.

You can also tell Access to jump to a specific place in your code. Here's an example:

```
On Error Goto ErrorHandlingCode
```

This example tells Access to jump to the section named ErrorHandlingCode as soon as it encounters any problem. You need to identify this section by adding the section name, followed by a colon (:) on a separate line, like this:

```
ErrorHandlingCode:

    ' If an error occurs, Access starts running your code here.
```

You can most easily understand how this error-handling system works when you consider how you can use it in the ValidateCard function:

```
Function ValidateCard(CardNumber As String)

On Error Goto ErrorHandlingCode

    ' (The code for Luhn's algorithm goes here.)

    Exit Function
```

```
ErrorHandlingCode:
    MsgBox "Oops. Did your credit card number have letters?"
    ValidateCard = False

End Function
```

Here are several important details. First, the On Error statement is placed at the very beginning of the code routine, so you can catch mistakes in any of the code that follows. Second, notice that after the number-checking code finishes, an Exit Function statement ends the routine. That statement prevents Access from drifting into the error-handling code that follows if an error hasn't happened. Finally, the error-handling code shows a message box that explains that something went wrong and returns a result that clearly indicates the problem. People most often handle errors this way. Just remember to always use an Exit Sub or Exit Function statement to make sure you don't run your error-handling code by accident.

> **NOTE** As written, the person using the AddCreditCard form may get two error messages—one explaining the letters-or-punctuation problem, and the second stating the obvious fact that validation failed. If this message seems like unnecessary punishment, you can move the error-handling code out of the ValidateCard function and into the On Update event handler code, which is where it really belongs. That way, the On Update event handler can choose exactly how to deal with the problem. To see the slightly rearranged code, check out the downloadable samples for this chapter (*www.missingmanuals.com/cds/access2013mm*).

You have only one other option for handling errors. You can tell Access to stop immediately and enter Debug mode by using this statement:

```
On Error Goto 0
```

Of course, this behavior is already the standard error-handling behavior. You need to use this statement only if you're switching back and forth between different error-handling approaches in the same routine.

Launching Other Windows Programs

How do I open Word (or Excel, or Notepad, or Dance Dance Revolution)?

Visual Basic includes a function named Shell that lets you launch another program. To use the Shell function, you need to supply the complete path that points to the program file. Here's an example that runs the Windows Calculator:

```
Shell "C:\Windows\Calc.exe"
```

When you use Shell, Windows launches the program you asked for, and your code keeps running. However, your code doesn't have any way to actually *interact* with the program. You can't force it to do something or find out if it's been closed.

Shell seems like a convenient function, but it has a major problem. To use the Shell function, you need to know exactly where a program is. You can't just say, "Launch Microsoft Word" or "Open this document." Instead, you need to dig down deep into your hard drive to find the program file you need (which is usually somewhere in the Program Files area of your computer). Even worse, once you get the Shell function working on your computer, there's no guarantee it'll work on someone else's—after all, the same program could be installed somewhere completely different.

So what can you do instead? You could use a hyperlink (page 443), which launches the right program automatically when it's clicked. But some programs, including the other members of the Microsoft Office family, give you a much better option. They provide their own objects that you can manipulate in Visual Basic code. With these objects, you can use these programs without worrying about where they're installed. You can also do way more with them by setting different properties and calling various methods. You can tell Word to open a document, add some text to it, send 10 copies to the printer, and then quit.

The objects that make this process work are beyond the scope of this book, but here's a very simple example that launches Word, shows the Word window, and then loads a document that's named GothicWedding.doc:

```
Dim Word As Object
Set Word = CreateObject("Word.Application")
Word.Visible = True
Word.Documents.Open CurrentProject.Path &_
  "\GothicWedding.doc"
```

If this technique intrigues you, check out the resources for Word programming in Microsoft's Office Developer Center at *http://tinyurl.com/vba-for-word*.

Deeper into Objects

There comes a point in every Access programmer's life when you realize you've learned enough about the VB language to get by. From that point on, you spend most of your time learning about different *objects*, which is a much larger task.

Access has several dozen built-in objects which, taken together, make up what programmers call an *object model*. Along with the control and form objects you know so well, it has objects representing queries, projects, reports, smart tags, printers, and much more. You can't cover all these objects in a single chapter. Even if you could, you'd find that many of them just don't interest you. However, you need to know enough so that you can hunt down the features you need when you're tackling a particularly sticky VB challenge.

You can explore the Access object model by using Microsoft's online VBA (Visual Basic for Applications) reference at *http://tinyurl.com/accessVBA*. Click "How do I" in the table contents to read how-to topics for a variety of Access tasks, with copious code. Or, click "Access object model reference" to get a lower-level look at the Access objects you can manipulate in code.

Even if you work your way through the sprawling Access object model, many more objects are still out there. If you're a black-belt VB programmer, then you may choose to create your own objects. And even if you aren't, you may decide to use another *component* that gives you even more objects to play with.

NOTE In programmer-speak, a component is just a file that has some objects you can use in your code. The file *acedao.dll* has the objects you can use to interact directly with your database (see page 633).

Later in this chapter, you'll learn how to use DAO (the *data access objects*) to interact with your database. DAO is such a common part of Access programming that most people treat it as a built-in part of the Access object model. But technically, DAO consists of a set of objects provided by a separate component, which Access provides. Many more components are waiting for you to discover them.

To use a new component, you need to add a reference to that component in your database. To do so, in the Visual Basic editor's menu, choose Tools→References. You'll see the References window shown in *Figure 18-7*.

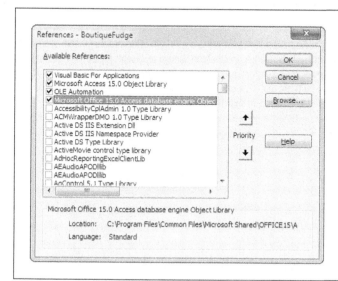

FIGURE 18-7

To add a reference to a component you want to use, find it in the list, and then place a checkmark next to it. The currently referenced components appear at the top of the list. Here, you can see the objects that are automatically referenced in every database—the objects built in Visual Basic, those that come with Access, and the data access objects you can use to read and edit the database directly (page 633).

The problem with the References window is that you need to know exactly what component you want to use. The Available References list is full of neat-sounding components that aren't designed for use in Access and that won't work right with your code. Among the components you can use are ones from Microsoft that let you interact with files, show web pages, and interact with other Office applications. However, you won't get far experimenting on your own. Instead, you'll need to find sample code on the Web.

The DoCmd Object

The DoCmd object is perhaps the single most useful object in the Access programming world. It provides one-stop shopping for a variety of tasks, like opening forms and reports, launching other programs, finding records, and running macros.

Unlike the objects you've seen so far, the DoCmd object doesn't have any properties. Instead, it's made up of methods that perform different actions. If you want to open a form named ProductCatalog, you can use the OpenForm method like this:

```
DoCmd.OpenForm "ProductCatalog"
```

Like most of the DoCmd methods, OpenForm can use several optional parameters. Visual Basic prompts you by showing the list of possible parameters as you type. Here's an example that skips over the second and third parameters (note the commas with no values in between) but supplies a filter in the fourth parameter, and a data mode in the fifth parameter:

```
DoCmd.OpenForm "ProductCatalog", , ," ID=5", acFormReadOnly
```

This command opens the ProductCatalog form, applies a filter to show only the record with the ID of 5, and uses read-only mode to prevent any changes.

NOTE This example uses an acFormReadOnly, which is a *constant*. Constants are numeric values that are given more helpful names. So instead of remembering that the number represents read-only mode, you can use the more readable acFormReadOnly constant. Anytime you see a variable that starts with *ac* or *vb* and you haven't created it yourself, the odds are that it's a constant. Of course, you still need to know the constant names to use them, but IntelliSense can help you, as shown in *Figure 18-8*.

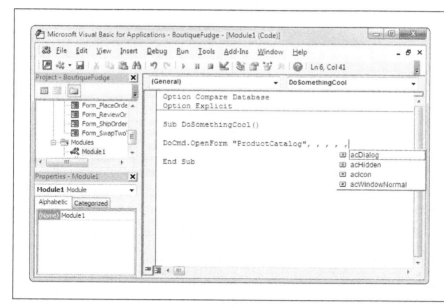

FIGURE 18-8

When you get to the data mode parameter, the Visual Basic editor pops up a list of all the valid constants that you can use. To find out what they really mean (if it's not obvious), you need to consult the Microsoft's Visual Basic reference (see the box on page 566).

If the OpenForm method looks familiar, that's because you've already seen the same functions with the OpenForm macro action (page 519). In fact, all the methods of the DoCmd object line up with the macro actions you learned about in Chapter 15. Table 18-1 lists the most useful ones.

TABLE 18-1 *Useful Methods of the DoCmd Object*

METHOD	DESCRIPTION
ApplyFilter	Applies a filter to a table, form, query, or report, to focus on the records you're interested in.
Beep	Makes some noise. Usually, you use this to get attention if a problem occurs.
Close	Closes the current database object (or a specific one you indicate).
CopyDatabaseFile	Gives you a quick way to make a database backup.
FindRecord, FindNext, and GoToRecord	Gives you different ways to search for the record you want.
Hourglass	Switches on or off the "please-wait" mouse pointer, which looks more like a swirl than an hourglass in modern versions of Windows. You can use this method to let someone know there's a time-consuming task underway, and she should chill.

METHOD	DESCRIPTION
OpenForm, OpenQuery, OpenReport, and OpenTable	Opens the appropriate database object, in whatever view mode you want, with filter settings and other optional details. As you learned in Chapter 15, you can also use OpenReport to print a report, and OpenQuery to run an action query.
PrintOut	Offers one way to print the data from the current database object.
Quit	Exits Access.
RunCommand	A fill-in-the-gaps command that lets you run various Access commands available on the ribbon. You just need to supply the right constant. Page 630 shows an example that uses RunCommand to save the current record immediately.
RunMacro	Runs a macro.
RunSQL	Executes a raw SQL statement (see page 220). You can't use this command to get information out of your database. Instead, it lets you run commands that change records or tables.
ShowAllRecords	Removes the current filter settings so you can see all the records in a table, form, query, or report.

Converting a Macro to VB Code

If you want to learn a little more about Visual Basic and the DoCmd object, you can take an existing macro and convert it into a pure code subroutine. Here's how:

1. **In the navigation pane, right-click the macro you want to use and choose Design.**

   This opens the macro in Design view.

2. **Choose File→Save As.**

   This takes you to backstage view.

3. **In the list on the left, choose Save Object As, then click the Save As button on the right.**

   A simplified Save As window appears, with two settings. Ordinarily, you use this window to create duplicate copies of database objects.

   TIP You can also convert the embedded macros in a form. To do so, open the form in Design view, choose Form Design Tools | Design→Tools→Convert Form's Macros to Visual Basic, and skip to step 6.

4. **In the second box, choose Module (rather than Macro, which is the only other option).**

The Module setting tells Access that you want to perform a macro conversion, not create a macro copy. Don't worry about the name in the first text box—it's used when copying a macro object, and has no effect when you're converting a macro to code.

5. **Click OK.**

   A window with two options appears (*Figure 18-9*).

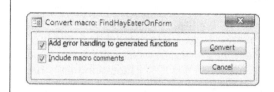

FIGURE 18-9

You see this tiny window if you ask Access to convert the FindHa-yEaterOnForm *macro.*

6. **If you want to add basic error-handling (as described on page 609), make sure "Add error handling to generated functions" is turned on.**

   A little bit of error handling is always a good idea.

7. **If you want to turn your macro comments into VB comments, make sure "Include macro comments" is selected.**

   If you've taken the time to add some explanatory text, it's worth keeping it around.

8. **Click Convert.**

   Access creates a new module for the converted code and gives it a name like "Converted Macro-[YourMacroName]." Inside the module, Access creates a function with the same name as your macro. If you convert a macro that contains submacros (page 524), Access adds one function for each submacro.

   Once the conversion process is complete, Access opens your module in the Visual Basic editor so you can review the code.

The following example shows the result of converting a macro from Chapter 15 (shown on page 519) that searches for specific text in the AnimalTypes table:

```
Function FindHayEater()

On Error GoTo FindHayEater_Err

    DoCmd.OpenForm "AnimalTypes", acNormal, "", "", , acNormal
    DoCmd.GoToControl "Diet"
    DoCmd.FindRecord "="""hay""""", acAnywhere, False, , _
      False, acCurrent, False
```

```
    FindHayEater_Exit:
        Exit Function

    FindHayEater_Err:
        MsgBox Error$
        Resume FindHayEater_Exit


    End Function
```

You'll notice that the converted code makes heavy use of the DoCmd object—in fact, almost every line uses the DoCmd object. First, it uses the OpenForm method to open a form, then it uses the GoToControl method to switch to the Diet field, and finally it looks for the first record that has the text "hay." This line looks a little weird because it doubles up its quotation marks (to make "=""hay"""). Quotation marks have a special meaning to Visual Basic (they show where text begins and ends). If you actually want to insert a quotation mark in your text, you need to put two quotation mark characters in a row. Strange, but true.

The code ends with an error-handling routine named FindHayEater_Err, which simply shows the problem in a message box and then ends the routine.

NOTE When you convert a macro into code, Access always generates a function (page 599), not a subroutine. However, the function doesn't return a result, so it's not really necessary. (Presumably, Access works this way to give you the flexibility to decide later on that you want to return a value.)

Using VB to Run a Better Business

Over the last 17 chapters, you've come to know and love the Boutique Fudge database, which demonstrates a practical sales database that tracks customers, products, and orders. However, although the Boutique Fudge database stores all the information you need, it still doesn't integrate seamlessly into company life. And before you can fix it, you need to understand why it comes up short.

Most people who work in a business like Boutique Fudge aren't thinking about tables and data operations (like inserting, updating, and deleting records). Instead, they're thinking about *tasks*, like placing an order, shipping an order, and handling a customer complaint.

Many tasks match quite closely with a data operation, in which case you really don't have a problem. The "register a new customer" task is clearly just a matter of opening the Customers table, and then inserting a new record. You can take care of it with a simple form. However, the "place an order" task is a little trickier. This task involves inserting records in more than one table (the Orders and OrderDetails tables), and using data from related tables (the Products and Customers tables) to complete the order. You can create an ordinary form to do the job, but the form doesn't quite work the way salespeople want (see *Figure 18-10*).

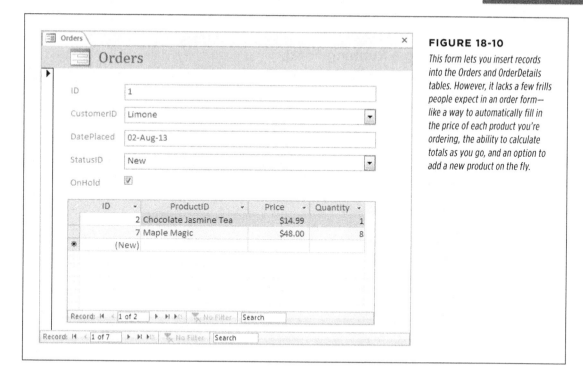

FIGURE 18-10

*This form lets you insert records
into the Orders and OrderDetails
tables. However, it lacks a few frills
people expect in an order form—
like a way to automatically fill in
the price of each product you're
ordering, the ability to calculate
totals as you go, and an option to
add a new product on the fly.*

The same is true when it comes to the "ship an order" task. This task requires several steps—changing the status of the order, logging the shipment, and updating the units-in-stock numbers. You could deal with this task as several separate data operations, but it's a lot nicer if you create a single form that takes care of the whole process.

Now your VB skills are truly useful. With the right code, you can design an intelligent form that fits the way people work. An intelligent form isn't just a way to add, edit, and insert records in a table—it's a tool that helps run your business.

In the following sections, you'll consider how to build better forms with some code-powered features. The following forms are covered:

- **PlaceOrder** lets you create a new order. It works in conjunction with the PlaceOrder_Subform, which lets you add individual items to the order.

- **AddProduct** lets you create a new product. You can use it directly from the PlaceOrder form to add a product in mid-order.

- **ShipOrders** lets you update an order with shipment information. It also works with a form named ReviewOrderDetails to show the items in the order.

You can check out the final result with the downloadable databases for this chapter.

TIP It's always a good idea to name your form according to the task it performs (placing an order, shipping a task, and so on), rather than the table it uses. This design helps you remember who's using each form, so you can tailor it to the right audience.

Keeping a Running Total

Few souls are brave enough to place an order without knowing exactly how much it costs. A typical order form shows how much each line item costs (by multiplying the price and quantity information) and the ever-important grand total (*Figure 18-11*).

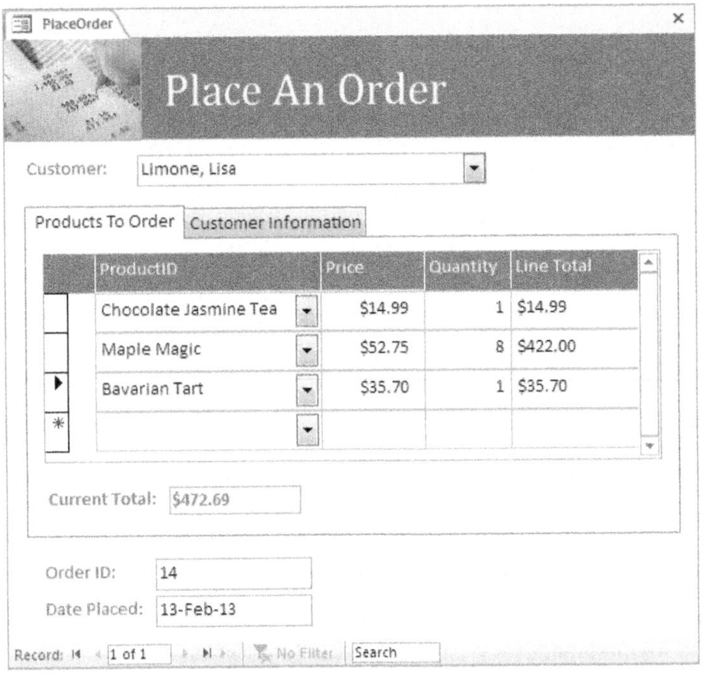

FIGURE 18-11

The PlaceOrder form, with subtotals and a grand total.

NOTE The PlaceOrder form also introduces a few refinements you already know about, like putting customer address information on a separate tab, moving the automatically generated fields (the order ID and the order date) to the bottom of the window where they won't distract anyone, and setting their `Locked` property to `Yes` to prevent changes. The form also has its `Data Entry` property set to `Yes`, so you start creating a new order as soon as you open the form.

The line total is the only detail that *doesn't* require code. In fact, you can solve this problem by adding a text box that uses the following expression to the PlaceOrder_Subform:

```
=Quantity * Price
```

This expression works because the fields you need (Price and Quantity) are located on the same form as the calculated field. However, the grand total isn't as straight-forward.

You can combine the line total expression with the Format function (page 250) to make sure you get the right number of decimal places and a currency symbol ($):

```
=Format(Quantity * Price, "Currency")
```

To calculate the grand total, you can use the Quantity and Price information in the OrderDetails table. Unfortunately, the PlaceOrder form doesn't have any easy way to get this information. Not only is this information shown somewhere else (in a subform), but it also involves several *separate* records. Even if you retrieve the Quantity and Price information from the subform, you can get only the values for the current record, not for the whole list of ordered items.

To solve this problem, you need to use a specialized Access function called a *domain function*. A domain function can process an entire table and return a single piece of information. (To learn more, see the box below.)

To calculate the total of all the items in an order, you use the DSum function. The information you need is in the OrderDetails table, but you want to select only those records where the OrderID field matches the current order. Finally, you need to add together the cost of each item. And as you know from before, you calculate the cost of a line by multiplying together the Price and Quantity fields.

UP TO SPEED

Become a Master of Your Domain (Functions)

The domain functions are like the grouping functions you use in a totals query (page 263). These functions take a range of records, and then perform a calculation or lookup to arrive at a single value.

Access includes eight domain functions:

- **DSum** calculates the sum of multiple values. You can use it to calculate an order's total price.

- **DAvg** calculates the average of multiple values. You can use it to calculate a product's average price.

- **DCount** counts the number of matching records. You can use it to count the number of items in an order, or the number of orders a customer made.

- **DMin** and **DMax** find the smallest or largest value in a series. You can use these functions to find bargain-basement or top-priced products.

- **DFirst** and **DLast** extract the first or last value in a series. If you sort a list of orders by date, you can get the oldest or most recent order.

- **DLookup** finds a value that meets specific criteria. You can use it to hunt through a table and find the product name for a given product ID.

All the domain functions take the same three parameters. The first parameter is the field (or calculated expression) you want to retrieve or use in your calculation. The second parameter is the table or query you're using. The third parameter contains any filter conditions you want to use to narrow down the number of rows. If you're trying to find the average price of all the beverages sold by Boutique Fudge, you use the Price field (as the first parameter), the Products table (the second parameter), and use the Beverages category (the third parameter) as a filter to include just the products you want.

With this information in mind, you can create the following calculated field:

```
=DSum("Price*Quantity","OrderDetails","OrderID=" & [ID])
```

The first argument is the calculated field that you're taking from each record. The second argument is the name of the table you're using. The third argument filters out just those records that match the current order. If the current order has an ID of 455, the final parameter matches all OrderDetails records where OrderID=455. Once again, you can wrap the whole thing with the Format function if you want the final number to look like a currency value.

This calculated field does the trick, but you need one more enhancement. Ordinarily, Access computes calculated fields the first time a record is shown. However, you need to make sure that the grand total is recalculated and redisplayed every time you make a change in the list of ordered items. To accomplish this, you need to call the Forms.Recalc method when an OrderDetails record is inserted, updated, or deleted. Here's the code that does the trick:

```
Private Sub Form_AfterInsert()
    Forms("PlaceOrder").Recalc
End Sub

Private Sub Form_AfterUpdate()
    Forms("PlaceOrder").Recalc
End Sub

Private Sub Form_AfterDelConfirm(Status As Integer)
    Forms("PlaceOrder").Recalc
End Sub
```

This code uses a new technique. Specifically, it runs in one form (PlaceOrder_Subform) but triggers an action in another form (PlaceOrder). In order to pull off this feat, it needs the object that represents the PlaceOrder form. The code finds the object it needs by searching inside the Forms collection for a form named "PlaceOrder." The box on page 623 analyzes this technique in closer detail.

Interacting with Other Forms

Not only can you retrieve and set the properties of the current form, you can also retrieve and set the properties of any other forms that are currently open. The trick is that you need to explicitly tell Access what form you're trying to use.

Suppose you want to change the color of the Price control on a form named Product when you click a button on a form named PriceChanger. This code doesn't work, because Access looks for a Price control on the PriceChanger form, which doesn't exist:

```
Price.BackColor = vbRed
```

However, this code does the trick nicely, by directing Access to the right form:

```
Forms("Product").Price.BackColor = vbRed
```

Technically, this code tells Access to look in the Forms *collection*, which keeps track of all the currently open forms. (If Product isn't currently open, this statement fails.) It grabs the form named Product from the collection, reaches into the form to get its Price control, and then digs into the Price control to find the BackColor property.

You actually have two ways to write this same line of logic. Old-school Access programmers use a wacky syntax with exclamation marks that looks like this:

```
Forms!Product!Price!BackColor = vbRed
```

Access interprets both lines of code in the same way. It's really just a matter of taste. However, you should be familiar with both approaches, in case you should see bizarre!code!with!exclamation!marks!

If you're troubled that this technique causes an error if the form you need isn't open, two techniques can help you out. On page 626, you'll learn how to open a form at will.

Getting Price Information

As you learned in Chapter 5, sometimes a table needs to store *point-in-time* data—information that's copied from one table to another because it might change over time. A good example is product prices, which evolve over time. ("Evolve" is a polite way to say, "increase relentlessly.") So a product's current price isn't necessarily the price at which you ordered it last week. To keep track of how much you owe the company, the selling price of a product needs to be stored in the OrderDetails table.

However, this system creates a headache when you fill out an order. Choosing an order item is easy enough—you just need to select the product from a lookup list. However, the lookup list sets the ProductID field only for the OrderDetails record. It's up to you to figure out the correct price, and then copy it from the Products table to your new record.

Fortunately, you can make this much easier. You can react to the On Change event in the ProductID list, which is triggered every time a product is selected. Then, you can use the DLookup domain function to find the corresponding price, and insert it in the Price field automatically. Here's the code that does it:

```
Private Sub ProductID_Change()
    Price = DLookup("Price", "Products", "ID=" & ProductID)
    Quantity = 1
End Sub
```

This code also sets the Quantity field to 1, which is a reasonable starting point. If necessary, you can edit the Price and Quantity fields after you pick your product. Or, to create a more stringent form, you can set the Locked property of the Price control to Yes, so that no price changes are allowed (as in the Boutique Fudge database). This way, when you create an order, you're forced to use the price that's currently in effect, with no discounting allowed.

> **TIP** You can use the same technique to fill in other point-in-time data. For example, you can grab the address information for the current customer, and use that as a starting point for the shipping address. And you can even use the DLookup function to create more sophisticated validation routines. You could use this technique with the Cacophoné Music School database, to look up prerequisites and maximum class sizes before letting a student enroll in a class.

Adding a New Product During an Order

Boutique Fudge is a customer-driven company. If someone wants an innovative product that's not yet in the product catalog (like fudge-dunked potatoes), the company's willing to create it on demand.

Ordinarily, the ProductID lookup list doesn't allow this sort of on-the-fly product creation. If you try to type in a product that doesn't exist, you get a stern reprimand from Access. However, adding new list items on the go is a common Access programming technique, and there's a dedicated event that's designed to help you out: the On Not In List event.

If you type in a product that doesn't exist and you're using the On Not In List event, Access starts by running your event-handling code. You can create the item if you want, show a different message, or correct the problem before Access complains.

The On Not In List event has two parameters: NewData and Response. NewData is the information that was typed into the list box that isn't found in the list. Response is a value you supply to tell Access how to deal with the problem.

Here's the basic skeleton of the subroutine that Access creates if you choose to handle the On Not In List event for the field named ProductID:

```
Private Sub ProductID_NotInList(NewData As String, Response As Integer)
End Sub
```

When the On Not In List event occurs, you should first ask the person using the form if they meant to enter a product that doesn't exist. You can take this step using the familiar MsgBox function in a slightly different way. First, you need to add a second parameter that tells Access to create a message box with Yes and No buttons. Then, you need to get hold of the return value from the MsgBox function to find out which button was clicked:

```
Dim ButtonClicked
ButtonClicked = MsgBox("Do you want to add a new product?", vbYesNo)
```

This code creates a variable named ButtonClicked and then shows the message. When the person closes the message box (by clicking Yes or No), Visual Basic puts a number into the ButtonClicked variable that tells you what happened. The number is 6 if Yes was clicked, or 7 if No was clicked. But rather than deal directly with these numbers and risk making a mistake, you can use the helpful constants vbYes (which equals 6) and vbNo (which equals 7).

Here's the partially completed code for the On Not In List event handler. It shows the message asking if a new item should be added (*Figure 18-12*), and then cancels the edit if the person using the form chooses No:

```
Private Sub ProductID_NotInList(NewData As String, Response As Integer)

    ' Show a Yes/No message and get the result.
    Dim ButtonClicked
    ButtonClicked = MsgBox("Do you want to add a new product for " & _
      NewData & "?", vbYesNo)

    ' Visual Basic gives you vbYes and vbNo constants
    ' that you can use to find out what button was clicked.
    If ButtonClicked = vbNo Then

        ' Cancel the edit.
        ProductID.Undo

        ' Tell Access not to show the error message.
        ' You've already dealt with it.
        Response = acDataErrContinue

    Else
        ' (Put some code here to add a new product.)
    End If
End Sub
```

Then you supply the code that adds the new product. In this example, it doesn't make sense for your code to add the product completely on its own—after all, a product needs other information (like price and category details) before it's considered valid. Instead, you need to show another form for adding products. The DoCmd.OpenForm method is the key:

```
' Tell Access not to worry, because you're adding the missing item.
Response = acDataErrAdded

' Open the AddProduct form, with three additional arguments.
DoCmd.OpenForm "AddProduct", , , , , acDialog, NewData
```

The two additional arguments you use with the OpenForm method are quite important:

- **acDialog** opens the form in Dialog mode, which means Access puts the code in the ProductID_NotInList on hold until the AddProduct form is closed. That step is important because once the adding process is finished, you'll need to run more code to update the PlaceOrder form.

- **NewData** takes the newly typed-in information and sets it in the AddProduct. OpenArgs property. That way, the AddProduct form can retrieve this information when it starts up, and then adjust itself accordingly.

FIGURE 18-12

Fudge-Dunked Potatoes isn't a currently offered product. When you type it in and then press Enter, your code asks whether you really intend to add this product.

Here's the code you need in the AddProduct form to copy the newly entered product name (the value you passed using the NewData variable in the previous code snippet) into the ProductName field when AddProduct first loads:

```
Private Sub Form_Open(Cancel As Integer)
    ProductName = Form.OpenArgs

End Sub
```

Figure 18-13 shows what this form looks like.

FIGURE 18-13

The AddProduct form lets you supply the rest of the information for the new product you want to create. Notice how the form opens as a pop-up form, and Access automatically assumes you're inserting a new record (not reviewing existing products). Access acts this way because the Pop Up and Data Entry properties of the form are both set to Yes. This type of form is also known as a modal form, and you can create one quickly by choosing Create→Forms→More Forms→Modal Dialog from the ribbon.

Once you finish entering all the product information, you can close the AddProduct form. At that point, a little more code runs in the ProductID_NotInList subroutine. This code is placed immediately after the DoCmd.OpenForm statement. Its job is to update the new order item to use the product you've just entered:

```
' Cancel the edit. That's because you need to refresh the list
' before you can select the new product.
ProductID.Undo

' Refresh the list.
ProductID.Requery

' Now find the ProductID for the newly added item using DLookup.
ProductID = DLookup("ID", "Products", "ProductName='" & NewData & "'")
```

NOTE This code works even if you cancel the new product in the AddProduct form by pressing the Esc key. In this case, the DLookup function can't find anything, so it returns a null (empty value) to the ProductID field. As a result, you get the familiar Access warning message telling you the product you picked isn't in the list.

There's one more detail. By the time the On Not In List event occurs, the On Change event has already taken place. So you just missed your chance to run the code you used earlier to insert the corresponding price into the Price field in the list of order items.

Fortunately, you can solve this problem quite easily. You just need to add one more line of code that tells Access to go ahead and run the event handler (the ProductID_Change subroutine) again:

```
ProductID_Change
```

To see the complete code for this example in one place, refer to the sample Boutique Fudge database for this chapter.

Managing Order Fulfillment

Now that you've perfected the ordering process, you can turn your attention to what happens next.

In the Boutique Fudge database, every record in the Orders table has an Order-Status field that keeps track of the, well, status. Newly created order records have a New status. In the stock room, the warehouse workers look for orders with the New status and pick one to start working on. At that point, they change the status of this order to In Progress, so nobody else tries to ship it at the same time. Finally, when the order is complete, they change it to Shipped, and then record the exact time in the ShipDate field.

Logically, this model makes sense. However, it's a bit tricky using ordinary tables and forms. To follow this workflow, the warehouse staff needs to modify the status of an order record several times, remember to record the ship date, and avoid changing other details. If they miss a step—say they never put the order into In Progress status—it's possible that more than one employee could try to complete the same order.

The solution is to create a ShipOrders form that guides the warehouse workers through the right steps. Initially, this form shows a list of orders with minimal information (*Figure 18-14*).

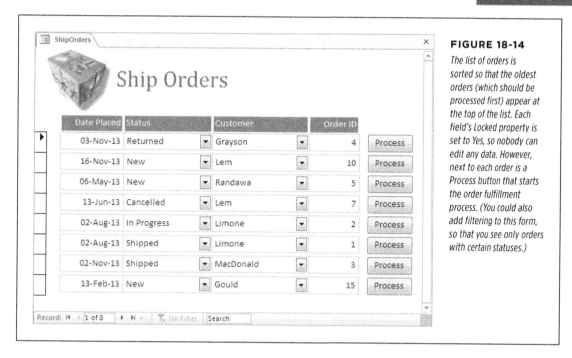

FIGURE 18-14

FIGURE 18-14

The list of orders is sorted so that the oldest orders (which should be processed first) appear at the top of the list. Each field's Locked property is set to Yes, so nobody can edit any data. However, next to each order is a Process button that starts the order fulfillment process. (You could also add filtering to this form, so that you see only orders with certain statuses.)

When someone clicks the Process button, several steps need to take place. Here's a step-by-step walkthrough of the code, one chunk at a time.

First, your code needs to refresh the record. That step catches whether someone else has started processing the order on another computer:

```
Private Sub ProcessOrder_Click()

    Form.Refresh
```

Next, your code needs to check the record's status. If it's anything other than New, that order isn't available for processing:

```
' The StatusID for New is 2.
If StatusID <> 2 Then
    MsgBox "This order is not available."
```

Otherwise, you need to switch the status to In Progress and save the record right away, to make sure no else tries to get it:

```
Else
    ' The StatusID for In Progress is 3.
    StatusID = 3

    ' Save the change.
    DoCmd.RunCommand acCmdSaveRecord
```

> **NOTE** It's extremely important to save the record (using the DoCmd.RunCommand method, as shown here) in this sort of situation. Otherwise, the order record remains in Edit mode, and the new status isn't saved in the database. Other people might start processing it, because they have no way of knowing that you've changed the status.

Now it's time to launch the ReviewOrderDetails form, which displays a read-only view of all the items in the order (*Figure 18-15*). The form is opened in Dialog mode, which locks up the ShipOrders form until the order fulfillment process is complete:

```
        DoCmd.OpenForm "ReviewOrderDetails", , , _
            "OrderID =" & ID, , acDialog
    End If


End Function
```

The ReviewOrderDetails form gives the warehouse staff two choices. If they click Ship, Access changes the order status to Shipped, and the process is complete:

```
Private Sub Ship_Click()
    ' Close this form.
    DoCmd.Close

    ' Switch back to the ShipOrders form.
    DoCmd.OpenForm "ShipOrders"

    ' Update the order.
    ' The StatusID for Shipped is 4.
    Forms("ShipOrders").StatusID = 4
    DoCmd.RunCommand acCmdSaveRecord
End Sub
```

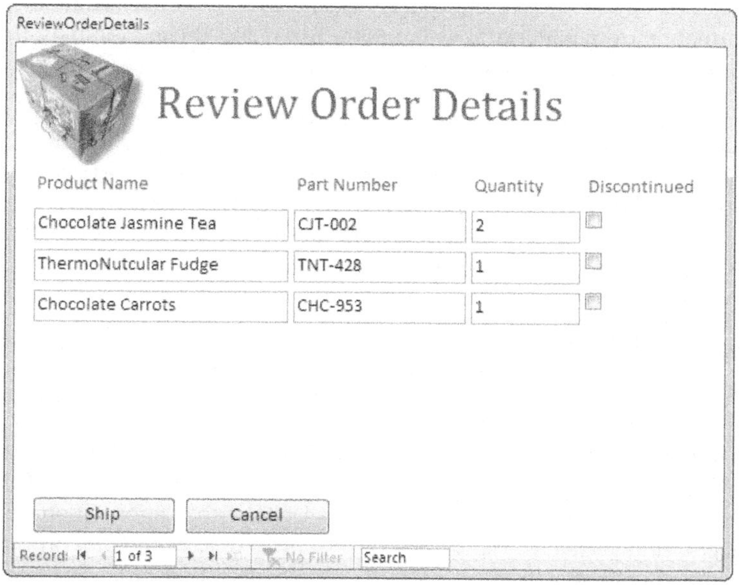

FIGURE 18-15

You don't need to include pricing details in the ReviewOrderDetails form. It's simply designed to give the warehouse people the information they need as efficiently as possible. The ReviewOrderDetails form also uses a query join to get some related data, like the PartNumber, from the Products table.

In the ReviewOrderDetails form, the properties Control Box and Close Button are both set to No. That way, the window doesn't give the warehouse staff any way to close it except to click the Ship or Cancel buttons. (If you don't use this approach, you need to write extra code that resets the order's status if someone clicks the X icon in the top-right corner to close the ReviewOrderDetails form.)

> **TIP** This spot is also a good place to use DoCmd.OpenReport to print a report that creates a shipping insert with a list of all the products in the order.

But if they click Cancel (perhaps because they've discovered they don't have the right items in stock), similar code is used to return the order to New status:

```vb
Private Sub Cancel_Click()
    ' Close this form.
    DoCmd.Close

    ' Switch back to the ShipOrders form.
    DoCmd.OpenForm "ShipOrders"

    ' Update the order.
    Forms("ShipOrders").StatusID = 2
```

```
        DoCmd.RunCommand acCmdSaveRecord
    End Sub
```

This part completes the code you need to coordinate order processing. Like the forms you learned about in Part Four of this book, the forms in this example draw all their information from your database's tables. But unlike those examples, these use code to perform some of the work automatically. This difference changes your forms from mere data-entry tools into supercharged *workflow* tools.

TIP You could also create a special status value to denote orders that have been attempted but couldn't be completed (like On Hold or Waiting For Stock). That way, the warehouse employees would know not to keep trying the same orders. If you take this step, make sure you modify the code in the `ProcessOrder_Click` subroutine so people can process orders with this status.

Updating Stock Numbers

Thanks to the ever-so-smart ShipOrders form you saw in the previous section, business is running smoothly at Boutique Fudge. However, suppose one day the warehouse employees come to senior management with a complaint. Although orders are sailing through without a hiccup, the product inventory information isn't keeping up. No one remembers to adjust the UnitsInStock information, so it's becoming increasingly useless. This challenge is entirely unlike the other problems you've solved in this chapter, because it forces you to make a change in a completely different set of records—records that aren't being displayed in any form.

UP TO SPEED

Code vs. Data Macros

One possible solution to the stock number problem is to use a data macro. You saw an example of this technique in Chapter 16, with a data macro that could react to changes in the OrderDetails table, and update the UnitsInStock field accordingly (page 556).

Even though the data macro approach is easy and automated, it creates a tight relationship that isn't always appropriate. Perhaps you modify the OrderDetails table for a variety of reasons—to log old purchases that have already been shipped, to correct errors—and you don't want Access to change the stock numbers in response to all of these actions. Or perhaps you want to take other details into account, analyze your

data, deal with obvious inconsistencies (like negative stock numbers), or even get the user's feedback before you update the stock numbers. Whatever the reason, if you want more flexibility, you can take control of the entire update process with some industrial-strength VB code.

If you're still interested in comparing the data macro approach, check out the downloadable samples for this chapter (*www.missingmanuals.com/cds/access2013mm*). They include the form-and-code approach that's described in this section *and* a data macro that does the same job. It's up to you which strategy fits best.

You already know that you can use the domain functions (page 621) to retrieve information from other tables. Unfortunately, Access doesn't have a similar set of functions that lets you make changes. Instead, you need to turn to a completely new set of objects, called the *data access objects* (DAO for short).

DAO lets you perform any data task you want, independent of your forms. However, DAO is a bit complex. If you use the DAO methods in the wrong order or leave out a step, you'll run into an error. Often, it's easiest to start with an example that works (like the sample code included with this chapter), copy it, and then alter it as needed. Usually, you'll use DAO in conjunction with SQL statements that fetch your data and update your tables. (For a quick refresher on how to write basic SQL commands, see page 220.)

DAO involves two essential techniques. First, there's the CurrentDb.Execute method, which lets you run a direct SQL command by supplying it in a string:

```
CurrentDb.Execute MyUpdateCommand
```

This method is a quick and dirty way to make database changes, like sweeping update, delete, or insert operations.

The second essential technique is to retrieve records by using a specialized object called the Recordset. To use a Recordset, you must begin by using the CurrentDb.OpenRecordset method, and supplying a string with a SQL select command:

```
Dim Recordset
Set Recordset = CurrentDb.OpenRecordset(MySelectCommand)
```

The Recordset represents a group of records, but it lets you access only one at a time. To move from one record to the next, you use the Recordset.MoveNext method. To check if you've reached the end, you examine the Recordset.EOF property (EOF stands for "end of file"). When this property is True, you've passed the last record.

You most often use a Recordset in a loop. You can use Recordset.EOF as the loop condition, so that the loop ends as soon as Access reaches the end of the Recordset. Inside the loop, you can retrieve field values for the current record. At the end of each pass, you must call MoveNext to move on:

```
Do While Recordset.EOF = False

  ' Display the value of the ProductName field.
  MsgBox Recordset("ProductName")

  ' Move to the next record.
  Recordset.MoveNext

Loop
```

With these bare essentials in mind, you can make your way through the following code, which adjusts the product stock values based on a recently shipped order. (A line-by-line analysis follows the code.)

```
1 Sub UpdateStock()
```

```
            ' If an error occurs, jump down to the DataAccessError section.
2           On Error GoTo DataAccessError

            ' Create a SELECT command.
3           Dim Query
4           Query = "SELECT ProductID, Quantity FROM OrderDetails WHERE OrderID=" & ID

            ' Get a recordset using this command.
5           Dim Recordset
6           Set Recordset = CurrentDb.OpenRecordset(Query)

            ' Move through the recordset, looking at each record.
            ' Each record is a separate item in the order.
7           Do Until Recordset.EOF

                ' For each item, get the product ID and quantity details.
8               Dim ProductID, Quantity
9               ProductID = Recordset("ProductID")
10              Quantity = Recordset("Quantity")

                ' Using this information, create an UPDATE command that
                ' changes the stock levels.
11              Dim UpdateCommand
12              UpdateCommand = "UPDATE Products SET UnitsInStock = UnitsInStock-" & _
13                  Quantity & " WHERE ID=" & ProductID

                ' Run the command.
14              CurrentDb.Execute UpdateCommand

                ' Move to the next order item (if there is one).
15              Recordset.MoveNext
16          Loop

            ' Time to clean up.
17          Recordset.Close
18          CurrentDb.Close

19          Exit Sub

20      DataAccessError:

            ' You only get here if an error occurred.
            ' Show the error.
21          MsgBox Err.Description

22      End Sub
```

Here's what takes place:

- **Line 1** declares a new subroutine. Because this code is fairly complex, it makes sense to put it in a separate subroutine, which you can call when the Ship button is clicked and the order is shipped.

- **Line 2** tells Access to head down to the end of the subroutine if an error takes place. Errors are always possible with data access code, so it's good to be on guard.

- **Lines 3–4** create the SQL command you need to select the OrderDetails records for the current order. (See page 220 for more about the SQL select command.)

- **Lines 5–6** execute that command and get all the matching records in a Recordset.

- **Line 7** begins a loop that moves through the entire Recordset.

- **Lines 8–10** get the ProductID and Quantity fields for the current OrderDetails record (the first one in the Recordset).

- **Lines 11–13** use this information to build a SQL update command. The command subtracts the number of items ordered from the total number in stock. A sample completed command looks like this: UPDATE Products SET UnitsInStock = UnitsInStock-4 WHERE ID=14. This subtracts 4 units from product 14.

- **Line 14** performs the update.

- **Lines 15–16** move to the next record and repeat the update process (until no more order items remain in the Recordset).

- **Lines 17–18** perform cleanup.

- **Line 19** exits the procedure. If you made it here, congratulations—everything worked without a hitch!

- **Lines 20–22** are only processed if an error occurs somewhere. In this case, the error description is shown in a message box.

This code is a fair bit more ambitious than anything you've seen so far. However, it builds on all the skills you've honed over the last three chapters. Once again, the best way to get comfortable with this code is to download the sample database, see it in action, and try changing it. Happy experimenting!

DAO vs. ADO

In an effort to make life more confusing, Microsoft introduced a second data access technology named ADO many moons ago. Both DAO and ADO let you perform data tasks by using handy objects. The key difference between them is that Microsoft designed ADO to be an all-purpose data access technology that works with other database products, like SQL Server, while DAO is strictly an Access-only affair.

Some Access programmers think (incorrectly) ADO is the successor to DAO, and a better choice when writing code for an Access database. (In fact, Microsoft may even have said that at one point, but they've destroyed all the evidence.) Today, the official story is that DAO is the better way to go, because it's fine-tuned for Access. That means DAO is easier to use and offers better performance in most cases. The only people who use ADO are seasoned VB programmers who already know how it works and don't want to bother learning DAO, or people who need an exotic feature that ADO provides but DAO doesn't.

Going Large: Access Databases for Many Users

Sharing a Database on Your Network

N ow that you've created the perfect database, you'd probably like to *share* it with friends and colleagues. In the hands of a single person, Access is a top-notch tool for managing information. But when you share the love with a group of people, it becomes an even better way to work together.

Sharing databases is particularly important if your database plays a behind-the-scenes role in an organization. Imagine you create a database that tracks company projects and their due dates. (Often, a database like this starts out as a timesaving convenience in the hands of an Access fan with a little too much free time.) Before long, other departments want in so they can keep track of their own projects. And the possibilities don't stop there; if you share the database with a wide enough audience, you can link together all sorts of related tasks. Employees can log the hours they work on each project. Product testers can submit outstanding issues that affect a project. Team leaders can identify time-taxing projects, head honchos can calculate salary bonuses, and the CEO can get a bird's-eye view of all the work that's taking place in the company. Before long, it becomes difficult to imagine life without your Access database.

In this chapter, you'll learn how to share your database with a small team. You'll consider the potential pitfalls, and you'll learn what you need to do to keep everything running smoothly.

■ Opening Up Your Database to the World

When you decide to share your data, the first decision you need to make is whether other people need to *change* any of the information. As you'll see, passing copies of your database around is easy. But getting people to work on the same database file at the same time is a trickier proposition.

If all you need to do is distribute a copy of your database for other people to review, you might try one of these two super-simple approaches:

- **Copy your database**. You can give others *a copy* of your database file. For example, if Uncle Earl has a copy of Access, you can email him your list of family addresses. The limitation with this approach is that there's no easy way to sync up the changes in different copies. If Uncle Earl adds a few new people to your database, your original remains the same. If you change the original, Uncle Earl's copy is out of date.

- **Export your data**. You can take the data in your database and *export* it to another format (like an HTML web page or an Excel spreadsheet). This is the way to go if the people who need to see your data don't have Access. You'll learn how to export data in Chapter 23.

On the other hand, if you want a crowd of people to be able to enter data and see each other's changes, all in real time, you need to step up your game. There are several potential solutions, and each one has its own drawbacks:

- **Use the multiuser features in Access**. You can place your database in a shared location (like a network drive) so several people can use it *simultaneously*. This way, everyone's working with the same set of data (and Uncle Earl's changes don't get lost). With this method, Access has to keep everyone's work coordinated. If your group is small—say, with no more than 40 people using your database at once—multiuser sharing should work. But if your group is large, Access isn't the best choice. Instead, you need a server product that's built from the ground up for high volume, multiuser access. (The next section gives you a handy checklist to help you decide if this approach is for you.)

- **Create a web app.** Here's the good news: with web apps, you can let other people view and edit your database over the Web, from any location, using any web browser. And here's the bad news: web apps are limited to a subset of Access's full feature set, and you'll need a SharePoint server or one of Microsoft's Office 365 hosting plans to get your work online. Web apps are Microsoft's preferred choice for solving the challenges of a multiuser database, but they aren't for everyone. You'll learn more about them in the next chapter.

- **Store your data somewhere else, and *link* to it.** Here, the idea is to use an industrial-strength server product like SQL Server or SharePoint to store all your data. You then use Access as a tool for retrieving and editing your data. The advantages of this approach are significant: first, you can keep using all your favorite Access tools, including forms, reports, and VBA code; and second, your database can stand up to a virtually unlimited number of users without a hiccup. The drawback is complexity—setting up either SQL Server or SharePoint is an ambitious task, even for technically savvy people. You'll try them out in Chapter 21 (SQL Server) and Chapter 22 (SharePoint).

This chapter focuses exclusively on the first item in the list—the multiuser support that's hardwired into Access. But before you get started, it's important to understand the limits you'll face so you can assess whether Access sharing can meet your needs.

How Access Sharing Works

The database-sharing features in Access are easy to understand. First, you place your database file in a location where everyone can get to it—like a folder you're sharing on your computer, or (better yet) a spot on a server computer on your company network. Now, anyone who wants to use the database simply needs to open the database file.

Sounds easy, right? Not so fast. Before you rearrange your entire company around a single database file, you need to crunch a few numbers. Here are some indications that suggest Access sharing will work for you:

- **No more than 40 people use the database at once**. The key part is how many people are using the database at once. You're free to share the same database with hundreds of users, so long as they don't all open it at the same time.

NOTE This number (40) is a sensible recommendation, not a set-in-stone rule. Some Access gurus have designed databases that can withstand 90 to 100 simultaneous users. However, without some serious (and complex) optimizations, you're likely to hit a brick wall much sooner.

- **No more than 15 people change the database at the same time**. Reading the database is easy, but updating it presents some serious challenges. One obvious problem occurs if more than one person tries to change the same record at the same time, but in different ways. And because of the way Access is designed, even changes that shouldn't clash with one another can slow down your overall performance. You'll tackle this issue later in this chapter when you consider locks (page 663).

NOTE This number (15) is just a conservative guideline. If different people are making changes in completely different tables, you may be able to squeeze in more updates at once. Conversely, if everyone wants to change the same few records, you may run into trouble even earlier. If in doubt, try it out.

- **The structure of the database changes infrequently**. In other words, you don't expect to regularly redesign your tables, add new fields, or tweak relationships. Ideally, you'll perfect all your tables before you share the database. And for best results, only one person should have the role of Chief Table Designer and be responsible for changing the database structure when needed.

- **Different people tend to work with different tables**. If everyone who uses the database is performing the same task (and accessing the same table), you've got a problem. But if one person maintains the product catalog, five more enter orders, and another six log shipments, you're in a much better situation. Even though everyone's using the same database at once, their work doesn't overlap.

- **Your database isn't mission-critical**. Data is always important. But if you're running an e-commerce company with a website that's live 24 hours a day, you can't afford even a momentary glitch. Unfortunately, Access can't guarantee that kind of stability. Although it's rare, a sudden network problem or a computer failure that happens while someone's in the middle of making a change could conceivably damage your database.

> **TIP** All Access fans should perform regular database backups throughout the day. You can use a scheduling tool (like Windows Task Scheduler) to automate this process.

It's no exaggeration to say that shared Access databases are the backbone of many small companies. But if you've reviewed the limitations of Access sharing and decided that Access can't fill your needs, it's time to step up to web apps (Chapter 20) or SQL Server (Chapter 21).

On the other hand, if Access does fit your needs, congratulations—you're moments away from transforming your lonely, single-person database into a resource your entire company can use. Just read on.

■ Preparing Your Database

If you've made it this far, you've decided that the multiuser features in Access are everything you need. However, before your database goes public, you may want to make a few changes. The most important of these is *splitting the database*—a critical but often overlooked step that gives your shared database extra reliability.

> **TIP** When you're sharing your data, it's essential to use a split database. Sharing an ordinary database can lead to all sorts of odd quirks that will make your database go wonky.

Understanding Split Databases

A split database is a database that has its objects divided into two separate files:

- **The back-end database** contains the raw data—in other words, the tables and nothing but.

- **The front-end database** contains everything you use to work with the tables. This includes all the other types of database objects, like queries, reports, forms, and macros.

Once you've split your database, you place the back-end database in a shared location (like a network drive). However, the front-end database works a little differently. You copy it to every computer that's going to use the back-end database. *Figure 19-1* shows how it works.

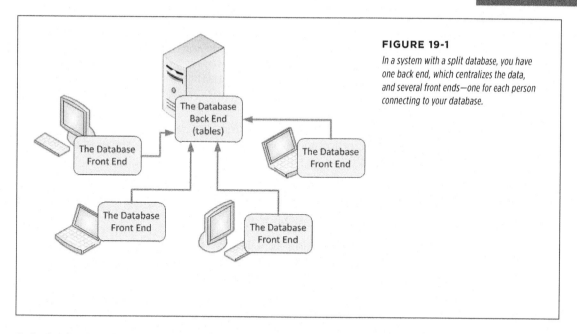

FIGURE 19-1

In a system with a split database, you have one back end, which centralizes the data, and several front ends—one for each person connecting to your database.

Split databases offer several advantages:

- **Performance**. When you use a split database, each client has a copy of the objects they need to use—like forms—ready and waiting on their computer. That means you don't need to retrieve the same information from the shared database, which would take more time (and generate more traffic on your network). Instead, the only thing you need to get from the shared database is the data you want to work with.

- **Easier updating**. It's relatively safe for people to change the data in a shared database, but Access isn't as good at sorting out the confusion if multiple people try to change the *design* of your database objects. A split database avoids this problem, because the objects that need to be tweaked most often, like queries, reports, and forms, are located in the front end. If you want to modify these objects (or add new ones), you can safely change the front end on one computer, and then distribute it to everyone who needs it. This approach isn't just easier—it's also more reliable, because there's no chance of an unsettling phenomenon called *data corruption* occurring (page 666).

- **Different people, different front ends**. When you use a shared database, you can create different front ends for different types of people—for example, the marketing department needs reports that show sales information, and the warehouse people need a form that shows outstanding orders. You can even use this approach to make sure people don't see forms, reports, and tables that don't apply to them, which reduces the risk of minor errors (like when the CEO accidentally wipes out the entire product catalog). But don't go too wild—the more front ends you create, the more you'll need to maintain.

> **NOTE** Technically speaking, you won't make your database more secure by giving people less capable front ends. After all, savvy Access users could just create their own front ends and use them to get unlimited access to the back-end database. However, even though the front end can't stop a malicious attacker, it can minimize the danger of a careless or overly curious user.

You have two ways to split a database. You can use a wizard, or you can do it by hand using the importing and exporting features in Access. The next sections describe both methods.

WORD TO THE WISE

Finding a Home for Your Database on the Network

Before you split your database, you should know where you want to place the back-end database file. One (somewhat risky) option is to share it directly from your own computer. The problem with this approach is that your computer isn't an ideal network server. If you turn off your computer to go on vacation, everyone is abruptly locked out of your database. Similarly, if you're busy running *Revenge of the Demon Spawn Legion Part IV* while other people are trying to use your database, their database performance (and your gaming experience) suffers. An even more serious problem occurs if you reboot your computer, at which point everyone who is currently using the database is rudely disconnected. This is guaranteed to lose somebody's work, and it may even cause data corruption (page 666).

For all these reasons, it's strongly recommended that you place your database on a server computer. A *server computer* isn't necessarily any different from your computer—in fact, it may just be an ordinary Windows computer that's plugged into the network. The difference is that no one uses this computer directly. Instead, it's left alone so it can concentrate on the important job of doling out data to everyone who needs it.

Splitting a Database with the Wizard

The easiest way to split a database is to use the handy wizard that Access includes for just this purpose. The wizard creates a new back-end database and moves all the tables out of the current database and into the back end. The current file is left with all the other database objects, so it becomes the front end.

Here's how to use the wizard:

1. **Open any database that has both tables and some other objects (like queries, reports, or forms).**

   You can try these steps with the Boutique Fudge and Cacophoné Studios databases you used in previous chapters.

2. **Before you begin, it's a good idea to make a database backup.**

   Hey, you never know when something could go wrong. To make your backup, choose File→Save & Publish and double-click Back Up Database.

3. **Choose Database Tools→Move Data→Access Database.**

The first window of the Database Splitter wizard appears (see *Figure 19-2*).

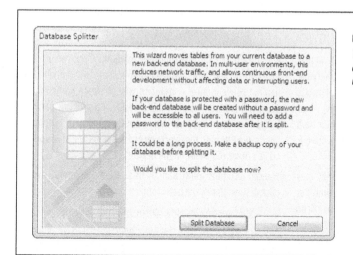

FIGURE 19-2

The first step of the wizard is fairly unremarkable. It describes how the wizard works and reminds you to make a backup before you go any further.

4. **Click Split Database.**

A window appears that prompts you to pick a location and file name for the back-end database.

Remember, you need to choose a location that everyone in your company or organization can access. (See the box on page 646 for some tips.)

NOTE Alternatively, you can save the back end on your computer for the time being, and then move it to the shared location later on (at which point you'll need to update the table links, as described on page 649).

Pointing to a Network Location

You have two ways to point to a place on a network. The first option is to use a *mapped network drive*, which takes a network location and gives it a drive letter on your computer. Mapped network drives look just the same as ordinary drives—for example, you can have a drive C: that represents your hard drive, a drive D: that represents your CD-ROM, and a drive F: that represents a place on the network.

The problem with mapped network drives is that they may be configured differently depending on the computer. For example, the drive you think of as F: may appear as drive H: on someone else's computer. As a result, the front-end database that works on one computer won't be able to find the back-end database it needs on another. Fortunately, this problem is easy to fix. You just need to point the front end to the appropriate back-end location, as described on page 649.

If you want to avoid this confusion altogether, you can use a *UNC path* instead of a mapped network drive. UNC (universal naming convention) is a standard way to create paths that point to locations on the network. The advantage of UNC paths is that they don't vary from one computer to the next. In other words, the UNC path that works on one computer will also work on any other computer on the network.

You can recognize a UNC path by its starting characters—two backslashes. Here's the basic form:

\\NetworkedComputerName\SharedFolderName

An example of a UNC path is *\\SalesComputer\Database*. When you browse to a computer through My Network Places, Access creates a UNC path that points to the location you choose.

5. **Choose a file name for the back-end database, and then click Split (*Figure 19-3*).**

    Access begins *exporting* the tables—in other words, copying them from the current database to the new back-end database file. This could take some time.

    When Access is finished, it shows the message "Database successfully split." It has successfully created the back-end database. The database that you started with (the one that's currently open) is now the front-end database. It no longer contains the tables with all the data; instead, it has a set of table links that let you pull the data out of the back-end database. (You'll learn how these table links work in the following section.)

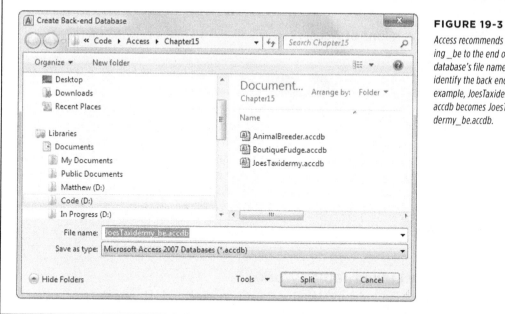

FIGURE 19-3

Access recommends adding _be to the end of your database's file name to identify the back end. For example, JoesTaxidermy. accdb becomes JoesTaxidermy_be.accdb.

6. **Now it's time to distribute the front end to everyone who needs to use the database.**

It's up to you how you want to share your front end. You could email it, burn it on a CD and hand it out, or just pop it in a shared location. However, it's important that everyone understand they need to copy the front end to their computer before they use it.

> **NOTE** If you distribute the front end by placing it on the network, you run the risk that people will launch the front end straight from the network, without copying it to their computers first. Left unchecked, this introduces all the problems of ordinary (non-split) databases, like hampered performance and greater risk for errors.

What About Old Versions of Access?

What happens if some of my coworkers have older versions of Access?

In an ideal world, everyone has a copy of the latest and greatest version of Access—Access 2013. In the real world, you're likely to find low-tech renegades who still love Windows XP.

If people with Access 2010 need to use your database, you won't have a problem, because Access 2010 shares the same database format as Access 2013 (.accdb). The same is true for Access 2007, but with a caveat—there are a small number of Access features that were introduced in Access 2010 and don't work in Access 2007. The most notable omission is the data

macro feature (page 544). If you use an unsupported feature in your database, Access 2007 folks will be able to read but not edit your tables.

If you need to support Access 2003 lovers, you need to store the back end in the Access 2003 format. (See page 42 for information about how to save a copy of your database in a different format.) As for the front end, you'll probably want to keep two versions—one for the Access 2007-or-later club and another for Access 2003 folks. You'll lose out on some features in the Access 2003 format, but you don't need to lock the technologically challenged out of your database.

How Linked Tables Work

The concept of a split database seems straightforward enough. One file (the back end) stores the raw data, while another (the front end) gives you the tools for working with it. But there's one detail that you haven't considered yet—namely, how does the front end get access to the tables in the back end? The secret is *table linking*.

Linking lets one database see a table in another database file. You can use linking in any database—in fact, you can choose to use it even if you won't be sharing your database. For example, you can divide your tables into two or more database files to get around the size limit, which is 2 GB (gigabytes), per database file. Or, you can use it to help you organize a sprawling database with dozens of tables. Finally, you may also find it helps you separate public information from supersecret details. If you put the tables with the secret information in a separate database, you're free to share copies of your main database without worrying about sensitive data getting into the wrong hands.

Thanks to linking, all the back-end tables still appear in the front-end database (see *Figure 19-4*). However, the actual data is in a separate file. When you open or otherwise interact with a linked table, Access heads to the linked file to get the information you need.

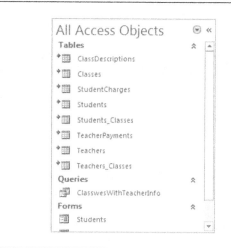

FIGURE 19-4

These tables have an arrow icon next to them, which indicates they're linked tables. They aren't actually stored in the current database file, but Access knows where to find the information when it needs it.

The only disadvantage to linked tables is that Access might go looking for a linked table in another database file but not be able to find it. This happens if the back-end database file is moved to another folder or if it's renamed.

> **NOTE** If your database has a bad link, when you attempt to open the table (or another object that uses the table, like a query or a report), you get a message informing you that Access can't find the file you need.

Fortunately, it's easy to update your links. Here's how:

1. **Choose External Data→Import & Link→Linked Table Manager (or right-click any linked table, and then choose Linked Table Manager).**

   The Linked Table Manager window appears, with a list of all the linked tables in your database (*Figure 19-5*).

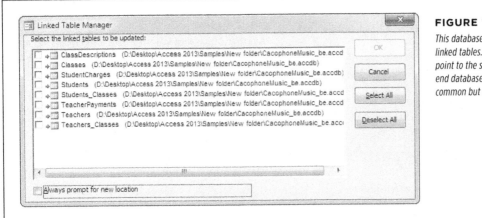

FIGURE 19-5

This database has eight linked tables. All the links point to the same back-end database, which is common but isn't required.

2. **Place a checkmark next to each link you need to change.**

If you need to update all your links, click Select All.

In most cases, all your links will point to the same database file. But if you need to point your tables to different files, select "Always prompt for new location."

3. **Click OK.**

Access pops open the familiar file selection window. Browse to the database file that has your linked tables, select it, and then click OK.

If you choose "Always prompt for new location," Access shows a separate file selection window for each link. Look at the window title to find out what table you're updating. If you didn't choose "Always prompt for new location," you can update all your links in one step.

The Mysterious "File Already in Use" Error

Now that you've created a shared database, you expect it to support a whole crowd of people. That's why it comes as quite a shock when you get the cryptic "file already in use" error. After all, aren't shared databases supposed to remain available even when someone else is using them?

This error occurs because someone has already opened the database in Exclusive mode. *Exclusive mode* (discussed on page 665) lets a single person tie up the database and lock out everyone else. The problem is that under certain circumstances, Access can use Exclusive mode even when you don't tell it to.

The most common problem occurs when someone doesn't have the correct permissions for the shared folder where the shared database is stored. (*Permissions* are a Windows security concept that determines how users are allowed to use files and folders.) Specifically, a problem occurs if you're the first person to open the database, and you don't have permission to *create new files*. In this situation, Access can't create the .laccdb file that tracks locks (see page 42). Without the .laccdb file, Access has no way to coordinate multiple users. Instead, it quietly switches to Exclusive mode, which freezes out everyone else.

The obvious solution is to identify everyone who needs to use the database, and then make sure they're allowed to create new files in the shared folder. Of course, this problem wouldn't be nearly as confusing if Access could warn you when it's not able to open a database normally and needs to use Exclusive mode.

Manually Splitting a Database

You don't need to use the wizard to split your database. You can move tables into a separate database file on your own, and then create links by hand. The main reason that you'd use this approach is because you want to split your database into more pieces—for example, you want one front-end and four back-end files.

There are some good reasons for subdividing your back end. They include:

- **Better reliability**. Essentially, if one file is damaged, the others will still live on unaffected.

- **Better security**. Using the tools of the Windows operating system, you can control who can open a specific file. You can use this to your advantage with split databases to lock people out of parts of the back end where they don't belong.

- **Leaving room to grow**. As mentioned earlier, Access limits databases to 2 GB. If you plan to store large numbers of records with attachments (like pictures), it's a good idea to make sure plenty of space is available now and for the foreseeable future.

To split a database by hand, you need to use the importing and exporting features in Access. The following steps show you how to split the Boutique Fudge database into three separate pieces so you can keep the credit card information separate from the rest of the data. (If you want to follow along, you can find the database with the sample content on the Missing CD page at *www.missingmanuals.com/cds/access2013mm*.)

1. **Create the back-end databases that you need.**

In this example, you need two back ends: one for the credit card details (call this BoutiqueFudgeSecrets_be.accdb) and one for all the other details (named BoutiqueFudge_be.accdb). Before you go any further, create both of these databases in Access and place them in the shared location, but leave them empty for now.

2. **Open the back-end database file.**

The next task is to add the correct tables to each back-end database. You do this by using Access's Import wizard.

Start with BoutiqueFudgeSecrets_be.accdb. It's easy because it requires just a single table.

3. **Choose External Data→Import & Link→Access.**

The Import wizard begins (see *Figure 19-6*).

NOTE In this example, you're importing the tables you need into the back end. You could also try the same trick in reverse, by exporting the tables out of the front end. However, export operations are more limited than import operations, because they let you transfer only a single table at a time.

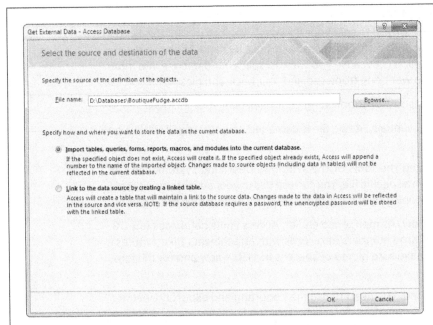

FIGURE 19-6

In the first step of the Import wizard, you choose the file that has the tables you want to import, and then you decide whether to copy the tables or just create links.

4. **Specify the location of your front-end database in the "File name" box.**

In this example, that's BoutiqueFudge.accdb, which currently contains the whole shebang (tables, queries, forms, and reports).

5. **Choose the first option, "Import tables... into the current database."**

The second option lets you create linked tables. You'll use it later in this process.

6. **Click OK.**

The Import Objects window appears, with a list of everything in your database (see *Figure 19-7*).

7. **Select the tables you want to import, and then click OK.**

The BoutiqueFudgeSecrets_be database needs just a single table: CreditCards.

Once you click OK, Access copies the tables into your database. You can now close the database file.

FIGURE 19-7

The Tables tab lists all the tables in your database. Select the ones you want to import by clicking each one once, so it becomes highlighted.

8. **Repeat steps 2 to 7 for any other back-end database files.**

In this example, you need to open BoutiqueFudge_be.accdb, and import all the tables *except* CreditCards.

Once you've finished transferring the data to your back ends, its time to update the front end.

9. **Open the front-end database.**

In this example, that's BoutiqueFudge.accdb.

10. **Delete all the tables.**

Don't be shy—after all, you've already copied them to their new homes in the back-end files. Once you're finished, it's time to take the last step and create the links you need in your front end. (Remember, if you're deleting tables that use relationships, then you need to delete the child tables first.)

11. **Choose External Data→Import & Link→Access.**

    The Import wizard starts again.

12. **Point the Import wizard to your first back-end file, choose "Link to the data source," and then click OK.**

    Start with the BoutiqueFudgeSecrets_be.accdb file.

13. **Choose all the tables and then click OK.**

    Access creates the corresponding linked tables in your database. Each table appears with the telltale arrow icon next to it in the navigation pane to let you know it uses a link.

14. **Repeat steps 11 to 13 for every back-end database.**

    If you started with BoutiqueFudgeSecrets_be, it's time to move on to BoutiqueFudge_be, which contains all the other tables you need.

If you follow all these steps, you wind up with three database files that work together: BoutiqueFudgeSecrets_be.accdb with the credit card information, BoutiqueFudge_be.accdb with the rest of the tables, and BoutiqueFudge.accdb with the queries, forms, and reports. If you want to see the finished product, check out the downloadable samples for this chapter. And jump ahead to page 668 to learn how you can apply different security settings to the different back ends.

Locking Down Your Front End

Before you let your database out into the wild, you need to think about what can go wrong. In the hands of less savvy Access users, your lovingly crafted forms and reports can get scrambled. It's a common complaint with multiuser Access databases: Sooner or later, a curious or careless person changes something that's better left alone, and that person's front end stops working.

Although you can't look over everyone's shoulder, you can prevent mischief by locking down your front end. That way, other folks won't be allowed to modify the design of forms and reports. (Of course, they can still use the front end to review and edit data.)

The secret to locking down your front end is to change the front-end database from an .accdb file to an .accde file. Although there's only one letter of difference, the .accde format restricts people in several ways:

- They can't modify forms or reports. In fact, they can't even open these objects in Design view.

- They can't create new forms and reports.

- They can't rename existing forms and reports (although they can delete them).
- They can't edit or even look at your VBA code and macros. In fact, all code is *compiled*, which means it's converted from the code statements you learned about in Chapter 17 and Chapter 18 to a shorthand that only the computer can understand.

NOTE Access gives you the same feature for the older .mdb database format. To lock down changes in an .mdb, you create an .mde file.

Making an .accde file is as easy as can be. Just follow these steps:

1. **Open your front-end database.**

   Your database must be running in full trust mode. (Usually, that means you clicked Enable Content the first time you opened the database on your computer. Page 512 has the full details about trusted databases.)

2. **Choose File→Save & Publish and double-click Make ACCDE.**

   The Save As window appears.

3. **Supply the file name for your .accde file.**

   Access won't change your original database—instead, it makes a copy in the new format.

When you create an .accde file, make sure you keep the original .accdb. That's because sooner or later you'll need to make changes. Access doesn't give you any way to change an .accde file back to its original format, so your only choice is to go back to the original format, make your changes, and then export a new .accde file.

TIP If you lose your original .accdb file, there's no way to change your forms and reports. You're stuck with a database that's frozen in time. However, as a last resort, you can try the Web, where other companies provide utilities that can (usually) transform an .accde file back to an .accdb file.

FREQUENTLY ASKED QUESTION

When Not to Use an ACCDE

Is the .accde format for front ends only?

You can turn any database into an .accde file. However, you should think twice before using this approach on anything other than a front end. That's because it's difficult to update an .accde file that has data.

To understand the problem, imagine you create an .accde file for an all-in-one database that sells discount hair care products. This database includes all the raw data—customer lists, available services, and invoices—and it contains the forms and reports that make your life easier. There's no division between the back end and front end.

A few weeks later, you decide to add a new report that shows customers subgrouped by the color of their highlights.

Of course, you can't edit the .accde file directly, so you polish off the report in the original .accdb file and create a new .accde. But wait—there's a problem. Your original .accdb file still has the old data. You're now stuck with two incomplete files: an .accde with the new data but the old forms and reports, and a new .accde with the right forms and reports but the wrong data. To remedy this situation, you need to perform a time-consuming import operation, as described earlier.

To avoid these data synchronization headaches, use the .accde format the way it's intended to be used—to lock down front ends that don't have any tables.

Sharing a Database with People Who Don't Own Access

Wouldn't it be nice if people could work with your data and use your forms and reports without needing the full Access software on their computers? It may seem like just a dream, but there are actually two possible solutions.

One option is to use the web app feature, described in Chapter 20, which makes your database available to anybody on almost any type of computer. The drawbacks are the hosting requirements (page 677), and the fact that web apps don't let you use all of Access's features

The other option is to ask the people who want to use your database to install a scaled-down version of Access that's called the Access *runtime engine*. The good news is that the Access runtime engine is free; the bad news is that they still need to go through the effort of downloading and installing it. Using Access runtime, other people can load up your database and use its forms and reports to review and edit data.

The Access runtime engine lets you use macros, Visual Basic code, and anything you can stuff in a form or report. However, Access runtime doesn't include the ribbon or the navigation pane. In fact, it doesn't provide *any* way for people to change the configuration or design of the database. (That's a job for you, the database designer.) The only thing they can do with the Access runtime is use the forms and reports that you've included in your front end. In fact, when using a well-designed front end with the Access runtime, people may not even realize that they're running Access.

The Access runtime engine is a truly useful way to share your databases without buying a zillion Access licenses and confusing people with all the features of the full Access user interface. If you're using Access to coordinate life in a small business, check it out.

So how can you get your hands on the Access runtime engine? At the time of this writing, it was only available in beta version. But the quickest way to track it down is to head to the Microsoft Download Center at *www.microsoft.com/downloads* and type *access runtime* in the search box.

> **NOTE** Microsoft typically releases the Access runtime about six months after it releases Access. At the time of this writing, the Access 2013 runtime wasn't yet available, although the Access 2010 runtime was. Because both Access 2013 and Access 2010 use the same database format, and because Access 2013 hasn't introduced any new features for desktop databases, you can use the Access 2010 runtime for an Access 2013 database in a pinch.

In the meantime, you can see what a database looks like when it's in the hands of the runtime engine. Here's how:

1. **Open your database and make sure it has a startup form (page 472).**

   The Access runtime engine doesn't have a navigation pane, so you need to have a startup form in order for the user to be able to do anything. That startup form will probably be a navigation form (page 479) with buttons that lead to other forms.

   To set the startup form, choose File→Options. Pick the Current Database section on the left. Finally, set the Display Form setting to the form you want to show automatically when the database is opened.

   The Current Database section has two other options you may want to use with .accdr files. Use Application Text to set the text that Access shows in the title bar, and use Application Icon to set the tiny icon graphic that Access shows in the top-left corner of the window.

2. **Rename your database's file extension from .accdb to .accdr.**

   Presumably, the r stands for runtime.

3. **Double-click your database to run it in Runtime mode.**

   You'll see your startup form, but no ribbon or navigation pane (*Figure 19-8*).

   Don't worry. You can rename your Access file to .accdb to get it back to normal.

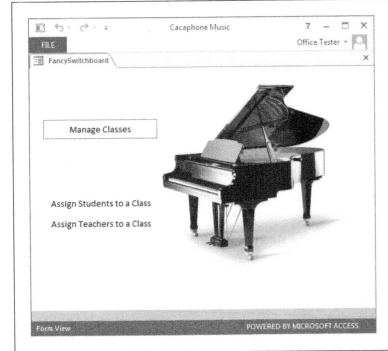

FIGURE 19-8

This .accdr file uses the fancy switchboard you saw on page 471. Note the lack of a ribbon. Similarly, the File menu is stripped down to just three commands: Print, Privacy Options, and Exit.

TIP Access doesn't use the trusted database system with .accdr files. Every time you open one, you get a stern security message, and you must click Open to continue. Fortunately, if the security message is wasting your time or intimidating other people, you can remove it. The trick is to designate the *folder* that holds the .accdr file as a trusted location, using the steps described on page 517. That way, Access automatically trusts all the databases in that folder, no matter what specific file type they use.

Playing Well with Others

Multiuser access is a perpetual juggling act. If all people want to do is read information, life is easy. But some significant challenges appear the moment people want to make changes. For example, what happens when two people try to change the same record at the same time? Or when you try to change a record while someone else tries to delete it? Or, if you want to read the latest information while an update is in progress?

Clearly, Access needs a way to manage the chaos. In this section, you'll learn what Access does to keep everything under control, and how you can adjust its settings. You'll also learn how to stave off the dangers of data corruption.

Seeing Changes as They Happen

Picture the following scenario. You're on the phone with a big-spending customer of Boutique Fudge. Using your trusty Access database, you run through the products that are available, giving your customer the price of each one. But unbeknownst to you, the head chef is looking at the same table at the same time—and raising the prices on the most popular dishes. The question is this: When do you notice the price increase?

Access deals with situations like this by using *automatic refreshes*. Once every 60 seconds, Access checks the back-end database to find out what's changed. Access then updates the corresponding information on your screen, whether you're looking at a form, a query, or directly at a table. In the Boutique Fudge example, the new prices appear the next time Access performs a refresh—and no later than 60 seconds after the changes are made.

A few exceptions to the refresh rule:

- When you start editing a record (by clicking inside one of the fields), Access immediately refreshes just that record. This ensures that you always start with the most up-to-date copy of a record before you begin making changes.

- If you can't wait 60 seconds, and you're getting nervous that something has changed since the last refresh, you can trigger an immediate refresh using the Home→Records→Refresh All command. And, if you click the down arrow part of this button, you can choose to refresh only the current record where your cursor is positioned (choose Refresh instead of Refresh All).

- Reports don't use automatic refreshes. If you run a report, wait, and then decide you want to update your results, you have two choices. You can close the report and reopen it, or you can use the Refresh button.

If you don't like the 60-second rule, you can fine-tune how often Access performs its automatic refreshes. To do so, choose File→Options. In the Access Options window, choose the Client Settings category, scroll down to the Advanced section, and look for the "Refresh interval" box (*Figure 19-9*).

NOTE The refresh interval is an Access setting that affects all the shared databases you open on that computer. If you want everyone to use the same refresh interval, you need to tell them all to update their Access settings.

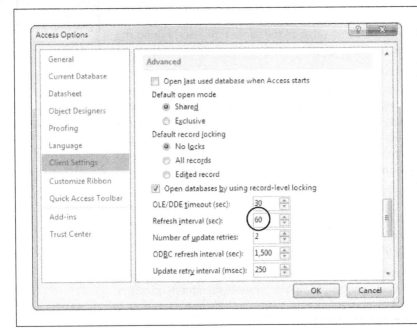

FIGURE 19-9

The refresh interval controls how often Access checks a shared database for changes. You can choose a value (in seconds) from 1 to 32,766.

The shorter the refresh interval, the faster you'll see other people's changes. However, shorter refresh intervals also create more network traffic. Most Access fans find they can safely lower the refresh interval without a problem, unless they're using a slow network. But keep in mind that the refresh interval affects all databases, not just the one that's currently open.

Dealing with Editing Conflicts

Shared databases are a bit of a free-for-all. Ordinarily, Access doesn't impose any limits on multiuser changes. If you're lucky, people will make their changes in an orderly fashion, one after the other. But sooner or later, changes will overlap, with potentially frustrating consequences.

Here's an example that shows what happens when two changes overlap:

1. You open a query that shows all the products in the Boutique Fudge database.

2. You find a record—a top-selling cheesecake known as The Chocolate Abyss—that needs changing. You click inside the Description field to start your edit.

3. At the same time, Bill Evans in the sales department fires up a form that also uses the Products table. He browses to the same record, and—realizing the potential for better profits—starts to change the price. Now two people are currently working with the same record. What happens next depends on who commits their change first.

4. Assume Bill gets the job done first. Quick as a flash he raises the price, and then heads on to another record.

5. Back on your computer, you've finished touching up the Description field. You move to another record. Ordinarily, this is the point where Access commits your edit, saving it to the back-end database. But in this case, Access notices a conflict—namely, the version of the record you're working with isn't the same as the version that's currently in the database.

6. Access warns you about the problem, and gives you three options (see *Figure 19-10*).

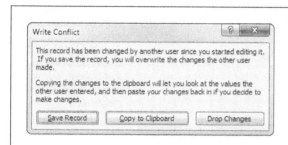

FIGURE 19-10

Between the time you started the edit and the time you tried to apply it, someone else made changes. Access lets you choose how you handle the conflict.

You have three ways to resolve a conflict:

- **Save Record** is the easiest and most reckless option. If you choose it, Access overwrites the record in the database with your version. The problem is that this option obliterates the changes that the other person made. In the previous example, the new description is saved in the database, but the price change is lost because Access reapplies your old, out-of-date price.

- **Drop Changes** cancels your edit. Access will refresh the record to show the most recent information, and then you can try making your change all over again. This option is reasonable if you can repeat the edit easily—it's not as good an option if you've finished a detailed revision of a large text field.

- **Copy to Clipboard** cancels your edit, just like Drop Changes. However, the values you changed are copied to the Clipboard, which makes it easier to reapply them, as shown in *Figure 19-11*.

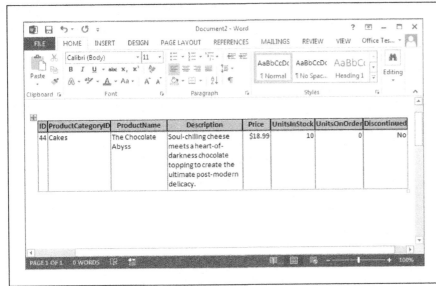

FIGURE 19-11

If you copied your last edit to the Clipboard, you need two steps to put it back into place. First, paste it into another program (like Word, shown here). Then, select just the data you want to use, and copy it back to the Clipboard by pressing Ctrl+C. Finally, switch back to Access, head over to the field you want to change, and then paste the new value by pressing Ctrl+V.

The best of the three choices is usually to copy changes to the Clipboard and try to repeat the edit. Unfortunately, you can't force people to do the right thing. Lazy workers may choose the quicker Save Record option, which quietly wipes out some-one else's work. Worst of all, the person who made the original change has no way of knowing it's been thrown away. If you have a high number of overlapping edits in your organization, you'll need to spend a good bit of time teaching everyone the right way to handle them.

> **NOTE** Access fans often wish they had a way to *merge* changes—that is, to update only the fields you changed. In the previous example, this option would let you apply a new description without disturbing the previous user's price change, because both updates affect different fields. However, Access doesn't provide this option. One reason is that there's no way to know if the two sets of changes will be *consistent*. And there's nothing worse than having a record that contradicts itself.

Splitting Tables for Safer Edits

One way to reduce the number of overlapping edits is to split tables into smaller pieces. The basic idea is to take a single table that has lots of fields, and divide it into two smaller tables, each containing only some of the fields. For example, you can take a Customers table and divide it into a CustomerAddress table and a CustomerFinancial table. Every record in CustomerAddress is linked to a single record in CustomerFinancial, using a one-to-one relationship (page 184). You'll need both records to get all the customer information.

The best time to split a table is when you know that a typical edit will involve the fields in just one table. Maybe you know that customer service often needs to update address information, while the billing department works with the financial information, so splitting the table is a great idea. The customer service department will use the Customer-Address table almost exclusively, and the billing department will use the CustomerFinancial table. The chance of overlapping edits is greatly reduced, because the work is split between two tables.

Using Locks to Stop Overlapping Edits

If overlapping changes are causing too many headaches, you have an option. You can use a software trick called a *lock* to prevent overlapping edits.

Essentially, a lock uses the same concept that protects two people from ending up in the same bathroom stall. When one person enters, she switches on the lock, and everyone else has to wait until the deed is done. Similarly, when a person attempts to change a record, Access starts by grabbing a lock on that record. Anyone else who wants to make a change is forced to wait until the first operation is finished.

The easiest way to use locks is to switch them on through the Access settings. To do so, choose File→Options. Then, choose the Client Settings category, scroll down to the Advanced section, and look for the "Default record locking" setting. You have three choices:

- **No locks** is the standard setting in Access. When you use this option, Access won't use locking at all, and overlapping edits are possible.

- **All records** tells Access to lock the entire table whenever someone begins editing a record. This setting is extremely rare. Because it locks every record, it prevents anyone else from working with the table when just one edit is taking place. This limitation can bring any organization to a grinding halt.

- **Edited record** locks individual records as they're being edited. This prevents overlapping edits.

The last option is the most common locking choice. When you use individual record locking, Access won't let you begin editing a record if someone else is currently modifying it. When you try, Access displays an icon that indicates the record is locked, as shown in *Figure 19-12*.

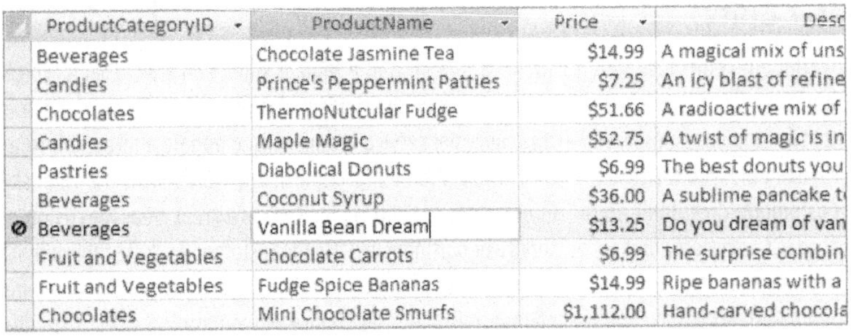

ProductCategoryID	ProductName	Price	Desc
Beverages	Chocolate Jasmine Tea	$14.99	A magical mix of uns
Candies	Prince's Peppermint Patties	$7.25	An icy blast of refine
Chocolates	ThermoNutcular Fudge	$51.66	A radioactive mix of
Candies	Maple Magic	$52.75	A twist of magic is in
Pastries	Diabolical Donuts	$6.99	The best donuts you
Beverages	Coconut Syrup	$36.00	A sublime pancake t
⊘ Beverages	Vanilla Bean Dream	$13.25	Do you dream of van
Fruit and Vegetables	Chocolate Carrots	$6.99	The surprise combin
Fruit and Vegetables	Fudge Spice Bananas	$14.99	Ripe bananas with a
Chocolates	Mini Chocolate Smurfs	$1,112.00	Hand-carved chocola

FIGURE 19-12

The don't-go-there symbol warns you to wait rather than edit a record that's already in use. If you still try to type in the field, Access stubbornly ignores you.

Locks prevent your database from becoming a mess of scrambled information, but they impose other headaches. It takes extra work for Access to keep track of everyone's lock—it has to play the role of an overworked washroom attendant who doles out the washroom keys. Access keeps track of locks by creating a .laccdb file. For example, the first time someone opens the shared database BoutiqueFudge_be.accdb, Access creates a file named BoutiqueFudge_be.laccdb. (The "l" stands for locking.) When the last person closes the database, Access removes the locking file.

> **TIP** If you look in the shared folder and don't see a .laccdb file, you know that no one is currently using the database, or someone's opened it in Exclusive mode (page 665).

Locks also slow other people down, forcing them to wait for the information they want. A careless user can tie up a record indefinitely, leaving it in Edit mode.

> **NOTE** If you head out for a lunch break, you could tie up the entire company without even knowing it. Even worse, although other would-be editors will see that the record is locked, they have no way of knowing who the culprit is. Their only recourse is to wait...and wait.

If you decide to use locking, it's a much better idea to apply it through individual forms, rather than switch it on for every database, by using the Access options. You could use the standard "No locks" setting for your entire database, but configure all the forms that use a particularly important table—say, Invoices—to use locking. To change the way a form works with locking, open the Property Sheet and look for the Record Locks property. It supports the same three settings: No Locks (the default), All Records, and Edited Record.

NOTE This trick leaves an open back door. If someone decides to make a change by directly opening the table, he'll bypass the locking that you've implemented in your forms. As always, it's easy to guide people to the right path but harder to force them to stay on it.

Opening a Database in Exclusive Mode

One of the limitations of shared databases is that you can't change the design of your tables while other people are using the database. Before you can make more radical alterations, you need to open the database in *Exclusive mode*.

Exclusive mode temporarily restricts a shared database to a single person. While you have the database open in Exclusive mode, no one else is able to access it, no matter what front-end database they use. You have a few precious moments to make the more radical changes that you wouldn't normally be able to do.

Here's how to open a database in Exclusive mode:

1. **Tell everyone else to close the database.**

   You can't open a database in Exclusive mode if it's currently in use. In a big company, this is the hardest part. System administrators sometimes resort to mass emailing to let everyone know that it's time to shut down. Another choice is to teach the people who use your database to close it every night before they leave, which lets you slip in a late-night update without disruption.

2. **Choose File→Open.**

   The Open window appears.

3. **Select the database file you want to open, and then click the drop-down arrow on the Open button.**

   A list of specialized options appears for opening your file, as shown in *Figure 19-13*.

4. **Choose Open Exclusive.**

   Access opens the database. You can now make changes with no restrictions. But work fast—the longer you keep the database open in Exclusive mode, the longer other people will need to wait to get on with their work.

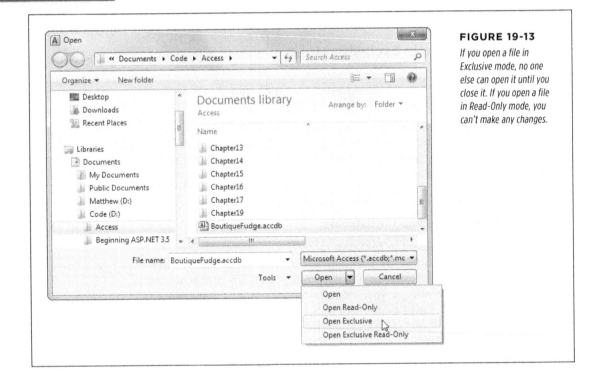

FIGURE 19-13

If you open a file in Exclusive mode, no one else can open it until you close it. If you open a file in Read-Only mode, you can't make any changes.

Data Corruption

Data corruption—the term strikes fear into the heart of the hardiest Access guru. Hopefully, the people who use your database will be well behaved, the network it sits on will remain reliable, and your database will never be in danger. But just in case life isn't that kind to you, it's important to be prepared.

Data corruption is a catch-all term that describes what happens when part of a database file is damaged. Imagine Jessica Baxter is in the middle of applying a large update when a power failure hits (or an office prankster pulls out her network cable). The back-end database will be left in an invalid state, because only part of Jessica's information will have been successfully received. As a result, the record she was working with may be scrambled beyond recognition. And if you're particularly unlucky, the problem can affect more than one record or even make the whole database act a little odd.

Diagnosing (and Fixing) Corrupt Databases

Every Access expert should have basic data corruption survival skills. First, you need to be able to spot when a database has gone bad. Here are some telltale signs:

- **Cryptic error messages that appear for no good reason, like "out of memory."** (Keep in mind that you shouldn't confuse this with the always-common category of cryptic error messages that appear for a legitimate reason, like the "file already in use" error described on page 651.)

- **Rows that contain gibberish, like ### or ???**. Often, you'll find these values in the last few rows of a corrupted database, which indicates that the rest of the data is probably kosher—it's just the new additions that ran into trouble.

- **A complete inability to use the database**. If you get the dreaded "unrecognizable database format" error, you know disaster has struck.

Once you identify that a database is corrupted, it's time to nurse it back to health. The first resort is always the *compact and repair* feature, which cleans up a host of problems and shrinks large, bloated databases back to more reasonable sizes. To try out this feature, open your database in Exclusive mode (page 665), and then choose File→Info and click Compact & Repair Database. The process could take some time, particularly with a large database.

The compact and repair feature fixes only tables, not forms or reports. However, if you've been sensible and have created a split database, the back end won't have any of these types of objects anyway.

TIP   Before you try to fix a corrupt database, make an immediate backup. That way you can try several repair strategies.

Sometimes, the compact and repair feature won't solve the problem, or it may just partly rehabilitate your database file. At this point, it's time to try other repair techniques. If the remaining problems are relatively minor (like a few rows with suspicious data), you may be able to simply delete the offending information and recreate it. But sometimes Access refuses to show corrupted records without bombarding you with error messages. If this is the case, select all the good records and copy them to another table. Then, delete the table with the corrupt data and rename your copy to take its place.

Finally, you can create a new blank database, and try to import the tables from the back end, using the importing technique described on page 797. This forces Access to recreate each object and rebuild every index. Even if this doesn't work completely, you may find that you can import most of the tables.

If all else fails, you'll need to revert back to the last backup. You do keep backups, right?

Preventing Corruption

As scary as data corruption is, following a few guidelines can ensure it remains a rare occurrence:

- **Stick to the sensible guidelines described on page 641.** If dozens of people try to make changes at once, you multiply the chances of a problem.

- **Always split your database (page 642)** to lighten the load on your back end and to keep forms and reports out of harm's way.

- **Use a reliable network.** If your network connection isn't dependable, an update can get interrupted, which is a prime cause of data corruption.

- **Protect your server with an uninterruptible power supply (UPS).** This relatively cheap device acts like a giant battery, supplying emergency power for several minutes or more in the case of an outage.

- **Teach people to close the database when they're finished using it**—or even when they're taking a lunch break.

- **Use the compact and repair feature** on your back-end database regularly (choose File→Info and click Compact & Repair Database). As more and more people make changes, database files grow larger and more disorganized. The compact and repair command rearranges your database to be more efficient, smaller, and less likely to run into trouble.

- **Make backups as often as possible.** Depending on how quickly you make changes, a daily backup may be sufficient. But you can make a backup every hour or even more often if needed.

> **TIP** Make sure you keep a collection of the most recent backups. If you keep only a single backup file, you run the risk that you may back up a database that's already corrupted, and you won't have an older copy to fall back on.

■ Securing Your Database

In most shared databases, different people perform different tasks. The easiest way to keep everyone on the right track is to create several distinct front ends, one for each group of people. This lets you gently guide people along in the tasks they perform.

However, customizing the front end doesn't restrict the abilities of a determined troublemaker. In a large company that relies on a multiuser database, you don't just think about guiding people—you also worry about restricting them.

Sadly, Access provides a limited security model. You have the ability to lock strangers out of a database with a password, but you don't have the more fine-grained features you need to restrict a single user from using certain tables or performing certain actions. As you'll see in the following sections, you can use some workarounds, but none works as well as the security provided by a server-side database product like SQL Server.

NOTE Once again, Access gives you just enough to make shared databases work, but not much more. It's up to you to decide whether Access works for your organization. Small outfits are likely to find that it's perfectly fine, while large organizations may want a server product.

Password-Protecting Your Database

The password protection feature in Access offers simple, no-frills security. You choose a single password for your database, and from that point on it can't be opened without the password. Even better, the data in your database file is scrambled using a key that's generated from your password. This ensures that even if high-tech hackers peer directly into your database file with a specialized tool, they won't be able to retrieve any data.

NOTE Access is serious about password protection. Access uses state-of-the-art encryption to ensure that skilled hackers can't crack open your files with specialized tools—at least not unless they're willing to devote a huge amount of time to the task.

It's ridiculously easy to apply a password. Here's how:

1. **Choose File→Open.**

   To apply a password, you need to open your database in Exclusive mode. This step is necessary because Access can't encrypt a database while it's in use.

2. **Select the file you want to open, click the drop-down arrow on the Open button, and then choose Open Exclusive.**

   Access opens the database in Exclusive mode.

3. **Choose File→Info and click Encrypt with Password.**

   Access asks you to supply a password (*Figure 19-14*).

FIGURE 19-14

Just to be sure, Access asks you to enter the password twice.

4. **Enter your password, verify it, and then click OK.**

   To ensure that your database is secure, you need to choose a strong password. Good passwords are long (10 letters or more), can't be found in the dictionary (because attackers use dictionaries to launch automated attacks), use mixed case, and include special characters (like numbers, punctuation, and other symbols). The password *hellodata* is a poor choice, while *wOnDER_wh@t_32* is much more reliable.

Access uses the password to encrypt your database and then saves the modified database automatically. Now, the next time you open your database you'll be asked to supply the password first.

If you decide later that you don't need password protection, choose File→Info and click Decrypt Database.

Passwords and Split Databases

It's fairly obvious how passwords work with ordinary databases, but a few interesting quirks are at work with split databases.

The first step is to decide which of the two database files you'll encrypt. Usually, you'll choose to encrypt both the front-end database *and* the back-end database. Here's why:

- If you encrypt only the front-end database, people can still muck up all the data by opening the back-end database directly. And even if you trust their intentions, it's amazing what people can do by accident.

- If you encrypt only the back-end database, people can still access the database through the front end. That's because when a front-end database links to a password-protected back end, Access quietly and automatically stores the back-end password in the front-end file.

> **NOTE**   Depending on your goal, you might choose to password-protect the back-end database only. This works well if you simply want to force people to use the front end, and prevent them from directly opening the back end. But if you're after stricter security, and you want to make sure that unauthorized people can't make *any* changes to your database, you need to password-protect both files.

There's no point in applying the password before you split the database—if you do, Access uses that password for the front end but not the back end, which isn't what you want. Instead, follow these steps:

1. **Split the database.**

   Follow the same process you used on page 644.

2. **Close the front-end and open the back-end database in Exclusive mode. Encrypt it with a password.**

   Use the same steps you applied on page 669.

3. **Now close the back-end database and open the front-end database in Exclusive mode.**

   Here's where things get a bit ugly. Adding a password to the back-end database has broken all your front-end links. If you try to open a linked table, you'll receive an "invalid password" error message. The only way to correct this problem is to remove your linked tables from the front end, and add them again. Sadly, the Database Splitter wizard doesn't have an elegant way to handle this problem.

4. **In your front-end database, delete all the linked tables.**

   Don't delete any other database objects—keep your queries, reports, forms, and macros.

5. **Choose External Data | Import & Link→Access.**

   The Import wizard starts up.

6. **Enter the file name of your back-end database.**

   You can type the file name, but it's easier to click Browse, find your back-end database file, select it, and then click Open.

7. **Click the "Link to the data source by creating a linked table" option, and then click OK.**

   Access prompts you to enter the back-end database password.

8. **Type the password and Click OK.**

   The Import Objects window appears.

9. **In the Tables tab, click Select All to grab all the tables, and then OK.**

   Access adds the linked tables to your database. It uses the same names, which ensures that your front-end database objects (queries, reports, and forms) will work properly.

   After all the linked tables have been created, the final step of the Import wizard appears.

10. **Click Close.**

    If you only want to protect the back-end database, you can stop here. People who don't know your password won't be able to open the back-end database, but they will be able to open and use the frontend database. That's why this technique is good for forcing ordinary people to stick with your front-end, preventing accidental disasters. However, this model doesn't provide industrial-strength security, since a crafty hacker could steal the password by digging through the front-end database file.

If you want to stop sneaky hackers, you can follow the next step to add a second password to your front-end database file. This part is easy.

11. **Close the back-end database and open the front-end database in Exclusive mode. Encrypt it with a password.**

    Again, use the steps you applied on page 669. Make sure you choose a different password than the one you used for your back-end database. This way, you can authorize people to use your front end without giving them unfettered access to your back end.

Using Windows File Security

Password protection isn't your only security choice. You can also use Windows security to specifically set which users and groups can access a file.

With an ordinary database (or a basic split database), this technique is a bit clumsy. The problem is that you have just two choices: Give someone complete control over your database file, or stop them from using it altogether. But you can apply more nuanced security settings. The trick is to split your back end into more than one file. Then, once the files are in the shared folder, you can configure exactly who is allowed to access each one. Presto—you can lock some people out of specific tables.

For best results, you'll need to have a network administrator help you set up the security settings you need. The basic process works like this:

1. **Using Windows Explorer, right-click the database file you want to protect, and then choose Properties.**

    The Properties window appears, with several tabs of information about the file.

2. **Choose the Security tab (*Figure 19-15*).**

    Windows keeps track of people in two ways—it identifies them uniquely by *user name*, and it categorizes entire groups of people by *group name*. For example, you can log in as MarkHamlon and be a member of several groups, including Users, Administrators, SalesDepartment, and so on. That gives an administrator the ability to change the security settings for a single individual or for a whole crowd of people with one rule.

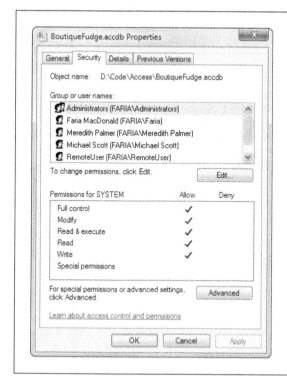

FIGURE 19-15

The Security tab lists all the people (and groups) who are allowed to use this file, and it indicates what they're allowed to do. In this example, every user and group name is preceded by the term FARIA\ because the name of the computer where the user accounts are defined is FARIA.

3. **To change permissions, click Edit.**

4. **To change what a person or group can do with the file, select them in the list, and then change the Allow or Deny options (*Figure 19-16*).**

   Say you don't want the people in the Users group to be able to use this file; select the Users group in the list, and then place a checkmark in the Deny column next to each permission.

   NOTE The Deny options always take precedence. For example, if a person is a member of two groups, and one group is allowed to use a file but the other isn't, the Deny setting overrides everything else.

5. **If you want to add a new group or person to the list, click the Add button, fill in the user or group name, and then click OK.**

You may decide you don't want to lock out an entire group but you want to single out a specific person.

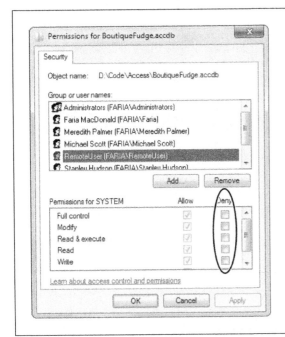

FIGURE 19-16

If the checkbox is grayed out, that's because the setting is inherited—in other words, it's based on the folder that contains this file. For example, you can't change the Allow settings of the Users group, because they're inherited. However, you can add Deny settings (as shown here with the user named RemoteUser). The Deny settings always overpower the Allow settings.

Windows file security gives you a very basic level of security. It isn't really designed to work with Access databases. To use it at all, you need to split your database into smaller and smaller pieces, which can be difficult to manage. You also can't control what actions a person is allowed to perform—the file security either locks people out entirely or gives them full control to add, delete, update, and redesign the information in your database.

If you need real user-level security, you're better off with a server product like SQL Server. However, if you just need the ability to keep some sensitive information out of reach, the Access file-based security features can help you out.

Building an Access Web App

A web app is a database that lives in the great Internet cloud. People who need to view or change the information in a web app database do so using an ordinary web browser, with no Access required. In fact, they can even use a tablet computer like the iPad.

Access web apps are hosted by Microsoft SharePoint, the server-based software that many companies use to collaborate, store documents, and host simple web applications. The web app's data is stored by SQL Server, the industrial-strength database software that NASDAQ uses to power thousands of transactions per second. But you don't need to be seasoned SQL Server administrator, because Access and SharePoint take care of all the details for you. All you need to provide is a server running the latest and greatest version of SharePoint (that's SharePoint 2013), or a SharePoint hosting plan (typically, through Microsoft's Office 365 hosting program).

In this chapter, you'll explore the features and limitations of web apps and their inherent compromises. You'll see why web apps just might be the boldest step forward for Access in years—and why they won't satisfy everyone.

NOTE Microsoft probably would have called the web app feature *web databases*, but it had already used the term for a now-abandoned feature that it introduced in Access 2010 (see the box on page 677 for the full scoop).

■ Assessing Web Apps

Web apps are the most hyped new feature in Access 2013. In fact, aside from the occasional bit of fine-tuning and error-fixing, web apps are the *only* new feature that Access 2013 offers.

On the face of it, the web app feature sounds great. Its advantages are obvious:

- **Portability.** You can get at your web app anywhere that has a web connection. Folks can even use your web app on a Mac or in an Internet café. Best of all, the web app feature doesn't require plug-ins, browser extensions, or an extra download.

- **Manageability.** When you update the data or design of your web app, everyone sees the changes immediately. There's no need to send everyone an Access front end (a file that has the queries, forms, and reports for your database).

- **Performance.** Because web apps use SQL Server, they're guaranteed to be blazingly fast, no matter how much data you store or how many people want to use it at once. Get a few hundred people working on an ordinary Access database, and you have no such guarantee.

- **Future-proofing.** Because your data is in a SQL Server database, hotshot programmers can create applications that access it in a variety of languages, from Java to C#. And if you need to chew through the ginormous mountains of data in your web app, you can use some of the sophisticated analysis and reporting tools that are built for SQL Server. You could even transition away from your Access front end to a custom-programmed solution, some day in the distant future.

Despite all these benefits, the web app feature is far from perfect. Nothing comes for free, and hardcore Access fans will discover that the web app feature has two potentially deal-breaking limitations:

- **Missing features.** Traditional Access databases, which are sometimes called *desktop databases*, have features aplenty. But in order to make web apps work in everyone's browser, on every web-connected computer, with no extra help, Microsoft had to sacrifice many of these capabilities. Reports, VB code, and form customization are just a few features that are absent in the web app world.

- **Web hosting.** For a web app to work, it must be hosted on a specially equipped computer. Ordinary web servers—the sort that you can use to host a website— can't host Access databases because they don't have a properly configured SharePoint 2013 server. Web apps will be out of your reach unless your company is using a SharePoint server (and has a qualified person to manage it), Microsoft's Office 365 subscription service (which isn't cheap), or a SharePoint hosting service from another company. You'll get the full details in the next section.

This combination of benefits and drawbacks adds up to a bit of a foggy future for web apps. Web app aficionados believe that web apps are the future of Access. Microsoft touts them on its Access blog (*http://blogs.office.com/b/microsoft-access*) and puts them front-and-center in the Access interface. As you may have already noticed, the "Custom web app" button appears *before* the "Blank desktop database" button in Access's backstage view.

Old-hand Access pros, however, are reluctant to abandon their favorite Access features. And they know web apps aren't an option for clients who don't have a SharePoint server or who don't want to use SharePoint in their business.

Perhaps the best way to see web apps is as a useful tool that lets you dramatically expand the reach of an Access database. If your database needs to support hundreds of people or needs to be available across the country, web apps are the easiest and most practical choice. In this situation, an ordinary Access desktop database won't cut it, and the alternatives that you'll consider in later chapters—storing your data in SharePoint or SQL Server and linking to it in Access—have plenty of headaches of their own.

NOSTALGIA CORNER

Web Databases, Take Three

Microsoft may promote web apps as a new and exciting feature, but it's actually the company's third attempt to push Access databases onto the Web. The previous two fizzled out, which highlights the risks of any new and exciting technology.

Microsoft's first attempt to webify Access was with a grafted-on feature called *Access data pages*. Included in Access 2000 and Access 2003, this feature let people review and edit the data in an Access database from the comfort of a browser window. The catch? Users needed to stick to Internet Explorer and they needed to have a special ActiveX control, which was bundled with Office. Even worse, Access data pages didn't address Access's scalability issues, which meant that a poorly designed (or very popular) database could crash under the weight of too many users. For all these reasons, Microsoft retired the feature in Access 2007.

Microsoft introduced a completely different approach in Access 2010, called *web databases*. Like web apps, web databases require SharePoint, which handles all the heavy lifting. Surprisingly, the web database feature has several advantages over the Access 2013 web app feature—in particular, it gives database designers more flexibility to customize their forms, and it supports reports (albeit without pictures). The key limitation: web databases are tied so closely to SharePoint that it's difficult to open them up to other applications and tools. By comparison, every web app uses a real SQL Server database, with the exact structure that you define for your data. As a result, your future is full of possibilities. Any tool or program that can interact with SQL Server can also connect to your web app and work with its data.

Access 2013 lets you open existing Access 2010 web databases and modify them, but it doesn't let you create new ones. If you want the portability, manageability, and performance of a web-based solution, the only option in Access 2013 is web apps.

Preparing for Web Apps

Before you can create a web app, you need to have a place to host it. Unfortunately, Access won't allow you to build even a trial web app unless you have a SharePoint server to help you out.

There are three ways to get the SharePoint hosting you need for a web app:

- **Use a SharePoint server in your company.** Access requires the full version of SharePoint 2013 (not the free, feature-reduced SharePoint Foundation 2013 or the older SharePoint 2010). Unfortunately, the licensing system for SharePoint is complex and expensive, and setting it up requires the work of a skilled network administrator. If your company isn't using SharePoint, you're probably out of luck.

- **Use an Office 365 subscription plan.** The cheapest Office 365 plans don't include SharePoint, but if your company uses the small business plan or one of the enterprise plans, you have everything you need to create web apps. However, everyone who needs to access your web app (either to review data or to edit it) will also need an Office 365 subscription. (If you have no idea what an Office 365 hosting plan, read the brief overview on page 14.)

- **Get SharePoint 2013 hosting from another company.** This option is far easier than setting up your own SharePoint server, and cheaper than paying for a pile of Office 365 subscriptions. However, you need to have full confidence in the hosting company you use, because it has the responsibility of storing *your* data. One company that specializes in SharePoint 2013 hosting for Access databases in Access Hosting (*http://accesshosting.com*).

No matter which approach you use, you'll need three pieces of information before you continue. First, you need the web address of your SharePoint site. This Internet location is where you'll host your web apps. Second, you need to know the user name and password to log into that site (which you get from your network admin or hosting company). Once you have these details, you're ready to read the next section.

Building a Simple Web App

There are two ways to create a web app. The most common way is to do it from inside Access. The other way is to do it in your browser when you visit the SharePoint site. Both approaches are equivalent, and usually you'll use the Access method, because you need to design the database in Access anyway—SharePoint doesn't have any tools that let you do that job online.

On the other hand, there are some situations where you may want to create your web app by using the SharePoint web interface. For example, the person creating the database may not be the same as the person who's designing it, and the database creator may not have a copy of Access handy. Also, in SharePoint you can easily create several web apps at once, without having to pause and edit each one. And, occasionally, some SharePoint web hosts *require* you to use the SharePoint approach for creating web apps; they may not allow you to create a web app through Access.

Creating a Web App in Access

Creating a web app in Access is much like creating a desktop database. You can create a web app from the welcome page, which appears when you first start Access, or by choosing File→New if you're currently working on another database. Either way, you'll see a list of templates that you can use to create new web apps and desktop databases. To create a web app, click the "Custom web app" template instead of "Blank desktop database."

When you click "Custom web app," Access asks you for two key details (*Figure 20-1*):

- **The app name.** Provide a descriptive name that will identity your database to other people (like "SalesTracker" or "Premium Toy Catalog").

- **The web address.** Fill in the URL that points to your SharePoint site (for example, *http://tigersharpinc.sharepoint.com*). This part differs slightly depending on exactly how Access is configured. For example, if you installed Access with Office 365, or if you've successfully created a web app in the past, you'll probably see the location you want in the Available Locations list. You can then click to select it. If Access doesn't show you the Available Locations list, or the list doesn't have the address of your SharePoint site, you'll need to type the address into the Web Location box underneath.

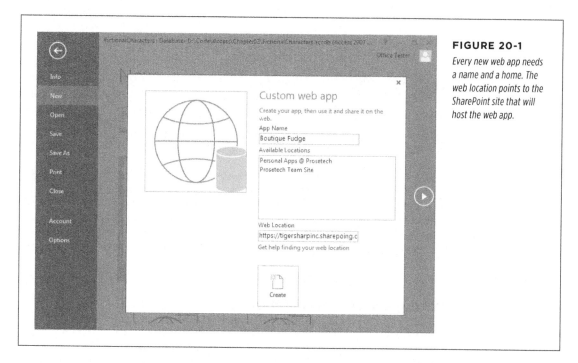

FIGURE 20-1
Every new web app needs a name and a home. The web location points to the SharePoint site that will host the web app.

Once you've filled in these two details, click Create. At this point, Access will ask for your login credentials (*Figure 20-2*).

FIGURE 20-2

Depending on how you're hosting your web app, Access may ask you what type of account you're using (left). Choose "Microsoft account" if you're using Office 365, or "Organizational account" if you're using a SharePoint server provided by your company or another SharePoint hosting company. Either way, the next step is to fill in your user name and password (right).

Once you've provided the right user name and password, Access creates the web app. It will take a few seconds to get the job done, because Access needs to communicate with the SharePoint server while it creates the web app.

Once Access is finished creating your web app, it opens it in the main Access window. Skip ahead to page 683 to learn how to add your first table.

> **NOTE** Web apps are always online, which means you never need to upload your work. Instead, every time you make a change or add a record, it's automatically reflected in the online copy of your database that everyone else sees. The disadvantage to this system is that you're always working without a safety net. The situation is quite different from when you're developing a desktop database, where you can test your changes (on a master copy of the database front end) before you go live with them (by distributing the new front end to everybody else).

Creating a Web App in SharePoint

It's just as easy to create a web app using the SharePoint web interface. Here's how:

1. **In a web browser, go to your SharePoint site and log in.**

   If you know very little about SharePoint, you may appreciate the quick SharePoint site tour on page 764. Read it to get your bearings, and then return back here.

2. **Click the Site Content link in the navigation menu (on the left).**

   A page appears with a list of items you can add to the site.

3. **Click the first icon, "add an app."**

   SharePoint shows a list of different apps you can add.

4. **In the "Find an app" search box, type access app.** Click the magnifying glass.

   Rather than hunt through the long list of potential apps, it's easier to search for what you need.

5. **When the Access App picture appears, click it.**

   Access pop up a box that asks for the name of your new app (*Figure 20-3*).

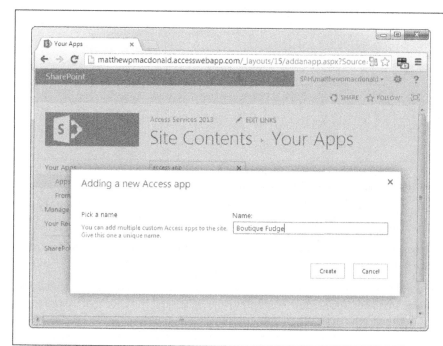

FIGURE 20-3

SharePoint doesn't provide any tools for designing Access web apps, but it has no problem creating a new blank web app with the name you choose.

6. **Fill in a name for your web app, and then click Create.**

   SharePoint takes you back to the Site Contents page. In the meantime, your app is being created in the background. You'll see an icon for it in the list, followed by the text "We're adding your app" (*Figure 20-4*).

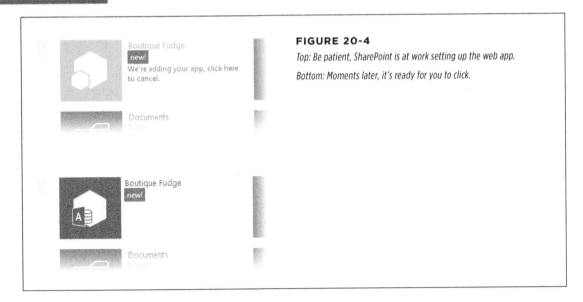

FIGURE 20-4

Top: Be patient, SharePoint is at work setting up the web app.

Bottom: Moments later, it's ready for you to click.

7. **When the app icon turns solid red, click it.**

   You'll see a welcome page that informs you that your app is ready but doesn't have any tables yet (*Figure 20-5*).

8. **To open your web app in Access, click the link "Open this app in Access to start adding tables."**

   Your browser will ask you to download a small file with the extension .accdw. This file is small because it doesn't contain any data—just the URL that points to the SharePoint web app. When you open this file, Access reads the URL, contacts the SharePoint server, downloads all the information it needs, and opens your web app. You can then begin designing the database.

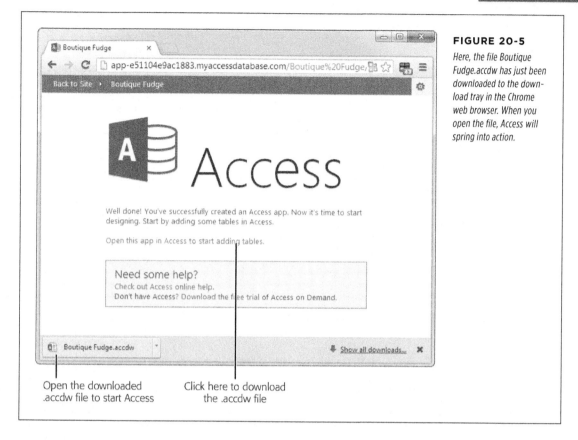

FIGURE 20-5

*Here, the file Boutique
Fudge.accdw has just been
downloaded to the down-
load tray in the Chrome
web browser. When you
open the file, Access will
spring into action.*

Open the downloaded
.accdw file to start Access

Click here to download
the .accdw file

Adding a Table

The first thing you'll notice when you create a new web app is the startlingly stripped-
down Access interface. The ribbon has just a single tab, named Home. Underneath
is the web app's *home tab*, where you begin creating your first table (*Figure 20-6*).

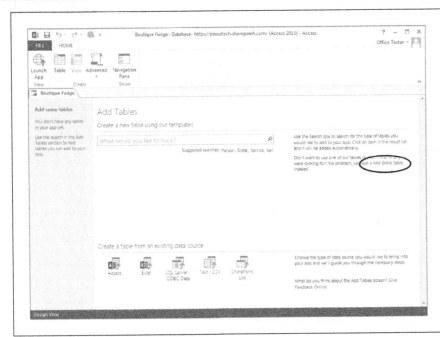

FIGURE 20-6

Here, the home tab is named Boutique Fudge, because that's the name of the web app you just created. Inside the tab are a number of links for creating new tables, including the useful but somewhat hidden "add a new blank table" link (circled).

Access gives you three ways to add a table to a web app:

- **From scratch.** The same way you design the tables in desktop databases.

- **From a template.** You search for the type of data you want to store (customers, products, clients, and so on), and Access suggests a ready-made table that fits the bill.

- **From another data source.** You import a table that you've already designed. Usually, you'll load a batch of tables from an Access desktop database, but you can also pull a table out of an Excel file, a text file in CSV format (page 803), a SQL Server database, or a SharePoint list.

The best way to get started is to create a blank table from scratch. To do that, click the "add a new blank table" link shown in *Figure 20-6*. Access loads up a new tab for your table in Design view, so you can add the fields you want (*Figure 20-7*).

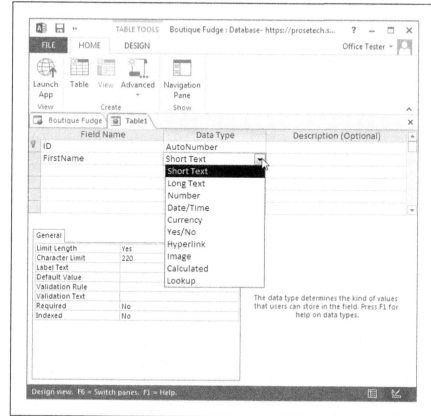

FIGURE 20-7

The Design view that you use to create a table in a web app closely resembles the design view that you use in a desktop database.

Initially, you'll start with just one field: an AutoNumber field named ID, which uniquely identifies each row in the table. You're already in the habit of adding an ID field to your own tables, but web apps *require* this best practice. Every table in a web app includes an ID field, and you can't delete or modify it.

As you add more fields, you'll find that you can choose from a similar set of data types as when creating a desktop database. However, because your data is actually stored in a SQL Server database, the data types need to play by the rules of SQL Server. This requirement introduces a few subtle differences—for example, the Attachment data type is replaced with the less-powerful Image data type, and the old-fashioned OLE Object data type is gone altogether. You'll also notice that the list of field properties you can customize for each data type is far smaller than with a desktop database. For example, you can't use the nifty custom format string feature (page 72) for any data type.

Table 20-1 details the most important difference and tells you what data type SQL Server is really using to store each type of data, behind the scenes.

TABLE 20-1 *Data Types in a Web App*

DATA TYPE	ACTUAL SQL SERVER DATA TYPE	KEY DIFFERENCES
Short Text	nvarchar	This field works the same in desktop databases and web apps.
Long Text	nvarchar(MAX)	Web apps don't offer the option of storing formatted HTML text. (Of course, you could store HTML markup in a Long Text field, but the formatting won't have any effect when someone views or edits the data—it'll just show up as extra tags sandwiched inside your field.)
Number	int, float, or decimal	In a web app, the exact data type depends on the Number Subtype setting, which lets you choose between whole numbers, floating point numbers that can have any number of decimal places, and decimal numbers that are allowed exactly six decimal places. The Display Format setting lets you choose how the number appears to someone using the database—for example, you can show a fixed number of decimal places or display the number as a percent value.
Date/Time	date, time, or datetime	In a web app, the exact data type depends on the subtype setting, which lets you to store just the date information, just the time information, or both. Unfortunately, you're limited to just two date formats, which you set using the Display Format property. You can use the standard short date format, which appears like 11/22/2013 on a computer with U.S. regional settings (page 75) or the standard long format, which appears like November 22, 2013.
Currency	money	As with desktop databases, web apps let you set how many decimal places are shown for a currency value. Web apps also include a property named Currency Symbol, which lets you choose from an exhaustive list of different countries' currency symbols.
Yes/No	bit	Once again, web apps lock down your format choices. With Yes/No fields, you don't get any other display options (which isn't a big deal, because most people don't bother to change the Format field for a Yes/No field in a desktop database anyway).
Hyperlink	nvarchar	Web apps and desktop databases treat hyperlinks the same way—they assume they're URLs and turn them into clickable links when they display them as part of a record. But in the database, a hyperlink is just an ordinary piece of text.

DATA TYPE	ACTUAL SQL SERVER DATA TYPE	KEY DIFFERENCES
Image	varbinary(MAX)	The web app Image field actually uses a SQL Server *varbinary* field, which gives it the ability to store an arbitrarily big block of binary data—in other words, any content from a picture to a video file. However, web apps *assume* the Image field is used for images. (When a web form has an Image field on it, the web app attempts to convert the data inside the field into a picture, which it then shows on the page. And when you edit a record that contains an Image field, the web app lets you upload a new picture file, which it then stores in the field.) The closest desktop equivalent is the attachment field, which is far more freewheeling—it allows any type of file and accepts multiple files in a single field.
Calculated		Web apps and desktop databases work the same way, letting you create an expression that performs a calculation (page 85).
Lookup		As in desktop databases, a Lookup is a feature, not a data type. It lets you provide a set of possible choices for a field or, more commonly, create a relationship between tables. Because Access web apps don't use the Relationships window, creating a lookup is the only way to create a relationship.

As with a desktop database, you can write field validation rules that reject bad data (page 146). You can also write data macros that perform more complex error checking. Macros work essentially the same as in a desktop database—you check for an error with the If action, and then cancel the insert, update, or delete operation with the RaiseError action, as explained on page 547. The chief difference is that you use the On Insert, On Update, and On Delete data macros in a web app, while a desktop database performs the same logic with the Before Change and Before Delete data macros.

Once you've finished entering all the fields for your table, it's time to save it. Press Ctrl+S or click the Save icon the Quick Access toolbar. Then, enter a name for your table and click OK.

When you save a table in a web app, Access communicates with the SharePoint server and pushes your new creation online. After a slight delay Access shows its friendly "Hang on while we save your changes message." Once the process is complete, your app will be live on the SharePoint server. You (or anyone else) can now log into SharePoint and start entering data.

Creating a Table from a Template

There's nothing particularly special about Access's ability to create a web app from a template. Using this feature is easy enough—you start by typing a word that describes the type of data you want to store (like "customers," "log," or "purchases") in the "What would you like to track" box in the home tab (*Figure 20-6*). Press Enter, and Access shows you a list of premade tables that include all the fields you're likely to need. Click one of them, and Access creates the table for you, without even taking you into design mode. Access may even create *multiple* tables if it concludes that the table you picked requires other related information to be tracked in another linked table.

Table templates are a good starting point if you're not sure of all the data you want to track. However, if you create a table from a template, you'll almost certainly have some fields that you don't need, or some that don't exactly match the type of data you want to track. To clean up these issues, you'll need to edit the table in Design view. To do that, right-click the table name in list on the left side of the web app's home tab, and choose Edit Table.

Entering Data in a Table

As with an Access desktop database, you can use Datasheet view to add or edit the records in your table. To switch into Datasheet view, right-click the tab for your table (for example, the Customers tab) and choose Datasheet View. Or, you can use the familiar View button in the ribbon. Either way, once you switch to the Datasheet view, you'll notice that it doesn't look quite the same as it does for a desktop database (*Figure 20-8*).

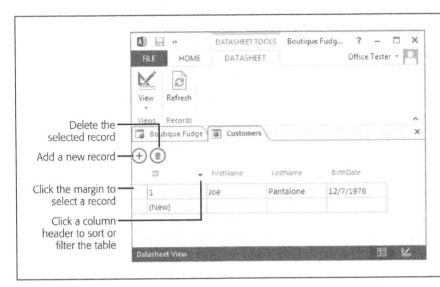

FIGURE 20-8

The Datasheet view for a web app has almost all the same features as the Datasheet view for a desktop app. However, some of the details have been restyled and rearranged.

Now's a good time to try adding a record. You'll find that the web app datasheet behaves much like the datasheet for a desktop database. Here are some examples:

- You can adjust the width of columns.

- You can rearrange the order of columns. Just hover over one until you see the four-way-arrow pointer; then drag.

- You can hide a column. Hover over the column header until you see the drop-down arrow, click it, and then choose Hide Column.

- You can sort by any field. Hover over a column header, click the drop-down arrow, and choose Sort Ascending or Sort Descending.

- You can show or hide records that have specific values. Hover over a column header, click the drop-down arrow, and add a checkmark next to the items you want to see (or choose Remove Filter to see everything).

- A calendar icon appears when you move to a field that uses the Date/Time data type (like BirthDate field in *Figure 20-8*). Click it to pop up a month-by-month calendar view, where you can find exactly the date you want.

One notably missing feature is the ability to search for a record. But as you'll see later, web apps have another way to accomplish that (page 695).

Given that the features of the Datasheet view are so similar in web apps as they are in desktop apps, you might wonder why the Datasheet view *looks* so different. The reason is that the Datasheet view in a web app is actually a piece of a web page. When you edit your table online, you use the same grid of records, with all the same buttons and features, except your interaction takes place inside your favorite web browser. (You'll see this happen a bit later, on page 691.)

This minor miracle works because of a subtle shift in the way the Datasheet view is created. In a desktop database, Access creates the grid of records. But in a web app, SharePoint generates the Datasheet view. It uses a mixture of HTML markup and some carefully crafted JavaScript code to simulate the desktop editing experience. In fact, even when you're working with your web app inside Access, exactly the same process is taking place—SharePoint is creating the Datasheet view, and Access is simply showing that bit of web content inside its main window.

Back to the Home Tab

Every web app has a built-in navigation system. As you add tables, your web app creates a menu that includes a link to each one. SharePoint shows this menu on the home page for your web app. Access shows what this menu looks like on the web app's home tab—the same place where you started out before you added your first table.

Initially, the home tab showed the helpful Add Tables page (*Figure 20-6*). But now that you've added a table, Access uses the home tab to show the home page of your web app (*Figure 20-9*).

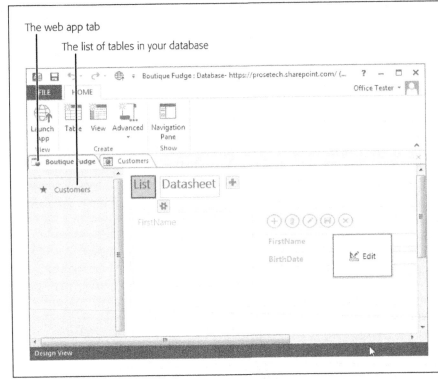

The web app tab

The list of tables in your database

FIGURE 20-9

When people use your web app online, they'll start out at a page that looks like this. On the left is a menu that lets them jump from one table to the next. Right now there's just one table, which is named Customers. On the right are the controls that let them edit the table's data.

Few databases have just a single table, and web apps are no exception. To add a new table, choose Home→Create→Table from the ribbon. This action doesn't actually create a table; instead it takes you back to the home tab and loads up the Add Tables page that you used earlier. Now you can click the "add a new blank table" link to create another new table, which Access will open in another new tab. Each time you create a new table, Access adds it to the list of tables, which it shows on the left of the home tab.

As you'll soon see, you can change the menu on your web app home page, and you can change the controls it uses to let people edit data. But before you start changing the web app home page, you need to get a better feel for how it works, and to do that you need to view your web app in a browser. The next section shows you how.

Running Your Web App

A web app with a single table may not seem like much (and, truthfully, it isn't that impressive yet). But before you ramp up your efforts, you need to see what your web app looks like to other people.

Launching your web app is easy. In Access, choose Home→View→Launch App. Access opens your default browser and sends it to the web app home page. If you aren't already logged in to your SharePoint site, you might be asked to enter your user name and password now.

Once you're logged in, you'll see the live version of your web app. It looks a lot like the web app's home tab in Access (*Figure 20-10*). Get comfortable—you'll spend the next few pages decoding this compact data display.

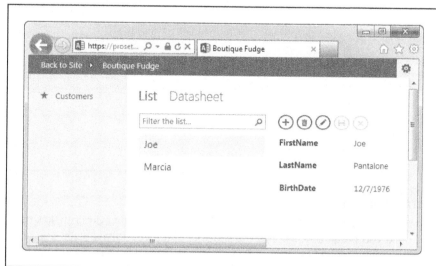

FIGURE 20-10

When folks visit your web app in a browser, they'll land at the home page shown here.

How to Visit Your Web App Online

The quickest way to get to your web app is to use the ribbon and choose Home→View→Launch App. But what if you need to tell someone else how to find your web app, or you need to reach it from a computer that doesn't have Access?

There are two ways to find your site online:

- **Use the direct link.** Type the right address into a browser, and you go straight to your web app's doorstep, with no extra steps (aside from logging in). However, web apps usually have ugly automatically generated addresses, like *https://prosetech-115e31b4ee2a78.sharepoint.com*. These URLs aren't exactly easy to remember, although

you can get around that by adding them to your web browser bookmarks, or emailing the link to the people with whom you want to share the app. To get hold of the correct, shortest possible URL for your web app, open it in Access and choose File→Info (*Figure 20-11*).

- **Browse to it in SharePoint.** Remember, your web app is part of a SharePoint site, and you can find it in the same way that you find any other SharePoint app. Start by logging into your SharePoint site, and then click the Site Contents link in the navigation menu (on the left). Scroll down until you find your web app, and then click it once to open it in the browser.

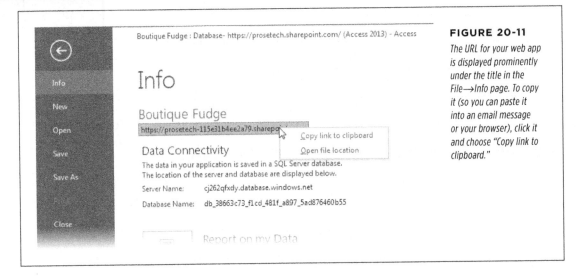

FIGURE 20-11

The URL for your web app is displayed prominently under the title in the File→Info page. To copy it (so you can paste it into an email message or your browser), click it and choose "Copy link to clipboard."

Editing Data in a Web App

At first glance, the home page may seem a bit puzzling. However, it makes more sense once you break it down into the series of steps you follow when you use a web app. Here's how the process unfolds:

1. **Pick the table you want to work on from the list on the left.**

   On the right, Access loads the views for that table. At the top, above the editing controls, you'll see the links for different views. Every new table in a web app starts its life with two views: List and Datasheet.

> **NOTE** A *view* is the web app equivalent of a form in a desktop database. As you'll see later in this chapter, you can create your own views and customize them to present data in the way you want. However, Access's view-tweaking abilities are far more modest than its form-building features.

2. **Pick the view you want to use by clicking the corresponding link.**

   You start at the List view, but you can switch to the Datasheet view with a single click (*Figure 20-12*).

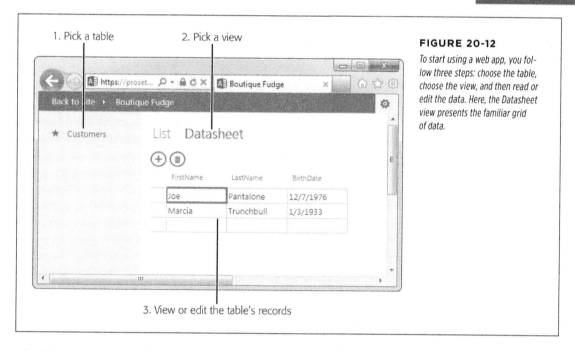

1. Pick a table

2. Pick a view

3. View or edit the table's records

FIGURE 20-12

To start using a web app, you follow three steps: choose the table, choose the view, and then read or edit the data. Here, the Datasheet view presents the familiar grid of data.

3. **Use the controls underneath to review and edit your data.**

As soon as you make changes, SharePoint commits them to its SQL Server database so everyone else can see them. This process is nearly instantaneous, unlike with shared desktop databases, which refresh themselves every 60-or-so seconds (page 659).

When you create a new table, Access creates a List view and a Datasheet view to help you edit it. If you choose to do your work in the Datasheet view (*Figure 20-12*), you won't have any trouble interpreting its compact grid of records. In fact, you've already seen this view in Access, where you used it to add the first record to your table (page 688). Using the Datasheet, you can edit, delete, and create records, and you can resize and rearrange columns. If you hover over a column header and click the drop-down arrow, you get a menu that lets you apply basic sorting and filtering.

If you choose the List view (*Figure 20-13*), you may need a bit of help finding your way around. List view lets you view and edit just one record at a time. That means it can present the data more effectively, especially if the database contains pictures, long text descriptions, or a huge number of fields. To pick which record you see, you find it in the list, which runs along the left side of view. To add, edit, or delete records, you use the icons that appear just above the record data (*Figure 20-14*).

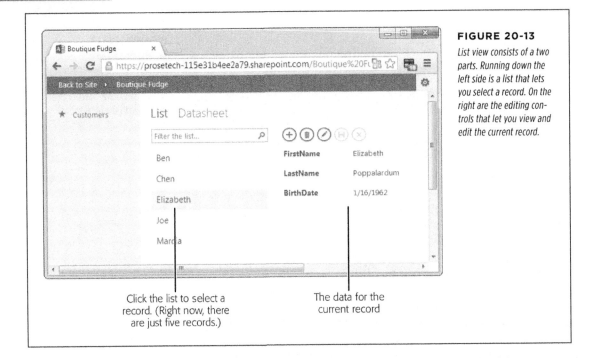

FIGURE 20-13

List view consists of a two parts. Running down the left side is a list that lets you select a record. On the right are the editing controls that let you view and edit the current record.

Click the list to select a record. (Right now, there are just five records.)

The data for the current record

NOTE By default, the list uses the first field in your table (not including the ID number). In the case of the Customers table, that means you see a list of first names, which isn't nearly as useful as seeing a list of full names. Fortunately, you'll find that it's easy to change the data in the list when you start editing your view (page 703).

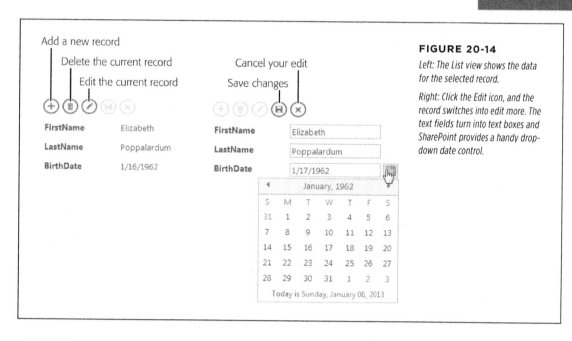

Add a new record

Delete the current record

Edit the current record

Cancel your edit

Save changes

FIGURE 20-14

Left: The List view shows the data for the selected record.

Right: Click the Edit icon, and the record switches into edit more. The text fields turn into text boxes and SharePoint provides a handy drop-down date control.

FirstName	Elizabeth
LastName	Poppalardum
BirthDate	1/16/1962

FirstName	Elizabeth
LastName	Poppalardum
BirthDate	1/17/1962

January, 1962

S	M	T	W	T	F	S
31	1	2	3	4	5	6
7	8	9	10	11	12	13
14	15	16	17	18	19	20
21	22	23	24	25	26	27
28	29	30	31	1	2	3

Today is Sunday, January 06, 2013

TIP SharePoint attempts to make your life easier with keyboard shortcuts. Using them, you can quickly create a new record (press N), delete the current record (press the Delete key), switch the current record into edit mode (press E), cancel your changes (press Esc), or save them (Ctrl+S).

GEM IN THE ROUGH

Searching and Filtering

Keen eyes will notice the "Filter the list" box that sits above the list of records in List view (*Figure 20-13*). If you have a table that's packed with records, this can help you find the ones you want.

To use the filter box, click inside it and type the text you want to match, and then press Enter. Access trim downs the list to show only the matching records. To remove a filter, click the tiny X icon in the filter box.

When you filter the list, you need to be aware of two quirks. First, Access matches the text you type to *any* part of a value. That means that typing "be" will match "*Betty*" and "*Verbeek*." Second, Access searches *all* the text values in your table, not just the field that appears in the list. If you have plenty of text values, you may get more matches than you expect—or want. Although there's no way to change Access's filtering style, you can create queries that filter data more stringently, as you'll see on page 710.

Understanding the Web App Navigation System

As you know, you can add as many tables as you want to a web app; you simply choose Home→Create→Table and then click the "add a new blank table" link. Every time you create a table, Access adds a matching link to the navigation menu on the left side of the home page. So if you add three tables to your web app, Access creates three links, and the person using your database can skip from one table to another by clicking these links.

You can also use the navigation menu when you're editing your web app in Access. On the home tab, right-click the table you want to work with. Access gives you several options: Choose View Data to open a Datasheet view on your table; use Edit Table to open the table in Design view; or click Delete to remove the table altogether.

You can customize the navigation menu, but only slightly. If you yearn to give it a new look, move it to a new place, or change the way it works, you're out of luck. But here are several less dramatic but still practical changes you can make to your navigation menu:

- **Change the order of menu items.** It makes sense to group related tables together and put the most commonly edited ones at the top. To change the menu order, just drag items up or down. When folks load up your app, SharePoint starts out showing them the first table in the list.

- **Change a menu item's text.** Right-click the item, choose Rename, and then type whatever you want to use. Unfortunately, you can't change the navigation menu's width, and SharePoint can only accommodate about 15 letters in its fixed layout, so don't use long names like "New Product Catalog."

- **Change the icon that appears next to the menu item.** Ordinarily, each table has a star on the left side, but you can replace this with a different tiny picture. You can't use your own handcrafted icon, but you can choose from over 150 readymade icons, including such mystifying choices as a miniature snowman and a soccer ball. To change the icon, select the menu item, and then click the tiny Formatting icon that appears to the right of it (*Figure 20-15*).

- **Hide a menu item.** If you've created a table that you don't want people to edit, right-click it and choose Hide. You'll still see the menu item in the home tab in Access, with a dashed line around it to indicate its hidden status. But when you run the web app online, you won't see the link at all.

> **NOTE** Hiding is a handy way to *guide* people to the right tables, but it isn't a bulletproof way to protect your data. For example, if someone adds a bookmark to one of your tables, and then you hide the link to that table, that person can still use the bookmark to return to the table and edit it.

Currently, web apps don't provide any user-level security to ensure that different groups of people can only perform certain types of tasks or edit certain types of tables. This is a clear limitation of the web app model, and possibly one that Microsoft will address in the future.

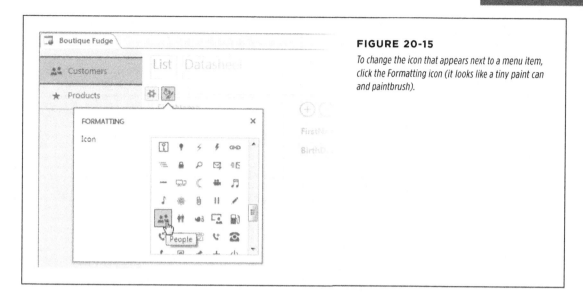

FIGURE 20-15

To change the icon that appears next to a menu item, click the Formatting icon (it looks like a tiny paint can and paintbrush).

At this point, you might be wondering what happened to the traditional navigation pane, which shows all the database objects in a desktop database. When you create a web app, Access hides the navigation pane, to prevent less experienced Access users from confusing it with the navigation menu. However, you can show the navigation pane whenever you need it by choosing Home→Show→Navigation Pane (*Figure 20-16*).

One reason to reveal the navigation pane is so you can see, at a glance, all the views that Access has created for your web app, without browsing through every table in the home tab. You can also use the pane to rename a table. (When you right-click the table in the navigation menu and choose Rename, you rename the navigation link, not the table.) And there are other good reasons to call up the navigation panel, like viewing the queries you've created and finding views and macros that aren't linked to any table. You'll use the navigation panel later in this chapter when you create a filtering query (page 710).

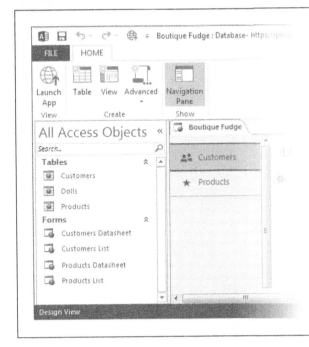

FIGURE 20-16

The navigation panel shows all the objects that are currently in the Boutique Fudge database: two tables and the four views that Access creates automatically to let people edit these tables. Oddly enough, Access calls them forms in the navigation pane, even though it calls them views everywhere else.

■ Customizing Views

You now have a simple web app that lets other people view data and edit it online. However, the editing experience falls short from what most hardcore database-crafters expect. Access's automatically generated list view is a nice enough starting point, but it's rarely perfect. For example, Access won't necessarily put related fields close together, because Access follows the order in which table fields are defined. And Access often fails to give each field the best size, making some boxes unnecessarily big (for example, dates), while placing long text values in cramped boxes. Fortunately, it's easy to fix these problems by taking control of your views.

Modifying a View

To modify a view, you need to open it up in Access. Here's how:

1. **In Access, switch to the web app's home tab.**

   Remember, the home tab uses the web app's name—in the current example, the home tab is named Boutique Fudge.

2. **In the list on the left, click the table.**

In this example, that's the Customers table.

3. **Choose the view you want to edit by clicking the view button at the top.**

Access lets you modify the List view *and* the Datasheet view. You might choose to make minor changes in the Datasheet view (for example, removing columns or changing their order), but you're likely to spend most of your time perfecting the more detailed List view.

4. **Click the floating Edit button to open the view.**

Alternatively, you can double-click the view button. Either way, Access opens the view in a new tab (*Figure 20-17*).

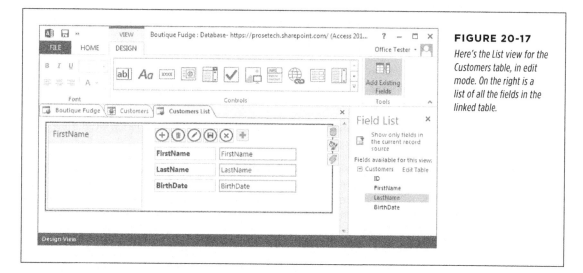

FIGURE 20-17

Here's the List view for the Customers table, in edit mode. On the right is a list of all the fields in the linked table.

5. **Edit the view.**

The following sections explore the changes you can make when editing a view.

6. **When you're finished, press Ctrl+S or click the Save button in the Quick Access toolbar.**

Access publishes your changes to the SharePoint server. If you already have the view open in a web browser, refresh your page to see your changes.

The Two Meanings of "View"

Access's web app terminology can be a bit confusing, because the word "view" has two different meanings. The first meaning is the traditional one: a view is a way that you can look at a database object. For example, a table can be in Design view or Datasheet view. The second meaning is the new web app use of the word: a view is a way to present data online—essentially, it's the web app equivalent of a form.

Sometimes, Access uses both meanings for the word "view" at once. For example, when you open the List view in *Figure 20-17*, the Access status bar notes that you're currently editing the List view in Design view.

Rearranging Controls

Editing a view in a web app is like editing a form in Layout view, but simpler. There's no Property Sheet of settings, for example, and there's no way for you to actually *see* the layout that Access is using. Instead, Access creates the layout automatically as you move your fields around.

The best way to understand how view editing works is to give it a whirl. Here are a few basic tasks to try:

- **To resize a control**, move the mouse over one of the edges. The mouse pointer will turn into a two-way arrow. Then, drag the edge up, down, or to the side. The resizing process doesn't affect other controls, which is different from the way forms work in a desktop database. In a desktop database, most forms use layouts. If you change the width of one control in a layout, Access then resizes all the other controls that are in the same layout to match.

> **NOTE** You can widen an ordinary single-line text box, but you can't make it any taller—for that, you need a multiline textbox. Access automatically uses a single-line text box for Short Text fields and a multiline text box for Long Text fields, but page 705 explains how you can change a field to use a different type of control.

- **To move a control**, position your mouse over the control so the pointer changes into a four-way arrow. Then, drag the control to a new place. As long as you don't overlap controls, you can place them almost anywhere. Access creates new rows and columns as needed (*Figure 20-18*).

- **To move a whole bunch of controls**, click in an empty space inside the view, and then drag to draw a selection box. When you release the mouse button, you've selected all the controls that are inside the box and you can drag them around en masse. If you find this technique too tricky to master, you can select specific controls one after the other by holding down the Ctrl key as you click them.

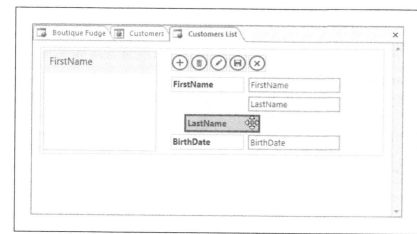

FIGURE 20-18

Here's what happens if you click the LastName label and drag it downwards. As you move the control, Access bumps everything else out of the way. It won't let you overlap controls, although you can place them unevenly, so their left and right edges don't line up.

TIP In a web app, fields and their associated labels don't stick together. If you want to move both at once, hold down Ctrl, click both, and *then* drag the pair where you want them.

Rearranging controls is the simplest improvement you can make to any view. You can do helpful things like putting related fields (say, FirstName and LastName) close together, and enlarging image fields and text fields so you have enough room to read long text and view big pictures.

Configuring Controls

When you get tired of moving the controls around your view, you might want to start changing them. Access doesn't provide anywhere near the level of control-customization in a web app view as it does in a desktop database form, but there are still plenty of useful modifications you can make. Here are two of the most basic:

- **To change the text in a label**, double-click it and then type the new text you want. Ordinarily, Access uses the unvarnished field names from the underlying table. You may prefer to replace a field name like "BirthDate" with a caption like "Birth Date" or "Date of Birth."

- **To format the text in a control**, select it and use the buttons in the View | Design→Font section of the ribbon. This trick works equally well with label controls (which are used for field captions) and text box controls (which are used to show field values). You can change the color, size, and justification of the text, and you can add bold, italic, and underlining. But that's it—so give up hope of ever getting exotic typefaces, fancy borders, or background fills.

Every control also has a small set of configurable settings that are tucked out of view. To see them, start by clicking the control you want to change. You'll see three tiny icons appear next to it (*Figure 20-19*):

- **Data.** Click this icon to link the control to a data field or change the control's name (which might be useful if you want to use a clearly descriptive name when you refer to it in a macro). You can also set a default value for your field.

- **Formatting.** Click here to change the control's tooltip, hide it, or disable it. If you're looking for fancier styling options, you'll need to use the View | Design→Font section of the ribbon instead.

- **Actions.** Click here to attach a data macro to the On Click event (which occurs when someone clicks the control) or the After Update event (which occurs when someone edits the value in the field).

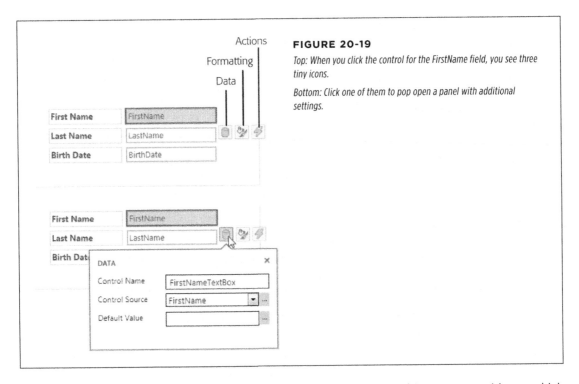

FIGURE 20-19

Top: When you click the control for the FirstName field, you see three tiny icons.

Bottom: Click one of them to pop open a panel with additional settings.

One of the most useful ways to improve a view is to add some user guidance, which you can do via tooltips and input hints. *Tooltips* are the brief pop-up messages that explain an onscreen item. You can use them, for example, to provide more details about what kind of information a field should hold. An *input hint* is the text that SharePoint displays in a text box when the corresponding field is empty and awaiting some data. You can use an input hint to suggest the proper format for a text value, as *Figure 20-20* demonstrates (bottom). To add both these details, select a field, click the Formatting icon, and then type some text in the Tooltip and Input Hint boxes.

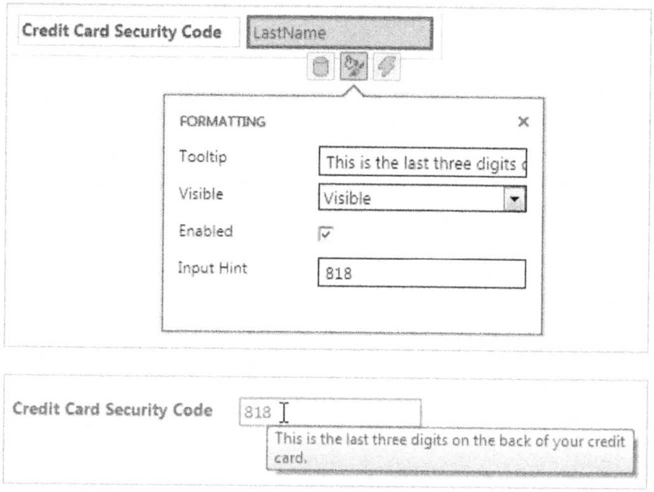

FIGURE 20-20

Top: You configure tooltip and input hint using the Data icon.

Bottom: The input hint appears when the text box is being edited, if the field is empty. The tooltip appears when the mouse moves over the text box.

TIP If you need to add a long or particularly important instruction, a tooltip isn't the best choice. Instead, put your message in a label that's always visible. Choose View | Design→Controls→Label to add another label to your view.

Changing the List

The list in List view is a special case. It's a control that does double-duty: not only does it display a list of values, but it also lets you jump from one record to another by clicking those values.

When Access creates the List view for a table, it grabs the first field (not including the ID field), and uses that to fill the list. As a result, the list may not have enough information to properly identify each record. For example, it may show the FirstName field, even though first names aren't unique and there may be many people with the same first name in your table. The list may even use a field that has blank values, in which case you'll need to click the blank spaces in the list to load those records. Clearly, this situation is far from ideal.

To configure the list control, select it and click the Data icon. (This is the only icon that appears, because you can't change the appearance of the record-selection list or react to its events.) When you click Data, you'll see a panel with several useful settings, including Primary, Secondary, and Thumbnail (all of which set the data that appears in the list) and Sort Field and Sort Order (which control how the items in the list are ordered).

There are three different approaches you can use to improve your list:

- **Set both a Primary and a Secondary field.** In the current Customers view, Primary is set to FirstName, and Secondary is not set. But if you set Primary to LastName and Secondary to FirstName, you'll see both bits of information in the list, one on top of the other (*Figure 20-21*).

- **Use an expression for the Primary field.** This is the standard approach you'd use in a desktop database. Click the ellipsis (...) next to the Primary setting, and type in an expression like FirstName + " " + LastName (if you want names to show up as "Matthew Malone") or LastName + ", " + FirstName (for "Malone, Matthew"). Don't set a Secondary field, unless you want to list to show even more information.

- **Add a thumbnail.** If your table includes a field with the Image data type, you can set it for the Thumbnail setting. Then, SharePoint will show a tiny thumbnail of your picture in the list, next to each item. This approach works best with pictures that are small and distinctive, like company logos.

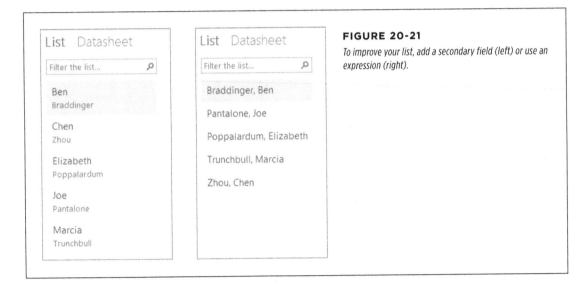

FIGURE 20-21

To improve your list, add a secondary field (left) or use an expression (right).

> **TIP** Even if you only need the primary field to identify your items, you can still put the secondary field to good use by showing some other information that lets users figure out which records they want to review. For example, if your view shows a list of projects, you might use the primary field to provide the unique project name, and the secondary field to show some important information, like the project's current status or its due date.

Once you make sure the list includes the data you want, you can set the Sort Field and Sort Order settings to make sure your list puts its values in the right order. The Sort Field is the field Access uses to sort the list (like LastName) and Sort Order lets you choose between an ascending or descending order. To avoid confusion, you should sort on the same field that you display. For example, if you show last names first, it makes sense to sort on LastName, whereas if you show first names first it's clearer to sort on FirstName. If the sort order isn't obvious by looking at the list, the people using your view may assume the list isn't sorted at all.

Adding and Removing Controls

As you may expect, you can easily add or delete the controls in a view.

To delete a control, click it and then press the Delete key. Alternatively, you can *hide* the control. That way it isn't visible (or usable) online, but you can unhide it if you want to add it back in the future. To hide a control, select it, click the Formatting icon, and change the Visible setting to Hidden.

Access gives you two ways to add a control. The quickest approach is to drag the field in from the Field List panel. Access adds a label for the caption and adds a control that matches the field type. For example, you get a text box for a field with the Short Text data type, a hyperlink control for a field with the Hyperlink data type, a checkbox for a Yes/No field, and so on.

The other way to add a control is to double-click the exact control you want in the View | Design→Controls section of the ribbon. Access then adds it to your layout. You'll need to drag it to the right place, and (optionally) connect it to a field in your database. To do that, select it, click the Data icon, and pick the field you want to use.

Now that you know how to add and delete controls, you also know how to *replace* one control with another. It's simply a matter of deleting the control you have now, adding a different control to take its place, and connecting it to the right field. Strange as it may seem at first, there are several good reasons to replace a control. Here are some examples:

- **You want to show a field but not let anyone edit it.** You could click the Formatting icon and turn off the Enabled checkbox. But another approach is to replace your text box with a label. When you edit a record, disabled fields appear faded, while labels stay the same, looking like ordinary pieces of text.

- **You want to restrict editing choices for a field to a few known values.** In this case, swap your text box for a combo box, click the Data icon, set Row Source Type to Value List, and enter the list of acceptable values in the Row Source box. Now when someone edits the record, he'll need to pick one of the values you've defined. But be careful—if you need to add more than a few values, you're probably better off putting your values in a separate table and creating a lookup (page 156).

- **You want to show a web page in your view.** As you already know, you can place web addresses in a Hyperlink control. They then become clickable links in your view. However, if you replace your Hyperlink control with a Web Browser control, SharePoint will show the referenced web page in the view, using a box that you can make as big or as small as you want. The only caveat—and it's a significant one—is that for security reasons, this trick only works with secure addresses that start with *https://*, not regular URLs that begin with *http://*.

Using the techniques you've learned up to this point, you can polish a view into sparkling form. You don't have the fine control of a desktop database for things like exact grid placement and heavy formatting, but you do have enough to get by, most of the time. *Figure 20-22* shows a customized view that uses many of the tricks you've considered.

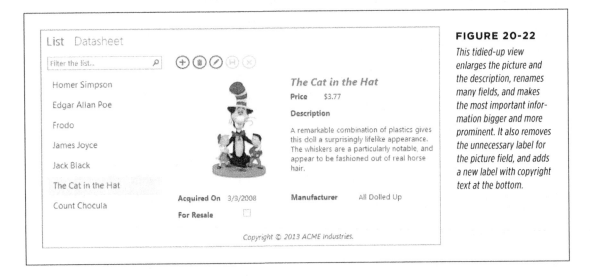

FIGURE 20-22

This tidied-up view enlarges the picture and the description, renames many fields, and makes the most important information bigger and more prominent. It also removes the unnecessary label for the picture field, and adds a new label with copyright text at the bottom.

■ Creating More Advanced Views

So far, you've spent your time customizing a single view. However, there's no reason to stop there. Access lets you create as many views as you want. For example, you might create different views to satisfy different editing tasks or to suit different users. Each view can show a different subset of your data, arranged in a different way, and with only certain fields editable. In this section, you'll learn how to create a new view, and then you'll see how you can use these skills to filter data, deal with linked tables, and launch simple macros.

Adding a New View

To add a new view, follow these steps:

1. **Click the web app's home tab, and then choose the table you want to work with from the list on the left.**

   The table appears in the main part of the window.

2. **Click the green plus (+) icon, which is just to the right of the list of views.**

Access pops open a panel where you can enter the settings for your new view (*Figure 20-23*).

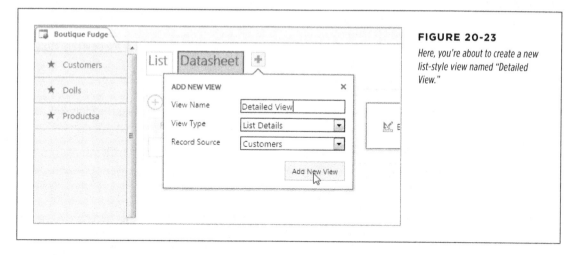

FIGURE 20-23

Here, you're about to create a new list-style view named "Detailed View."

3. **Give your view a name.**

   The convention that SharePoint uses when it names its views is to use the name of the table, followed by a space, followed by the name of the view, as in "Dolls List" and "Dolls Datasheet." However, you're free to use any name you'd like.

   The view *link* (the text the user clicks to see the view) doesn't need to match the view *name* (the name of the object you're creating now). You'll see how to change the view name in step 8.

4. **Choose the View Type.**

   You can start with a completely blank slate (choose Blank), a view that resembles the standard List view (List Details), a view that resembles the standard Datasheet view (Datasheet), or a view that's tailored for grouping records and showing totals (Summary).

5. **Choose the Record Source.**

   This is where the view gets its data. You aren't limited to the current table—a new view can use any table for its data source. You can also create queries (as you'll see on page 710) and use them as the foundation for views.

6. **Click Add New View.**

   Access creates the view and adds a link for your view next to links for the pre-built List and Datasheet view.

7. **If you want to change the text of the view link, right-click it and choose "rename."**

Initially, the view link matches the view name, but you can use whatever you want. You can also rearrange the order of view links (by dragging them), delete a view you don't want (right-click and choose Delete), and create a copy of a view to use as a starting point for a new view (right-click and choose Duplicate). You *can't* change the appearance of view links, move the group of view links to another place, or hide a view link without deleting the associated view, so don't bother trying.

8. **Once you've created a view, you can edit it.**

   Open your new view in the normal way: by double-clicking the view link.

Reports with a Web App

It's easy enough to create views, which are the web app equivalent of forms. But what about reports?

SharePoint web apps don't provide a reporting feature. This is partly due to the complexity of creating rich, formatted printer output on the Web.

Despite this limitation, Access has a way for you to have your web app and your reports too. The slightly cumbersome technique involves creating a linked desktop database that grabs the most recent information from the web app tables, but doesn't let you modify it. With this desktop database, you can create desktop reports and use them to print the data from the web app's tables.

To create a desktop database for reporting, follow these steps:

1. Open your web app in Access.

2. Choose File→Info.

3. Click the big Create Reports button.

   Access prompts you to save the local copy of your database somewhere on your computer.

4. Choose a location, type in a file name, and click Save.

   Access opens the reporting database in a new window. You'll see all the web app tables listed in the navigation. When you open one, Access fetches the current data from the web app, and displays it.

5. You can now create a report in the usual way, using the linked tables.

Super-pro users can use their own SQL Server-friendly reporting software, and connect directly to the web app's database. The sidebar on page 724 explains how to perform this expert feat.

Using a View to Create a Welcome Page

Here's a novel use for a custom view: creating an introductory message that welcomes people to your web app.

Right now, new visitors begin in the thick of things. SharePoint loads up the views for the first table in the navigation menu, creating a dense display that can be dizzying at first glance. Compare that to the web app in *Figure 20-24*, which uses a special screen to explain what's going on.

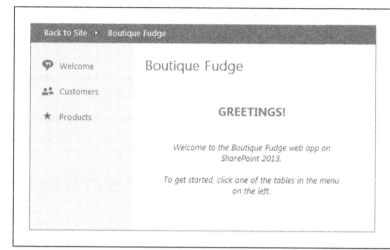

FIGURE 20-24

New visitors will appreciate a welcome page explaining what to do, although it forces experienced users to waste a click getting to the table they want.

Custom views make this frill possible, although it's a bit more work than you'd expect (and much more awkward than in a desktop database). The following list of steps takes you through the whole process:

1. **Create a new table named Welcome.**

   Each link in the navigation menu must correspond to a real table. So, to show a welcome message, you need a table, even though you don't plan to store any data in it. What you name this table doesn't matter, because you can rename the navigation menu link, but it makes sense to use a name that indicates its purpose.

2. **Add a field named Message to the Welcome table, with the data type Long Text.**

   This field will hold the welcome message that's shown on the welcome page. Strictly speaking, you don't need to use this approach; instead, you could type the text you want directly into your view. However, your Welcome table *does* need at least one row, because otherwise SharePoint will show a "no items" message instead of your view. So seeing as you need a record in the Welcome table, you may as well use it for something.

3. **Switch the Welcome table to Datasheet view. Then, add a single record, and type the welcome text in the Message field.**

   In this example, that's the two italicized paragraphs shown in *Figure 20-24*. Because you're using the Long Text data type, you can press Enter once to start a new paragraph and twice to add a blank line.

4. **Go to the home tab, and then drag the navigation link for the Welcome table to the top of the list.**

That way, SharePoint will load it up first.

5. **Delete the two automatically created views for the Welcome table.**

   Simply select the view link for each one and press Delete.

6. **Add a new view named Boutique Fudge. Choose Blank for the View Type and Welcome for the Record Source.**

   Or, you can use a different name, in which case you'll simply need to rename the view link text to Boutique Fudge, as shown in *Figure 20-24*.

   It makes sense to use a blank view, because you don't want a list or any other automatically generated controls.

7. **Double-click the view link to edit your new view.**

   You'll see that the view has just one ingredient: the action bar (the toolbar with editing icons).

8. **Delete the icons in the action bar.**

   Click one, press Delete, and then repeat the process until all the buttons are gone.

9. **Drag the Message field from the Field List panel (on the left) and drop it onto the view.**

   This field shows the welcome message you created in step 3.

10. **Perfect your form.**

    You can edit or remove the caption that comes with the Message field, add more labels with additional text, and change the color and size of each bit of text. When it's perfect, save it and view the results in the browser. You'll probably need several tries to get it right.

NOTE There are still a few quirks with this workaround. For example, there's no way to reclaim the space the action bar takes, even once you've deleted its icon, and you can't control the text spacing and formatting with complete precision.

Views That Use Queries

Custom views become more interesting when you combine them with another database ingredient—queries. Your query can filter out specific records, join tables together, and use expressions to manipulate individual fields. Your view shows the data that the query retrieves.

For example, consider the records in the Orders table from the desktop version of the Boutique Fudge database. You may want to create a view that shows only those orders that are currently in progress. On its own, a view can't accomplish this feat. But with a query, it's Access 101. You simply need to write a filter condition that matches records that have a status of In Progress.

To create a query, choose Home→Create→Advanced→Query. Access opens the familiar query designer, where you can create your query in the formal way, by picking fields and typing in your filters (*Figure 20-25*).

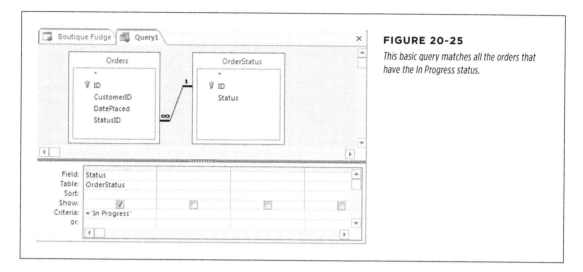

FIGURE 20-25

This basic query matches all the orders that have the In Progress status.

When you're finished creating your query, press Ctrl+S to save it or close the query tab, in which case Access will prompt you to save changes. Choose a descriptive name for your query, like InProgressOrders.

NOTE Make sure your query include the unique ID field of the table. Without this detail, SharePoint won't allow you to edit any of the data in the query results, because it won't know which record to update.

The web app query designer looks strikingly similar to the query designer in a desktop database. As with a desktop database, you can create a query that groups data, calculates totals, joins tables, requires parameters, and uses expressions. However, certain features are missing, such as action queries, Datasheet view (for testing a query), and SQL view (for editing the underlying SQL command).

Queries don't appear in the home tab. If you want to edit a query, or just reassure yourself that it's stored in your database, you need to show the navigation pane by choosing Home→Show→Navigation Pane.

Once you've created a query, you can use it as the basis for a new view. Follow the normal instructions for creating a view (page 706), but in the Record Source setting, choose the query you just created. Using the query from *Figure 20-25*, you can create a list-style view that lets users review and edit in-progress orders.

Views That Use Related Tables

Web apps are surprisingly adept at dealing with table relationships. If there's a relationship between your tables, Access pays attention, and uses that relationship to create a better view (*Figure 20-26*).

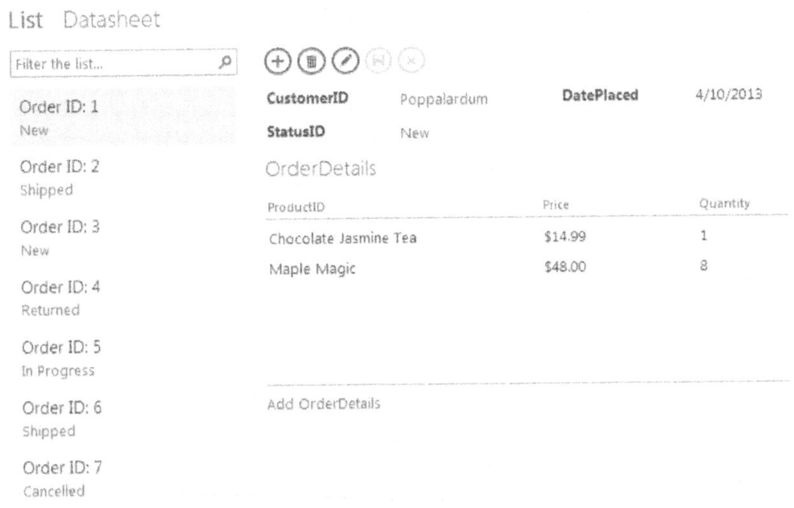

FIGURE 20-26

If your table is the parent in a one-to-many relationship, Access shows related items in the automatically generated List view. Here, the List view for the Orders table shows all the items in the current order, by getting the related records from the OrderDetails table.

> **TIP** When you use relationships, you display the data from multiple tables in one place. In many cases, there's no reason to show the child table separately. For example, it makes sense to view and edit Orders and OrderDetails records together, but there's probably no need to edit the OrderDetails table directly. To streamline your database, you should hide the OrderDetails table from the navigation menu (page 696).

Creating Table Relationships

Access doesn't provide the handy Relationships window in a web app. To link tables, you need to add a lookup that binds the two tables together. This is a technique you first considered on page 180.

For example, consider the relationship between the OrderDetails and the Orders table shown in *Figure 20-26*. To create this relationship, you add a field named OrderID to the OrderDetails table. The OrderID field links each order item to its associated order.

To create the relationship, choose Lookup for the data type of the OrderID field. Access shows a revamped version of the Lookup Wizard that has all its settings crammed into a single window (*Figure 20-27*). Here, you choose the linked table (Orders). When you've finished configuring the lookup, click OK to create the relationship between the two tables.

There's one alternative way to create a table relationship: you can import already-linked tables from an Access desktop database. You'll use this approach on page 718.

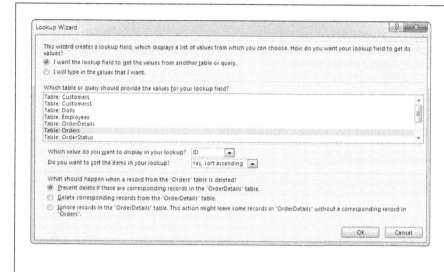

FIGURE 20-27

You don't need to tell Access what field to use in the parent table. Every table in a web app includes the unique ID field, so Access uses that automatically. However, you can choose what value Access displays in the lookup, which is handy if you want to show a customer name, say, instead of the customer ID. (Sadly, you can't use an expression that combines more than one field.) Finally, the setting at the bottom lets you choose how you want to enforce referential integrity (page 173).

To show related records, Access uses the Related Items control—a new control that's available only in web apps. And although Access' automatically created List views make good use of the Related Items control, you'll often want to tweak your views to improve the way your data is displayed. Here are some reasons to crack open a view and fine-tune the Related Items control:

- **To show different fields from the related table.** In the OrderDetails example shown in *Figure 20-26*, the Related Items control has room to show every field from the OrderDetails table. But if the OrderDetails record had more fields, Access would choose to show only some of them, and they might not be the ones you want.

- **To show records from a different table.** The Order table is the parent table in just one relationship, so it's obvious that the Related Items control should use the OrderItems table. But other tables are not so simple. For example, a customer can be linked to order records and invoice records. When Access creates a view for the Customers table, it may use the Related Items control to show linked records from the Orders table, when you would prefer to see linked records from the Invoices table.

- **To show records from multiple tables.** In much the same way that you add views for a table, you can add pages to the Related Items control. Each page can then show the related records from a different table.

To try out these techniques, open a view that uses the Related Items control, like the List view for the Orders table. You'll see the Related Items control, which looks like a big blank box (*Figure 20-28*).

NOTE You can the Related Items control to an existing view by choosing View | Design→Controls→Related Items Control. When added in this way, the Related Items control starts out completely empty, and you need to click the plus (+) icon to add the first page.

To fine-tune the settings for the Related Items control, start by clicking the heading inside it, which corresponds to the child table. In the orders example, the heading is named OrderDetails. Three icons will appear.

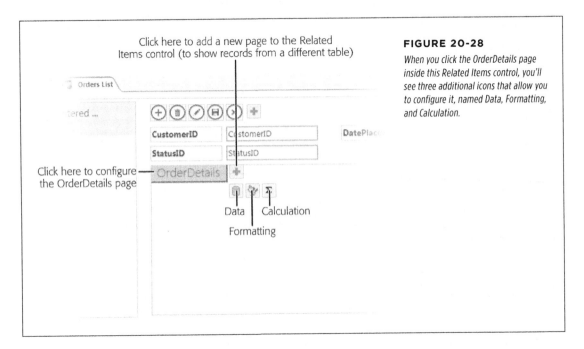

Click here to add a new page to the Related Items control (to show records from a different table)

Click here to configure the OrderDetails page

Data | Calculation

Formatting

FIGURE 20-28

When you click the OrderDetails page inside this Related Items control, you'll see three additional icons that allow you to configure it, named Data, Formatting, and Calculation.

Out of the three icons, the Data icon is the most important. It lets you choose the table that the Related Items control uses, and the fields that it shows (*Figure 20-29*). The Formatting tab lets you change the page title (for example, you could rename OrderDetails to "Order Contents"). The Calculation tab lets you pick a field that will be added, counted, or averaged—the result is displayed at the bottom of the list of related records. Unfortunately, the Calculation tab isn't nearly as useful as it seems, because it doesn't support expressions. That means there's no way to calculate the total cost of an order, for example, by multiplying the cost and quantity of each item.

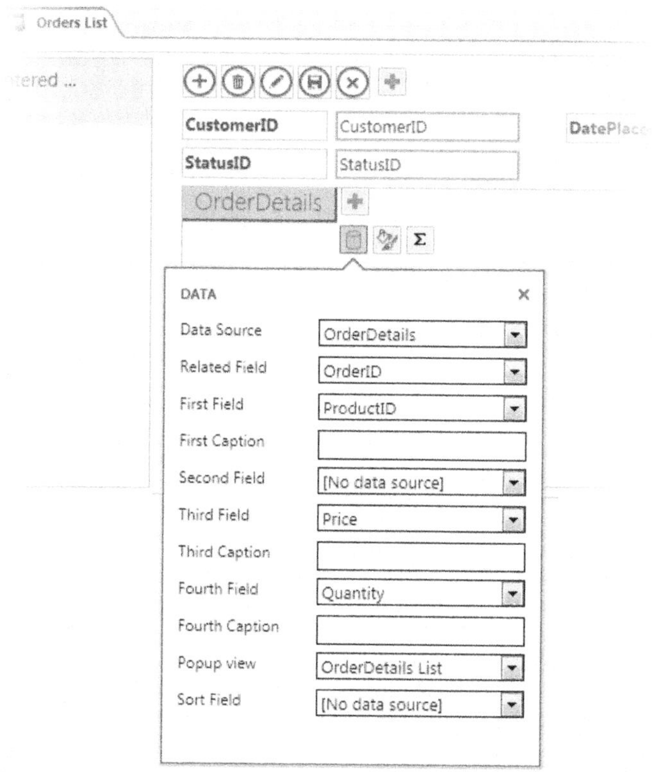

FIGURE 20-29

For each page in the Related Items control, you choose the table, you specify how it's related, and you choose up to four fields that will be shown. Optionally, you can give those fields a new caption, if the field name isn't clear enough. Don't worry about the "Popup view" setting for now—you'll consider that on page 716.

If you don't need four fields, it helps to be strategic about where you place your fields. Each field is given the same fixed amount of space, so if you have a long value, you can give it more space if you don't use the slot that follows it. The example in *Figure 20-29* uses this technique to give extra space to product names (the first field) by leaving the second field unoccupied.

◼ ADDING CHILD RECORDS

The Related Items control has another trick in store. While you're viewing a parent table (like Orders), you can use the Related Items control to add a record to the child table (in this case, OrderDetails). The secret is the tiny link that appears at the bottom of the Related Items control. You'll recognize it because it starts with the word "Add" (like "Add OrderDetails" in *Figure 20-26*).

When you click the record-adding link, the Related Items control opens a popup window with a new view that lets you add a record to the child table (*Figure 20-30*).

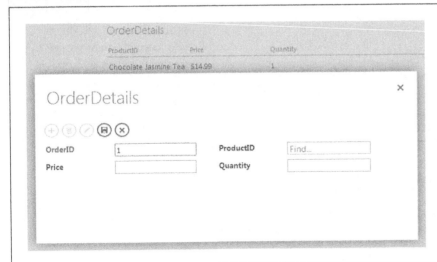

FIGURE 20-30

Click the "Add OrderDetails" link and Access pops open a basic view that you can use to add new order items. This view lacks some of the convenience you'd get in a desktop database (for example, when you pick a product it would be nice to fill in the corresponding price automatically, as you did on page 620), but it gets the job done.

By default, Access uses the List view for the corresponding table. So if you click Add OrderDetails, you'll see the OrderDetails List view. However, you can choose a different view by configuring the Related Items control and changing the "Popup view" setting (*Figure 20-29*).

This convenience does a lot to centralize the functionality in a web app, and it reduces the number of times you need to hop around from view to view while you're editing data. In the current example, it lets someone add a new order and fill out all the linked order items in one place, rather than having to edit two separate tables.

Access pros often create a new custom view—one that's not explicitly linked to any table in the navigation list—to use with the Related Items popup. Choose Home→Create→Advanced and pick Blank View or List View. Once you save the view, you'll be able to pick it in the "Popup view" setting. If you need to edit or delete the view later, you can find it in the navigation pane (choose Home→Show→Navigation Pane).

■ ADDING PARENT RECORDS

Web apps introduce a second new control that simplifies editing with related tables: the Autocomplete control.

The Autocomplete control takes the place of the traditional Combo Box control. In a desktop database, you see plenty of Combo Box controls, because they let you pick a parent record when editing a child record. For example, you might use a Combo Box to choose the product for a given order item, as shown in *Figure 20-31*.

Web apps also support the Combo Box. But when Access creates a view, it assumes you would prefer to use the new Autocomplete control, which works a little differently. In the Autocomplete control, you begin typing part of text from the item you want to match (in this case, the product name). As you type, SharePoint shows potential matches, which you can click to select. But if you don't find what you want, you can make use of an additional option, "< Add a new item >," which appears at the top of the list (*Figure 20-31*). Click that, and SharePoint opens *another* popup view where you can add the parent record you want.

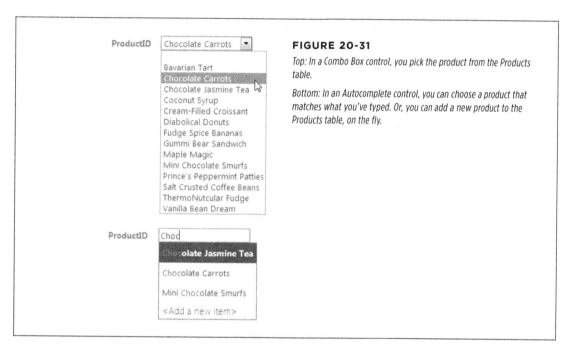

FIGURE 20-31

Top: In a Combo Box control, you pick the product from the Products table.

Bottom: In an Autocomplete control, you can choose a product that matches what you've typed. Or, you can add a new product to the Products table, on the fly.

In some cases, you may not want to use the Autocomplete control that Access has given you. Perhaps you worry that it may lead novice users to accidentally create new products rather than pick the one correct record that already exists in the table. The solution in this case is easy—edit the view, delete the Autocomplete control, and add a Combo Box control in its place.

Tutorial: Creating a Web App from an Access Database

You've covered a lot of ground in your web app exploration. Throughout, the theme has been the same: web apps are a gently scaled down version of desktop databases. They don't provide the same features—in fact, sometimes their omissions are downright maddening. But, overall, they give you the features you need put your data online. Even better, when they work, they're easy. Because of their strict limits on customization, there isn't much chance to spend hours fiddling with finicky details or debugging an intricate code routine.

By the same token, if you need to use a web app with a larger, more complex database, you may run into some headaches. In the final section of this chapter, you'll see an example with the sprawling Cacophoné Studios database. You'll learn how to use the tables in the desktop version of the database as the starting point for a web app (easy) and how to deal with the challenges of many-to-many relationships (more difficult). Along the way, you'll learn about a final web app feature—macros.

Creating a Web App Based on a Desktop Database

If you already have the perfect set of tables in a desktop database, there's no need to recreate them by hand in a web app. Instead, you can use a nifty import feature to transfer their tables to your web app, with or without their data. Obviously, some tables can cause problems (for example, ones that use the unsupported Attachment data type) and other database objects, like queries, forms, and reports, won't come along for the ride. But overall, the database import feature works surprisingly well.

To import the tables from a database, follow these steps:

1. **Choose Home→Create→Table from the ribbon.**

   This brings you to the Home tab and shows you the Add Tables page. At the bottom of the Add Tables page, you'll find a series of icons for importing data from different sources.

   In this example, you'll import data from an Access desktop database, which is the most useful option. However, you can import data from several other locations, such as a text file or an Excel spreadsheet. When importing these types of data, Access uses the Import wizard described in Chapter 23.

> **NOTE** When importing from SharePoint or SQL Server, Access lets you create *linked* tables—tables that are permanently connected to the SharePoint list or SQL Server database you specify. Linked tables fetch the most recent data every time you open them. (You'll learn about linking to SQL Server and SharePoint in Chapter 20 and Chapter 21, respectively.) However, there's a significant limitation. In a web app, linked tables are always read-only, which means you can't modify any of the linked data.

2. **Click the Access icon.**

   Access opens the Get External Data window.

3. **Pick your desktop database file.**

   You can type it into the "File name" box, or you can click the Browse button and navigate to it.

4. **Click OK.**

   Access opens the Import Objects window (*Figure 20-32*).

5. **Select the tables you want to import.**

By importing multiple tables at once, you can keep their relationships intact. (You can always delete unwanted tables from your web app after you import them.)

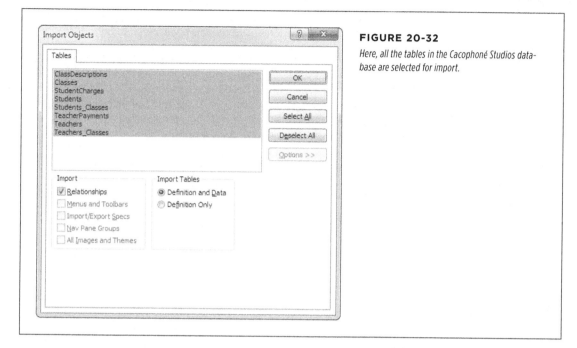

FIGURE 20-32

Here, all the tables in the Cacophoné Studios database are selected for import.

6. **Optionally, you can choose to import the tables but not the data.**

To do that, click the Options button and then click Definition Only.

7. **Click OK to begin the import process.**

Access transfers the tables to the web app and adds them to the navigation list, exactly as though you were creating each one from scratch. When Access finishes, it informs you of any issues.

The database import process works without a hitch for the Cacophoné Studios database. However, if you attempt to import a table that causes a problem (for example, one with unsupported data types or table validation rules), Access ignores the details it doesn't support, imports the table as best as it can, and then informs you of what it left out.

Dealing with a Many-to-Many Relationship

The Cacophoné Studios database uses several many-to-many relationships. For example, there's a many-to-many relationship between teachers and classes—one teacher may teach several classes, and the same class may be taught by more than one teacher. Similarly, there's a many-to-many relationship between students and classes, because one student can be enrolled in multiple classes and a single class holds a number of students.

To create many-to-many relationships, you create a junction table that sits between the two tables you want to link (page 186). For example, to link teachers and classes, you can create a table named Teachers_Classes. Each record pairs up one teacher with one class. (To review how junction tables work in closer detail, and to review all the relationships in the Cacophoné Studios database, refer to page 190.)

The problem with many-to-many relationships is that they confuse the Related Items control. It displays the related records from the junction table, but it doesn't get any of the information from the table that sits on the other side of the relationship. That means if you're looking at a teacher record, you'll see a list of all classes taught by that teacher, but you won't see the rest of the class information, such as the start date, class description, and so on (*Figure 20-33*).

FIGURE 20-33

The List view for the Customers table indicates that Donald teaches four classes. Thanks to the lookup that binds the Teachers_Classes records to the Classes table, you can see the name of each class. However, other information is off limits, because it's part of the Classes table, not the Teachers_Classes table.

There's no way to solve this problem by using the Related Items control, because you can't control what data it shows. However, there are two approaches that work around this problem:

- **Use the Subview control.** The Subview control is the web app equivalent of the Subform control (page 455). It shows another view of your choice, *inside* the current view, and with the filtering criteria you choose.

- **Create a Popup.** As you've already seen (page 715), a popup is a view that appears on top of your current view, temporarily obscuring it. To show a popup view, you need to create a macro.

Either way, you follow essentially the same steps. First, you create a query that fetches all the data you want to display (not just the limited details that the Related Items control shows on its own). Second, you create a view that uses your query. Third, you show your view as a popup or with the help of the Subview control. This example uses the popup approach, which requires slightly more work but provides a nicer viewing experience.

CREATING A QUERY TO GET RELATED DATA

The first step is to create a query that gets the data you need. This query needs two join two tables: the junction table (like Teachers_Classes) and the table on the other side of the relationship (Classes). You use the Teachers_Classes table to get the TeacherID field, and you use the TeacherID field to filter out the classes that belong to a specific teacher. Then, you use the Classes table to get the class data that you want to show.

Creating a query like this is a quick bit of work. Just choose Home→Create→ Advanced→Query, add the two tables you need, and choose the fields you want to show (*Figure 20-34*). Don't worry about the filter criteria yet—that part will be set by your view. Instead, save your query with a name that communicates its role (like ClassesByTeacher).

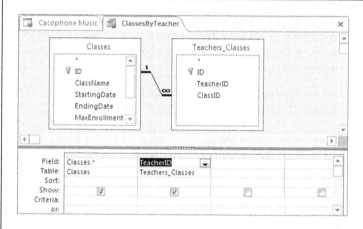

FIGURE 20-34

This straightforward query links the Teachers_Classes table to the Classes table in order to get the class information.

CREATING A VIEW FOR YOUR QUERY

The next step is to build a view that uses this query, so you can show your data when you need it. You don't want this view to be linked to any of the tables in the navigation menu, so you should create it using the Home→Create→Advanced→List View command.

Initially, your view is empty, but you can quickly attach it to your query (*Figure 20-35*). After that it's simply a matter of dragging the fields you want to show from the Field List pane onto your new view, and arranging them. Save your view with a name that matches the query (like ClassesByTeacherView).

FIGURE 20-35

To set the data for a new view, click the outer box that wraps around the empty view, and then click the Data icon. You can choose your newly created query from the Record Source list.

Now it's time to return to the original view that started this odyssey. In this example, it's the Customers List view. Delete the Related Items control, so you have room to implement your improved solution.

You can then put your newly created view to work in a Subview control or using a popup window, as explained in the next section.

■ SHOWING YOUR VIEW IN A POPUP

To show your view, you need two ingredients that work together: a button and a macro. The button sits on your form, waiting for someone to click it. When it's clicked, the button triggers your macro, which opens a popup window and shows ClassesByTeacherView.

Adding a button is easy: it's one of the small set of controls you can find in the View | Design→Controls section of the ribbon. Once you've added the button, click the tiny Actions icon to show the events you can react to. In the case of a button, there's just one: the On Click event that fires when the button is clicked (*Figure 20-36*).

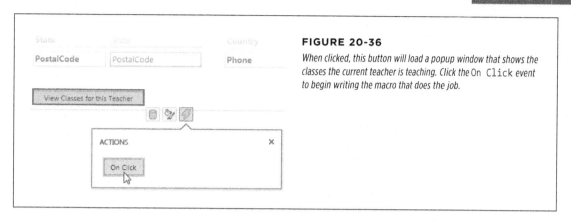

FIGURE 20-36

When clicked, this button will load a popup window that shows the classes the current teacher is teaching. Click the On Click event to begin writing the macro that does the job.

The final step is to create the macro that shows the popup window. Creating a macro in a web app is identical to creating one in a desktop database, except you have far fewer commands to work with. In this case, you need to use the OpenPopup command, and specify two arguments. The first argument is View, the view that you want to open (in this case, that's ClassesByTeacherView). The second argument is Where, which sets a filter condition that cuts the results down to just the matching records. What's needed here is an expression that matches the current teacher ID (provided by the ID field) with the TeacherID that's stored in the Teachers_Classes table and returned by the ClassesByTeacher query. Here's the expression that does the trick:

```
TeacherID=ID
```

Figure 20-37 shows the finished macro.

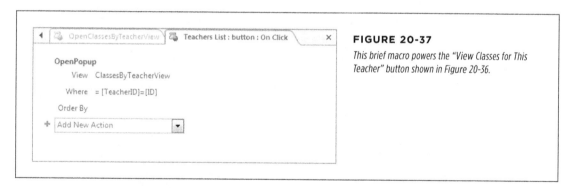

FIGURE 20-37

This brief macro powers the "View Classes for This Teacher" button shown in Figure 20-36.

This example is notable because it takes you through all the features of a web app. You create a custom query that's shown in a custom view, and you call that custom view into action with a macro. The end result is a polished experience, and a decent impersonation of an Access database in a browser.

NOTE This example suffers from one limitation. Because of the join, SharePoint won't let you edit the class information. If you need to make changes, you need to go directly to the Class table and use one of its views.

Opening Up Your Database to the World

At the beginning of this chapter, you learned that one of the advantages of the web app model is that it uses a standard SQL Server database, which means custom written programs and all-purpose reporting tools can connect directly to your database. Now that you've reached the end of your web app exploration, one question remains: how do you do it?

To let other programs talk to your database, you need to take two steps. First, you need to tell SharePoint that it should allow this sort of direct connection. (Otherwise, it will refuse to let anyone talk to the database, unless they go through the web app.) Second, you need to get the connection details that will tell that other piece of software how to find your database on the Internet.

You can take care of both details by choosing File→Info and clicking the big Manage button. It pops open a large menu of options (*Figure 20-38*).

First you need to decide whether you want to allow people to connect to your SQL Server database from any computer or just from the current computer (where you're working right now). Depending on your choice, choose either From My Location or From Any Location in the menu.

Next, you need to allow connections. You can tell SharePoint to allow read-only connections (which let you see data but not make changes) by clicking Enable Read-Only Connection. Or, you can tell SharePoint to allow full connections that can read *and* change data by clicking Enable Read-Write Connection.

Now you need to collect the connection information. Choose either View Read Only-Connection Information or View Read-Write Connection Information to open a new window that has all the information a SQL Server expert needs, including the server's network address, the database name, and the user name password. All of these details are computer-generated, so you'll need to copy the strings of gibberish-like characters to a text file or email message.

If at some point you decide to lock down your database, you can choose Disable All Connections. Or, if you want to continue allowing connections but you want to generate new passwords, so no one can gain access to your database with the old information, click either Reset Read-Only Connection Password or Reset Read-Write Connection Password.

Connections
Currently, connections are enabled to your application.

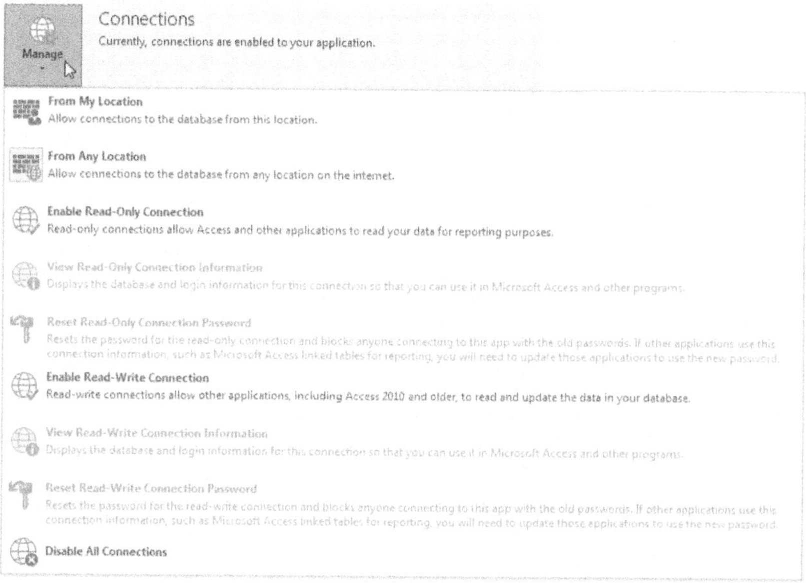

Manage

 From My Location
Allow connections to the database from this location.

 From Any Location
Allow connections to the database from any location on the internet.

 Enable Read-Only Connection
Read-only connections allow Access and other applications to read your data for reporting purposes.

 View Read-Only Connection Information
Displays the database and login information for this connection so that you can use it in Microsoft Access and other programs.

 Reset Read-Only Connection Password
Resets the password for the read-only connection and blocks anyone connecting to this app with the old passwords. If other applications use this connection information, such as Microsoft Access linked tables for reporting, you will need to update those applications to use the new password.

 Enable Read-Write Connection
Read-write connections allow other applications, including Access 2010 and older, to read and update the data in your database.

 View Read-Write Connection Information
Displays the database and login information for this connection so that you can use it in Microsoft Access and other programs.

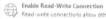 Reset Read-Write Connection Password
Resets the password for the read-write connection and blocks anyone connecting to this app with the old passwords. If other applications use this connection information, such as Microsoft Access linked tables for reporting, you will need to update those applications to use the new password.

 **Disable All Connections**

FIGURE 20-38

*The Manage button has
a slew of options that let
you control who can talk
directly to your SQL Server
database.*

Linking Access to SQL Server

A s you probably know, Access isn't the only game in town. SQL Server is Microsoft's *other* relational database system. And while Access is known as a friendly desktop database and a great tool for quickly building small-business solutions, SQL Server is the high-powered (and massively complex) software that you'll find powering the back end of an e-commerce shop or tracking financial records at a multinational bank.

Most of the time, Access and SQL Server stand on opposite sides of the room. People and businesses choose one or the other, depending on their needs, skills, and time constraints. If Access meets your needs, you'll find that it's the quickest, easiest way to create a database and get on with your life. Not only is Access easy to set up (it's a regular Windows application, after all), it bundles together features like reports and forms in one place. If you were to use a SQL Server database, you'd need to use another tool to view and edit your data. Or—more commonly—you'd need a programmer to create a custom program that does those tasks. (Flip back to page 5 for more details about the difference between client-side databases and server-side databases.)

Despite their differences, Access and SQL Server can work together. In fact, this combination gives you the best of both worlds. You get to use a supremely reliable database engine (that's SQL Server), without giving up the friendly user interface that makes it easy to get things done (that's Access). Best of all, you can start using a free version of SQL Server so you don't need to shell out a single cent.

How Access and SQL Server Can Work Together

The magic that allows Access and SQL Server to interact is an Access feature called *linking*. The idea behind linking is simple: your data lives in SQL Server, but you have the opportunity to look at it and manipulate it in Access.

There are two common reasons that you might decide to use linking with SQL Server:

- Your company has some data in SQL Server, and you want to make use of it in Access. For example, maybe you're building a quick-and-dirty project management tool in Access, and you want to get a list of all the people in your company from a central SQL Server database. Or maybe your company has a SQL Server database with all the data, and you just want to use Access's handy reporting tools to print it up.

- You want to replace your Access database with a SQL Server solution. Usually, you'll go this route because you have a database that exceeds the multiuser guidelines set out on page 641—either there are too many people trying to edit records at once, or you need to store a ridiculous amount of data. The basic strategy in this situation is to move all your data to SQL Server, but to connect to SQL Server *through Access*. That way, you can keep using your favorite Access queries, forms, and reports. The people using your database don't even need to realize that SQL Server is involved at all.

In this chapter, you'll learn enough to use both approaches. The second option is the most ambitious—used properly, it gives Access superpowers, with Access acting as the front end for a massive database that would ordinarily be beyond its abilities to manage.

However, there's a minor problem. Microsoft has recently reduced its focus on the integration between Access and SQL Server. That's because Microsoft believes that the best and easiest way to upsize an Access database is to replace it with a web app, as described in Chapter 20. Microsoft has even gone so far as to remove some of the conveniences that made it easy for Access and SQL Server to work together in previous versions of Access (see the box on page 728 for more about that). However, if you're not put off by the prospect of a little extra work, Access and SQL Server can still get along quite nicely. In fact, many companies and organizations depend on this feature to run their everyday business.

The Death of the Access Data Project

In previous versions of Access, SQL Server fans could use an innovative feature called Access Data Projects (ADPs). An ADP is a special type of Access project that can connect to a SQL Server database. When you open a table in an ADP, Access fetches the records from the SQL Server database. And when you make a change to a record, Access updates the data in SQL Server. In this respect, ADPs are just like the table-linking feature you'll use in this chapter.

The key difference is that ADPs let you *manage* a SQL Server database. Using an ADP, you could create SQL Server tables and change their design, all from right inside Access. Linked tables don't give you that power. Instead, you need to create your tables, using a SQL Server management tool. Only then can you use them in Access.

Sadly, Microsoft has completely removed the ADP feature from Access 2013. You can't even open old ADP project files. Instead, if you want to use an ADP with Access 2013, you need to switch to the linked table approach by following a tedious migration strategy: First, create a new database in Access 2010 or 2007.

Add the SQL Server tables that you need to use as linked tables in this new database. Then, import your other database objects (like forms and reports) into that file, using the Access import feature (page 797).

Along with the removal of the ADP feature, Microsoft has also cut out another convenience—the SQL Server upsizing wizard. In previous versions of Access, this wizard could analyze an ordinary Access database and move its tables and data to SQL Server. (Oddly enough, Microsoft still includes an upsizing feature for SharePoint lists, as you'll see on page 783.) However, there's a workaround: you can use a free utility called the Microsoft SQL Server Migration Assistant for Access, which does the same job. You'll try it out on page 758.

The bottom line is: Access and SQL Server still pair up nicely, and once you've set up linked tables, you can use them just as easily as an Access database. But before you get to that point, you'll need to spend some additional time getting comfortable with SQL Server's management utilities.

Should You Switch to SQL Server?

In Chapter 19, you learned how to share your prized database with other people. For some, this is Access paradise. Teams of people can collaborate, small businesses can take care of day-to-day workflow, and everyone can work happily ever after. But if you make serious demands on your database—for example, you want it to store millions of records or serve hundreds of people—sharing your database file on a network is a recipe for big-time headaches.

There's no absolute rule that decides who can use Access's built-in sharing feature successfully and who can't. You find extremes—a Fortune 500 company with thousands of workers probably can't use Access sharing, while a five-person interior design team won't face any problems. Successful sharing depends on a number of factors: how many people need to make changes at once, how extensive their changes tend to be, how long they keep their records in Edit mode, and how much data you're storing (for example, ginormous Long Text and Attachment fields are much harder to manage in a multiuser database than basic text and number fields).

Some factors are beyond the control of Access—like a slow or unreliable company network that can derail database sharing. Page 641 has some good guidelines that describe when sharing may fall short. However, if you're setting up an Access database for a small business, you may need to test out database sharing yourself.

If you decide to use database sharing, some typical symptoms will alert you if it's not working out. Here are some key danger signs:

- **Your edits often overlap with someone else's**. In this situation, Access keeps asking you what to do about the conflict (page 660). This problem is one of the most common, and while it won't crash your database, conflicting edits can lead to legitimate changes getting blown out by someone else's work.

- **You can't edit the records you want**. This problem occurs when Access uses *locks* (page 663) to prevent simultaneous changes. Locks let Access dodge the overlapping edit problem but at a price: Every other process that uses the record grinds to a halt. Again, this occurrence isn't dangerous—just a triple-aspirin aggravation.

- **Data gets corrupted**. This occurrence is both the least common and the most serious. But even though it's rare (and it gets rarer with each new release of Access), it can still happen. You'll know you have a problem when garbled data appears in a field, or Access gives you a bizarre error message (like "too many indexes") when you try to open a database object. Page 666 explains the problem and gives some safety tips.

> **NOTE** Data corruption can happen through no fault of Access. For example, if Zoe loses her network connection while she's in the middle of saving a change, Access can leave the shared database in an inconsistent state. The only way that you can prevent problems like these is to have a powerful database program running on the server that does all the work. That's the idea behind SQL Server. When you use SQL Server, no one changes the database directly. Instead, people make polite requests to the always-running SQL Server engine, which then does the work in a safe and controlled manner.

If you run into any of these problems, you may want to consider combining Access with a high-powered server-side database product like SQL Server. Using SQL Server obviously adds more complexity (meaning you'll spend more time setting up your system and making sure it's running properly), but it gives you ironclad support for sharing data safely and efficiently.

The Top Reasons to Switch to SQL Server

You have a lot of reasons to like SQL Server. But when diehard Access fans switch over, they usually have one of the following reasons in mind:

- **Lots and lots of people**. As you've learned, Access doesn't do so well if you need to share one database file with a few hundred people.

- **Lots and lots of data**. Access doesn't let you make a database bigger than 2 GB (gigabytes). The full version of SQL Server lets you create databases that swallow entire hard drives whole.

- **Performance**. As your database grows, you'll probably find that it doesn't retrieve your data quite as speedily as it used to. Although indexes can help to a certain extent (see page 135), SQL Server is able to do much more. It keeps recently used information in a vast pool of memory and doles that information out to whomever needs it. This technique alone saves oodles of time.

- **Real security**. Access doesn't offer a fine-grained security model that lets you lock specific people out of specific database objects. (It used to, but Microsoft pulled that feature out of Access 2007 because it wasn't secure

enough.) But SQL Server has bulletproof security that can be as fine-grained as you want.

- **Transactions**. In complex database systems, many tasks consist of several separate database operations that happen one after the other. For example, a money transfer of $500 involves two correlated actions—one account gets a $500 credit, and the other gets a $500 debit. SQL Server lets you put this sequence of steps in a *transaction,* which ensures that if any one of these actions fails, the whole shebang is canceled. In other words, even if lightning strikes and your server reboots in the middle of its work, SQL Server can restore the system to the moment just before the account transfer (and you'll never wind up with $500 winking out of existence).

Although these features are great, most of them are beyond the scope of this book. To learn more, you need to track down a dedicated book about SQL Server. One good choice is *Beginning Microsoft SQL Server 2012 Programming* (Paul Atkinson and Robert Vieira, Wrox). (Don't be put off by the word "programming," because this book covers the essentials of database design, optimization, and maintenance.)

How Access and SQL Server Work Together

Before you prance into the land of SQL Server, you need to know a little bit more about how it works. *Figure 21-1* shows how SQL Server and Access interact. In this example, several people are using the SQL Server database at once, each with a separate copy of Access to help them out.

> **NOTE** This is actually how *any* server-side database works, including competing database products like Oracle and DB2. However, other server-side databases don't have the nifty Access integration that you'll learn about in this chapter, so clients need to use another front-end (usually, a custom-built application).

This figure just may look familiar—after all, this is more or less the same way that database sharing works. Each person gets a copy of the front end with the forms and reports, and the back end (which actually stores the data) is placed on another computer (the server) and made available to all.

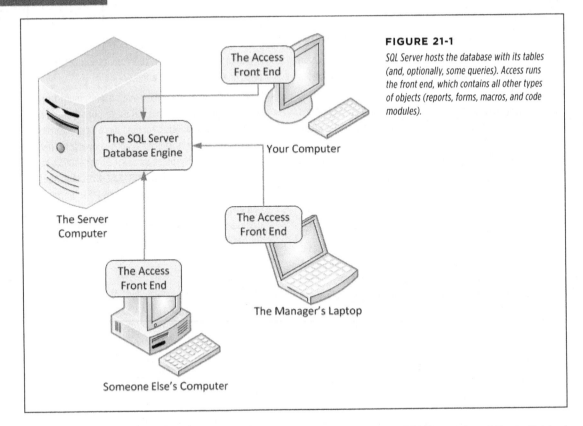

FIGURE 21-1

SQL Server hosts the database with its tables (and, optionally, some queries). Access runs the front end, which contains all other types of objects (reports, forms, macros, and code modules).

The Access Front End

The SQL Server Database Engine

Your Computer

The Server Computer

The Access Front End

The Manager's Laptop

The Access Front End

Someone Else's Computer

However, there's also a significant difference here. In SQL Server Land, the individual front ends do less work. Instead of modifying the database on their own, they contact SQL Server (which is really just a program that runs in the background on the server computer). Essentially, you've given Access a demotion. It's now responsible for eye candy, macros, and printouts, but it doesn't do the heavy lifting (like inserting, updating, and deleting records) anymore.

A Cheaper SQL Server

At this point, you're probably wondering how much that part in the center of *Figure 21-1*—the SQL Server database engine—actually costs. Microsoft sets the price using a complex licensing scheme that ratchets up the cost depending on how many people use the database at once. Usually, it runs into thousands of dollars, and it's not uncommon for a big business to shell out $20,000 or more.

But before you skip this chapter in disgust, there's something you should know: A completely *free* version of SQL Server is out there waiting for you. Amazingly enough, it's almost as powerful as the one that costs thousands of dollars and requires you to pledge your first-born child to Microsoft.

This version is called *SQL Server Express*, and you'll learn how to download and install it in the next section. If you compare it with the full version of SQL Server, you'll find it has three limitations:

- **It supports just one CPU (computer processor)**. More CPUs make for more powerful computers, and this limit prevents SQL Server Express from being quite as powerful as its big non-Express brother.

- **It can use only 1 GB of RAM memory**. If your server has more, use it for something else.

- **Each database you create tops out at 10 GB**. No problem here—Access itself tops out at 2 GB database files. If you avoid storing pictures and other large content in the database, you'll be good for a while.

What's more noteworthy is all the stuff that *isn't* left out. SQL Server Express is a full-fledged version of SQL Server, with exactly the same high-powered engine under the hood. If you need to upsize your Access database, it's a great deal.

NOTE Everything you learn in this chapter about Access and SQL Server Express also applies to the full version of SQL Server.

FREQUENTLY ASKED QUESTIONS

Can You Trust Microsoft?

Why would Microsoft give anything away for free?

Savvy computer users are suspicious of anything that seems too good to be true. They're worried that Microsoft's SQL Server deal may be a crafty bait-and-switch tactic—in other words, just enough to entice you to use SQL Server but not enough to meet your needs.

Fortunately, you have no reason to worry. If you decide to use SQL Server Express, you can stick with it happily for years without ever finding a reason to upgrade to the retail version.

So why does Microsoft offer a product they can't make any money on? It's simple—they're after the big fish. They know that a small company may start out with SQL Server Express and then grow into a large enterprise that's happy to pay the extra money to get a version that's even more powerful. This is particularly true if that company is using SQL Server to power a so-called web application (an online shopping site, for example). If that website becomes the next eBay, the company running it will need some serious database horsepower (like a server computer that has multiple CPUs and a ton of memory). To support this hardware, they'll need the full version of SQL Server.

Finally, offering a free version of SQL Server helps Microsoft by enticing more people to design fancy database systems using SQL Server. A techie may come to know and love SQL Server Express, and then recommend the full version to a deep-pocketed company.

■ Getting Started with SQL Server Express

Before you can start using SQL Server Express, you need to install it. This process is long and it involves downloading some very big files—a typical install requires a whopping 1 GB download.

If you plan to run SQL Server Express on a server computer and share it with a bunch of people, the setup process can be a bit challenging. Simply installing SQL Server Express isn't enough; you also need to configure it so other people can access it over a network, and then to grant these people permission to use specific databases. The following sections provide a basic overview of the steps. If your goal is to experiment with SQL Server and practice your Access upsizing skills, this chapter is quite possibly all the information you need to get started. But if you're trying to set up a *production server*—that is, an instance of SQL Server that hosts real data and runs a real application on a company network—get a skilled network administrator to help you out.

NOTE You may not need to install SQL Server. Perhaps you work in a company that already has a SQL Server database up and running, and you just want to use Access to view, edit, or analyze that data. In this case, you can save some time by jumping straight to page 752, where you'll learn to connect Access to an existing SQL Server database.

Preparing for SQL Server Express

You install SQL Server on the computer where you plan to place the shared database. Typically, this is a computer on the network that no one uses for anything else. (If someone's using the computer, there's the risk that they'll shut it down, restart it, tie it up with other work, or do something else that will affect everyone's ability to get the information they need.) You *don't* need to install SQL Server on the computers that run the Access front end, although obviously they all need to have a copy of Access (or the Access runtime; see page 656).

However, if you're still in the process of designing and fine-tuning your database, you may decide to try it on your own computer first. In that case, install SQL Server on your computer. Then, when you're ready to start sharing, install SQL Server on the server computer and move your database there. In fact, if you're new to SQL Server, it's probably best if you try it on your computer *first*. That's because you need to tweak a few finicky settings to let other people access SQL Server from other computers. You'll probably prefer to see how everything works before you start messing around with those details.

The system requirements for SQL Server are pretty modest. (Shockingly enough, most of the requirements are less stringent than the system requirements for running Access.) You can find the exact specifications at *http://tinyurl.com/aflkq8*. You'll find that any relatively modern computer can run SQL Server, but you should need to make sure your operating system has the latest updates and service packs.

To find out which service packs are installed on your computer in Windows 7, click Start and then, in the right-hand column, right-click Computer and choose Properties. A window appears with system information (*Figure 21-2*). Windows 8 makes you work a bit harder. In the Start screen, move to the bottom-right corner and click the Search button. Then, type "system info" in the search box, and click the System Information icon when it appears.

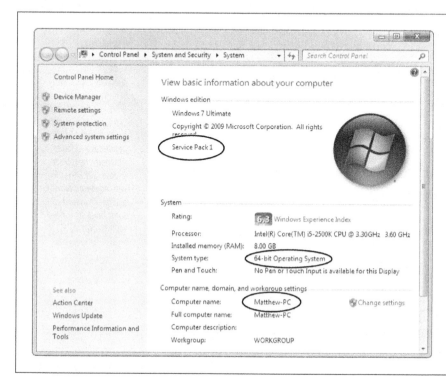

FIGURE 21-2

This Windows 7 computer has Service Pack 1 installed, so it's ready for SQL Server Express. This window also shows other important details, such as whether your version of Windows is 32-bit or 64-bit, and what name your computer has on the network. You'll use this information later in the setup process.

Downloading SQL Server Express

Before you begin installing SQL Server Express, clear your schedule and grab a coffee. Both the download and the installation can take considerable time.

Here's what you need to do first:

1. **Open your favorite browser and go to the SQL Server Express website at** ***http://tinyurl.com/sql2012express.***

   You arrive at a web page that describes SQL Server Express and lets you install it.

2. **Click the red "Download SQL Server 2012 Express" button.**

   Microsoft gives you the choice of several different packages (*Figure 21-3*). You can install just the database engine, just the management tools, or a combination.

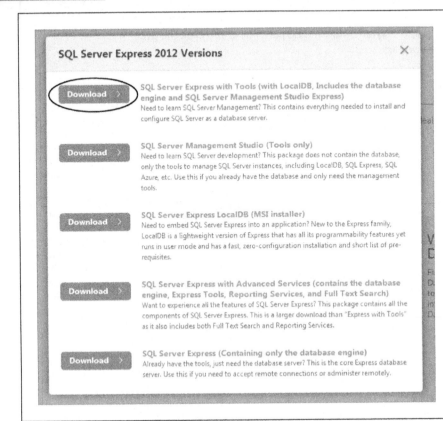

FIGURE 21-3

You can download SQL Server Express in several different packages. All of them are free, but the package you choose depends on the tools you need. The best choice is usually "SQL Server Express with Tools," which gives you the database and the management tools you need to create databases and tables. Alternatively, you can choose "SQL Server Express with Advanced Tools" for a larger download with some more specialized tools thrown in.

3. **Click the Download button next to the package you want to install.** If you aren't sure, click the first button, "SQL Server Express with Tools."

   Next, you'll see a page that asks you to pick the type of operating system you're using (32-bit or 64-bit) and the language.

4. **Next to the appropriate version of Windows, choose the language for your version of SQL Server.**

   For example, pick English from the 64-bit list if you're installing SQL Server on a 64-bit version of Windows. If you're not sure what type of operating system you're running, you can find out by reviewing your system properties (*Figure 21-2*).

5. **Click the Download link.**

   If you're using Chrome or Firefox, your browser begins downloading the giant installation file. Put it somewhere where you can easily find it later (your desktop, for example).

If you're using Internet Explorer, it will ask you to install a specialized download manager (*Figure 21-4*). This tool supports pausing and restarting, so if you don't get the chance to download the entire file in one go, you can restart your computer and pick up where you left off later on.

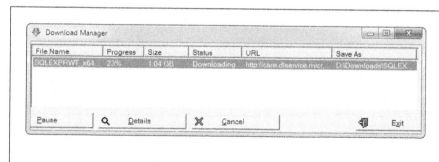

FIGURE 21-4

Here, the Microsoft Download Manager has downloaded 23% of the 1 GB installation file. When it finishes, the Pause button becomes a Launch button that lets you start the setup.

Installing SQL Server Express

When the download is complete, you're ready to run the SQL Server Express setup. But you'll face more than a few questions on the way. Here's how to navigate the occasionally cryptic setup wizard:

1. **Double-click the downloaded setup file to run it. Or, if you used the Download Manager, just click the Launch button.**

   If you're having trouble finding the setup file, look for a file with a name like SQLEXPRWT_x64_ENU.exe (that translates to SQL Server Express, with tools, 64-bit, English edition, if you're curious).

   Once the setup process finishes initializing, you'll see the SQL Server Installation Center window (*Figure 21-5*).

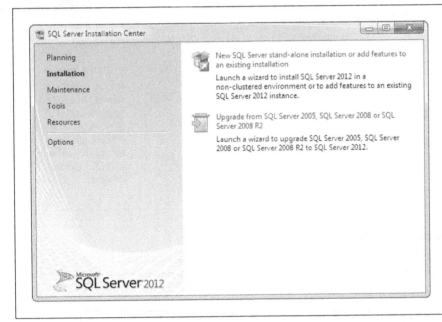

FIGURE 21-5

The Installation Center lets you install SQL Server for the first time (which is what you want to do), upgrade from an older version of SQL Server, or check for updates for an existing installation.

2. **Click the first link: "New SQL Server stand-alone installation."**

   After a short delay, a setup wizard appears, ready to take you through the rest of the process.

3. **Turn on the "I accept the license terms" checkbox and click Next to start the installation.**

   The license agreement contains the standard computer legalese, restricting you from making unauthorized copies of the software, hacking it, and generally just getting into trouble.

   After you agree, the setup wizard does some work and then asks you to pick what features you want to install.

4. **There's no need to change any settings in this step. Click Next to keep going.**

   Ordinarily, the setup installs everything, which is the safest choice. However, if you feel an urge to customize, you can remove features by clearing the corresponding checkbox—at the risk of leaving out something SQL Server might need.

   You can also use this step to change the installation folder for SQL Server, but you're best off leaving this option alone as well. SQL Server can pick a perfectly good home for itself on its own.

The next step asks you to pick an *instance name* for your installation of SQL Server (*Figure 21-6*).

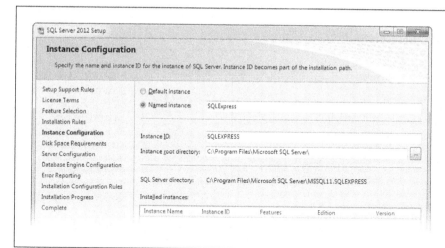

FIGURE 21-6

The instance name is the name that you use when you connect to this installation of SQL Server. Thanks to instance names, the same computer can run several different copies (or instances) of SQL Server, while keeping them completely separate. Here, the instance name is SQLExpress, which is the most common choice.

5. **Click Next to continue with the instance name SQLExpress.**

The instance name you choose isn't important, as long as you remember to use it when you connect to SQL Server. The standard value, SQLExpress, is easy to remember. Alternatively, you can choose the "Default instance" option, in which case your SQL Server installation won't use an instance name at all, and people can connect to it by using only the name of the computer where it's installed. (That's how the full-fledged, non-Express version of SQL Server is usually configured.)

The next step asks you to configure two SQL services (*Figure 21-7*).

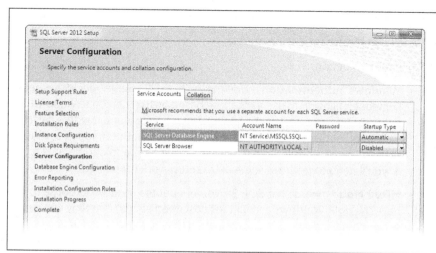

FIGURE 21-7

The SQL Server Database Engine service runs quietly in the background of the computer, doing all the database work. Without it, your database won't work. The SQL Server Browser service lets people on other computers connect to a SQL Server database.

6. **If you want to let other people access your database over the network, change the Startup Type of the SQL Server Browser to Automatic. Click Next.**

The next step asks you to choose the security settings for SQL Server (*Figure 21-8*).

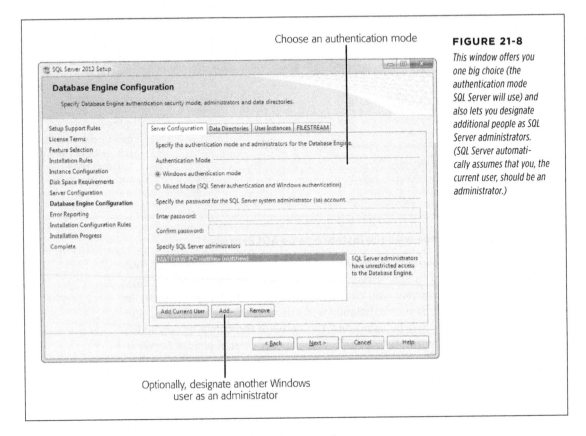

Choose an authentication mode

FIGURE 21-8

This window offers you one big choice (the authentication mode SQL Server will use) and also lets you designate additional people as SQL Server administrators. (SQL Server automatically assumes that you, the current user, should be an administrator.)

Optionally, designate another Windows user as an administrator

7. **Choose your authentication mode.**

You have two options:

- **Windows authentication** mode means that SQL Server decides whether someone's allowed to use a database based on that person's Windows user account. This approach is the best and most secure, and it works perfectly well if you're the only person using the database. But if you're setting up SQL Server on a server and you want a crowd of people to be able to use it, you'll need to perform some extra setup work (page 741).

- **Mixed Mode** means that SQL Server lets people use the database if they have the right Windows account (as described above) *or* if they can supply a user name and password combination that you've defined. If you choose Mixed Mode, you need to supply a password for a special SQL Server account known as *sa* (system administrator). Anyone who logs in with this user name and password is given complete control of every database on the server. Mixed Mode saves you some configuration hassle, but it's much less secure. (For one thing, you need to pass this information—the user name and password you want people to use—around the office.)

8. **Click Next to continue.**

   The last question the setup wizard asks is whether you want to have SQL Server automatically send error reports to Microsoft. No, the company isn't offering to help you out. This feature is designed solely to help Microsoft improve future versions of SQL Server by determining what problems are commonly occurring. It's entirely up to you whether to switch this setting on.

9. **Click Next.**

   The setup wizard continues its work, without asking for any more input from you.

10. **Click Close to exit the setup program.**

    If you're installing SQL Server on your computer, you can start using it as soon as the setup wizard finishes its work. Jump ahead to page 742 to carry on.

    If you're installing SQL Server on a server computer, you still have more setup steps to complete. The next section has the details.

Putting SQL Server on the Network

When you first install SQL Server, it's usable only from the current computer—that is, other computers can't log into the server and use any of its databases.

At first glance, this appears to defeat the whole purpose of using SQL Server. (On second glance, it does, too.) However, Microsoft knows that if they release a product that's wide open to the rest of the world, with its hackers, crackers, and all-around computer bad guys, someone somewhere will shout at them. For that reason, SQL Server takes the safest approach—it limits itself to the current computer until you give it the go-ahead to accept outside calls.

To open up SQL Server to the outside world, you need to take a few highly technical steps. Odds are you'll need a network administrator to help you navigate this process.

First, you need to switch on the TCP/IP protocol, which gives SQL Server the *ability* to talk to other computers. Second, you need to add an exception to the Windows Firewall, which gives SQL Server the *permission* to socialize. Microsoft provides a sprawling reference for SQL Server network configuration that covers both topics at *http://tinyurl.com/sqlnetwork*. You can use the list of steps in the "Enable or Disable a Server Network Protocol" page and the "Configure a Windows Firewall for Database Engine Access" page.

Once you've made these changes, other people will finally be able to contact SQL Server and try to log in. However, the party's not on yet. SQL Server may still refuse them. That's because SQL Server won't let anyone in that it doesn't trust.

So who does SQL Server trust? Here's the lowdown:

- When you install SQL Server, you get the chance to specify one or more administrators (see *Figure 21-8*). People signed in with one of these Windows accounts are allowed to do anything to any database.

- If you configured SQL Server to use mixed mode authentication (page 740), it lets in anyone who supplies the user name *sa* and the password you specified during the install. Any person who does this gets the wide-ranging abilities of an administrator.

If you want SQL Server to trust more people, you have some extra work to do. Usually, you make sure that everyone who needs to use SQL Server belongs to a single Windows *group* (a group is a collection of users and has a descriptive name, like Guests, Administrators, DatabaseLovers, and so on). This job is a Windows setup task, so consult your network administrator to get it done.

Once you've done that, you need to tell SQL Server to trust your group. You can use several approaches to take this step, but the easiest is to use the SQL Server Management Studio tool, which you downloaded with SQL Server Express. For more information, look for a dedicated book about SQL Server administration.

> **NOTE** By this point, you're probably wondering why SQL Server makes life so difficult. The reason is because SQL Server is designed to be extremely flexible. Its security model seems ridiculously complex when you're just trying to let people use your database, but it's indispensable if you need to control exactly what different people are allowed to do.

■ Building a SQL Server Database

You've suffered through the long and grueling installation process. Now it's time to reap the rewards of your labor and create your first SQL Server database.

Although Access can use a SQL Server database, it can't create one on its own. To get the job done, you need to turn to another tool—the all-purpose utility called SQL Server Management Studio. To start it, choose All Programs→Microsoft SQL Server 2012®SQL Server Management Studio in the Start menu, or search your computer for "sql management."

When you start SQL Server Management Studio, you need to connect to your database before you can see or do anything (*Figure 21-9*). Click Connect to continue.

FIGURE 21-9

To connect to a SQL Server database, you need to supply the server name, which is the computer's network name, followed by a backslash, followed by the SQL Server instance name (page 739). Fortunately SQL Server Management Studio is smart enough to suggest the instance of SQL Server that you just installed.

The main SQL Server Management Studio window is split into two parts. On the left is a tree of database servers. You can expand this tree to see all the databases that each instance of SQL Server holds (*Figure 21-10*). On the right is the blank space where you do your work.

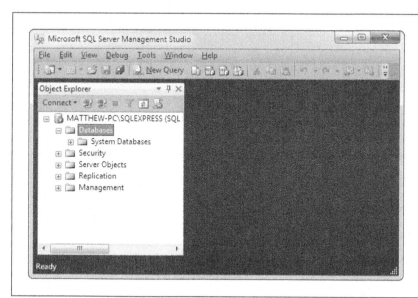

FIGURE 21-10

Right now, there's only one instance of SQL Server that SQL Server Management Studio knows about—the one you just installed. Because it's new, it doesn't contain any databases, aside from the system databases, which keep track of information the SQL Server needs to function, and are strictly off limits.

Creating a New Database

Before you get take advantage of any SQL Server goodness, you need a database. Fortunately, it takes mere seconds to get one. Here's what to do:

1. **Expand the tree on the left (by clicking the plus boxes) so you can see the Databases item, as shown in *Figure 21-10*.**

2. **Right click the Databases item and choose New Database.**

   The New Database window appears (*Figure 21-11*).

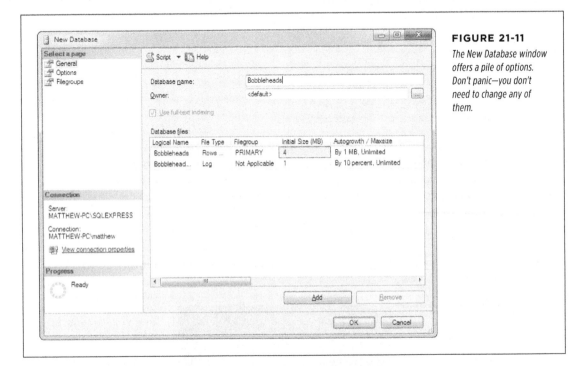

FIGURE 21-11

The New Database window offers a pile of options. Don't panic—you don't need to change any of them.

3. **In the "Database name" box, type a name for your database.**

   Good database names are like good table names—keep them short and leave out spaces and other punctuation. BoutiqueFudge or CustomerSales are sensible names, while MyData is not.

4. **Click OK.**

   If you're a SQL Server guru, you can adjust other settings, such as how big to let the database get. By default, it starts out at 4 MB but it's allowed to grow as big as you need. For most people, the default settings are the best choices.

   You'll see your new database in the tree (*Figure 21-12*).

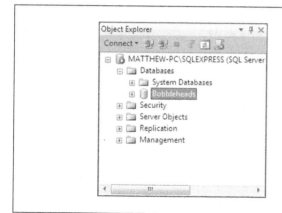

FIGURE 21-12

The new Bobbleheads database starts out its life empty.

In Access Land, it's easy to delete, move, or back up a database. All you need to do is find the corresponding .accdb file and use a file management tool like Windows Explorer to create a backup file. But SQL Server doesn't work this way. It handles databases by files behind the scenes, and stores them in a large centralized catalog, without even revealing their file names. For example, the Bobbleheads database shown in *Figure 21-12* is probably stored using two files (Bobbleheads.mdf and Bobbleheads_log.ldf) in a folder like *c:\Program Files\Microsoft SQL Server\ MSSQL11.SQLEXPRESS\MSSQL\DATA*. But knowing this location isn't much help, because you can't directly work with these files. There's no way to open them without SQL Server, and if you want to perform database management tasks like deleting, moving, or backing up a database, you need to go through SQL Server, so it can move the files *and* update its database catalog.

Adding a Table

A blank database isn't much good to anyone. If you plan to store some data, you need to add one or more tables. Here are the steps to follow in SQL Server Management Studio:

1. **Expand the item for your database by clicking the plus box next to it.**

   In the current example, that means expanding the Bobbleheads item (*Figure 21-13*). Inside, you'll see many more groups for storing different types of database objects, including tables. Right now these groups are all empty, aside from some hard-wired system information.

FIGURE 21-13

*The Tables group shows all the tables that belong to this database.
Right-click it and you'll get the option to add a new table.*

2. **Right-click the Tables group and choose New Table.**

On the right, the SQL Server table designer appears.

The SQL Server table designer is similar to the Design view you use to create tables in ordinary Access databases. You add a list of fields from top to bottom, and configure the name and data type. (SQL Server calls them columns instead of fields, but there's really no difference.)

To add a new field, you must supply three pieces of information:

- **Column Name**. A name that identifies the field (just as it does in a normal Access table). To avoid headaches, don't use spaces or special characters.

- **Data Type**. The type of information the field can store (just as it does in a normal Access table). However, the set of data types that SQL Server provides is different from the set that Access uses—more on that issue on page 748.

- **Allow Nulls**. Corresponds to the Required field property in Access (page 130). If a checkmark is in this column, you're telling SQL Server that blank values are acceptable, which means the database user can leave this field empty.

The first field you need to add is the ID field that uniquely identifies each record. In an Access database, you use the AutoNumber data type to get this result. SQL Server has a similar feature called *identity values*.

3. **Add a new field named ID. In the Data Type column, choose "int." And in the Allow Nulls column, remove the checkmark.**

ID values are stored in an *int* column, which is a numeric field type that accepts whole numbers only. Blank values are obviously not acceptable.

Once you've added the ID field, you still need to switch on the identity feature. You'll do that next, using the Column Properties tab that sits just underneath the list of fields.

4. **In the Column Properties tab, scroll down until you see the Identity Specification setting, and expand it. Then, click in the box next to "(Is Identity)" and change No to Yes (*Figure 21-14*).**

Underneath are two more identity-related settings that you can adjust if you want:

- **Identity Seed** is the starting value. This property is a sorely missed feature in Access, which always starts its AutoNumber values at 1. (You may remember the complex workaround on page 295.)

- **Identity Increment** is the amount SQL Server increases in between values. For example, if the Identity Increment is 5, you may see numbers like 1, 6, 11, 16, and so on. Of course, SQL Server is free to skip over a number for a variety of reasons, just like Access does.

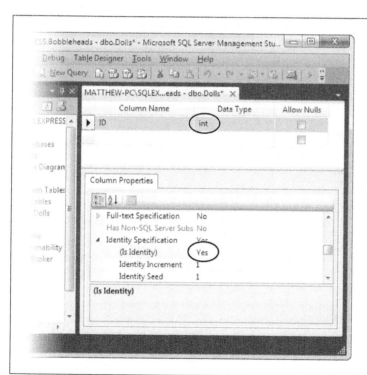

FIGURE 21-14

To create an ID field, you need to choose the int data type and turn the "(Is Identity)" property on.

5. **Add the other fields you need.**

The only trick in adding more fields is picking the right data type. SQL Server has a different set of data types than Access, although there are some close correspondences between the two. Consult Table 21-1 to figure out which SQL Server data types to use. If you want to supply a default value, go to the Column Properties box and set it in the Default Value box.

When you're finished adding fields (*Figure 21-15*), continue to the next step.

TABLE 21-1 *SQL Server and Access Data Types Compared*

IF YOU WANT THIS ACCESS DATA TYPE...	USE THIS SQL SERVER DATA TYPE
Short Text	nvarchar(255) The number in brackets indicates the maximum number of characters that the field can hold. You can increase this number all the way to 4,000 characters, which is also represented as nvarchar(MAX).
Long Text	text
Number (with a Field Size of Integer)	smallint
Number (with a Field Size of Long Integer)	int
Number (with a Field Size of Single)	real
Number (with a Field Size of Double)	float
Number (with a Field Size of Decimal)	decimal
Number (with a Field Size of Byte)	tinyint
Number (with a Field Size of ReplicationID)	uniqueidentifier
Date/Time	datetime But if you want to store just a date, use the date data type, and if you want to store just a time, use the time data type.
Currency	money
AutoNumber	int But you must turn on the "(Is Identity)" setting.
Yes/No	bit But make sure to turn off Allow Nulls and set the Default Value setting to 0 or 1, to avoid the bug explained in the box on page 749.

IF YOU WANT THIS ACCESS DATA TYPE...	USE THIS SQL SERVER DATA TYPE
Hyperlink	There's no equivalent. You must store the value as ordinary text.
Attachment	There's no equivalent. You can create a varbinary(MAX) field that holds a block of binary data, and use that to store the file you want. However, you won't have any way to edit it in Access. There are some third-party Access controls available (for a modest cost) that let you retrieve pictures from a binary field and display or edit them in a form.

NOTE SQL Server has still more data types that aren't shown in this table and that don't map directly to Access data types. However, the data types shown here are by far the most common.

TROUBLESHOOTING MOMENT

The Bizarre Bit Type Bug

There's a strange bug in the way Access deals with bit fields (the Access equivalent of a Yes/No field) that can cause mysterious problems. The most common manifestation is that Access will prevent you from editing a record, and warn that the record currently being edited by another user—even when it isn't.

Rather than attempt to diagnose this odd situation, you can avoid the problem entirely by using the bit field carefully. When you use it, *always* remove the Allows Null checkmark, and then set a default value of 0 (for False) or 1 (for True). To set the default value, scroll through the settings in the Column Properties tab until you see the "Default Value or Binding" setting, and type it in there.

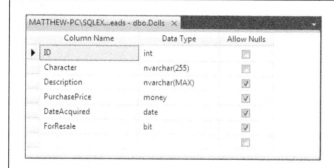

FIGURE 21-15

This example shows the familiar Dolls table from the Bobblehead database, SQL Server style.

6. **It's time to set the primary key. Right-click the ID field and choose Set Primary Key.**

   The primary key indexes your table (page 88) so individual records can be speedily retrieved.

7. Press Ctrl+S to save your table. When asked, type in a name for your table and click OK.

You may not see the table appear immediately in the tree on the left. To show it, right-click the Tables item and choose Refresh.

> **NOTE** Tables in SQL Server use a two-part naming syntax. The first part of the name is the owner of the table, and the second part is the actual table name. In most databases, the first part is *dbo*, which represents the *database owner*. Don't think too hard about this convention, because you can ignore it most of the time, and use the second part of the table name when you need to refer to the table in a query, report, or form.

SQL Server Management Studio is the place to go for all your table management. To edit a previously created table later on, simply right-click the table name in the tree and choose Design. To change a table's name or remove it from your database, right-click it and choose Rename or Delete. And to back up your data (which is always a good idea), right-click the name of the database (not an individual table) and choose Tasks→Back Up.

SQL Server Management Studio also includes a basic data-entry feature. To use it, right-click your table and choose "Edit Top 200 rows." A datasheet will appear on the right that shows the first 200 records and lets you edit them or, if you scroll to the bottom, add a new one. (The 200-row limit is there to prevent careless administrators from deciding to view and edit *all* the records in the database, which could slow down other people who are currently using the same table.)

Creating Relationships Between Tables

As you learned in Chapter 5, every respectable database has lots of table relationships. In Access, you have two speedy ways to build a relationship: use the database diagram tool, or create a lookup on a field. But in SQL Server, neither of those features is available. Instead, you need to define the relationship by hand in the design window for your table.

Here's how to do it:

1. Identify which table is the parent and which table is the child. Right-click the child table and choose Design to begin editing its structure.

For example, some versions of the Bobblehead database include both a parent table of manufacturers and a child table with bobbleheads dolls. It's always the responsibility of the child table (Dolls) to link to the parent (Manufacturers).

2. Add a field in the child table that will point to the parent table.

For example, in the Bobblehead database you would add a field to the Dolls table named ManufacturerID. This field must use the int data type (page 748), because it must match the data type that's used for the ID field in the parent.

3. Choose Table Designer→Relationships from the menu.

The Foreign Key relationships window appears, but it's currently blank.

4. **Click Add.**

This adds a new relationship. Now you need to configure it.

5. **In the list of settings on the right, click to select the "Tables and Columns Specifications" box. Then, click the ellipsis button (*Figure 21-16*).**

Now a new window appears where you can pair up the two fields that need to be linked (for example, the ManufacturerID field in the Dolls table and the ID field in the Manufacturers table).

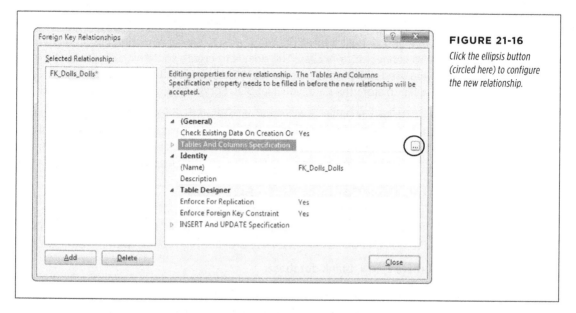

FIGURE 21-16

Click the ellipsis button (circled here) to configure the new relationship.

6. **In the list box under the heading "Primary key table," pick the parent table.**

In the Bobblehead example, that's the Manufacturers table.

7. **In the first row underneath, pick the ID field.**

You have several rows here because it's possible to create relationships based on several fields, although it's rarely done.

8. **Click OK.**

This returns you to the Foreign Key Relationships window shown in (*Figure 21-16*). Now you have the option of setting a few more settings:

- **Check Existing Data on Creation.** If you don't want to check your existing records to make sure they live up to the rules of this relationship, change this setting to No. If you don't have any data in the table yet, it doesn't matter what you choose.

- **Enforce Foreign Key Constraint.** If for some reason you don't want to enforce the rules of referential integrity (page 173), change this setting to No.

- **INSERT and UPDATE Specification.** If you want to use cascading deletes, expand this section and set the Delete Rule to Cascade, Set Null, or Set Default. Page 174 has more about these choices.

9. **Click Close.**

   Now your relationship is in place. Press Ctrl+S to save the table and make it permanent.

■ Editing SQL Server Tables in Access

Now that you've built a basic database in SQL Server Management Studio, you're ready to connect it to Access. The goal is to create something similar to the front ends you used with the split databases in Chapter 19. But instead of using a separate Access file to store the data, you'll let SQL Server take care of that responsibility.

Editing SQL Server tables in Access is easy enough, once you've set up the Access-to-SQL Server connection. However, the linking process is convoluted. As you'll see, it forces you to jump through window after window of settings, even though you rarely need to change anything. The following section leads you through the process.

Setting Up a Connection to SQL Server

Access isn't as intelligent as the SQL Server Management Studio. It can't spot your SQL Server database unless you're willing to give it detailed information about where to go and how to connect. Here are the steps you need to follow in Access:

1. **Create a new, blank database.**

   Here's where you'll create your linked tables.

2. **Choose External Data→Import & Link→ODBC Database.**

   ODBC is a standard for connecting to databases. Access can connect to database that has an *ODBC driver*, although SQL Server is the clear favorite.

   The first question Access asks is whether you want to import the data from SQL Server (in other words, create a copy of the tables inside your Access database), or create true linked tables. If you want to stay plugged in to SQL Server, so that your changes are reflected in the SQL Server database and visible to everyone else, you need to use linked tables. (For more about plain Jane imports, see Chapter 23.)

3. **Click "Link to the data source by creating a linked table" and then click OK.**

   The Select Data Source window appears. You start out at the File Data Source tab, which isn't much help, because you can't load a SQL Server database from a file.

4. **Switch to the Machine Data Source tab.**

   Here you'll see a list of preconfigured data sources (*Figure 21-17*).

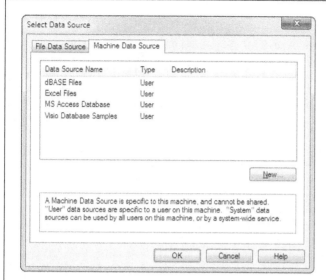

FIGURE 21-17

The Machine Data Source tab lists a few data sources, but the one you need—a connection to your new SQL Server database—isn't here. You'll need to add it yourself.

5. **Click New.**

   At this point, Access will show a warning explaining that you aren't running Access as an administrator and, for that reason, other people won't be able to use the connection you create. This isn't a problem, so click OK to carry on.

   The Create New Data Source wizard starts. The first step asks you whether you want to create a user data source (for just yourself) or a system data source (for everyone who uses that computer). But because you aren't running Access as an administrator, only the first option is available.

6. **Click Next to continue.**

   You'll see a list of drivers for different types of databases.

7. **Pick the latest SQL Server driver, which will have a name like SQL Server Native Client 11.0. Then click Next.**

   You've reached the end of the Create New Data Source wizard.

8. **Click Finish.**

   Now Access knows what driver to use when it connects to your database, but it doesn't know where to *find* your database. In the next step, you'll fill in that missing information (*Figure 21-18*).

9. **Enter a name for your connection and the server location.**

The name is what you'll see when your data source is listed in the Select Data Source window, so anything descriptive goes. The server location is the critical bit—if you aren't sure what to put there, refer to the box below.

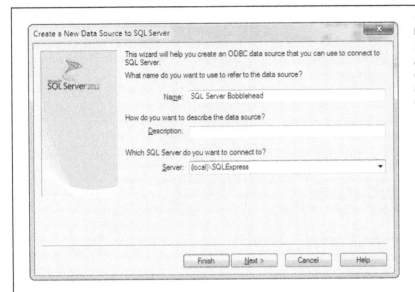

Know Your Server Name

The server name consists of the name of the computer that's running SQL Server, followed by a backslash (\), followed by *SqlExpress* (although the capitalization doesn't matter). So, if the computer that's running SQL Server is named BigServer, you'd find your database at BigServer\SqlExpress. If you're connecting to the full version of SQL Server (not the Express edition), you usually don't need the second part, so just BigServer would do. Consult with your database administrator for help.

If the SQL Server database is on your current computer (in other words, the same computer that you're using to run Access), you can use the text "(local)" as a shortcut to refer to your computer. For example, if you've installed SQL Server Express on your computer, you can connect to *(local)\SqlExpress*. And if you'd like to find out the name of your computer, refer to the computer information you saw in *Figure 21-2*.

10. **Click Next.**

    The next step asks you what security model you want to use when you log in.

11. **Keep the "With Integrated Windows Authentication" setting and click Next.**

    Now you'll see another page of settings. There's one important detail hidden here—you need to tell Access what database to use when it connects to your server.

12. **Turn on the "Change the default database to" setting. Then, pick the database you want to use from the list below.**

    In this example, that database is Bobbleheads.

13. **Click Next.**

    You'll see yet another page of settings, but this one doesn't include anything you need to change.

14. **Click Finish.**

    Access provides a summary of all the settings you chose.

15. **Click OK to continue and create the connection.**

    Now you'll end up back at the Select Data Source window, only now there's a connection for your SQL Server database there (*Figure 21-19*).

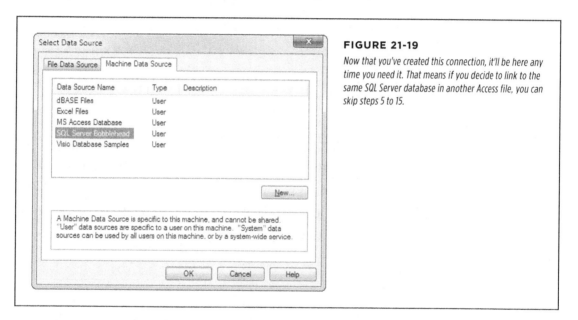

FIGURE 21-19

Now that you've created this connection, it'll be here any time you need it. That means if you decide to link to the same SQL Server database in another Access file, you can skip steps 5 to 15.

16. **Select the newly created connection to SQL Server, and click OK.**

    Access shows a list of all the tables in your SQL Server database (*Figure 21-20*). You'll see many more tables here than you've actually created, because Access lists all the automatically generated system tables (which aren't true tables at all).

FIGURE 21-20

In this long list of tables, you've only created the two at the top. You can recognize the tables you've created because they'll begin with dbo, which stands for database owner.

17. **Select the tables you want (just the ones you've created), and click OK.**

    For each table you're linking, Access will ask you to identify the unique field.

18. **Choose the ID field at the top of the list (but no other fields), and click OK.**

    Access adds each linked table to your database. You'll see them appear in the navigation pane (*Figure 21-21*).

FIGURE 21-21

These don't look like ordinary Access tables. The arrow-and-globe icon indicates that these are linked tables, and their data isn't stored in Access.

Managing Linked Tables

Now that you have your linked tables in Access, you have nearly all the options of an ordinary Access database. You can start looking at your data and editing in the datasheet by double-clicking the table. Or, you can use them to write queries and build full-featured forms and reports. The difference is that now your copy of Access is communicating with SQL Server to get the information it needs and make changes.

If other Access users need to use the SQL Server database, you can give them a copy of your Access front end. However, they'll need to be able to connect to the database from their computers, as described on page 741. If you attempt to open a linked table and Access fails to connect, it shows an error message and then asks you to type in a new server name (page 754), so you can make the connection you need.

The one thing you can't do in Access is change the design of your linked tables. (You *can* open them in Design view to see their fields and settings, but you can't make any changes.) Instead, you need to change your tables in SQL Server Management Studio, and then refresh the linked tables in Access to make sure you're seeing the latest version. To perform a refresh, right-click any one of your linked tables and choose Linked Table Manager. In the Linked Table Manager window, choose the tables you want to refresh, and click OK (*Figure 21-22*).

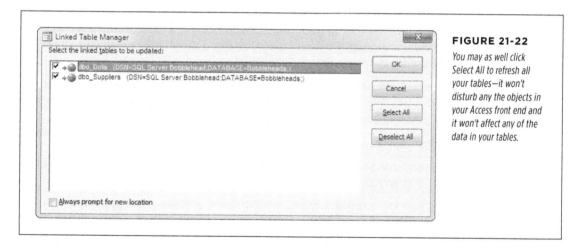

FIGURE 21-22

You may as well click Select All to refresh all your tables—it won't disturb any the objects in your Access front end and it won't affect any of the data in your tables.

TIP If you want to connect the tables to a database in a different instance of SQL Server (for example, you're moving from a locally installed version of SQL Server Express to a copy that's running on a network server, turn on the "Always prompt for new location" setting. When you perform you update, Access will show the familiar Select Data Source window where you can pick your database (page 753).

Finally, if at some point you want to disconnect from SQL Server, you can copy the data into ordinary Access tables. For example, imagine that you're using Access to create reports for last year's sales totals. In this situation, you don't need the latest and most up-to-date information, and you don't need to be able to change any of the data. By converting your linked tables to local tables, you'll be able to do your work anywhere, without having a live connection to SQL Server.

To create a local copy of a linked table, right-click the table and choose "Convert to Local Table." Or, hold down Ctrl, select as many tables as you want, then right-click and choose "Convert to Local Table" to transfer them all at once.

Migrating an Access Database to SQL Server

If you already have a thriving Access database, you don't want to be saddled with the hard work of recreating each table from scratch (not to mention the hassle of exporting all the data). Fortunately, there's a tool that can help you out. It's called the SQL Server Migration Assistant for Access (SSMA for short), and Microsoft offers it free of charge. Less fortunately, using the SSMA tool is frequently painful. Installing it is a lot of work, and navigating the awkward 80s-style interface is likely to confuse even Access pros. But SSMA does what it promises, and if you need a way to move a large number of tables, it's an indispensable tool.

Installing SSMA

You can download SSMA from *http://tinyurl.com/ssma-access*. You'll get a ZIP file that contains a setup program inside. The setup program is a standard affair—run it, choose the defaults, and you'll be all set.

However, SSMA has one extra installation requirement: it needs a license. Microsoft provides this license free of charge, but in order to get it you need to surrender a bit of personal information. Here's the quickest way to get your license:

1. **Start SSMA.**

   Search the Start menu until you find the long-winded "Microsoft SQL Server Migration Assistant for Access" entry.

   When the program starts, you'll see the License Management window (*Figure 21-23*).

2. **Click the "license registration page" link.**

   SSMA launches a new browser window where you can request your license. You'll need to sign in with a Microsoft account (the same one you use for Hotmail or Office 365). If you don't have one, you can sign up *www.live.com*.

3. **Confirm your personal information, and then click Finish.**

   Your browser then downloads a small license file.

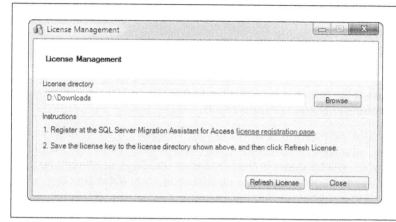

FIGURE 21-23

In order to run SSMA, you need to download a license file, and you need to tell SSMA where to find that License file. Here, it's in the d:\Downloads directory.

4. **In the License Management window, click Browse, and then find the folder that contains the license file.**

   Its name is *access-ssma.license*.

5. **Click Refresh License.**

   SSMA checks for the license. Assuming the license checks out, SSMA shows you a confirmation.

6. **Click OK to continue to the program.**

   Now that the licensing is out of the way, you can get started with the migration in the next section.

Transferring an Access Database to SQL Server

When you first start SSMA, it launches a Migration Wizard. You don't need to use the wizard, but it's the simplest way to get the job done without drowning in extra settings (and losing your way in the far-from-intuitive interface). Here are the steps that take you through it:

1. **Click Next to get started. Optionally, choose the name of your SSMA project and the folder where it should be stored.**

   The SSMA project stores the migration settings that you're about to enter. This step is helpful if you're trying out a complex import and you need several tries to get it right. (To retry the import at a later time, you simply open the SSMA project you've created.) But in most cases, you won't need to reuse the SSMA project once you've finished transferring your tables.

2. **Click Next.**

   Time to tell SSMA where to find your Access database.

3. **Click Add Database, browse to your database file, and click Open.**

You can transfer multiple Access databases at once, all to the same SQL Server, but it's easier to just do one at a time.

4. **Click Next.**

Now's your chance to choose which objects you want to transfer from the Access database.

5. **If there are some tables you don't want to transfer to SQL Server, clear the corresponding checkbox (*Figure 21-24*).**

At first, SSMA, selects all the tables in your database, which is usually what you want. Optionally, you can also convert your Access queries to SQL Server queries, which will be stored in the SQL Server database, but there's no need to do so. You don't get the option of transferring other database objects, like reports and forms, because only Access can use those.

SSMA also attempt to convert other details that go along with your table, like indexes, relationships, default values, and validation rules.

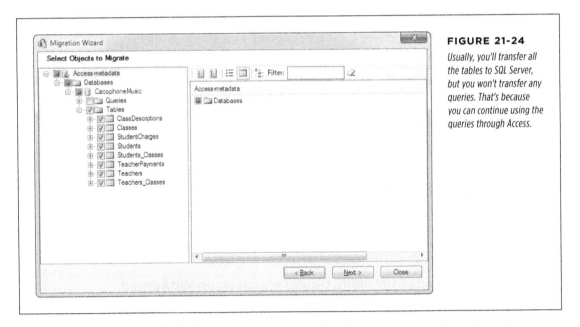

FIGURE 21-24

Usually, you'll transfer all the tables to SQL Server, but you won't transfer any queries. That's because you can continue using the queries through Access.

6. **Click Next**

Next, you need to tell SSMA where to find your instance of SQL Server (*Figure 21-25*).

7. **Enter the server name.**

For example, *(local)\SQLExpress* is the default name for a copy of SQL Server Express on the current computer. The box on page 754 explains more.

8. **In the Database box, type the name you want to use for your SQL Server database.**

You can also pick an existing database. But it's more likely that you'll choose a new database, which SSMA will then create for you.

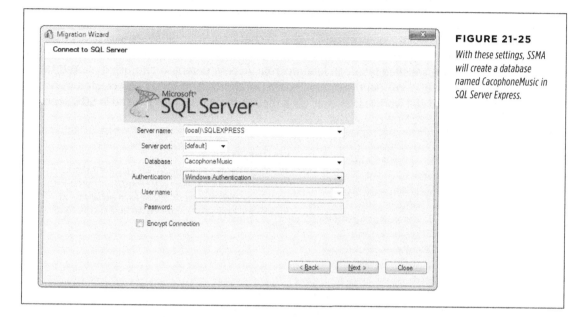

FIGURE 21-25

With these settings, SSMA will create a database named CacophoneMusic in SQL Server Express.

9. **Click Next.**

SSMA offers to change your Access database, so that the local tables become linked tables after the migration move.

10. **Turn on the "Link tables" checkbox.**

This option saves you the work of creating the linked tables by hand. SSMA is extra careful when you turn this on—it still keeps all the original tables, but it renames them. So if you import a table named Classes and opt for linked tables, your Access database will get a linked table named Classes and a backed-up copy of the ordinary table named SSMA$Classes$local. That way, you still have the original table and original data to compare against the new database. (If everything checks out, you should delete these extra tables to avoid confusion.)

11. **Click Next.**

Now SSMA starts the migration. If it encounters any problems, it reports them as it goes along. When SSMA has finished transferring the tables, it shows you a double tree view that compares the structure of the new SQL Server database (on the left) with the original Access database (on the right)

12. **Click OK.**

SSMA continues to perform some final operations.

13. **When SSMA finishes the migration, click Close.**

This returns you to the main SSMA window, where you can explore the new and old databases, or tweak the migration settings.

At this point, you'll probably want to check out your database in SQL Server Management Studio to see if there are any other adjustments you need to make. When you're satisfied, you can load up your Access database and use its linked tables (*Figure 21-26*). All the original queries, reports, and forms you created in Access should still work just as well, even though the data is now housed in SQL Server.

FIGURE 21-26

After a migration, this Access database has a batch of backup tables (they start with SSMA$), followed by the linked tables that connect to SQL Server. Underneath are the original forms and reports—untouched—which will automatically draw their data from the linked tables.

NOTE The SSMA program is packed full of options that may appeal to serious database migrators. For example, you can bypass its built-in rules and tell it exactly what SQL Server data types you want it to use for given Access data types. These features are far beyond the scope of this book, but you can learn more from the official SSMA documentation at *http://tinyurl.com/ssma-docs*.

Linking Access
to SharePoint

E ven in the most dysfunctional companies, people need to get along. Businesses
that have efficient ways to share information are more successful than those
that keep quiet. SharePoint is a Microsoft product that's explicitly designed for
this sort of office teamwork, and you'll find it at work in many blue-chip businesses.

You already met SharePoint in Chapter 20, when you learned to create Access web
apps. Web apps use a single, specialized SharePoint 2013 feature, called Access
Web Services. But Access also has a simpler and more general ability that lets you
edit SharePoint *lists*.

SharePoint users create lists whenever they need to store any sort of structured
information. For example, a manager might create a list of prioritized tasks for a
project, while a sales person might compile a list of potential customers at a sales
conference. In fact, a list is much like an Access table, but dressed up a little differently.

Here's where Access's list linking feature comes in. Using Access, you can retrieve
the data from any SharePoint list, and edit it without leaving the comfort of the Access window. Even better, you can view, analyze, and manipulate list data by using
your favorite Access tools, including queries, reports, and forms. In this chapter,
you'll learn how.

> **NOTE** Unlike the web app feature, which requires SharePoint 2013, Access's list-linking feature works with
> the free version of SharePoint (called SharePoint Foundation) and the older 2010 editions of SharePoint, as well
> as SharePoint 2013. The box on page 772 gives a closer look at the differences between web apps and list linking.

Understanding SharePoint

SharePoint is a server-based program that helps groups of people collaborate, letting them share information and documents through a centralized website.

SharePoint is a bit of an oddity: Even though it's one of the fastest-growing products in Microsoft's history, many ordinary people have never heard of it, and even its longtime fans have a difficult time describing what it actually does. Fortunately, the basic idea behind SharePoint is pretty straightforward. First, your team gets together and sets up a SharePoint website. The SharePoint site is usually hosted on a server computer on your company's network, although you can also use a third-party hosting company (like *www.fpweb.net*). As part of the setup process, you decide who's allowed to access the SharePoint site and what they're allowed to do on it.

> **NOTE** Microsoft uses thousands of SharePoint sites to coordinate its own teams, including the one that created Access.

Once your SharePoint site is set up, every team member can access it. To take a look, fire up a web browser, surf to the SharePoint site, and log in with your user name and password. You'll see a customizable home page that can include uploaded documents, recent news, and other links (*Figure 22-1*).

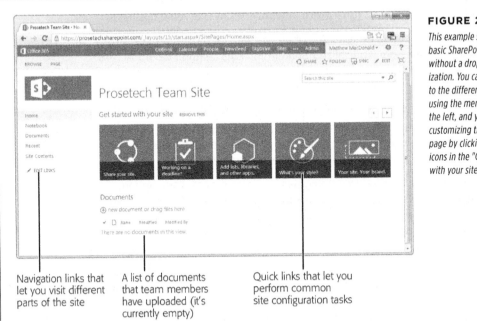

FIGURE 22-1

This example shows a basic SharePoint 2013 site without a drop of customization. You can navigate to the different areas by using the menu of links on the left, and you can start customizing the home page by clicking one of the icons in the "Get started with your site" section.

Navigation links that let you visit different parts of the site

A list of documents that team members have uploaded (it's currently empty)

Quick links that let you perform common site configuration tasks

> **NOTE** Although SharePoint 2013 and 2010 have a similar set of features for customizing a site and creating lists, the way the commands are organized and the way the pages look is drastically different. The examples in this chapter use SharePoint 2013. If you want to learn more about SharePoint's web interface, pick up a book that covers your version, like *Microsoft SharePoint 2010 Plain & Simple*, by Jonathan Lightfoot and Chris Beckett.

Customizing a SharePoint Site

A brand new SharePoint site is a rather boring thing. To personalize a brand new SharePoint 2013 site so that it better suits your business, team, or project, you can start out with the handy links in the "Get started with your site" section on the home page. Start with these three:

- **"Your site. Your brand."** Click here to set the site title, add a site description, and upload a picture for your site. This is the very least information that any SharePoint site needs to distinguish itself.

- **"What's your style?"** Click here to pick a different theme for your site. You can customize the color scheme, layout, and fonts of the theme you choose.

- **"Add lists, libraries, and other apps."** Click here to start adding SharePoint apps, the building blocks of functionality that lets your site *do* things. Clicking here is equivalent to clicking Site Contents in the navigation menu, and then choosing "add an app." You'll learn more on page 767.

Once you've done a decent bit of customization, it's time to remove the "Get started with your site" section. To do that, click the "Remove This" link next to the heading. That way it won't distract the other people who are using your site.

What You Can Do in SharePoint

Here are some things that SharePoint lets you do:

- Share Office documents (like reports you've written in Word and spreadsheets from Excel). Different people can supply edited versions, and team leaders can reject ones they don't like.

- Assign tasks to different people, and find out when they're finished.

- Keep an eye on important dates by using a team calendar.

- Post messages on a team discussion board.

- Create and edit lists to store important information (*Figure 22-2*). For example, you can use a list to store top customer complaints that need to be addressed or the food items that employees are bringing to the company potluck.

The last task is where Access fits in. Even though you can create and manage a list of information in SharePoint through your browser, you may want to *use* that list in Access. Maybe you have a form, query, or code routine that needs to take that information into account. Or perhaps you're just more comfortable editing data in the familiar Access interface.

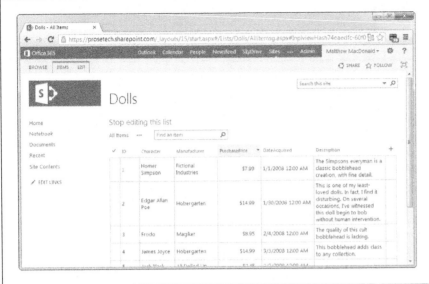

FIGURE 22-2

*This example shows a
SharePoint list that duplicates the infamous Dolls
table from the Bobblehead
database.*

A SharePoint *list* is analogous to an Access *table*. Although both names refer to
the same thing, a SharePoint list is slightly more limited than an Access table. For
example, SharePoint lists don't support the full range of Access data types, and
they're a bit clumsier when dealing with related data.

SharePoint is well suited to informal lists and ad hoc scraps of information that you
need to pass between colleagues, like a list of team tasks or a signup sheet for the
company baseball team. SharePoint is also a good way to share simply structured
data that everyone needs—think, for example, of a list of office phone numbers. Finally, SharePoint provides a great way to gather data from a large number of people.
For example, you might use it to collect expense reports that you later import into
the stricter tables of an Access database.

On the other hand, SharePoint isn't necessarily the best place to store critical business information, like customer lists, product catalogs, and invoices. If you use it for
these purposes, you'll need to live with some compromises.

Adding an App to a SharePoint Site

The first thing you should understand about a SharePoint site is that it's ridiculously
customizable. If you're the site owner, you choose what content appears on the site,
and how it's arranged.

Initially, you won't see much more than a section where site members can upload
documents. However, it won't take you long to start adding new ingredients. The
ingredients you add to a SharePoint site are called *apps*. (At least they are in

SharePoint 2013. In earlier versions, the same ingredients were usually called *web parts*.) To add an app, you first click Site Contents in the navigation menu on the left side of the home page. You'll see the Site Contents page, which lists everything the site contains, including documents, hand-crafted web pages, and the currently installed apps.

To add something new, click the first icon, named "add an app." Now you'll see a much longer list that details all the components you can add to a SharePoint site (*Figure 22-3*).

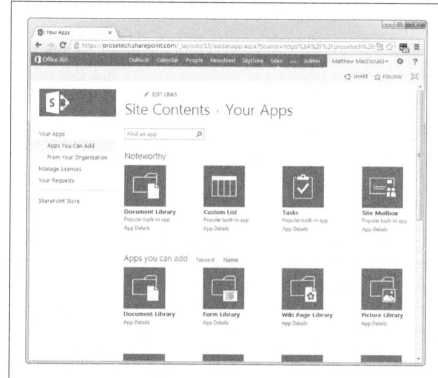

FIGURE 22-3

SharePoint sites gain features through apps—small bits of software that you can plug in at will. For example, you could add the Tasks app (shown here) to assign a list of work items to different people, or the Discussion Board app to let team members share their thoughts.

To get a taste of SharePoint apps, why not install the Tasks app, which sits at the top of the list? Here's how:

1. **Click the icon for the Tasks app.**

   SharePoint pops open a new window that lets you name your task (*Figure 22-4*).

   TIP If you want to add an app, but you're having trouble finding it, type the first part of its name (say, cal) in the "Find an app" box, and then press Enter. SharePoint will show you just the apps that match your criteria.

2. Type a name for your app.

If you plan to use a task list for everyone's tasks, a generic name like Tasks is fine. But you might also consider adding more than one copy of the Tasks app and giving each one a different name to represent a specific project (like "Maher Account Tasks" and "Office Christmas Party").

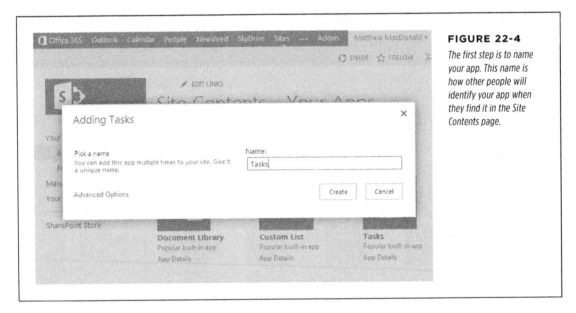

FIGURE 22-4

The first step is to name your app. This name is how other people will identify your app when they find it in the Site Contents page.

3. Optionally, click the Advanced Options link to see what else you can change.

Many apps have other useful settings, but the Tasks app lets you set just one additional detail: a detailed description of your task list.

4. Click Create.

SharePoint adds the app to your site and returns you to the Site Contents page, where you'll see it listed. You'll also see your new app in the Recent section of the navigation menu. Click either spot and you'll load up the task list (*Figure 22-5*).

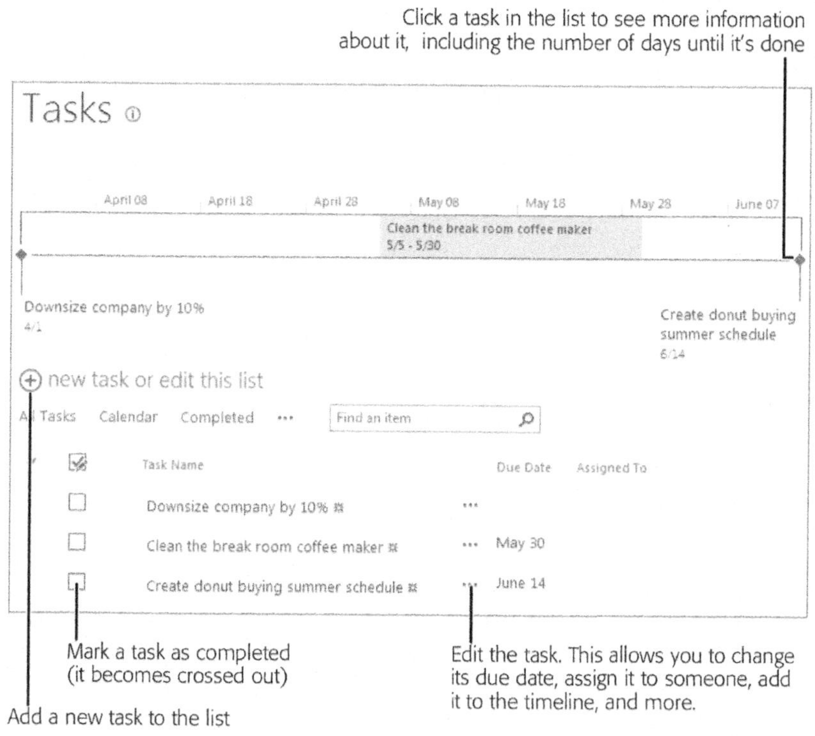

Click a task in the list to see more information
about it, including the number of days until it's done

FIGURE 22-5

FIGURE 22-5

*This task list has three
tasks. Above the task list
is a timeline—you can
add tasks here to get a
graphical representation of
how much time you have.
In this example, all three
tasks have been added to
the timeline. The middle
task ("Clean the break
room coffee maker") has
a start and end date, and
so shows up as a band
spanning 25 days.*

Tasks ⓘ

| April 08 | April 18 | April 28 | May 08 | May 18 | May 28 | June 07 |

Clean the break room coffee maker
5/5 - 5/30

Downsize company by 10%
4/1

Create donut buying
summer schedule
6/14

⊕ new task or edit this list

All Tasks   Calendar   Completed   ••• | Find an item   🔍 |

☑	Task Name		Due Date	Assigned To
☐	Downsize company by 10% ✕	•••		
☐	Clean the break room coffee maker ✕	•••	May 30	
☐	Create donut buying summer schedule ✕	•••	June 14	

Mark a task as completed
(it becomes crossed out)

Edit the task. This allows you to change
its due date, assign it to someone, add
it to the timeline, and more.

Add a new task to the list

TIP   Two of the most useful apps are the Tasks app (which lets you assign and track important jobs) and the Calendar app (which lets you schedule events). To add both these apps to a new site, complete with Quick Launch links, click Home to go to the home page, and then click the "Working on a deadline?" icon. (It appears in the "Get started with your site section" shown in *Figure 22-1*.)

5. Optionally, add a permanent link to your app in the navigation menu.

SharePoint calls this menu the Quick Launch, because it has links that let you quickly access whatever apps you deem most important. You can add your app to the Quick Launch menu by finding it in the Site Contents section and changing its settings. But here's an easier approach: click Edit Links, which appears just under your menu. This switches the menu into edit mode. In edit mode, you can remove any link (click the X next to it) and drag links around the menu to rearrange them (*Figure 22-6*). When you're finished, click the Save button under the navigation menu to make your changes permanent.

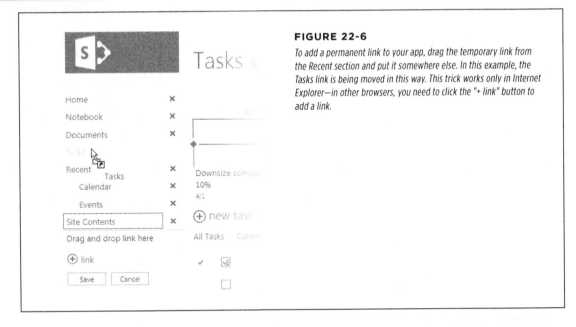

FIGURE 22-6

To add a permanent link to your app, drag the temporary link from the Recent section and put it somewhere else. In this example, the Tasks link is being moved in this way. This trick works only in Internet Explorer—in other browsers, you need to click the "+ link" button to add a link.

To remove an app you don't want, click Site Contents and hover over the app. An ellipsis (...) will appear in the top-right corner of the box that has the list information. Click the ellipsis, and SharePoint pops open a box with the full description of the app (if you wrote one in step 3) and the links that let you configure how it works (Settings) and wipe it from your site (Remove).

Five Fun Features to Try in SharePoint

The rest of this chapter focuses on the SharePoint features that work with Access—namely, lists. However, you don't need to stop your SharePoint exploration here. If you're still curious, be sure to check out the following SharePoint features:

- **Share a document**. Often, teams need to send specifications, reports, and other business documents through a review chain. SharePoint makes it easy. You've already seen the Shared Documents app that sits on the site's home page, which lets you browse shared documents and upload your own work (click the "new document" link). If you're somewhere else in the site, you can get to the Shared Document section in a hurry by clicking Documents in the navigation menu.

- **Book a meeting**. If you've added the Calendar app, you can use it to schedule a meeting. Click the Calendar link, browse to the month and day you want, and click a specific time slot to begin creating a new event. You can fill in the title, description, location, and time for your meeting.

- **Assign a task**. When there's work to be done, it helps to have an efficient way to coordinate who's doing what. In SharePoint, that means clicking the Tasks link in the navigation panel to see the lists of outstanding jobs. You can create and assign new tasks with a wealth of important tracking information (like priority, status, percent complete, start date, due date, and even an attached file).

- **Talk with colleagues**. Sometimes, the fastest way to sort out a problem is to collaborate in a free-flowing discussion. If you've added the Discussion Board app, you can use it add new posts and make replies, just like any other forum you've used on the Web.

- **Create a custom web page**. Even if you don't know a lick of HTML, you can create your own custom page and put it on your SharePoint site, where others can view it. To get started, click Site Contents, and then click Site Pages. You'll see a list of static HTML pages—and a link that lets you add a new one, with the help of SharePoint's integrated HTML editor (it runs right in your browser). When you're finished, you can use the menu shown in *Figure 22-6* to add the page to your navigation menu. When the menu is in edit mode, drag the page from the list of pages and drop it onto the menu.

SharePoint and Access

SharePoint works perfectly well without Access—in fact, all you need is a decent web browser. Using your browser you can log into your team's SharePoint site, review the latest information, upload documents, and edit lists of data. For many SharePoint users, this is more than enough. But with Access, you get two more options. You can:

- **Transfer data into and out of SharePoint**. This trick is useful if some people in your company use Access and others use SharePoint. Of course, it's up to you to make sure you keep everyone's data up-to-date.

- **Use Access as a front end for SharePoint**. This is the same technique you used in Chapter 21 to interact with SQL Server. It lets you work with tables of information in the familiar Access environment but *store* these tables on the SharePoint server. The advantage is that your data is available to much larger numbers of people at once, and for those who don't have Access, it's available through the web pages on your SharePoint site.

NOTE It's important not to confuse any of these linking techniques with the Access web app feature discussed in Chapter 20, which also uses SharePoint. If you're still confused, the following box has a detailed breakdown of the differences.

The Difference Between Web Apps and List Linking

Access web apps use SharePoint. Access's list-linking feature uses SharePoint. Beyond that superficial similarity, the two features really don't have much in common. Here's a rundown that crystalizes the differences:

- **System requirements.** Access's web app feature requires the full version of SharePoint 2013. Access's list-linking feature works with just about any version of SharePoint, including the older 2010 editions and the scaled-down SharePoint Foundation software, which is free.

- **Type of storage.** Web apps store data in SQL Server tables. You define the structure of these tables, and, once you've created them, you can use other tools to connect to these tables directly. The result is a whole universe of integration possibilities. When you store data in a SharePoint list, you don't have this ability. SharePoint still enlists the help of SQL Server to store list data (behind the scenes), but it uses a limited set of data types and its own quirky data encoding rules.

- **The online editing experience.** The only way for

SharePoint users to view the data in a web app, or change it, is to use one of the views you've created. The goal is to make a web app seem like a webified version of an Access database. But with SharePoint lists, you have no way to change the editing experience. When folks edit a list in SharePoint, they use a SharePoint web page (page 780), which isn't quite like the Access datasheet.

- **The desktop editing experience.** Web apps can only be edited online. There is no Access database that acts as a front end. With SharePoint lists, you can create a front end by using the regular set of desktop features, like forms and reports. However, if you want someone else to use it, it's up to you to distribute the Access file.

The most important difference is conceptual. Access web apps are an attempt to make an Access-style database that works on the Web. Access list linking is simply a way for Access fans to get at the data in a SharePoint list.

Creating a List in SharePoint

SharePoint lists are designed to help you track any kind of miscellaneous information that you need to share with your colleagues. Some of SharePoint's basic features—like links, announcements, tasks, contacts, and even the calendar—use premade lists. However, you'll probably want to create custom lists to store your own specific types of data.

Creating a list by using SharePoint's web page interface is nearly as easy as building a table in Access. Here's how to do it:

1. **In the navigation menu, click Site Contents.**

2. **Click the "add an app" icon, at the top of the list.**

A page appears with a long list of ready-made list types.

3. **Click the Custom List template.**

   SharePoint shows a popup asking for your list's name.

4. **Enter a name for your list.**

   For example, you could create a list named "Cafeteria Menu Ideas" that lists the items people would like to see for sale in the company canteen. Or, use "Dodgeball Team Assignment" to find out who's going to square off against the boss.

5. **Click Create.**

   SharePoint creates the list and returns you to the Site Contents page. You'll see your new list there, along with all the other apps you've added to your site. But before you can start adding items to your list, you need to tweak it into the shape you want.

6. **Hover over your custom list, and click the ellipsis (...) in the top-right corner. Then, click Settings (*Figure 22-7*).**

   This opens the list settings page, which is chock-full of list-configuring tools.

FIGURE 22-7

To fine-tune your list, click the ellipsis, and then click Settings. This step opens the list settings page Figure 22-8), where you can perform a variety of useful tune-ups.

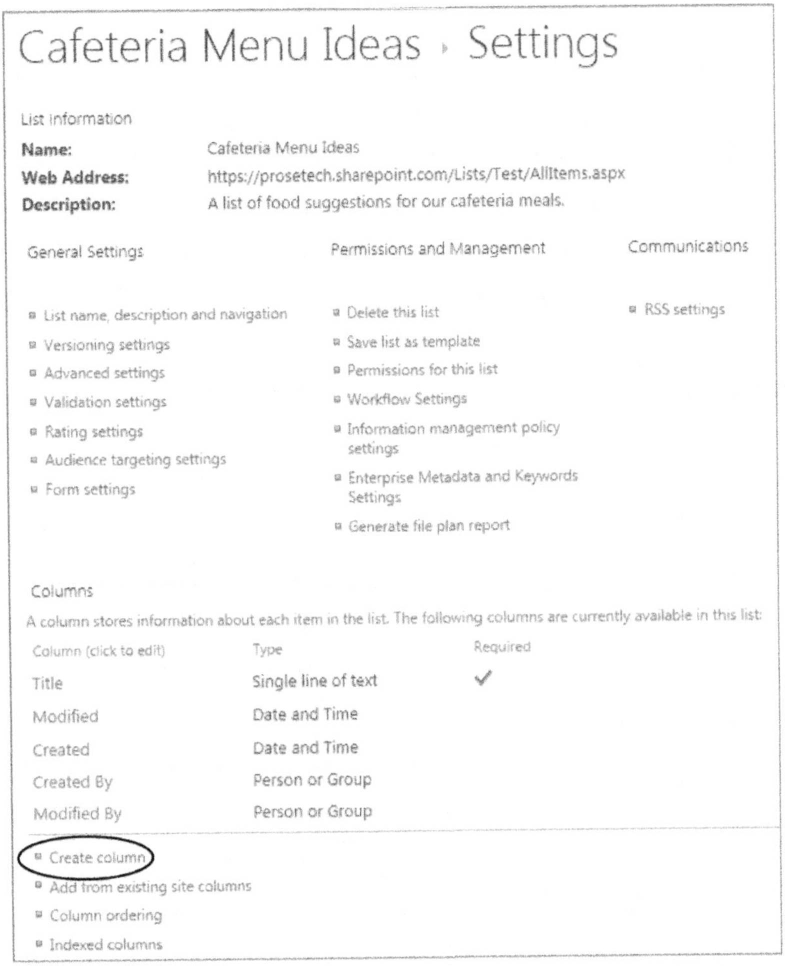

Cafeteria Menu Ideas › Settings

List Information

Name: Cafeteria Menu Ideas

Web Address: https://prosetech.sharepoint.com/Lists/Test/AllItems.aspx

Description: A list of food suggestions for our cafeteria meals.

General Settings	Permissions and Management	Communications
▫ List name, description and navigation	▫ Delete this list	▫ RSS settings
▫ Versioning settings	▫ Save list as template	
▫ Advanced settings	▫ Permissions for this list	
▫ Validation settings	▫ Workflow Settings	
▫ Rating settings	▫ Information management policy settings	
▫ Audience targeting settings		
▫ Form settings	▫ Enterprise Metadata and Keywords Settings	
	▫ Generate file plan report	

Columns

A column stores information about each item in the list. The following columns are currently available in this list:

Column (click to edit)	Type	Required
Title	Single line of text	✓
Modified	Date and Time	
Created	Date and Time	
Created By	Person or Group	
Modified By	Person or Group	

▫ Create column

▫ Add from existing site columns

▫ Column ordering

▫ Indexed columns

FIGURE 22-8

The first section of the list settings page reports a few important pieces of information including the list name, description, and the URL you can use to go directly to it. Underneath this is a set of links that lets you configure various list options. Beneath that is a Columns section, which lists the columns in your list and includes the all-important "Create column" link. Finally, at the bottom of the page (not shown here) is a section that lets you review the current views and create your own.

7. **Scroll down to the Columns section.**

New custom lists start out with several columns, but only one of them—the Title column—is displayed and can be edited. If possible, you should use the Title column to store an important piece of text that describes your item. The Title column can't be removed from a list (although it can be hidden).

Every SharePoint list also has several columns that it maintains behind the scenes. For example, each list item has a unique, hidden ID, and columns that track who inserted an item and the last time a change was made to it.

8. Click the "Create column" link under the list of columns.

SharePoint shows the Create Column page (*Figure 22-9*).

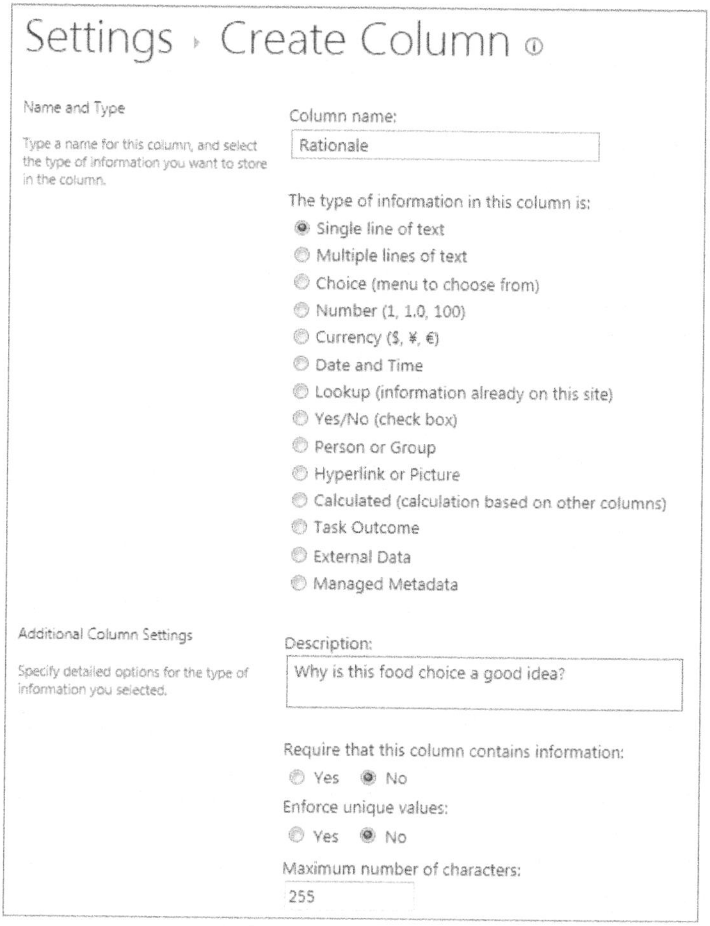

Settings › Create Column ⓘ

Name and Type

Type a name for this column, and select the type of information you want to store in the column.

Column name:

Rationale

The type of information in this column is:

◉ Single line of text
○ Multiple lines of text
○ Choice (menu to choose from)
○ Number (1, 1.0, 100)
○ Currency ($, ¥, €)
○ Date and Time
○ Lookup (information already on this site)
○ Yes/No (check box)
○ Person or Group
○ Hyperlink or Picture
○ Calculated (calculation based on other columns)
○ Task Outcome
○ External Data
○ Managed Metadata

Additional Column Settings

Specify detailed options for the type of information you selected.

Description:

Why is this food choice a good idea?

Require that this column contains information:
○ Yes ◉ No

Enforce unique values:
○ Yes ◉ No

Maximum number of characters:
255

FIGURE 22-9

The SharePoint data types for lists correspond to the Access data types for tables (although you don't have quite as many choices as you get with Access). If you want to draw the values from another table, then create a lookup column, and indicate the list that you want to link to.

9. Fill out all the information for your new column. When you're finished, click OK to add the column and return to the list settings.

This includes its name, a description, and the type of data. You can also set a maximum length, supply a default value, and indicate if the field is required (and can't be left blank).

NOTE At the bottom of the list of column settings is a Column Validation section where you can supply a validation expression and an error message that's shown when someone tries to enter an invalid value. However, the syntax for SharePoint validation expressions is different from the one Access uses. Fortunately, if you export an Access table to SharePoint (as described in the next section), Access automatically converts your table validation rules to the corresponding SharePoint validation expressions.

10. **Repeat steps 8 and 9 until you've added all the columns you need for your list.**

    If you want to edit a column, click its name in the Columns section, adjust its settings, and then click OK.

    If you want to delete a column, click its name in the Columns section, and then click the Delete button at the bottom of the page.

11. **When you're finished creating the columns you want, you may want to change some of the other list settings.**

    The most useful links on the list settings page are:

    - **List name, description, and navigation** lets you modify the information you supplied when you created the list, and (optionally) add the list to the Quick Launch navigation menu that sits at the left of your site.

    - **Advanced settings** lets you control whether list users are restricted to reading and modifying their own entries. You can also turn off the attachment feature (which lets users tack on their own files with an item), and turn on the folder feature (which lets users create subfolders to better organize list items).

    - **Delete this list** does the obvious.

    - **Permissions for this list** lets you control who's allowed to edit the list and what they're allowed to do. Ordinarily, site owners have *full control* permission (meaning they can do anything, including changing the list settings), normal members have *contribute* permission (meaning they can add, edit, and delete items), and visitors have *read* permission (meaning they can only look at the existing information).

SharePoint Views = Access Queries

In SharePoint lingo, a *view* is a customizable way to look at the data in a list. Views can show a subset of the full range of columns, and they can use filters to cut down the list to just those rows that interest you. You can also use sorting, grouping, and totals. In essence, a SharePoint view plays the same role as the versatile Access select query that you mastered in Chapter 6.

You can create new views for your list using the list settings page. Scroll to the bottom to see the current views and add new ones. Newly created lists have only a single view, called the *default view*.

When you create a new column, you also see an "Add to default view" checkbox. The default view is the view you start in when you first open the list. If you don't add your column to the default view, you won't see it at all (unless you create a new view that includes the column).

Optionally, you can create additional views, which can include just a subset of columns. You might use this approach to let different people work with different data from your list items, in much the same way that you use different reports and forms in an Access database. Click the "Create view" link at the bottom of the list settings page to get started experimenting with this feature.

12. **When you're finished configuring your list, it's time enter your data. Click the name of the list at the top of the list settings page.**

    SharePoint whisks you off to the list page, which shows all the list items. At first, this list is empty.

    You can also get to your custom list by clicking the link for it in the navigation menu, or finding it in the Site Contents page and clicking it there.

13. **Add your list items.**

    To add a new item, click the "new item" link at the top of the list. SharePoint shows a data entry page, with a box for each column that accepts a value (*Figure 22-10*). Once you've filled in your data, click Save.

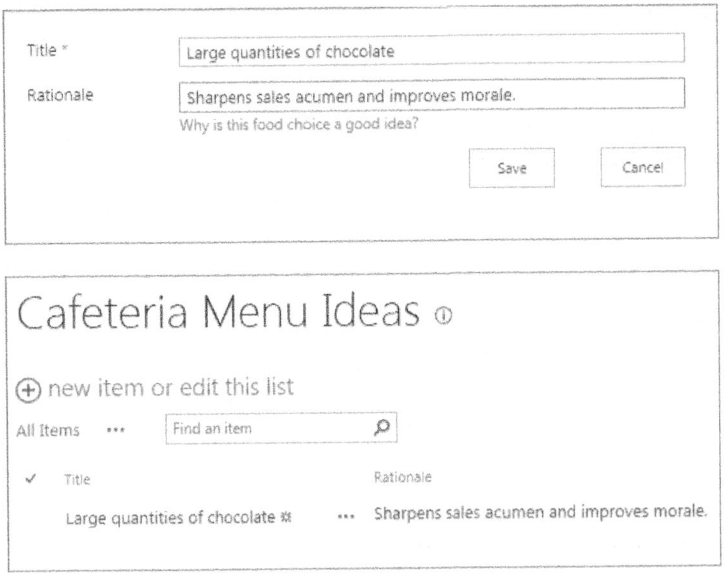

FIGURE 22-10

Top: Here's a new item for the Cafeteria Menu Ideas list.

Bottom: Now the list has one item. Click "new item" to add another one.

NOTE SharePoint is designed for use by large numbers of people at once (also known as *concurrency*), so it's quite conceivable that you won't be the only person editing a list. To see any recent changes and additions made by other people, just refresh the list page in your browser.

SharePoint's concurrency features are relatively unsophisticated. If two people edit the same list item at once, the one who tries to save the change last gets an error message rejecting the edit. (The situation is better if you're using Access to make your edit, as described on page 787.)

Exporting a Table to SharePoint

You have another way to build a SharePoint list. You can start with an Access table and *export* it to SharePoint. The disadvantage of this approach is that a bit of conversion is involved to turn the Access data types into SharePoint data types. Some of the finer points (like validation rules and input masks) will be lost, so it's not worth customizing any of these details in Access. However, exporting a table from Access is a great technique if you have some existing data that you need to transfer to a SharePoint site so more people can use it.

Here's how to export a table to SharePoint:

1. **Open your Access database.**

2. **Select the table you want to export in the navigation pane.**

If you export a child table, Access will also export all the linked parent tables automatically. For example, if you export Products, ProductCategories comes along for the ride.

3. **Choose External Data→Export→More→SharePoint List from the ribbon.**

   The Export window appears (*Figure 22-11*).

4. **Enter the URL for the SharePoint site, the name you want to use for the list, and (optionally) a description.**

   These are the basic details that identify a SharePoint list.

5. **If you want to see the list in SharePoint when the process is finished, choose "Open the list when finished."**

   It's always a good idea to review your list after a transfer operation to make sure it worked as you expected.

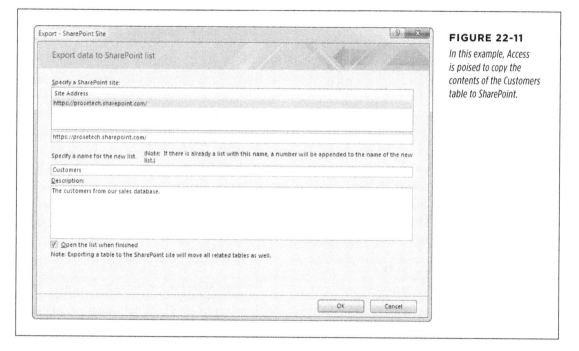

FIGURE 22-11

In this example, Access is poised to copy the contents of the Customers table to SharePoint.

6. **Click OK.**

   If you need a password to access your SharePoint site, you need to supply it now. Then, Access creates the new SharePoint list and fills it with data. Your Access database isn't modified in any way.

   If you chose "Open the list when finished" in step 5, Access launches a browser window to show you the new list when the process is complete (*Figure 22-12*).

When the export is finished, Access asks if you want to save your export steps. If you do, you can repeat the same export operation later on (presumably, to move the latest copy of your data to the server). You can learn more about this feature on page 807.

> **NOTE** If you export the same table to SharePoint more than once, Access gives it a new name by appending a number (like Customers1, Customers2, and so on). If you want to replace a SharePoint list, you need to remove the list first. To do that, click Site Contents, and find the offending list. Hover over it, and an ellipsis (...) will appear in the top-right next to the list information. Click that, and you'll see a pop up menu with extra choices, including a Remove link that will send the list to the site's recycle bin.

FIGURE 22-12

Here's the exported Customers table, as a SharePoint list, and in the process of being edited online.

When you export your data to SharePoint, you create a *copy* of that data. That means if someone edits the SharePoint list, your database won't get the change. Similarly, if you change the database, it won't appear in SharePoint unless you export it all over again. If this isn't what you want, consider storing the data in SharePoint and managing it in Access by using linked tables.

Access provides an easy way to export your data and to create a linked table in one step. It's the Database Tools→Move Data→SharePoint command, which you'll use on page 784. But before you tackle this technique, it's time to consider how you can use a quick-and-dirty import operation to snatch data out of a SharePoint list and transfer it to an Access table.

How Access Deals with SharePoint Incompatibilities

Most of the time, data follows a seamless path from the world of Access tables to the land of SharePoint lists. For example, Access can export tables that have default values and tables that use relationships without a problem. It can also convert most validation rules and calculated fields to the equivalent SharePoint expressions.

But Access and SharePoint don't always see eye-to-eye, and some table features can trip up your exports:

- **Ignored features.** Access cheerily ignores data macros, input masks, and multi-columned lookup lists when exporting data. If your tables use these features, Access makes no attempt to transfer them to the exported list, and no attempt to notify you that your exported list has lost some of the functionality of the original Access table. Life gets even trickier if you're using validation rules or calculated fields, because Access can convert most, but

not all, of these expressions. Once again, Access doesn't inform you if it fails to convert an expression (for example, if you have a validation rule that uses the keyword Between, which doesn't work in SharePoint). For reasons like these, you should test your newly exported list in SharePoint, and see whether it catches invalid values.

- **Error-causing features.** A few features can cause more obvious problems. Examples include tables with more than one attachment field, tables with compound indexes (indexes that use multiple fields), and fields that use reserved SharePoint names. If possible, Access exports the valid parts of the table, but leaves out the offending fields. Access also logs these errors to a table called Move To SharePoint Issues, which appears in the navigation pane after a failed or partially failed export. Each record in this table describes a problem and the reason why it occurred.

Importing a List in Access

It's just as easy to perform the reverse operation, and download a list from a SharePoint site into an Access table. Here's how:

1. **Open a database in Access (or create a new one).**

2. **Choose External Data→Import & Link→More→SharePoint List.**

   The Get External Data window appears.

3. **Specify the SharePoint site, and choose whether you want to import a copy of the data or create linked tables.**

   Your choice depends on how to plan to make changes to the information later:

   - **With a copy**, you have two separate sets of data that can be changed independently (the SharePoint list, and the table in your database). You can't synchronize these two pieces. The advantage of this option is that you don't need to keep connecting to the SharePoint server to apply your changes.

   - **With a linked table**, the data is always stored in SharePoint. You simply use Access to modify it. That way, only one copy of the information exists, and everyone's changes are made in the same place.

TIP A linked table is a great tool if you want to transfer data from SharePoint to Access regularly. For example, you might create a linked table for a SharePoint list named CustomerProspects, where salespeople enter information about potential customers. Every week, you could then run an action query, macro, or code routine that transfer the data from the linked table to an ordinary Access table named MailingList. This extra step may seem like more work, but it gives you a great way to check data before letting it into the inner sanctum of your business. Essentially, it means you're using SharePoint to collect information and Access to store it for the long haul.

4. **Click Next.**

   Access shows you all the lists that are available on the SharePoint site (*Figure 22-13*).

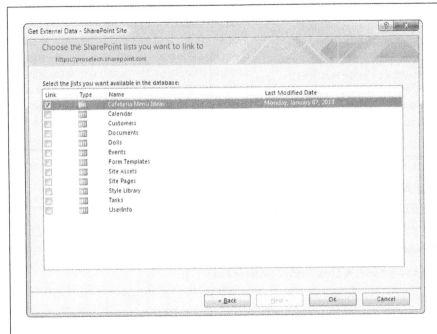

FIGURE 22-13

The Cafeteria Menu Ideas table is being imported from the SharePoint site. You can use this window to import more than one table at the same time. And if you imported and linked some of these tables in a previous import operation, they'll appear in the list with checkmarks already next to them. You can then remove the linked table from your Access database by clearing the checkmark. (This is a neat trick, but it's no different from just deleting a linked table, which you can do easily enough from the navigation pane.)

5. **Place a checkmark next to each list that you want to import or link, and click OK.**

6. **Access creates the tables in your database (*Figure 22-14*).**

   Along with the table you picked (in step 1), SharePoint also exports a table named UserInfo, which appears in your database. This table lists the members of your SharePoint site.

When you import a table from a SharePoint list, it comes with a whole whack of hidden fields that track extra information. Two examples are the hidden fields Created By and Modified By that indicate who created and last modified an item in the list. You don't need to worry about these details, because Access maintains them automatically. In fact, you won't even see them in the datasheet unless you use the Home→Records→More→Unhide Fields command.

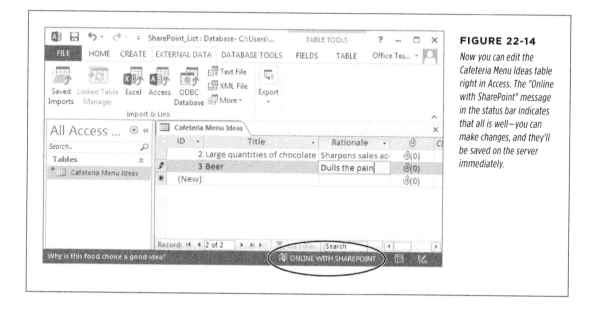

FIGURE 22-14

Now you can edit the Cafeteria Menu Ideas table right in Access. The "Online with SharePoint" message in the status bar indicates that all is well—you can make changes, and they'll be saved on the server immediately.

NOTE SharePoint allows you to attach files to any list. Access supports this feature by adding an Attachment field to the end of every SharePoint table. Add files here, and they'll be uploaded to the SharePoint server and attached to the corresponding list item so others can see them.

However, if you import a table to Access and then export it back to SharePoint (which is generally not the easiest way to manage your data), you'll get a number of error messages in the Move To SharePoint Issues table explaining that Access can't transfer these fields. The problem is that SharePoint automatically creates these fields for every new list, and the copies you're trying to export conflict with the new fields that SharePoint has already created. Fortunately, this error is harmless.

Moving a Whole Database to SharePoint

Why stop at a single table? Using Access, you can convert an entire database to a set of SharePoint lists. This is a great way to *upsize* your database. For example, if you have a successful database that's being used in your company, but you want to make sure it can handle more people (including those who don't have Access), it makes good sense to hand it off to SharePoint. You can perform this task by using the handy "Export Tables to SharePoint" Wizard, which carries out the following tasks:

- Creates a backup of your database (just in case you want to get back to the original, non-SharePoint version).

- Creates a SharePoint list for every table in the database.

- Removes your tables and replaces them with linked tables that get their information from SharePoint. That way, all the data is in the capable hands of the SharePoint server.

- Optionally uploads a copy of this converted database to the SharePoint site. Other Access users may want to use this database if they need your queries, forms, reports, or code routines.

The following steps walk you through the whole process:

1. **In Access, open the database you want to convert.**

2. **Choose Database Tools→Move Data→SharePoint.**

   The wizard starts (*Figure 22-15*).

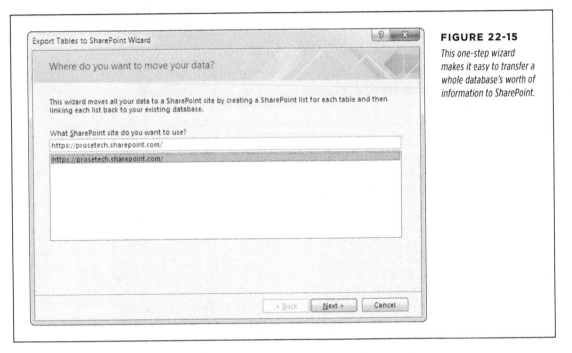

FIGURE 22-15

This one-step wizard makes it easy to transfer a whole database's worth of information to SharePoint.

3. **Enter the URL for your SharePoint site and Click Next.**

   If you need a password to access your SharePoint site, supply it now. Then, Access begins the transfer process, which can take some time for a large database. A progress indicator will keep you up-to-date on how much of the job remains.

   When Access finishes, you see a final confirmation window.

4. **Turn on Show Details to see exactly what Access did (*Figure 22-16*).**

   By reviewing the details, you can catch obvious errors. For example, you can see whether the exported tables had conflicting names and had to be renamed.

   If any problems occur during the conversion process, Access creates a table named "Move to SharePoint Site Issues" and adds one record that describes each problem.

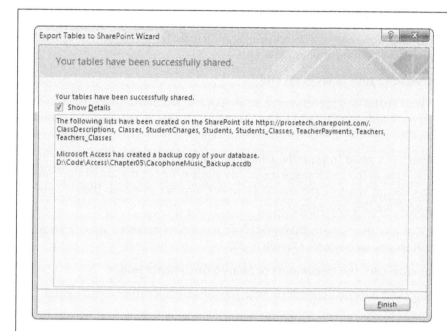

FIGURE 22-16

In this example, Access generated eight lists without a hitch and created a backup copy of the database.

5. **Click Finish.**

   You'll notice that your database has been changed. All the tables have been changed to linked tables that connect to the corresponding SharePoint lists. (The telltale sign is the yellow table-with-an-arrow icon that appears next to each table in the Access navigation pane.)

> **TIP** Access gives you easy access to a few common SharePoint settings. To see them, right-click a linked table, and choose the More Options submenu. You'll see commands that let you modify the table, tweak its permissions, or set up alerts that notify you when certain data is changed. When you choose one of these options, Access launches your web browser and points it to the appropriate SharePoint page.

Even after you've moved your data to SharePoint, it's still up to you to distribute the front end—the Access database that has the linked tables and any other Access objects you've created, like queries, reports, and forms.

One option is to publish this front end to the Shared Documents section of your SharePoint site. That way, the people who need it can download it from SharePoint. To quickly upload an Access database to a SharePoint site, follow these steps:

1. **Choose File→Save As.**

   Access enters Backstage view.

2. **In the "Save Database As" list on the right, choose SharePoint.**

3. **Click the big Save As button.**

   The "Save to SharePoint" window appears. It looks like an ordinary Save window, except it's pointed at your network.

4. **Browse to your SharePoint site.**

   If your SharePoint server is on a local network, you may be able to see it in the network listing provided by the "Save to SharePoint" window. If so, double-click it.

   If not, you need to type the URL that points to your SharePoint site. To do that, click in the blank space inside the address box at the top of the "Save to SharePoint" window; the word "Network" becomes selected. Then type in the SharePoint URL and press Enter.

   Either way, the "Save to SharePoint" window will contact your SharePoint server and display its contents (*Figure 22-17*).

5. **Double-click the Documents or Shared Documents folder.**

   The exact naming depends on how your SharePoint server is configured.

6. **Click Save.**

   Access uploads your database to SharePoint. To see it, visit the SharePoint site and click the Documents link in the navigation panel.

No matter how you distribute your database front end, you'll face the usual problems if you need to change it. For example, if you add a handy new form, it's up to you to upload a new version of the front-end database to the SharePoint site, tell everyone about it, and hope they download it and start using it right away. This coordination is a major headache if you change your front end often, and it's one of the key advantages of the web database feature described in Chapter 20.

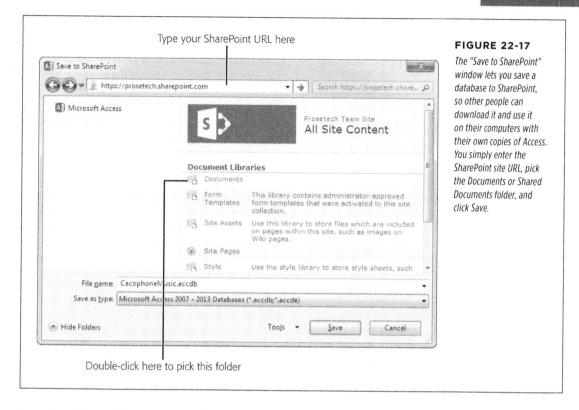

Type your SharePoint URL here

FIGURE 22-17

The "Save to SharePoint" window lets you save a database to SharePoint, so other people can download it and use it on their computers with their own copies of Access. You simply enter the SharePoint site URL, pick the Documents or Shared Documents folder, and click Save.

Double-click here to pick this folder

Editing Your SharePoint Data in Access

Whenever you commit a change in a linked table (for example, by making an edit and moving to another row), Access sends the new values to the SharePoint server. The only thing you aren't allowed to do is modify the design of the table. To do that, you need to use SharePoint. (One quick way to jump to the right web page is to right-click the table in Access, and then choose More Options→Modify Columns and Settings.)

> **TIP** You can use the Home→Records→Refresh All command to show the latest information in your datasheet at any time.

If you're unlucky, you can modify a record at the same time that someone else is changing it. If you complete your edit first, you won't be aware of the conflict. (Instead, the other person's change will be rolled back.) But if you're caught on the losing side and you complete your change *after* the record has already been modified by someone else, you'll get the message shown in *Figure 22-18*, which lets you decide what to do.

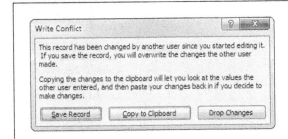

FIGURE 22-18

This message tells you that someone else has already modified the record you're using. You can click Save Record to blindly overwrite the other person's changes (which is always a risky move), or click Drop Changes to cancel your edits. But the most interesting choice is "Copy to Clipboard," which copies your values to the Windows Clipboard and cancels your edit. You can then look over the current record and paste back part or all of your changes.

TIP When you use "Copy to Clipboard," Access copies the entire row. If you want to paste just a couple values, you can paste the whole selection in another program (like a text editor), and then copy only the value you need.

Importing and Exporting Data

An Access database is like a carefully built fort. It takes strictly organized and error-tested information and locks it up tight. Very few programs guard their data as protectively as database software does. Word processors and spreadsheet programs accept just about any content and let you build your document structure on the fly. Databases aren't nearly as freewheeling.

Most of the time, databases live in an independent world. But every once in a while, you need to bridge the gap in one of two ways:

- You want to take the information from another program and *import* it—basically, stuff it into your database.

- You want to take some of the information in an Access database and *export* it, so you can work with it in another program.

Access has several different options for transferring information. You can use the lowly Clipboard, Access's standard import and export features, or the universal XML standard. In this chapter, you'll learn about all your options.

■ Case for Importing and Exporting

If you haven't thought much about importing and exporting, it's probably because you don't need to use these features—yet. Many databases are completely happy living a quiet, solitary life. However, importing and exporting might come in handy for a few reasons. Sooner or later, one of these reasons will apply to you.

Understanding Exports

Exporting is the easier part of the equation. Exporting is simpler than importing, because it involves moving information from a stricter storage location (the database) to one with fewer rules (another type of document).

> **NOTE** Exporting is a way to transfer a copy of your information to another location. The original copy always remains in Access. There's no point in changing the exported copy. Instead, if you need changes, make them in the database, and then perform the export operation again.

Here are some of the most common reasons people decide to export information:

- **You want to email some information to a friend**. You don't want to send the Access database because your friend doesn't have a copy of Access, or you want him to see only some—not all—of the data.

- **You're creating a presentation in PowerPoint**. The easiest way to dazzle and convince your peers is to show them some impressive information from your database.

> **NOTE** Access stores huge volumes of information, which is often more than other programs can handle. You'd never be able to copy a table into a PowerPoint presentation—at most, a slide can fit a handful of records. However, you might choose to show the results of a totals query (page 263) that uses grouping to boil down the results to a few subtotals.

- **You want to analyze the information in Excel**. Access is great for storing and managing your data, but it doesn't give you the tools to help you figure out what it all means. If you want to crunch the numbers with heavy-duty formulas and slick charting features, it makes sense to move it to Excel.

Some programs are intelligent enough to pull the information out of an Access database all on their own. One example is Word, which provides a *mail merge* feature that lets you take a list of names and addresses from a database, and then use them to create mailing labels, personalized forms, or any other sort of batch paperwork. When using this feature, you don't need to perform any exporting—instead, you can just point Word to your Access database file.

Understanding Imports

You need importing whenever there's information outside your database that belongs inside it. Suppose you create a state-of-the-art e-commerce database for your buffalo farm. However, some of your sales associates still fill out forms by using an old Excel spreadsheet. Now, you need a way to get the information out of the Excel spreadsheet and into your database.

> **NOTE** Your sales staff has let you down. They really shouldn't enter data into a document for another program. Instead, they should use a form that's designed for logging sales, as described in Chapter 12.

Import operations have two key challenges. The first is making sure the data fits the database's strict requirements. As you learned in Chapter 1, databases are rule-crazy, and they rudely toss out any information that doesn't fit (for example, text in a date field). The second challenge is dealing with information that doesn't quite line up—in other words, its representation in the database doesn't match its representation in the external document. This headache is more common than you may think.

In your database, you might use status codes (like 4302), while the spreadsheet you want to import uses status *names* (like High Priority). Or, you may need to break the information you're importing into more than one linked table, even though it's stored together in a single document. The customer order spreadsheet for your buffalo farm could include customer information (which corresponds to the Customers table) and order information (for the Orders table). Sadly, you don't have any easy way to solve these problems. If the external data doesn't match the representation in the database *exactly*, you'll need to change it by hand before or after the import operation.

Experts occasionally try to solve problems like these by writing Visual Basic code that reads the data and creates the appropriate records. (To do this, you'd need to use the DAO objects described on page 633.) While the code approach is infinitely flexible, it can quickly become a nightmare to write and maintain, so avoid it if at all possible.

■ Using the Clipboard

Anyone who's spent much time using a Windows computer is familiar with the Clipboard—a behind-the-scenes container that temporarily stores information so you can transfer it from one program to another. Using the Clipboard, you can copy a snippet of text in a Word document, and then paste it into a field in an Access table, or vice versa. That much is easy. But you probably don't realize that you can copy an entire *table* of information.

TIP Almost all Windows programs respect the same shortcut keys for the Clipboard. Use Ctrl+C to copy information, Ctrl+X to cut it (copy and delete it), and Ctrl+V to paste it.

Before you try out this trick, you need to understand two key facts about the Clipboard:

- **The Clipboard can store many different types of information**. Most of the time, you're using it to copy plain text. However, depending on the program you're using, you can also copy shapes, pictures, tables, and more.

- **Some types of information can convert themselves to other types**. If you copy a selection of cells in Excel, then you can paste it as a formatted table in a word processing program like Word or WordPerfect. Of course, if you copy a diagram in Visio, then you can paste it as a picture in Paint. In both examples, you copy a specialized type of object (Excel cells or a Visio diagram) to the Windows Clipboard. However, this object can *downgrade* itself when it needs to. You can paste a full-fledged copy of the object in the original program without losing anything, or you can paste and convert it to something simpler in a less powerful program.

This flexibility is the secret to transferring data to and from Access. The following sections explain how it works.

NOTE The Clipboard approach is simpler than the import and export features in Access. As a result, it's a faster choice (with fewer steps). Of course, it also gives you fewer choices and doesn't work with all programs.

Copying a Table from Access to Somewhere Else

Access lets you copy a selection of rows or an entire table to another program, without going through the hassle of the Export wizard. Access copies these rows to the Clipboard as an intelligent object that can convert itself into a variety of software-friendly formats. You can paste them as Excel cells, HTML text (the formatting language of the Web), or RichText (a formatting standard created by Microsoft and supported by all major word processors). Since HTML and RichText are so widely supported, you'll almost never have a problem copying your rows into another program when you use this technique.

Here's how to try it out:

1. **If you want to copy an entire table, then, in the navigation pane, select the table. If you want to copy only a few rows, then select them in the Datasheet view, as shown in *Figure 23-1*.**

   You're not limited to copying tables. You can also copy a query's results. Just select the query in the navigation pane. You can't copy data from reports or forms, however.

   When you copy rows or an entire table, Access takes your column-hiding settings (page 102) into account. If you've hidden a column so it doesn't appear in the datasheet (by selecting it, and then choosing Home→Records→More→Hide Fields), Access doesn't copy it to the Clipboard. This technique helps you leave out information you don't want to copy.

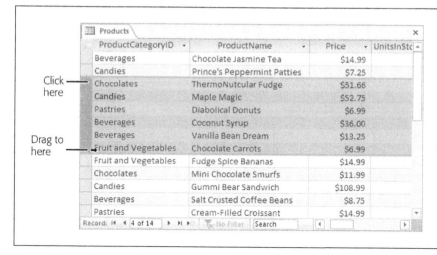

FIGURE 23-1

When selecting rows in the datasheet, click the gray margin just to the left of the first row you want to select. Then, drag down to select as many rows as you want. If you don't want to take your hand off the mouse, then you can copy these rows by holding down the Ctrl key, and right-clicking one of them. Then, from the popup menu, choose Copy.

NOTE　You can copy only a contiguous selection of rows, which is a fancy way of saying you can copy only rows that are right next to each other. If you have 10 rows in a table, then you can copy rows 3–6, but you can't copy just the first and last rows. (Of course, you can use several smaller copy operations to get the stragglers.)

---

2. **Press Ctrl+C to copy your selection.**

   This action places the records on the Windows Clipboard. You can now paste them inside Access or in another program.

3. **Switch to the program where you want to paste your information.**

   If you're just trying this feature for the first time, then take a whirl with Excel or Word (shown in *Figure 23-2*).

4. **Press Ctrl+V to paste your selection (see *Figure 23-2*).**

   Access pastes the rows from your selection, complete with column headers. If you've applied formatting to the datasheet (page 98), then most of that formatting comes along.

   Depending on the program where you paste your records, you might see a smart tag icon appear at your newly pasted content's right-hand corner. In Office applications, you can use this smart tag to change options about how the data is pasted (for example, with or without formatting).

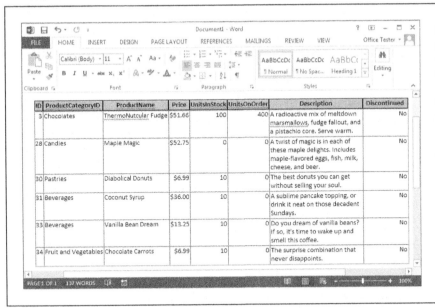

FIGURE 23-2

*Using cut and paste, you
can transform a database
table into a table in a
Word document (shown
here). Once you've pasted
the content, you may need
to fiddle with column
widths to make sure it all
looks right.*

NOTE Copying text, numbers, and dates is easy. However, some data types don't make the transition as well. If you copy an attachment field, then the pasted content shows the number of attachment fields, but the files themselves are left out.

TIMESAVING TIP

Copying from One Database to Another

You can also use a copying trick to transfer data from one Access database to another Access database that's open in a separate window. However, it works only if you're copying a complete table (or other object), not a selection of rows.

To try it out, right-click the object you want in the navigation pane and choose Copy. Then, switch to the second Access database, right-click in the empty space in its navigation pane, and choose Paste. Access asks you what you want to name the pasted table and gives you three pasting options:

- **Structure** creates the table structure, but leaves it empty.
- **Structure and Data** creates an exact duplicate of the table, with all the data.
- **Append Data to Existing Table** doesn't create a new table—instead, it adds the data to the table that you specify. For this to work, the table must have the same structure as the one you've copied.

This trick also lets you create a duplicate copy of a table (or other object) in the same database.

Copying Cells from Excel into Access

You can copy information from Access into another program easily enough, but you probably don't expect to be able to do the reverse. After all, a database is a strict, rigorously structured collection of information. If you try to copy a table from a word processing program, then you'll lack vital information, like the data types of each column. For that reason, Access doesn't allow it.

However, Access makes a special exception for everyone's favorite spreadsheet program, Excel. You can copy a selection of cells in Excel, and then paste them into Access to create a new table. This procedure works because Excel *does* distinguish between different types of data (although it isn't nearly as picky as Access). For example, Excel treats numbers, dates, text, and TRUE/FALSE values differently.

Here's how to use this feature:

1. **In Excel, select the cells you want to copy.**

   If your spreadsheet includes column titles, then include those headers in the selection. Access can use the titles as field names.

   NOTE It doesn't matter what version of Excel you have—this trick works with them all.

2. **Press Ctrl+C to copy your selection.**

3. **Switch to Access.**

4. **Click anywhere in the navigation pane, and then press Ctrl+V.**

   Access notices that you're trying to paste a group of Excel cells, and it tries to transform them into a table. First, it asks if the first row in your selection includes column titles.

5. **If you selected the column titles in step 1, then choose Yes. Otherwise, choose No.**

   If you choose Yes, then Access doesn't need to create random field names—instead, it can use your headers.

   Access creates a new table to deal with the new data. This table is named after the Excel sheet. If your sheet is named Sheet1 (as so many are in Excel), you now have a Sheet1 table.

   Once Access finishes the paste, it shows a confirmation message to let you know everything is finished successfully.

6. **Click OK.**

   Now you can refine your table to make sure the data types and field names are exactly what you want.

■ Import and Export Operations

Although the Clipboard cut-and-paste approach is neat, it doesn't always work out. If you need to export data to a file and you don't have the corresponding program installed on your computer (or you just don't want to bother running it), then you need a different way to transfer your information. Similarly, if you're downloading data from the Web or fetching information from a program that doesn't support Windows cut-and-paste, you need the full-fledged Access import feature.

You can do all the importing and exporting you want from a single ribbon tab, which is named External Data (*Figure 23-3*).

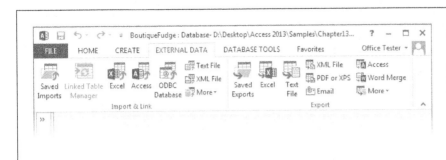

FIGURE 23-3

The External Data tab's Import & Link section lets you pipe data into Access by using a variety of formats. The Export section does the reverse—it takes your table and exports it in a bunch of different flavors.

> **TIP** The Import & Link and Export sections have easy-to-access buttons for the most popular file formats. If you don't see what you want, then click the More button to see an expanded list of choices.

Whether you're importing or exporting data, the process is essentially the same. You answer a few questions about what file you want to use and how you want to make the conversion, and then Access does your bidding.

Once you finish performing an import or export operation, Access gives you the option of saving all your steps. If you do, you can reuse them later on (see page 807). This method is a great way to save time if you need to perform the same export or import process again (like if you need to import some data every day, or export a summary at the end of every month).

Importable File Types

Most of the time, you'll import data that's in one of these four common formats:

- **Excel**. Pulls the data from an Excel spreadsheet.

- **Access**. When you use this option, you aren't performing a conversion. Instead, you're taking a database object from another Access database file, and copying it into the current database. You used this option in Chapter 19 when building a front-end database.

- **Text File**. Pulls the data out of a plain text file. Typically, plain text files use some sort of character (like a comma) to separate field values. This universally understood format is supported by many programs, including just about every piece of spreadsheet software ever written. When you use this option, Access takes a look at the text file to figure out how it's organized. However, you get the chance to confirm or correct the hunch before you import any data, as described on page 803.

- **XML File**. Pulls the data out of a structured XML file. XML is a cross-platform format used to represent any type of information. However, you can't successfully import all XML files—for the import feature to have any chance of success, the XML file must use a table-like structure. You'll learn more about this option on page 819.

Access also provides several other, more exotic import choices. Most of them don't appear until you click the More button. They include:

- **ODBC Database**. Grabs information from just about any database product, provided it has an ODBC driver. You used this feature in Chapter 21 to get data out of SQL Server.

- **Data Services**. Gets data from a web service running on a web server on your company's network. To use this feature, a programmer needs to create the web service and generate a file called a *data services connection definition*. You give Access the file, and then it knows how to contact the web service and ask it for some information.

- **SharePoint List**. Pulls the data from a list that's hosted on a SharePoint server. You don't need to import SharePoint information to work with it. You can also edit SharePoint lists directly in Access. Chapter 22 has much more about getting Access and SharePoint to work together.

- **HTML Document**. Extracts information from a list or a table in an HTML web page. Since HTML is a standard that's notoriously loose (and at times downright sloppy), you should try to avoid this option. You're likely to have importing problems.

- **Outlook Folder**. Pulls information out of a folder in Outlook.

NOTE If you're an Access veteran, don't bother hunting around for an option for importing from dBase files. Microsoft removed the feature from Access 2013. You'll need Access 2010 if you want to pull information out of a file created with this Paleolithic database program.

Importing Data

No matter what type of data you want to import, you'll go through the same basic steps. Here's an overview:

1. **In the ribbon's External Data→Import & Link section, click the button that corresponds to the type of file you want to import.**

When you choose a format, Access launches the Import wizard (*Figure 23-4*).

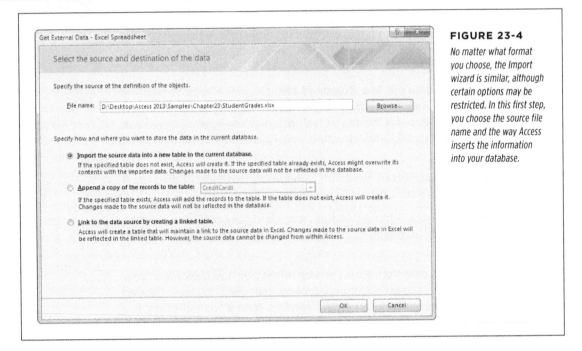

FIGURE 23-4

No matter what format you choose, the Import wizard is similar, although certain options may be restricted. In this first step, you choose the source file name and the way Access inserts the information into your database.

2. **Enter the name of the file you want to import.**

   If you don't remember the file path (or you just don't want to type it in by hand), then click Browse and navigate to the right place in the File Open window. Once you find the file, double-click it.

3. **Choose where to place the imported content in your database.**

   You have three possible choices for placing your data. Depending on the file format you're using, all these may not be available.

   - **Create a new table.** This option creates a fresh new table for the data you're importing, which saves you the headache of worrying about conflicting records. However, if a table of the same name already exists in the Access database, then this option wipes it out.

   - **Append to an existing table.** This option takes the rows you're importing and adds them to an existing table. For this option to work, the structure of the data you're importing must match the structure of the table you're using. For example, the field names must match exactly. However, the data you're importing can leave out fields that aren't required (page 130) or have default values (page 133).

- **Create a linked table.** If you use this approach, then Access doesn't actually transfer the information into your database. Instead, every time you view the linked table, Access checks the original file to get the most recent information. The neat thing here is that your linked table always shows the most recent information. With any other option, the imported table is left untouched if you change the original file. However, linked tables are also risky, because you don't have any guarantee that the file won't travel to another location on your hard drive (where Access can't find it). You used linked tables to create a split database in Chapter 19.

> **TIP** Linked tables are a good way to bridge the gap between different Access databases or other databases (like SQL Server). However, they don't work well with other more limited formats, like text files.

4. **Click OK.**

   A wizard launches that collects the remaining information that Access needs. If you're importing an Excel file, then Access asks you which worksheet to use. If you're importing a text file, then Access asks you how the fields are separated.

5. **Answer all questions in the wizard to tell Access what it needs to know about the structure of the data you're importing.**

   Once you're finished with this stage, Access asks you its final question—whether you want to save your import steps.

6. **If you want to perform this import again later on, then select "Save import steps." Then, click Close.**

   Page 807 shows how to reuse a saved import.

> **NOTE** If Access finds any errors while importing your data, then it creates another table with the same name as the table you're importing to, with _ImportErrors tacked on the end. Access adds one record to that table for each problem. If you try to import a bunch of information into a table named SalesData, and Access can't convert the values to the data type you want (for example, text is in a column that should only hold numbers), you get a table named SalesData_ImportErrors.

The following sections walk you through the specifics for two common data formats that need a few extra steps: Excel workbooks and text files.

The Danger of Duplicates

If your import is adding (otherwise known as *appending*) records to an existing table, then you're in danger of every importer's worst nightmare: *duplication*.

Quite simply, Access has no way of telling whether it's already imported the same information. If you've set Access to automatically fill in an autonumbered ID value for each record, then it cheerily adds the same data several times, with a different ID value each time. On the other hand, if you aren't using autonumbered ID values and the data you're importing contains the primary key, then Access can't import the new data at all. Obviously, neither outcome is ideal.

If you're in the import business for the long term, then the only solution is to be very careful. Here are some tips:

• If you want to reuse a file after you've imported the data

it contains, then make sure you delete all the information you've already imported right away.

• If you suspect you might have imported the same information twice, then use a query to check. You can create your own, or you can use the Find Duplicates query that the Query Wizard creates (page 216).

• Perform small updates frequently, rather than less frequent large updates. That way, you'll catch mistakes faster, and have an easier time tracking them down.

• If you really need a more robust solution, then you need to build it yourself. You can use Visual Basic code to control exactly how Access transfers data (which is a lot more work).

Importing from an Excel File

To import from an Excel file, your data should be organized in a basic table. Ideally, you have column headings that match the fields in your database. You should trim out any data that you don't want to import (like other cells under the table that aren't a part of the table). You may also decide to remove values that are calculated using Excel formulas. If possible, it's better to recalculate this information whenever you need it by using an expression in a query (page 237). That way, there's no danger that your calculated values will become inconsistent or out of date.

> **NOTE** Earlier in this chapter, you learned how to take Excel data and cut and paste your way to an Access table. However, when you perform a full-fledged import, you get the opportunity to change field names, fine-tune data types, and use indexing.

Once you have a cleaned-up table of data in an Excel file, you're ready to start the import process:

1. **Choose External Data→Import & Link→Excel, choose your Excel file, and then specify how you want to add the imported information to your database. Then, click OK.**

   You learned how to make these decisions in steps 1 to 3 starting on page 797.

2. **If your Excel file has more than one worksheet, choose the one that houses your data (*Figure 23-5*).**

Many Excel files have more than one worksheet. (In fact, spreadsheets created in older versions of Excel begin with three worksheets. Most people plop their data on the first one, which is initially named Sheet1.)

If you're an Excel expert, then you might have designated a section of a more complex worksheet as a *named range*. If so, you can choose the Show Named Ranges option and then pick that named range from the list.

If your Excel file has just a single worksheet and no named ranges, there's nothing for you to choose, and you won't see this part of the wizard. Instead, skip to step 4.

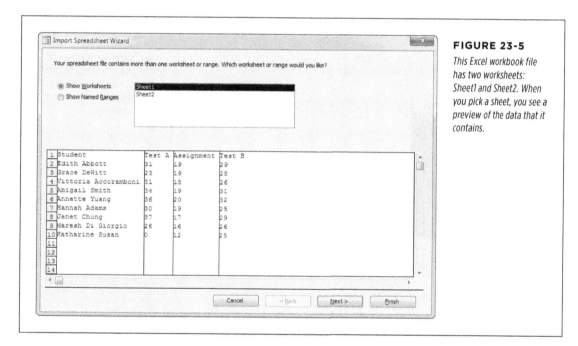

FIGURE 23-5

This Excel workbook file has two worksheets: Sheet1 and Sheet2. When you pick a sheet, you see a preview of the data that it contains.

3. **Click Next.**

4. **If your Excel data has a row with column headings, then choose First Row Contains Column Headings.**

These headings become the starting point for your field names. If you don't choose First Row Contains Column Headings, then Excel treats the first row as an ordinary record.

5. **Click Next.**

If you're creating a new table for your imported records, then Access asks you to configure the fields you're creating. If you're appending the records to an existing table, then skip ahead to step 7.

6. **For each field, you can choose a field name, the data type, and whether the field should be indexed (page 134). Then, click Next.**

   Access makes some intelligent guesses based on the data that's there, but it's up to you to fine-tune the details. For example, if you have a column with whole numbers, you may want to change the data type from Double (which supports fractional numbers) to Integer, as shown in *Figure 23-6*.

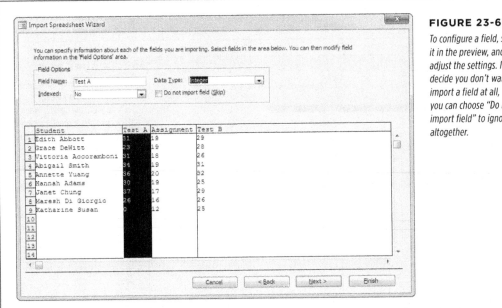

FIGURE 23-6

To configure a field, select it in the preview, and then adjust the settings. If you decide you don't want to import a field at all, then you can choose "Do not import field" to ignore it altogether.

7. **Choose whether you want Access to create the primary key.**

   Choose "Let Access add primary key" if you'd like Access to create an autonumbered ID field (which is generally a good idea). If the data you're importing already includes a field you want to use as a key, then select "Choose my own primary key," and then pick the right field.

8. **In the "Import to Table" text box, type the name of the table you want to create or add your records to.**

   You can also switch on the option "I would like a wizard to analyze my table after importing the data." If you do, after the import is finished, Access runs the Table Analyzer Wizard. The goal of the Table Analyzer Wizard is to split your imported data into multiple tables, so you can avoid the many problems of bad database design (page 89).

> **TIP** Although this is a fantastic idea in theory, it's a bit clumsy in practice. The Table Analyzer isn't clever enough to find anything you can't spot yourself, and it has a bad habit of finding problems that don't exist.

9. **Click Finish to finalize your choices.**

   Once the import is complete, you can choose whether to save your import steps for reuse.

You'll find some potential stumbling blocks when importing data from Excel. Blank values and fields, the commonest problems, occur when the Import wizard assumes there's data in a part of your worksheet that doesn't contain any information. (This could happen if there's a cell with just a space somewhere on your worksheet, or even if you have a cell that used to contain data but that has since been deleted.) The best approach is to prevent as many problems as possible by tidying up your worksheet (for example, removing extra cells and unneeded columns) before you perform an import operation. But if some issues slip through, you may need to clean up the imported table by deleting empty fields and records.

Importing from a Text File

Text files are the lowest common denominator for data exchange. If you're using a program that creates files Access can't import, then plain text may be your only avenue.

Once again, you start by choosing your file, and then choosing how you want to add the information to your database. Then, the Import wizard takes you through a few more steps:

1. **Specify the type of text file.**

   Access can import from two types of text files:

   - **Delimited text files** use some sort of separator to indicate where each field ends. For example, *Joe,Piscapone,43* is a line of text you may find in a delimited text file—it's three field values separated by commas.

   - **Fixed-width text files** separate a record into separate fields by position. Each field has a certain number of characters allocated to it, and if you don't use them all, Access fills the remaining space (up until the next field) with space characters.

> **TIP** Delimited text files are more flexible than fixed-width text files (because they can accommodate data values of vastly different lengths). They're also more common.

2. **Click Next.**

   If you're importing delimited text, Access asks you what character is the *delimiter*—in other words, what character separates the fields (*Figure 23-7*). Commas and tabs are common delimiters.

If you're importing fixed-width text, Access lets you set the field boundaries by dragging column lines to the right position in the preview window.

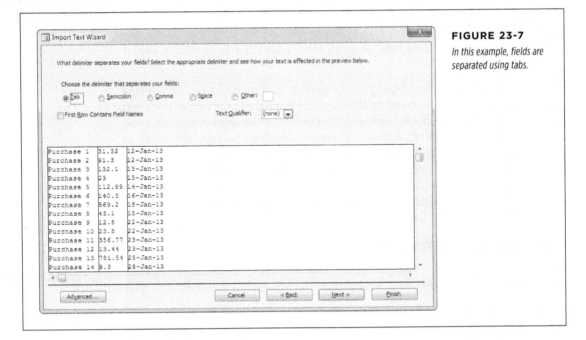

FIGURE 23-7

In this example, fields are separated using tabs.

3. **Complete the wizard.**

The rest of the wizard unfolds in exactly the same way as it does for Excel data.

If you're creating a new table to hold your imported data, then the next step asks you to configure the fields you want to create by setting their names, data types, and indexing options (*Figure 23-6*). Once you've finished this part, you can choose whether you want Access to create an autonumbered ID field, and then use it as the primary key.

Finally, in the last step, you need to enter the name of the table you want to create or add to. You can then click Finish (and, optionally, choose to save your import steps for later reuse).

Exportable File Types

Just as you can import information from other files and pop it into your database, you can also take the existing information and ship it out to another format. You'll most often undertake this step to let some other person or program use your information without needing to go through Access.

When exporting your data, you can use all the same formats that you can use in an import operation, plus a few more. Here's a rundown of the most popular choices:

- **Excel**. Puts the data into the cells of an Excel worksheet. Perfect if you want to use Excel's tools to analyze a sales trend or plot a profit chart.

- **Text File**. Dumps the data into a plain text file, with tabs and spaces used to arrange the data. You lose colors, fonts, borders, and other formatting details. This format isn't very useful—think of it as a last resort to transfer data to another program if none of the other export options work.

- **XML File**. Saves the data in a text .xml file, without any formatting. This option makes sense if you're using some sort of automated program that can read the exported XML file and process the data. (See page 810 for more information about XML and detailed export steps.)

- **PDF or XPS**. Creates a print-ready PDF file with the exact formatting and lay-out you'd see if you sent the table to your printer. Unlike with Excel or Word documents, you can't edit a PDF file—you're limited to reviewing the report and printing it.

- **Access**. Transfers the Access table (or a different type of object) to another Access database file. This feature isn't as powerful as importing Access objects, because you're limited to one object at a time. For that reason, people don't use it as often.

- **Word Merge**. Puts the data into a Word document by using Word's mail merge feature, which is designed to organize address information into printable labels, envelopes, and form letters. This option isn't just a straight transfer. Instead, the Word document stores the details about your database (like the name of the database file and the table you're using), so it can grab updated information and repeat the mail merge later.

- **Word**. Puts the data into a Word document, separating each column with tabs and each line with a hard return. This format leaves a lot to be desired, because it's difficult to rearrange the data after the fact in Word. (A nicer export feature would put the report data into a Word table, which would make it far easier to work with.)

- **HTML Document**. Creates a web-ready HTML web page that you can post to a website or a company intranet. The HTML format that Access generates looks remarkably like your real, printed report.

Exporting Data

To perform an export operation, follow these steps:

1. **In the navigation pane, select the table you want to export.**

   Unfortunately, you can't export more than one table at once. However, you can export just a *portion* of a table. One way to do this partial export is to open the table, and then select the rows you want to export. (Once you start the export process, you see an option that lets you export just the selected rows.) You can also create a query that gets just the rows you want. You can export the query results by selecting the query in the navigation pane instead of the underlying table.

2. **Click the button that corresponds to the type of file you want to export.**

When you choose a format, Access launches the Export wizard (*Figure 23-8*).

3. **Enter the name of the file you want to create.**

Access creates this file during the export operation. In some cases, you may have a choice of file format. For example, if you're exporting to Excel you can use the newer XML-based spreadsheet format (the .xlsx standard), or the older .xls standard that supports older versions, like Excel 97.

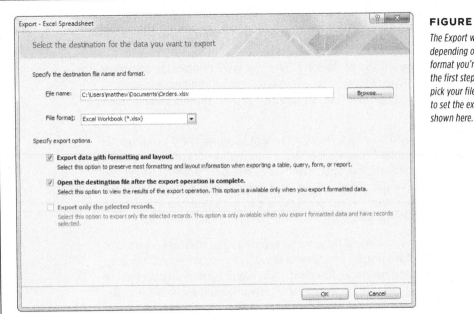

FIGURE 23-8

The Export wizard varies depending on the export format you're using. But the first step is always to pick your file, and then to set the export options shown here.

4. **If you want to keep the formatting that's in your database, then choose "Export data with formatting and layout."**

If you've tailored the datasheet with fancy fonts and colors (as described on page 98), Access preserves these details in the exported file. Obviously, this option doesn't work for all formats. For example, simple text files can't handle any formatting.

5. **If you want to double-check your exported document, then choose "Open the destination file after the export operation is complete."**

It's always a good idea to make sure you got the data and the formatting you expect. If you use this option, then Access launches the exported file, opening it in the program that owns it (Excel for spreadsheets, Notepad for text files, and so on). Of course, this method works only if you have that application on your computer.

6. **If you've selected only a few records in a table, then choose "Export only the selected records."**

    This way, Access exports the current selection, not the entire table or query.

7. **Click OK to perform the export.**

    Access may ask you for additional details if it needs any more information about how to create the exported file.

    Once you've finished this stage, Access asks you its final question—whether you want to save your export steps.

8. **If you want to perform this export again later on, select "Save export steps." Then, click Close.**

    The following section explains how to use a saved export.

> **NOTE** Do you need to export the same database object to the same file with the same options over and over again? Consider using the ExportWithFormatting macro action, which is a great way to take care of daily or weekly export jobs.

GEM IN THE ROUGH

Exporting Reports

Tables and queries aren't the only database objects you can export. Access also lets you export your reports. If you choose to keep the formatting and layout, then Access tries to make sure the exported file looks just like the printed report.

This choice is great if you want to pass along a report to someone who doesn't have Access. If you simply want to share the report data, then you can use Word. If you want to preserve the formatting exactly so that it can be printed later on, then

the PDF format makes more sense. Page 323 discusses in detail how to export a report.

Access also lets you export a form, but you probably won't get the results you want. Access uses the formatting and layout from the Datasheet view. Most forms use a carefully laid out set of controls in Form view and rarely use the Datasheet view. However, when Access exports a form, it ignores the Form view altogether.

Reusing Import and Export Settings

In some situations, you'll find you need to perform regular import or export operations. You may need to dump the data from an Excel spreadsheet into your database once a week. Or maybe you need to produce a monthly PDF report with a sales summary. In these cases, it's quite time-consuming to go through the entire wizard. This is especially true if you're performing an import, because you might need to choose which columns you want to import, set the appropriate data types, and then adjust other settings the exact way you did the first time you performed the operation.

Fortunately, Access has a solution for times like these. You can save all the settings you chose in the Import or Export wizard and store them in your current database. Then, when you need to repeat the process, you can use these settings to do it with just a couple of clicks (with no brainpower needed).

To save your steps, just turn on the "Save import steps" or "Save export steps" checkbox at the end of the process the first time you import or export your data. You'll need to choose a descriptive name for your settings, as shown in *Figure 23-9*, and then click Save Import.

NOTE If you're saving an import operation, think carefully about whether you choose to create a new table or append to an existing table. If you create a new table, then every time you run the import, Access overwrites that table with a new table that has all new data. But if you append to an existing table, Access adds the new data to whatever data you've already got. (In this case, you need to be on the lookout for duplicate data; see the box on page 800.)

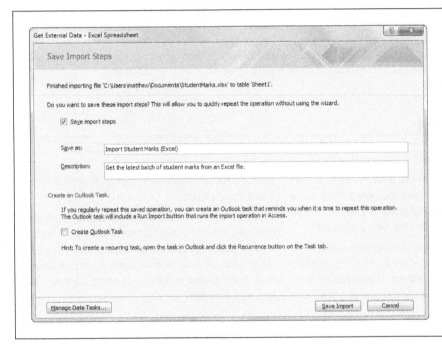

FIGURE 23-9

Here, an import process is being saved for later use. You can fill in an optional description for this operation to help you remember what it's all about.
And if you're using the popular Microsoft Outlook email program, then you can turn on Create Outlook Task to create an automatic reminder that tells you when it's time to perform your import or export.

At some future point, you can rerun your import or export operation. If you want to repeat an import, then choose External Data→Import & Link→Saved Imports. To repeat an export, choose External Data→Export→Saved Exports. Either way, you get to the Manage Data Tasks window (*Figure 23-10*), at either the Saved Imports or Saved Exports tab. These tabs list the import and export operations you've saved for this database.

Here's what you can do in the Manage Data Tasks window:

- **Run the operation again**. Select it in the list, and then click Run. Access warns you if it needs to overwrite an existing table (in an import) or file (in an export). Other than that, the whole process happens in a flash.

- **Delete your saved operation**. Just select it, and then click Delete.

- **Create an Outlook Task for the operation**. You can use this feature to remind yourself to perform this operation at some future scheduled time (or at regular intervals). To do so, click the Create Outlook Task button to create the task, and then find and configure that task in Outlook. When the reminder occurs, it includes a handy Run Import button that you can click to launch the import operation in Access right away.

- **Change some aspects of your operation**. You can modify the name, the description, and the file name by clicking the appropriate detail in the Manage Data Tasks window (*Figure 23-10*). This way, you can start out importing *C:\ My Documents\FancyFiles\WildExpenses.xlsx*, but then use the same settings to import *D:\HankSmith\EvenMoreExpenses.xlsx*. You can't change any other details, like the source or destination table in Access, or the field data types.

When you're finished using the Manage Data Tasks window, click Close to get back to Access.

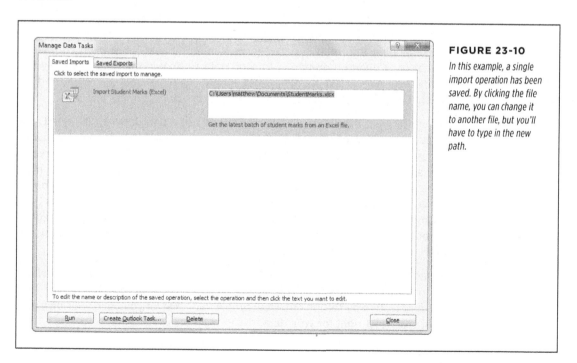

FIGURE 23-10

In this example, a single import operation has been saved. By clicking the file name, you can change it to another file, but you'll have to type in the new path.

■ Access and XML

XML (extensible markup language) is an all-purpose way of exchanging information between different programs. Access supports XML with its import and export features, where XML shows up as just one more supported format. However, importing and exporting XML isn't like importing and exporting other types of data. In particular, Access can only understand XML files that have certain types of structure—throw in something different, and Access won't know what to do. To make the most of Access's XML features and avoid these problems, you need to understand a bit more about what XML really is and how the XML features in Access work.

What Is XML, Really?

XML alone *sounds* pretty modest. People often describe it as a format for storing information. For example, instead of saving data in Word documents, Excel spreadsheets, or ordinary text files, you can save data in an XML file. This simplicity is deceiving, and two factors make XML really special:

- **XML is flexible**. You can tailor XML to store pretty much any type of information: pictures, product catalogs, invoice data, receipts, catalog listings, the maintenance specs for every Dodge Minivan ever built, and on and on.

- **XML is widespread**. Computer applications written in different programming languages (like Java, Visual Basic, or C++), or running on different operating systems and computer hardware (like Windows, Mac, or Linux), can all use XML in exactly the same way. That quality makes XML a perfect solution for exchanging information between people, companies, and even computers that have been programmed to send data to one another automatically (it's features like this last one that cause supply-chain management types to drool when they talk about XML).

Contrary to what many people believe, XML is *not* a data format (like HTML, the format used to create web pages). If XML were an ordinary data format, it wouldn't be nearly as useful because, no matter how good a format is, it can't suit everyone. For example, even though almost every company needs to create invoices, most companies wouldn't be happy with a generic format for storing invoice information. One company may need to track customer names, while another might track customer ID numbers. The bottom line is that most companies need to store slightly different data in slightly different ways. That means a one-size-fits-all solution is pretty much always doomed to failure.

So if XML isn't a data format, what is it? Technically, XML is a *meta-language*, which is a fancy way of saying that XML is a language for creating *other* languages. XML does this creating by setting out a few simple rules that let you build your *own* data format that's just right for *your* data.

For example, Acme Company can build an XML format for invoices, and call it Acme-Invoice. Meanwhile, Budget Company can build *its* own XML invoice format and call it BudgetInvoice. Even though both these formats are designed to store invoice information, they can contain completely different kinds of data. XML's flexibility is its strength.

At the same time, XML's flexibility can create problems. Suppose a bank named Worldwide Green sets up a system to automatically process XML invoices in a specific format. The system works smoothly until Acme Corporation sends along its own homegrown invoice. Even though Acme's invoice uses XML, it doesn't conform to the XML that the bank expects, so it gums up the bank's automated invoice-processing application. Suddenly, XML doesn't look so useful.

The bottom line: XML holds the *promise* of universal data sharing—but if you don't create some rules and follow them, then you're left with a bunch of incompatible formats.

NOTE XML is really quite simple. However, a slew of other standards with names like XML Schema and XSLT work in conjunction with XML and provide solutions for validating XML, searching XML, transforming XML, and so on. These other standards are quite complex and aren't discussed in this book. For more information, refer to a book like *Learning XML* by Erik Ray (O'Reilly), or the website *www.w3schools.com/xml*.

Three Rules of XML

To get a better understanding of how to configure Access to handle XML, look at a simple example. Technically, you don't need to know what XML looks like to use the XML features in Access, but the more you understand, the less confusing life will be. In this section, you'll learn the three most important rules that shape all XML documents. If you already know a little about XML, feel free to skip ahead.

By the way, good news before you even start: XML is written in a text-based, human-readable format. So you can use a program like Notepad to crack open an existing XML file, and get a basic idea of its format and structure. You can even write an XML file from scratch by using Notepad. You can't do the same with the average Access database, because it's stored in a binary format that you can read only when you're looking at the data in Access. (If you try to open a database in Notepad, you'll see a jumble of indecipherable symbols.)

■ THE PROLOG

All respectable XML documents start with something called a *document prolog*. This bit simply announces that what you're looking at is an XML document. It can also indicate the *encoding* of the document, which sometimes specifies that the document uses a special character set (like a non-English alphabet).

Here's a typical document prolog, indicating that this document uses Version 1.0 of the XML standard (the most prevalent version):

```
<?xml version="1.0" ?>
```

If you're creating an XML document by hand, then you should make sure you place the document prolog as the very first line of the file.

ELEMENTS

The basic building block of any XML document is the *element*. Elements are information containers. For example, if you wanted to store a person's name, you could create an element called Name. (For more on the infinite variety of elements that anyone can create, see the box below.)

A typical element is composed of a start tag and an end tag. The actual information goes between these two tags. You can easily recognize start tags and end tags because they use angle brackets <>. Here's one possible start tag:

```
<Name>
```

This tag marks the start of the Name element. The end tag looks almost identical, except it begins with the characters </ instead of just <. Here's what you need to end the Name element:

```
</Name>
```

To actually store some information in an XML document, just insert the content between the start and end tags of an element. Here's how you might store someone's name in an XML document:

```
<Name>Patrick</Name>
```

You could create a list of names by putting one <Name> element after the other, or you could add other elements that store different types of information, like address, title, employer, and so on. You put all these tags together in a file to make an XML document.

UP TO SPEED

A Closer Look at Tags

Tags follow fairly strict naming rules. Tags can be of any length, are case-sensitive, include any alphanumeric character and hyphens (-), underscores (_), and periods (.). You can't use other special characters, including spaces, and the tag name *must* start with an underscore or letter. XML documents also support characters from non-English alphabets.

The most important thing you should understand about tags is that it's up to you to create them. If you decide that you need to store a list of names, you may create an XML format that uses a <Name> tag. Meanwhile, someone else may decide to track name information by creating another XML format that uses elements like <firstName> and <lastName>.

These two elements may store the same type of information as your <Name> element, but they're different, and a document written with the <firstName> and <lastName> tags isn't compatible with your documents.

Since there are so many possible XML formats, many intelligent people have invested a lot of time and energy in trying to create ways to define and manage different XML formats. Also, companies and organizations have come together to define specific XML standards for different industries. If you search on the Internet, you'll find predefined XML formats for law, science, real estate, and much more.

NESTING

So far, you've seen examples of XML elements that contain text. You can also create an element that contains one or more additional elements. This is a basic principle for organizing information in XML.

Suppose you want to keep track of several people's names and ages. The following format isn't especially clear because it's hard to tell which person connects to which age:

```
<Name>Lisa Chen</Name>
<Age>19</Age>
<Name>Bill Harrison</Name>
<Age>48</Age>
```

A better solution is to group the <Name> and <Age> elements together for each person, and to put them inside *another* element. Here's an example:

```
<Person>
    <Name>Lisa Chen</Name>
    <Age>19</Age>
</Person>

<Person>
    <Name>Bill Harrison</Name>
    <Age>48</Age>
</Person>
```

Here, the two <Person> elements each represent a distinct individual. Information about each person is stored in <Name> and <Age> elements that are *nested* inside the appropriate <Person> element.

There's no limit to how many layers deep you can nest information, making this method of organizing information extremely flexible. In fact, it's part of the reason that XML can work with so many different types of data.

XML imposes one more rule. Every document must start with a single element that you place right after the document prolog. You place all the other content inside this element, which is called the *root or document element*. So far, the examples you've seen are only excerpts of XML. The following listing shows a complete, valid XML document—a list with information about two people—that starts off with the document element <PeopleList>:

```
<?xml version="1.0" ?>
<PeopleList>
    <Person>
        <Name>Lisa Chen</Name>
        <Age>19</Age>
    </Person>
```

```
<Person>
    <Name>Bill Harrison</Name>
    <Age>48</Age>
</Person>
</PeopleList>
```

You could enhance this document by adding more <Person> elements or different elements to track additional information about each person.

You've probably noticed that these XML examples indent each level of elements. That indentation makes the overall structure easier to read, but it's not required. In fact, applications that read XML (including Access) ignore all the white space between elements, so it doesn't matter if you add spaces, tabs, and blank lines. In fact, as far as computers are concerned, the document above is exactly the same as the following, much less human-friendly, version:

```
<?xml version="1.0" ?>
<PeopleList><Person><Name>Lisa Chen</Name><Age>19</
Age></Person><Person><Name>Bill Harrison</Name><Age>48
</Age></Person></PeopleList>
```

XML Files and Schemas

As you've already learned, a file is one place you can store XML documents. But you can just as easily place XML documents in databases or other storage locations. In fact, sometimes XML data isn't stored anywhere—instead, people just use it to send information between applications over the Internet. However, when you use XML with Access, you're always using XML files (unless your company has created a custom solution by using the heavy-duty programming features in Access).

Most XML files have the extension .xml. For example, it makes perfect sense to take the person list document shown earlier and place it in a text file named PersonList.xml.

Another type of XML document is extremely important: XML *schemas*. Schemas are designed to solve a common problem—namely, defining the rules for a specific XML-based format. For example, a schema indicates the element names you can use, how you can arrange the elements, and the type of information each element can contain. An XML-friendly application can use the schema to verify that an XML document uses the right structure and contains the appropriate content. In an ideal world, every time a company created an XML format, they'd write an XML schema that defines it. (You probably won't be surprised to learn this doesn't always happen.)

To use a schema, you simply need to have a copy of it in a file. (Schemas themselves are complex and ugly and beyond the scope of what a typical office needs—or wants—to learn.) Usually, schema files have the extension .xsd.

TIP For a more comprehensive beginner's introduction to XML and XML schemas, see the excellent online tutorial provided by W3 Schools at *www.w3schools.com/schema*.

The Access XML Story

XML is a great way to exchange data between different computer programs. But what does that have to do with Access, which already has its own perfectly good way of storing data? Here's the deal: More and more companies today use XML to pass data back and forth. When companies exchange business orders, for instance, or news organizations post stories, or real estate firms list properties for sale, chances are they're using an XML-based format. If you want to send your Access data to these systems, then you need a way to take it out of the specialized .accdb database format, and put it in clear-as-a-bell XML.

Unfortunately, the XML support in Access is still quite limited. The problem is that Access doesn't let you pick the XML format you want. Instead, it creates a custom format that closely matches your table. Consider the table in *Figure 23-11*. (When exporting XML, you always export a complete table.)

	ProductID	Name	ProductNumber	SafetyStockLevel	ReorderPoint
+	371	Thin-Jam Hex Nut 7	HJ-7161	1000	750
+	372	Thin-Jam Hex Nut 8	HJ-7162	1000	750
+	373	Thin-Jam Hex Nut 12	HJ-9080	1000	750
+	374	Thin-Jam Hex Nut 11	HJ-9161	1000	750
+	375	Hex Nut 5	HN-1024	1000	750
+	376	Hex Nut 6	HN-1032	1000	750
+	377	Hex Nut 16	HN-1213	1000	750
+	378	Hex Nut 17	HN-1220	1000	750
+	379	Hex Nut 7	HN-1224	1000	750
+	380	Hex Nut 8	HN-1420	1000	750
+	381	Hex Nut 9	HN-1428	1000	750
+	382	Hex Nut 22	HN-3410	1000	750

FIGURE 23-11

Some sample data, ready for a new life in XML format.

When you export this table, Access creates an XML document that looks like this:

```
<dataroot>
    <Product>
        <ProductID>371</ProductID>
        <Name>Thin-Jam Hex Nut 7</Name>
        <ProductNumber>HJ-7161</ProductNumber>
        <SafetyStockLevel>1000</SafetyStockLevel>
        <ReorderPoint>750</ReorderPoint>
    </Product>
    <Product>
        <ProductID>372</ProductID>
        <Name>Thin-Jam Hex Nut 8</Name>
        <ProductNumber>HJ-7162</ProductNumber>
        <SafetyStockLevel>1000</SafetyStockLevel>
        <ReorderPoint>750</ReorderPoint>
    </Product>

    ...
</dataroot>
```

No matter what table you export, Access always follows the same rules:

- The document's root element is named <dataroot>.

- Access creates a separate element for each row in the table, using the table name. In this example, that system means you end up with one <Product> element for each record.

- Inside each record, Access creates a separate element for each field. In this example, you end up with fields like <Name>, <ProductNumber>, and so on.

There's nothing particularly *wrong* with structuring XML in this way. However, since you can't change the structure, you'll run into trouble if you want to use another program that expects XML in a different format. For example, your program may expect the root element to be named <ProductRecords> instead of <dataroot>, or it may assume a slightly different nesting. Minor quibbles like these can completely derail an XML-processing application.

Sadly, there's no way around this problem. To use Access XML, you must specifically design a program that recognizes this structure, or you must use another tool to convert the XML to the standard you *really* want. Access's XML export feature is enough to get you started, but it doesn't take your data all the way.

TIP If all you need to do is filter out records or fields that don't interest you, or give fields different names, then you can solve the problem with a query. Just create a query that presents the information the way you want it, and then export its results (rather than the whole table).

The same limitations appear when you import XML content. Access expects to find XML content in the rigid table-like format it expects. If you try to feed it a different type of XML, then you get an error.

Exporting to an XML File

Now that you've learned about XML and considered its limitations in Access, you're ready to try it out for yourself. The following steps lead you through the process:

1. **Choose External Data→Export→XML File.**

   The familiar export process begins.

2. **Supply the name of the file you want to create, and then click OK.**

   Access suggests you use the table name. For example, if you're exporting the Orders table, it recommends an XML file named Orders.xml.

3. **Choose what file types you want to create (*Figure 23-12*):**

   - **Data (XML)** creates the XML file that has the actual content from all records in your table.

   - **Schema (XSD)** creates an .xsd schema file. The schema doesn't contain any data, but it stores a concise definition that describes your table and the fields it contains. The schema has two purposes—you can pass it along to expert programmers so they know what type of XML to expect from Access, or you can use it to create a new, empty table in another Access database.

   - **Presentation (XSL)** creates a .xsl transform file. This file defines how a browser can convert the raw data in the XML file into an HTML web page suitable for display in a browser. When you choose this option, Access also creates an .htm file that *uses* the .xsl file. For example, if you're exporting the Products table, you wind up with a Products.htm web page—open this in your browser, and it uses the Products.xsl file to display the data in Products.xml.

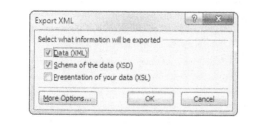

FIGURE 23-12

Usually, you'll want to create the XML file that stores the actual data from your table. In addition, you can create two more support files.

4. **If you want to export related tables in the same XML document, then click More Options.**

An Export XML window with additional options appears. Most of these options are best left for XML gurus. However, the Data tab is more interesting—it lets you export related tables (*Figure 23-13*).

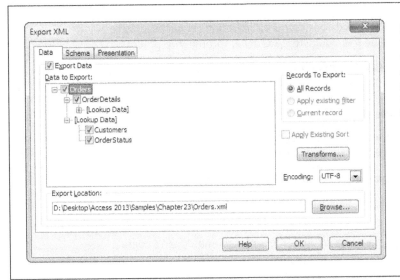

FIGURE 23-13

The Data tab shows a tree that starts with the table you're exporting, and branches out to other related tables. If you want to include the data from these related tables, simply add a checkmark next to each one.

For example, if you're exporting the Orders table, you have two options:

- **Export other child tables.** You could also export the OrderDetails records for each order. Access nests the OrderDetails elements inside the corresponding Orders element in the XML.

- **Export the related records from a parent table.** You could, for instance, also export records from the Customers and OrderStatus tables. These records appear under the heading [Lookup Data] because they provide more data that's linked to an order (in this case, the current status of the order, and the credit card used to pay for an order).

NOTE When you export parent tables, the records aren't nested in the XML, because that could lead to duplication (for example, if more than one order has the same status or uses the same credit card). Instead, they're added after the main table you're exporting.

5. **Click OK.**

   Access creates the files you chose in step 3.

6. **If you want to repeat the export process another time, then choose "Save export steps."**

   Click Close to return to Access.

Importing from an XML File

Access makes it just as easy to import XML data, provided it's in the structure Access expects. To try it out, take the table you just exported, and then re-import it into a new database. Here's how to do it:

1. **Choose External Data→Import & Link→XML File.**

   The familiar import process begins.

2. **If you're creating a new table and you have a schema for your data, then supply the schema file's name. If you already have the tables that you want to use, or you don't have a schema handy, then jump straight to step 6.**

   You can import straight from the XML file, but it's always better to use the schema if you need to create the table for the first time, because the schema stores information about each field's data types. This information ensures that the table you create is a closer match to the original table you exported.

3. **Click OK.**

   Access scans the schema and displays the structure of the tables it'll create (*Figure 23-14*).

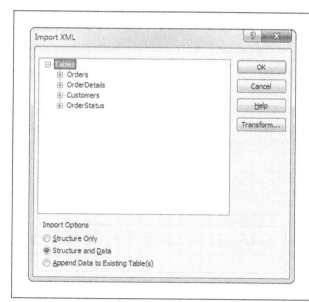

FIGURE 23-14

In this example, Access correctly identifies that your schema file defines the structure for the Orders, OrderDetails, Customers, and OrderStatus tables. You can expand each table to see what fields it contains.

4. **Click OK.**

   Using the schema information, Access creates a new, blank table with the correct structure. Now you're ready to fill it with data.

NOTE If a table already exists with the same name, Access adds a number to the end to distinguish it (such as Products1, Products2, and so on).

5. **Click Close to return to Access.**

6. **Choose External Data→Import & Link→XML File.**

   Now that you've created your tables, you're ready to import the actual data.

7. **Supply the name of the XML file that has the data you want to import, and then click OK.**

   Access shows the structure of the table, based on the XML data in your file. This structure should *exactly* match the structure of the table you want to create or add to.

8. **Choose one of the three import options:**

   • **Append Data to Existing Table(s)** tells Access to find the table with the same name, and then add all the data to this table. Use this option if the table you're using already exists. But remember, Access won't overwrite existing values. If you try to import a record that has the same value as an existing record in a field that doesn't allow duplicates (like an ID field), your import will fail.

   • **Structure and Data** creates the table and then fills it with all the data.

   • **Structure Only** creates the table if it doesn't already exist, but doesn't import any data.

NOTE If you need to create a new table as part of your import process, it's always best to use the schema file to create the table (as described in steps 1 to 5), because the schema file has more precise information about data types.

9. **Click OK.**

   Access fills the tables with data from your XML file.

If you want to repeat the import process another time, then choose "Save import steps."

Appendix

APPENDIX A:
Customizing Access

Customizing Access

When Microsoft introduced the ribbon in Office 2007, they clamped down on customization. Quite simply, the designers of Office were concerned that overly creative Office fans would replace the standard arrangement of buttons with a jumble of personal favorites. Their worst fear was that Access customizers would transform Access so completely that no one else would be able to use it, and the instructions in books like this one would be useless. To prevent this crisis, Microsoft made it extremely difficult to customize the ribbon. The only people who could do it were programming gearheads who were willing to work with the intimidating RibbonX standard.

Access 2013 isn't nearly as paranoid. It lets you rename or hide tabs, and add and remove groups. It even lets you create an entirely new tab with your own button selections. When used carefully, this feature gives you a great way to speed up your work and put your favorite commands in a central spot. But if you get carried away, you can end up causing confusion for friends, family, coworkers, and even yourself.

Along with its surprisingly powerful ribbon customization ability, Access 2013 also lets you customize the Quick Access toolbar—the sequence of tiny buttons that sits just above the ribbon and its tabs. If you don't have the ambition to create your own custom tab, you may find it easier to stick your absolute favorite buttons in the Quick Access toolbar, which is the first task described in this appendix. (And if you're itching to give the Access ribbon a radical revamp, you'll get the details for that, too, starting on page 829.)

■ Adding Your Favorites to the QAT

You've already seen the Quick Access toolbar (known to Access nerds as the QAT). It's the micro-sized toolbar that sits above the ribbon. The Quick Access toolbar has only icons, but you can hover over a button if you want to see a label describing what it does.

When you first start out with Access, the Quick Access toolbar is a lonely place, with buttons for quickly saving the current database object and undoing or redoing the last action. However, Access gives you complete control over this space, including the ability to add new buttons. The quickest way to add buttons is by clicking the downward-pointing arrow shown in *Figure A-1*.

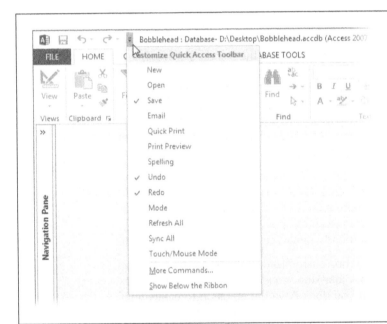

FIGURE A-1

When you click the drop-down arrow on the Quick Access toolbar, Access shows a list of often-used commands that you can add just by clicking them. These commands include ones for creating a new database, opening an existing database, sending the current database object (the one that's selected in the navigation pane) to the printer with no questions asked, emailing the data from the current database object, and firing up the spell checker. But to see all your possibilities, you need to choose More Commands.

You can add buttons to the Quick Access toolbar for two reasons:

- **To make it easier to get to a command you use frequently**. If it's in the Quick Access toolbar, then you don't need to memorize a keyboard shortcut or switch to a different tab in the ribbon.

- **To get to a command that the ribbon doesn't provide**. Access has a small set of less popular commands that it lets you use but that it doesn't keep in the ribbon. Some of these commands are holdovers from previous versions of Access. If you have a long-lost favorite Access feature that's missing, it just may be available using the Quick Access toolbar's extra buttons. (The next section shows you how to peruse the full complement of available buttons.)

Keyboard lovers can also trigger the commands in the Quick Access toolbar with lightning speed, thanks to Access's KeyTips feature (page 10). When you press the Alt key, Access displays a number superimposed over every command in the Quick Access toolbar (starting at 1 and going up from there). You can then press the number to trigger the command. So in the Quick Access toolbar shown in *Figure A-1*, Alt+1 saves the currently open database object, Alt+2 triggers the Undo command, and so on.

> **TIP** If you want to add a command that duplicates something that's already in the ribbon, here's a shortcut: Find the command in the ribbon, right-click it, and then choose "Add to Quick Access Toolbar."

Adding Buttons

To add a button to the Quick Access toolbar, follow these steps:

1. **Click the drop-down arrow on the Quick Access toolbar, and then choose More Commands.**

   The Access Options window opens and positions you at the Customize section (*Figure A-2*).

2. **Choose a category from the "Choose commands from" list.**

   The library of commands that you can add to the Quick Access toolbar is enormous. To make it easier to find what you want, Access divides your choices into a collection of categories. Many of the categories overlap—Access simply provides them to make finding what you want easier. Here are the top choices:

   - **Popular Commands** gives you a short list of commands that Access jockeys love. If you're trying to get quick access to a commonly used feature, you'll probably find it here.

   - **Commands Not in the Ribbon** provides all the leftovers—commands that Microsoft didn't consider useful enough to include in the ribbon. This list holds some commands that are superseded or partially duplicated by other commands, commands that are included in other windows, and commands that were used in previous versions of Access and put out to pasture in this release.

- **All Commands** includes the full list of choices. As with the other categories, it's ordered alphabetically.

- **Macros** shows all the macros in the currently open database. However, there's a problem here: If you add a macro command to the Quick Access toolbar, it won't work in other databases because they don't have the same macro. The solution is to use another Access feature that lets you customize how the Quick Access toolbar appears in a *specific database*. Full details are in the next section.

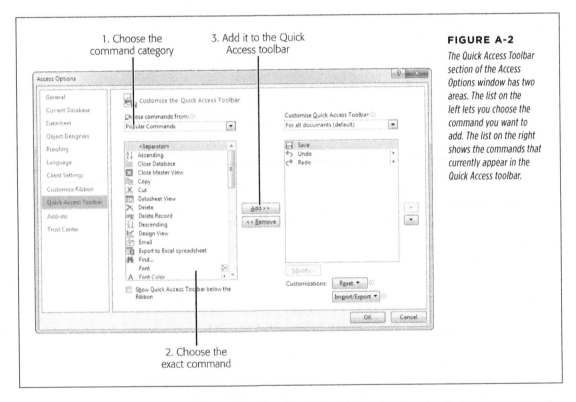

1. Choose the command category

3. Add it to the Quick Access toolbar

2. Choose the exact command

FIGURE A-2

The Quick Access Toolbar section of the Access Options window has two areas. The list on the left lets you choose the command you want to add. The list on the right shows the commands that currently appear in the Quick Access toolbar.

Under these categories are several additional categories that correspond to the File menu and various tabs in the ribbon. For example, you can choose the Create tab to see all the commands that appear in the ribbon's Create tab. At the top of the tab list is the File tab, which has the commands from the File menu and backstage view. At the bottom of the list are the Tools tabs—tabs that appear only when certain objects are selected, such as charts, pictures, or images.

3. **Once you've chosen the category you want, pick the command from the list below, and then click Add.**

   The command moves from the list on the left to the list on the right, placing it on the Quick Access toolbar (*Figure A-3*).

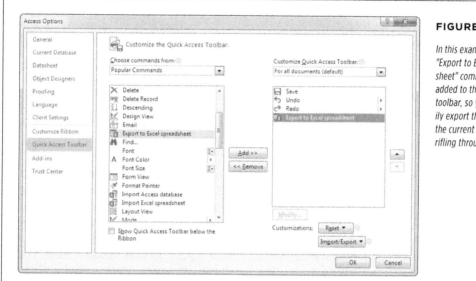

FIGURE A-3

In this example, the "Export to Excel spreadsheet" command is being added to the Quick Access toolbar, so you can speedily export the contents of the current table without rifling through the ribbon.

4. **You can repeat this process (starting at step 2) to add more commands.**

   Optionally, you can rearrange the order of items in the Quick Access toolbar. Just pick a command, and then use the up and down arrow buttons to move it. The topmost commands in the list are displayed to the left on the Quick Access toolbar.

TIP If you've customized the heck out of your Quick Access toolbar and want to go back to a simpler way of life, just click the Reset button.

---

5. **When you're finished, click OK to return to Access with the revamped Quick Access toolbar.**

   Adding a Quick Access toolbar isn't a lifetime commitment. To get rid of a command you don't want anymore, right-click it, and then choose "Remove from Quick Access Toolbar."

NOTE You may notice the tempting Modify button, which lets you change a command's name and picture. Unfortunately, it works only for macro commands.

Customizing Specific Databases

Do you have a button or two that you're using incessantly, but just for a specific database? In this situation, it may not make sense to customize the Quick Access toolbar in the normal way. If you do, then you'll get your extra buttons in *every* database you use, including those where the commands aren't useful.

Access has a great feature to help you out in this situation. You can customize the Quick Access toolbar for an individual database. That way, whenever you open that database, the buttons you need appear in the Quick Access toolbar. When you close it (or open another database in a separate window), the buttons disappear.

NOTE Customizing individual databases has advantages and disadvantages. The disadvantage is that you need to perform this task separately for every database, which can take a lot of time. The advantage is that your customizations are recorded right in your database file. As a result, they stick around even if you open the database on someone else's computer (or if you log onto your computer as a different user).

To customize the toolbar for a single database, follow the same steps that you used in the previous section. Start by clicking the Quick Access toolbar's drop-down arrow, and then choose More Commands. However, before you add any commands, change the selection in the Customize Quick Access Toolbar drop-down menu, which appears just above the list of commands in the Quick Access toolbar. Instead of using "For all documents (default)," choose your database's name (as in "For C:\ MyFiles\SecretSanta.accdb"). This list starts off empty. Then, follow the normal steps to add buttons.

When Access displays the Quick Access toolbar, it combines the standard buttons (as configured in the previous section) with any buttons you've defined for the current database. *Figure A-4* shows an example.

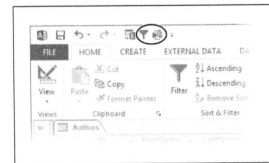

FIGURE A-4

The database-specific buttons (circled) always appear after the standard buttons in the Quick Access toolbar.

Customizing the Quick Access toolbar for a specific database is a useful trick. It makes great sense with macros, because it lets you create a single database that has a useful set of macros *and* handy buttons for running them. For example, you could create macros that show specific forms in your database, and then add them to the Quick Access toolbar. That way, a person can zip around your database without using the navigation pane.

■ Personalizing the Ribbon

Retooling the ribbon is a more complex affair than customizing the Quick Access toolbar, but it lets you make more radical changes. So if you think you could become more productive with a ribbon that's tailored to the tasks you perform most often, then ribbon customization is the way to go.

As with the QAT, you make changes to the ribbon in the Access Options window. The easiest way to get there is to right-click the ribbon and choose Customize Ribbon. Access opens the Access Options window and sends you straight to the Customize Ribbon section (*Figure A-5*).

FIGURE A-5

Customizing the ribbon is much like customizing the Quick Access toolbar. The most obvious difference is that there's a lot more information on the right side of the window, because this list includes all the ribbon tabs. To see the groups in each tab, and the commands in each group, click the tiny plus (+) icon next to the appropriate item. For example, here the Home tab is expanded to show all its groups, and the Records group is expanded to show the buttons it contains.

There's a lot you can do to fine-tune your ribbon. The next sections show you how.

> **NOTE** The ribbon changes you make are linked to your Windows user account. People who log onto your computer with a different user name and run Access get the standard ribbon.

Changing Existing Tabs

Tired of Access's standard tabs? Surprisingly, you can do quite a bit to change them. But why bother?

You might, for example, embark on this path if you want to cut down the wealth of Access commands to a small, more manageable set of essentials for an Access newbie. Or, you might want your favorite command to sit on your most frequently used tab, to reduce the amount of tab switching you do. Or, maybe something about the standard arrangement of buttons really rubs you the wrong way, and you feel the burning desire to reorganize. In all of these cases, Access is surprisingly accommodating.

TIP Of course, just because you *can* make sweeping changes in the ribbon doesn't mean you *should*. You may end up hiding something you need and making Access more difficult to use. If you go too far, Access lets you return the ribbon to its original state. Just click the Reset button and choose "Reset all customizations." Alternatively, you can reset a single tab—just select it in the list, click the Reset button, and choose "Reset only selected Ribbon tab."

For advice on which kinds of ribbon changes are most likely to succeed, see the box on page 831.

Here are the changes you can make to an existing tab:

- **Hide a tab**. If you're absolutely positive you don't need any of the commands in a tab, or if you're a system administrator trying to prevent your users from messing up spreadsheets with the wrong features, you can remove the tab from the ribbon. To do so, clear the checkbox next to the tab name. To restore it at a later time, add the checkmark back.

- **Remove a group**. A similar, but more fine-grained, strategy is to remove a section of a tab. This leaves more room for the rest of the buttons (which, presumably, are ones that are more useful to you). To remove a group, click the plus (+) icon to expand the tab that has it, select the group, and then click the Remove button (which appears between the two lists).

- **Change the order of tabs**. If you use one tab far more than another, you might decide to change the tab order. Click to select the tab you want to move, and click the up arrow button (to move the tab toward the left side, or start, of the ribbon), or click the down arrow button (to move the tab toward the right side, or end, of the ribbon). You can find both arrow buttons just to the right of the list.

- **Change the order of groups in a tab**. This maneuver works in the same way as changing the tab order, but it lets you rearrange the sections inside a tab. Click the plus (+) icon to expand the appropriate tab, select the group you want to move, and use the up and down arrows to shuffle its position. But be warned: Though this seems like a small change, it can seriously throw off anyone using your copy of Access, because people tend to remember the general position of the commands they use.

NOTE If you keep pressing the up arrow when you reach the top of the tab's group list (or the down arrow when you reach the bottom), Access moves the group to the next adjacent tab.

- **Rename a tab or group**. Select either a tab or a single group. (You can't rename individual buttons.) Then click the Rename button under the list. A small window pops up where you can type the new name.

- **Add a new group to an existing tab**. Expand the tab where you want to place your group. Select an existing group, and then click the New Group button. Your new group is placed immediately after the group you selected, but you can use the arrow buttons to move it. Now give your group a good name (click Rename) and fill it up. To do that, select the command you want in the list on the left and click Add, just as you did when adding commands to the Quick Access toolbar.

And here's the much smaller list of changes Access doesn't let you make:

- **Delete or rearrange commands in a standard group**. You can take a standard group or leave it, but you can't change what's inside. Of course, nothing stops you from removing a standard group and creating a custom group that has just the commands you want.

- **Add custom commands to a standard group**. If you want to add new commands, you need to place them in a custom group in a standard tab or, even better, in a custom group in a custom tab.

UP TO SPEED

Ribbon Tweaking: Too Much of a Good Thing?

Before you begin a wild bout of customization, it's worth asking which customizations are really worth the effort. Here's the rundown:

- Hiding tabs and removing groups makes sense if you're trying to simplify Access. However, you risk losing features you'll need later, which is usually far more inconvenient.

- Changing tab and group names doesn't make you more efficient and could confuse other people, so it's usually a bad idea.

- Rearranging groups is a worthwhile strategy if you want to move the features you never use to the far right end of the tab, so they won't distract you.

- Adding new groups is a great way to get important features at your fingertips, but it probably makes even more sense to put your custom-picked buttons on a brand-new tab you've added from scratch (which you'll learn to do in the next section).

Any ribbon customization is a tradeoff between personalization and consistency. You already know that a revamped ribbon can confuse other Accesslians when they use your computer. But you might not have realized the more insidious reverse effect—namely, you'll be embarrassingly slow when you switch over to a normal Access installation on a colleague's computer or at the local copy shop. For that reason, it's best to practice a bit of restraint and follow these ribbon-customization guidelines:

- Customize only when you're absolutely sure it will make your life easier and more convenient.

- If you want to add more than two or three new commands to the ribbon, consider putting them all into a new tab, so they're cleanly separate from the standard buttons.

- If you want to customize something just so you can express your own personal design aesthetic, stick to your computer's background wallpaper and desktop icons.

Creating Your Own Tab

The safest way to customize the ribbon is to put your custom buttons on a completely separate tab. This way, you can keep the rest of the Access user interface in its normal state. It's also oddly satisfying to have a ribbon tab all to yourself, to fill with your favorite shortcuts, as shown in *Figure A-6*.

FIGURE A-6

You can fit quite a bit more into a custom ribbon tab than you can fit in the Quick Access toolbar. Here, the custom tab (named Favorites) has a few items from Backstage view, such as New (to create a new database), Open, Close Database, Save As (which pops open a small menu of format choices), and Back Up Database.

You probably already know how to create and fill a custom tab. But if you're unsure, just follow this sequence of steps:

1. **In the Access Options window, select the last tab in the list, and then click the New Tab button.**

   Access adds a new tab named "New Tab" at the end of the ribbon. (You can move it by selecting it and using the arrow buttons.) Inside the new tab, Access adds a single new group named "New Group."

2. **Change the tab and group names.**

   First, select the new tab, click Rename, and fill in a new name. Then, select the new group, click Rename, and give it a new name. For example, in *Figure A-6* the tab is named Favorites and the first group is named File.

3. **Now add your favorite commands.**

   The Customize Ribbon section of the Access Options window works the same as the Quick Access Toolbar section. You pick commands in the list on the left and click Add to transfer them over to the currently selected custom group.

   For example, to add the Open command shown in *Figure A-5*, start by picking "File Tab" from the "Choose commands from" list. Then, select Open and click the Add button.

> **NOTE** The command list includes many variations of each command. For example, along with Save, you'll find Save As, Save As Local Database, Save As Other Format, and so on. Although you can do just about everything with Save As, these variations will be slightly more convenient for different saving tasks. You may want to explore a little and try the different variations before you settle on the exact commands you want.

4. **Optionally, add more groups.**

   To make a complete tab, you'll probably want several groups of commands. To create each new group, click Add Group. You can use the arrow buttons to rearrange them appropriately.

5. **Once you're finished, consider saving your ribbon for posterity (as described in the next section).**

Saving and Reusing Your Custom Ribbon

After you've spent a lot of effort getting exactly the right arrangement of tabs and buttons, it's natural to wonder if you can reuse your custom ribbon on another computer. Fortunately, Access has an export feature that preserves all your hard ribbon-customization work. It copies your ribbon settings to a special file (with the clunky file extension *.exportedUI*), which you can then apply to a copy of Access that's installed somewhere else.

Here's how to use Access's ribbon export feature:

1. **When you're finished perfecting your ribbon in the Access Options window, click the Import/Export button, and choose "Export all customizations."**

   A File Save window appears.

2. **Browse to the folder where you want to place your file, and give it a suitable name, like DavesCustomRibbon.exportedUI. Then click Save.**

   This file contains your ribbon customizations in portable form. You can transfer it to another computer by email, USB drive, and so on.

3. **Go to the other computer where you want to replicate your ribbon, and take your file with you. In the Access Options window, click the Import/Export button, and choose "Import customization file."**

   A File Open window appears.

4. **Browse to your ribbon file, select it, and click Open.**

   Before it imports your ribbon, Access gives you a last-minute confirmation warning. That's because the settings that are stored in your file will overwrite any custom ribbon settings in that copy of Access.

5. **Click Yes to seal the deal and import your custom ribbon.**

   Presto—Access replaces the standard-issue ribbon with your personalized version.

Index

Access 2013

THE MISSING CD

There's no
CD with this book;
you just saved $5.00.

Instead, every single Web address, practice file, and
piece of downloadable software mentioned in this
book is available at *missingmanuals.com*
(click the Missing CD icon).
There you'll find a tidy list of links,
organized by chapter.

Don't miss a thing!
Sign up for the free Missing
Manual email announcement
list at missingmanuals.com.
We'll let you know when we
release new titles, make
free sample chapters available,
and update the features and
articles on the Missing Manual
website.

CPSIA information can be obtained at www.ICGtesting.com
Printed in the USA
BVOW08s2345231214

380610BV00007B/15/P